The Andrew Murray Collection

MW00386710

Abide in Christ

Preface

During the life of Jesus on earth, the word He chiefly used when speaking of the relations of the disciples to Himself was: "Follow me." When about to leave for heaven, He gave them a new word, in which their more intimate and spiritual union with Himself in glory should be expressed. That chosen word was: "Abide in me."

It is to be feared that there are many earnest followers of Jesus from whom the meaning of this word, with the blessed experience it promises, is very much hidden. While trusting in their Saviour for pardon and for help, and seeking to some extent to obey Him, they have hardly realized to what closeness of union, to what intimacy of fellowship, to what wondrous oneness of life and interest, He invited them when He said, "Abide in me." This is not only an unspeakable loss to themselves, but the Church and the world suffer in what they lose.

If we ask the reason why those who have indeed accepted the Saviour, and been made partakers of the renewing of the Holy Ghost, thus come short of the full salvation prepared for them, I am sure the answer will in very many cases be, that ignorance is the cause of the unbelief that fails of the inheritance. If, in our orthodox Churches, the abiding in Christ, the living union with Him, the experience of His daily and hourly presence and keeping, were preached with the same distinctness and urgency as His atonement and pardon through His blood, I am confident that many would be found to accept with gladness the invitation to such a life, and that its influence would be manifest in their experience of the purity and the power, the love and the joy, the fruit-bearing, and all the blessedness which the Saviour connected with the abiding in Him.

It is with the desire to help those who have not yet fully understood what the Saviour meant with His command, or who have feared that it was a life beyond their reach, that these meditations are now published. It is only by frequent repetition that a child learns its lessons. It is only by continuously fixing the mind for a time on some one of the lessons of faith, that the believer is gradually helped to take and thoroughly assimilate them. I have the hope that to some, especially young believers, it will be a help to come and for a month day after day spell over the precious words, "Abide in me," with the lessons connected with them in the parable of the Vine. Step by step we shall get to see how truly this promise-precept is meant for us, how surely grace is provided to enable us to obey it, how indispensable the experience of its blessing is to a healthy Christian life, and how unspeakable the blessings are that flow from it. As we listen, and meditate, and pray--as we surrender ourselves, and accept in faith the whole Jesus as He offers

Himself to us in it--the Holy Spirit will make the word to be spirit and life; this word of Jesus, too, will become to us the power of God unto salvation, and through it will come the faith that grasps the long desired blessing.

I pray earnestly that our gracious Lord may be pleased to bless this little book, to help those who seek to know Him fully, as He has already blessed it in its original issue in a different (the Dutch) language. I pray still more earnestly that He would, by whatever means, make the multitudes of His dear children who are still living divided lives, to see how He claims them wholly for Himself, and how the wholehearted surrender to abide in Him alone brings the joy unspeakable and full of glory. Oh, let each of us who has begun to taste the sweetness of this life, yield himself wholly to be a witness to the grace and power of our Lord to keep us united with Himself, and seek by word and walk to win others to follow Him fully. It is only in such fruitbearing that our own abiding can be maintained.

In conclusion, I ask to be permitted to give one word of advice to my reader. It is this. It needs time to grow into Jesus the Vine: do not expect to abide in Him unless you will give Him that time. It is not enough to read God's Word, or meditations as here offered, and when we think we have hold of the thoughts, and have asked God for His blessing, to go out in the hope that the blessing will abide. No, it needs day by day time with Jesus and with God. We all know the need of time for our meals each day--every workman claims his hour for dinner; the hurried eating of so much food is not enough. If we are to live through Jesus, we must feed on Him (John 6:57); we must thoroughly take in and assimilate that heavenly food the Father has given us in His life. Therefore, my brother, who would learn to abide in Jesus, take time each day, ere you read, and while you read, and after you read, to put yourself into living contact with the living Jesus, to yield yourself distinctly and consciously to His blessed influence; so will you give Him the opportunity of taking hold of you, of drawing you up and keeping you safe in His almighty life.

And now, to all God's children whom He allows me the privilege of pointing to the Heavenly Vine, I offer my fraternal love and salutations, with the prayer that to each one of them may be given the rich and full experience of the blessedness of abiding in Christ. And may the grace of Jesus, and the love of God, and the fellowship of the Holy Spirit, be their daily portion. Amen.

Chapter 1: ALL YOU WHO HAVE COME TO HIM

"Come unto me."--MATT.11:28

"Abide in me."--JOHN 15:4

IT IS to you who have heard and hearkened to the call, "Come unto me," that this new invitation comes, "Abide in me." The message comes from the same loving Saviour. You doubtless have never repented having come at His call. You experienced that His word was truth; all His promises He fulfilled; He made you partakers of the blessings and the joy of His love. Was not His welcome most hearty, His pardon full and free, His love most sweet and precious? You more than once, at your first coming to Him, had reason to say, "The half was not told me."

And yet you have had to complain of disappointment: as time went on, your expectations were not realized. The blessings you once enjoyed were lost; the love and joy of your first meeting with your Saviour, instead of deepening, have become faint and feeble. And often you have wondered what the reason could be, that with such a Saviour, so mighty and so loving, your experience of salvation should not have been a fuller one.

The answer is very simple. You wandered from Him. The blessings He bestows are all connected with His "Come to ME," and are only to be enjoyed in close fellowship with Himself. You either did not fully understand, or did not rightly remember, that the call meant, "Come to me to stay with me." And yet this was in very deed His object and purpose when first He called you to Himself. It was not to refresh you for a few short hours after your conversion with the joy of His love and deliverance, and then to send you forth to wander in sadness and sin. He had destined you to something better than a short-lived blessedness, to be enjoyed only in times of special earnestness and prayer, and then to pass away, as you had to return to those duties in which far the greater part of life has to be spent. No, indeed; He had prepared for you an abiding dwelling with Himself, where your whole life and every moment of it might be spent, where the work of your daily life might be done, and where all the while you might be enjoying unbroken communion with Himself. It was even this He meant when to that first word, "Come to me," He added this, "Abide in me." As earnest and faithful, as loving and tender, as the compassion that breathed in that blessed "Come," was the grace that added this no less blessed "Abide." As mighty as the attraction with which that first word drew you, were the bonds with which this second, had you but listened to it, would have kept you. And as great as were the blessings with which that coming was rewarded, so large, yea, and much greater, were the treasures to which that abiding would have given you access.

And observe especially, it was not that He said, "Come to me and abide with me," but, "Abide in me." The intercourse was not only to be unbroken, but most intimate and complete. He opened His arms, to press you to His bosom; He opened His heart, to welcome you there; He opened up all His divine fulness of life and love, and offered to take you up into its fellowship, to make you wholly one with Himself. There was a depth of meaning you cannot yet realize in His words: "Abide IN ME."

And with no less earnestness than He had cried, "Come to me," did He plead, had you but noticed it, "Abide in me." By every motive that had induced you to come, did He beseech you to abide. Was it the fear of sin and its curse that first drew you? the pardon you received on first coming could, with all the blessings flowing from it, only be confirmed and fully enjoyed on abiding in Him. Was it the longing to know and enjoy the Infinite Love that was calling you? the first coming gave but single drops to taste--'tis only the abiding that can really satisfy the thirsty soul, and give to drink of the rivers of pleasure that are at His right hand. Was it the weary longing to be made free from the bondage of sin, to become pure and holy, and so to find rest, the rest of God for the soul? this too can only be realized as you abide in Him--only abiding in Jesus gives rest in Him. Or if it was the hope of an inheritance in glory, and an everlasting home in the presence of the Infinite One: the true preparation for this,as well as its blessed foretaste in this life, are granted only to those who abide in Him. In very truth, there is nothing that moved you to come, that does not plead with thousandfold greater force: "Abide in Him." You did well to come; you do better to abide. Who would, after seeking the King's palace, be content to stand in the door, when he is invited in to dwell in the King's presence, and share with Him in all the glory of His royal life? Oh, let us enter in and abide, and enjoy to the full all the rich supply His wondrous love hath prepared for us!

And yet I fear that there are many who have indeed come to Jesus, and who yet have mournfully to confess that they know but little of this blessed abiding in Him. With some the reason is, that they never fully understood that this was the meaning of the Saviour's call. With others, that though they heard the word, they did not know that such a life of abiding fellowship was possible, and indeed within their reach. Others will say that, though they did believe that such a life was possible, and seek after it, they have never yet succeeded discovering the secret of its attainment. And others, again, alas! will confess that it is their own unfaithfulness that has kept them from the enjoyment of the blessing. When the Saviour would have kept them, they were not found ready to stay; they were not prepared to give up everything, and always, only, wholly to abide in Jesus.

To all such I come now in the name of Jesus, their Redeemer and mine, with the blessed message: "Abide in me." In His name I invite them to come, and for a season meditate with me daily on its meaning, its lessons, its claims, and its promises. I know how many, and, to the young believer, how difficult, the questions are which suggest themselves in connection with it. There is especially the question, with its various aspects, to the possibility, in the midst of wearying work and continual distraction, of keeping up, or rather being kept in, the abiding communion. I do not undertake to remove all difficulties; this Jesus Christ Himself alone must do by His Holy Spirit. But what I would fain by the grace of God be permitted to do is, to repeat day by day the Master's blessed command, "Abide in me," until it enter the heart and find a place there, no more to be forgotten or neglected. I would fain that in the light of Holy Scripture we should Meditate on its meaning, until the understanding, that gate to the heart, opens to apprehend something of what it offers and expects. So we shall discover the means of its attainment, and learn to know what keeps us from it, and what can help us to it. So we shall feel its claims, and be compelled to acknowledge that there can be no true allegiance to our King without simply and heartily accepting this one, too, of His commands. So we shall gaze on its blessedness, until desire be inflamed, and the will with all its energies be roused to claim and possess the unspeakable blessing.

Come, my brethren, and let us day by day set ourselves at His feet, and meditate on this word of His, with an eye fixed on Him alone. Let us set ourselves in quiet trust before Him, waiting to hear His holy voice-- the still small voice that is mightier than the storm that rends the rocks- -breathing its quickening spirit within us, as He speaks: "Abide in me." The soul that truly hears Jesus Himself speak the word, receives with the word the power to accept and to hold the blessing He offers.

And it may please Thee, blessed Saviour, indeed, to speak to us; let each of us hear Thy blessed voice. May the feeling of our deep need, and the faith of Thy wondrous love, combined with the sight of the wonderfully blessed life Thou art waiting to bestow upon us, constrain us to listen and to obey, as often as Thou speakest: "Abide in me." Let day by day the answer from our heart be clearer and fuller: "Blessed Saviour, I do abide in Thee. "

Chapter 2: AND YOU SHALL FIND REST TO YOUR SOULS

"Come unto me, and I will give you rest. Take my yoke upon you, and learn of me; and ye shall find rest to your souls -MATT.11:28-29

REST for the soul: Such was the first promise with which the Saviour sought to win the heavy-laden sinner. Simple though it appears, the promise is indeed as large and comprehensive as can be found. Rest for the soul--does it not imply deliverance from every fear, the supply of every want, the fulfilment of every desire? And now nothing less than this is the prize with which the Saviour woos back the wandering one-- who is mourning that the rest has not been so abiding or so full as it had hoped--to come back and abide in Him. Nothing but this was the reason that the rest has either not been found, or, if found, has been disturbed or lost again: you did not abide with, you did not abide in Him.

Have you ever noticed how, in the original invitation of the Saviour to come to Him, the promise of rest was repeated twice, with such a variation in the conditions as might have suggested that abiding rest could only be found in abiding nearness. First the Saviour says, "Come unto me, and I will give you rest"; the very moment you come, and believe, I will give you rest--the rest of pardon and acceptance--the rest in my love. But we know that all that God bestows needs time to become fully our own; it must be held fast, and appropriated, and assimilated into our inmost being; without this not even Christ's giving can make it our very own, in full experience and enjoyment. And so the Saviour repeats His promise, in words which clearly speak not so much of the initial rest with which He welcomes the weary one who comes, but of the deeper and personally appropriated rest of the soul that abides with Him. He now not only says, "Come unto me," but "Take my yoke upon you and learn of me"; become my scholars, yield ourselves to my training, submit in all things to my will, let your whole life be one with mine--in other words, Abide in me. And then He adds, not only, "I will give," but "ye shall find rest to your souls." The rest He gave at coming will become something you have really found and made your very own--the deeper the abiding rest which comes from longer acquaintance and closer fellowship, from entire surrender and deeper sympathy. "Take my yoke, and learn of me," "Abide in me"-- this is the path to abiding rest.

Do not these words of the Saviour discover what you have perhaps often sought in vain to know, how it is that the rest you at times enjoy is so often lost. It must have been this: you had not understood how entire surrender to Jesus is the secret of perfect rest. Giving up one's whole life to Him, for Him alone to rule and order it; taking up His yoke, and submitting to be led and taught, to learn of Him; abiding in

Him, to be and do only what He wills--these are the conditions of discipleship without which there can be no thought of maintaining the rest that was bestowed on first coming to Christ. The rest is in Christ, and not something He gives apart from Himself, and so it is only in having Him that the rest can really be kept and enjoyed.

It is because so many a young believer fails to lay hold of this truth that the rest so speedily passes away. With some it is that they really did not know; they were never taught how Jesus claims the undivided allegiance of the whole heart and life; how there is not a spot in the whole of life over which He does not wish to reign; how in the very least things His disciples must only seek to please Him. They did not know how entire the consecration was that Jesus claimed. With others, who had some idea of what a very holy life a Christian ought to lead, the mistake was a different one: they could not believe such a life to be a possible attainment. Taking, and bearing, and never for a moment laying aside the yoke of Jesus, appeared to them to require such a strain of effort, and such an amount of goodness, as to be altogether beyond their reach. The very idea of always, all the day, abiding in Jesus, was too high--something they might attain to after a life of holiness and growth, but certainly not what a feeble beginner was to start with. They did not know how, when Jesus said, "My yoke is easy," He spoke the truth; how just the yoke gives the rest, because the moment the soul yields itself to obey, the Lord Himself gives the strength and joy to do it. They did not notice how, when He said, "Learn of me," He added, "I am meek and lowly in heart," to assure them that His gentleness would meet their every need, and bear them as a mother bears her feeble child. Oh, they did not know that when He said, "Abide in me," He only asked the surrender to Himself, His almighty love would hold them fast, and keep and bless them. And so, as some had erred from the want of full consecration, so these failed because they did not fully trust. These two, consecration and faith, are the essential elements of the Christian life--the giving up all to Jesus, the receiving all from Jesus. They are implied in each other; they are united in the one word-- surrender. A full surrender is to obey as well as to trust, to trust as well as to obey.

With such misunderstanding at the outset, it is no wonder that the disciple life was not one of such joy or strength as had been hoped. In some things you were led into sin without knowing it, because you had not learned how wholly Jesus wanted to rule you, and how you could not keep right for a moment unless you had Him very near you. In other things you knew what sin was, but had not the power to conquer, because you did not know or believe how entirely Jesus would take charge of you to keep and to help you. Either way, it was not long before the bright joy of your first love was lost, and your path, instead of being like the path of the just, shining more and more unto the perfect day, became like Israel's wandering in the desert--ever on the way, never very far, and yet always coming short of the promised rest. Weary soul, since so many years driven to and fro like the panting hart, O come and learn this day the lesson that there is a spot where safety and victory, where peace and rest, are always sure, and that that spot is always open to thee--the heart of Jesus.

But, alas! I hear someone say, it is just this abiding in Jesus, always bearing His yoke, to learn of Him, that is so difficult, and the very effort to attain to this often disturbs the rest even more than sin or the world. What a mistake to speak thus, and yet how often the words are heard! Does it weary the traveller to rest in the house or on the bed where he seeks repose from his fatigue? Or is it a labour to a little child to rest in its mother's arms? Is it not the house that keeps the traveller within its shelter? do not the arms of the mother sustain and keep the little one? And so it is with Jesus. The soul has but to yield itself to Him, to be still and rest in the confidence that His love has undertaken, and that His faithfulness will perform, the work of keeping it safe in the shelter of His bosom. Oh, it is because the blessing is so great that our little hearts cannot rise to apprehend it; it is as if we cannot believe that Christ, the Almighty One, will in very deed teach and keep us all the day. And yet this is just what He has promised, for without this He cannot really give us rest. It is as our heart takes in this truth that, when He says, "Abide in me," "Learn of me," He really means it, and that it is His own work to keep us abiding when we yield ourselves to Him, that we shall venture to cast ourselves into the arms of His love, and abandon ourselves to His blessed keeping. It is not the yoke, but resistance to the yoke, that makes the difficulty; the whole-hearted surrender to Jesus, as at once our Master and our Keeper, finds and secures the rest.

Come, my brother, and let us this very day commence to accept the word of Jesus in all simplicity. It is a distinct command this: "Take my yoke, and learn of me, " "Abide in me. " A command has to be obeyed. The obedient scholar asks no questions about possibilities or results; he accepts every order in the confidence that his teacher has provided for all that is needed. The power and the perseverance to abide in the rest, and the blessing in abiding--it belongs to the Saviour to see to this; 'tis mine to obey, 'tis His to provide. Let us this day in immediate obedience accept the command, and answer boldly, "Saviour, I abide in Thee. At Thy bidding I take Thy yoke; I undertake the duty without delay; I abide in Thee." Let each consciousness of failure only give new urgency to the command, and teach us to listen more earnestly than ever till the Spirit again give us to hear the voice of Jesus saying, with a love and authority that inspire both hope and obedience, "Child, abide in me." That word, listened to as coming from Himself, will be an end of all doubting--a divine promise of what shall surely be granted. And with ever-increasing simplicity its meaning will be interpreted. Abiding in Jesus is nothing but the giving up of oneself to be ruled and taught and led, and so resting in the arms of Everlasting Love.

Blessed rest! the fruit and the foretaste and the fellowship of God's own rest! found of them who thus come to Jesus to abide in Him. It is the peace of God, the great calm of the eternal world, that passeth all understanding, and that keeps the heart and mind. With this grace secured, we have strength for every duty, courage for every struggle, a blessing in every cross, and the joy of life eternal in death itself.

O my Saviour! if ever my heart should doubt or fear again, as if the blessing were too great to expect, or too high to attain, let me hear Thy voice to quicken my faith and obedience: "Abide in me"; "Take my yoke upon you, and learn of me; ye shall find rest to your souls."

Chapter 3: TRUSTING HIM TO KEEP YOU

"I follow after, if that I may apprehend that for which I also am apprehended of Christ Jesus."--PHIL.3:12

MORE than one admits that it is a sacred duty and a blessed privilege to abide in Christ, but shrinks back continually before the question: Is it possible, a life of unbroken fellowship with the Saviour? Eminent Christians, to whom special opportunities of cultivating this grace have been granted, may attain to it; for the large majority of disciples, whose life, by a divine appointment, is so fully occupied with the affairs of this life, it can scarce be expected. The more they hear of this life, the deeper their sense of its glory and blessedness, and there is nothing they would not sacrifice to be made partakers of it. But they are too weak, too unfaithful--they never can attain to it.

Dear souls! how little they know that the abiding in Christ is just meant for the weak, and so beautifully suited to their feebleness. It is not the doing of some great thing, and does not demand that we first lead a very holy and devoted life. No, it is simply weakness entrusting itself to a Mighty One to be kept--the unfaithful one casting self on One who is altogether trustworthy and true. Abiding in Him is not a work that we have to do as the condition for enjoying His salvation, but a consenting to let Him do all for us, and in us, and through us. It is a work He does for us--the fruit and the power of His redeeming love. Our part is simply to yield, to trust, and to wait for what He has engaged to perform.

It is this quiet expectation and confidence, resting on the word of Christ that in Him there is an abiding place prepared, which is so sadly wanting among Christians. They scarce take the time or the trouble to realize that when He says "Abide IN ME," He offers Himself, the Keeper of Israel that slumbers not nor sleeps, with all His power and love, as the living home of the soul, where the mighty influences of His grace will be stronger to keep than all their feebleness to lead astray. The idea they have of grace is this--that their conversion and pardon are God's work, but that now, in gratitude to God, it is their work to live as Christians, and follow Jesus. There is always the thought of a work that has to be done, and even though they pray for help, still the work is theirs. They fail continually, and become hopeless; and the despondency only increases the helplessness. No, wandering one; as it was Jesus who drew you when He spake "Come," so it is Jesus who keeps you when He says "Abide." The grace to come and the grace to abide are alike from Him alone. That word Come, heard, meditated on, accepted, was the cord of love that drew you nigh; that word Abide is even so the band with which He holds you fast and binds you to Himself. Let the soul but take time to listen to the voice of Jesus. "In me," He says, "is thy place--in my almighty arms. It is I who love thee so, who speak Abide in me; surely thou canst trust me." The voice of Jesus entering and dwelling in the soul cannot but call for the response: "Yes, Saviour, in Thee I can, I will abide."

Abide in me: These words are no law of Moses, demanding from the sinful what they cannot perform. They are the command of love, which is ever only a promise in a different shape. Think of this until all feeling of burden and fear and despair pass away, and the first thought that comes as you hear of abiding in Jesus be one of bright and joyous hope: it is for me, I know I shall enjoy it. You are not under the law, with its inexorable Do, but under grace, with its blessed Believe what Christ will do for you. And if the question be asked, "But surely there is something for us to do?" the answer is, "Our doing and working are but the fruit of Christ's work in us." It is when the soul becomes utterly passive, looking and resting on what Christ is to do, that its energies are stirred to their highest activity, and that we work most effectually because we know that He works in us. It is as we see in that word IN ME the mighty energies of love reaching out after us to have us and to hold us, that all the strength of our will is roused to abide in Him.

This connection between Christ's work and our work is beautifully expressed in the words of Paul: "I follow after, if that I may apprehend that whereunto I also am apprehended of Christ Jesus." It was because he knew that the mighty and the faithful One had grasped him with the glorious purpose of making him one with Himself, that he did his utmost to grasp the glorious prize. The faith, the experience, the full assurance, "Christ hath apprehended me," gave him the courage and the strength to press on and apprehend that whereunto he was apprehended. Each new insight of the great end for which Christ had apprehended and was holding him, roused him afresh to aim at nothing less.

Paul's expression, and its application to the Christian life, can be best understood if we think of a father helping his child to mount the side of some steep precipice. The father stands above, and has taken the son by the hand to help him on. He points him to the spot on which he will help him to plant his feet, as he leaps upward. The leap would be too high and dangerous for the child alone; but the father's hand is his trust, and he leaps to get hold of the point for which his father has taken hold of him. It is the father's strength that secures him and lifts him up, and so urges him to use his utmost strength.

Such is the relation between Christ and you, O weak and trembling believer! Fix first your eyes on the whereunto for which He has apprehended you. It is nothing less than a life of abiding, unbroken fellowship with Himself to which He is seeking to lift you up. All that you have already received--pardon and peace, the Spirit and His grace--

are but preliminary to this. And all that you see promised to you in the future--holiness and fruitfulness and glory everlasting--are but its natural outcome. Union with Himself, and so with the Father, is His highest object. Fix your eye on this, and gaze until it stand out before you clear and unmistakeable: Christ's aim is to have me abiding in Him.

And then let the second thought enter your heart: Unto this I am apprehended of Christ. His almighty power hath laid hold on me, and offers now to lift me up to where He would have me. Fix your eyes on Christ. Gaze on the love that beams in those eyes, and that asks whether you cannot trust Him, who sought and found and brought you nigh, now to keep you. Gaze on that arm of power, and say whether you have reason to be assured that He is indeed able to keep you abiding in Him.

And as you think of the spot whither He points--the blessed whereunto for which He apprehended you--and keep your gaze fixed on Himself, holding you and waiting to lift you up, O say, could you not this very day take the upward step, and rise to enter upon this blessed life of abiding in Christ? Yes, begin at once, and say, "O my Jesus, if Thou biddest me, and if Thou engagest to lift and keep me there, I will venture. Trembling, but trusting, I will say: Jesus, I do abide in Thee. " My beloved fellow-believer, go, and take time alone with Jesus, and say this to Him. I dare not speak to you about abiding in Him for the mere sake of calling forth a pleasing religious sentiment. God's truth must at once be acted on. O yield yourself this very day to the blessed Saviour in the surrender of the one thing He asks of you: give up yourself to abide in Him. He Himself will work it in you. You can trust Him to keep you trusting and abiding.

And if ever doubts again arise, or the bitter experience of failure tempt you to despair, just remember where Paul found His strength: "I am apprehended of Jesus Christ." In that assurance you have a fountain of strength. From that you can look up to the whereunto on which He has set His heart, and set yours there too. From that you gather confidence that the good work He hath begun He will also perform. And in that confidence you will gather courage, day by day, afresh to say, " `I follow on, that I may also apprehend that for which I am apprehended of Christ Jesus.' It is because Jesus has taken hold of me, and because Jesus keeps me, that I dare to say: Saviour, I abide in Thee. "

Chapter 4: AS THE BRANCH IN THE VINE

"I am the vine, ye are the branches."-JOHN 15:5

IT WAS in connection with the parable of the Vine that our Lord first used the expression, "Abide in me." That parable, so simple, and yet so rich in its teaching, gives us the best and most complete illustration of the meaning of our Lord's command, and the union to which He invites us.

The parable teaches us the nature of that union. The connection between the vine and the branch is a living one. No external, temporary union will suffice; no work of man can effect it: the branch, whether an original or an engrafted one, is such only by the Creator's own work, in virtue of which the life, the sap, the fatness, and the fruitfulness of the vine communicate themselves to the branch. And just so it is with the believer too. His union with his Lord is no work of human wisdom or human will, but an act of God, by which the closest and most complete life-union is effected between the Son of God and the sinner. "God hath sent forth the Spirit of His Son into your hearts." The same Spirit which dwelt and still dwells in the Son, becomes the life of the believer; in the unity of that one Spirit, and the fellowship of the same life which is in Christ, he is one with Him. As between the vine and branch, it is a life-union that makes them one.

The parable teaches us the completeness of the union. So close is the union between the vine and the branch, that each is nothing without the other, that each is wholly and only for the other.

Without the vine the branch can do nothing. To the vine it owes its right of place in the vineyard, its life and its fruitfulness. And so the Lord says, "Without me ye can do nothing." The believer can each day be pleasing to God only in that which he does through the power of Christ dwelling in him. The daily inflowing of the life-sap of the Holy Spirit is his only power to bring forth fruit. He lives alone in Him and is for each moment dependent on Him alone.

Without the branch the vine can also do nothing. A vine without branches can bear no fruit. No less indispensable than the vine to the branch, is the branch to the vine. Such is the wonderful condescension of the grace of Jesus, that just as His people are dependent on Him, He has made Himself dependent on them. Without His disciples He cannot dispense His blessing to the world; He cannot offer sinners the grapes of the heavenly Canaan. Marvel not! It is His own appointment; and this is the high honour to which He has called His redeemed ones, that as indispensable as He is to them in heaven, that from Him their fruit may be found, so indispensable are they to Him on earth, that through them His fruit may be found. Believers, meditate on this, until your soul bows to worship in presence of the mystery of the perfect union between Christ and the believer.

There is more: as neither vine nor branch is anything without the other, so is neither anything except for the other.

All the vine possesses belongs to the branches. The vine does not gather from the soil its fatness and its sweetness for itself--all it has is at the disposal of the branches. As it is the parent, so it is the servant of the branches. And Jesus, to whom we owe our life, how completely does He give Himself for us and to us: "The glory Thou gavest me, I have given them"; "He that believeth in me, the works that I do shall he do also; and greater works shall he do." All His fullness and all His riches are for thee, O believer; for the vine does not live for itself, keeps nothing for itself, but exists only for the branches. All that Jesus is in heaven, He is for us: He has no interest there separate from ours; as our representative He stands before the Father.

And all the branch possesses belongs to the vine. The branch does not exist for itself, but to bear fruit that can proclaim the excellence of the vine: it has no reason of existence except to be of service to the vine. Glorious image of the calling of the believer, and the entireness of his consecration to the service of his Lord. As Jesus gives Himself so wholly over to him, he feels himself urged to be wholly his Lord's. Every power of his being, every moment of his life, every thought and feeling, belong to Jesus, that from Him and for Him he may bring forth fruit. As he realizes what the vine is to the branch, and what the branch is meant to be to the vine, he feels that he has but one thing to think of and to live for, and that is, the will, the glory, the work, the kingdom of his blessed Lord--the bringing forth of fruit to the glory of His name.

The parable teaches us the object of the union. The branches are for fruit and fruit alone. "Every branch that beareth not fruit He taketh away." The branch needs leaves for the maintenance of its own life, and the perfection of its fruit: the fruit itself it bears to give away to those around. As the believer enters into his calling as a branch, he sees that he has to forget himself, and to live entirely for his fellowmen. To love them, to seek for them, and to save them, Jesus came: for this every branch on the Vine has to live as much as the Vine itself. It is for fruit, much fruit, that the Father has made us one with Jesus.

Wondrous parable of the Vine-unveiling the mysteries of the Divine love, of the heavenly life, of the world of Spirit--how little have I understood thee! Jesus the living Vine in heaven, and I the living branch on earth! How little have I understood how great my need, but also how perfect my claim, to all His fullness! How little understood, how great His need, but also how perfect His claim, to my emptiness! Let me, in its beautiful light, study the wondrous union between Jesus and His people, until it becomes to me the guide into full communion with my beloved Lord. Let me listen and believe, until my whole being cries out, "Jesus is indeed to me the True Vine, bearing me, nourishing me, supplying me, using me, and filling me to the full to make me bring forth fruit abundantly." Then shall I not fear to say, "I am indeed a branch to Jesus, the True Vine, abiding in Him, resting on Him, waiting for Him, serving Him, and living only that through me, too, He may show forth the riches of His grace, and give His fruit to a perishing world."

It is when we try thus to understand the meaning of the parable, that the blessed command spoken in connection with it will come home to us in its true power. The thought of what the vine is to the branch, and Jesus to the believer, will give new force to the words, "Abide in me!" It will be as if He says, "Think, soul, how completely I belong to thee. I have joined myself inseparably to thee; all the fulness and fatness of the Vine are thine in very deed. Now thou once art in me, be assured that all I have is wholly thine. It is my interest and my honour to have thee a fruitful branch; only Abide in me. Thou art weak, but I am strong; thou art poor, but I am rich. Only abide in me; yield thyself wholly to my teaching and rule; simply trust my love, my grace, my promises. Only believe; I am wholly thine; I am the Vine, thou art the branch. Abide in me."

What sayest thou, 0 my soul? Shall I longer hesitate, or withhold consent? Or shall I not, instead of only thinking how hard and how difficult it is to live like a branch of the True Vine, because I thought of it as something I had to accomplish--shall I not now begin to look upon it as the most blessed and joyful thing under heaven? Shall I not believe that, now I once am in Him, He Himself will keep me and enable me to abide? On my part, abiding is nothing but the acceptance of my position, the consent to be kept there, the surrender of faith to the strong Vine still to hold the feeble branch. Yes, I will, I do abide in Thee, blessed Lord Jesus.

O Saviour, how unspeakable is Thy love! "Such knowledge is too wonderful for me: it is high, I cannot attain unto it." I can only yield myself to Thy love with the prayer that, day by day, Thou wouldest unfold to me somewhat of its precious mysteries, and so encourage and strengthen Thy loving disciple to do what his heart longs to do indeed-- ever, only, wholly to abide in Thee.

Chapter 5: AS YOU CAME TO HIM, BY FAITH

"As ye have received Christ Jesus the Lord, so walk ye in Him: rooted and built up in Him, and stablished in the faith, abounding therein. "COL.2:6-7

IN THESE words the apostle teaches us the weighty lesson, that it is not only by faith that we first come to Christ and are united to Him, but that it is by faith that we are to be rooted and established in our union with Christ. Not less essential than for the commencement, is faith for the progress of the spiritual life. Abiding in Jesus can only be by faith. There are earnest Christians who do not understand this; or, if they admit it in theory, they fail to realize its application in practice. They are very zealous for a free gospel, with our first acceptance of Christ, and justification by faith alone. But after this they think everything depends on our diligence and faithfulness. While they firmly grasp the truth, "The sinner shall be justified by faith," they have hardly found a place in their scheme for the larger truth, "The just shall live by faith." They have never understood what a perfect Saviour Jesus is, and how He will each day do for the sinner just as much as He did the first day when he came to Him. They know not that the life of grace is always and only a life of faith, and that in the relationship to Jesus the one daily and unceasing duty of the disciple is to believe, because believing is the one channel through which divine grace and strength flow out into the heart of man. The old nature of the believer remains evil and sinful to the last; it is only as he daily comes, all empty and helpless, to his Saviour to receive of His life and strength, that he can bring forth the fruits of righteousness to the glory of God. Therefore it is: "As ye have received Christ Jesus the Lord, so walk ye in Him: rooted in Him, and stablished in the faith, abounding therein." As you came to Jesus, so abide in Him, by faith.

And if you would know how faith is to be exercised in thus abiding in Jesus, to be rooted more deeply and firmly in Him, you have only to look back to the time when first you received Him. You remember well what obstacles at that time there appeared to be in the way of your believing. There was first your vileness and guilt: it appeared impossible that the promise of pardon and love could be for such a sinner. Then there was the sense of weakness and death: you felt not the power for the surrender and the trust to which you were called. And then there was the future: you dared not undertake to be a disciple of Jesus while you felt so sure that you could not remain standing, but would speedily again be unfaithful and fall. These difficulties were like mountains in your way. And how were they removed? Simply by the word of God. That word, as it were, compelled you to believe that, notwithstanding guilt in the past, and weakness in the present, and unfaithfulness in the future, the promise was sure that Jesus would accept and save you. On that word you ventured to come, and were not deceived: you found that Jesus did indeed accept and save.

Apply this, your experience in coming to Jesus, to the abiding in Him. Now, as then, the temptations to keep you from believing are many. When you think of your sins since you became a disciple, your heart is cast down with shame, and it looks as if it were too much to expect that Jesus should indeed receive you into perfect intimacy and the full enjoyment of His holy love. When you think how utterly, in times past, you have failed in keeping the most sacred vows, the consciousness of present weakness makes you tremble at the very idea of answering the Saviour's command with the promise, "Lord, from henceforth I will abide in Thee. " And when you set before yourself the life of love and joy, of holiness and fruitfulness, which in the future are to flow from abiding in Him, it is as if it only serves to make you still more hopeless: you, at least, can never attain to it. You know yourself too well. It is no use expecting it, only to be disappointed; a life fully and wholly abiding in Jesus is not for you.

Oh that you would learn a lesson from the time of your first coming to the Saviour! Remember, dear soul, how you then were led, contrary to all that your experience, and your feelings, and even your sober judgment said, to take Jesus at His word, and how you were not disappointed. He did receive you, and pardon you; He did love you, and save you--you know it. And if He did this for you when you were an enemy and a stranger, what think you, now that you are His own, will He not much more fulfil His promise? Oh that you would come and begin simply to listen to His word, and to ask only the one question: Does He really mean that I should abide in Him? The answer His word gives is so simple and so sure: By His almighty grace you now are in Him; that same almighty grace will indeed enable you to abide in Him. By faith you became partakers of the initial grace; by that same faith you can enjoy the continuous grace of abiding in Him. And if you ask what exactly it is that you now have to believe that you may abide in Him, the answer is not difficult. Believe first of all what He says: "I am the Vine." The safety and the fruitfulness of the branch depend upon the strength of the vine. Think not so much of yourself as a branch, nor of the abiding as your duty, until you have first had your soul filled with the faith of what Christ as the Vine is. He really will be to you all that a vine can be--holding you fast, nourishing you, and making Himself every moment responsible for your growth and your fruit. Take time to know, set yourself heartily to believe: My Vine, on whom I can depend for all I need, is Christ. A large, strong vine bears the feeble branch, and holds it more than the branch holds the vine.

Ask the Father by the Holy Ghost to reveal to you what a glorious, loving, mighty Christ this is, in whom you have your place and your life; it is the faith in what Christ is, more than anything else, that will keep you abiding in Him. A soul filled with large thoughts of the Vine will be a strong branch, and will abide confidently in Him. Be much occupied with Jesus, and believe much in Him, as the True Vine.

And then, when Faith can well say, "He is my Vine," let it further say, "I am His branch, I am in Him." I speak to those who say they are Christ's disciples, and on them I cannot too earnestly press the importance of exercising their faith in saying, "I am in Him." It makes the abiding so simple. If I realize clearly as I meditate: Now I am in Him, I see at once that there is nothing wanting but just my consent to be what He has made me, to remain where He has placed me. I am in Christ: This simple thought, carefully, prayerfully, believingly uttered, removes all difficulty as if there were some great attainment to be reached. No, I am in Christ, my blessed Saviour. His love has prepared a home for me with Himself, when He says, "Abide in my love"; and His power has undertaken to keep the door, and to keep me in, if I will but consent. I am in Christ: I have now but to say, "Saviour, I bless Thee for this wondrous grace. I consent; I yield myself to Thy gracious keeping; I do abide in Thee."

It is astonishing how such a faith will work out all that is further implied in abiding in Christ. There is in the Christian life great need of watchfulness and of prayer, of self-denial and of striving, of obedience and of diligence. But "all things are possible to him that believeth." "This is the victory that overcometh, even our faith." It is the faith that continually closes its eyes to the weakness of the creature, and finds its joy in the sufficiency of an Almighty Saviour, that makes the soul strong and glad. It gives itself up to be led by the Holy Spirit into an ever deeper appreciation of that wonderful Saviour whom God hath given us--the Infinite Immanuel. It follows the leading of the Spirit from page to page of the blessed Word, with the one desire to take each revelation of what Jesus is and what He promises as its nourishment and its life. In accordance with the promise, "If that which ye have heard from the beginning abide in you, ye shall also abide in the Father and the Son," it lives by every word that proceedeth out of the mouth of God. And so it makes the soul strong with the strength of God, to be and to do all that is needed for abiding in Christ.

Believer, you would abide in Christ: only believe. Believe always; believe now. Bow even now before your Lord, and say to Him in childlike faith, that because He is your Vine, and you are His branch, you will this day abide in Him.

NOTE

" `I am the True Vine.' He who offers us the privilege of an actual union with Himself is the great I AM, the almighty God, who upholds all things by the word of His power. And this almighty God reveals Himself as our perfect Saviour, even to the unimaginable extent of seeking to renew our fallen natures by grafting them into His own Divine nature.

"To realize the glorious Deity of Him whose call sounds forth to longing hearts with such exceeding sweetness, is no small step towards gaining the full privilege to which we are invited. But longing is by itself of no use; still less can there be any profit in reading of the blessed results to be gained from a close and personal union with our Lord, if we believe that union to be practically beyond our reach. His words are meant to be a living, an eternal, precious reality. And this they can never become unless we are sure that we may reasonably expect their accomplishment. But what could make the accomplishment of such an idea possible--what could make it reasonable to suppose that we poor, weak, selfish creatures, full of sin and full of failures, might be saved out of the corruption of our nature and made partakers of the holiness of our Lord--except the fact, the marvellous, unalterable fact, that He who proposes to us so great a transformation is Himself the everlasting God, as able as He is willing to fulfil His own word. In meditating, therefore, upon these utterances of Christ, containing as they do the very essence of His teaching, the very concentration of His love, let us, at the outset, put away all tendency to doubt. Let us not allow ourselves so much as to question whether such erring disciples as we are can be enabled to attain the holiness to which we are called through a close and intimate union with our Lord. If there be any impossibility, any falling short of the proposed blessedness, it will arise from the lack of earnest desire on our part. There is no lack in any respect on His part who puts forth the invitation; with GOD there can be no shortcoming in the fulfilment of His promise."--The Life of Fellowship; Meditations on John 15:1,11 by A. M. James.

It is perhaps necessary to say, for the sake of young or doubting Christians, that there is something more necessary than the effort to exercise faith in each separate promise that is brought under our notice. What is of even greater importance is the cultivation of a trustful disposition towards God, the habit of always thinking of Him, of His ways and His works, with bright confiding hopefulness. In such soil alone can the individual promises strike root and grow up. In a little work published by the Tract Society, Encouragements to Faith, by James Kimball, there will be found many most suggestive and helpful thoughts, all pleading for the right God has to claim that He shall be trusted. The Christian's Secret of a Happy Life is another little work that has been a great help to many. Its bright and buoyant tone, its loving and unceasing repetition of the keynote--we may indeed depend on Jesus to do all He has said, and more than we can think --has breathed hope and joy into many a heart that was almost ready to despair of ever getting on. In Frances Havergal's Kept for the Master's Use, there is the same healthful, hope-inspiring tone.

Chapter 6: GOD HIMSELF HAS UNITED YOU TO HIM

"OF GOD ARE YE IN CHRIST JESUS, who was made unto us
wisdom from God, both righteousness and sanctification, and
redemption."--I COR.1:30 (R.V. marg.).
"My Father is the husbandman."--JOHN 15:1
"Ye ARE in Christ Jesus." The believers at Corinth were still feeble
and carnal, only babes in Christ. And yet Paul wants them, at the outset
of his teaching, to know distinctly that they are in Christ Jesus. The
whole Christian life depends on the clear consciousness of our position
in Christ. Most essential to the abiding in Christ is the daily renewal of
our faith's assurance, "I am in Christ Jesus." All fruitful preaching to
believers must take this as its startingpoint: "Ye are in Christ Jesus."
But the apostle has an additional thought, of almost greater importance:
"OF GOD are ye in Christ Jesus." He would have us not only
remember our union to Christ, but specially that it is not our own
doing, but the work of God Himself. As the Holy Spirit teaches us to
realize this, we shall see what a source of assurance and strength it
must become to us. If it is of God alone that I am in Christ, then God
Himself, the Infinite One, becomes my security for all I can need or
wish in seeking to abide in Christ.
Let me try to understand what it means, this wonderful "OF GOD in
Christ." In becoming partakers of the union with Christ, there is a work
God does and a work we have to do. God does His work by moving us
to do our work. The work of God is hidden and silent; what we do is
something distinct and tangible. Conversion and faith, prayer and
obedience, are conscious acts of which we can give a clear account;
while the spiritual quickening and strengthening that come from above
are secret and beyond the reach of human sight. And so it comes that
when the believer tries to say, "I am in Christ Jesus," he looks more to
the work he did, than to that wondrous secret work of God by which he
was united to Christ. Nor can it well be otherwise at the
commencement of the Christian course. "I know that I have believed,"
is a valid testimony. But it is of great consequence that the mind should
be led to see that at the back of our turning, and believing, and
accepting of Christ, there was God's almighty power doing its work--
inspiring our will, taking possession of us, and carrying out its own
purpose of love in planting us into Christ Jesus. As the believer enters
into this, the divine side of the work of salvation, he will learn to praise
and to worship with new exultation, and to rejoice more than ever in
the divineness of that salvation he has been made partaker of. At each
step he reviews, the song will come, "This is the Lord's doing"--Divine
Omnipotence working out what Eternal Love had devised. "OF GOD I

am in Christ Jesus."

The words will lead him even further and higher, even to the depths of eternity. "Whom He hath predestinated, them He also called." The calling in time is the manifestation of the purpose in eternity. Ere the world was, God had fixed the eye of His sovereign love on you in the election of grace, and chosen you in Christ. That you know yourself to be in Christ, is the stepping-stone by which you rise to understand in its full meaning the word, "OF GOD I am in Christ Jesus." With the prophet, your language will be, "The Lord hath appeared of old unto me: yea, I have loved thee with an everlasting love, therefore with loving-kindness have I drawn thee." And you will recognise your own salvation as a part of that "mystery of His will, according to the good pleasure of His will which He purposed in Himself," and join with the whole body of believers in Christ as these say, "In whom we also have obtained an inheritance, being predestinated according to the purpose of Him who worketh all things after the counsel of His own will." Nothing will more exalt free grace, and make man bow very low before it, than this knowledge of the mystery "OF GOD in Christ."

It is easy to see what a mighty influence it must exert on the believer who seeks to abide in Christ. What a sure standing-ground it gives him, as he rests his right to Christ and all His fulness on nothing less than the Father's own purpose and work! We have thought of Christ as the Vine, and the believer as the branch; let us not forget that other precious word, "My Father is the husbandman." The Saviour said, "Every plant which my heavenly Father hath not planted, shall be rooted up"; but every branch grafted by Him in the True Vine, shall never be plucked out of His hand. As it was the Father to whom Christ owed all He was, and in whom He had all His strength and His life as the Vine, so to the Father the believer owes his place and his security in Christ. The same love and delight with which the Father watched over the beloved Son Himself, watch over every member of His body, every one who is in Christ Jesus.

What confident trust this faith inspires--not only as to the being kept in safety to the end, but specially as to the being able to fulfil in every point the object for which I have been united to Christ. The branch is as much in the charge and keeping of the husbandman as the vine; his honour as much concerned in the wellbeing and growth of the branch as of the vine. The God who chose Christ to be Vine fitted Him thoroughly for the work He had as Vine to perform. The God who has chosen me and planted me in Christ, has thereby engaged to secure, if I will but let Him, by yielding myself to Him, that I in every way be worthy of Jesus Christ. Oh that I did but fully realize this! What confidence and urgency it would give to my prayer to the God and

Father of Jesus Christ! How it would quicken the sense of dependence, and make me see that praying without ceasing is indeed the one need of my life--an unceasing waiting, moment by moment, on the God who has united me to Christ, to perfect His own divine work, to work in me both to will and to do of His good pleasure.

And what a motive this would be for the highest activity in the maintenance of a fruitful branch-life! Motives are mighty powers; it is of infinite importance to have them high and clear. Here surely is the highest: "You are God's workmanship, created in Christ Jesus unto good works": grafted by Him into Christ, unto the bringing forth of much fruit. Whatever God creates is exquisitely suited to its end. He created the sun to give light: how perfectly it does its work! He created the eye to see: how beautifully it fulfils its object! He created the new man unto good works: how admirably it is fitted for its purpose.

OF GOD I am in Christ: created anew, made a branch of the Vine, fitted for fruit-bearing. Would to God that believers would cease looking most at their old nature, and complaining of their weakness, as if God called them to what they were unfitted for! Would that they would believingly and joyfully accept the wondrous revelation of how God, in uniting them to Christ, has made Himself chargeable for their spiritual growth and fruitfulness! How all sickly hesitancy and sloth would disappear, and under the influence of this mighty motive--the faith in the faithfulness of Him of whom they are in Christ--their whole nature would rise to accept and fulfil their glorious destiny!

O my soul! yield yourself to the mighty influence of this word: "OF GOD ye are in Christ Jesus." It is the same GOD OF WHOM Christ is made all that He is for us, OF WHOM we also are in Christ, and will most surely be made what we must be to Him. Take time to meditate and to worship, until the light that comes from the throne of God has shone into you, and you have seen your union to Christ as indeed the work of His almighty Father. Take time, day after day, and let, in your whole religious life, with all it has of claims and duties, of needs and wishes, God be everything. See Jesus, as He speaks to you, "Abide in me," pointing upward and saying, "My FATHER IS THE HUSBANDMAN. Of Him you are in me, through Him you abide in me, and to Him and to His glory shall be the fruit you bear." And let your answer be, Amen, Lord! So be it. From eternity Christ and I were ordained for each other; inseparably we belong to each other: it is God's will; I shall abide in Christ. It is of God I am in Christ Jesus.

Chapter 7: AS YOUR WISDOM

"Of God are ye in Christ Jesus, who was made unto us WISDOM from God, both righteousness and sanctification, and redemption."--I COR. 1:30 (R.V. marg.).

JESUS CHRIST is not only Priest to purchase, and King to secure, but also Prophet to reveal to us the salvation which God hath prepared for them that love Him. Just as at the creation the light was first called into existence, that in it all God's other works might have their life and beauty, so in our text wisdom is mentioned first as the treasury in which are to be found the three precious gifts that follow. The life is the light of man; it is in revealing to us, and making us behold the glory of God in His own face, that Christ makes us partakers of eternal life. It was by the tree of knowledge that sin came; it is through the knowledge that Christ gives that salvation comes. He is made of God unto us wisdom. In Him are hid all the treasures of wisdom and knowledge.

And of God you are in Him, and have but to abide in Him, to be made partaker of these treasures of wisdom. In Him you are, and in Him the wisdom is; dwelling in Him, you dwell in the very fountain of all light; abiding in Him, you have Christ the wisdom of God leading your whole spiritual life, and ready to communicate, in the form of knowledge, just as much as is needful for you to know. Christ is made unto us wisdom: you are in Christ.

It is this connection between what Christ has been made of God to us, and how we have it only as also being in Him, that we must learn to understand better. We shall thus see that the blessings prepared for us in Christ cannot be obtained as special gifts in answer to prayer apart from the abiding in Him. The answer to each prayer must come in the closer union and the deeper abiding in Him; in Him, the unspeakable gift, all other gifts are treasured up, the gift of wisdom and knowledge too.

How often have you longed for wisdom and spiritual understanding that you might know God better, whom to know is life eternal! Abide in Jesus: your life in Him will lead you to that fellowship with God in which the only true knowledge of God is to be had. His love, His power, His infinite glory will, as you abide in Jesus, be so revealed as it hath not entered into the heart of man to conceive. You may not be able to grasp it with the understanding, or to express it in words; but the knowledge which is deeper than thoughts or words will be given--the knowing of God which comes of being known of Him. "We preach Christ crucified unto them which are called, Christ the power of God, and the wisdom of God."

Or you would fain count all things but loss for the excellency of the knowledge of Jesus Christ your Lord. Abide in Jesus, and be found in Him. You shall know Him in the power of His resurrection and the fellowship of His sufferings. Following Him, you shall not walk in darkness, but have the light of life. It is only when God shines into the heart, and Christ Jesus dwells there, that the light of the knowledge of God in the face of Christ can be seen.

Or would you understand his blessed work, as He wrought it on earth, or works it from heaven by His Spirit? Would you know how Christ can become our righteousness, and our sanctification, and redemption? It is just as bringing, and revealing, and communicating these that He is made unto us wisdom from God. There are a thousand questions that at times come up, and the attempt to answer them becomes a weariness and a burden. It is because you have forgotten you are in Christ, whom God has made to be your wisdom. Let it be your first care to abide in Him in undivided fervent devotion of heart; when the heart and the life are right, rooted in Christ, knowledge will come in such measure as Christ's own wisdom sees meet. And without such abiding in Christ the knowledge does not really profit, but is often most hurtful. The soul satisfies itself with thoughts which are but the forms and images of truth, without receiving the truth itself in its power. God's way is ever first to give us, even though it be but as a seed, the thing itself, the life and the power, and then the knowledge. Man seeks the knowledge first, and often, alas! never gets beyond it. God gives us Christ, and in Him hid the treasures of wisdom and knowledge. O let us be content to possess Christ, to dwell in Him, to make Him our life, and only in a deeper searching into Him, to search and find the knowledge we desire. Such knowledge is life indeed.

Therefore, believer, abide in Jesus as your wisdom, and expect from Him most confidently whatever teaching you may need for a life to the glory of the Father. In all that concerns your spiritual life, abide in Jesus as your wisdom. The life you have in Christ is a thing of infinite sacredness, far too high and holy for you to know how to act it out. It is He alone who can guide you, as by a secret spiritual instinct, to know what is becoming your dignity as a child of God, what will help and what will hinder your inner life, and specially your abiding in Him. Do not think of it as a mystery or a difficulty you must solve. Whatever questions come up as to the possibility of abiding perfectly and uninterruptedly in Him, and of really obtaining all the blessing that comes from it, always remember: He knows, all is perfectly clear to Him, and He is my wisdom. Just as much as you need to know and are capable of apprehending, will be communicated, if you only trust Him. Never think of the riches of wisdom and knowledge hid in Jesus as treasures without a key, or of your way as a path without a light. Jesus your wisdom is guiding you in the right way, even when you do not see it.

In all your intercourse with the blessed Word, remember the same truth: abide in Jesus, your wisdom. Study much to know the written Word; but study more to know the living Word, in whom you are of God. Jesus, the wisdom of God, is only known by a life of implicit confidence and obedience. The words He speaks are spirit and life to those who live in Him. Therefore, each time you read, or hear, or meditate upon the Word, be careful to take up your true position. Realize first your oneness with Him who is the wisdom of God; know yourself to be under His direct and special training; go to the Word abiding in Him, the very fountain of divine light--in His light you shall see light.

In all your daily life, its ways and its work, abide in Jesus as your wisdom. Your body and your daily life share in the great salvation: in Christ, the wisdom of God, provision has been made for their guidance too. Your body is His temple, your daily life the sphere for glorifying Him: it is to Him a matter of deep interest that all your earthly concerns should be guided aright. Only trust His sympathy, believe His love, and wait for His guidance--it will be given. Abiding in Him, the mind will be calmed and freed from passion, the judgment cleared and strengthened, the light of heaven will shine on earthly things, and your prayer for wisdom, like Solomon's, will be fulfilled above what you ask or think.

And so, especially in any work you do for God, abide in Jesus as your wisdom. "We are created in Christ Jesus unto good works, which God hath before ordained that we should walk in them"; let all fear or doubt lest we should not know exactly what these works are, be put far away. In Christ we are created for them: He will show us what they are, and how to do them. Cultivate the habit of rejoicing in the assurance that the divine wisdom is guiding you, even where you do not yet see the way.

All that you can wish to know is perfectly clear to Him. As Man, as Mediator, He has access to the counsels of Deity, to the secrets of Providence, in your interest, and on your behalf. If you will but trust Him fully, and abide in Him entirely, you can be confident of having unerring guidance.

Yes, abide in Jesus as your wisdom. Seek to maintain the spirit of waiting and dependence, that always seeks to learn, and will not move but as the heavenly light leads on. Withdraw yourself from all needless distraction, close your ears to the voices of the world, and be as a docile learner, ever listening for the heavenly wisdom the Master has to teach. Surrender all your own wisdom; seek a deep conviction of the utter blindness of the natural understanding in the things of God; and both as to what you have to believe and have to do, wait for Jesus to teach and to guide. Remember that the teaching and guidance come not from without: it is by His life in us that the divine wisdom does His work. Retire frequently with Him into the inner chamber of the heart, where the gentle voice of the Spirit is only heard if all be still. Hold fast with unshaken confidence, even in the midst of darkness and apparent desertion, His own assurance that He is the light and the leader of His own. And live, above all, day by day in the blessed truth that, as He Himself, the living Christ Jesus, is your wisdom, your first and last care must ever be this alone--to abide in Him. Abiding in Him, His wisdom will come to you as the spontaneous outflowing of a life rooted in Him. I am, I abide in Christ, who was made unto us wisdom from God; wisdom will be given me.

Chapter 8: AS YOUR RIGHTEOUSNESS

"Of God are ye in Christ Jesus, who was made unto us wisdom from God, both RIGHTEOUSNESS and sanctification, and redemption."-I Cor.1:30 (R.V. marg.).

THE first of the great blessings which Christ our wisdom reveals to us as prepared in Himself, is --righteousness. It is not difficult to see why this must be first.

There can be no real prosperity or progress in a nation, a home, or a soul, unless there be peace. As not even a machine can do its work unless it be in rest, secured on a good foundation, quietness and assurance are indispensable to our moral and spiritual well-being. Sin had disturbed all our relations; we were out of harmony with ourselves, with men, and with God. The first requirement of a salvation that should really bring blessedness to us was peace. And peace can only come with right. Where everything is as God would have it, in God's order and in harmony with His will, there alone can peace reign. Jesus Christ came to restore peace on earth, and peace in the soul, by restoring righteousness. Because He is Melchizedek, King of righteousness, He reigns as King of Salem, King of peace (Heb.7:2). He so fulfils the promise the prophets held out: "A king shall reign in righteousness: and the work of righteousness shall be peace, and the effect of righteousness, quietness and assurance for ever" (Isa.32:1,17). Christ is made of God unto us righteousness; of God we are in Him as our righteousness; we are made the righteousness of God in Him. Let us try to understand what this means.

When first the sinner is led to trust in Christ for salvation, he, as a rule, looks more to His work than His person.

As he looks at the Cross, and Christ suffering there, the Righteous One for the unrighteous, he sees in that atoning death the only but sufficient foundation for his faith in God's pardoning mercy. The substitution, and the curse-bearing, and the atonement of Christ dying in the stead of sinners, are what give him peace. And as he understands how the righteousness which Christ brings becomes his very own, and how, in the strength of that, he is counted righteous before God, he feels that he has what he needs to restore him to God's favour: "Being justified by faith, we have peace with God." He seeks to wear this robe of righteousness in the ever renewed faith in the glorious gift of righteousness which has been bestowed upon him.

But as time goes on, and he seeks to grow in the Christian life, new needs arise. He wants to understand more fully how it is that God can thus justify the ungodly on the strength of the righteousness of another. He finds the answer in the wonderful teaching of Scripture as to the true union of the believer with Christ as the second Adam. He sees that it is because Christ had made Himself one with His people, and they were one with Him; that it was in perfect accordance with all law in the kingdom of nature and of heaven, that each member of the body should have the full benefit of the doing and the suffering as of the life of the head. And so he is led to feel that it can only be in fully realizing his personal union with Christ as the Head, that he can fully experience the power of His righteousness to bring the soul into the full favour and fellowship of the Holy One. The work of Christ does not become less precious, but the Person of Christ more so; the work leads up into the very heart, the love and the life of the God-man.

And this experience sheds its light again upon Scripture. It leads him to notice, what he had scarce remarked before, how distinctly the righteousness of God, as it becomes ours, is connected with the Person of the Redeemer. "This is His name whereby HE shall be called, JEHOVAH OUR RIGHTEOUSNESS." "IN JEHOVAH have I righteousness and strength." "Of God is HE made unto us righteousness." "That we might be made the righteousness of God IN HIM." "That I may be found IN HIM, having the righteousness of God." He sees how inseparable righteousness and life in Christ are from each other: "The righteousness of one comes upon all unto justification of life." "They which receive the gift of righteousness shall reign in life by one, Jesus Christ." And he understands what deep meaning there is in the key-word of the Epistle to the Romans: "The righteous shall live by faith." He is not now content with only thinking of the imputed righteousness as his robe; but, putting on Jesus Christ, and seeking to be wrapped up in, to be clothed upon with Himself and His life, he feels how completely the righteousness of God is his, because the Lord our righteousness is his. Before he understood this, he too often felt it difficult to wear his white robe all the day: it was as if he specially had to put it on when he came into God's presence to confess his sins, and seek new grace. But now the living Christ Himself is his righteousness--that Christ who watches over, and keeps and loves us as His own; it is no longer an impossibility to walk all the day enrobed in the loving presence with which He covers His people.

Such an experience leads still further. The life and the righteousness are inseparably linked, and the believer becomes more conscious than before of a righteous nature planted within him. The new man created in Christ Jesus, is "created in righteousness and true holiness." "He that doeth righteousness is righteous, even as He is righteous." The union to Jesus has effected a change not only in the relation to God, but in the personal state before God. And as the intimate fellowship to which the union has opened up the way is maintained, the growing renewal of the whole being makes righteousness to be his very nature.

To a Christian who begins to see the deep meaning of the truth, "HE is made to us righteousness," it is hardly necessary to say, "Abide in Him." As long as he only thought of the righteousness of the substitute, and our being counted judicially righteous for His sake, the absolute necessity of abiding in Him was not apparent. But as the glory of "Jehovah our righteousness" unfolds to the view, he sees that abiding in Him personally is the only way to stand, at all times, complete and accepted before God, as it is the only way to realize how the new and righteous nature can be strengthened from Jesus our Head. To the penitent sinner the chief thought was the righteousness which comes through Jesus dying for sin; to the intelligent and advancing believer, Jesus, the Living One, through whom the righteousness comes, is everything, because having Him he has the righteousness too.

Believer, abide in Christ as your righteousness. You bear about with you a nature altogether corrupt and vile, ever seeking to rise up and darken your sense of acceptance, and of access to unbroken fellowship with the Father. Nothing can enable you to dwell and walk in the light of God, without even the shadow of a cloud between, but the habitual abiding in Christ as your righteousness. To this you are called. Seek to walk worthy of that calling. Yield yourself to the Holy Spirit to reveal to you the wonderful grace that permits you to draw nigh to God, clothed in a divine righteousness. Take time to realize that the King's own robe has indeed been put on, and that in it you need not fear entering His presence. It is the token that you are the man whom the King delights to honour. Take time to remember that as much as you need it in the palace, no less do you require it when He sends you forth into the world, where you are the King's messenger and representative. Live your daily life in the full consciousness of being righteous in God's sight, an object of delight and pleasure in Christ. Connect every view you have of Christ in His other graces with this first one: "Of God He is made to you righteousness." This will keep you in perfect peace. Thus shall you enter into, and dwell in, the rest of God. So shall your inmost being be transformed into being righteous and doing righteousness. In your heart and life it will become manifest where you dwell; abiding in Jesus Christ, the Righteous One, you will share His position, His character, and His blessedness: "Thou lovest righteousness, and hatest iniquity: therefore God, thy God, hath anointed thee with the oil of gladness above thy fellows." Joy and gladness above measure will be your portion.

Chapter 9: AS YOUR SANCTIFICATION

"Of God are ye in Christ Jesus, who has made unto us wisdom from God, both righteousness and SANCTIFICATION, and redemption." I COR.1:30(R.V. marg.).

"PAUL, unto the Church of God which is at Corinth to them that are sanctified in Christ Jesus, called to be saints";--thus the chapter opens in which we are taught that Christ is our sanctification. In the Old Testament, believers were called the righteous; in the New Testament they are called saints, the holy ones, sanctified in Christ Jesus. Holy is higher than righteous.[1] Holy in God has reference to His inmost being; righteous, to His dealings with His creatures. In man, righteousness is but a tepping-stone to holiness. It is in this he can approach most near to the perfection of God (comp. Matt.5:48; I Pet.1:16). In the Old Testament righteousness was found, while holiness was only typified; in Jesus Christ, the Holy One, and in His people, His saints or holy ones, it is first realized.

As in Scripture, and in our text, so in personal experience righteousness precedes holiness. When first the believer finds Christ as his righteousness, he has such joy in the new-made discovery that the study of holiness hardly has a place. But as he grows, the desire for holiness makes itself felt, and he seeks to know what provision his God has made for supplying that need. A superficial acquaintance with God's plan leads to the view that while justification is God's work, by faith in Christ, sanctification is our work, to be performed under the influence of the gratitude we feel for the deliverance we have experienced, and by the aid of the Holy Spirit. But the earnest Christian soon finds how little gratitude can supply the power. When he thinks that more prayer will bring it, he finds that, indispensable as prayer is, it is not enough. Often the believer struggles hopelessly for years, until he listens to the teaching of the Spirit, as He glorifies Christ again, and reveals Christ, our anctification, to be appropriated by faith alone.

Christ is made of God unto us sanctification. Holiness is the very nature of God, and that alone is holy which God takes possession of and fills with Himself. God's answer to the question, How could sinful man become holy? is, "Christ, the Holy One of God." In Him, whom the Father sanctified and sent into the world, God's holiness was revealed incarnate, and brought within reach of man. "I sanctify myself for them, that they also may be sanctified in truth." There is no other way of our becoming holy, but by becoming partakers of the holiness of Christ. [2] And there is no other way of this taking place than by our personal spiritual union with Him, so that through His Holy Spirit His holy life flows into us. "Of God are ye in Christ, who is made unto us sanctification." Abiding by faith in Christ our sanctification is the simple secret of a holy life. The measure of sanctification will depend on the measure of abiding in Him; as the soul learns wholly to abide in Christ, the promise is increasingly fulfilled: "The very God of peace sanctify you wholly."

To illustrate this relation between the measure of the abiding and the measure of sanctification experienced,let us think of the grafting a tree, that instructive symbol of our union to Jesus. The illustration is suggested by the Saviour's words, "Make the tree good, and his fruit good." I can graft a tree so that only a single branch bears good fruit, while many of the natural branches remain, and bear their old fruit--a type of believer in whom a small part of the life is sanctified, but in whom, from ignorance or other reasons, the carnal life still in many respects has full dominion. I can graft a tree so that every branch is cut off, and the whole tree becomes renewed to bear good fruit; and yet, unless I watch over the tendency of the stems to give sprouts, they may again rise and grow strong, and, robbing the new graft of the strength it needs, make it weak. Such are Christians who, when apparently powerfully converted, forsake all to follow Christ, and yet after a time, through unwatchfulness, allow old habits to regain their power, and whose Christian life and fruit are but feeble. But if I want a tree wholly made good, I take it when young, and, cutting the stem clean off on the ground, I graft it just where it emerges from the soil. I watch over every bud which the old nature could possibly put forth, until the flow of sap from the old roots into the new stem is so complete, that the old life has, as it were, been entirely conquered and covered by the new. Here I have a tree entirely renewed--emblem of the Christian who has learnt in entire consecration to surrender everything for Christ, and in a whole-hearted faith wholly to abide in Him.

If, in this last case, the old tree were a reasonable being that could co-operate with the gardener, what would his language be to it? Would it not be this: "Yield now yourself entirely to this new nature with which I have invested you; repress every tendency of the old nature to give buds or sprouts; let all your sap and all your life-powers rise up into this graft from yonder beautiful tree, which I have put on you; so shall you bring forth sweet and much fruit." And the language of the tree to the gardener would be: "When you graft me, O spare not a single branch; let everything of the old self, even the smallest bud, be destroyed, that I may no longer live in my own, but in that other life that was cut off and brought and put upon me, that I might be wholly new and good." And, once again, could you afterwards ask the renewed tree, as it was bearing abundant fruit, what it could say of itself, its answer would be this: "In me, that is, in my roots, there dwells no good thing. I am ever inclined to evil; the sap I collect from the soil is in its

nature corrupt, and ready to show itself in bearing evil fruit. But just when the sap rises into the sunshine to ripen into fruit, the wise gardener has clothed me with a new life, through which my sap is purified, and all my powers are renewed to the bringing forth of good fruit. I have only to abide in that which I have received. He cares for the immediate repression and removal of every bud which the old nature still would
put forth."

Christian, fear not to claim God's promises to make you holy. Listen not to the suggestion that the corruption of your old nature would render holiness an impossibility. In your flesh dwells no good thing, and that flesh, though crucified with Christ, is not yet dead, but will continually seek to rise and lead you to evil. But the Father is the Husbandman. He has grafted the life of Christ on your life. That holy life is mightier than your evil life; under the watchful care of the Husbandman, that new life can keep down the workings of the evil life within you. The evil nature is there, with its unchanged tendency to rise up and show itself. But the new nature is there too--the living Christ, your sanctification, is there--and through Him all your powers can be sanctified as they rise into life, and be made to bear fruit to the glory of the Father.

And now, if you would live a holy life, abide in Christ your sanctification. Look upon Him as the Holy One of God, made man that He might communicate to us the holiness of God. Listen when Scripture teaches that there is within you a new nature, a new man, created in Christ Jesus in righteousness and true holiness. Remember that this holy nature which is in you is singularly fitted for living a holy life, and performing all holy duties, as much so as the old nature is for doing evil. Understand that this holy nature within you has its root and life in Christ in heaven, and can only grow and become strong as the intercourse between it and its source is uninterrupted. And above all, believe most confidently that Jesus Christ Himself delights in maintaining that new nature within you, and imparting to it His own strength and wisdom for its work. Let that faith lead you daily to the surrender of all self-confidence, and the confession of the utter corruption of all there is in you by nature. Let it fill you with a quiet and assured confidence that you are indeed able to do what the Father expects of you as His child, under the covenant of His grace, because you have Christ strengthening you. Let it teach you to lay yourself and your services on the altar as spiritual sacrifices, holy and acceptable in His sight, a sweet-smelling savour. Look not upon a life of holiness as a strain and an effort, but as the natural outgrowth of the life of Christ within you. And let ever again a quiet, hopeful, gladsome faith hold itself assured that all you need for a holy life will most assuredly be given you out of the holiness of Jesus. Thus will you understand and prove what it is to abide in Christ our sanctification.

NOTE

The thought that in the personal holiness of our Lord a new holy nature was formed to be communicated to us, and that we make use of it by faith, is the central idea of Marshall's invaluable work, The Gospel Mystery of Sanctcation:

"One great mystery is, that the holy frame and disposition whereby our souls are furnished and enabled for immediate practice of the law, must be obtained by receiving it out of Christ's fulness, as a thing already prepared and brought to an existence for us in Christ, and treasured up in Him; and that, as we are justified by a righteousness wrought out in Christ, and imputed to us, so we are sanctified by such an holy frame and qualification as are first wrought out and completed in Christ for us, and then imparted to us. As our natural corruption was produced originally in the first Adam, and propagated from him to us, so our new nature and holiness is first produced in Christ, and derived from Him to us, or, as it were, propagated. So that we are not at all to work together with Christ in making or producing that holy frame in us, but only to take it to ourselves, and use it in our holy practice, as made ready to our hands. Thus we have fellowship with Christ, in receiving that holy frame of spirit that was originally in Him; for fellowship is where several persons have the same things in common. This mystery is so great, that notwithstanding all the light of the Gospel, we commonly think that we must get an holy frame by producing it anew in ourselves, and by pursuing it and working it out of our own heart" (see chap. 3). [3]

Footnotes:

1. "Holiness may be called spiritual perection, as righteousnes is legal completeness." --Horatius Bonar in God's Way of Holiness.

2. See note at end of chapter.

3. I have felt so strongly that the teaching of Marshall is just what the Church needs to bring out clearly what the Scripture path of holiness is, that I have prepared an abridgment (all in the author's own words) of his work. By leaving out what was not essential to his argument, and shortening when he appeared diffuse, I hoped to bring his book within reach of many who might never read the larger work. It is published by Nisbet & Co. under the title, The Highway of Holiness. I cannot too earnestly urge every student of theology, and of Scripture, and of the art of holy living, to make himself master of the teaching of Marshall's third, fourth, and twelfth chapters.

Chapter 10: AS YOUR REDEMPTION

"Of God are ye in Christ Jesus, who was made unto us wisdom from God, both righteousness and sanctification, and REDEMPTION."--I COR.1:30(R.V. marg.).

HERE we have the top of the ladder, reaching into heaven--the blessed end to which Christ and life in Him is to lead. The word redemption, though sometimes applied to our deliverance from the guilt of sin, here refers to our complete and final deliverance from all its consequences, when the Redeemer's work shall become fully manifest, even to the redemption of the body itself (comp. Rom.8:21-23; Eph.1.14; 4:30). The expression points us to the highest glory to be hoped for in the future, and therefore also to the highest blessing to be enjoyed in the present in Christ. We have seen how, as a Prophet, Christ is our wisdom, revealing to us God and His love, with the nature and conditions of the salvation that love has prepared. As a Priest, He is our righteousness, restoring us to right relations to God, and securing us His favour and friendship. As a King, He is our sanctification, forming and guiding us into the obedience to the Father's holy will. As these three offices work out God's one purpose, the grand consummation will be reached,the complete deliverance from sin and all its effects be accomplished, and ransomed humanity regain all that it had ever lost. Christ is made of God unto us redemption. The word invites us to look upon Jesus, not only as He lived on earth, teaching us by word and example, as He died, to reconcile us with God, as He lives again, a victorious King, rising to receive His crown, but as, sitting at the right hand of God, He takes again the glory which He had with the Father, before the world began, and holds it there for us. It consists in this, that there His human nature, yea, His human body, freed from all the consequences of sin to which He once had been exposed, is now admitted to share the divine glory. As Son of Man, He dwells on the throne and in the bosom of the Father: the deliverance from what He had to suffer from sin is complete and eternal. The complete redemption is found embodied in His own Person: what He as man is and has in heaven is the complete redemption. HE is made of God to us redemption.

We are in Him as such. And the more intelligently and believingly we abide in Him as our redemption, the more shall we experience, even here, of "the powers of the world to come." As our communion with Him becomes more intimate and intense, and we let the Holy Spirit reveal Him to us in His heavenly glory, the more we realize how the life in us is the life of One who sits upon the throne of heaven. We feel the power of an endless life working in us. We taste the eternal life. We have the foretaste of the eternal glory.

The blessings flowing from abiding in Christ as our redemption are great. The soul is delivered from all fear of death. There was a time when even the Saviour feared death. But now no longer. He has triumphed over death; even His body has entered into the glory. The believer who abides in Christ as his full redemption, realizes even now his spiritual victory over death. It becomes to him the servant that removes the last rags of the old carnal vesture, ere he be clothed upon with the new body of glory. It carries the body to the grave, to lie there as the seed whence the new body will arise the worthy companion of the glorified spirit. The resurrection of the body is no longer a barren doctrine, but a living expectation, and even an incipient experience, because the Spirit of Him that raised Jesus from the dead, dwells in the body as the pledge that even our mortal bodies shall be quickened (Rom.8:11-23). This faith exercises its sanctifying influence in the willing surrender of the sinful members of the body to be mortified and completely subjected to the dominion of the Spirit, as preparation for the time when the frail body shall be changed and fashioned like to His glorious body.

This full redemption of Christ as extending to the body, has a depth of meaning not easily expressed. It was of man as a whole, soul and body that it is said that he was made in the image and likeness of God. In the angels, God had created spirits without material bodies; in the creation of the world, there was matter without spirit. Man was to be the highest specimen of divine art: the combination in one being, of matter and spirit in perfect harmony, as type of the most perfect union between God and His own creation. Sin entered in, and appeared to thwart the divine plan: the material obtained a fearful supremacy over the spiritual. The Word was made flesh, the divine fulness received an embodiment in the humanity of Christ, that the redemption might be a complete and perfect one; that the whole creation, which now groaneth and travaileth in pain together, might be delivered from the bondage of corruption into the liberty of the glory of the children of God. God's purpose will not be accomplished, and Christ's glory will not be manifested fully, until the body, with that whole of nature of which it is part and head, has been transfigured by the power of the spiritual life, and made the transparent vesture for showing forth the glory of the Infinite Spirit. Then only shall we understand: "Christ Jesus is made unto us (complete) redemption."

Meantime we are taught to believe: "Of God are ye in Christ, as your redemption." This is not meant as a revelation, to be left to the future; for the full development of the Christian life, our present abiding in Christ must seek to enter into and appropriate it. We do this as we learn to triumph over death. We do it as we learn to look upon Christ as the

Lord of our body, claiming its entire consecration, securing even here, if faith will claim it (Mark 16:17-18), victory over the terrible dominion sin hath had in the body. We do this as we learn to look on all nature as part of the Kingdom of Christ, destined, even though it be through a baptism of fire, to partake in His redemption. We do it as we allow the powers of the coming world to possess us, and to lift us up into a life in the heavenly places, to enlarge our hearts and our views, to anticipate, even here, the things which have never entered into the heart of man to conceive.

Believer, abide in Christ as your redemption. Let this be the crown of your Christian life. Seek it not first or only, apart from the knowledge of Christ in His other relations. But seek it truly as that to which they are meant to lead you up. Abide in Christ as your redemption. Nothing will fit you for this but faithfulness in the previous steps of the Christian life. Abide in Him as your wisdom, the perfect revelation of all that God is and has for you. Follow, in the daily ordering of the inner and the outer life, with meek docility His teaching, and you shall be counted worthy to have secrets revealed to you which to most disciples are a sealed book. The wisdom will lead you into the mysteries of complete redemption. Abide in Him as your righteousness, and dwell clothed upon with Him in that inner sanctuary of the Father's favour and presence to which His righteousness gives you access. As you rejoice in your reconciliation, you shall understand how it includes all things, and how they too wait the full redemption; "for it pleased the Father by Him to reconcile all things unto Himself; by Him, I say, whether they be things on earth or things in heaven." And abide in Him as your sanctification; the experience of His power to make you holy, spirit and soul and body, will quicken your faith in a holiness that shall not cease its work until the bells of the horses and every pot in Jerusalem shall be holiness to the Lord. Abide in Him as your redemption, and live, even here, as the heir of the future glory. And as you seek to experience in yourself to the full, the power of His saving grace, your heart shall be enlarged to realize the position man has been destined to occupy in the universe, as having all things made subject to him, and you shall for your part be fitted to live worthy of that high and heavenly calling.

Chapter 11: THE CRUCIFIED ONE

"I am crucified with Christ: nevertheless I live; yet not I, but Christ liveth in me."--GAL.2:20.

"We have been planted together in the likeness of his death. "--Rom.6:5

"I AM crucified with Christ." Thus the apostle expresses his assurance of his fellowship with Christ in His sufferings and death, and his full participation in all the power and the blessing of that death. And so really did he mean what he said, and know that he was now indeed dead, that he adds: "It is no longer I that live, but Christ that liveth in me."How blessed must be the experience of such a union with the Lord Jesus! To be able to look upon His death as mine, just as really as it was His--upon His perfect obedience to God, His victory over sin, and complete deliverance from its power, as mine; and to realize that the power of that death does by faith work daily with a divine energy in mortifying the flesh, and renewing the whole life into the perfect conformity to the resurrection life of Jesus! Abiding in Jesus, the Crucified One, is the secret of the growth of that new life which is ever begotten of the death of nature.

Let us try to understand this. The suggestive expression, "Planted into the likeness of His death," will teach us what the abiding in the Crucified One means. When a graft is united with the stock on which it is to grow, we know that it must be kept fixed, it must abide in the place where the stock has been cut, been wounded, to make an opening to receive the graft. No graft without wounding--the laying bare and opening up of the inner life of the tree to receive the stranger branch. It is only through such wounding that access can be obtained to the fellowship of the sap and the growth and the life of the stronger stem. Even so with Jesus and the sinner. Only when we are planted into the likeness of His death shall we also be in the likeness of His resurrection, partakers of the life and the power there are in Him. In the death of the Cross Christ was wounded, and in His opened wounds a place prepared where we might be grafted in. And just as one might say to a graft, and does practically say as it is fixed in its place, "Abide here in the wound of the stem, that is now to bear you"; so to the believing soul the message comes, "Abide in the wounds of Jesus; there is the place of union, and life, and growth. There you shall see how His heart was opened to receive you; how His flesh was rent that the way might be opened for your being made one with Him, and having access to all the blessings flowing from His divine nature."

You have also noticed how the graft has to be torn away from the tree where it by nature grew, and to be cut into conformity to the place prepared for it in the wounded stem. Even so the believer has to be made conformable to Christ's death--to be crucified and to die with

Him. The wounded stem and the wounded graft are cut to fit into each other, into each other's likeness. There is a fellowship between Christ's sufferings and your sufferings. His experiences must become yours. The disposition He manifested in choosing and bearing the cross must be yours. Like Him, you will have to give full assent to the righteous judgment and curse of a holy God against sin. Like Him, you have to consent to yield your life, as laden with sin and curse,to death, and through it to pass to the new life. Like Him, you shall experience that it is only through the self-sacrifice of Gethsemane and Calvary that the path is to be found to the joy and the fruit-bearing of the resurrection life. The more clear the resemblance between the wounded stem and the wounded graft, the more exactly their wounds fit into each other, the surer and the easier, and the more complete will be the union and the growth.

It is in Jesus, the Crucified One, I must abide. I must learn to look upon the Cross as not only an atonement to God, but also a victory over the devil--not only a deliverance from the guilt, but also from the power of sin. I must gaze on Him on the Cross as wholly mine, offering Himself to receive me into the closest union and fellowship, and to make me partaker of the full power of His death to sin, and the new life of victory to which it is but the gateway. I must yield myself to Him in an undivided surrender, with much prayer and strong desire, imploring to be admitted into the ever closer fellowship and conformity of His death, of the Spirit in which He died that death.

Let me try and understand why the Cross is thus the place of union. On the Cross the Son of God enters into the fullest union with man--enters into the fullest experience of what it says to have become a son of man, a member of a race under the curse. It is in death that the Prince of life conquers the power of death; it is in death alone that He can make me partaker of that victory. The life He imparts is a life from the dead; each new experience of the power of that life depends upon the fellowship of the death. The death and the life are inseparable. All the grace which Jesus the Saving One gives is given only in the path of fellowship with Jesus the Crucified One. Christ came and took my place; I must put myself in His place, and abide there. And there is but one place which is both His and mine--that place is the Cross. His in virtue of His free choice; mine by reason of the curse of sin. He came there to seek me; there alone I can find Him. When He found me there, it was the place of cursing; this He experienced, for "cursed is every one that hangeth on a tree." He made it a place of blessing; this I experienced, for Christ has delivered us from the curse, being made a curse for us. When Christ comes in my place, He remains what He was, the beloved of the Father; but in the fellowship with me He shares my curse and dies my death. When I stand in His place, which is still always mine, I am still what I was by nature, the accursed one, who deserves to die; but as united to Him, I share His blessing, and receive His life. When He came to be one with me He could not avoid the Cross, for the curse always points to the Cross as its end and fruit. And when I seek to be one with Him, I cannot avoid the Cross either, for nowhere but on the Cross are life and deliverance to be found. As inevitably as my curse pointed Him to the Cross as the only place where He could be fully united to me, His blessing points me to the Cross too as the only place where I can be united to Him. He took my cross for His own; I must take His Cross as my own; I must be crucified with Him. It is as I abide daily, deeply in Jesus the Crucified One, that I shall taste the sweetness of His love, the power of His life, the completeness of His salvation.

Beloved believer! it is a deep mystery, this of the Cross of Christ. I fear there are many Christians who are content to look upon the Cross, with Christ on it dying for their sins, who have little heart for fellowship with the Crucified One. They hardly know that He invites them to it. Or they are content to consider the ordinary afflictions of life, which the children of the world often have as much as they, as their share of Christ's Cross. They have no conception of what it is to be crucified with Christ, that bearing the cross means likeness to Christ in the principles which animated Him in His path of obedience. The entire surrender of all self-will, the complete denial to the flesh of its every desire and pleasure, the perfect separation from the world in all its ways of thinking and acting, the losing and hating of one's life, the giving up of self and its interests for the sake of others--this is the disposition which marks him who has taken up Christ's Cross, who seeks to say, "I am crucified with Christ; I abide in Christ, the Crucified One."

Would you in very deed please your Lord, and live in as close fellowship with Him as His grace could maintain you in? O pray that His Spirit lead you into this blessed truth: this secret of the Lord for them that fear Him. We know how Peter knew and confessed Christ as the Son of the living God while the Cross was still an offence (Matt.16:16,17,21,23). The faith that believes in the blood that pardons, and the life that renews, can only reach its perfect growth as it abides beneath the Cross, and in living fellowship with Him seeks for perfect conformity with Jesus the Crucified.

O Jesus, our crucified Redeemer, teach us not only to believe on Thee, but to abide in Thee, to take Thy Cross not only as the ground of our pardon, but also as the law of our life. O teach us to love it not only because on it Thou didst bear our curse, but because on it we enter into the closest fellowship with Thyself, and are crucified with Thee. And teach us, that as we yield ourselves wholly to be possessed of the Spirit in which Thou didst bear the Cross, we shall be made partakers of the power and the blessing to which the Cross alone gives access.

Chapter 12: GOD HIMSELF WILL STABLISH YOU IN HIM

"He which stablisheth us with you in Christ, is God."-2 COR.1:21

THESE words of Paul teach us a much needed and most blessed truth--
that just as our first being united with Christ was the work of divine
omnipotence, so we may look to the Father, too, for being kept and
being fixed more firmly in Him. "The Lord will perfect that which
concerneth me"--this expression of confidence should ever accompany
the prayer, "Forsake not the work of Thine own hands." In all his
longings and prayers to attain to a deeper and more perfect abiding in
Christ, the believer must hold fast his confidence: "He which hath
begun a good work in you, will perform it until the day of Jesus
Christ." There is nothing that will so help to root and ground him in
Christ as this faith: "He which stablisheth us in Christ is God."

How many there are who can witness that this faith is just what they
need! They continually mourn over the variableness of their spiritual
life. Sometimes there are hours and days of deep earnestness, and even
of blessed experience of the grace of God. But how little is needed to
mar their peace, to bring a cloud over the soul! And then, how their
faith is shaken! All efforts to regain their standing appear utterly
fruitless; and neither solemn vows, nor watching and prayer, avail to
restore to them the peace they for a while had tasted. Could they but
understand how just their own efforts are the cause of their failure,
because it is God alone who can establish us in Christ Jesus. They
would see that just as in justification they had to cease from their own
working, and to accept in faith the promise that God would give them
life in Christ, so now, in the matter of their sanctification, their first
need is to cease from striving themselves to establish the connection
with Christ more firmly, and to allow God to do it. "God is faithful, by
whom ye were called unto the fellowship of His Son Jesus Christ."
What they need is the simple faith that the stablishing in Christ, day by
day, is God's work--a work that He delights to do, in spite of all our
weakness and unfaithfulness, if we will but trust Him for it.

To the blessedness of such a faith, and the experience it brings, many
can testify. What peace and rest, to know that there is a Husbandman
who cares for the branch, to see that it grows stronger, and that its
union with the Vine becomes more perfect, who watches over every
hindrance and danger, who supplies every needed aid! What peace and
rest, fully and finally to give up our abiding into the care of God, and
never have a wish or thought, never to offer a prayer or engage in an
exercise connected with it, without first having the glad remembrance
that what we do is only the manifestation of what God is doing in us!
The establishing in Christ is His work: He accomplishes it by stirring
us to watch, and wait, and work. But this He can do with power only as

we cease interrupting Him by our self-working--as we accept in faith the dependent posture which honours Him and opens the heart to let Him work. How such a faith frees the soul from care and responsibility! In the midst of the rush and bustle of the world's stirring life, amid the subtle and ceaseless temptations of sin, amid all the daily cares and trials that so easily distract and lead to failure, how blessed it would be to be an established Christian--always abiding in Christ! How blessed even to have the faith that one can surely become it--that the attainment is within our reach!

Dear believer, the blessing is indeed within your reach. He that stablisheth you with us in Christ is God. What I want you to take in is this--that believing this promise will not only give you comfort, but will be the means of your obtaining your desire. You know how Scripture teaches us that in all God's leadings of His people faith has everywhere been the one condition of the manifestation of His power. Faith is the ceasing from all nature's efforts, and all other dependence; faith is confessed helplessness casting itself upon God's promise, and claiming its fulfilment; faith is the putting ourselves quietly into God's hands for Him to do His work. What you and I need now is to take time, until this truth stands out before us in all its spiritual brightness: It is God Almighty, God the Faithful and Gracious One, who has undertaken to stablish me in Christ Jesus.

Listen to what the Word teaches you:--"The Lord shall establish thee an holy people unto Himself"; "O Lord God, stablish their heart unto Thee"; "Thy God loved Israel, to establish them for ever"; "Thou wilt establish the heart of the humble"; "Now to Him that is of power to establish you, be glory for ever"; "To the end He may establish your hearts unblameable in holiness" ; "THE LORD IS FAITHFUL, who shall stablish you and keep you from all evil"; "The God of all grace, who hath called us in Christ Jesus, make you perfect, stablish, strengthen, settle you." Can you take these words to mean anything less than that you too--however fitful your spiritual life has hitherto been, however unfavourable your natural character or your circumstances may appear--can be established in Christ Jesus--can become an established Christian? Let us but take time to listen, in simple childlike teachableness, to these words as the truth of God, and the confidence will come: As surely--as I am in Christ, I shall also, day by day, be established in Him.

The lesson appears so simple; and yet the most of us take so long to learn it. The chief reason is, that the grace the promise offers is so large, so God-like, so beyond all our thoughts, that we do not take it really to mean what it says. The believer who has once come to see and accept what it brings, can bear witness to the wonderful change there comes over the spiritual life. Hitherto he had taken charge of his own welfare; now he has a God to take charge of it. He now knows himself to be in the school of God, a Teacher who plans the whole course of study for each of His pupils with infinite wisdom, and delights to have them come daily for the lessons He has to give. All he asks is to feel himself constantly in God's hands, and to follow His guidance, neither lagging behind nor going before. Remembering that it is God who worketh both to will and to do, he sees his only safety to be in yielding himself to God's working. He lays aside all anxiety about his inner life and its growth, because the Father is the Husbandman under whose wise and watchful care each plant is well secured. He knows that there is the prospect of a most blessed life of strength and fruitfulness to every one who will take God alone and wholly as his hope.

Believer, you cannot but admit that such a life of trust must be a most blessed one. You say, perhaps, that there are times when you do, with your whole heart, consent to this way of living, and do wholly abandon the care of your inner life to your Father. But somehow it does not last. You forget again; and instead of beginning each morning with the joyous transference of all the needs and cares of your spiritual life to the Father's charge, you again feel anxious, and burdened, and helpless. Is it not, perhaps, my brother, because you have not committed to the Father's care this matter of daily remembering to renew your entire surrender? Memory is one of the highest powers in our nature. By it day is linked to day, the unity of life through all our years is kept up, and we know that we are still ourselves. In the spiritual life, recollection is of infinite value. For the sanctifying of our memory, in the service of our spiritual life, God has provided most beautifully. The Holy Spirit is the remembrancer, the Spirit of recollection. Jesus said, "He shall bring all things to your remembrance." "He which stablisheth us with you in Christ is God, who hath also sealed us, and given the earnest of the Spirit in our hearts." It is just for the stablishing that the Holy Remembrancer has been given. God's blessed promises, and your unceasing acts of faith and surrender accepting of them--He will enable you to remember these each day. The Holy Spirit is--blessed be God-- the memory of the new man.

Apply this to the promise of the text: "He that stablisheth us in Christ is God." As you now, at this moment, abandon all anxiety about your growth and progress to the God who has undertaken to stablish you in the Vine, and feel what a joy it is to know that God alone has charge, ask and trust Him by the Holy Spirit ever to remind you of this your blessed relation to Him. He will do it; and with each new morning your faith may grow stronger and brighter: I have a God to see that each day I become more firmly united to Christ.

And now, beloved fellow-believer, "the God of all grace, who hath called us in Christ Jesus, make you perfect, stablish, strengthen, settle you." What more can you desire? Expect it confidently, ask it fervently. Count on God to do His work. And learn in faith to sing the song, the notes of which each new experience will make deeper and sweeter: "Now to Him, that is of power to establish you, be glory for ever. Amen." Yes, glory to God, who has undertaken to establish us in Christ!

Chapter 13: EVERY MOMENT

"In that day sing ye unto her, A vineyard of red wine. I the Lord do keep it; I will water it every moment: lest any hurt it, I will keep it night and day."--ISA.27:2,3.

THE vineyard was the symbol of the people of Israel, in whose midst the True Vine was to stand. The branch is the symbol of the individual believer, who stands in the Vine. The song of the vineyard is also the song of the Vine and its every branch. The command still goes forth to the watchers of the vineyard--would that they obeyed it, and sang till every feeble-hearted believer had learned and joined the joyful strain-- "Sing ye unto her: I, JEHOVAH, Do KEEP IT; I will water it every moment: lest any hurt it, I WILL KEEP it night and day."

What an answer from the mouth of God Himself to the question so often asked: Is it possible for the believer always to abide in Jesus? Is a life of unbroken fellowship with the Son of God indeed attainable here in this earthly life? Truly not, if the abiding is our work, to be done in our strength. But the things that are impossible with men are possible with God. If the Lord Himself will keep the soul night and day, yea, will watch and water it every moment, then surely the uninterrupted communion with Jesus becomes a blessed possibility to those who can trust God to mean and to do what He says. Then surely the abiding of the branch of the vine day and night, summer and winter, in a never-ceasing life-fellowship, is nothing less than the simple but certain promise of your abiding in your Lord.

In one sense, it is true, there is no believer who does not always abide in Jesus; without this there could not be true life. "If a man abide not in me, he is cast forth." But when the Saviour gives the command, "Abide in me," with the promise, "He that abideth in me bringeth forth much fruit," He speaks of that willing, intelligent, and whole-hearted surrender by which we accept His offer, and consent to the abiding in Him as the only life we choose or seek. The objections raised against our right to expect that we shall always be able thus voluntarily and consciously to abide in Jesus are chiefly two.

The one is derived from the nature of man. It is said that our limited powers prevent our being occupied with two things at the same moment. God's providence places many Christians in business, where for hours at a time the closest attention is required to the work they have to do. How can such a man, it is asked, with his whole mind in the work he has to do, be at the same time occupied with Christ, and keeping up fellowship with Him? The consciousness of abiding in Jesus is regarded as requiring such a strain, and such a direct occupation of the mind with heavenly thoughts, that to enjoy the blessing would imply a withdrawing of oneself from all the ordinary avocations of life. This is the same error as drove the first monks into the wilderness.

Blessed be God, there is no necessity for such a going out of the world. Abiding in Jesus is not a work that needs each moment the mind to be engaged, or the affections to be directly and actively occupied with it. It is an entrusting of oneself to the keeping of the Eternal Love, in the faith that it will abide near us, and with its holy presence watch over us and ward off the evil, even when we have to be most intently occupied with other things. And so the heart has rest and peace and joy in the consciousness of being kept when it cannot keep itself.

In ordinary life, we have abundant illustration of the influence of a supreme affection reigning in and guarding the soul, while the mind concentrates itself on work that requires its whole attention. Think of the father of a family, separated for a time from his home, that he may secure for his loved ones what they need. He loves his wife and children, and longs much to return to them. There may be hours of intense occupation when he has not a moment to think of them, and yet his love is as deep and real as when he can call up their images; all the while his love and the hope of making them happy urge him on, and fill him with a secret joy in his work. Think of a king: in the midst of work, and pleasure, and trial, he all the while acts under the secret influence of the consciousness of royalty, even while he does not think of it. A loving wife and mother never for one moment loses the sense of her relation to the husband and children: the consciousness and the love are there, amid all her engagements. And shall it be thought impossible for the Everlasting Love so to take and keep possession of our spirits, that we too shall never for a moment lose the secret consciousness: We are in Christ, kept in Him by His almighty power. Oh, it is possible; we can be sure it is. Our abiding in Jesus is even more than a fellowship of love--it is a fellowship of life. In work or in rest, the consciousness of life never leaves us. And even so can the mighty power of the Eternal Life maintain within us the consciousness of its presence. Or rather, Christ, who is our life, Himself dwells within us, and by His presence maintains our consciousness that we are in Him.

The second objection has reference to our sinfulness. Christians are so accustomed to look upon sinning daily as something absolutely inevitable, that they regard it as a matter of course that no one can keep up abiding fellowship with the Saviour: we must sometimes be unfaithful and fail. As if it was not just because we have a nature which is naught but a very fountain of sin, that the abiding in Christ has been ordained for us as our only but our sufficient deliverance! As if it were not the Heavenly Vine, the living, loving Christ, in whom we have to abide, and whose almighty power to hold us fast is to be the measure of our expectations! As if He would give us the command, "Abide in me," without securing the grace and the power to enable us to perform it! As if, above all, we had not the Father as the Husbandman to keep us from falling, and that not in a large and general sense, but according to His own precious promise: "Night and day, every moment!" Oh, if we will but look to our God as the Keeper of Israel, of whom it is said, "Jehovah shall keep thee from all evil; He shall keep thy soul," we shall learn to believe that conscious abiding in Christ every moment, night and day, is indeed what God has prepared for them that love Him.

My beloved fellow-Christians, let nothing less than this be your aim. I know well that you may not find it easy of attainment; that there may come more than one hour of weary struggle and bitter failure. Were the Church of Christ what it should be--were older believers to younger converts what they should be, witnesses to God's faithfulness, like Caleb and Joshua, encouraging their brethren to go up and possess the land with their, "We are well able to overcome; if the Lord delight in us, then HE WILL BRING us into this land"--were the atmosphere which the young believer breathes as he enters the fellowship of the saints that of a healthy, trustful, joyful consecration, abiding in Christ would come as the natural outgrowth of being in Him. But in the sickly state in which such a great part of the body is, souls that are pressing after this blessing are sorely hindered by the depressing influence of the thought and the life around them. It is not to discourage that I say this, but to warn, and to urge to a more entire casting of ourselves upon the word of God Himself. There may come more than our hour in which you are ready to yield to despair; but be of good courage. Only believe. He who has put the blessing within your reach will assuredly lead to its possession.

The way in which souls enter into the possession may differ. To some it may come as the gift of a moment. In times of revival, in the fellowship with other believers in whom the Spirit is working effectually, under the leading of some servant of God who can guide, and sometimes in solitude too, it is as if all at once a new revelation comes upon the soul. It sees, as in the light of heaven, the strong Vine holding and bearing the feeble branches so securely, that doubt becomes impossible. It can only wonder how it ever could have understood the words to mean aught else than this: To abide unceasingly in Christ is the portion of every believer. It sees it; and to believe, and rejoice, and love, come as of itself.

To others it comes by a slower and more difficult path. Day by day, amid discouragement and difficulty, the soul has to press forward. Be of good cheer; this way too leads to the rest. Seek but to keep your heart set upon the promise: "I THE LORD DO KEEP IT, night and day." Take from His own lips the watchword: "Every moment." In that you have the law of His love, and the law of your hope. Be content with nothing less. Think no longer that the duties and the cares, that the sorrows and the sins of this life must succeed in hindering the abiding life of fellowship. Take rather for the rule of your daily experience the language of faith: I am persuaded that neither death with its fears, nor life with its cares, nor things present with their pressing claims, nor things to come with their dark shadows, nor height of joy, nor depth of sorrow, nor any other creature, shall be able, for one single moment, to separate us from the love of God which is in Christ Jesus our Lord, and in which He is teaching me to abide. If things look dark and faith would fail, sing again the song of the vineyard: "I the Lord do keep it; I will water it every moment: lest any hurt it, I will keep it night and day." And be assured that, if Jehovah keep the branch night and day, and water it every moment, a life of continuous and unbroken fellowship with Christ is indeed our privilege.

Chapter 14: DAY BY DAY

"And the people shall go out and gather the portion of a day in his day."-Ex.16:4(marg.).

THE day's portion in its day: Such was the rule for God's giving and man's working in the ingathering of the manna. It is still the law in all the dealings of God's grace with His children. A clear insight into the beauty and application of this arrangement is a wonderful help in understanding how one, who feels himself utterly weak, can have the confidence and the perseverance to hold on brightly through all the years of his earthly course. A doctor was once asked by a patient who had met with a serious accident: "Doctor, how long shall I have to lie here?" The answer, "Only a day at a time," taught the patient a precious lesson. It was the same lesson God had recorded for His people of all ages long before: The day's portion in its day.

It was, without doubt, with a view to this and to meet man's weakness, that God graciously appointed the change of day and night. If time had been given to man in the form of one long unbroken day, it would have exhausted and overwhelmed him; the change of day and night continually recruits and recreates his powers. As a child, who easily makes himself master of a book, when each day only the lesson for the day is given him, would be utterly hopeless if the whole book were given him at once; so it would be with man, if there were no divisions in time. Broken small and divided into fragments, he can bear them; only the care and the work of each day have to be undertaken--the day's portion in its day. The rest of the night fits him for making a fresh start with each new morning; the mistakes of the past can be avoided, its lessons improved. And he has only each day to be faithful for the one short day, and long years and a long life take care of themselves, without the sense of their length or their weight ever being a burden.

Most sweet is the encouragement to be derived from this truth in the life of grace. Many a soul is disquieted with the thought as to how it will be able to gather and to keep the manna needed for all its years of travel through such a barren wilderness. It has never learnt what unspeakable comfort there is in the word: The day's portion for its day. That word takes away all care for the morrow most completely. Only to-day is yours; to-morrow is the Father's. The question: What security have you that during all the years in which you have to contend with the coldness, or temptations, or trials of the world, you will always abide in Jesus? is one you need, yea, you may not ask. Manna, as your food and strength, is given only by the day; faithfully to fill the present is your only security for the future. Accept, and enjoy, and fulfil with your whole heart the part you have this day to perform. His presence and grace enjoyed to-day will remove all doubt whether you can entrust the morrow to Him too.

How great the value which this truth teaches us to attach to each single day! We are so easily led to look at life as a great whole, and to neglect the little to-day, to forget that the single days do indeed make up the whole, and that the value of each single day depends on its influence on the whole. One day lost is a link broken in the chain, which it often takes more than another day to mend. One day lost influences the next,and makes its keeping more difficult. Yea, one day lost may be the loss of what months or years of careful labour had secured. The experience of many a believer could confirm this.

Believer! would you abide in Jesus, let it be day by day. You have already heard the message: Moment by moment; the lesson of day by day has something more to teach. Of the moments there are many where there is no direct exercise of the mind on your part; the abiding is in the deeper recesses of the heart, kept by the Father, to whom you entrusted yourself. But just this is the work that with each new day has to be renewed for the day--the distinct renewal of surrender and trust for the life of moment by moment. God has gathered up the moments and bound them up into a bundle, for the very purpose that we might take measure of them. As we look forward in the morning, or look back in the evening, and weigh the moments, we learn how to value and how to use them rightly. And even as the Father, with each new morning, meets you with the promise of just sufficient manna for the day for yourself and those who have to partake with you, meet Him with the bright and loving renewal of your acceptance of the position He has given you in His beloved Son. Accustom yourself to look upon this as one of the reasons for the appointment of day and night. God thought of our weakness, and sought to provide for it. Let each day have its value from your calling to abide in Christ. As its light opens on your waking eyes, accept it on these terms: A day, just one day only, but still a day, given to abide and grow up in Jesus Christ. Whether it be a day of health or sickness, joy or sorrow, rest or work, of struggle or victory, let the chief thought with which you receive it in the morning thanksgiving be this: "A day that the Father gave; in it I may, I must become more closely united to Jesus." As the Father asks, "Can you trust me just for this one day to keep you abiding in Jesus, and Jesus to keep you fruitful?" you cannot but give the joyful response: "I will trust and not be afraid."

The day's portion for its day was given to Israel in the morning very early. The portion was for use and nourishment during the whole day, but the giving and the getting of it was the morning's work. This suggests how greatly the power to spend a day aright, to abide all the day in Jesus, depends on the morning hour. If the first-fruits be holy, the lump is holy. During the day there come hours of intense occupation in the rush of business or the throng of men, when only the Father's keeping can maintain the connection with Jesus unbroken. The morning manna fed all the day; it is only when the believer in the morning secures his quiet time in secret to renew distinctly and effectually loving fellowship with his Saviour, that the abiding can be kept up all the day. But what cause for thanksgiving that it may be done! In the morning, with its freshness and quiet, the believer can look out upon the day. He can consider its duties and its temptations, and pass them through beforehand, as it were, with his Saviour, throwing all upon Him who has undertaken to be everything to him. Christ is his manna, his nourishment, his strength, his life: he can take the day's portion for the day, Christ as his for all the needs the day may bring, and go on in the assurance that the day will be one of blessing and of growth.

And then, as the lesson of the value and the work of the single day is being taken to heart, the learner is all unconsciously being led on to get the secret of "day by day continually" (Ex.29:38). The blessed abiding grasped by faith for each day apart is an unceasing and ever-increasing growth. Each day of faithfulness brings a blessing for the next; makes both the trust and the surrender easier and more blessed. And so the Christian life grows: as we give our whole heart to the work of each day, it becomes all the day, and from that every day. And so each day separately, all the day continually, day by day successively, we abide in Jesus. And the days make up the life: what once appeared too high and too great to attain, is given to the soul that was content to take and use "every day his portion" (Ezra 3:4), "as the duty of every day required." Even here on earth the voice is heard: "Well done, good and faithful servant, thou hast been faithful over few, I will make thee ruler over many: enter thou into the joy of thy Lord." Our daily life becomes a wonderful interchange of God's daily grace and our daily praise: "Daily He loadeth us with His benefits"; "that I may daily perform my vows." We learn to understand God's reason for daily giving, as He most certainly gives, only enough, but also fully enough, for each day. And we get into His way, the way of daily asking and expecting only enough, but most certainly fully enough, for the day. We begin to number our days not from the sun's rising over the world, or by the work we do or the food we eat, but the daily renewal of the miracle of the manna--the blessedness of daily fellowship with Him who is the Life and the Light of the world. The heavenly life is as unbroken and continuous as the earthly; the abiding in Christ each day has for that day brought its blessing; we abide in Him every day, and all the day. Lord, make this the portion of each one of us.

Chapter 15: AT THIS MOMENT

"Behold, NOW is the accepted time; behold, NOW is the day of salvation." 2 Cor 6:2

THE thought of living moment by moment is of such central importance--looking at the abiding in Christ from our side--that we want once more to speak of it. And to all who desire to learn the blessed art of living only a moment at a time, we want to say: The way to learn it is to exercise yourself in living in the present moment. Each time your attention is free to occupy itself with the thought of Jesus-- whether it be with time to think and pray, or only for a few passing seconds--let your first thought be to say: Now, at this moment, I do abide in Jesus. Use such time, not in vain regrets that you have not been abiding fully, or still more hurtful fears that you will not be able to abide, but just at once take the position the Father has given you: "I am in Christ; this is the place God has given me. I accept it; here I rest; I do now abide in Jesus." This is the way to learn to abide continually. You may be yet so feeble as to fear to say of each day, "I am abiding in Jesus"; but the feeblest can, each single moment, say, as he consents to occupy his place as a branch in the vine, "Yes, I do abide in Christ." It is not a matter of feeling--it is not a question of growth or strength in the Christian life--it is the simple question whether the will at the present moment desires and consents to recognise the place you have in your Lord, and to accept it. If you are a believer, you are in Christ. If you are in Christ, and wish to stay there, it is your duty to say, though it be but for a moment, "Blessed Saviour, I abide in Thee now; Thou keepest me now."

It has been well said that in that little word now lies one of the deepest secrets of the life of faith. At the close of a conference on the spiritual life, a minister of experience rose and spoke. He did not know that he had learnt any truth he did not know before, but he had learnt how to use aright what he had known. He had learnt that it was his privilege at each moment, whatever surrounding circumstances might be, to say, "Jesus saves me now." This is indeed the secret of rest and victory. If I can say, "Jesus is to me at this moment all that God gave Him to be-- life, and strength, and peace"--I have but as I say it to hold still, and rest, and realize it, and for that moment I have what I need. As my faith sees how of God I am in Christ, and takes the place in Him my Father has provided, my soul can peacefully settle down: Now I abide in Christ.

Believer! when striving to find the way to abide in Christ from moment to moment, remember that the gateway is: Abide in Him at this present moment. Instead of wasting effort in trying to get into a state that will last, just remember that it is Christ Himself, the living, loving Lord, who alone can keep you, and is waiting to do so. Begin at once and act faith in Him for the present moment: this is the only way to be kept the next. To attain the life of permanent and perfect abiding is not ordinarily given at once as a possession for the future: it comes mostly step by step. Avail yourself, therefore, of every opportunity of exercising the trust of the present moment. Each time you bow in prayer, let there first be an act of simple devotion: "Father, I am in Christ; I now abide in Him." Each time you have, amidst the bustle of duty, the opportunity of self-recollection, let its first involuntary act be: "I am still in Christ, abiding in Him now." Even when overtaken by sin, and the heart within is all disturbed and excited, O let your first look upwards be with the words: "Father, I have sinned; and yet I come-- though I blush to say it--as one who is in Christ. Father! here I am; I can take no other place; of God I am in Christ; I now abide in Christ." Yes, Christian, in every possible circumstance, every moment of the day, the voice is calling: Abide in me, do it now. And even now, as you are reading this, O come at once and enter upon the blessed life of always abiding, by doing it at once: do it now.

In the life of David there is a beautiful passage which may help to make this thought clearer (2 Sam.3:17,18). David had been anointed king in Judah. The other tribes still followed Ish-bosheth, Saul's son. Abner, Saul's chief captain, resolves to lead the tribes of Israel to submit to David, the God-appointed king of the whole nation. He speaks to the elders of Israel: "Ye sought for David in times past to be king over you; now, then, do it, for Jehovah hath spoken of David, saying, By the hand of my servant David will I save my people Israel out of the hand of the Philistines, and out of the hand of all their enemies." And they did it, and anointed David a second time to be king, now over all Israel, as at first only over Judah (2 Sam.5:3)--a most instructive type of the way in which a soul is led to the life of entire surrender and undivided allegiance, to the full abiding.

First you have the divided kingdom: Judah faithful to the king of God's appointment; Israel still clinging to the king of its own choosing. As a consequence, the nation divided against itself, and no power to conquer the enemies. Picture of the divided heart. Jesus accepted as King in Judah, the place of the holy mount, in the inner chamber of the soul; but the surrounding territory, the every-day life, not yet brought to subjection; more than half the life still ruled by self-will and its hosts. And so no real peace within and no power over the enemies.

Then there is the longing desire for a better state: "Ye sought for David in times past to be king over you." There was a time, when David had conquered the Philistines, that Israel believed in him; but they had been led astray. Abner appeals to their own knowledge of God's will, that

David must rule over all. So the believer, when first brought to Jesus, did indeed want Him to be Lord over all, had hoped that He alone would be King. But, alas! unbelief and self-will had come in, and Jesus could not assert His power over the whole life. And yet the Christian is not content. How he longs--sometimes without daring to hope that it can be--for a better time.

Then follows God's promise. Abner says: "The Lord hath spoken, By the hand of David I will save my people from the hand of all their enemies." He appeals to God's promise: as David had conquered the Philistines, the nearest enemy in time past, so he alone could conquer those farther off. He should save Israel from the hand of all their enemies. Beautiful type of the promise by which the soul is now invited to trust Jesus for the victory over every enemy, and a life of undisturbed fellowship. "The Lord hath spoken"--this is our only hope. On that word rests the sure expectation (Luke 1:70-75): "As He spake, That we should be saved from the hand of all that hate us, to perform the oath which He sware, that He would grant unto us that we, being delivered from the hand of our enemies, should serve Him without fear, in holiness and righteousness before Him, all the days of our life." David reigning over every corner of the land, and leading a united and obedient people on from victory to victory: this is the promise of what Jesus can do for us, as soon as in faith in God's promise all is surrendered to Him, and the whole life given up to be kept abiding in Him.

"Ye sought for David in times past to be king over you," spake Abner, and added, "Then do it now." Do it now is the message that this story brings to each one of us who longs to give Jesus unreserved supremacy. Whatever the present moment be, however unprepared the message finds you, however sad the divided and hopeless state of the life may be, still I come and urge Christ's claim to an immediate surrender--this very moment. I know well that it will take time for the blessed Lord to assert His power, and order all within you according to His will--to conquer the enemies and train all your powers for His service. This is not the work of a moment. But there are things which are the work of a moment--of this moment. The one is--your surrender of all to Jesus; your surrender of yourself entirely to live only in Him. As time goes on, and exercise has made faith stronger and brighter, that surrender may become clearer and more intelligent. But for this no one may wait. The only way ever to attain to it is to begin at once. Do it now. Surrender yourself this very moment to abide wholly, only, always in Jesus. It is the work of a moment. And just so, Christ's renewed acceptance of you is the work of a moment. Be assured that He has you and holds you as His own, and that each new "Jesus, I do abide in Thee," meets with an immediate and most hearty response from the Unseen One. No act of faith can be in vain. He does indeed anew take hold on us and draw us close to Himself. Therefore, as often as the message comes, or the thought of it comes, Jesus says: Abide in me, do it at once. Each moment there is the whisper: Do it now.

Let any Christian begin, then, and he will speedily experience how the blessing of the present moment is passed on to the next. It is the unchanging Jesus to whom he links himself; it is the power of a divine life, in its unbroken continuity, that takes possession of him. The do it now of the present moment--a little thing though it seems--is nothing less than the beginning of the ever-present now, which is the mystery and the glory of eternity. Therefore, Christian, abide in Christ: do it now.

Chapter 16: FORSAKING ALL FOR HIM

"I have suffered the loss of all things, and do count them but dung, that I may win Christ, and be found IN HIM.+--PHIL.3:8-9.

WHEREVER there is life, there is a continual interchange of taking in and giving out, receiving and restoring. The nourishment I take is given out again in the work I do; the impressions I receive, in the thoughts and feelings I express. The one depends on the other--the giving out ever increases the power of taking in. In the healthy exercise of giving and taking is all the enjoyment of life.

It is so in the spiritual life too. There are Christians who look on its blessedness as consisting all in the privilege of ever receiving; they know not how the capacity for receiving is only kept up and enlarged by continual giving up and giving out--how it is only in the emptiness that comes from the parting with what we have, that the divine fulness can flow in. It was a truth our Saviour continually insisted on. When He spoke of selling all to secure the treasure, of losing our life to find it, of the hundred-fold to those who forsake all, He was expounding the need of self-sacrifice as the law of the Kingdom for Himself as well as for His disciples. If we are really to abide in Christ, and to be found in Him--to have our life always and wholly in Him--we must each in our measure say with Paul, "I count all things but loss for the excellency of the knowledge of Christ Jesus my Lord, that I may win Christ, and be FOUND IN Him."

Let us try and see what there is to be forsaken and given up. First of all, there is sin. There can be no true conversion without the giving up of sin. And yet, owing to the ignorance of the young convert of what really is sin, of what the claims of God's holiness are, and what the extent to which the power of Jesus can enable us to conquer sin, the giving up of sin is but partial and superficial. With the growth of the Christian life there comes the want of a deeper and more entire purging out of everything that is unholy. And it is specially when the desire to abide in Christ uninterruptedly, to be always found in Him, becomes strong, that the soul is led to see the need of a new act of surrender, in which it afresh accepts and ratifies its death to sin in Christ, and parts indeed with everything that is sin. Availing himself, in the strength of God's Spirit, of that wonderful power of our nature by which the whole of one's future life can be gathered up and disposed of in one act of the will, the believer yields himself to sin no more--to be only and wholly a servant of righteousness. He does it in the joyful assurance that every sin surrendered is gain indeed--room for the inflowing of the presence and the love of Christ.

Next to the parting with unrighteousness, is the giving up of self-righteousness. Though contending most earnestly against our own works or merits, it is often long before we come really to understand what it is to refuse self the least place or right in the service of God. Unconsciously we allow the actings of our own mind and heart and will free scope in God's presence. In prayer and worship, in Bible reading and working for God, instead of absolute dependence on the Holy Spirit's leading, self is expected to do a work it never can do. We are slow to learn the lesson, "In me, that is, in my flesh, dwelleth no good thing." As it is learnt, and we see how corruption extends to everything that is of nature, we see that there can be no entire abiding in Christ without the giving up of all that is of self in religion--without giving it up to the death, and waiting for the breathings of the Holy Spirit as alone able to work in us what is acceptable in God's sight. Then, again, there is our whole natural life, with all the powers and endowments bestowed upon us by the Creator, with all the occupations and interests with which Providence has surrounded us. It is not enough that, when once you are truly converted, you have the earnest desire to have all these devoted to the service of the Lord. The desire is good, but can neither teach the way nor give the strength to do it acceptably. Incalculable harm has been done to the deeper spirituality of the Church, by the idea that when once we are God's children the using of our gifts in His service follows as a matter of course. No; for this there is indeed needed very special grace. And the way in which the grace comes is again that of sacrifice and surrender. I must see how all my gifts and powers are, even though I be a child of God, still defiled by sin, and under the power of the flesh. I must feel that I cannot at once proceed to use them for God's glory. I must first lay them at Christ's feet, to be accepted and cleansed by Him. I must feel myself utterly powerless to use them aright. I must see that they are most dangerous to me, because through them the flesh, the old nature, self, will so easily exert its power. In this conviction I must part with them, giving them entirely up to the Lord. When He has accepted them, and set His stamp upon them, I receive them back, to hold them as His property, to wait on Him for the grace to use them aright day by day, and to have them act only under His influence. And so experience proves it true here too, that the path of entire consecration is the path of full salvation. Not only is what is thus given up received back again to become doubly our own, but the forsaking all is followed by the receiving all. We abide in Christ more fully as we forsake all and follow Him. As I count all things loss for His sake, I am found IN Him. The same principle holds good of all the lawful occupations and possessions with which we are entrusted of God. Such were the fish-nets on the Sea of Galilee, and the household duties of Martha of Bethany--the home and the friends of many a one among Jesus' disciples. Jesus taught them in very deed to forsake all for Him. It was no arbitrary command, but the simple application of a law in nature to the Kingdom of His grace--that the more perfectly the old occupant is cast out, the more complete can be the possession of the new, and the more entire the renewal of all within.

This principle has a still deeper application. The truly spiritual gifts which are the working of God's own Holy Spirit within us--these surely need not be thus given up and surrendered? They do indeed; the interchange of giving up and taking in is a life process, and may not cease for a moment. No sooner does the believer begin to rejoice in the possession of what he has, than the inflow of new grace is retarded, and stagnation threatens. It is only into the thirst of an empty soul that the streams of living waters flow. Ever thirsting is the secret of never thirsting. Each blessed experience we receive as a gift of God, must at once be returned back to Him from whom it came, in praise and love, in self-sacrifice and service; so only can it be restored to us again, fresh and beautiful with the bloom of heaven. Is not this the wonderful lesson Isaac on Moriah teaches us? Was he not the son of promise, the God-given life, the wonder-gift of the omnipotence of Him who quickeneth the dead? (Rom.4:17). And yet even he had to be given up, and sacrificed, that he might be received back again a thousandfold more precious than before--a type of the Only-begotten of the Father, whose pure and holy life had to be given up ere He could receive it again in resurrection power, and could make His people partakers of it. A type, too, of what takes place in the life of each believer, as, instead of resting content with past experiences or present grace, he presses on, forgetting and giving up all that is behind, and reaches out to the fullest possible apprehension of Christ His life.

And such surrender of all for Christ, is it a single step, the act and experience of a moment, or is it a course of daily renewed and progressive attainment? It is both. There may be a moment in the life of a believer when he gets a first sight, or a deeper insight, of this most blessed truth, and when, made willing in the day of God's power, he does indeed, in an act of the will, gather up the whole of life yet before him into the decision of a moment, and lay himself on the altar a living and an acceptable sacrifice. Such moments have often been the blessed transition from a life of wandering and failure to a life of abiding and power divine. But even then his daily life becomes, what the life must be of each one who has no such experience, the unceasing prayer for more light on the meaning of entire surrender, the ever-renewed offering up of all he has to God.

Believer, would you abide in Christ, see here the blessed path. Nature shrinks back from such self-denial and crucifixion in its rigid application to our life in its whole extent. But what nature does not love and cannot perform, grace will accomplish, and make to you a life of joy and glory. Do you but yield up yourself to Christ your Lord; the conquering power of His incoming presence will make it joy to cast out all that before was most precious. "A hundredfold in this life": this word of the Master comes true to all who, with whole-hearted faithfulness, accept His commands to forsake all. The blessed receiving soon makes the giving up most blessed too. And the secret of a life of close abiding will be seen to be simply this: As I give myself wholly to Christ, I find the power to take Him wholly for myself; and as I lose myself and all I have for Him, He takes me wholly for Himself, and gives Himself wholly to me.

Chapter 17: THROUGH THE HOLY SPIRIT

"The anointing which ye have received of him, abideth in you; and even as it hath taught you, ye shall abide in him."--I JOHN 2:27.

How beautiful the thought of a life always abiding in Christ! The longer we think of it, the more attractive it becomes. And yet how often it is that the precious words, "Abide in me," are heard by the young disciple with a sigh! It is as if he understands so little what they really mean, and can realize so little how this full enjoyment can be attained. He longs for some one who could make it perfectly clear, and continually again remind him that the abiding is in very deed within his reach. If such an one would but listen to the word we have from John this day, what hope and joy it would bring! It gives us the divine assurance that we have the anointing of the Holy Spirit to teach us all things, also to teach us how to abide in Christ.

Alas! someone answers, this word does not give me comfort, it only depresses me more. For it tells of another privilege I so little know to enjoy: I do not understand how the teaching of the Spirit is given-- where or how I can discern His voice. If the Teacher is so unknown, no wonder that the promise of His teaching about the abiding does not help me much.

Thoughts like these come from an error which is very common among believers. They imagine that the Spirit, in teaching them, must reveal the mysteries of the spiritual life first to their intellect, and afterwards in their experience. And God's way is just the contrary of this. What holds true of all spiritual truth is specially true of the abiding in Christ: We must live and experience truth in order to know it. Life-fellowship with Jesus is the only school for the science of heavenly things. "What I do, thou knowest not now, but thou shalt know hereafter," is a law of the Kingdom, specially true of the daily cleansing of which it first was spoken, and the daily keeping. Receive what you do not comprehend, submit to what you cannot understand, accept and expect what to reason appears a mystery, believe what looks impossible, walk in a way which you know not--such are the first lessons in the school of God. "If ye abide in my word, ye shall understand the truth": in these and other words of God we are taught that there is a habit of mind and life which precedes the understanding of the truth. True discipleship consists in first following, and then knowing the Lord. The believing surrender to Christ, and the submission to His word to expect what appears most improbable, is the only way to the full blessedness of knowing Him.

These principles hold specially good in regard to the teaching of the Spirit. That teaching consists in His guiding the spiritual life within us to that which God has prepared for us, without our always knowing how. On the strength of God's promise, and trusting in His faithfulness, the believer yields himself to the leading of the Holy Spirit, without claiming to have it first made clear to the intellect what He is to do, but consenting to let Him do His work in the soul, and afterwards to know what He has wrought there. Faith trusts the working of the Spirit unseen in the deep recesses of the inner life. And so the word of Christ and the gift of the Spirit are to the believer sufficient guarantee that He will be taught of the Spirit to abide in Christ. By faith he rejoices in what he does not see or feel: he knows, and is confident that the blessed Spirit within is doing His work silently but surely, guiding him into the life of full abiding and unbroken communion. The Holy Spirit is the Spirit of life in Christ Jesus; it is His work, not only to breathe, but ever to foster and strengthen, and so to perfect the new life within. And just in proportion as the believer yields himself in simple trust to the unseen, but most certain law of the Spirit of life working within him, his faith will pass into knowledge. It will be rewarded by the Spirit's light revealing in the Word what has already been wrought by the Spirit's power in the life.

Apply this now to the promise of the Spirit's teaching us to abide in Christ. The Holy Spirit is indeed the mighty power of God. And He comes to us from the heart of Christ, the bearer of Christ's life, the revealer and communicator of Christ Himself within us. In the expression, "the fellowship of the Spirit," we are taught what His highest work is. He is the bond of fellowship between the Father and the Son: by Him they are one. He is the bond of fellowship between all believers: by Him they are one. Above all, He is the bond of fellowship between Christ and believers ; He is the life-sap through which Vine and branch grow into real and living oneness: by Him we are one. And we can be assured of it, that if we do but believe in His presence and working, if we do but watch not to grieve Him, because we know that He is in us, if we wait and pray to be filled with Him, He will teach us how to abide. First guiding our will to a whole-hearted cleaving to Christ, then quickening our faith into ever larger confidence and expectation, then breathing into our hearts a peace and joy that pass understanding, He teaches us to abide, we scarce know how. Then coming through the heart and life into the understanding, He makes us know the truth--not as mere thought-truth, but as the truth which is in Christ Jesus, the reflection into the mind of the light of what He has already made a reality in the life. "The life was the light of men."

In view of such teaching, it is clear how, if we would have the Spirit to guide us into the abiding life, our first need is--quiet restful faith. Amid all the questions and difficulties that may come up in connection with our striving to abide in Christ--amid all the longing we may sometimes feel to have a Christian of experience to aid us--amid the frequent painful consciousness of failure, of ignorance, of helplessness--do let us hold fast the blessed confidence: We have the unction of the Holy One to teach us to abide in Him. "THE ANOINTING which ye have received of Him, ABIDETH IN you; and even as it hath taught you, YE SHALL ABIDE IN Him." Make this teaching of His in connection with the abiding a matter of special exercise of faith. Believe that as surely as you have part in Christ, you have His Spirit too. Believe that He will do His work with power, if only you do not hinder Him. Believe that He is working,even when you cannot discern it. Believe that He will work mightily if you ask this from the Father. It is impossible to live the life of full abiding without being full of the the Holy Spirit; believe that the fulness of the Spirit is indeed your daily portion. Be sure and take time in prayer to dwell at the footstool of the throne of God and the Lamb, whence flows the river of the water of life. It is there, and only there, that you can be filled with the Spirit. Cultivate carefully the habit of daily, yea, continually honouring Him by the quiet, restful confidence that He is doing His work within. Let faith in His indwelling make you jealous of whatever could grieve Him--the spirit of the world or the actings of self and the flesh. Let that faith seek its nourishment in the Word and all it says of the Spirit, His power, His comfort, and His work. Above all, let that faith in the Spirit's indwelling lead you specially, to look away to Jesus; as we have received the anointing of Him, it comes in ever stronger flow from Him as we are occupied with Him alone. Christ is the Anointed One. As we look up to Him, the holy anointing comes, "the precious ointment upon the head of Aaron, that went down to the skirts of his garments." It is faith in Jesus that brings the anointing; the anointing leads to Jesus, and to the abiding in Him alone.

Believer, abide in Christ, in the power of the Spirit. What think you, ought the abiding longer to be a fear or a burden? Surely not. Oh, if we did but know the graciousness of our Holy Comforter, and the blessedness of wholly yielding ourselves to His leading, we should indeed experience the divine comfort of having such a teacher to secure our biding in Christ. The Holy Spirit was given for this one purpose-- that the glorious redemption and life in Christ might with divine power be conveyed and communicated to us. We have the Holy Spirit to make the living Christ, in all His saving power, and in the completeness of His victory over sin, ever present within us. It is this that constitutes Him the Comforter: with Him we need never mourn an absent Christ. Let us therefore, as often as we read, or meditate, or pray in connection with this abiding in Christ, reckon upon it as a settled thing that we have the Spirit of God Himself within us, teaching, and guiding, and working. Let us rejoice in the confidence that we must succeed in our desires, because the Holy Spirit is working all the while with secret but divine power in the soul that does not hinder Him by its unbelief.

Chapter 18: IN STILLNESS OF SOUL

"In returning and rest shall ye be saved; in quietness and confidence shall be your strength."--Isaih 30:15

"Be silent to the Lord, and wait patiently for him."--Ps.37:7 (marg.)

"Truly my soul is silent unto God."--Ps.62:1 (marg.)

THERE is a view of the Christian life that regards it as a sort of partnership, in which God and man have each to do their part. It admits that it is but little that man can do, and that little defiled with sin; still he must do his utmost--then only can he expect God to do His part. To those who think thus,it is extremely difficult to understand what Scripture means when it speaks of our being still and doing nothing, of our resting and waiting to see the salvation of God. It appears to them a perfect contradiction, when we speak of this quietness and ceasing from all effort as the secret of the highest activity of man and all his powers. And yet this is just what Scripture does teach. The explanation of the apparent mystery is to be found in this, that when God and man are spoken of as working together, there is nothing of the idea of a partnership between two partners who each contribute their share to a work. The relation is a very different one. The true idea is that of cooperation founded on subordination. As Jesus was entirely dependent on the Father for all His words and all His works, so the believer can do nothing of himself. What he can do of himself is altogether sinful. He must therefore cease entirely from his own doing, and wait for the working of God in him. As he ceases from self-effort, faith assures him that God does what He has undertaken, and works in him. And what God does is to renew, to sanctify, and waken all his energies to their highest power. So that just in proportion as he yields himself a truly passive instrument in the hand of God, will he be wielded of God as the active instrument of His almighty power. The soul in which the wondrous combination of perfect passivity with the highest activity is most completely realized, has the deepest experience of what the Christian life is.

Among the lessons to be learnt of those who are studying the blessed art of abiding in Christ, there is none more needful and more profitable than this one of stillness of soul. In it alone can we cultivate that teachableness of spirit, to which the Lord will reveal His secrets--that meekness to which He shows His ways. It is the spirit exhibited so beautifully in all the three Marys: In her whose only answer to the most wonderful revelation ever made to human being was, "Behold the handmaid of the Lord; be it unto me according to Thy word"; and of whom, as mysteries multiplied around her, it is written: "Mary kept all these things and pondered them in her heart." And in her who "sat at Jesus' feet, and heard His word," and who showed, in the anointing

Him for His burial, how she had entered more deeply into the mystery of His death than even the beloved disciple. And in her, too, who sought her Lord in the house of the Pharisee, with tears that spake more than words. It is a soul silent unto God that is the best preparation for knowing Jesus, and for holding fast the blessings He bestows. It is when the soul is hushed in silent awe and worship before the Holy Presence that reveals itself within, that the still small voice of the blessed Spirit will be heard.

Therefore, beloved Christian, as often as you seek to understand better the blessed mystery of abiding in Christ, let this be your first thought (Ps.62:5, marg.): "My soul, only be silent unto God; for my expectation is from Him." Do you in very deed hope to realize the wondrous union with the Heavenly Vine? Know that flesh and blood cannot reveal it unto you, but only the Father in heaven. "Cease from thine own wisdom." You have but to bow in the confession of your own ignorance and impotence; the Father will delight to give you the teaching of the Holy Spirit. If but your ear be open, and your thoughts brought into subjection, and your heart prepared in silence to wait upon God, and to hear what He speaks, He will reveal to you His secrets. And one of the first secrets will be the deeper insight into the truth, that as you sink low before Him in nothingness and helplessness, in a silence and a stillness of soul that seeks to catch the faintest whisper of His love, teachings will come to you which you had never heard before for the rush and noise of your own thoughts and efforts. You shall learn how your great work is to listen, and hear, and believe what He promises; to watch and wait and see what He does; and then, in faith, and worship, and obedience, to yield yourself to His working who works in you mightily.

One would think that no message could be more beautiful or welcome than this, that we may rest and be quiet, and that our God will work for us and in us. And yet how far this is from being the case! And how slow many are to learn that quietness is blessedness, that quietness is strength, that quietness is the source of the highest activity--the secret of all true abiding in Christ! Let us try to learn it, and to watch against whatever interferes with it. The dangers that threaten the soul's rest are not a few.

There is the dissipation of soul which comes from entering needlessly and too deeply into the interests of this world. Every one of us has his divine calling; and within the circle pointed out by God Himself, interest in our work and its surroundings is a duty. But even here the Christian needs to exercise watchfulness and sobriety. And still more do we need a holy temperance in regard to things not absolutely imposed upon us by God. If abiding in Christ really be our first aim, let us beware of all needless excitement. Let us watch even in lawful and necessary things against the wondrous power these have to keep the soul so occupied, that there remains but little power or zest for fellowship with God. Then there is the restlessness and worry that come of care and anxiety about earthly things; these eat away the life of trust, and keep the soul like a troubled sea. There the gentle whispers of the Holy Comforter cannot be heard.

No less hurtful is the spirit of fear and distrust in spiritual things; with its apprehensions and its efforts, it never comes really to hear what God has to say. Above all, there is the unrest that comes of seeking in our own way and in our own strength the spiritual blessing which comes alone from above. The heart occupied with its own plans and efforts for doing God's will, and securing the blessing of abiding in Jesus, must fail continually. God's work is hindered by our interference. He can do His work perfectly only when the soul ceases from its work. He will do His work mightily in the soul that honours Him by expecting Him to work both to will and to do.

And, last of all, even when the soul seeks truly to enter the way of faith, there is the impatience of the flesh, which forms its judgment of the life and progress of the soul not after the divine but the human standard.

In dealing with all this, and so much more, blessed the man who learns the lesson of stillness, and fully accepts God's word: "In quietness and confidence shall be your strength." Each time he listens to the word of the Father, or asks the Father to listen to his words, he dares not begin his Bible reading or prayer without first pausing and waiting, until the soul be hushed in the presence of the Eternal Majesty. Under a sense of the divine nearness, the soul, feeling how self is always ready to assert itself, and intrude even into the holiest of all with its thoughts and efforts, yields itself in a quiet act of self-surrender to the teaching and working of the divine Spirit. It is still and waits in holy silence, until all is calm and ready to receive the revelation of the divine will and presence. Its reading and prayer then indeed become a waiting on God with ear and heart opened and purged to receive fully only what He says.

"Abide in Christ!" Let no one think that he can do this if he has not daily his quiet time, his seasons of meditation and waiting on God. In these a habit of soul must be cultivated, in which the believer goes out into the world and its distractions, the peace of God, that passeth all understanding, keeping the heart and mind. It is in such a calm and restful soul that the life of faith can strike deep root, that the Holy Spirit can give His blessed teaching, that the Holy Father can accomplish His glorious work. May each one of us learn every day to say, "Truly my soul is silent unto God." And may every feeling of the difficulty of attaining this only lead us simply to look and trust to Him whose presence makes even the storm a calm. Cultivate the quietness as a means to the abiding in Christ; expect the ever deepening quietness and calm of heaven in the soul as the fruit of abiding in Him.

Chapter 19: IN AFFLICTION AND TRIAL

"Every branch that bearest fruit, he purgeth it, that it may bring forth more fruit."--JOHN 15:2.

IN THE whole plant world there is not a tree to be found so specially suited to the image of man in his relation to God, as the vine. There is none of which the fruit and its juice are so full of spirit, so quickening and stimulating. But there is also none of which the natural tendency is so entirely evil--none where the growth is so ready to run into wood that is utterly worthless except for the fire. Of all plants, not one needs the pruning knife so unsparingly and so unceasingly. None is so dependent on cultivation and training, but with this none yields a richer reward to the husbandman. In His wonderful parable, the Saviour, with a single word, refers to this need of pruning in the vine, and the blessing it brings. But from that single word what streams of light pour in upon this dark world, so full of suffering and of sorrow to believers! What treasures of teaching and comfort to the bleeding branch in its hour of trial: "Every branch that beareth fruit, He purgeth it, that it may bring forth more fruit." And so He has prepared His people, who are so ready when trial comes to be shaken in their confidence, and to be moved from their abiding in Christ, to hear in each affliction the voice of a messenger that comes to call them to abide still more closely. Yes, believer, most specially in times of trial,abide in Christ.

Abide in Christ! This is indeed the Father's object in sending the trial. In the storm the tree strikes deeper roots in the soil; in the hurricane the inhabitants of the house abide within, and rejoice in its shelter. So by suffering the Father would lead us to enter more deeply into the love of Christ. Our hearts are continually prone to wander from Him; prosperity and enjoyment all too easily satisfy us, dull our spiritual perception, and unfit us for full communion with Himself. It is an unspeakable mercy that the Father comes with His chastisement, makes the world round us all dark and unattractive, leads us to feel more deeply our sinfulness, and for a time lose our joy in what was becoming so dangerous. He does it in the hope that, when we have found our rest in Christ in time of trouble, we shall learn to choose abiding in Him as our only portion; and when the affliction is removed, have so grown more firmly into Him, that in prosperity He still shall be our only joy. So much has He set His heart on this, that though He has indeed no pleasure in afflicting us, He will not keep back even the most painful chastisement if He can but thereby guide His beloved child to come home and abide in the beloved Son. Christian! pray for grace to see in every trouble, small or great, the Father's finger pointing to Jesus, and saying, Abide in Him.

Abide in Christ: so will you become partaker of all the rich blessings

God designed for you in the affliction. The purposes of God's wisdom will become clear to you, your assurance of the unchangeable love become stronger, and the power of His Spirit fulfil you the promise: "He chasteneth us for our profit, that we might be partakers of His holiness." Abide in Christ: and your cross becomes the means of fellowship with His cross, and access into its mysteries--the mystery of the curse which He bore for you, of the death to sin in which you partake with Him, of the love in which, as sympathizing High Priest, He descended into all your sorrows. Abide in Christ: growing in conformity to your blessed Lord in His sufferings, deeper experience of the reality and the tenderness of His love will be yours. Abide in Christ: in the fiery oven, one like the Son of Man will be seen as never before; the purging away of the dross and the refining of the gold will be accomplished, and Christ's own likeness reflected in you. O abide in Christ: the power of the flesh will be mortified, the impatience and self-will of the old nature be humbled, to make place for the meekness and gentleness of Christ. A believer may pass through much affliction, and yet secure but little blessing from it all. Abiding in Christ is the secret of securing all that the Father meant the chastisement to bring us. Abide in Christ: in Him you shall find sure and abundant consolation. With the afflicted comfort is often first, and the profit of the affliction second. The Father loves us so, that with Him our real and abiding profit is His first object, but He does not forget to comfort too. When He comforts it is that He may turn the bleeding heart to Himself to receive the blessing in fellowship with Him; when He refuses comfort, His object is still the same. It is in making us partakers of His holiness that true comfort comes. The Holy Spirit is the Comforter, not only because He can suggest comforting thoughts of God's love, but far more, because He makes us holy, and brings us into close union with Christ and with God. He teaches us to abide in Christ; and because God is found there, the truest comfort will come there too. In Christ the heart of the Father is revealed, and higher comfort there cannot be than to rest in the Father's bosom. In Him the fulness of the divine love is revealed, combined with the tenderness of a mother's compassion--and what can comfort like this? In Him you see a thousand times more given you than you have lost; see how God only took from you that you might have room to take from Him what is so much better. In Him suffering is consecrated, and becomes the foretaste of eternal glory; in suffering it is that the Spirit of God and of glory rests on us. Believer! would you have comfort in affliction?--Abide in Christ.

Abide in Christ: so will you bear much fruit. Not a vine is planted but the owner thinks of the fruit, and the fruit only. Other trees may be planted for ornament, for the shade, for the wood--the vine only for the fruit. And of each vine the husbandman is continually asking how it can bring forth more fruit, much fruit. Believer! abide in Christ in times of affliction, and you shall bring forth more fruit. The deeper experience of Christ's tenderness and the Father's love will urge you to live to His glory. The surrender of self and selfwill in suffering will prepare you to sympathize with the misery of others, while the softening that comes of chastisement will fit you for becoming, as Jesus was, the servant of all. The thought of the Father's desire for fruit in the pruning will lead you to yield yourself afresh, and more than ever, to Him, and to say that now you have but one object in life-- making known and conveying His wonderful love to fellow-men. You shall learn the blessed art of forgetting self, and, even in affliction, availing yourself of your separation from ordinary life to plead for the welfare of others. Dear Christian, in affliction abide in Christ. When you see it coming, meet it in Christ; when it is come, feel that you are more in Christ than in it, for He is nearer you than affliction ever can be; when it is passing, still abide in Him. And let the one thought of the Saviour, as He speaks of the pruning, and the one desire of the Father, as He does the pruning, be yours too: "Every branch that beareth fruit, He purgeth, that it may bring forth more fruit."

So shall your times of affliction become your times of choicest blessing--preparation for richest fruitfulness. Led into closer fellowship with the Son of God, and deeper experience of His love and grace-- established in the blessed confidence that He and you entirely belong to each other--more completely satisfied with Him and more wholly given up to Him than ever before--with your own will crucified afresh, and the heart brought into deeper harmony with God's will--you shall be a vessel cleansed, meet for the Master's use, prepared for every good work. True believer! O try and learn the blessed truth, that in affliction your first, your only, your blessed calling is to abide in Christ. Be much with Him alone. Beware of the comfort and the distractions that friends so often bring. Let Jesus Christ Himself be your chief companion and comforter. Delight yourself in the assurance that closer union with Him, and more abundant fruit through Him, are sure to be the results of trial, because it is the Husbandman Himself who is pruning, and will ensure the fulfilment of the desire of the soul that yields itself lovingly to His work.

Chapter 20: THAT YOU MAY BEAR MUCH FRUIT

"He that abideth in me, and I in him, the same bringeth forth much fruit. Herein is my Father glorified, that ye bear much fruit."--JOHN 15:5,8.

WE ALL know what fruit is. The produce of the branch, by which men are refreshed and nourished. The fruit is not for the branch, but for those who come to carry it away. As soon as the fruit is ripe, the branch gives it off, to commence afresh its work of beneficence, and anew prepare its fruit for another season. A fruit-bearing tree lives not for itself, but wholly for those to whom its fruit brings refreshment and life. And so the branch exists only and entirely for the sake of the fruit. To make glad the heart of the husbandman is its object, its safety, and its glory.

Beautiful image of the believer, abiding in Christ! He not only grows in strength, the union with the Vine becoming ever surer and firmer, he also bears fruit, yea, much fruit. He has the power to offer that to others of which they can eat and live. Amid all who surround him he becomes like a tree of life, of which they can taste and be refreshed. He is in his circle a centre of life and of blessing, and that simply because he abides in Christ, and receives from Him the Spirit and the life of which he can impart to others. Learn thus, if you would bless others, to abide in Christ, and that if you do abide, you shall surely bless. As surely as the branch abiding in a fruitful vine bears fruit, so surely, yea, much more surely, will a soul abiding in Christ with His fulness of blessing be made a blessing.

The reason of this is easily understood. If Christ, the heavenly Vine, has taken the believer as a branch, then He has pledged Himself, in the very nature of things, to supply the sap and spirit and nourishment to make it bring forth fruit. "From ME is thy fruit found": these words derive new meaning from our parable. The soul need but have one care--to abide closely, fully, wholly. He will give the fruit. He works all that is needed to make the believer a blessing.

Abiding in Him, you receive of Him His Spirit of love and compassion towards sinners, making you desirous to seek their good. By nature the heart is full of selfishness. Even in the believer, his own salvation and happiness are often too much his only object. But abiding in Jesus, you come into contact with His infinite love; its fire begins to burn within your heart; you see the beauty of love; you learn to look upon loving and serving and saving your fellow-men as the highest privilege a disciple of Jesus can have. Abiding in Christ, your heart learns to feel the wretchedness of the sinner still in darkness, and the fearfulness of the dishonour done to your God. With Christ you begin to bear the burden of souls, the burden of sins not your own. As you are more closely united to Him, somewhat of that passion for souls which urged Him to Calvary begins to breathe within you, and you are ready to follow His footsteps, to forsake the heaven of your own happiness, and devote your life to win the souls Christ has taught you to love. The very spirit of the Vine is love; the spirit of love streams into the branch that abides in Him.

The desire to be a blessing is but the beginning. As you undertake to work, you speedily become conscious of your own weakness and the difficulties in your way. Souls are not saved at your bidding. You are ready to be discouraged, and to relax your effort. But abiding in Christ, you receive new courage and strength for the work. Believing what Christ teaches, that it is HE who through you will give His blessing to the world, you understand that you are but the feeble instrument through which the hidden power of Christ does its work, that His strength may be perfected and made glorious in your weakness. It is a great step when the believer fully consents to his own weakness, and the abiding consciousness of it, and so works faithfully on, fully assured that his Lord is working through him. He rejoices that the excellence of the power is of God, and not of us. Realizing his oneness with his Lord, he considers no longer his own weakness, but counts on the power of Him of whose hidden working within he is assured. It is this secret assurance that gives a brightness to his look, and a gentle firmness to his tone, and a perseverance to all his efforts, which of themselves are great means of influencing those he is seeking to win. He goes forth in the spirit of one to whom victory is assured; for this is the victory that overcometh, even our faith. He no longer counts it humility to say that God cannot bless his unworthy efforts. He claims and expects a blessing, because it is not he, but Christ in him, that worketh. The great secret of abiding in Christ is the deep conviction that we are nothing, and He is everything. As this is learnt, it no longer seems strange to believe that our weakness need be no hindrance to His saving power. The believer who yields himself wholly up to Christ for service in the spirit of a simple, childlike trust, will assuredly bring forth much fruit. He will not fear even to claim his share in the wonderful promise: "He that believeth on me, the works that I do shall he do also; and greater works than these shall he do, because I go to the Father." He no longer thinks that He cannot have a blessing, and must be kept unfruitful, that he may be kept humble. He sees that the most heavily laden branches bow the lowest down. Abiding in Christ, he has yielded assent to the blessed agreement between the Vine and the branches, that of the fruit all the glory shall be to the Husbandman, the blessed Father.

Let us learn two lessons. If we are abiding in Jesus, let us begin to work. Let us first seek to influence those around us in daily life. Let us accept distinctly and joyfully our holy calling, that we are even now to live as the servants of the love of Jesus to our fellow-men. Our daily life must have for its object the making of an impression favourable to Jesus. When you look at the branch, you see at once the likeness to the Vine. We must live so that somewhat of the holiness and the gentleness of Jesus may shine out in us. We must live to represent Him. As was the case with Him when on earth, the life must prepare the way for the teaching. What the Church and the world both need is this: men and women full of the Holy Ghost and of love, who, as the living embodiments of the grace and power of Christ, witness for Him, and for His power on behalf of those who believe in Him. Living so, with our hearts longing to have Jesus glorified in the souls He is seeking after, let us offer ourselves to Him for direct work. There is work in our own home. There is work among the sick, the poor, and the outcast. There is work in a hundred different paths which the Spirit of Christ opens up through those who allow themselves to be led by Him. There is work perhaps for us in ways that have not yet been opened up by others. Abiding in Christ, let us work. Let us work, not like those who are content if they now follow the fashion, and take some share in religious work. No; let us work as those who are growing more like Christ, because they are abiding in Him, and who, like Him, count the work of winning souls to the Father the very joy and glory of heaven begun on earth.

And the second lesson is: If you work, abide in Christ. This is one of the blessings of work if done in the right spirit--it will deepen your union with your blessed Lord. It will discover your weakness, and throw you back on His strength. It will stir you to much prayer; and in prayer for others is the time when the soul, forgetful of itself, unconsciously grows deeper into Christ. It will make clearer to you the true nature of branch-life; its absolute dependence, and at the same time its glorious sufficiency--independent of all else, because dependent on Jesus. If you work, abide in Christ. There are temptations and dangers. Work for Christ has sometimes drawn away from Christ, and taken the place of fellowship with Him. Work can sometimes give a form of godliness without the power. As you work, abide in Christ. Let a living faith in Christ working in you be the secret spring of all your work; this will inspire at once humility and courage. Let the Holy Spirit of Jesus dwell in you as the Spirit of His tender compassion and His divine power. Abide in Christ, and offer every faculty of your nature freely and unreservedly to Him, to sanctify it for Himself. If Jesus Christ is really to work through us, it needs an entire consecration of ourselves to Him, daily renewed. But we understand now, just this is abiding in Christ; just this it is that constitutes our highest privilege and happiness. To be a branch bearing much fruit--nothing less, nothing more--be this our only joy.

Chapter 21: SO WILL YOU HAVE POWER IN PRAYER

"If ye abide in me, and my words abide in you, ye shall ask what ye will, and it shall be done unto you. "-- JOHN 15:7.

PRAYER is both one of the means and one of the fruits of union to Christ. As a means it is of unspeakable importance. All the things of faith, all the pleadings of desire, all the yearnings after a fuller surrender, all the confessions of shortcoming and of sin, all the exercises in which the soul gives up self and clings to Christ, find their utterance in prayer. In each meditation on abiding in Christ, as some new feature of what Scripture teaches concerning this blessed life is apprehended, the first impulse of the believer is at once to look up to the Father and pour out the heart into His, and ask from Him the full understanding and the full possession of what he has been shown in the Word. And it is the believer, who is not content with this spontaneous expression of his hope, but who takes time in secret prayer to wait until he has received and laid hold of what he has seen, who will really grow strong in Christ. However feeble the soul's first abiding, its prayer will be heard, and it will find prayer one of the great means of abiding more abundantly.

But it is not so much as a means, but as a fruit of the abiding, that the Saviour mentions it in the parable of the Vine. He does not think so much of prayer--as we, alas! too exclusively do--as a means of getting blessing for ourselves, but as one of the chief channels of influence by which, through us as fellow-workers with God, the blessings of Christ's redemption are to be dispensed to the world. He sets before Himself and us the glory of the Father, in the extension of His Kingdom, as the object for which we have been made branches; and He assures us that if we but abide in Him, we shall be Israels, having power with God and man. Ours shall be the effectual, fervent prayer of the righteous man, availing much, like Elijah's for ungodly Israel. Such prayer will be the fruit of our abiding in Him, and the means of bringing forth much fruit. To the Christian who is not abiding wholly in Jesus, the difficulties connected with prayer are often so great as to rob him of the comfort and the strength it could bring. Under the guise of humility, he asks how one so unworthy could expect to have influence with the Holy One. He thinks of God's sovereignty, His perfect wisdom and love, and cannot see how his prayer can really have any distinct effect. He prays, but it is more because he cannot rest without prayer, than from a loving faith that the prayer will be heard. But what a blessed release from such questions and perplexities is given to the soul who is truly abiding in Christ! He realizes increasingly how it is in the real spiritual unity with Christ that we are accepted and heard. The union with the Son of God is a life union: we are in very deed one with Him--our prayer ascends as His prayer. It is because we abide in Him that we can ask what we will, and it is given to us.

There are many reasons why this must be so. One is, that abiding in Christ, and having His words abiding in us, teach us to pray in accordance with the will of God. With the abiding in Christ our self-will is kept down, the thoughts and wishes of nature are brought into captivity to the thoughts and wishes of Christ; likemindedness to Christ grows upon us--all our working and willing become transformed into harmony with His. There is deep and oft-renewed heart-searching to see whether the surrender has indeed been entire; fervent prayer to the heart-searching Spirit that nothing may be kept back. Everything is yielded to the power of His life in us, that it may exercise its sanctifying influence even on ordinary wishes and desires. His Holy Spirit breathes through our whole being; and without our being conscious how, our desires, as the breathings of the divine life, are in conformity with the divine will, and are fulfilled. Abiding in Christ renews and sanctifies the will: we ask what we will, and it is given to us.

In close connection with this is the thought, that the abiding in Christ teaches the believer in prayer only to seek the glory of God. In promising to answer prayer, Christ's one thought (see John 14:13) is this, "that the Father may be glorified in the Son." In His intercession on earth (John 17), this was His one desire and plea; in His intercession in heaven, it is still His great object. As the believer abides in Christ, the Saviour breathes this desire into him. The thought, ONLY THE GLORY of GOD, becomes more and more the keynote of the life hid in Christ. At first this subdues, and quiets, and makes the soul almost afraid to dare entertain a wish, lest it should not be to the Father's glory. But when once its supremacy has been accepted, and everything yielded to it, it comes with mighty power to elevate and enlarge the heart, and open it to the vast field open to the glory of God. Abiding in Christ, the soul learns not only to desire, but spiritually to discern what will be for God's glory; and one of the first conditions of acceptable prayer is fulfilled in it when, as the fruit of its union with Christ, the whole mind is brought into harmony with that of the Son as He said: "Father, glorify Thy name."

Once more: Abiding in Christ, we can fully avail ourselves of the name of Christ. Asking in the name of another means that that other authorized me and sent me to ask, and wants to be considered as asking himself: he wants the favour done to him. Believers often try to think of the name of Jesus and His merits, and to argue themselves into the faith that they will be heard, while they painfully feel how little they have of the faith of His name. They are not living wholly in Jesus' name; it is only when they begin to pray that they want to take up that name and use it. This cannot be. The promise "Whatsoever ye ask in my name," may not be severed from the command, "Whatsoever ye do, do all in the name of the Lord Jesus." If the name of Christ is to be wholly at my disposal, so that I may have the full command of it for all I will, it must be because I first put myself wholly at His disposal, so that He has free and full command of me. It is the abiding in Christ that gives the right and power to use His name with confidence. To Christ the Father refuses nothing. Abiding in Christ, I come to the Father as one with Him. His righteousness is in me, His Spirit is in me; the Father sees the Son in me, and gives me my petition. It is not--as so many think--by a sort of imputation that the Father looks upon us as if we were in Christ, though we are not in Him. No; the Father wants to see us living in Him: thus shall our prayer really have power to prevail. Abiding in Christ not only renews the will to pray aright, but secures the full power of His merits to us.

Again: Abiding in Christ also works in us the faith that alone can obtain an answer. "According to your faith be it unto you": this is one of the laws of the kingdom. "Believe that ye receive, and ye shall have." This faith rests upon, and is rooted in the Word, but is something infinitely higher than the mere logical conclusion: God has promised, I shall obtain. No; faith, as a spiritual act, depends upon the words abiding in us as living powers, and so upon the state of the whole inner life. Without fasting and prayer (Mark 9:29), without humility and a spiritual mind (John 5:44), without a wholehearted obedience (1 John 3:22), there cannot be this living faith. But as the soul abides in Christ, and grows into the consciousness of its union with Him, and sees how entirely it is He who makes it and its petition acceptable, it dares to claim an answer because it knows itself one with Him. It was by faith it learnt to abide in Him; as the fruit of that faith, it rises to a larger faith in all that God has promised to be and to do. It learns to breathe its prayers in the deep, quiet, confident assurance: We know we have the petition we ask of Him.

Abiding in Christ, further, keeps us in the place where the answer can be bestowed. Some believers pray earnestly for blessing; but when God comes and looks for them to bless them, they are not to be found. They never thought that the blessing must not only be asked, but waited for, and received in prayer. Abiding in Christ is the place for receiving answers. Out of Him the answer would be dangerous--we should consume it on our lusts (Jas. 4:3). Many of the richest answers--say for spiritual grace, or for power to work and to bless--can only come in the shape of a larger experience of what God makes Christ to us. The fulness is IN Him; abiding in Him is the condition of power in prayer, because the answer is treasured up and bestowed in Him.

Believer, abide in Christ, for there is the school of prayer--mighty, effectual, answer-bringing prayer. Abide in Him, and you shall learn what to so many is a mystery: That the secret of the prayer of faith is the life of faith--the life that abides in Christ alone.

Chapter 22: AND IN HIS LOVE

"As the Father hath loved me, so have I loved you: abide ye in my love."--John 15:9.[1]

BLESSED Lord, enlighten our eyes to see aright the glory of this wondrous word. Open to our meditation the secret chamber of THY LOVE, that our souls may enter in, and find there their everlasting dwelling-place. How else shall we know aught of a love that passeth knowledge?

Before the Saviour speaks the word that invites us to abide in His love, He first tells us what that love is. What He says of it must give force to His invitation, and make the thought of not accepting it an impossibility: "As the Father hath loved me, so I have loved you!"

"As the Father hath loved me." How shall we be able to form right conceptions of this love? Lord, teach us. God is love. Love is His very being. Love is not an attribute, but the very essence of His nature, the centre round which all His glorious attributes gather. It was because He was love that He was the Father, and that there was a Son. Love needs an object to whom it can give itself away, in whom it can lose itself, with whom it can make itself one. Because God is love, there must be a Father and a Son. The love of the Father to the Son is that divine passion with which He delights in the Son, and speaks, "My beloved Son, in whom I am well pleased." The divine love is as a burning fire; in all its intensity and infinity it has but one object and but one joy, and that is the only-begotten Son. When we gather together all the attributes of God--His infinity, His perfection, His immensity, His majesty, His omnipotence--and consider them but as the rays of the glory of His love, we still fail in forming any conception of what that love must be. It is a love that passeth knowledge.

And yet this love of God to His Son must serve, O my soul, as the glass in which you are to learn how Jesus loves you. As one of His redeemed ones, you are His delight, and all His desire is to you, with the longing of a love which is stronger than death, and which many waters cannot quench. His heart yearns after you, seeking your fellowship and your love. Were it needed, He could die again to possess you. As the Father loved the Son, and could not live without Him, could not be God the blessed without Him-so Jesus loves you. His life is bound up in yours; you are to Him inexpressibly more indispensable and precious than you ever can know. You are one with Himself. "As the Father hath loved me, so have I loved you." What a love!

It is an eternal love. From before the foundation of the world-God's Word teaches us this-the purpose had been formed that Christ should be the Head of His Church, that He should have a body in which His glory could be set forth. In that eternity He loved and longed for those who had been given Him by the Father; and when He came and told His disciples that He loved them, it was indeed not with a love of earth and of time, but with the love of eternity. And it is with that same infinite love that His eye still rests upon each of us here seeking to abide in Him, and in each breathing of that love there is indeed the power of eternity. "I have loved thee with an everlasting love."

It is a perfect love. It gives all, and holds nothing back. "The Father loveth the Son, and hath given all things into His hand." And just so Jesus loves His own: all He has is theirs. When it was needed, He sacrificed His throne and crown for you: He did not count His own life and blood too dear to give for you. His righteousness, His Spirit, His glory, even His throne, all are yours. This love holds nothing, nothing back, but, in a manner which no human mind can fathom, makes you one with itself. O wondrous love! to love us even as the Father loved Him, and to offer us this love as our everyday dwelling.

It is a gentle and most tender love. As we think of the love of the Father to the Son, we see in the Son everything so infinitely worthy of that love. When we think of Christ's love to us, there is nothing but sin and unworthiness to meet the eye. And the question comes: How can that love within the bosom of the divine life and its perfections be compared to the love that rests on sinners? Can it indeed be the same love? Blessed be God, we know it is so. The nature of love is always one, however different the objects. Christ knows of no other law of love but that with which His Father loved Him. Our wretchedness only serves to call out more distinctly the beauty of love, such as could not be seen even in heaven. With the tenderest compassion He bows to our weakness, with patience inconceivable He bears with our slowness, with the gentlest loving-kindness He meets our fears and our follies. It is the love of the Father to the Son, beautified, glorified, in its condescension, in its exquisite adaptation to our needs.

And it is an unchangeable love. "Having loved His own which were in the world, He loved them to the end." "The mountains shall depart, and the hills be removed, but my kindness shall not depart from thee." The promise with which it begins its work in the soul is this: "I shall not leave thee, until I have done that which I have spoken to thee of." And just as our wretchedness was what first drew it to us, so the sin, with which it is so often grieved, and which may well cause us to fear and doubt, is but a new motive for it to hold to us all the more. And why? We can give no reason but this: "As the Father hath loved me, so I have loved you."

And now, does not this love suggest the motive, the measure, and the means of that surrender by which we yield ourselves wholly to abide in Him?

This love surely supplies a motive. Only look and see how this love stands and pleads and prays. Gaze, O gaze on the divine form, the eternal glory, the heavenly beauty, the tenderly pleading gentleness of the crucified love, as it stretches out its pierced hands and says, "Oh, wilt thou not abide with me? wilt thou not come and abide in me?" It points you up to the eternity of love whence it came to seek you. It points you to the Cross, and all it has borne to prove the reality of its affection, and to win you for itself. It reminds you of all it has promised to do for you, if you will but throw yourself unreservedly into its arms. It asks you whether, so far as you have come to dwell with it and taste its blessedness, it has not done well by you. And with a divine authority, mingled with such an inexpressible tenderness that one might almost think he heard the tone of reproach in it, it says, "Soul, as the Father hath loved me, so I have loved you: abide in my love." Surely there can be but one answer to such pleading: Lord Jesus Christ! here I am. Henceforth Thy love shall be the only home of my soul: in Thy love alone will I abide.

That love is not only the motive, but also the measure, of our surrender to abide in it. Love gives all, but asks all. It does so, not because it grudges us aught, but because without this it cannot get possession of us to fill us with itself. In the love of the Father and the Son, it was so. In the love of Jesus to us, it was so. In our entering into His love to abide there, it must be so too; our surrender to it must have no other measure than its surrender to us. O that we understood how the love that calls us has infinite riches and fulness of joy for us, and that what we give up for its sake will be rewarded a hundredfold in this life! Or rather, would that we understood that it is a LOVE with a height and a depth and a length and a breadth that passes knowledge! How all thought of sacrifice or surrender would pass away, and our souls be filled with wonder at the unspeakable privilege of being loved with such a love, of being allowed to come and abide in it for ever.

And if doubt again suggest the question: But is it possible, can I always abide in His love? listen how that love itself supplies the only means for the abiding in Him: It is faith in that love which will enable us to abide in it. If this love be indeed so divine, such an intense and burning passion, then surely I can depend on it to keep me and to hold me fast. Then surely all my unworthiness and feebleness can be no hindrance. If this love be indeed so divine, with infinite power at its command, I surely have a right to trust that it is stronger than my weakness; and that with its almighty arm it will clasp me to its bosom, and suffer me to go out no more. I see how this is the one thing my God requires of me. Treating me as a reasonable being endowed with the wondrous power of willing and choosing, He cannot force all this blessedness on me, but waits till I give the willing consent of the heart. And the token of this consent He has in His great kindness ordered faith to be-that faith by which utter sinfulness casts itself into the arms of love to be saved, and utter weakness to be kept and made strong. O Infinite Love! Love with which the Father loved the Son! Love with which the Son loves us! I can trust thee, I do trust thee. O keep me abiding in Thyself. [1] It is difficult to understand why in our English Bible one Greek word should in the first sixteen verses of John 15 have had three different translations: abide in ver. 4, continue in ver. 9, and remain in vers. 11 and 16. The Revised Version has of course kept the one word, abide.

Chapter 23: AS CHRIST IN THE FATHER

"As the Father hath loved me, so I have loved you. Abide in my love, even as I abide in my Father's love."-JOHN 15:9,10.

CHRIST had taught His disciples that to abide in Him was to abide in His love. The hour of His suffering is nigh, and He cannot speak much more to them. They doubtless have many questions to ask as to what that abiding in Him and His love is. He anticipates and meets their wishes, and gives them HIS OWN LIFE as the best exposition of His command. As example and rule for their abiding in His love, they have to look to His abiding in the Father's love. In the light of His union with the Father, their union with Him will become clear. His life in the Father is the law of their life in Him.

The thought is so high that we can hardly take it in, and is yet so clearly revealed, that we dare not neglect it. Do we not read in John 6 (ver.57), "As I live by the Father, even so he that eateth me, he shall live by me"? And the Saviour prays so distinctly (John 17:22), "that they may be one even as we are one: I in them, and Thou in me." The blessed union of Christ with the Father and His life in Him is the only rule of our thoughts and expectations in regard to our living and abiding in Him.

Think first of the origin of that life of Christ in the Father. They were ONE--one in life and one in love. In this His abiding in the Father had its root. Though dwelling here on earth, He knew that He was one with the Father; that the Father's life was in Him, and His love on Him. Without this knowledge, abiding in the Father and His love would have been utterly impossible. And it is thus only that you can abide in Christ and His love. Know that you are one with Him--one in the unity of nature. By His birth He became man, and took your nature that He might be one with you. By your new birth you become one with Him, and are made partaker of His divine nature. The link that binds you to Him is as real and close as bound Him to the Father--the link of a divine life. Your claim on Him is as sure and always availing as was His on the Father. Your union with Him is as close.

And as it is the union of a divine life, it is one of an infinite love. In His life of humiliation on earth He tasted the blessedness and strength of knowing Himself the object of an infinite love, and of dwelling in it all the day; from His own example He invites you to learn that herein lies the secret of rest and joy. You are one with Him: yield yourself now to be loved by Him; let your eyes and heart open to the love that shines and presses in on you on every side. Abide in His love.

Think then too of the mode of that abiding in the Father and His love which is to be the law of your life. "I kept my Father's commandments and abide in His love." His was a life of subjection and dependence and yet most blessed. To our proud self-seeking nature the thought of dependence and subjection suggests the idea of humiliation and servitude; in the life of love which the Son of God lived, and to which He invite us, they are the secret of blessedness. The Son is not afraid of losing aught by giving up all to the Father, for He knows that the Father loves Him, and can have no interest apart from that of the beloved Son. He knows that as complete as is the dependence on His part is the communication on the part of the Father of all He possesses. Hence when He had said, "The Son can do nothing of Himself, except He see the Father do it," He adds at once, "Whatsoever things the Father doeth, them also doeth the Son likewise: for the Father loveth the Son, and showeth Him all things that Himself doeth." The believer who studies this life of Christ as the pattern and the promise of what his may be, learns to understand how the "Without me ye can do nothing," is but the forerunner of "I can do all things through Christ who strengtheneth me." We learn to glory in infirmities, to take pleasure in necessities and distresses for Christ's sake; for "when I am weak, then am I strong." He rises above the ordinary tone in which so many Christians speak of their weakness, while they are content to abide there, because he has learnt from Christ that in the life of divine love the emptying of self and the sacrifice of our will is the surest way to have all we can wish or will. Dependence, subjection, self-sacrifice, are for the Christian as for Christ the blessed path of life. Like as Christ lived through and in the Father, even so the believer lives through and in Christ.

Think of the glory of this life of Christ in the Father's love. Because He gave Himself wholly to the Father's will and glory, the Father crowned Him with glory and honour. He acknowledged Him as His only representative; He made Him partaker of His power and authority; He exalted Him to share His throne as God. And even so will it be with him who abides in Christ's love. If Christ finds us willing to trust ourselves and our interests to His love, if in that trust we give up all care for our own will and honour, if we make it our glory to exercise and confess absolute dependence on Him in all things, if we are content to have no life but in Him, He will do for us what the Father did for Him. He will lay of His glory on us: As the name of our Lord is Jesus is glorified in us, we are glorified in Him (2 Thess.1:12). He acknowledges us as His true and worthy representatives; He entrusts us with His power; He admits us to His counsels, as He allows our intercession to influence His rule of His Church and the world; He makes us the vehicles of His authority and His influence over men. His Spirit knows no other dwelling than such, and seeks no other instruments for His divine work. Blessed life of love for the soul that abides in Christ's love, even as He in the Father's!

Believer! abide in the love of Christ. Take and study His relation to the Father as pledge of what thine own can become. As blessed, as mighty, as glorious as was His life in the Father, can yours be in Him. Let this truth, accepted under the teaching of the Spirit in faith, remove every vestige of fear, as if abiding in Christ were a burden and a work. In the light of His life in the Father, let it henceforth be to you a blessed rest in the union with Him, an overflowing fountain of joy and strength. To abide in His love, His mighty, saving, keeping, satisfying love, even as He abode in the Father's love--surely the very greatness of our calling teaches us that it never can be a work we have to perform; it must be with us as with Him, the result of the spontaneous outflowing of a life from within, and the mighty inworking of the love from above. What we only need is this: to take time and study the divine image of this life of love set before us in Christ. We need to have our souls still unto God, gazing upon that life of Christ in the Father until the light from heaven falls on it, and we hear the living voice of our Beloved whispering gently to us personally the teaching He gave to the disciples. Soul, be still and listen; let every thought be hushed until the word has entered your heart too: "Child! I love thee, even as the Father loved me. Abide in my love, even as I abide in the Father's love. Thy life on earth in me is to be the perfect counterpart of mine in the Father."

And if the thought will sometimes come: Surely this is too high for us; can it be really true? only remember that the greatness of the privilege is justified by the greatness of the object He has in view. Christ was the revelation of the Father on earth. He could not be this if there were not the most perfect unity, the most complete communication of all the Father had to the Son. He could be it because the Father loved Him, and He abode in that love. Believers are the revelation of Christ on earth. They cannot be this unless there be perfect unity, so that the world can know that He loves them and has sent them. But they can be it if Christ loves them with the infinite love that gives itself and all it has, and if they abide in that love.

Lord, show us Thy love. Make us with all the saints to know the love that passeth knowledge. Lord, show us in Thine own blessed life what it is to abide in Thy love. And the sight shall so win us, that it will be impossible for us one single hour to seek any other life than the life of abiding in Thy love.

Chapter 24: OBEYING HIS COMMANDMENTS

"If ye keep my commandments, ye shall abide in my love; even as I kept my Father's commandments, and abide in his love."--JOHN 15:10.

How clearly we are taught here the place which good works are to occupy in the life of the believer! Christ as the beloved Son was in the Father's love. He kept His commandments, and so He abode in the love. So the believer, without works, receives Christ and is in Him; he keeps the commandments, and so abides in the love. When the sinner, in coming to Christ, seeks to prepare himself by works, the voice of the Gospel sounds, "Not of works." When once in Christ, lest the flesh should abuse the word, "Not of works," the Gospel lifts its voice as loud: "Created in Christ Jesus unto good works" (see Eph.2:9,10). To the sinner out of Christ, works may be his greatest hindrance, keeping him from the union with the Saviour. To the believer in Christ, works are strength and blessing, for by them faith is made perfect (Jas.2:22), the union with Christ is cemented, and the soul established and more deeply rooted in the love of God. "If a man love me, he will keep my words, and my Father will love him." "If ye keep my commandments, ye shall abide in my love."

The connection between this keeping the commandments and the abiding in Christ's love is easily understood. Our union with Jesus Christ is not a thing of the intellect or sentiment, but a real vital union in heart and life. The holy life of Jesus, with His feelings and. disposition, is breathed into us by the Holy Spirit. The believer's calling is to think and feel and will just what Jesus thought and felt and willed. He desires to be partaker not only of the grace but also of the holiness of His Lord; or rather, he sees that holiness is the chief beauty of grace. To live the life of Christ means to him to be delivered from the life of self; the will of Christ is to him the only path of liberty from the slavery of his own evil self-will.

To the ignorant or slothful believer there is a great difference between the promises and commands of Scripture. The former he counts his comfort and his food; but to him who is really seeking to abide in Christ's love, the commands become no less precious, As much as the promises they are the revelation of the divine love, guides into the deeper experience of the divine life, blessed helpers in the path to a closer union with the Lord. He sees how the harmony of our will with His will is one of the chief elements of our fellowship with Him. The will is the central faculty in the Divine as in the human being. The will of God is the power that rules the whole moral as well as the natural world. How could there be fellowship with Him without delight in His will? It is only as long as salvation is to the sinner nothing but a personal safety, that he can be careless or afraid of the doing of God's will. No sooner is it to him what Scripture and the Holy Spirit reveal it to be--the restoration to communion with God and conformity to Him--than he feels that there is no law more natural or more beautiful than this: Keeping Christ's commandments the way to abide in Christ's love. His inmost soul approves when he hears the beloved Lord make the larger measure of the Spirit, with the manifestation of the Father and the Son in the believer, entirely dependent upon the keeping of His commandments (John 14:15,16,21,23).

There is another thing that opens to him a deeper insight and Secures a still more cordial acceptance of this truth. It is this, that in no other way did Christ Himself abide in the Father's love. In the life which Christ led upon earth, obedience was a solemn reality. The dark and awful power that led man to revolt from his God, came upon Him too, to tempt Him. To Him as man its offers of self-gratification were not matters of indifference; to refuse them, He had to fast and pray. He suffered, being tempted. He spoke very distinctly of not seeking to do His own will, as a surrender He had continually to make. He made the keeping of the Father's commandments the distinct object of His life, and so abode in His love. Does He not tell us, "I do nothing of myself, but as the Father taught me, I speak these things. And He that sent me is with me; He hath not left me alone; for I do always the things that are pleasing to Him." He thus opened to us the only path to the blessedness of a life on earth in the love of heaven; and when, as from our vine, His Spirit flows in the branches, this keeping the commands is one of the surest and highest elements of the life He inspires.

Believer! would you abide in Jesus, be very careful to keep His commandments. Keep them in the love of your heart. Be not content to have them in the Bible for reference, but have them transferred by careful study, by meditation and by prayer, by a loving acceptance, by the Spirit's teaching, to the fleshy tables of the heart. Be not content with the knowledge of some of the commands, those most commonly received among Christians, while others lie unknown and neglected. Surely, with your New Covenant privileges, you would not be behind the Old Testament saints who spoke so fervently: "I esteem all thy precepts concerning all things to be right." Be assured that there is still much of your Lord's will that you do not yet understand. Make Paul's prayer for the Colossians yours for yourself and all believers, "that you might be filled with the knowledge of His will in all wisdom and spiritual understanding"; and that of wrestling Epaphras, "that you may stand perfect and complete in all the will of God." Remember that this is one of the great elements of spiritual growth--a deeper insight into the will of God concerning you. Imagine not that entire consecration is the end--it is only the beginning--of the truly holy life. See how Paul, after having (Rom. 12:1) taught believers to lay themselves upon the altar, whole and holy burnt-offerings to their God, at once proceeds (ver. 2) to tell them what the true--altar-life is: being ever more and more "renewed in their mind to prove what is the good and perfect and acceptable will of God." The progressive renewal of the Holy Spirit leads to growing like-mindedness to Christ; then comes a delicate power of spiritual perception--a holy instinct--by which the soul "quick of understanding (marg. quick of scent) in the fear of the Lord," knows to recognise the meaning and the application of the Lord's commands to daily life in a way that remains hidden to the ordinary Christian. Keep them dwelling richly within you, hide them within your heart, and you shall taste the blessedness of the man whose "delight is in the law of the Lord, and in His law doth he meditate dayand night." Love will assimilate into your inmost being the commands as food from heaven. They will no longer come to you as a law standing outside and against you, but as the living power which has transformed your will into perfect harmony with all your Lord requires.

And keep them in the obedience of your life. It has been your solemn vow--has it not?--no longer to tolerate even a single sin: "I have sworn, and I will perform it, that I will keep Thy righteous judgments." Labour earnestly in prayer to stand perfect and complete in all the will of God. Ask earnestly for the discovery of every secret sin--of anything that is not in perfect harmony with the will of God. Walk up to the light you have faithfully and tenderly, yielding yourself in an unreserved surrender to obey all that the Lord has spoken. When Israel took that vow (Exodus 19:8, 24:7), it was only to break it all too soon. The New Covenant gives the grace to make the vow and to keep it too (Jer.31). Be careful of disobedience even in little things. Disobedience dulls the conscience, darkens the soul, deadens our spiritual energies--therefore keep the commandments of Christ with implicit obedience. Be a soldier that asks for nothing but the orders of the commander.

And if even for a moment the commandments appear grievous, just remember whose they are. They are the commandments of Him who loves you. They are all love, they come from His love, they lead to His love. Each new surrender to keep the commandments, each new sacrifice in keeping them, leads to deeper union with the will, the spirit, and the love of the Saviour. The double recompense of reward shall be yours--a fuller entrance into the mystery of His love--a fuller conformity to His own blessed life. And you shall learn to prize these words as among your choicest treasures: "If ye keep my commandments, ye shall abide in my love, EVEN AS I have kept my Father's commandments and abide in His love."

Chapter 25: THAT YOUR JOY MAY BE FULL

"These things have I spoken unto you, that my joy might abide in you, and that your joy might be full." --JOHN 15:11

ABIDING fully in Christ is a life of exquisite and overflowing happiness. As Christ gets more complete possession of the soul, it enters into the joy of its Lord. His own joy, the joy of heaven, becomes its own, and that in full measure, and as an ever-abiding portion. Just as joy on earth is everywhere connected with the vine and its fruit, so joy is an essential characteristic of the life of the believer who fully abides in Christ, the heavenly Vine.

We all know the value of joy. It alone is the proof that what we have really satisfies the heart. As long as duty, or self-interest, or other motives influence me, men cannot know what the object of my pursuit or possession is really worth to me. But when it gives me joy, and they see me delight in it, they know that to me at least it is a treasure. Hence there is nothing so attractive as joy, no preaching so persuasive as the sight of hearts made glad. Just this makes gladness such a mighty element in the Christian character: there is no proof of the reality of God's love and the blessing He bestows, which men so soon feel the force of, as when the joy of God overcomes all the trials of life. And for the Christian's own welfare, joy is no less indispensable: the joy of the Lord is his strength; confidence, and courage, and patience find their inspiration in joy. With a heart full of joy no work can weary, and no burden can depress; God Himself is strength and song.

Let us hear what the Saviour says of the joy of abiding in Him. He promises us His own joy: "My joy." As the whole parable refers to the life His disciples should have in Him when ascended to heaven, the joy is that of His resurrection life. This is clear from those other words of His (John 16:22): "I will see you again, and your heart shall rejoice, and your joy shall no man take from you." It was only with the resurrection and its glory that the power of the never-changing life began, and only in it that the never-ceasing joy could have its rise. With it was fulfilled the word: "Therefore thy God hath anointed thee with the oil of gladness above thy fellows." The day of His crowning was the day of the gladness of His heart. That joy of His was the joy of a work fully and for ever completed, the joy of the Father's bosom regained, and the joy of souls redeemed. These are the elements of His joy; of them the abiding in Him makes us partakers. The believer shares so fully His victory and His perfect redemption, that his faith can without ceasing sing the conqueror's song: "Thanks be to God, who always causeth me to triumph." As the fruit of this, there is the joy of the undisturbed dwelling in the light of the Father's love--not a cloud to intervene if the abiding be unbroken. And then, with this joy in the love of the Father, as a love received, the joy of the love of souls, as love going out and rejoicing over the lost. Abiding in Christ, penetrating into the very depths of His life and heart, seeking for the most perfect oneness, these the three streams of His joy flow into our hearts. Whether we look backward and see the work He has done, or upward and see the reward He has in the Father's love that passeth knowledge, or forward in the continual accessions of joy as sinners are brought home, His joy is ours. With our feet on Calvary, our eyes on the Father's countenance, and our hands helping sinners home, we have His joy as our own.

And then He speaks of this joy as abiding--a joy that is never to cease or to be interrupted for a moment: "That my joy might abide in you." "Your joy no man taketh from you." This is what many Christians cannot understand. Their view of the Christian life is that it is a succession of changes, now joy and now sorrow. And they appeal to the experiences of a man like the Apostle Paul, as a proof of how much there may be of weeping, and sorrow, and suffering. They have not noticed how just Paul gives the strongest evidence as to this unceasing joy. He understood the paradox of the Christian life as the combination at one and the same moment of all the bitterness of earth and all the joy of heaven. "As sorrowful, yet always rejoicing": these precious golden words teach us how the joy of Christ can overrule the sorrow of the world, can make us sing while we weep, and can maintain in the heart, even when cast down by disappointment or difficulties, a deep consciousness of a joy that is unspeakable and full of glory. There is but one condition: "I will see you again, and your heart shall rejoice, and your joy shall no man take from you." The presence of Jesus, distinctly manifested, cannot but give joy. Abiding in Him consciously, how can the soul but rejoice and be glad? Even when weeping for the sins and the souls of others, there is the fountain of gladness springing up in the faith of His power and love to save.

And this His own joy abiding with us, He wants to be full. Of the full joy our Saviour spoke thrice on the last night. Once here in the parable of the Vine: "These things have I spoken unto you that your joy might be full"; and every deeper insight into the wonderful blessedness of being the branch of such a Vine confirms His Word. Then He connects it (John 16:24) with our prayers being answered: "Ask and ye shall receive, that your joy may be full." To the spiritual mind, answered prayer is not only a means of obtaining certain blessings, but something infinitely higher. It is a token of our fellowship with the Father and the Son in heaven, of their delight in us, and our having been admitted and having had a voice in that wondrous interchange of love in which the Father and the Son hold counsel, and decide the daily guidance of the children on earth. To a soul abiding in Christ, that longs for manifestations of His love, and that understands to take an answer to prayer in its true spiritual value, as a response from the throne to all its utterances of love and trust, the joy which it brings is truly unutterable. The word is found true: "Ask and ye shall receive, and your joy shall be full." And then the Saviour says, in His highpriestly prayer to the Father (John 17:13), "These things I speak, that they might have my joy fulfilled in themselves." It is the sight of the great High Priest entering the Father's presence for us, ever living to pray and carry on His blessed work in the power of an endless life, that removes every possible cause of fear or doubt, and gives us the assurance and experience of a perfect salvation. Let the believer who seeks, according to the teaching of John 15, to possess the full joy of abiding in Christ, and according to John 16, the full joy of prevailing prayer, press forward to John 17. Let him there listen to those wondrous words of intercession spoken, that his joy might be full. Let him, as he listens to those words, learn the love that even now pleads for him in heaven without ceasing, the glorious objects for which it is pleading, and which through its all-prevailing pleading are hourly being realized, and Christ's joy will be fulfilled in him.

Christ's own joy, abiding joy, fulness of joy--such is the portion of the believer who abides in Christ. Why, O why is it that this joy has so little power to attract? The reason simply is: Men, yea, even God's children, do not believe in it. Instead of the abiding in Christ being looked upon as the happiest life that ever can be led, it is regarded as a life of self-denial and of sadness. They forget that the self-denial and the sadness are owing to the not abiding, and that to those who once yield themselves unreservedly to abide in Christ as a bright and blessed life, their faith comes true--the joy of the Lord is theirs. The difficulties all arise from the want of the full surrender to a full abiding.

Child of God, who seekest to abide in Christ, remember what the Lord says. At the close of the parable of the Vine He adds these precious words: "These things have I spoken unto you, that my joy might abide in you, and that your joy might be full." Claim the joy as part of the branch life--not the first or chief part, but as the blessed proof of the sufficiency of Christ to satisfy every need of the soul. Be happy. Cultivate gladness. If there are times when it comes of itself, and the heart feels the unutterable joy of the Saviour's presence, praise God for it, and seek to maintain it. If at other times feelings are dull, and the experience of the joy not such as you could wish it, still praise God for the life of unutterable blessedness to which you have been redeemed. In this, too, the word holds good: "According to your faith be it unto you." As you claim all the other gifts in Jesus, ever claim this one too--

not for your own sake, but for His and the Father's glory. "My joy in you"; "that my joy may abide in you"; "my joy fulfilled in themselves"--these are Jesus' own words. It is impossible to take Him wholly and heartily, and not to get His joy too. Therefore, "Rejoice in the Lord alway; and again I say, Rejoice."

Chapter 26: AND IN LOVE TO THE BRETHREN

"This is my commandment, That ye love one another, as I have loved you."--JOHN 15:12.

"Like as the Father loved me, EVEN so I have loved you; LIKE AS I have loved you, EVEN SO love ye one another." God became man; divine love began to run in the channel of a human heart; it becomes the love of man to man. The love that fills heaven and eternity is ever to be daily seen here in the life of earth and of time.

"This is my commandment," the Saviour says, "That ye love one another, as I have loved you." He sometimes spoke of commandments, but the love, which is the fulfilling of the law, is the all-including one, and therefore is called His commandment--the new commandment. It is to be the great evidence of the reality of the New Covenant, of the power of the new life revealed in Jesus Christ. It is to be the one convincing and indisputable token of discipleship: "Hereby shall all men know that ye are my disciples"; "That they may be one in us, that the world may believe"; "That they may be made perfect in one, that the world may know that Thou hast loved them, as Thou hast loved me." To the believer seeking perfect fellowship with Christ, the keeping of this commandment is at once the blessed proof that he is abiding in Him, and the path to a fuller and more perfect union.

Let us try to understand how this is so. We know that God is love, and that Christ came to reveal this, not as a doctrine but as a life. His life, in its wonderful self-abasement and self-sacrifice, was, above everything, the embodiment of divine love, the showing forth to men, in such human manifestations as they could understand, how God loves. In His love to the unworthy and the ungrateful, in His humbling Himself to walk among men as a servant, in His giving Himself up to death, He simply lived and acted out the life of the divine love which was in the heart of God. He lived and died to show us the love of the Father.

And now, just as Christ was to show forth God's love, believers are to show forth to the world the love of Christ. They are to prove to men that Christ loves them, and in loving fills them with a love that is not of earth. They, by living and by loving just as He did, are to be perpetual witnesses to the love that gave itself to die. He loved so that even the Jews cried out, as at Bethany, "Behold how He loved!" Christians are to live so that men are compelled to say, "See how these Christians love one another." In their daily intercourse with each other, Christians are made a spectacle to God, and to angels, and to men; and in the Christlikeness of their love to each other, are to prove what manner of spirit they are of. Amid all diversity of character or of creed, of language or of station, they are to prove that love has made them members of one body, and of each other, and has taught them each to forget and sacrifice self for the sake of the other. Their life of love is the chief evidence of Christianity, the proof to the world that God sent Christ, and that He has shed abroad in them the same love with which He loved Him. Of all the evidences of Christianity, this is the mightiest and most convincing.

This love of Christ's disciples to each other occupies a central position between their love to God and to all men. Of their love to God, whom they cannot see, it is the test. The love to one unseen may so easily be a mere sentiment, or even an imagination; in the intercourse with God's children, love to God is really called into exercise, and shows itself in deeds that the Father accepts as done to Himself. So alone can it be proved to be true. The love to the brethren is the flower and fruit of the root, unseen in the heart, of love to God. And this fruit again becomes the seed of love to all men: intercourse with each other is the school in which believers are trained and strengthened to love their fellow-men, who are yet out of Christ, not simply with the liking that rests on points of agreement, but with the holy love that takes hold of the unworthiest, and bears with the most disagreeable for Jesus' sake. It is love to each other as disciples that is ever put in the foreground as the link between love to God alone and to men in general.

In Christ's intercourse with His disciples this brotherly love finds the law of its conduct. As it studies His forgiveness and forbearance towards His friends, with the seven times seven as its only measure--as it looks to His unwearied patience and His infinite humility--as it sees the meekness and lowliness with which He seeks to win for Himself a place as their servant, wholly devoted to their interests--it accepts with gladness His command, "Ye should do as I have done" (John 13:15). Following His example, each lives not for Himself but for the other. The law of kindness is on the tongue, for love has vowed that never shall one unkind word cross its lips. It refuses not only to speak, but even to hear or to think evil; of the name and character of the fellow-Christian it is more jealous than of its own. My own good name I may leave to the Father; my brother's my Father has entrusted to me. In gentleness and loving kindness, in courtesy and generosity, in self-sacrifice and beneficence, in its life of blessing and of beauty, the divine love, which has been shed abroad in the believer's heart, shines out as it shone in the life of Jesus.

Christian! what say you of this your glorious calling to love like Christ? Does not your heart bound at the thought of the unspeakable privilege of thus showing forth the likeness of the Eternal Love? Or are you rather ready to sigh at the thought of the inaccessible height of perfection to which you are thus called to climb? Brother, sigh not at what is in very deed the highest token of the Father's love, that He has called us to be like Christ in our love, just as He was like the Father in His love. Understand that He who gave the command in such close connection with His teaching about the Vine and the abiding in Him, gave us in that the assurance that we have only to abide in Him to be able to love like Him. Accept the command as a new motive to a more full abiding in Christ. Regard the abiding in Him more than ever as an abiding in His love; rooted and grounded daily in a love that passeth knowledge, you receive of its fulness, and learn to love. With Christ abiding in you, the Holy Spirit sheds abroad the love of God in your heart, and you love the brethren, the most trying and unloveable, with a love that is not your own, but the love of Christ in you. And the command about your love to the brethren is changed from a burden into a joy, if you but keep it linked, as Jesus linked it, to the command about His love to you: "Abide in my love; love one another, as I have loved you."

"This is my commandment, That ye love one another, as I have loved you." Is not this now some of the much fruit that Jesus has promised we shall bear--in very deed a cluster of the grapes of Eshcol, with which we can prove to others that the land of promise is indeed a good land? Let us try in all simplicity and honesty to go out to our home to translate the language of high faith and heavenly enthusiasm into the plain prose of daily conduct, so that all men can understand it. Let our temper be under the rule of the love of Jesus: He can not alone curb it-- He can make us gentle and patient. Let the vow, that not an unkind word about others shall ever be heard from our lips, be laid trustingly at His feet. Let the gentleness that refuses to take offence, that is always ready to excuse, to think and hope the best, mark our intercourse with all. Let the love that seeks not its own, but ever is ready to wash others' feet, or even to give its life for them, be our aim as we abide in Jesus. Let our life be one of self-sacrifice, always studying the welfare of others, finding our highest joy in blessing others. And let us, in studying the divine art of doing good, yield ourselves as obedient learners to the guidance of the Holy Spirit. By His grace, the most commonplace life can be transfigured with the brightness of a heavenly beauty, as the infinite love of the divine nature shines out through our frail humanity. Fellow-Christian, let us praise God! We are called to love as Jesus loves, as God loves.

"Abide in my love, and love as I have loved." Bless God, it is possible. The new holy nature we have, and which grows ever stronger as it abides in Christ the Vine, can love as He did. Every discovery of the evil of the old nature, every longing desire to obey the command of our Lord, every experience of the power and the blessedness of loving with Jesus' love, will urge us to accept with fresh faith the blessed injunctions: "Abide in me, and I in you"; "Abide in my love."

Chapter 27: THAT YOU MAY NOT SIN

"In him is no sin. Whosoever abideth in him sinneth not."--1 JOHN 3:5,6.

"YE KNOW," the apostle had said, "that He was manifested to take away our sin," and had thus indicated salvation from sin as the great object for which the Son was made man. The connection shows clearly that the taking away has reference not only to the atonement and freedom from guilt, but to deliverance from the power of sin, so that the believer no longer does it. It is Christ's personal holiness that constitutes His power to effect this purpose. He admits sinners into life union with Himself; the result is, that their life becomes like His. "In Him is no sin. Whosoever abideth in Him sinneth not." As long as he abides, and as far as he abides, the believer does not sin. Our holiness of life has its roots in the personal holiness of Jesus. "If the root be holy, so also are the branches."

The question at once arises: How is this consistent with what the Bible teaches of the abiding corruption of our human nature, or with what John himself tells of the utter falsehood of our profession, if we say that we have no sin, that we have not sinned? (see I John 1:8,10). It is just this passage which, if we look carefully at it, will teach us to understand our text aright. Note the difference in the two statements (ver. 8), "If we say that we have no sin," and (ver.10), "If we say that we have not sinned." The two expressions cannot be equivalent; the second would then be an unmeaning repetition of the first. Having sin in verse 8 is not the same as doing sin in verse 10. Having sin is having a sinful nature. The holiest believer must each moment confess that he has sin within him--the flesh, namely, in which dwelleth no good thing. Sinning or doing sin is something very different: it is yielding to indwelling sinful nature, and falling into actual transgression. And so we have two admissions that every true believer must make. The one is that he has still sin within him (ver. 8); the second, that that sin has in former times broken out into sinful actions (ver.10). No believer can say either, "I have no sin in me," or "I have in time past never sinned." If we say we have no sin at present, or that we have not sinned in the past, we deceive ourselves. But no confession, though we have sin in the present, is demanded that we are doing sin in the present too; the confession of actual sinning refers to the past. It may, as appears from chapter 2:2, be in the present also, but is expected not to be. And so we see how the deepest confession of sin in the past (as Paul's of his having been a persecutor), and the deepest consciousness of having still a vile and corrupt nature in the present, may consist with humble but joyful praise to Him who keeps from stumbling.

But how is it possible that a believer, having sin in him--sin of such intense vitality, and such terrible power as we know the flesh to have--that a believer having sin should yet not be doing sin? The answer is: "In Him is no sin. He that abideth in Him sinneth not." When the abiding in Christ becomes close and unbroken, so that the soul lives from moment to moment in the perfect union with the Lord its keeper, He does, indeed, keep down the power of the old nature, so that it does not regain dominion over the soul. We have seen that there are degrees in the abiding. With most Christians the abiding is so feeble and intermittent, that sin continually obtains the ascendency, and brings the soul into subjection. The divine promise given to faith is: "Sin shall not have dominion over you." But with the promise is the command: "Let not sin reign in your mortal body." The believer who claims the promise in full faith has the power to obey the command, and sin is kept from asserting its supremacy. Ignorance of the promise, or unbelief, or unwatchfulness, opens the door for sin to reign. And so the life of many believers is a course of continual stumbling and sinning. But when the believer seeks full admission into, and a permanent abode in Jesus, the Sinless One, then the life of Christ keeps from actual transgression. "In Him is no sin. He that abideth in Him sinneth not. " Jesus does indeed save him from his sin--not by the removal of his sinful nature, but by keeping him from yielding to it.

I have read of a young lion whom nothing could awe or keep down but the eye of his keeper. With the keeper you could come near him, and he would crouch, his savage nature all unchanged, and thirsting for blood --trembling at the keeper's feet. You might put your foot on his neck, as long as the keeper was with you. To approach him without the keeper would be instant death. And so it is that the believer can have sin and yet not do sin. The evil nature, the flesh, is unchanged in its enmity against God, but the abiding presence of Jesus keeps it down. In faith the believer entrusts himself to the keeping, to the indwelling, of the Son of God; he abides in Him, and counts on Jesus to abide in Him too. The union and fellowship is the secret of a holy life: "In Him is no sin; he that abideth in Him sinneth not."

And now another question will arise: Admitted that the complete abiding in the Sinless One will keep from sinning, is such abiding possible? May we hope to be able so to abide in Christ, say, even for one day, that we may be kept from actual transgressions? The question has only to be fairly stated and considered-- it will suggest its own answer. When Christ commanded us to abide in Him, and promised us such rich fruit-bearing to the glory of the Father, and such mighty power in our intercessions, can He have meant anything but the healthy, vigorous, complete union of the branch with the vine? When He promised that as we abide in Him He would abide in us, could He mean anything but that His dwelling in us would be a reality of divine power and love? Is not this way of saving from sin just that which will glorify Him?--keeping us daily humble and helpless in the consciousness of the evil nature, watchful and active in the knowledge of its terrible power, dependent and trustful in the remembrance that only His presence can keep the lion down. O let us believe that when Jesus said, "Abide in me, and I in you," He did indeed mean that, while we were not to be freed from the world and its tribulation, from the sinful nature and its temptations, we were at least to have this blessing fully secured to us--grace to abide wholly, only, even in our Lord. The abiding in Jesus makes it possible to keep from actual sinning; and Jesus Himself makes it possible to abide in Him.

Beloved Christian! I do not wonder if the promise of the text appears almost too high. Do not, I pray, let your attention be diverted by the question as to whether it would be possible to be kept for your whole life, or for so many years, without sinning. Faith has ever only to deal with the present moment. Ask this: Can Jesus at the present moment, as I abide in Him, keep me from those actual transgressions which have been the stain and the weariness of my daily life? You cannot but say: Surely He can. Take Him then at this present moment, and say, "Jesus keeps me now, Jesus saves me now." Yield yourself to Him in the earnest and believing prayer to be kept abiding, by His own abiding in you--and go into the next moment, and the succeeding hours, with this trust continually renewed. As often as the opportunity occurs in the moments between your occupations, renew your faith in an act of devotion: Jesus keeps me now, Jesus saves me now. Let failure and sin, instead of discouraging you, only urge you still more to seek your safety in abiding in the Sinless One. Abiding is a grace in which you can grow wonderfully, if you will but make at once the complete surrender, and then persevere with ever larger expectations. Regard it as His work to keep you abiding in Him, and His work to keep you from sinning. It is indeed your work to abide in Him; but it is that, only because it is His work as Vine to bear and hold the branch. Gaze upon His holy human nature as what He prepared for you to be partaker of with Himself, and you will see that there is something even higher and better than being kept from sin--that is but the restraining from evil: there is the positive and larger blessing of being now a vessel purified and cleansed, of being filled with His fulness, and made the channel of showing forth His power, His blessing, and His glory.

NOTE

IS DAILY SINNING AN INEVITABLE NECESSITY?

"Why is it that, when we possess a Saviour whose love and lower are infinite, we are so often filled with fear and despondency? We are wearied and faint in our minds, because we do not look stedfastly unto Jesus, the author and finisher of faith, who is set down at the right hand of God--unto Him whose omnipotence embraces both heaven and earth, who is strong and mighty in His feeble saints.

"While we remember our weakness, we forget His all-sufficient power. While we acknowledge that apart from Christ we can do nothing, we do not rise to the height or depth of Christian humility: I can do all things through Christ which strengtheneth me. While we trust in the power of the death of Jesus to cancel the guilt of sin, we do not exercise a reliant and appropriating faith in the omnipotence of the living Saviour to deliver us from the bondage and power of sin in our daily life. We forget that Christ worketh in us mightily, and that, one with Him, we possess strength sufficient to overcome every temptation. We are apt either to forget our nothingness, and imagine that in our daily path we can live without sin, that the duties and trials of our everyday life can be performed and borne in our own strength; or we do not avail ourselves of the omnipotence of Jesus, who is able to subdue all things to Himself, and to keep us from the daily infirmities and falls which we are apt to imagine an inevitable necessity. If we really depended in all things and at all times on Christ, we would in all things and at all times gain the victory through Him whose power is infinite, and who is appointed by the Father to be the Captain of our salvation. Then all our deeds would be wrought, not merely before, but in God. We would then do all things to the glory of the Father, in the all-powerful name of Jesus, who is our sanctification. Remember that unto Him all power is given in heaven and on earth, and live by the constant exercise of faith in His power. Let us most fully believe that we have and are nothing, that with man it is impossible, that in ourselves we have no life which can bring forth fruit; but that Christ is all--that abiding in Him, and His word dwelling in us, we can bring forth fruit to the glory of the Father"--From Christ and the Church. Sermons by Adolph Saphir. The italics are not in the original.

Chapter 28: AS YOUR STRENGTH

"All power is given UNTO ME in heaven and in earth."--MATT.28:18.
[1]

"Be strong IN THE LORD, and in the power of his might."--EPH.6.10.

"My power is made perfect in weakness."--2 COR.12:9 (R.V.).

THERE is no truth more generally admitted among earnest Christians than that of their utter weakness. There is no truth more generally misunderstood and abused. Here, as elsewhere, God's thoughts are heaven-high above man's thoughts.

The Christian often tries to forget his weakness: God wants us to remember it, to feel it deeply. The Christian wants to conquer his weakness and to be freed from it: God wants us to rest and even rejoice in it. The Christian mourns over his weakness: Christ teaches His servant to say, "I take pleasure in infirmities; most gladly will I glory in my infirmities." The Christian thinks his weakness his greatest hindrance in the life and service of God: God tells us that it is the secret of strength and success. It is our weakness, heartily accepted and continually realized, that gives us our claim and access to the strength of Him who has said, "My strength is made perfect in weakness."

When our Lord was about to take His seat upon the throne, one of His last words was: "All power is given unto me in heaven and on earth." Just as His taking His place at the right hand of the power of God was something new and true--a real advance in the history of the God-man-- so was this clothing with all power. Omnipotence was now entrusted to the man Christ Jesus, that from henceforth through the channels of human nature it might put forth its mighty energies. Hence He connected with this revelation of what He was to receive, the promise of the share that His disciples would have in it: When I am ascended, ye shall receive power from on high (Luke 24:49; Acts 1:8). It is in the power of the omnipotent Saviour that the believer must find his strength for life and for work.

It was thus with the disciples. During ten days they worshipped and waited at the footstool of His throne. They gave expression to their faith in Him as their Saviour, to their adoration of Him as their Lord, to their love to Him as their Friend, to their devotion and readiness to work for Him as their Master. Jesus Christ was the one object of thought, of love, of delight. In such worship of faith and devotion their souls grew up into intensest communion with Him upon the throne, and when they were prepared, the baptism of power came. It was power within and power around.

The power came to qualify for the work to which they had yielded themselves--of testifying by life and word to their unseen Lord. With some the chief testimony was to be that of a holy life, revealing the heaven and the Christ from whom it came. The power came to set up the Kingdom within them, to give them the victory over sin and self, to fit them by living experience to testify to the power of Jesus on the throne, to make men live in the world as saints. Others were to give themselves up entirely to the speaking in the name of Jesus. But all needed and all received the gift of power, to prove that now Jesus had received the Kingdom of the Father, all power in heaven and earth was indeed given to Him, and by Him imparted to His people just as they needed it, whether for a holy life or effective service. They received the gift of power, to prove to the world that the Kingdom of God, to which they professed to belong, was not in word but in power. By having power within, they had power without and around. The power of God was felt even by those who would not yield themselves to it (Acts 2.43; 4:13; 5:13).

And what Jesus was to these first disciples, He is to us too. Our whole life and calling as disciples find their origin and their guarantee in the words: "All power is given to me in heaven and on earth." What He does in and through us, He does with almighty power. What He claims or demands, He works Himself by that same power. All He gives, He gives with power. Every blessing He bestows, every promise He fulfils, every grace He works--all, all is to be with power. Everything that comes from this Jesus on the throne of power is to bear the stamp of power. The weakest believer may be confident that in asking to be kept from sin, to grow in holiness, to bring forth much fruit, be may count upon these his petitions being fulfilled with divine power. The power is in Jesus; Jesus is ours with all His fulness; it is in us His members that the power is to work and be made manifest.

And if we want to know how the power is bestowed, the answer is simple: Christ gives His power in us by giving His life in us. He does not, as so many believers imagine, take the feeble life He finds in them, and impart a little strength to aid them in their feeble efforts. No; it is in giving His own life in us that He gives us His power. The Holy Spirit came down to the disciples direct from the heart of their exalted Lord, bringing down into them the glorious life of heaven into which He had entered. And so His people are still taught to be strong in the Lord and in the power of His might. When He strengthens them, it is not by taking away the sense of feebleness, and giving in its place the feeling of strength. By no means. But in a very wonderful way leaving and even increasing the sense of utter impotence, He gives them along with it the consciousness of strength in Him. "We have this treasure in earthen vessels, that the excellency of the power may be of God and not of us." The feebleness and the strength are side by side; as the one grows, the other too, until they understand the saying, "When I am weak, then am I strong; I glory in my infirmities, that the power of Christ may rest on me."

The believing disciple learns to look upon Christ on the throne, Christ the Omnipotent, as his life. He studies that life in its infinite perfection and purity, in its strength and glory; it is the eternal life dwelling in a glorified man. And when he thinks of his own inner life, and longs for holiness, to live wellpleasing unto God, or for power to do the Father's work, he looks up, and, rejoicing that Christ is his life, he confidently reckons that that life will work mightily in him all he needs. In things little and things great, in the being kept from sin from moment to moment for which he has learned to look, or in the struggle with some special difficulty or temptation, the power of Christ is the measure of his expectation. He lives a most joyous and blessed life, not because he is no longer feeble, but because, being utterly helpless, he consents and expects to have the mighty Saviour work in him.

The lessons these thoughts teach us for practical life are simple, but very precious. The first is, that all our strength is in Christ, laid up and waiting for use. It is there as an almighty life, which is in Him for us, ready to flow in according to the measure in which it finds the channels open. But whether its flow is strong or feeble, whatever our experience of it be, there it is in Christ: All power in heaven and earth. Let us take time to study this. Let us get our minds filled with the thought: That Jesus might be to us a perfect Saviour, the Father gave Him all power. That is the qualification that fits Him for our needs: All the power of heaven over all the powers of earth, over every power of earth in our heart and life too.

The second lesson is: This power flows into us as we abide in close union with Him. When the union is feeble, little valued or cultivated, the inflow of strength will be feeble. When the union with Christ is rejoiced in as our highest good, and everything sacrificed for the sake of maintaining it, the power will work: "His strength will be made perfect in our weakness." Our one care must therefore be to abide in Christ as our strength. Our one duty is to be strong in the Lord,and in the power of His might. Let our faith cultivate large and clear apprehensions of the exceeding greatness of God's power in them that believe, even that power of the risen and exalted Christ by which He triumphed over every enemy (Eph. 1: 19-21). Let our faith consent to God's wonderful and most blessed arrangement: nothing but feebleness in us as our own, all the power in Christ, and yet within our reach as surely as if it were in us. Let our faith daily go out of self and its life into the life of Christ, placing our whole being at His disposal for Him to work in us. Let our faith, above all, confidently rejoice in the assurance that He will in very deed, with His almighty power, perfect

His work in us. As we thus abide in Christ, the Holy Spirit, the Spirit of His power, will work mightily in us, and we too shall sing, "JEHOVAH is my strength and song: IN JEHOVAH I have righteousness and strength." "I can do all things through Christ, which strengtheneth me."

[1] The word power in this verse is properly authority (R.V.), but the two ideas are so closely linked, and the authority as a living divine reality is so inseparable from the power, that I have felt at liberty to retain the word power.

Chapter 29: AND NOT IN SELF

"In me, that is, in my flesh, dwelleth no good thing." --Rom. 7:18.

TO HAVE life in Himself is the prerogative of God alone, and of the Son, to whom the Father hath also given it. To seek life, not in itself, but in God, is the highest honour of the creature. To live in and to himself is the folly and guilt of sinful man; to live to God in Christ, the blessedness of the believer. To deny, to hate, to forsake, to lose his own life, such is the secret of the life of faith. "I live, yet NOT I, but Christ liveth in me"; "NOT I, but the grace of God which is with me": this is the testimony of each one who has found out what it is to give up his own life, and to receive instead the blessed life of Christ within us. There is no path to true life, to abiding in Christ, than that which our Lord went before us--through death.

At the first commencement of the Christian life, but few see this. In the joy of pardon, they feel constrained to live for Christ, and trust with the help of God to be enabled to do so. They are as yet ignorant of the terrible enmity of the flesh against God, and its absolute refusal in the believer to be subject to the law of God. They know not yet that nothing but death, the absolute surrender to death of all that is of nature, will suffice, if the life of God is to be manifested in them with power. But bitter experience of failure soon teaches them the insufficiency of what they have yet known of Christ's power to save, and deep heart-longings are awakened to know Him better. He lovingly points them to His cross. He tells them that as there, in the faith of His death as their substitute, they found their title to life, so there they shall enter into its fuller experience too. He asks them if they are indeed willing to drink of the cup of which He drank--to be crucified and to die with Him. He teaches them that in Him they are indeed already crucified and dead--all unknowing, at conversion they became partakers of His death. But what they need now is to give a full and intelligent consent to what they received ere they understood it, by an act of their own choice to will to die with Christ.

This demand of Christ's is one of unspeakable solemnity. Many a believer shrinks back from it. He can hardly understand it. He has become so accustomed to a low life of continual stumbling, that he hardly desires, and still less expects, deliverance. Holiness, perfect conformity to Jesus, unbroken fellowship with His love, can scarcely be counted distinct articles of his creed. Where there is not intense longing to be kept to the utmost from sinning, and to be brought into the closest possible union with the Saviour, the thought of being crucified with Him can find no entrance. The only impression it makes is that of suffering and shame: such a one is content that Jesus bore the cross, and so won for him the crown he hopes to wear. How different the light in which the believer who is really seeking to abide fully in Christ looks upon it. Bitter experience has taught him how, both in the matter of entire surrender and simple trust, his greatest enemy in the abiding life, is SELF. Now it refuses to give up its will; then again, by its working, it hinders God's work. Unless this life of self, with its willing and working, be displaced by the life of Christ, with His willing and working, to abide in Him will be impossible. And then comes the solemn question from Him who died on the cross: "Are you ready to give up self to the death?" You yourself, the living person born of God, are already in me dead to sin and alive to God; but are you ready now, in the power of this death, to mortify your members, to give up self entirely to its death of the cross, to be kept there until it be wholly destroyed? The question is a heart-searching one. Am I prepared to say that the old self shall no longer have a word to say; that it shall not be allowed to have a single thought, however natural--not a single feeling, however gratifying--not a single wish or work, however right?

Is this in very deed what He requires? Is not our nature God's handiwork, and may not our natural powers be sanctified to His service? They may and must indeed. But perhaps you have not yet seen how the only way they can be sanctified is that they be taken from under the power of self, and brought under the power of the life of Christ. Think not that this is a work that you can do, because you earnestly desire it, and are indeed one of His redeemed ones. No, there is no way to the altar of consecration but through death. As you yielded yourself a sacrifice on God's altar as one alive from the dead (Rom.6:13, 7:1), so each power of your nature--each talent, gift, possession, that is really to be holiness to the Lord--must be separated from the power of sin and self, and laid on the altar to be consumed by the fire that is ever burning there. It is in the mortifying, the slaying of self, that the wonderful powers with which God has fitted you to serve Him, can be set free for a complete surrender to God, and offered to Him to be accepted, and sanctified, and used. And though, as long as you are in the flesh, there is no thought of being able to say that self is dead, yet when the life of Christ is allowed to take full possession, self can be so kept in its crucifixion place, and under its sentence of death, that it shall have ho dominion over you, not for a single moment. Jesus Christ becomes your second self.

Believer! would you truly and fully abide in Christ, prepare yourself to part for ever from self, and not to allow it, even for a single moment, to have aught to say in your inner life. If you are willing to come entirely away out of self, and to allow Jesus Christ to become your life within you, inspiring all your thinking, feeling, acting, in things temporal and spiritual, He is ready to undertake the charge. In the fullest and widest sense the word life ever can have, He will be your life, extending His interest and influence to each one, even the minutest, of the thousand things that make up your daily life. To do this He asks but one thing: Come away out of self and its life, abide in Christ and the Christ life, and Christ will be your life. The power of His holy presence will cast out the old life.

To this end give up self at once and for ever. If you have never yet dared to do it, for fear you might fail of your engagement, do it now, in view of the promise Christ gives you that His life will take the place of the old life. Try and realize that though self is not dead, you are indeed dead to self. Self is still strong and living, but it has no power over you. You, your renewed nature--you, your new self, begotten again in Jesus Christ from the dead--are indeed dead to sin and alive to God. Your death in Christ has freed you completely from the control of self: it has no power over you, except as you, in ignorance, or unwatchfulness, or unbelief, consent to yield to its usurped authority. Come and accept by faith simply and heartily the glorious position you have in Christ. As one who, in Christ, has a life dead to self, as one who is freed from the dominion of self, and has received His divine life to take the place of self, to be the animating and inspiring principle of your life, venture boldly to plant the foot upon the neck of this enemy of yours and your Lord's. Be of good courage, only believe; fear not to take the irrevocable step, and to say that you have once for all given up self to the death for which it has been crucified in Christ (Rom.6:6). And trust Jesus the Crucified One to hold self to the cross, and to fill its place in you with His own blessed resurrection life.

In this faith, abide in Christ! Cling to Him; rest on Him; hope on Him. Daily renew your consecration; daily accept afresh your position as ransomed from your tyrant, and now in turn made a conqueror. Daily look with holy fear on the enemy, self, struggling to get free from the cross, seeking to allure you into giving it some little liberty, or else ready to deceive you by its profession of willingness now to do service to Christ. Remember, self seeking to serve God is more dangerous than self refusing obedience. Look upon it with holy fear, and hide yourself in Christ: in Him alone is your safety. Abide thus in Him; He has promised to abide in you. He will teach you to be humble and watchful. He will teach you to be happy and trustful. Bring every interest of your life, every power of your nature, all the unceasing flow of thought, and will, and feeling, that makes up life, and trust Him to take the place that self once filled so easily and so naturally. Jesus Christ will indeed take possession of you and dwell in you; and in the restfulness and peace and grace of the new life you shall have unceasing joy at the wondrous exchange that has been made--the coming out of self to abide in Christ alone.

NOTE

In his work on Sanctification, Marshall, in the twelfth chapter, on "Holiness through faith alone," puts with great force the danger in which the Christian is of seeking sanctification in the power of the flesh, with the help of Christ, instead of looking for it to Christ alone, and receiving it from Him by faith. He reminds us how there are two natures in the believer, and so two ways of seeking holiness, according as we allow the principles of the one or other nature to guide us. The one is the carnal way, in which we put forth our utmost efforts and resolutions, trusting Christ to help us in doing so. The other the spiritual way, in which, as those who have died, and can do nothing, our one care is to receive Christ day by day, and at every step to let Him live and work in us.

"Despair of purging the flesh or natural man of its sinful lusts and inclinations, and of practising holiness by your willing and resolving to do the best that lieth in your own power, and trusting on the grace of God and Christ to help you in such resolutions and endeavours. Rather resolve to trust on Christ to work in you to will and to do by His own power according to His own good pleasure. They that are convinced of their own sin and misery do commonly first think to tame the flesh, and to subdue and root out its lusts, and to make their corrupt nature to be better-natured and inclined to holiness by their struggling and wrestling with it; and if they can but bring their hearts to a full purpose and resolution to do the best that lieth in them, they hope that by such a resolution they shall be able to achieve great enterprises in the conquests of their lusts and performance of the most difficult duties. It is the great work of some zealous divines in their preachings and writings to stir up people to this resolution, wherein they place the chiefest turningpoint from sin to godliness. And they think that this is not contrary to the life of faith, because they trust in the grace of God through Christ to help them in all such resolutions and endeavours. Thus they endeavour to reform their old state, and to be made perfect in the flesh, instead of putting it off and walking according to the new state in Christ. They trust on low carnal things for holiness, and upon the acts of their own will, their purposes, resolutions, and endeavours, instead of Christ; and they trust to Christ to help them in this carnal way; whereas true faith would teach them that they are nothing, and that they do but labour in vain."

Chapter 30: AS THE SURETY OF THE COVENANT

"Jesus was made a surety of a better testament."--Heb 7:22

OF THE old Covenant, Scripture speaks as not being faultless, and God complains that Israel had not continued in it; and so He regarded them not (Heb.8:7-9). It had not secured its apparent object, in uniting Israel and God: Israel had forsaken Him, and He had not regarded Israel. Therefore God promises to make a New Covenant, free from the faults of the first, and effectual to realize its purpose. If it were to accomplish its end, it would need to secure God's faithfulness to His people, and His people's faithfulness to God. And the terms of the New Covenant expressly declare that these two objects shall be attained. "I will put my laws into their mind": thus God proposes to secure their unchanging faithfulness to Him. "Their sins I will remember no more" (see Heb.8:10-12): thus He assures His unchanging faithfulness to them. A pardoning God and an obedient people: these are the two parties who are to meet and to be eternally united in the New Covenant.

The most beautiful provision of this New Covenant is that of the surety in whom its fulfilment on both parts is guaranteed. Jesus was made the surety of the better covenant. To man He became surety that God would faithfully fulfil His part, so that man could confidently depend upon God to pardon, and accept, and never more forsake. And to God He likewise became surety that man would faithfully fulfil his part, so that God could bestow on him the blessing of the covenant. And the way in which He fulfils His suretyship is this: As one with God, and having the fulness of God dwelling in His human nature, He is personally security to men that God will do what He has engaged. All that God has is secured to us in Him as man. And then, as one with us, and having taken us up as members into His own body, He is security to God that His interests shall be cared for. All that man must be and do is secured in Him. It is the glory of the New Covenant that it has in the Person of the God-man its living surety, its everlasting security. And it can easily be understood how, in proportion as we abide in Him as the surety of the covenant, its objects and its blessings will be realized in us.

We shall understand this best if we consider it in the light of one of the promises of the New Covenant. Take that in Jer.32:40 : "I will make an everlasting covenant with them, that I will not turn away from them, to do them good; but I will put my fear in their hearts, that they shall not depart from me."

With what wonderful condescension the infinite God here bows Himself to our weakness! He is the Faithful and Unchanging One, whose word is truth; and yet more abundantly to show to the heirs of the promise the immutability of His counsel, He binds Himself in the covenant that He will never change: "I will make an everlasting covenant, that I will not turn away from them." Blessed the man who has thoroughly appropriated this, and finds his rest in the everlasting covenant of the Faithful One!

But in a covenant there are two parties. And what if man becomes unfaithful and breaks the covenant? Provision must be made, if the covenant is to be well ordered in all things and sure, that this cannot be, and that man too remain faithful. Man never can undertake to give such an assurance. And see, here God comes to provide for this too. He not only undertakes in the covenant that He will never turn from His people, but also to put His fear in their heart, that they do not depart from Him. In addition to His own obligations as one of the covenanting parties, He undertakes for the other party too: "I WILL CAUSE you to walk in my statutes, and ye shall keep my judgments and do them" (Ezek.36:27). Blessed the man who understands this half of the covenant too! He sees that his security is not in the covenant which he makes with His God, and which he would but continually break again. He finds that a covenant has been made, in which God stands good, not only for Himself, but for man too. He grasps the blessed truth that his part in the covenant is to accept what God has promised to do, and to expect the sure fulfilment of the divine engagement to secure the faithfulness of His people to their God: "I will put my fear in their hearts, that they shall not depart from me."

It is just here that the blessed work comes in of the surety of the covenant, appointed of the Father to see to its maintenance and perfect fulfilment. To Him the Father hath said, "I have given thee for a covenant of the people." And the Holy Spirit testifies, "All the promises of God IN Him are yea, and in Him are Amen, to the glory of God by us." The believer who abides in Him hath a divine assurance for the fulfilment of every promise the covenant ever gave.

Christ was made surety of a better testament. It is as our Melchisedec that Christ is surety (see Heb.7). Aaron and his sons passed away; of Christ it is witnessed that He liveth. He is priest in the power of an endless life. Because He continueth ever, He hath an unchangeable priesthood. And because He ever liveth to make intercession, He can save to the uttermost, He can save completely. It is because Christ is the Ever-living One that His suretyship of the covenant is so effectual. He liveth ever to make intercession, and can therefore save completely. Every moment there rise up from His holy presence to the Father, the unceasing pleadings which secure to His people the powers and the blessings of the heavenly life. And every moment there go out from Him downward to His people, the mighty influences of His unceasing intercession, conveying to them uninterruptedly the power of the heavenly life. As surety with us for the Father's favour, He never ceases to pray and present us before Him; as surety with the Father for us, He never ceases to work, and reveal the Father within us.

The mystery of the Melchisedec priesthood, which the Hebrews were not able to receive (Heb.5:10-14), is the mystery of the resurrection life. It is in this that the glory of Christ as surety of the covenant consists: He ever liveth. He performs His work in heaven in the power of a divine, an omnipotent life. He ever liveth to pray; not a moment that as surety His prayers do not rise Godward to secure the Father's fulfilment to us of the covenant. He performs His work on earth in the power of that same life; not a moment that His answered prayers--the powers of the heavenly world--do not flow downward to secure for His Father our fulfilment of the covenant. In the eternal life there are no breaks--never a moment's interruption; each moment has the power of eternity in it. He ever, every moment, liveth to pray. He ever, every moment, liveth to bless. He can save to the uttermost, completely and perfectly, because He ever liveth to pray.

Believer! come and see here how the possibility of abiding in Jesus every moment is secured by the very nature of this ever-living priesthood of your surety. Moment by moment, as His intercession rises up, its efficacy descends. And because Jesus stands good for the fulfilment of the covenant--"I will put my fear in their heart, and they shall not depart from me"--He cannot afford to leave you one single moment to yourself. He dare not do so, or He fails of His undertaking. Your unbelief may fail of realizing the blessing; He cannot be unfaithful. If you will but consider Him, and the power of that endless life after which He was made and is a High Priest, your faith will rise to believe that an endless, ever-continuing, unchangeable life of abiding in Jesus, is nothing less than what is waiting you.

It is as we see what Jesus is, and is to us, that the abiding in Him will become the natural and spontaneous result of our knowledge of Him. If His life unceasingly, moment by moment, rises to the Father for us, and descends to us from the Father, then to abide moment by moment is easy and simple. Each moment of conscious intercourse with Him we simply say, "Jesus, surety, keeper, ever-living Saviour, in whose life I dwell, I abide in Thee." Each moment of need, or darkness, or fear, we still say, "O thou great High Priest, in the power of an endless, unchangeable life, I abide in Thee." And for the moments when direct and distinct communion with Him must give place to needful occupations, we can trust His suretyship, His unceasing priesthood, in its divine efficacy, and the power with which He saves to the uttermost, still to keep us abiding in Him.

Chapter 31: THE GLORIFIED ONE

"Your life is hid with Christ in God. When Christ, who is our life, shall appear, then shall ye also appear with him in glory."--COL.3:3-4

HE THAT abides in Christ the Crucified One, learns to know what it is to be crucified with Him, and in Him to be indeed dead unto sin. He that abides in Christ the Risen and Glorified One, becomes in the same way partaker of His resurrection life, and of the glory with which He has now been crowned in heaven. Unspeakable are the blessings which flow to the soul from the union with Jesus in His glorified life.

This life is a life of perfect victory and rest. Before His death, the Son of God had to suffer and to struggle, could be tempted and troubled by sin and its assaults: as the Risen One, He has triumphed over sin; and, as the Glorified One, His humanity has entered into participation of the glory of Deity. The believer who abides in Him as such, is led to see how the power of sin and the flesh are indeed destroyed: the consciousness of complete and everlasting deliverance becomes increasingly clear, and the blessed rest and peace, the fruit of such a conviction that victory and deliverance are an accomplished fact, take possession of the life. Abiding in Jesus, in whom he has been raised and set in the heavenly places, he receives of that glorious life streaming from the Head through every member of the body.

This life is a life in the full fellowship of the Father's love and holiness. Jesus often gave prominence to this thought with His disciples. His death was a going to the Father. He prayed: "Glorify me, O Father, with Thyself, with the glory which I had with Thee." As the believer, abiding in Christ the Glorified One, seeks to realize and experience what His union with Jesus on the throne implies, he apprehends how the unclouded light of the Father's presence is His highest glory and blessedness, and in Him the believer's portion too. He learns the sacred art of always, in fellowship with His exalted Head, dwelling in the secret of the Father's presence. Further, when Jesus was on earth, temptation could still reach Him: in glory, everything is holy, and in perfect harmony with the will of God. And so the believer who abides in Him experiences that in this high fellowship his spirit is sanctified into growing harmony with the Father's will. The heavenly life of Jesus is the power that casts out sin.

This life is a life of loving beneficence and activity. Seated on His throne, He dispenses His gifts, bestows His Spirit, and never ceases in love to watch and to work for those who are His. The believer cannot abide in Jesus the Glorified One, without feeling himself stirred and strengthened to work: the Spirit and the love of Jesus breathe the will and the power to be a blessing to others. Jesus went to heaven with the very object of obtaining power there to bless abundantly. He does this as the heavenly Vine only through the medium of His people as His branches. Whoever, therefore, abides in Him, the Glorified One, bears much fruit, for he receives of the Spirit and the power of the eternal life of his exalted Lord, and becomes the channel through which the fulness of Jesus, who hath been exalted to be a Prince and a Saviour, flows out to bless those around him.

There is one more thought in regard to this life of the Glorified One, and ours in Him. It is a life of wondrous expectation and hope. It is so with Christ. He sits at the right hand of God, expecting till all His enemies be made His footstool, looking forward to the time when He shall receive His full reward, when His glory shall be made manifest, and His beloved people be ever with Him in that glory. The hope of Christ is the hope of His redeemed: "I will come again and take you to myself, that where I am there ye may be also." This promise is as precious to Christ as it ever can be to us. The joy of meeting is surely no less for the coming bridegroom than for the waiting bride. The life of Christ in glory is one of longing expectation: the full glory only comes when His beloved are with Him.

The believer who abides closely in Christ will share with Him in this spirit of expectation. Not so much for the increase of personal happiness, but from the spirit of enthusiastic allegiance to his King, he longs to see Him come in His glory, reigning over every enemy, the fill revelation of God's everlasting love. "Till He come," is the watchword of every true-hearted believer. "Christ shall appear, and we shall appear with Him in glory."

There may be very serious differences in the exposition of the promises of His coming. To one it is plain as day that He is coming very speedily in person to reign on earth, and that speedy coming is his hope and his stay. To another, loving his Bible and his Saviour not less, the coming can mean nothing but the judgment day--the solemn transition from time to eternity, the close of history on earth, the beginning of heaven; and the thought of that manifestation of his Saviour's glory is no less his joy and his strength. It is Jesus, Jesus coming again, Jesus taking us to Himself, Jesus adored as Lord of all, that is to the whole Church the sum and the centre of its hope.

It is by abiding in Christ the Glorified One that the believer will be quickened to that truly spiritual looking for His coming, which alone brings true blessing to the soul. There is an interest in the study of the things which are to be, in which the discipleship of a school is often more marked than the discipleship of Christ the meek; in which contendings for opinions and condemnation of brethren are more striking than any signs of the coming glory. It is only the humility that is willing to learn from those who may have other gifts and deeper revelations of the truth than we, and the love that always speaks gently and tenderly of those who see not as we do, and the heavenliness that shows that the Coming One is indeed already our life, that will persuade either the Church or the world that this our faith is not in the wisdom of men, but in the power of God. To testify of the Saviour as the Coming One, we must be abiding in and bearing the image of Him as the Glorified One. Not the correctness of the views we hold, nor the earnestness with which we advocate them, will prepare us for meeting Him, but only the abiding in Him. Then only can our being manifested in glory with Him be what it is meant to be--a transfiguration, a breaking out and shining forth of the indwelling glory that had been waiting for the day of revelation.

Blessed life! "the life hid with Christ in God," "set in the heavenlies in Christ," abiding in Christ the glorified! Once again the question comes: Can a feeble child of dust really dwell in fellowship with the King of glory? And again the blessed answer has to be given: To maintain that union is the very work for which Christ has all power in heaven and earth at His disposal. The blessing will be given to him who will trust his Lord for it, who in faith and confident expectation ceases not to yield himself to be wholly one with Him. It was an act of wondrous though simple faith, in which the soul yielded itself at first to the Saviour. That faith grows up to clearer insight and faster hold of God's truth that we are one with Him in His glory. In that same wondrous faith, wondrously simple, but wondrously mighty, the soul learns to abandon itself entirely to the keeping of Christ's almighty power, and the actings of His eternal life. Because it knows that it has the Spirit of God dwelling within to communicate all that Christ is, it no longer looks upon it as a burden or a work, but allows the divine life to have its way, to do its work; its faith is the increasing abandonment of self, the expectation and acceptance of all that the love and the power of the Glorified One can perform. In that faith unbroken fellowship is maintained, and growing conformity realized. As with Moses, the fellowship makes partakers of the glory, and the life begins to shine with a brightness not of this world.

Blessed life! it is ours, for Jesus is ours. Blessed life! we have the possession within us in its hidden power, and we have the prospect before us in its fullest glory. May our daily lives be the bright and blessed proof that the hidden power dwells within, preparing us for the glory to be revealed. May our abiding in Christ the Glorified One be our power to live to the glory of the Father, our fitness to share to the glory of the Son.

AND NOW,
LITTLE CHILDREN,

ABIDE IN HIM,
THAT, WHEN HE SHALL APPEAR, WE MAY HAVE
CONFIDENCE, AND NOT BE ASHAMED
BEFORE HIM AT HIS COMING.

Absolute Surrender

"And Ben-hadad the king of Syria gathered all his host together: and there were thirty and two kings with him, and horses, and chariots: and he went up and besieged Samaria, and warred against it. And he sent messengers to Ahab king of Israel into the city, and said unto him, Thus saith Ben-hadad, Thy silver and thy gold is mine; thy wives also and thy children, even the goodliest, are mine. And the king of Israel answered and said, My lord, O king, according to thy saying, I am thine and all that I have" (1 Ki. 20:1-4).

What Ben Hadad asked was absolute surrender; and what Ahab gave was what was asked of him—absolute surrender. I want to use these words: "My lord, O king, according to thy saying, I am thine, and all that I have," as the words of absolute surrender with which every child of God ought to yield himself to his Father. We have heard it before, but we need to hear it very definitely—the condition of God's blessing is absolute surrender of all into His hands. Praise God! If our hearts are willing for that, there is no end to what God will do for us, and to the blessing God will bestow.

Absolute surrender—let me tell you where I got those words. I used them myself often, and you have heard them numberless times. But in Scotland once I was in a company where we were talking about the condition of Christ's Church, and what the great need of the Church and of believers is; and there was in our company a godly worker who has much to do in training workers, and I asked him what he would say was the great need of the Church, and the message that ought to be preached. He answered very quietly and simply and determinedly: "Absolute surrender to God is the one thing."

The words struck me as never before. And that man began to tell how, in the workers with whom he had to deal, he finds that if they are sound on that point, even though they be backward, they are willing to be taught and helped, and they always improve; whereas others who are not sound there very often go back and leave the work. The condition for obtaining God's full blessing is absolute surrender to Him.

And now, I desire by God's grace to give to you this message—that your God in Heaven answers the prayers which you have offered for blessing on yourselves and for blessing on those around you by this one demand: Are you willing to surrender yourselves absolutely into His hands? What is our answer to be? God knows there are hundreds of hearts who have said it, and there are hundreds more who long to say it but hardly dare to do so. And there are hearts who have said it, but who have yet miserably failed, and who feel themselves condemned because they did not find the secret of the power to live that life. May God have a word for all!

Let me say, first of all, that God claims it from us.

God Expects Your Surrender

Yes, it has its foundation in the very nature of God. God cannot do otherwise. Who is God? He is the Fountain of life, the only Source of existence and power and goodness, and throughout the universe there is nothing good but what God works. God has created the sun, and the moon, and the stars, and the flowers, and the trees, and the grass; and are they not all absolutely surrendered to God? Do they not allow God to work in them just what He pleases? When God clothes the lily with its beauty, is it not yielded up, surrendered, given over to God as He works in its beauty? And God's redeemed children, oh, can you think that God can work His work if there is only half or a part of them surrendered? God cannot do it. God is life, and love, and blessing, and power, and infinite beauty, and God delights to communicate Himself to every child who is prepared to receive Him; but ah! this one lack of absolute surrender is just the thing that hinders God. And now He comes, and as God, He claims it.

You know in daily life what absolute surrender is. You know that everything has to be given up to its special, definite object and service. I have a pen in my pocket, and that pen is absolutely surrendered to the one work of writing, and that pen must be absolutely surrendered to my hand if I am to write properly with it. If another holds it partly, I cannot write properly. This coat is absolutely given up to me to cover my body. This building is entirely given up to religious services. And now, do you expect that in your immortal being, in the divine nature that you have received by regeneration, God can work His work, every day and every hour, unless you are entirely given up to Him? God cannot. The Temple of Solomon was absolutely surrendered to God when it was dedicated to Him. And every one of us is a temple of God, in which God will dwell and work mightily on one condition—absolute surrender to Him. God claims it, God is worthy of it, and without it God cannot work His blessed work in us.

God not only claims it, but God will work it Himself.

God Accomplishes Your Surrender

I am sure there is many a heart that says: "Ah, but that absolute surrender implies so much!" Someone says: "Oh, I have passed through so much trial and suffering, and there is so much of the self-life still remaining, and I dare not face the entire giving of it up, because I know it will cause so much trouble and agony."

Alas! alas! that God's children have such thoughts of Him, such cruel thoughts. Oh, I come to you with a message, fearful and anxious one. God does not ask you to give the perfect surrender in your strength, or by the power of your will; God is willing to work it in you. Do we not read: "It is God that worketh in us, both to will and to do of his good pleasure" (Phil. 2:13)? And that is what we should seek for—to go on our faces before God, until our hearts learn to believe that the everlasting God Himself will come in to turn out what is wrong, to conquer what is evil, and to work what is well-pleasing in His blessed sight. God Himself will work it in you.

Look at the men in the Old Testament, like Abraham. Do you think it was by accident that God found that man, the father of the faithful and the Friend of God, and that it was Abraham himself, apart from God, who had such faith and such obedience and such devotion? You know it is not so. God raised him up and prepared him as an instrument for His glory.

Did not God say to Pharaoh: "For this cause have I raised thee up, for to show in thee my power" (Ex. 9:16)?

And if God said that of him, will not God say it far more of every child of His?

Oh, I want to encourage you, and I want you to cast away every fear. Come with that feeble desire; and if there is the fear which says: "Oh, my desire is not strong enough, I am not willing for everything that may come, I do not feel bold enough to say I can conquer everything"—I pray you, learn to know and trust your God now. Say: "My God, I am willing that Thou shouldst make me willing." If there is anything holding you back, or any sacrifice you are afraid of making, come to God now, and prove how gracious your God is, and be not afraid that He will command from you what He will not bestow.

God comes and offers to work this absolute surrender in you. All these searchings and hungerings and longings that are in your heart, I tell you they are the drawings of the divine magnet, Christ Jesus. He lived a life of absolute surrender, He has possession of you; He is living in your heart by His Holy Spirit. You have hindered and hindered Him terribly, but He desires to help you to get hold of Him entirely. And He comes and draws you now by His message and words. Will you not come and trust God to work in you that absolute surrender to Himself? Yes, blessed be God, He can do it, and He will do it.

God not only claims it and works it, but God accepts it when we bring it to Him.

God Accepts Your Surrender

God works it in the secret of our heart, God urges us by the hidden power of His Holy Spirit to come and speak it out, and we have to bring and to yield to Him that absolute surrender. But remember, when you come and bring God that absolute surrender, it may, as far as your feelings or your consciousness go, be a thing of great imperfection, and you may doubt and hesitate and say:

"Is it absolute?"

But, oh, remember there was once a man to whom Christ had said: "If thou canst believe, all things are possible to him that believeth" (Mark 9:23).

And his heart was afraid, and he cried out:

"Lord, I believe, help thou mine unbelief" (Mark 9:24).

That was a faith that triumphed over the Devil, and the evil spirit was cast out. And if you come and say: "Lord, I yield myself in absolute surrender to my God," even though it be with a trembling heart and with the consciousness: "I do not feel the power, I do not feel the determination, I do not feel the assurance," it will succeed. Be not afraid, but come just as you are, and even in the midst of your trembling the power of the Holy Spirit will work.

Have you never yet learned the lesson that the Holy Spirit works with mighty power, while on the human side everything appears feeble? Look at the Lord Jesus Christ in Gethsemane. We read that He, "through the eternal Spirit" (Heb. 9:14), offered Himself a sacrifice unto God. The Almighty Spirit of God was enabling Him to do it. And yet what agony and fear and exceeding sorrow came over Him, and how He prayed! Externally, you can see no sign of the mighty power of the Spirit, but the Spirit of God was there. And even so, while you are feeble and fighting and trembling, in faith in the hidden work of God's Spirit do not fear, but yield yourself.

And when you do yield yourself in absolute surrender, let it be in the faith that God does now accept of it. That is the great point, and that is what we so often miss—that believers should be thus occupied with God in this matter of surrender. I pray you, be occupied with God. We want to get help, every one of us, so that in our daily life God shall be clearer to us, God shall have the right place, and be "all in all." And if we are to have that through life, let us begin now and look away from ourselves, and look up to God. Let each believe—while I, a poor worm on earth and a trembling child of God, full of failure and sin and fear, bow here, and no one knows what passes through my heart, and while I in simplicity say, O God, I accept Thy terms; I have pleaded for blessing on myself and others, I have accepted Thy terms of absolute surrender—while your heart says that in deep silence, remember there is a God present that takes note of it, and writes it down in His book, and there is a God present who at that very moment takes possession of you. You may not feel it, you may not realize it, but God takes possession if you will trust Him.

God not only claims it, and works it, and accepts it when I bring it, but God maintains it.

God Maintains Your Surrender

That is the great difficulty with many. People say: "I have often been stirred at a meeting, or at a convention, and I have consecrated myself to God, but it has passed away. I know it may last for a week or for a month, but away it fades, and after a time it is all gone."

But listen! It is because you do not believe what I am now going to tell you and remind you of. When God has begun the work of absolute surrender in you, and when God has accepted your surrender, then God holds Himself bound to care for it and to keep it. Will you believe that? In this matter of surrender there are two: God and I—I a worm, God the everlasting and omnipotent Jehovah. Worm, will you be afraid to trust yourself to this mighty God now? God is willing. Do you not believe that He can keep you continually, day by day, and moment by moment?

Moment by moment I'm kept in His love;
Moment by moment I've life from above.

If God allows the sun to shine upon you moment by moment, without intermission, will not God let His life shine upon you every moment? And why have you not experienced it? Because you have not trusted God for it, and you do not surrender yourself absolutely to God in that trust.

A life of absolute surrender has its difficulties. I do not deny that. Yes, it has something far more than difficulties: it is a life that with men is absolutely impossible. But by the grace of God, by the power of God, by the power of the Holy Spirit dwelling in us, it is a life to which we are destined, and a life that is possible for us, praise God! Let us believe that God will maintain it.

Some of you have read the words of that aged saint who, on his ninetieth birthday, told of all God's goodness to him—I mean George Muller. What did he say he believed to be the secret of his happiness, and of all the blessing which God had given him? He said he believed there were two reasons. The one was that he had been enabled by grace to maintain a good conscience before God day by day; the other was, that he was a lover of God's Word. Ah, yes, a good conscience is complete obedience to God day by day, and fellowship with God every day in His Word, and prayer—that is a life of absolute surrender.

Such a life has two sides—on the one side, absolute surrender to work what God wants you to do; on the other side, to let God work what He wants to do.

First, to do what God wants you to do.

Give up yourselves absolutely to the will of God. You know something of that will; not enough, far from all. But say absolutely to the Lord

God: "By Thy grace I desire to do Thy will in everything, every moment of every day." Say: "Lord God, not a word upon my tongue but for Thy glory, not a movement of my temper but for Thy glory, not an affection of love or hate in my heart but for Thy glory, and according to Thy blessed will."

Someone says: "Do you think that possible?"

I ask, What has God promised you, and what can God do to fill a vessel absolutely surrendered to Him? Oh, God wants to bless you in a way beyond what you expect. From the beginning, ear hath not heard, neither hath the eye seen, what God hath prepared for them that wait for Him (1 Cor. 2:9). God has prepared unheard-of things, blessings much more wonderful than you can imagine, more mighty than you can conceive. They are divine blessings. Oh, say now:

"I give myself absolutely to God, to His will, to do only what God wants."

It is God who will enable you to carry out the surrender.

And, on the other side, come and say: "I give myself absolutely to God, to let Him work in me to will and to do of His good pleasure, as He has promised to do."

Yes, the living God wants to work in His children in a way that we cannot understand, but that God's Word has revealed, and He wants to work in us every moment of the day. God is willing to maintain our life. Only let our absolute surrender be one of simple, childlike, and unbounded trust.

God Blesses When You Surrender

This absolute surrender to God will wonderfully bless.

What Ahab said to his enemy, King Ben-hadad—"My lord, O king, according to thy word I am thine, and all that I have"—shall we not say to our God and loving Father? If we do say it, God's blessing will come upon us. God wants us to be separate from the world; we are called to come out from the world that hates God. Come out for God, and say: "Lord, anything for Thee." If you say that with prayer, and speak that into God's ear, He will accept it, and He will teach you what it means.

I say again, God will bless you. You have been praying for blessing. But do remember, there must be absolute surrender. At every tea-table you see it. Why is tea poured into that cup? Because it is empty, and given up for the tea. But put ink, or vinegar, or wine into it, and will they pour the tea into the vessel? And can God fill you, can God bless you if you are not absolutely surrendered to Him? He cannot. Let us believe God has wonderful blessings for us, if we will but stand up for God, and say, be it with a trembling will, yet with a believing heart: "O God, I accept Thy demands. I am thine and all that I have. Absolute surrender is what my soul yields to Thee by divine grace."

You may not have such strong and clear feelings of deliverances as you would desire to have, but humble yourselves in His sight, and acknowledge that you have grieved the Holy Spirit by your self-will, self-confidence, and self-effort. Bow humbly before him in the confession of that, and ask him to break the heart and to bring you into the dust before Him. Then, as you bow before Him, just accept God's teaching that in your flesh "there dwelleth no good thing" (Rom. 7:18), and that nothing will help you except another life which must come in. You must deny self once for all. Denying self must every moment be the power of your life, and then Christ will come in and take possession of you.

When was Peter delivered? When was the change accomplished? The change began with Peter weeping, and the Holy Spirit came down and filled his heart.

God the Father loves to give us the power of the Spirit. We have the Spirit of God dwelling within us. We come to God confessing that, and praising God for it, and yet confessing how we have grieved the Spirit. And then we bow our knees to the Father to ask that He would strengthen us with all might by the Spirit in the inner man, and that He would fill us with His mighty power. And as the Spirit reveals Christ to us, Christ comes to live in our hearts forever, and the self-life is cast out.

Let us bow before God in humility, and in that humility confess before Him the state of the whole Church. No words can tell the sad state of the Church of Christ on earth. I wish I had words to speak what I sometimes feel about it. Just think of the Christians around you. I do not speak of nominal Christians, or of professing Christians, but I speak of hundreds and thousands of honest, earnest Christians who are not living a life in the power of God or to His glory. So little power, so little devotion or consecration to God, so little perception of the truth that a Christian is a man utterly surrendered to God's will! Oh, we want to confess the sins of God's people around us, and to humble ourselves. We are members of that sickly body, and the sickliness of the body will hinder us, and break us down, unless we come to God, and in confession separate ourselves from partnership with worldliness, with coldness toward each other, unless we give up ourselves to be entirely and wholly for God.

How much Christian work is being done in the spirit of the flesh and in the power of self! How much work, day by day, in which human energy—our will and our thoughts about the work—is continually manifested, and in which there is but little of waiting upon God, and upon the power of the Holy Spirit! Let us make confession. But as we confess the state of the Church and the feebleness and sinfulness of work for God among us, let us come back to ourselves. Who is there who truly longs to be delivered from the power of the self-life, who truly acknowledges that it is the power of self and the flesh, and who is willing to cast all at the feet of Christ? There is deliverance.

I heard of one who had been an earnest Christian, and who spoke about the "cruel" thought of separation and death. But you do not think that, do you? What are we to think of separation and death? This: death was the path to glory for Christ. For the joy set before Him He endured the cross. The cross was the birthplace of His everlasting glory. Do you love Christ? Do you long to be in Christ, and not like Him? Let death be to you the most desirable thing on earth—death to self, and fellowship with Christ. Separation—do you think it a hard thing to be called to be entirely free from the world, and by that separation to be united to God and His love, by separation to become prepared for living and walking with God every day? Surely one ought to say: "Anything to bring me to separation, to death, for a life of full fellowship with God and Christ."

Come and cast this self-life and flesh-life at the feet of Jesus. Then trust Him. Do not worry yourselves with trying to understand all about it, but come in the living faith that Christ will come into you with the power of His death and the power of His life; and then the Holy Spirit will bring the whole Christ—Christ crucified and risen and living in glory—into your heart.

"THE FRUIT OF THE SPIRIT IS LOVE"

I want to look at the fact of a life filled with the Holy Spirit more from the practical side, and to show how this life will show itself in our daily walk and conduct.

Under the Old Testament you know the Holy Spirit often came upon men as a divine Spirit of revelation to reveal the mysteries of God, or for power to do the work of God. But He did not then dwell in them. Now, many just want the Old Testament gift of power for work, but know very little of the New Testament gift of the indwelling Spirit, animating and renewing the whole life. When God gives the Holy Spirit, His great object is the formation of a holy character. It is a gift of a holy mind and spiritual disposition, and what we need above everything else, is to say:

"I must have the Holy Spirit sanctifying my whole inner life if I am really to live for God's glory."

You might say that when Christ promised the Spirit to the disciples, He did so that they might have power to be witnesses. True, but then they received the Holy Spirit in such heavenly power and reality that He took possession of their whole being at once and so fitted them as holy men for doing the work with power as they had to do it. Christ spoke of power to the disciples, but it was the Spirit filling their whole being that worked the power.

I wish now to dwell upon the passage found in Gal. 5:22:

"The fruit of the Spirit is love."

We read that "Love is the fulfilling of the law" (Rom. 13:10), and my desire is to speak on love as a fruit of the Spirit with a twofold object. One is that this word may be a searchlight in our hearts, and give us a test by which to try all our thoughts about the Holy Spirit and all our experience of the holy life. Let us try ourselves by this word. Has this been our daily habit, to seek to be filled with the Holy Spirit as the Spirit of love? "The fruit of the Spirit is love." Has it been our experience that the more we have of the Holy Spirit the more loving we become? In claiming the Holy Spirit we should make this the first object of our expectation. The Holy Spirit comes as a Spirit of love. Oh, if this were true in the Church of Christ how different her state would be! May God help us to get hold of this simple, heavenly truth that the fruit of the Spirit is a love which appears in the life, and that just as the Holy Spirit gets real possession of the life, the heart will be filled with real, divine, universal love.

One of the great causes why God cannot bless His Church is the want of love. When the body is divided, there cannot be strength. In the time of their great religious wars, when Holland stood out so nobly against

Spain, one of their mottoes was: "Unity gives strength." It is only when God's people stand as one body, one before God in the fellowship of love, one toward another in deep affection, one before the world in a love that the world can see—it is only then that they will have power to secure the blessing which they ask of God. Remember that if a vessel that ought to be one whole is cracked into many pieces, it cannot be filled. You can take a potsherd, one part of a vessel, and dip out a little water into that, but if you want the vessel full, the vessel must be whole. That is literally true of Christ's Church, and if there is one thing we must pray for still, it is this: Lord, melt us together into one by the power of the Holy Spirit; let the Holy Spirit, who at Pentecost made them all of one heart and one soul, do His blessed work among us. Praise God, we can love each other in a divine love, for "the fruit of the Spirit is love." Give yourselves up to love, and the Holy Spirit will come; receive the Spirit, and He will teach you to love more.

God Is Love

Now, why is it that the fruit of the Spirit is love? Because God is love (1 John 4:8).

And what does that mean?

It is the very nature and being of God to delight in communicating Himself. God has no selfishness, God keeps nothing to Himself. God's nature is to be always giving. In the sun and the moon and the stars, in every flower you see it, in every bird in the air, in every fish in the sea. God communicates life to His creatures. And the angels around His throne, the seraphim and cherubim who are flames of fire—whence have they their glory? It is because God is love, and He imparts to them of His brightness and His blessedness. And we, His redeemed children—God delights to pour His love into us. And why? Because, as I said, God keeps nothing for Himself. From eternity God had His only begotten Son, and the Father gave Him all things, and nothing that God had was kept back. "God is love."

One of the old Church fathers said that we cannot better understand the Trinity than as a revelation of divine love—the Father, the loving One, the Fountain of love; the Son, the beloved one, the Reservoir of love, in whom the love was poured out; and the Spirit, the living love that united both and then overflowed into this world. The Spirit of Pentecost, the Spirit of the Father, and the Spirit of the Son is love. And when the Holy Spirit comes to us and to other men, will He be less a Spirit of love than He is in God? It cannot be; He cannot change His nature. The Spirit of God is love, and "the fruit of the Spirit is love."

Mankind Needs Love

Why is that so? That was the one great need of mankind, that was the thing which Christ's redemption came to accomplish: to restore love to this world.

When man sinned, why was it that he sinned? Selfishness triumphed—he sought self instead of God. And just look! Adam at once begins to accuse the woman of having led him astray. Love to God had gone, love to man was lost. Look again: of the first two children of Adam the one becomes a murderer of his brother.

Does not that teach us that sin had robbed the world of love? Ah! what a proof the history of the world has been of love having been lost! There may have been beautiful examples of love even among the heathen, but only as a little remnant of what was lost. One of the worst things sin did for man was to make him selfish, for selfishness cannot love.

The Lord Jesus Christ came down from Heaven as the Son of God's love. "God so loved the world that He gave His only begotten Son" (John 3:16). God's Son came to show what love is, and He lived a life of love here upon earth in fellowship with His disciples, in compassion over the poor and miserable, in love even to His enemies, and He died the death of love. And when He went to Heaven, whom did He send down? The Spirit of love, to come and banish selfishness and envy and pride, and bring the love of God into the hearts of men. "The fruit of the Spirit is love."

And what was the preparation for the promise of the Holy Spirit? You know that promise as found in the fourteenth chapter of John's Gospel. But remember what precedes in the thirteenth chapter. Before Christ promised the Holy Spirit, He gave a new commandment, and about that new commandment He said wonderful things. One thing was: "Even as I have loved you, so love ye one another." To them His dying love was to be the only law of their conduct and intercourse with each other. What a message to those fishermen, to those men full of pride and selfishness! "Learn to love each other," said Christ, "as I have loved you." And by the grace of God they did it. When Pentecost came, they were of one heart and one soul. Christ did it for them.

And now He calls us to dwell and to walk in love. He demands that though a man hate you, still you love him. True love cannot be conquered by anything in Heaven or upon the earth. The more hatred there is, the more love triumphs through it all and shows its true nature. This is the love that Christ commanded His disciples to exercise. What more did He say? "By this shall all men know that ye are my disciples, if ye have love one to another" (John 13:35).

You all know what it is to wear a badge. And Christ said to His disciples in effect: "I give you a badge, and that badge is love. That is to be your mark. It is the only thing in Heaven or on earth by which men can know me."

Do we not begin to fear that love has fled from the earth? That if we were to ask the world: "Have you seen us wear the badge of love?" the world would say: "No; what we have heard of the Church of Christ is that there is not a place where there is no quarreling and separation." Let us ask God with one heart that we may wear the badge of Jesus' love. God is able to give it.

Love Conquers Selfishness

"The fruit of the Spirit is love." Why? Because nothing but love can expel and conquer our selfishness.

Self is the great curse, whether in its relation to God, or to our fellow-men in general, or to fellow-Christians, thinking of ourselves and seeking our own. Self is our greatest curse. But, praise God, Christ came to redeem us from self. We sometimes talk about deliverance from the self-life—and thank God for every word that can be said about it to help us—but I am afraid some people think deliverance from the self-life means that now they are going to have no longer any trouble in serving God; and they forget that deliverance from self-life means to be a vessel overflowing with love to everybody all the day. And there you have the reason why many people pray for the power of the Holy Spirit, and they get something, but oh, so little! because they prayed for power for work, and power for blessing, but they have not prayed for power for full deliverance from self. That means not only the righteous self in intercourse with God, but the unloving self in intercourse with men. And there is deliverance. "The fruit of the Spirit is love." I bring you the glorious promise of Christ that He is able to fill our hearts with love.

A great many of us try hard at times to love. We try to force ourselves to love, and I do not say that is wrong; it is better than nothing. But the end of it is always very sad. "I fail continually," such a one must confess. And what is the reason? The reason is simply this: Because they have never learned to believe and accept the truth that the Holy Spirit can pour God's love into their heart. That blessed text; often it has been limited!—"The love of God is shed abroad in our hearts" (Rom. 5:5). It has often been understood in this sense: It means the love of God to me. Oh, what a limitation! That is only the beginning. The love of God is always the love of God in its entirety, in its fullness as an indwelling power, a love of God to me that leaps back to Him in love, and overflows to my fellow-men in love—God's love to me, and my love to God, and my love to my fellow-men. The three are one; you cannot separate them.

Do believe that the love of God can be shed abroad in your heart and mine so that we can love all the day.

"Ah!" you say, "how little I have understood that!"

Why is a lamb always gentle? Because that is its nature. Does it cost the lamb any trouble to be gentle? No. Why not? It is so beautiful and gentle. Has a lamb to study to be gentle? No. Why does that come so easy? It is its nature. And a wolf—why does it cost a wolf no trouble to be cruel, and to put its fangs into the poor lamb or sheep? Because that is its nature. It has not to summon up its courage; the wolf-nature is there.

And how can I learn to love? Never until the Spirit of God fills my heart with God's love, and I begin to long for God's love in a very different sense from which I have sought it so selfishly, as a comfort and a joy and a happiness and a pleasure to myself; never until I begin to learn that "God is love," and to claim it, and receive it as an indwelling power for self-sacrifice; never until I begin to see that my glory, my blessedness, is to be like God and like Christ, in giving up everything in myself for my fellow-men. May God teach us that! Oh, the divine blessedness of the love with which the Holy Spirit can fill our hearts! "The fruit of the Spirit is love."

Love Is God's Gift

Once again I ask, Why must this be so? And my answer is: Without this we cannot live the daily life of love.

How often, when we speak about the consecrated life, we have to speak about temper, and some people have sometimes said:

"You make too much of temper."

I do not think we can make too much of it. Think for a moment of a clock and of what its hands mean. The hands tell me what is within the clock, and if I see that the hands stand still, or that the hands point wrong, or that the clock is slow or fast, I say that something inside the clock is not working properly. And temper is just like the revelation that the clock gives of what is within. Temper is a proof whether the love of Christ is filling the heart, or not. How many there are who find it easier in church, or in prayer-meeting, or in work for the Lord—diligent, earnest work—to be holy and happy than in the daily life with wife and children; easier to be holy and happy outside the home than in it! Where is the love of God? In Christ. God has prepared for us a wonderful redemption in Christ, and He longs to make something supernatural of us. Have we learned to long for it, and ask for it, and expect it in its fullness?

Then there is the tongue! We sometimes speak of the tongue when we talk of the better life, and the restful life, but just think what liberty many Christians give to their tongues. They say:

"I have a right to think what I like."

When they speak about each other, when they speak about their neighbors, when they speak about other Christians, how often there are sharp remarks! God keep me from saying anything that would be unloving; God shut my mouth if I am not to speak in tender love. But what I am saying is a fact. How often there are found among Christians who are banded together in work, sharp criticism, sharp judgment, hasty opinion, unloving words, secret contempt of each other, secret condemnation of each other! Oh, just as a mother's love covers her children and delights in them and has the tenderest compassion with their foibles or failures, so there ought to be in the heart of every believer a motherly love toward every brother and sister in Christ. Have you aimed at that? Have you sought it? Have you ever pleaded for it? Jesus Christ said: "As I have loved you . . . love one another" (John 13:34). And He did not put that among the other commandments, but He said in effect:

"That is a new commandment, the one commandment: Love one another as I have loved you" (John 13:34).

It is in our daily life and conduct that the fruit of the Spirit is love. From that there comes all the graces and virtues in which love is manifested: joy, peace, longsuffering, gentleness, goodness; no sharpness or hardness in your tone, no unkindness or selfishness; meekness before God and man. You see that all these are the gentler virtues. I have often thought as I read those words in Colossians, "Put on therefore as the elect of God, holy and beloved, bowels of mercies, kindness, humbleness of mind, meekness, longsuffering" (Col. 3:12), that if we had written this, we should have put in the foreground the manly virtues, such as zeal, courage, and diligence; but we need to see how the gentler, the most womanly virtues are especially connected with dependence upon the Holy Spirit. These are indeed heavenly graces. They never were found in the heathen world. Christ was needed to come from Heaven to teach us. Your blessedness is longsuffering, meekness, kindness; your glory is humility before God. The fruit of the Spirit that He brought from Heaven out of the heart of the crucified Christ, and that He gives in our heart, is first and foremost—love.

You know what John says: "No man hath seen God at any time. If we love one another, God dwelleth in us" (1 John 4:12). That is, I cannot see God, but as a compensation I can see my brother, and if I love him, God dwells in me. Is that really true? That I cannot see God, but I must love my brother, and God will dwell in me? Loving my brother is the way to real fellowship with God. You know what John further says in that most solemn test, "If a man say, I love God, and hateth his brother, he is a liar; for he that loveth not his brother whom he hath seen, how can he love God whom he hath not seen?" (1 John 4:20). There is a brother, a most unlovable man. He worries you every time you meet him. He is of the very opposite disposition to yours. You are a careful businessman, and you have to do with him in your business. He is most untidy, unbusiness-like. You say:

"I cannot love him."

Oh, friend, you have not learned the lesson that Christ wanted to teach above everything. Let a man be what he will, you are to love him. Love is to be the fruit of the Spirit all the day and every day. Yes, listen! If a man loves not his brother whom he hath seen—if you don't love that unlovable man whom you have seen, how can you love God whom you have not seen? You can deceive yourself with beautiful thoughts about loving God. You must prove your love to God by your love to your brother; that is the one standard by which God will judge your love to Him. If the love of God is in your heart you will love your brother. The fruit of the Spirit is love.

And what is the reason that God's Holy Spirit cannot come in power? Is it not possible?

You remember the comparison I used in speaking of the vessel. I can dip a little water into a potsherd, a bit of a vessel; but if a vessel is to be full, it must be unbroken. And the children of God, wherever they come together, to whatever church or mission or society they belong, must love each other intensely, or the Spirit of God cannot do His work. We talk about grieving the Spirit of God by worldliness and ritualism and formality and error and indifference, but, I tell you, the one thing above everything that grieves God's Spirit is this lack of love. Let every heart search itself, and ask that God may search it.

Our Love Shows God's Power

Why are we taught that "the fruit of the Spirit is love"? Because the Spirit of God has come to make our daily life an exhibition of divine power and a revelation of what God can do for His children.

In the second and the fourth chapters of Acts we read that the disciples were of one heart and of one soul. During the three years they had walked with Christ they never had been in that spirit. All Christ's teaching could not make them of one heart and one soul. But the Holy Spirit came from Heaven and shed the love of God in their hearts, and they were of one heart and one soul. The same Holy Spirit that brought the love of Heaven into their hearts must fill us too. Nothing less will do. Even as Christ did, one might preach love for three years with the tongue of an angel, but that would not teach any man to love unless the power of the Holy Spirit should come upon him to bring the love of Heaven into his heart.

Think of the church at large. What divisions! Think of the different bodies. Take the question of holiness, take the question of the cleansing blood, take the question of the baptism of the Spirit—what differences are caused among dear believers by such questions! That there are differences of opinion does not trouble me. We do not have the same constitution and temperament and mind. But how often hate, bitterness, contempt, separation, unlovingness are caused by the holiest truths of God's Word! Our doctrines, our creeds, have been more important than love. We often think we are valiant for the truth and we forget God's command to speak the truth in love. And it was so in the time of the Reformation between the Lutheran and Calvinistic churches. What bitterness there was then in regard to the Holy Supper, which was meant to be the bond of union among all believers! And so, down the ages, the very dearest truths of God have become mountains that have separated us.

If we want to pray in power, and if we want to expect the Holy Spirit to come down in power, and if we want indeed that God shall pour out His Spirit, we must enter into a covenant with God that we love one another with a heavenly love.

Are you ready for that? Only that is true love that is large enough to take in all God's children, the most unloving and unlovable, and unworthy, and unbearable, and trying. If my vow—absolute surrender to God—was true, then it must mean absolute surrender to the divine love to fill me; to be a servant of love to love every child of God around me. "The fruit of the Spirit is love."

Oh, God did something wonderful when He gave Christ, at His right hand, the Holy Spirit to come down out of the heart of the Father and

His everlasting love. And how we have degraded the Holy Spirit into a mere power by which we have to do our work! God forgive us! Oh, that the Holy Spirit might be held in honor as a power to fill us with the very life and nature of God and of Christ!

Christian Work Requires Love

"The fruit of the Spirit is love." I ask once again, Why is it so? And the answer comes: That is the only power in which Christians really can do their work.

Yes, it is that we need. We want not only love that is to bind us to each other, but we want a divine love in our work for the lost around us. Oh, do we not often undertake a great deal of work, just as men undertake work of philanthropy, from a natural spirit of compassion for our fellow-men? Do we not often undertake Christian work because our minister or friend calls us to it? And do we not often perform Christian work with a certain zeal but without having had a baptism of love? People often ask: "What is the baptism of fire?"

I have answered more than once: I know no fire like the fire of God, the fire of everlasting love that consumed the sacrifice on Calvary. The baptism of love is what the Church needs, and to get that we must begin at once to get down upon our faces before God in confession, and plead:

"Lord, let love from Heaven flow down into my heart. I am giving up my life to pray and live as one who has given himself up for the everlasting love to dwell in and fill him."

Ah, yes, if the love of God were in our hearts, what a difference it would make! There are hundreds of believers who say:

"I work for Christ, and I feel I could work much harder, but I have not the gift. I do not know how or where to begin. I do not know what I can do."

Brother, sister, ask God to baptize you with the Spirit of love, and love will find its way. Love is a fire that will burn through every difficulty. You may be a shy, hesitating man, who cannot speak well, but love can burn through everything. God fill us with love! We need it for our work.

You have read many a touching story of love expressed, and you have said, How beautiful! I heard one not long ago. A lady had been asked to speak at a Rescue Home where there were a number of poor women. As she arrived there and got to the window with the matron, she saw outside a wretched object sitting, and asked:

"Who is that?"

The matron answered: "She has been into the house thirty or forty times, and she has always gone away again. Nothing can be done with her, she is so low and hard."

But the lady said: "She must come in."

The matron then said: "We have been waiting for you, and the company is assembled, and you have only an hour for the address."

The lady replied: "No, this is of more importance"; and she went outside where the woman was sitting and said:

"My sister, what is the matter?"

"I am not your sister," was the reply.

Then the lady laid her hand on her, and said: "Yes, I am your sister, and I love you"; and so she spoke until the heart of the poor woman was touched.

The conversation lasted some time, and the company were waiting patiently. Ultimately the lady brought the woman into the room. There was the poor wretched, degraded creature, full of shame. She would not sit on a chair, but sat down on a stool beside the speaker's seat, and she let her lean against her, with her arms around the poor woman's neck, while she spoke to the assembled people. And that love touched the woman's heart; she had found one who really loved her, and that love gave access to the love of Jesus.

Praise God! there is love upon earth in the hearts of God's children; but oh, that there were more!

O God, baptize our ministers with a tender love, and our missionaries, and our Bible-readers, and our workers, and our young men's and young women's associations. Oh, that God would begin with us now, and baptize us with heavenly love!

Love Inspires Intercession

Once again. It is only love that can fit us for the work of intercession. I have said that love must fit us for our work. Do you know what the hardest and the most important work is that has to be done for this sinful world? It is the work of intercession, the work of going to God and taking time to lay hold on Him.

A man may be an earnest Christian, an earnest minister, and a man may do good, but alas! how often he has to confess that he knows but little of what it is to tarry with God. May God give us the great gift of an intercessory spirit, a spirit of prayer and supplication! Let me ask you in the name of Jesus not to let a day pass without praying for all saints, and for all God's people.

I find there are Christians who think little of that. I find there are prayer unions where they pray for the members, and not for all believers. I pray you, take time to pray for the Church of Christ. It is right to pray for the heathen, as I have already said. God help us to pray more for them. It is right to pray for missionaries and for evangelistic work, and for the unconverted. But Paul did not tell people to pray for the heathen or the unconverted. Paul told them to pray for believers. Do make this your first prayer every day: "Lord, bless Thy saints everywhere."

The state of Christ's Church is indescribably low. Plead for God's people that He would visit them, plead for each other, plead for all believers who are trying to work for God. Let love fill your heart. Ask Christ to pour it out afresh into you every day. Try to get it into you by the Holy Spirit of God: I am separated unto the Holy Spirit, and the fruit of the Spirit is love. God help us to understand it.

May God grant that we learn day by day to wait more quietly upon Him. Do not wait upon God only for ourselves, or the power to do so will soon be lost; but give ourselves up to the ministry and the love of intercession, and pray more for God's people, for God's people round about us, for the Spirit of love in ourselves and in them, and for the work of God we are connected with; and the answer will surely come, and our waiting upon God will be a source of untold blessing and power. "The fruit of the Spirit is love."

Have you a lack of love to confess before God? Then make confession and say before Him, "O Lord, my lack of heart, my lack of love—I confess it." And then, as you cast that lack at His feet, believe that the blood cleanses you, that Jesus comes in His mighty, cleansing, saving power to deliver you, and that He will give His Holy Spirit.

SEPARATED UNTO THE HOLY GHOST

"Now there were in the church that was at Antioch certain prophets and teachers; as Barnabas, and Simeon that was called Niger, and Lucius of Cyrene, and Manaen . . . and Saul.

"As they ministered to the Lord, and fasted, the Holy Spirit said, Separate me Barnabas and Saul for the work whereunto I have called them.

"And when they had fasted and prayed, and laid their hands on them, they sent them away. So they, being sent forth by the Holy Spirit, departed unto Seleucia" (Acts 13:1-4).

In the story of our text we shall find some precious thoughts to guide us as to what God would have of us, and what God would do for us. The great lesson of the verses quoted is this: The Holy Spirit is the director of the work of God upon the earth. And what we should do if we are to work rightly for God, and if God is to bless our work, is to see that we stand in a right relation to the Holy Spirit, that we give Him every day the place of honor that belongs to Him, and that in all our work and (what is more) in all our private inner life, the Holy Spirit shall always have the first place. Let me point out to you some of the precious thoughts our passage suggests.

First of all, we see that God has His own plans with regard to His kingdom.

His church at Antioch had been established. God had certain plans and intentions with regard to Asia, and with regard to Europe. He had conceived them; they were His, and He made them known to His servants.

Our great Commander organizes every campaign, and His generals and officers do not always know the great plans. They often receive sealed orders, and they have to wait on Him for what He gives them as orders. God in Heaven has wishes, and a will, in regard to any work that ought to be done, and to the way in which it has to be done. Blessed is the man who gets into God's secrets and works under God.

Some years ago, at Wellington, South Africa, where I live, we opened a Mission Institute—what is counted there a fine large building. At our opening services the principal said something that I have never forgotten. He remarked:

"Last year we gathered here to lay the foundation-stone, and what was there then to be seen? Nothing but rubbish, and stones, and bricks, and ruins of an old building that had been pulled down. There we laid the foundation-stone, and very few knew what the building was that was to rise. No one knew it perfectly in every detail except one man, the architect. In his mind it was all clear, and as the contractor and the mason and the carpenter came to their work they took their orders from him, and the humblest laborer had to be obedient to orders, and the structure rose, and this beautiful building has been completed. And just so," he added, "this building that we open today is but laying the foundation of a work of which only God knows what is to become." But God has His workers and His plans clearly mapped out, and our position is to wait, that God should communicate to us as much of His will as each time is needful.

We have simply to be faithful in obedience, carrying out His orders. God has a plan for His Church upon earth. But alas! we too often make our plan, and we think that we know what ought to be done. We ask God first to bless our feeble efforts, instead of absolutely refusing to go unless God goes before us. God has planned for the work and the extension of His kingdom. The Holy Spirit has had that work given in charge to Him. "The work whereunto I have called them." May God, therefore, help us all to be afraid of touching "the ark of God" except as we are led by the Holy Spirit.

Then the second thought—God is willing and able to reveal to His servants what His will is.

Yes, blessed be God, communications still come down from Heaven! As we read here what the Holy Spirit said, so the Holy Spirit will still speak to His Church and His people. In these later days He has often done it. He has come to individual men, and by His divine teaching He has led them out into fields of labor that others could not at first understand or approve, into ways and methods that did not recommend themselves to the majority. But the Holy Spirit does still in our time teach His people. Thank God, in our foreign missionary societies and in our home missions, and in a thousand forms of work, the guiding of the Holy Spirit is known, but (we are all ready, I think, to confess) too little known. We have not learned enough to wait upon Him, and so we should make a solemn declaration before God: O God, we want to wait more for Thee to show us Thy Will.

Do not ask God only for power. Many a Christian has his own plan of working, but God must send the power. The man works in his own will, and God must give the grace—the one reason why God often gives so little grace and so little success. But let us all take our place before God and say:

"What is done in the will of God, the strength of God will not be withheld from it; what is done in the will of God must have the mighty blessing of God."

And so let our first desire be to have the will of God revealed.

If you ask me, Is it an easy thing to get these communications from Heaven, and to understand them? I can give you the answer. It is easy to those who are in right fellowship with Heaven, and who understand the art of waiting upon God in prayer.

How often we ask: How can a person know the will of God? And people want, when they are in perplexity, to pray very earnestly that God should answer them at once. But God can only reveal His will to a heart that is humble and tender and empty. God can only reveal His will in perplexities and special difficulties to a heart that has learned to obey and honor Him loyally in little things and in daily life.

That brings me to the third thought—Note the disposition to which the Spirit reveals God's will.

What do we read here? There were a number of men ministering to the Lord and fasting, and the Holy Spirit came and spoke to them. Some people understand this passage very much as they would in reference to a missionary committee of our day. We see there is an open field, and we have had our missions in other fields, and we are going to get on to that field. We have virtually settled that, and we pray about it. But the position was a very different one in those former days. I doubt whether any of them thought of Europe, for later on even Paul himself tried to go back into Asia, till the night vision called him by the will of God. Look at those men. God had done wonders. He had extended the Church to Antioch, and He had given rich and large blessing. Now, here were these men ministering to the Lord, serving Him with prayer and fasting. What a deep conviction they have—"It must all come direct from Heaven. We are in fellowship with the risen Lord; we must have a close union with Him, and somehow He will let us know what He wants." And there they were, empty, ignorant, helpless, glad and joyful, but deeply humbled.

"O Lord," they seem to say, "we are Thy servants, and in fasting and prayer we wait upon Thee. What is Thy will for us?"

Was it not the same with Peter? He was on the housetop, fasting and praying, and little did he think of the vision and the command to go to Caesarea. He was ignorant of what his work might be.

It is in hearts entirely surrendered to the Lord Jesus, in hearts separating themselves from the world, and even from ordinary religious exercises, and giving themselves up in intense prayer to look to their Lord—it is in such hearts that the heavenly will of God will be made manifest.

You know that word fasting occurs a second time (in the third verse): "They fasted and prayed." When you pray, you love to go into your closet, according to the command of Jesus, and shut the door. You shut out business and company and pleasure and anything that can distract, and you want to be alone with God. But in one way even the material world follows you there. You must eat. These men wanted to shut themselves out from the influences of the material and the visible, and they fasted. What they ate was simply enough to supply the wants of nature, and in the intensity of their souls they thought to give expression to their letting go of everything on earth in their fasting before God. Oh, may God give us that intensity of desire, that separation from everything, because we want to wait upon God, that the Holy Spirit may reveal to us God's blessed will.

The fourth thought—What is now the will of God as the Holy Spirit reveals it? It is contained in one phrase: Separation unto the Holy Spirit. That is the keynote of the message from Heaven.

"Separate me Barnabas and Saul for the work whereunto I have called them. The work is mine, and I care for it, and I have chosen these men and called them, and I want you who represent the Church of Christ upon earth to set them apart unto me."

Look at this heavenly message in its twofold aspect. The men were to be set apart to the Holy Spirit, and the Church was to do this separating work. The Holy Spirit could trust these men to do it in a right spirit. There they were abiding in fellowship with the heavenly, and the Holy Spirit could say to them, "Do the work of separating these men." And these were the men the Holy Spirit had prepared, and He could say of them, "Let them be separated unto me."

Here we come to the very root, to the very life of the need of Christian workers. The question is: What is needed that the power of God should rest upon us more mightily, that the blessing of God should be poured out more abundantly among those poor, wretched people and perishing sinners among whom we labor? And the answer from Heaven is: "I want men separated unto the Holy Spirit."

What does that imply? You know that there are two spirits on earth. Christ said, when He spoke about the Holy Spirit: "The world cannot receive him" (John 14:17). Paul said: "We have received not the spirit of the world, but the Spirit that is of God" (1 Cor. 2:12). That is the great want in every worker—the spirit of the world going out, and the Spirit of God coming in to take possession of the inner life and of the whole being.

I am sure there are workers who often cry to God for the Holy Spirit to come upon them as a Spirit of power for their work, and when they feel that measure of power, and get blessing, they thank God for it. But God wants something more and something higher. God wants us to seek for the Holy Spirit as a Spirit of power in our own heart and life, to conquer self and cast out sin, and to work the blessed and beautiful image of Jesus into us.

There is a difference between the power of the Spirit as a gift, and the power of the Spirit for the grace of a holy life. A man may often have a measure of the power of the Spirit, but if there is not a large measure of the Spirit as the Spirit of grace and holiness, the defect will be manifest in his work. He may be made the means of conversion, but he never will help people on to a higher standard of spiritual life, and when he passes away, a great deal of his work may pass away too. But a man who is separated unto the Holy Spirit is a man who is given up to say: "Father, let the Holy Spirit have full dominion over me, in my home, in my temper, in every word of my tongue, in every thought of my heart, in every feeling toward my fellow men; let the Holy Spirit have entire possession."

Is that what has been the longing and the covenant of your heart with your God—to be a man or a woman separated and given up unto the Holy Spirit? I pray you listen to the voice of Heaven. "Separate me," said the Holy Spirit. Yes, separated unto the Holy Spirit. May God grant that the Word may enter into the very depths of our being to search us, and if we discover that we have not come out from the world entirely, if God reveals to us that the self-life, self-will, self-exaltation are there, let us humble ourselves before Him.

Man, woman, brother, sister, you are a worker separated unto the Holy Spirit. Is that true? Has that been your longing desire? Has that been your surrender? Has that been what you have expected through faith in the power of our risen and almighty Lord Jesus? If not, here is the call of faith, and here is the key of blessing—separated unto the Holy Spirit. God write the word in our hearts!

I said the Holy Spirit spoke to that church as a church capable of doing that work. The Holy Spirit trusted them. God grant that our churches, our missionary societies, and our workers' unions, that all our directors and councils and committees may be men and women who are fit for the work of separating workers unto the Holy Spirit. We can ask God for that too.

Then comes my fifth thought, and it is this—This holy partnership with the Holy Spirit in this work becomes a matter of consciousness and of action.

These men, what did they do? They set apart Paul and Barnabas, and then it is written of the two that they, being sent forth by the Holy Spirit, went down to Seleucia. Oh, what fellowship! The Holy Spirit in Heaven doing part of the work, men on earth doing the other part. After the ordination of the men upon earth, it is written in God's inspired Word that they were sent forth by the Holy Spirit.

And see how this partnership calls to new prayer and fasting. They had for a certain time been ministering to the Lord and fasting, perhaps days; and the Holy Spirit speaks, and they have to do the work and to enter into partnership, and at once they come together for more prayer and fasting. That is the spirit in which they obey the command of their Lord. And that teaches us that it is not only in the beginning of our Christian work, but all along that we need to have our strength in prayer. If there is one thought with regard to the Church of Christ, which at times comes to me with overwhelming sorrow; if there is one thought in regard to my own life of which I am ashamed; if there is one thought of which I feel that the Church of Christ has not accepted it and not grasped it; if there is one thought which makes me pray to God: "Oh, teach us by Thy grace, new things"—it is the wonderful power that prayer is meant to have in the kingdom. We have so little availed ourselves of it.

We have all read the expression of Christian in Bunyan's great work, when he found he had the key in his breast that should unlock the dungeon. We have the key that can unlock the dungeon of atheism and of heathendom. But, oh! we are far more occupied with our work than we are with prayer. We believe more in speaking to men than we believe in speaking to God. Learn from these men that the work which the Holy Spirit commands must call us to new fasting and prayer, to new separation from the spirit and the pleasures of the world, to new consecration to God and to His fellowship. Those men gave themselves up to fasting and prayer, and if in all our ordinary Christian work there were more prayer, there would be more blessing in our own inner life. If we felt and proved and testified to the world that our only strength lay in keeping every minute in contact with Christ, every minute allowing God to work in us—if that were our spirit, would not, by the grace of God, our lives be holier? Would not they be more abundantly fruitful?

I hardly know a more solemn warning in God's Word than that which we find in the third chapter of Galatians, where Paul asked:

"Having begun in the Spirit, are ye now made perfect by the flesh?" (Gal. 3:3).

Do you understand what that means? A terrible danger in Christian work, just as in a Christian life that is begun with much prayer, begun in the Holy Spirit, is that it may be gradually shunted off on to the lines of the flesh; and the word comes: "Having begun in the Spirit, are ye now made perfect by the flesh?" In the time of our first perplexity and helplessness we prayed much to God, and God answered and God blessed, and our organization became perfected, and our band of workers became large; but gradually the organization and the work and the rush have so taken possession of us that the power of the Spirit, in which we began when we were a small company, has almost been lost.

Oh, I pray you, note it well! It was with new prayer and fasting, with more prayer and fasting, that this company of disciples carried out the command of the Holy Spirit, "My soul, wait thou only upon God." That is our highest and most important work. The Holy Spirit comes in answer to believing prayer.

You know when the exalted Jesus had ascended to the throne, for ten days the footstool of the throne was the place where His waiting disciples cried to Him. And that is the law of the kingdom—the King upon the throne, the servants upon the footstool. May God find us there unceasingly!

Then comes the last thought—What a wonderful blessing comes when the Holy Spirit is allowed to lead and to direct the work, and when it is carried on in obedience to Him!

You know the story of the mission on which Barnabas and Saul were sent out. You know what power there was with them. The Holy Spirit sent them, and they went on from place to place with large blessing. The Holy Spirit was their leader further on. You recollect how it was by the Spirit that Paul was hindered from going again into Asia, and was led away over to Europe. Oh, the blessing that rested upon that little company of men, and upon their ministry unto the Lord!

I pray you, let us learn to believe that God has a blessing for us. The Holy Spirit, into whose hands God has put the work, has been called "the executive of the Holy Trinity." The Holy Spirit has not only power, but He has the Spirit of love. He is brooding over this dark world and every sphere of work in it, and He is willing to bless. And why is there not more blessing? There can be but one answer. We have not honored the Holy Spirit as we should have done. Is there one who can say that that is not true? Is not every thoughtful heart ready to cry: "God forgive me that I have not honored the Holy Spirit as I should have done, that I have grieved Him, that I have allowed self and the flesh and my own will to work where the Holy Spirit should have been honored! May God forgive me that I have allowed self and the flesh and the will actually to have the place that God wanted the Holy Spirit to have."

Oh, the sin is greater than we know! No wonder that there is so much feebleness and failure in the Church of Christ!

PETER'S REPENTANCE

"And the Lord turned, and looked upon Peter. And Peter remembered the word of the Lord, how he had said unto him, Before the cock crow, thou shalt deny me thrice. And Peter went out, and wept bitterly" (Luke 22:61, 62).

That was the turning-point in the history of Peter. Christ had said to him: "Thou canst not follow me now" (John 13:36). Peter was not in a fit state to follow Christ, because he had not been brought to an end of himself; he did not know himself, and he therefore could not follow Christ. But when he went out and wept bitterly, then came the great change. Christ previously said to him: "When thou art converted, strengthen thy brethren." Here is the point where Peter was converted from self to Christ.

I thank God for the story of Peter. I do not know a man in the Bible who gives us greater comfort. When we look at his character, so full of failures, and at what Christ made him by the power of the Holy Spirit, there is hope for every one of us. But remember, before Christ could fill Peter with the Holy Spirit and make a new man of him, he had to go out and weep bitterly; he had to be humbled. If we want to understand this, I think there are four points that we must look at. First, let us look at Peter the devoted disciple of Jesus; next, at Peter as he lived the life of self; then at Peter in his repentance; and last, at what Christ made of Peter by the Holy Spirit.

Peter the Devoted Disciple of Christ

Christ called Peter to forsake his nets, and follow Him. Peter did it at once, and he afterward could say rightly to the Lord:
"We have forsaken all and followed thee" (Matt. 19:27).
Peter was a man of absolute surrender; he gave up all to follow Jesus. Peter was also a man of ready obedience. You remember Christ said to him, "Launch out into the deep, and let down the net." Peter the fisherman knew there were no fish there, for they had been toiling all night and had caught nothing; but he said: "At thy word I will let down the net" (Luke 5:4, 5). He submitted to the word of Jesus. Further, he was a man of great faith. When he saw Christ walking on the sea, he said: "Lord, if it be thou, bid me come unto thee" (Matt. 14:28); and at the voice of Christ he stepped out of the boat and walked upon the water.
And Peter was a man of spiritual insight. When Christ asked the disciples: "Whom do ye say that I am?" Peter was able to answer: "Thou art the Christ, the Son of the living God." And Christ said: "Blessed art thou, Simon Barjona; for flesh and blood hath not revealed it unto thee, but my Father which is in heaven." And Christ spoke of him as the rock man, and of his having the keys of the kingdom. Peter was a splendid man, a devoted disciple of Jesus, and if he were living nowadays, everyone would say that he was an advanced Christian. And yet how much there was wanting in Peter!

Peter Living the Life of Self

You recollect that just after Christ had said to him: "Flesh and blood hath not revealed it unto thee, but my Father which is in heaven," Christ began to speak about His sufferings, and Peter dared to say: "Be it far from thee, Lord; this shall not be unto thee." Then Christ had to say:

"Get thee behind me, Satan; for thou savorest not the things that be of God, but those that be of men" (Matt. 16:22-23).

There was Peter in his self-will, trusting his own wisdom, and actually forbidding Christ to go and die. Whence did that come? Peter trusted in himself and his own thoughts about divine things. We see later on, more than once, that among the disciples there was a questioning who should be the greatest, and Peter was one of them, and he thought he had a right to the very first place. He sought his own honor even above the others. It was the life of self strong in Peter. He had left his boats and his nets, but not his old self.

When Christ had spoken to him about His sufferings, and said: "Get thee behind me, Satan," He followed it up by saying: "If any man will come after me, let him deny himself, and take up his cross, and follow me" (Matt. 16:24). No man can follow Him unless he do that. Self must be utterly denied. What does that mean? When Peter denied Christ, we read that he said three times: "I do not know the man"; in other words: "I have nothing to do with Him; He and I are no friends; I deny having any connection with Him." Christ told Peter that he must deny self. Self must be ignored, and its every claim rejected. That is the root of true discipleship; but Peter did not understand it, and could not obey it. And what happened? When the last night came, Christ said to him: "Before the cock crow twice thou shalt deny me thrice."

But with what self-confidence Peter said: "Though all should forsake thee, yet will not I. I am ready to go with thee, to prison and to death" (Mark 14:29; Luke 22:33).

Peter meant it honestly, and Peter really intended to do it; but Peter did not know himself. He did not believe he was as bad as Jesus said he was.

We perhaps think of individual sins that come between us and God, but what are we to do with that self-life which is all unclean—our very nature? What are we to do with that flesh that is entirely under the power of sin? Deliverance from that is what we need. Peter knew it not, and therefore it was that in his self-confidence he went forth and denied his Lord.

Notice how Christ uses that word deny twice. He said to Peter the first time, "Deny self"; He said to Peter the second time, "Thou wilt deny me." It is either of the two. There is no choice for us; we must either deny self or deny Christ. There are two great powers fighting each other—the self-nature in the power of sin, and Christ in the power of God. Either of these must rule within us.

It was self that made the Devil. He was an angel of God, but he wanted to exalt self. He became a Devil in hell. Self was the cause of the fall of man. Eve wanted something for herself, and so our first parents fell into all the wretchedness of sin. We their children have inherited an awful nature of sin.

Peter's Repentance

Peter denied his Lord thrice, and then the Lord looked upon him; and that look of Jesus broke the heart of Peter, and all at once there opened up before him the terrible sin that he had committed, the terrible failure that had come, and the depth into which he had fallen, and "Peter went out and wept bitterly."

Oh! who can tell what that repentance must have been? During the following hours of that night, and the next day, when he saw Christ crucified and buried, and the next day, the Sabbath—oh, in what hopeless despair and shame he must have spent that day!

"My Lord is gone, my hope is gone, and I denied my Lord. After that life of love, after that blessed fellowship of three years, I denied my Lord. God have mercy upon me!"

I do not think we can realize into what a depth of humiliation Peter sank then. But that was the turning point and the change; and on the first day of the week Christ was seen of Peter, and in the evening He met him with the others. Later on at the Lake of Galilee He asked him: "Lovest thou me?" until Peter was made sad by the thought that the Lord reminded him of having denied Him thrice; and said in sorrow, but in uprightness:

"Lord, thou knowest all things; thou knowest that I love thee" (John 21:17).

Peter Transformed

Now Peter was prepared for deliverance from self, and that is my last thought. You know Christ took him with others to the footstool of the throne, and bade them wait there; and then on the day of Pentecost the Holy Spirit came, and Peter was a changed man. I do not want you to think only of the change in Peter, in that boldness, and that power, and that insight into the Scriptures, and that blessing with which he preached that day. Thank God for that. But there was something for Peter deeper and better. Peter's whole nature was changed. The work that Christ began in Peter when He looked upon him, was perfected when he was filled with the Holy Spirit.

If you want to see that, read the First Epistle of Peter. You know wherein Peter's failings lay. When he said to Christ, in effect: "Thou never canst suffer; it cannot be"—it showed he had not a conception of what it was to pass through death into life. Christ said: "Deny thyself," and in spite of that he denied his Lord. When Christ warned him: "Thou shalt deny me," and he insisted that he never would, Peter showed how little he understood what there was in himself. But when I read his epistle and hear him say: "If ye be reproached for the name of Christ, happy are ye, for the Spirit of God and of glory resteth upon you" (1 Pet. 4:14), then I say that it is not the old Peter, but that is the very Spirit of Christ breathing and speaking within him.

I read again how he says: "Hereunto ye are called, to suffer, even as Christ suffered" (1 Pet. 2:21). I understand what a change had come over Peter. Instead of denying Christ, he found joy and pleasure in having self denied and crucified and given up to the death. And therefore it is in the Acts we read that, when he was called before the Council, he could boldly say: "We must obey God rather than men" (Acts 5:29), and that he could return with the other disciples and rejoice that they were counted worthy to suffer for Christ's name.

You remember his self-exaltation; but now he has found out that "the ornament of a meek and quiet spirit is in the sight of God of great price." Again he tells us to be "subject one to another, and be clothed with humility" (1 Pet. 5:5).

Dear friend, I beseech you, look at Peter utterly changed—the self-pleasing, the self-trusting, the self-seeking Peter, full of sin, continually getting into trouble, foolish and impetuous, but now filled with the Spirit and the life of Jesus. Christ had done it for him by the Holy Spirit.

And now, what is my object in having thus very briefly pointed to the story of Peter? That story must be the history of every believer who is really to be made a blessing by God. That story is a prophecy of what everyone can receive from God in Heaven.

Now let us just glance hurriedly at what these lessons teach us.

The first lesson is this—You may be a very earnest, godly, devoted believer, in whom the power of the flesh is yet very strong.

That is a very solemn truth. Peter, before he denied Christ, had cast out devils and had healed the sick; and yet the flesh had power, and the flesh had room in him. Oh, beloved, we have to realize that it is just because there is so much of that self-life in us that the power of God cannot work in us as mightily as God is willing that it should work. Do you realize that the great God is longing to double His blessing, to give tenfold blessing through us? But there is something hindering Him, and that something is a proof of nothing but the self-life. We talk about the pride of Peter, and the impetuosity of Peter, and the self-confidence of Peter. It all rooted in that one word, self. Christ had said, "Deny self," and Peter had never understood, and never obeyed; and every failing came out of that.

What a solemn thought, and what an urgent plea for us to cry: O God, do reveal this to us, that none of us may be living the self-life! It has happened to many a one who had been a Christian for years, who had perhaps occupied a prominent position, that God found him out and taught him to find himself out, and he became utterly ashamed, falling down broken before God. Oh, the bitter shame and sorrow and pain and agony that came to him, until at last he found that there was deliverance! Peter went out and wept bitterly, and there may be many a godly one in whom the power of the flesh still rules.

And then my second lesson is—It is the work of our blessed Lord Jesus to reveal the power of self.

How was it that Peter, the carnal Peter, self-willed Peter, Peter with the strong self-love, ever became a man of Pentecost and the writer of his epistles? It was because Christ had him in charge, and Christ watched over him, and Christ taught and blessed him. The warnings that Christ had given him were part of the training; and last of all there came that look of love. In His suffering Christ did not forget him, but turned round and looked upon him, and "Peter went out and wept bitterly." And the Christ who led Peter to Pentecost is waiting today to take charge of every heart that is willing to surrender itself to Him.

Are there not some saying: "Ah! that is the mischief with me; it is always the self-life, and self-comfort, and self-consciousness, and self-pleasing, and self-will; how am I to get rid of it?"

My answer is: It is Christ Jesus who can rid you of it; none else but Christ Jesus can give deliverance from the power of self. And what does He ask you to do? He asks that you should humble yourself before Him.

IMPOSSIBLE WITH MAN, POSSIBLE WITH GOD

"And he said, The things which are impossible with men are possible with God" (Luke 18:27).

Christ had said to the rich young ruler, "Sell all that thou hast . . . and come, follow me." The young man went away sorrowful. Christ then turned to the disciples, and said: "How hardly shall they that have riches enter into the kingdom of God!" The disciples, we read, were greatly astonished, and answered: "If it is so difficult to enter the kingdom, who, then, can be saved?" And Christ gave this blessed answer:

"The things which are impossible with men are possible with God." The text contains two thoughts—that in religion, in the question of salvation and of following Christ by a holy life, it is impossible for man to do it. And then alongside that is the thought—What is impossible with man is possible with God.

The two thoughts mark the two great lessons that man has to learn in the religious life. It often takes a long time to learn the first lesson, that in religion man can do nothing, that salvation is impossible to man. And often a man learns that, and yet he does not learn the second lesson—what has been impossible to him is possible with God. Blessed is the man who learns both lessons! The learning of them marks stages in the Christian's life.

Man Cannot

The one stage is when a man is trying to do his utmost and fails, when a man tries to do better and fails again, when a man tries much more and always fails. And yet very often he does not even then learn the lesson: With man it is impossible to serve God and Christ. Peter spent three years in Christ's school, and he never learned that, It is impossible, until he had denied his Lord and went out and wept bitterly. Then he learned it.

Just look for a moment at a man who is learning this lesson. At first he fights against it; then he submits to it, but reluctantly and in despair; at last he accepts it willingly and rejoices in it. At the beginning of the Christian life the young convert has no conception of this truth. He has been converted, he has the joy of the Lord in his heart, he begins to run the race and fight the battle; he is sure he can conquer, for he is earnest and honest, and God will help him. Yet, somehow, very soon he fails where he did not expect it, and sin gets the better of him. He is disappointed; but he thinks: "I was not watchful enough, I did not make my resolutions strong enough." And again he vows, and again he prays, and yet he fails. He thought: "Am I not a regenerate man? Have I not the life of God within me?" And he thinks again: "Yes, and I have Christ to help me, I can live the holy life."

At a later period he comes to another state of mind. He begins to see such a life is impossible, but he does not accept it. There are multitudes of Christians who come to this point: "I cannot"; and then think God never expected them to do what they cannot do. If you tell them that God does expect it, it appears to them a mystery. A good many Christians are living a low life, a life of failure and of sin, instead of rest and victory, because they began to see: "I cannot, it is impossible." And yet they do not understand it fully, and so, under the impression, I cannot, they give way to despair. They will do their best, but they never expect to get on very far.

But God leads His children on to a third stage, when a man comes to take that, It is impossible, in its full truth, and yet at the same time says: "I must do it, and I will do it—it is impossible for man, and yet I must do it"; when the renewed will begins to exercise its whole power, and in intense longing and prayer begins to cry to God: "Lord, what is the meaning of this?—how am I to be freed from the power of sin?"

It is the state of the regenerate man in Romans 7. There you will find the Christian man trying his very utmost to live a holy life. God's law has been revealed to him as reaching down into the very depth of the desires of the heart, and the man can dare to say:

"I delight in the law of God after the inward man. To will what is good is present with me. My heart loves the law of God, and my will has chosen that law."

Can a man like that fail, with his heart full of delight in God's law and with his will determined to do what is right? Yes. That is what Romans 7 teaches us. There is something more needed. Not only must I delight in the law of God after the inward man, and will what God wills, but I need a divine omnipotence to work it in me. And that is what the apostle Paul teaches in Philippians 2:13:

"It is God which worketh in you, both to will and to do."

Note the contrast. In Romans 7, the regenerate man says: "To will is present with me, but to do—I find I cannot do. I will, but I cannot perform." But in Philippians 2, you have a man who has been led on farther, a man who understands that when God has worked the renewed will, God will give the power to accomplish what that will desires. Let us receive this as the first great lesson in the spiritual life: "It is impossible for me, my God; let there be an end of the flesh and all its powers, an end of self, and let it be my glory to be helpless."

Praise God for the divine teaching that makes us helpless!

When you thought of absolute surrender to God were you not brought to an end of yourself, and to feel that you could see how you actually could live as a man absolutely surrendered to God every moment of the day—at your table, in your house, in your business, in the midst of trials and temptations? I pray you learn the lesson now. If you felt you could not do it, you are on the right road, if you let yourselves be led. Accept that position, and maintain it before God: "My heart's desire and delight, O God, is absolute surrender, but I cannot perform it. It is impossible for me to live that life. It is beyond me." Fall down and learn that when you are utterly helpless, God will come to work in you not only to will, but also to do.

God Can

Now comes the second lesson. "The things which are impossible with men are possible with God."

I said a little while ago that there is many a man who has learned the lesson, It is impossible with men, and then he gives up in helpless despair, and lives a wretched Christian life, without joy, or strength, or victory. And why? Because he does not humble himself to learn that other lesson: With God all things are possible.

Your religious life is every day to be a proof that God works impossibilities; your religious life is to be a series of impossibilities made possible and actual by God's almighty power. That is what the Christian needs. He has an almighty God that he worships, and he must learn to understand that he does not need a little of God's power, but he needs—with reverence be it said—the whole of God's omnipotence to keep him right, and to live like a Christian.

The whole of Christianity is a work of God's omnipotence. Look at the birth of Christ Jesus. That was a miracle of divine power, and it was said to Mary: "With God nothing shall be impossible." It was the omnipotence of God. Look at Christ's resurrection. We are taught that it was according to the exceeding greatness of His mighty power that God raised Christ from the dead.

Every tree must grow on the root from which it springs. An oak tree three hundred years old grows all the time on the one root from which it had its beginning. Christianity had its beginning in the omnipotence of God, and in every soul it must have its continuance in that omnipotence. All the possibilities of the higher Christian life have their origin in a new apprehension of Christ's power to work all God's will in us.

I want to call upon you now to come and worship an almighty God. Have you learned to do it? Have you learned to deal so closely with an almighty God that you know omnipotence is working in you? In outward appearance there is often so little sign of it. The apostle Paul said: "I was with you in weakness and in fear and in much trembling, and . . . my preaching was . . . in demonstration of the Spirit and of power." From the human side there was feebleness, from the divine side there was divine omnipotence. And that is true of every godly life; and if we would only learn that lesson better, and give a wholehearted, undivided surrender to it, we should learn what blessedness there is in dwelling every hour and every moment with an almighty God. Have you ever studied in the Bible the attribute of God's omnipotence? You know that it was God's omnipotence that created the world, and created light out of darkness, and created man. But have you studied God's omnipotence in the works of redemption?

Look at Abraham. When God called him to be the father of that people out of which Christ was to be born, God said to him: "I am God Almighty, walk before me and be thou perfect." And God trained Abraham to trust Him as the omnipotent One; and whether it was his going out to a land that he knew not, or his faith as a pilgrim midst the thousands of Canaanites—his faith said: This is my land—or whether it was his faith in waiting twenty-five years for a son in his old age, against all hope, or whether it was the raising up of Isaac from the dead on Mount Moriah when he was going to sacrifice him—Abraham believed God. He was strong in faith, giving glory to God, because he accounted Him who had promised able to perform.

The cause of the weakness of your Christian life is that you want to work it out partly, and to let God help you. And that cannot be. You must come to be utterly helpless, to let God work, and God will work gloriously. It is this that we need if we are indeed to be workers for God. I could go through Scripture and prove to you how Moses, when he led Israel out of Egypt; how Joshua, when he brought them into the land of Canaan; how all God's servants in the Old Testament counted upon the omnipotence of God doing impossibilities. And this God lives today, and this God is the God of every child of His. And yet we are some of us wanting God to give us a little help while we do our best, instead of coming to understand what God wants, and to say: "I can do nothing. God must and will do all." Have you said: "In worship, in work, in sanctification, in obedience to God, I can do nothing of myself, and so my place is to worship the omnipotent God, and to believe that He will work in me every moment"? Oh, may God teach us this! Oh, that God would by His grace show you what a God you have, and to what a God you have entrusted yourself—an omnipotent God, willing with His whole omnipotence to place Himself at the disposal of every child of His! Shall we not take the lesson of the Lord Jesus and say: "Amen; the things which are impossible with men are possible with God"?

Remember what we have said about Peter, his self-confidence, self-power, self-will, and how he came to deny his Lord. You feel, "Ah! there is the self-life, there is the flesh-life that rules in me!" And now, have you believed that there is deliverance from that? Have you believed that Almighty God is able so to reveal Christ in your heart, so to let the Holy Spirit rule in you, that the self-life shall not have power or dominion over you? Have you coupled the two together, and with tears of penitence and with deep humiliation and feebleness, cried out: "O God, it is impossible to me; man cannot do it, but, glory to Thy name, it is possible with God"? Have you claimed deliverance? Do it now. Put yourself afresh in absolute surrender into the hands of a God of infinite love; and as infinite as His love is His power to do it.

God Works in Man

But again, we came to the question of absolute surrender, and felt that that is the want in the Church of Christ, and that is why the Holy Spirit cannot fill us, and why we cannot live as people entirely separated unto the Holy Spirit; that is why the flesh and the self-life cannot be conquered. We have never understood what it is to be absolutely surrendered to God as Jesus was. I know that many a one earnestly and honestly says: "Amen, I accept the message of absolute surrender to God"; and yet thinks: "Will that ever be mine? Can I count upon God to make me one of whom it shall be said in Heaven and on earth and in Hell, he lives in absolute surrender to God?" Brother, sister, "the things which are impossible with men are possible with God." Do believe that when He takes charge of you in Christ, it is possible for God to make you a man of absolute surrender. And God is able to maintain that. He is able to let you rise from bed every morning of the week with that blessed thought directly or indirectly: "I am in God's charge. My God is working out my life for me."

Some are weary of thinking about sanctification. You pray, you have longed and cried for it, and yet it appeared so far off! The holiness and humility of Jesus—you are so conscious of how distant it is. Beloved friends, the one doctrine of sanctification that is scriptural and real and effectual is: "The things which are impossible with men are possible with God." God can sanctify men, and by His almighty and sanctifying power every moment God can keep them. Oh, that we might get a step nearer to our God now! Oh, that the light of God might shine, and that we might know our God better!

I could go on to speak about the life of Christ in us—living like Christ, taking Christ as our Saviour from sin, and as our life and strength. It is God in Heaven who can reveal that in you. What does that prayer of the apostle Paul say: "That he would grant you according to riches of his glory"—it is sure to be something very wonderful if it is according to the riches of His glory—"to be strengthened with might by his Spirit in the inner man"? Do you not see that it is an omnipotent God working by His omnipotence in the heart of His believing children, so that Christ can become an indwelling Saviour? You have tried to grasp it and to seize it, and you have tried to believe it, and it would not come. It was because you had not been brought to believe that "the things which are impossible with men are possible with God."

And so, I trust that the word spoken about love may have brought many to see that we must have an inflowing of love in quite a new way; our heart must be filled with life from above, from the Fountain of everlasting love, if it is going to overflow all the day; then it will be just as natural for us to love our fellow men as it is natural for the lamb to be gentle and the wolf to be cruel. Until I am brought to such a state that the more a man hates and speaks evil of me, the more unlikable and unlovable a man is, I shall love him all the more; until I am brought to such a state that the more the obstacles and hatred and ingratitude, the more can the power of love triumph in me—until I am brought to see that, I am not saying: "It is impossible with men." But if you have been led to say: "This message has spoken to me about a love utterly beyond my power; it is absolutely impossible"—then we can come to God and say: "It is possible with Thee."

Some are crying to God for a great revival. I can say that that is the prayer of my heart unceasingly. Oh, if God would only revive His believing people! I cannot think in the first place of the unconverted formalists of the Church, or of the infidels and skeptics, or of all the wretched and perishing around me, my heart prays in the first place: "My God, revive Thy Church and people." It is not for nothing that there are in thousands of hearts yearnings after holiness and consecration: it is a forerunner of God's power. God works to will and then He works to do. These yearnings are a witness and a proof that God has worked to will. Oh, let us in faith believe that the omnipotent God will work to do among His people more than we can ask. "Unto him," Paul said, "who is able to do exceeding abundantly above all that we ask or think. . . . unto him be glory." Let our hearts say that. Glory to God, the omnipotent One, who can do above what we dare to ask or think!

"The things which are impossible with men are possible with God." All around you there is a world of sin and sorrow, and the Devil is there. But remember, Christ is on the throne, Christ is stronger, Christ has conquered, and Christ will conquer. But wait on God. My text casts us down: "The things which are impossible with men"; but it ultimately lifts us up high—"are possible with God." Get linked to God. Adore and trust Him as the omnipotent One, not only for your own life, but for all the souls that are entrusted to you. Never pray without adoring His omnipotence, saying: "Mighty God, I claim Thine almightiness." And the answer to the prayer will come, and like Abraham you will become strong in faith, giving glory to God, because you account Him who hath promised able to perform.

"O WRETCHED MAN THAT I AM!"

"O wretched man that I am! who shall deliver me from the body of this death? I thank God through Jesus Christ our Lord" (Romans 7:24, 25).

You know the wonderful place that this text has in the wonderful epistle to the Romans. It stands here at the end of the seventh chapter as the gateway into the eighth. In the first sixteen verses of the eighth chapter the name of the Holy Spirit is found sixteen times; you have there the description and promise of the life that a child of God can live in the power of the Holy Spirit. This begins in the second verse: "The law of the Spirit of life in Christ Jesus hath made me free from the law of sin and death" (Rom. 8:12). From that Paul goes on to speak of the great privileges of the child of God, who is to be led by the Spirit of God. The gateway into all this is in the twenty-fourth verse of the seventh chapter:

"O wretched man that I am!"

There you have the words of a man who has come to the end of himself. He has in the previous verses described how he had struggled and wrestled in his own power to obey the holy law of God, and had failed. But in answer to his own question he now finds the true answer and cries out: "I thank God through Jesus Christ our Lord." From that he goes on to speak of what that deliverance is that he has found.

I want from these words to describe the path by which a man can be led out of the spirit of bondage into the spirit of liberty. You know how distinctly it is said: "Ye have not received the spirit of bondage again to fear." We are continually warned that this is the great danger of the Christian life, to go again into bondage; and I want to describe the path by which a man can get out of bondage into the glorious liberty of the children of God. Rather, I want to describe the man himself.

First, these words are the language of a regenerate man; second, of an impotent man; third, of a wretched man; and fourth, of a man on the borders of complete liberty.

The Regenerate Man

There is much evidence of regeneration from the fourteenth verse of the chapter on to the twenty-third. "It is no more I that do it, but sin that dwelleth in me" (Rom. 7:17): that is the language of a regenerate man, a man who knows that his heart and nature have been renewed, and that sin is now a power in him that is not himself. "I delight in the law of the Lord after the inward man" (Rom. 7:22): that again is the language of a regenerate man. He dares to say when he does evil: "It is no more I that do it, but sin that dwelleth in me." It is of great importance to understand this.

In the first two great sections of the epistle, Paul deals with justification and sanctification. In dealing with justification, he lays the foundation of the doctrine in the teaching about sin, not in the singular, sin, but in the plural, sins—the actual transgressions. In the second part of the fifth chapter he begins to deal with sin, not as actual transgression, but as a power. Just imagine what a loss it would have been to us if we had not this second half of the seventh chapter of the Epistle to the Romans, if Paul had omitted in his teaching this vital question of the sinfulness of the believer. We should have missed the question we all want answered as to sin in the believer. What is the answer? The regenerate man is one in whom the will has been renewed, and who can say: "I delight in the law of God after the inward man."

The Impotent Man

Here is the great mistake made by many Christian people: they think that when there is a renewed will, it is enough; but that is not the case. This regenerate man tells us: "I will to do what is good, but the power to perform I find not." How often people tell us that if you set yourself determinedly, you can perform what you will! But this man was as determined as any man can be, and yet he made the confession: "To will is present with me; but how to perform that which is good, I find not" (Rom. 7:18).

But, you ask: "How is it God makes a regenerate man utter such a confession, with a right will, with a heart that longs to do good, and longs to do its very utmost to love God?"

Let us look at this question. What has God given us our will for? Had the angels who fell, in their own will, the strength to stand? Surely not. The will of the creature is nothing but an empty vessel in which the power of God is to be made manifest. The creature must seek in God all that it is to be. You have it in the second chapter of the epistle to the Philippians, and you have it here also, that God's work is to work in us both to will and to do of His good pleasure. Here is a man who appears to say: "God has not worked to do in me." But we are taught that God works both to will and to do. How is the apparent contradiction to be reconciled?

You will find that in this passage (Rom. 7:6-25) the name of the Holy Spirit does not occur once, nor does the name of Christ occur. The man is wrestling and struggling to fulfill God's law. Instead of the Holy Spirit and of Christ, the law is mentioned nearly twenty times. In this chapter, it shows a believer doing his very best to obey the law of God with his regenerate will. Not only this; but you will find the little words, I, me, my, occur more than forty times. It is the regenerate I in its impotence seeking to obey the law without being filled with the Spirit. This is the experience of almost every saint. After conversion a man begins to do his best, and he fails; but if we are brought into the full light, we need fail no longer. Nor need we fail at all if we have received the Spirit in His fullness at conversion.

God allows that failure that the regenerate man should be taught his own utter impotence. It is in the course of this struggle that there comes to us this sense of our utter sinfulness. It is God's way of dealing with us. He allows that man to strive to fulfill the law that, as he strives and wrestles, he may be brought to this: "I am a regenerate child of God, but I am utterly helpless to obey His law." See what strong words are used all through the chapter to describe this condition: "I am carnal, sold under sin" (Rom. 7:14); "I see another law in my members bringing me into captivity" (Rom. 7:23); and last of all, "O wretched man that I am! who shall deliver me from the body of this death?" (Rom. 7:24). This believer who bows here in deep contrition is utterly unable to obey the law of God.

The Wretched Man

Not only is the man who makes this confession a regenerate and an impotent man, but he is also a wretched man. He is utterly unhappy and miserable; and what is it that makes him so utterly miserable? It is because God has given him a nature that loves Himself. He is deeply wretched because he feels he is not obeying his God. He says, with brokenness of heart: "It is not I that do it, but I am under the awful power of sin, which is holding me down. It is I, and yet not I: alas! alas! it is myself; so closely am I bound up with it, and so closely is it intertwined with my very nature." Blessed be God when a man learns to say: "O wretched man that I am!" from the depth of his heart. He is on the way to the eighth chapter of Romans.

There are many who make this confession a pillow for sin. They say that if Paul had to confess his weakness and helplessness in this way, what are they that they should try to do better? So the call to holiness is quietly set aside. Would God that every one of us had learned to say these words in the very spirit in which they are written here! When we hear sin spoken of as the abominable thing that God hates, do not many of us wince before the word? Would that all Christians who go on sinning and sinning would take this verse to heart. If ever you utter a sharp word say: "O wretched man that I am!" And every time you lose your temper, kneel down and understand that it never was meant by God that this was to be the state in which His child should remain. Would God that we would take this word into our daily life, and say it every time we are touched about our own honor, and every time we say sharp things, and every time we sin against the Lord God, and against the Lord Jesus Christ in His humility, and in His obedience, and in His self-sacrifice! Would to God you could forget everything else, and cry out: "O wretched man that I am! who shall deliver me from the body of this death?"

Why should you say this whenever you commit sin? Because it is when a man is brought to this confession that deliverance is at hand.

And remember it was not only the sense of being impotent and taken captive that made him wretched, but it was above all the sense of sinning against his God. The law was doing its work, making sin exceedingly sinful in his sight. The thought of continually grieving God became utterly unbearable—it was this that brought forth the piercing cry: "O wretched man!" As long as we talk and reason about our impotence and our failure, and only try to find out what Romans 7 means, it will profit us but little; but when once every sin gives new intensity to the sense of wretchedness, and we feel our whole state as one of not only helplessness, but actual exceeding sinfulness, we shall be pressed not only to ask: "Who shall deliver us?" but to cry: "I thank God through Jesus Christ my Lord."

The Almost-Delivered Man

The man has tried to obey the beautiful law of God. He has loved it, he has wept over his sin, he has tried to conquer, he has tried to overcome fault after fault, but every time he has ended in failure.

What did he mean by "the body of this death"? Did he mean, my body when I die? Surely not. In the eighth chapter you have the answer to this question in the words: "If ye through the Spirit do mortify the deeds of the body, ye shall live." That is the body of death from which he is seeking deliverance.

And now he is on the brink of deliverance! In the twenty-third verse of the seventh chapter we have the words: "I see another law in my members, warring against the law of my mind, and bringing me into captivity to the law of sin which is in my members." It is a captive that cries: "O wretched man that I am! who shall deliver me from the body of this death?" He is a man who feels himself bound. But look to the contrast in the second verse of the eighth chapter: "The law of the Spirit of life in Christ Jesus hath made me free from the law of sin and death." That is the deliverance through Jesus Christ our Lord; the liberty to the captive which the Spirit brings. Can you keep captive any longer a man made free by the "law of the Spirit of life in Christ Jesus"?

But you say, the regenerate man, had not he the Spirit of Jesus when he spoke in the sixth chapter? Yes, but he did not know what the Holy Spirit could do for him.

God does not work by His Spirit as He works by a blind force in nature. He leads His people on as reasonable, intelligent beings, and therefore when He wants to give us that Holy Spirit whom He has promised, He brings us first to the end of self, to the conviction that though we have been striving to obey the law, we have failed. When we have come to the end of that, then He shows us that in the Holy Spirit we have the power of obedience, the power of victory, and the power of real holiness.

God works to will, and He is ready to work to do, but, alas! many Christians misunderstand this. They think because they have the will, it is enough, and that now they are able to do. This is not so. The new will is a permanent gift, an attribute of the new nature. The power to do is not a permanent gift, but must be each moment received from the Holy Spirit. It is the man who is conscious of his own impotence as a believer who will learn that by the Holy Spirit he can live a holy life. This man is on the brink of that great deliverance; the way has been prepared for the glorious eighth chapter. I now ask this solemn question: Where are you living? Is it with you, "O wretched man that I am! who shall deliver me?" with now and then a little experience of the power of the Holy Spirit? or is it, "I thank God through Jesus Christ! The law of the Spirit hath set me free from the law of sin and of death"?

What the Holy Spirit does is to give the victory. "If ye through the Spirit do mortify the deeds of the flesh, ye shall live" (Rom. 8:13). It is the Holy Spirit who does this—the third Person of the Godhead. He it is who, when the heart is opened wide to receive Him, comes in and reigns there, and mortifies the deeds of the body, day by day, hour by hour, and moment by moment.

I want to bring this to a point. Remember, dear friend, what we need is to come to decision and action. There are in Scripture two very different sorts of Christians. The Bible speaks in Romans, Corinthians and Galatians about yielding to the flesh; and that is the life of tens of thousands of believers. All their lack of joy in the Holy Spirit, and their lack of the liberty He gives, is just owing to the flesh. The Spirit is within them, but the flesh rules the life. To be led by the Spirit of God is what they need. Would God that I could make every child of His realize what it means that the everlasting God has given His dear Son, Christ Jesus, to watch over you every day, and that what you have to do is to trust; and that the work of the Holy Spirit is to enable you every moment to remember Jesus, and to trust Him! The Spirit has come to keep the link with Him unbroken every moment. Praise God for the Holy Spirit! We are so accustomed to think of the Holy Spirit as a luxury, for special times, or for special ministers and men. But the Holy Spirit is necessary for every believer, every moment of the day. Praise God you have Him, and that He gives you the full experience of the deliverance in Christ, as He makes you free from the power of sin. Who longs to have the power and the liberty of the Holy Spirit? Oh, brother, bow before God in one final cry of despair:

"O God, must I go on sinning this way forever? Who shall deliver me, O wretched man that I am! from the body of this death?"

Are you ready to sink before God in that cry and seek the power of Jesus to dwell and work in you? Are you ready to say: "I thank God through Jesus Christ"?

What good does it do that we go to church or attend conventions, that we study our Bibles and pray, unless our lives are filled with the Holy Spirit? That is what God wants; and nothing else will enable us to live a life of power and peace. You know that when a minister or parent is using the catechism, when a question is asked an answer is expected. Alas! how many Christians are content with the question put here: "O wretched man that I am! who shall deliver me from the body of this death?" but never give the answer. Instead of answering, they are silent. Instead of saying: "I thank God through Jesus Christ our Lord," they are forever repeating the question without the answer. If you want the path to the full deliverance of Christ, and the liberty of the Spirit, the glorious liberty of the children of God, take it through the seventh chapter of Romans; and then say: "I thank God through Jesus Christ our Lord." Be not content to remain ever groaning, but say: "I, a wretched man, thank God, through Jesus Christ. Even though I do not see it all, I am going to praise God."

There is deliverance, there is the liberty of the Holy Spirit. The kingdom of God is "joy in the Holy Spirit" (Rom. 14:17).

"HAVING BEGUN IN THE SPIRIT"

The words from which I wish to address you, you will find in the
epistle to the Galatians, the third chapter, the third verse; let us read the
second verse also: "This only would I learn of you, Received ye the
Spirit by the works of the law, or by the hearing of faith? Are ye so
foolish?" And then comes my text—"Having begun in the Spirit, are ye
now made perfect by the flesh?"

When we speak of the quickening or the deepening or the strengthening
of the spiritual life, we are thinking of something that is feeble and
wrong and sinful; and it is a great thing to take our place before God
with the confession:

"Oh, God, our spiritual life is not what it should be!"

May God work that in your heart, reader.

As we look round about on the church we see so many indications of
feebleness and of failure, and of sin, and of shortcoming, that we are
compelled to ask: Why is it? Is there any necessity for the church of
Christ to be living in such a low state? Or is it actually possible that
God's people should be living always in the joy and strength of their
God?

Every believing heart must answer: It is possible.

Then comes the great question: Why is it, how is it to be accounted for,
that God's church as a whole is so feeble, and that the great majority of
Christians are not living up to their privileges? There must be a reason
for it. Has God not given Christ His Almighty Son to be the Keeper of
every believer, to make Christ an ever-present reality, and to impart
and communicate to us all that we have in Christ? God has given His
Son, and God has given His Spirit. How is it that believers do not live
up to their privileges?

We find in more than one of the epistles a very solemn answer to that
question. There are epistles, such as the first to the Thessalonians,
where Paul writes to the Christians, in effect: "I want you to grow, to
abound, to increase more and more." They were young, and there were
things lacking in their faith, but their state was so far satisfactory, and
gave him great joy, and he writes time after time: "I pray God that you
may abound more and more; I write to you to increase more and more"
(1 Thes. 4:1,10). But there are other epistles where he takes a very
different tone, especially the epistles to the Corinthians and to the
Galatians, and he tells them in many different ways what the one
reason was, that they were not living as Christians ought to live; many
were under the power of the flesh. My text is one example. He reminds
them that by the preaching of faith they had received the Holy Spirit.
He had preached Christ to them; they had accepted that Christ and had

received the Holy Spirit in power. But what happened? Having begun in the Spirit, they tried to perfect the work that the Spirit had begun in the flesh by their own effort. We find the same teaching in the epistle to the Corinthians.

Now, we have here a solemn discovery of what the great want is in the church of Christ. God has called the church of Christ to live in the power of the Holy Spirit, and the church is living for the most part in the power of human flesh, and of will and energy and effort apart from the Spirit of God. I doubt not that that is the case with many individual believers; and oh, if God will use me to give you a message from Him, my one message will be this: "If the church will return to acknowledge that the Holy Spirit is her strength and her help, and if the church will return to give up everything, and wait upon God to be filled with the Spirit, her days of beauty and gladness will return, and we shall see the glory of God revealed among us." This is my message to every individual believer: "Nothing will help you unless you come to understand that you must live every day under the power of the Holy Spirit."

God wants you to be a living vessel in whom the power of the Spirit is to be manifested every hour and every moment of your life, and God will enable you to be that.

Now let us try to learn that this word to the Galatians teaches us—some very simple thoughts. It shows us how (1) the beginning of the Christian life is receiving the Holy Spirit. It shows us (2) what great danger there is of forgetting that we are to live by the Spirit, and not live after the flesh. It shows us (3) what are the fruits and the proofs of our seeking perfection in the flesh. And then it suggests to us (4) the way of deliverance from this state.

Receiving the Holy Spirit

First of all, Paul says: "Having begun in the Spirit." Remember, the apostle not only preached justification by faith, but he preached something more. He preached this—the epistle is full of it—that justified men cannot live but by the Holy Spirit, and that therefore God gives to every justified man the Holy Spirit to seal him. The apostle says to them in effect more than once:

"How did you receive the Holy Spirit? Was it by the preaching of the law, or by the preaching of faith?"

He could point back to that time when there had been a mighty revival under his teaching. The power of God had been manifested, and the Galatians were compelled to confess:

"Yes, we have got the Holy Spirit: accepting Christ by faith, by faith we received the Holy Spirit."

Now, it is to be feared that there are many Christians who hardly know that when they believed, they received the Holy Spirit. A great many Christians can say: "I received pardon and I received peace." But if you were to ask them: "Have you received the Holy Spirit?" they would hesitate, and many, if they were to say Yes, would say it with hesitation; and they would tell you that they hardly knew what it was, since that time, to walk in the power of the Holy Spirit. Let us try and take hold of this great truth: The beginning of the true Christian life is to receive the Holy Spirit. And the work of every Christian minister is that which was the work of Paul—to remind his people that they received the Holy Spirit, and must live according to His guidance and in His power.

If those Galatians who received the Holy Spirit in power were tempted to go astray by that terrible danger of perfecting in the flesh what had been begun in the Spirit, how much more danger do those Christians run who hardly ever know that they have received the Holy Spirit, or who, if they know it as a matter of belief, hardly ever think of it and hardly ever praise God for it!

Neglecting the Holy Spirit

But now look, in the second place, at the great danger.

You all know what shunting is on a railway. A locomotive with its train may be run in a certain direction, and the points at some place may not be properly opened or closed, and unobservingly it is shunted off to the right or to the left. And if that takes place, for instance, on a dark night, the train goes in the wrong direction, and the people might never know it until they have gone some distance.

And just so God gives Christians the Holy Spirit with this intention, that every day all their life should be lived in the power of the Spirit. A man cannot live one hour a godly life unless by the power of the Holy Spirit. He may live a proper, consistent life, as people call it, an irreproachable life, a life of virtue and diligent service; but to live a life acceptable to God, in the enjoyment of God's salvation and God's love, to live and walk in the power of the new life—he cannot do it unless he be guided by the Holy Spirit every day and every hour.

But now listen to the danger. The Galatians received the Holy Spirit, but what was begun by the Spirit they tried to perfect in the flesh. How? They fell back again under Judaizing teachers who told them they must be circumcised. They began to seek their religion in external observances. And so Paul uses that expression about those teachers who had them circumcised, that "they sought to glory in their flesh" (Gal. 6:13).

You sometimes hear the expression used, religious flesh. What is meant by that? It is simply an expression made to give utterance to this thought: My human nature and my human will and my human effort can be very active in religion, and after being converted, and after receiving the Holy Spirit, I may begin in my own strength to try to serve God.

I may be very diligent and doing a great deal, and yet all the time it is more the work of human flesh than of God's Spirit. What a solemn thought, that man can, without noticing it, be shunted off from the line of the Holy Spirit on to the line of the flesh; that he can be most diligent and make great sacrifices, and yet it is all in the power of the human will! Ah, the great question for us to ask of God in self-examination is that we may be shown whether our religious life is lived more in the power of the flesh than in the power of the Holy Spirit. A man may be a preacher, he may work most diligently in his ministry, a man may be a Christian worker, and others may tell of him that he makes great sacrifices, and yet you can feel there is a want about it. You feel that he is not a spiritual man; there is no spirituality about his life. How many Christians there are about whom no one would ever think of saying: "What a spiritual man he is!" Ah! there is the weakness of the Church of Christ. It is all in that one word—flesh. Now, the flesh may manifest itself in many ways. It may be manifested in fleshly wisdom. My mind may be most active about religion. I may preach or write or think or meditate, and delight in being occupied with things in God's Book and in God's Kingdom; and yet the power of the Holy Spirit may be markedly absent. I fear that if you take the preaching throughout the Church of Christ and ask why there is, alas! so little converting power in the preaching of the Word, why there is so much work and often so little result for eternity, why the Word has so little power to build up believers in holiness and in consecration—the answer will come: It is the absence of the power of the Holy Spirit. And why is this? There can be no other reason but that the flesh and human energy have taken the place that the Holy Spirit ought to have. That was true of the Galatians, it was true of the Corinthians. You know Paul said to them: "I cannot speak to you as to spiritual men; you ought to be spiritual men, but you are carnal." And you know how often in the course of his epistles he had to reprove and condemn them for strife and for divisions.

Lacking the Fruit of the Holy Spirit

A third thought: What are the proofs or indications that a church like the Galatians, or a Christian, is serving God in the power of the flesh—is perfecting in the flesh what was begun in the Spirit?

The answer is very easy. Religious self-effort always ends in sinful flesh. What was the state of those Galatians? Striving to be justified by the works of the law. And yet they were quarreling and in danger of devouring one another. Count up the expressions that the apostle uses to indicate their want of love, and you will find more than twelve—envy, jealousy, bitterness, strife, and all sorts of expressions. Read in the fourth and fifth chapters what he says about that. You see how they tried to serve God in their own strength, and they failed utterly. All this religious effort resulted in failure. The power of sin and the sinful flesh got the better of them, and their whole condition was one of the saddest that could be thought of.

This comes to us with unspeakable solemnity. There is a complaint everywhere in the Christian Church of the want of a high standard of integrity and godliness, even among the professing members of Christian churches. I remember a sermon which I heard preached on commercial morality. And, oh, if we speak not only of the commercial morality or immorality, but if we go into the homes of Christians, and if we think of the life to which God has called His children, and which He enables them to live by the Holy Spirit, and if we think of how much, nevertheless, there is of unlovingness and temper and sharpness and bitterness, and if we think how much there is very often of strife among the members of churches, and how much there is of envy and jealousy and sensitiveness and pride, then we are compelled to say: "Where are marks of the presence of the Spirit of the Lamb of God?" Wanting, sadly wanting!

Many people speak of these things as though they were the natural result of our feebleness and cannot well be helped. Many people speak of these things as sins, yet have given up the hope of conquering them. Many people speak of these things in the church around them, and do not see the least prospect of ever having the things changed. There is no prospect until there comes a radical change, until the Church of God begins to see that every sin in the believer comes from the flesh, from a fleshly life midst our religious activities, from a striving in self-effort to serve God. Until we learn to make confession, and until we begin to see, we must somehow or other get God's Spirit in power back to His Church, we must fail. Where did the Church begin in Pentecost? There they began in the Spirit. But, alas, how the Church of the next century went off into the flesh! They thought to perfect the Church in the flesh.

Do not let us think, because the blessed Reformation restored the great doctrine of justification by faith, that the power of the Holy Spirit was then fully restored. If it is our faith that God is going to have mercy on His Church in these last ages, it will be because the doctrine and the truth about the Holy Spirit will not only be studied, but sought after with a whole heart; and not only because that truth will be sought after, but because ministers and congregations will be found bowing before God in deep abasement with one cry: "We have grieved God's Spirit; we have tried to be Christian churches with as little as possible of God's Spirit; we have not sought to be churches filled with the Holy Spirit."

All the feebleness in the Church is owing to the refusal of the Church to obey its God.

And why is that so? I know your answer. You say: "We are too feeble and too helpless, and we try to obey, and we vow to obey, but somehow we fail."

Ah, yes, you fail because you do not accept the strength of God. God alone can work out His will in you. You cannot work out God's will, but His Holy Spirit can; and until the Church, until believers grasp this, and cease trying by human effort to do God's will, and wait upon the Holy Spirit to come with all His omnipotent and enabling power, the Church will never be what God wants her to be, and what God is willing to make of her.

Yielding to the Holy Spirit

I come now to my last thought, the question: What is the way to restoration?

Beloved friend, the answer is simple and easy. If that train has been shunted off, there is nothing for it but to come back to the point at which it was led away. The Galatians had no other way in returning but to come back to where they had gone wrong, to come back from all religious effort in their own strength, and from seeking anything by their own work, and to yield themselves humbly to the Holy Spirit. There is no other way for us as individuals.

Is there any brother or sister whose heart is conscious: "Alas! my life knows but little of the power of the Holy Spirit"? I come to you with God's message that you can have no conception of what your life would be in the power of the Holy Spirit. It is too high and too blessed and too wonderful, but I bring you the message that just as truly as the everlasting Son of God came to this world and wrought His wonderful works, that just as truly as on Calvary He died and wrought out your redemption by His precious blood, so, just as truly, can the Holy Spirit come into your heart that with His divine power He may sanctify you and enable you to do God's blessed will, and fill your heart with joy and with strength. But, alas! we have forgotten, we have grieved, we have dishonored the Holy Spirit, and He has not been able to do His work. But I bring you the message: The Father in Heaven loves to fill His children with His Holy Spirit. God longs to give each one individually, separately, the power of the Holy Spirit for daily life. The command comes to us individually, unitedly. God wants us as His children to arise and place our sins before Him, and to call upon Him for mercy. Oh, are ye so foolish? Having begun in the Spirit, are ye perfecting in the flesh that which was begun in the Spirit? Let us bow in shame, and confess before God how our fleshly religion, our self-effort, and self-confidence, have been the cause of every failure.

I have often been asked by young Christians: "Why is it that I fail so? I did so solemnly vow with my whole heart, and did desire to serve God; why have I failed?"

To such I always give the one answer: "My dear friend, you are trying to do in your own strength what Christ alone can do in you."

And when they tell me: "I am sure I knew Christ alone could do it, I was not trusting in myself," my answer always is:

"You were trusting in yourself or you could not have failed. If you had trusted Christ, He could not fail."

Oh, this perfecting in the flesh what was begun in the Spirit runs far deeper through us than we know. Let us ask God to reveal to us that it is only when we are brought to utter shame and emptiness that we shall be prepared to receive the blessing that comes from on high.

And so I come with these two questions. Are you living, beloved brother-minister—I ask it of every minister of the Gospel—are you living under the power of the Holy Spirit? Are you living as an anointed, Spirit-filled man in your ministry and your life before God? O brethren, our place is an awful one. We have to show people what God will do for us, not in our words and teaching, but in our life. God help us to do it!

I ask it of every member of Christ's Church and of every believer: Are you living a life under the power of the Holy Spirit day by day, or are you attempting to live without that? Remember you cannot. Are you consecrated, given up to the Spirit to work in you and to live in you? Oh, come and confess every failure of temper, every failure of tongue however small, every failure owing to the absence of the Holy Spirit and the presence of the power of self. Are you consecrated, are you given up to the Holy Spirit?

If your answer is No, then I come with a second question—Are you willing to be consecrated? Are you willing to give up yourself to the power of the Holy Spirit?

You well know that the human side of consecration will not help you. I may consecrate myself a hundred times with all the intensity of my being, and that will not help me. What will help me is this—that God from Heaven accepts and seals the consecration.

And now are you willing to give yourselves up to the Holy Spirit? You can do it now. A great deal may still be dark and dim, and beyond what we understand, and you may feel nothing; but come. God alone can effect the change. God alone, who gave us the Holy Spirit, can restore the Holy Spirit in power into our life. God alone can "strengthen us with might by his Spirit in the inner man." And to every waiting heart that will make the sacrifice, and give up everything, and give time to cry and pray to God, the answer will come. The blessing is not far off. Our God delights to help us. He will enable us to perfect, not in the flesh, but in the Spirit, what was begun in the Spirit.

KEPT BY THE POWER OF GOD

The words from which I speak, you will find in 1 Peter 1:5. The third, fourth and fifth verses are: "Blessed be the God and Father of our Lord Jesus Christ, which . . . hath begotten us again unto a lively hope by the resurrection of Jesus Christ from the dead, to an inheritance incorruptible . . . reserved in heaven for you, who are kept by the power of God through faith unto salvation." The words of my text are: "Kept by the power of God through faith."

There we have two wonderful, blessed truths about the keeping by which a believer is kept unto salvation. One truth is, Kept by the power of God; and the other truth is, Kept through faith. We should look at the two sides—at God's side and His almighty power, offered to us to be our Keeper every moment of the day; and at the human side, we having nothing to do but in faith to let God do His keeping work. We are begotten again to an inheritance kept in Heaven for us; and we are kept here on earth by the power of God. We see there is a double keeping—the inheritance kept for me in Heaven, and I on earth kept for the inheritance there.

Now, as to the first part of this keeping, there is no doubt and no question. God keeps the inheritance in Heaven very wonderfully and perfectly, and it is waiting there safely. And the same God keeps me for the inheritance. That is what I want to understand.

You know it is very foolish of a father to take great trouble to have an inheritance for his children, and to keep it for them, if he does not keep them for it. What would you think of a man spending his whole time and making every sacrifice to amass money, and as he gets his tens of thousands, you ask him why it is that he sacrifices himself so, and his answer is: "I want to leave my children a large inheritance, and I am keeping it for them"—if you were then to hear that that man takes no trouble to educate his children, that he allows them to run upon the street wild, and to go on in paths of sin and ignorance and folly, what would you think of him? Would not you say: "Poor man! he is keeping an inheritance for his children, but he is not keeping or preparing his children for the inheritance"! And there are so many Christians who think: "My God is keeping the inheritance for me"; but they cannot believe: "My God is keeping me for that inheritance." The same power, the same love, the same God doing the double work.

Now, I want to speak about a work God does upon us—keeping us for the inheritance. I have already said that we have two very simple truths: the one the divine side—we are kept by the power of God; the other, the human side—we are kept through faith.

Kept by the Power of God

Look at the divine side: Christians are kept by the power of God.

Keeping Includes All

Think, first of all, that this keeping is all-inclusive.

What is kept? You are kept. How much of you? The whole being. Does God keep one part of you and not another? No. Some people have an idea that this is a sort of vague, general keeping, and that God will keep them in such a way that when they die they will get to Heaven. But they do not apply that word kept to everything in their being and nature. And yet that is what God wants.

Here I have a watch. Suppose that this watch had been borrowed from a friend, and he said to me:

"When you go to Europe, I will let you take it with you, but mind you keep it safely and bring it back."

And suppose I damaged the watch, and had the hands broken, and the face defaced, and some of the wheels and springs spoiled, and took it back in that condition, and handed it to my friend; he would say:

"Ah, but I gave you that watch on condition that you would keep it."

"Have I not kept it? There is the watch."

"But I did not want you to keep it in that general way, so that you should bring me back only the shell of the watch, or the remains. I expected you to keep every part of it."

And so God does not want to keep us in this general way, so that at the last, somehow or other, we shall be saved as by fire, and just get into Heaven. But the keeping power and the love of God applies to every particular of our being.

There are some people who think God will keep them in spiritual things, but not in temporal things. This latter, they say, lies outside of His line. Now, God sends you to work in the world, but He did not say: "I must now leave you to go and earn your own money, and to get your livelihood for yourself." He knows you are not able to keep yourself. But God says: "My child, there is no work you are to do, and no business in which you are engaged, and not a cent which you are to spend, but I, your Father, will take that up into my keeping." God not only cares for the spiritual, but for the temporal also. The greater part of the life of many people must be spent, sometimes eight or nine or ten hours a day, amid the temptations and distractions of business; but God will care for you there. The keeping of God includes all.

There are other people who think: "Ah! in time of trial God keeps me, but in times of prosperity I do not need His keeping; then I forget Him and let Him go." Others, again, think the very opposite. They think: "In time of prosperity, when things are smooth and quiet, I am able to cling to God, but when heavy trials come, somehow or other my will rebels, and God does not keep me then."

Now, I bring you the message that in prosperity as in adversity, in the sunshine as in the dark, your God is ready to keep you all the time. Then again, there are others who think of this keeping thus: "God will keep me from doing very great wickedness, but there are small sins I cannot expect God to keep me from. There is the sin of temper. I cannot expect God to conquer that."

When you hear of some man who has been tempted and gone astray or fallen into drunkenness or murder, you thank God for His keeping power.

"I might have done the same as that man," you say, "if God had not kept me." And you believe He kept you from drunkenness and murder. And why do you not need believe that God can keep you from outbreaks of temper? You thought that this was of less importance; you did not remember that the great commandment of the New Testament is—"Love one another as I have loved you" (John 13:34). And when your temper and hasty judgment and sharp words came out, you sinned against the highest law—the law of God's love. And yet you say: "God will not, God cannot"—no, you will not say, God cannot; but you say, "God does not keep me from that." You perhaps say: "He can; but there is something in me that cannot attain to it, and which God does not take away."

I want to ask you, Can believers live a holier life than is generally lived? Can believers experience the keeping power of God all the day, to keep them from sin? Can believers be kept in fellowship with God? And I bring you a message from the Word of God, in these words: Kept by the power of God. There is no qualifying clause to them. The meaning is, that if you will entrust yourself entirely and absolutely to the omnipotence of God, He will delight to keep you.

Some people think that they never can get so far as that every word of their mouth should be to the glory of God. But it is what God wants of them, it is what God expects of them. God is willing to set a watch at the door of their mouth, and if God will do that, cannot He keep their tongue and their lips? He can; and that is what God is going to do for them that trust Him. God's keeping is all-inclusive, and let everyone who longs to live a holy life think out all their needs, and all their weaknesses, and all their shortcomings, and all their sins, and say deliberately: "Is there any sin that my God cannot keep me from?" And the heart will have to answer: "No; God can keep me from every sin."

Keeping Requires Power

Second, if you want to understand this keeping, remember that it is not only an all-inclusive keeping, but it is an almighty keeping.

I want to get that truth burned into my soul; I want to worship God until my whole heart is filled with the thought of His omnipotence. God is almighty, and the Almighty God offers Himself to work in my heart, to do the work of keeping me; and I want to get linked with Omnipotence, or rather, linked to the Omnipotent One, to the living God, and to have my place in the hollow of His hand. You read the Psalms, and you think of the wonderful thoughts in many of the expressions that David uses; as, for instance, when he speaks about God being our God, our Fortress, our Refuge, our strong Tower, our Strength and our Salvation. David had very wonderful views of how the everlasting God is Himself the hiding place of the believing soul, and of how He takes the believer and keeps him in the very hollow of His hand, in the secret of His pavilion, under the shadow of His wings, under His very feathers. And there David lived. And oh, we who are the children of Pentecost, we who have known Christ and His blood and the Holy Spirit sent down from Heaven, why is it we know so little of what it is to walk tremblingly step by step with the Almighty God as our Keeper?

Have you ever thought that in every action of grace in your heart you have the whole omnipotence of God engaged to bless you? When I come to a man and he bestows upon me a gift of money, I get it and go away with it. He has given me something of his; the rest he keeps for himself. But that is not the way with the power of God. God can part with nothing of His own power, and therefore I can experience the power and goodness of God only so far as I am in contact and fellowship with Himself; and when I come into contact and fellowship with Himself, I come into contact and fellowship with the whole omnipotence of God, and have the omnipotence of God to help me every day.

A son has, perhaps, a very rich father, and as the former is about to commence business the father says: "You can have as much money as you want for your undertaking." All the father has is at the disposal of the son. And that is the way with God, your Almighty God. You can hardly take it in; you feel yourself such a little worm. His omnipotence needed to keep a little worm! Yes, His omnipotence is needed to keep every little worm that lives in the dust, and also to keep the universe, and therefore His omnipotence is much more needed in keeping your soul and mine from the power of sin.

Oh, if you want to grow in grace, do learn to begin here. In all your judgings and meditations and thoughts and deeds and questionings and studies and prayers, learn to be kept by your Almighty God. What is Almighty God not going to do for the child that trusts Him? The Bible says: "Above all that we can ask or think" (Eph. 3:20). It is

Omnipotence you must learn to know and trust, and then you will live as a Christian ought to live. How little we have learned to study God, and to understand that a godly life is a life full of God, a life that loves God and waits on Him, and trusts Him, and allows Him to bless it! We cannot do the will of God except by the power of God. God gives us the first experience of His power to prepare us to long for more, and to come and claim all that He can do. God help us to trust Him every day.

Keeping Is Continuous

Another thought. This keeping is not only all-inclusive and omnipotent, but also continuous and unbroken.

People sometimes say: "For a week or a month God has kept me very wonderfully: I have lived in the light of His countenance, and I cannot say what joy I have not had in fellowship with Him. He has blessed me in my work for others. He has given me souls, and at times I felt as if I were carried heavenward on eagle wings. But it did not continue. It was too good; it could not last." And some say: "It was necessary that I should fall to keep me humble." And others say: "I know it was my own fault; but somehow you cannot always live up in the heights."

Oh, beloved, why is it? Can there be any reason why the keeping of God should not be continuous and unbroken? Just think. All life is in unbroken continuity. If my life were stopped for half an hour I would be dead, and my life gone. Life is a continuous thing, and the life of God is the life of His Church, and the life of God is His almighty power working in us. And God comes to us as the Almighty One, and without any condition He offers to be my Keeper, and His keeping means that day by day, moment by moment, God is going to keep us.

If I were to ask you the question: "Do you think God is able to keep you one day from actual transgression?" you would answer: "I not only know He is able to do it, but I think He has done it. There have been days in which He has kept my heart in His holy presence, when, though I have always had a sinful nature within me, He has kept me from conscious, actual transgression."

Now, if He can do that for an hour or a day, why not for two days? Oh! let us make God's omnipotence as revealed in His Word the measure of our expectations. Has God not said in His Word: "I, the Lord, do keep it, and will water it every moment" (Isa. 27:3)? What can that mean? Does "every moment" mean every moment? Did God promise of that vineyard or red wine that every moment He would water it so that the heat of the sun and the scorching wind might never dry it up? Yes. In South Africa they sometimes make a graft, and above it they tie a bottle of water, so that now and then there shall be a drop to saturate what they have put about it. And so the moisture is kept there unceasingly until the graft has had time to stroke, and resist the heat of the sun.

Will our God, in His tenderhearted love toward us, not keep us every moment when He has promised to do so? Oh! if we once got hold of the thought: Our whole spiritual life is to be God's doing—"It is God that worketh in us to will and to do of his good pleasure" (Phil. 2:13)—when once we get faith to expect that from God, God will do all for us. The keeping is to be continuous. Every morning God will meet you as you wake. It is not a question: If I forgot to wake in the morning with the thought of Him, what will come of it? If you trust your waking to God, God will meet you in the morning as you wake with His divine sunshine and love, and He will give you the consciousness that through the day you have got God to take charge of you continuously with His almighty power. And God will meet you the next day and every day; and never mind if in the practice of fellowship there comes failure sometimes. If you maintain your position and say: "Lord, I am going to expect Thee to do Thy utmost, and I am going to trust Thee day by day to keep me absolutely," your faith will grow stronger and stronger, and you will know the keeping power of God in unbrokenness.

Kept Through Faith

And now the other side—Believing. "Kept by the power of God through faith." How must we look at this faith?

Faith Implies Helplessness

Let me say, first of all, that this faith means utter impotence and helplessness before God.

At the bottom of all faith there is a feeling of helplessness. If I have a bit of business to transact, perhaps to buy a house, the lawyer must do the work of getting the transfer of the property in my name and making all the arrangements. I cannot do that work, and in trusting that agent I confess I cannot do it. And so faith always means helplessness. In many cases it means: I can do it with a great deal of trouble, but another can do it better. But in most cases it is utter helplessness; another must do it for me. And that is the secret of the spiritual life. A man must learn to say: "I give up everything; I have tried and longed and thought and prayed, but failure has come. God has blessed me and helped me, but still, in the long run, there has been so much of sin and sadness." What a change comes when a man is thus broken down into utter helplessness and self-despair, and says: "I can do nothing!" Remember Paul. He was living a blessed life, and he had been taken up into the third Heaven, and then the thorn in the flesh came, "a messenger of Satan to buffet me." And what happened? Paul could not understand it, and he prayed the Lord three times to take it away; but the Lord said, in effect:

"No; it is possible that you might exalt yourself, and therefore I have sent you this trial to keep you weak and humble."

And Paul then learned a lesson that he never forgot, and that was—to rejoice in his infirmities. He said that the weaker he was the better it was for him, for when he was weak, he was strong in his Lord Christ. Do you want to enter what people call "the higher life"? Then go a step lower down. I remember Dr. Boardman telling how that once he was invited by a gentleman to go to see a factory where they made fine shot, and I believe the workmen did so by pouring down molten lead from a great height. This gentleman wanted to take Dr. Boardman up to the top of the tower to see how the work was done. The doctor came to the tower, he entered by the door, and began going upstairs; but when he had gone a few steps the gentleman called out:

"That is the wrong way. You must come down this way; that stair is locked up."

The gentleman took him downstairs a good many steps, and there an elevator was ready to take him to the top; and he said:

"I have learned a lesson that going down is often the best way to get up."

Ah, yes, God will have to bring us very low down; there will have to come upon us a sense of emptiness and despair and nothingness. It is when we sink down in utter helplessness that the everlasting God will reveal Himself in His power, and that our hearts will learn to trust God alone.

What is it that keeps us from trusting Him perfectly?

Many a one says: "I believe what you say, but there is one difficulty. If my trust were perfect and always abiding, all would come right, for I know God will honor trust. But how am I to get that trust?"

My answer is: "By the death of self. The great hindrance to trust is self-effort. So long as you have got your own wisdom and thoughts and strength, you cannot fully trust God. But when God breaks you down, when everything begins to grow dim before your eyes, and you see that you understand nothing, then God is coming near, and if you will bow down in nothingness and wait upon God, He will become all."

As long as we are something, God cannot be all, and His omnipotence cannot do its full work. That is the beginning of faith—utter despair of self, a ceasing from man and everything on earth, and finding our hope in God alone.

Faith Is Rest

And then, next, we must understand that faith is rest.

In the beginning of the faith-life, faith is struggling; but as long as faith is struggling, faith has not attained its strength. But when faith in its struggling gets to the end of itself, and just throws itself upon God and rests on Him, then comes joy and victory.

Perhaps I can make it plainer if I tell the story of how the Keswick Convention began. Canon Battersby was an evangelical clergyman of the Church of England for more than twenty years, a man of deep and tender godliness, but he had not the consciousness of rest and victory over sin, and often was deeply sad at the thought of stumbling and failure and sin. When he heard about the possibility of victory, he felt it was desirable, but it was as if he could not attain it. On one occasion, he heard an address on "Rest and Faith" from the story of the nobleman who came from Capernaum to Cana to ask Christ to heal his child. In the address it was shown that the nobleman believed that Christ could help him in a general way, but he came to Jesus a good deal by way of an experiment. He hoped Christ would help him, but he had not any assurance of that help. But what happened? When Christ said to him: "Go thy way, for thy child liveth," that man believed the word that Jesus spoke; he rested in that word. He had no proof that his child was well again, and he had to walk back seven hours' journey to

Capernaum. He walked back, and on the way met his servant, and got the first news that the child was well, that at one o'clock on the afternoon of the previous day, at the very time that Jesus spoke to him, the fever left the child. That father rested upon the word of Jesus and His work, and he went down to Capernaum and found his child well; and he praised God, and became with his whole house a believer and disciple of Jesus.

Oh, friends, that is faith! When God comes to me with the promise of His keeping, and I have nothing on earth to trust in, I say to God: "Thy word is enough; kept by the power of God." That is faith, that is rest. When Canon Battersby heard that address, he went home that night, and in the darkness of the night found rest. He rested on the word of Jesus. And the next morning, in the streets of Oxford, he said to a friend: "I have found it!" Then he went and told others, and asked that the Keswick Convention might be begun, and those at the convention with himself should testify simply what God had done.

It is a great thing when a man comes to rest on God's almighty power for every moment of his life, in prospect of temptations to temper and haste and anger and unlovingness and pride and sin. It is a great thing in prospect of these to enter into a covenant with the omnipotent Jehovah, not on account of anything that any man says, or of anything that my heart feels, but on the strength of the Word of God: "Kept by the power of God through faith."

Oh, let us say to God that we are going to test Him to the very uttermost. Let us say: We ask Thee for nothing more than Thou canst give, but we want nothing less. Let us say: My God, let my life be a proof of what the omnipotent God can do. Let these be the two dispositions of our souls every day—deep helplessness, and simple, childlike rest.

Faith Needs Fellowship

That brings me to just one more thought in regard to faith—faith implies fellowship with God.

Many people want to take the Word and believe that, and they find they cannot believe it. Ah, no! you cannot separate God from His Word. No goodness or power can be received separate from God, and if you want to get into this life of godliness, you must take time for fellowship with God.

People sometimes tell me: "My life is one of such scurry and bustle that I have no time for fellowship with God." A dear missionary said to me: "People do not know how we missionaries are tempted. I get up at five o'clock in the morning, and there are the natives waiting for their orders for work. Then I have to go to the school and spend hours there;

and then there is other work, and sixteen hours rush along, and I hardly get time to be alone with God."

Ah! there is the lack. I pray you, remember two things. I have not told you to trust the omnipotence of God as a thing, and I have not told you to trust the Word of God as a written book, but I have told you to go to the God of omnipotence and the God of the Word. Deal with God as that nobleman dealt with the living Christ. Why was he able to believe the word that Christ spoke to him? Because in the very eyes and tones and voice of Jesus, the Son of God, he saw and heard something which made him feel that he could trust Him. And that is what Christ can do for you and me. Do not try to stir and arouse faith from within. How often I have tried to do that, and made a fool of myself! You cannot stir up faith from the depths of your heart. Leave your heart, and look into the face of Christ, and listen to what He tells you about how He will keep you. Look up into the face of your loving Father, and take time every day with Him, and begin a new life with the deep emptiness and poverty of a man who has got nothing, and who wants to get everything from Him—with the deep restfulness of a man who rests on the living God, the omnipotent Jehovah—and try God, and prove Him if He will not open the windows of Heaven and pour out a blessing that there shall not be room to receive it.

I close by asking if you are willing to experience to the very full the heavenly keeping for the heavenly inheritance? Robert Murray M'Cheyne says, somewhere: "Oh, God, make me as holy as a pardoned sinner can be made." And if that prayer is in your heart, come now, and let us enter into a covenant with the everlasting and omnipotent Jehovah afresh, and in great helplessness, but in great restfulness place ourselves in His hands. And then as we enter into our covenant, let us have the one prayer—that we may believe fully that the everlasting God is going to be our Companion, holding our hand every moment of the day; our Keeper, watching over us without a moment's interval; our Father, delighting to reveal Himself in our souls always. He has the power to let the sunshine of His love be with us all the day. Do not be afraid because you have got your business that you cannot have God with you always. Learn the lesson that the natural sun shines upon you all the day, and you enjoy its light, and wherever you are you have got the sun; God takes care that it shines upon you. And God will take care that His own divine light shines upon you, and that you shall abide in that light, if you will only trust Him for it. Let us trust God to do that with a great and entire trust.

Here is the omnipotence of God, and here is faith reaching out to the measure of that omnipotence. Shall we not say: "All that that omnipotence can do, I am going to trust my God for"? Are not the two sides of this heavenly life wonderful? God's omnipotence covers me, and my will in its littleness rests in that omnipotence, and rejoices in it!

Moment by moment, I'm kept in His love;
Moment by moment, I've life from above;
Looking to Jesus, the glory doth shine;
Moment by moment, Oh, Lord, I am Thine!

"YE ARE THE BRANCHES"

An Address to Christian Workers

Everything depends on our being right ourselves in Christ. If I want good apples, I must have a good apple tree; and if I care for the health of the apple tree, the apple tree will give me good apples. And it is just so with our Christian life and work. If our life with Christ be right, all will come right. There may be the need of instruction and suggestion and help and training in the different departments of the work; all that has value. But in the long run, the greatest essential is to have the full life in Christ—in other words, to have Christ in us, working through us. I know how much there often is to disturb us, or to cause anxious questionings; but the Master has such a blessing for every one of us, and such perfect peace and rest, and such joy and strength, if we can only come into, and be kept in, the right attitude toward Him.

I will take my text from the parable of the Vine and the Branches, in John 15:5: "I am the vine, ye are the branches." Especially these words: "Ye are the branches."

What a simple thing it is to be a branch, the branch of a tree, or the branch of a vine! The branch grows out of the vine, or out of the tree, and there it lives and grows, and in due time, bears fruit. It has no responsibility except just to receive from the root and stem sap and nourishment. And if we only by the Holy Spirit knew our relationship to Jesus Christ, our work would be changed into the brightest and most heavenly thing upon earth. Instead of there ever being soul-weariness or exhaustion, our work would be like a new experience, linking us to Jesus as nothing else can. For, alas! is it not often true that our work comes between us and Jesus? What folly! The very work that He has to do in me, and I for Him, I take up in such a way that it separates me from Christ. Many a laborer in the vineyard has complained that he has too much work, and not time for close communion with Jesus, and that his usual work weakens his inclination for prayer, and that his too much intercourse with men darkens the spiritual life. Sad thought, that the bearing of fruit should separate the branch from the vine! That must be because we have looked upon our work as something other than the branch bearing fruit. May God deliver us from every false thought about the Christian life.

Now, just a few thoughts about this blessed branch-life.

Absolute Dependence

In the first place, it is a life of absolute dependence. The branch has nothing; it just depends upon the vine for everything. Absolute dependence is one of the most solemn and precious of thoughts. A great German theologian wrote two large volumes some years ago to show that the whole of Calvin's theology is summed up in that one principle of absolute dependence upon God; and he was right. Another great writer has said that absolute, unalterable dependence upon God alone is the essence of the religion of angels, and should be that of men also. God is everything to the angels, and He is willing to be everything to the Christian. If I can learn every moment of the day to depend upon God, everything will come right. You will get the higher life if you depend absolutely upon God.

Now, here we find it with the vine and the branches. Every vine you ever see, or every bunch of grapes that comes upon your table, let it remind you that the branch is absolutely dependent on the vine. The vine has to do the work, and the branch enjoys the fruit of it.

What has the vine to do? It has to do a great work. It has to send its roots out into the soil and hunt under the ground—the roots often extend a long way out—for nourishment, and to drink in the moisture. Put certain elements of manure in certain directions, and the vine sends its roots there, and then in its roots or stems it turns the moisture and manure into that special sap which is to make the fruit that is borne. The vine does the work, and the branch has just to receive from the vine the sap, which is changed into grapes. I have been told that at Hampton Court, London, there is a vine that sometimes bore a couple of thousand bunches of grapes, and people were astonished at its large growth and rich fruitage. Afterward it was discovered what was the cause of it. Not so very far away runs the River Thames, and the vine had stretched its roots away hundreds of yards under the ground, until it had come to the riverside, and there in all the rich slime of the riverbed it had found rich nourishment, and obtained moisture, and the roots had drawn the sap all that distance up and up into the vine, and as a result there was the abundant, rich harvest. The vine had the work to do, and the branches had just to depend upon the vine, and receive what it gave.

Is that literally true of my Lord Jesus? Must I understand that when I have to work, when I have to preach a sermon, or address a Bible class, or to go out and visit the poor, neglected ones, that all the responsibility of the work is on Christ?

That is exactly what Christ wants you to understand. Christ wants that in all your work, the very foundation should be the simple, blessed consciousness: Christ must care for all.

And how does He fulfill the trust of that dependence? He does it by sending down the Holy Spirit—not now and then only as a special gift, for remember the relationship between the vine and the branches is such that hourly, daily, unceasingly there is the living connection maintained. The sap does not flow for a time, and then stop, and then flow again, but from moment to moment the sap flows from the vine to the branches. And just so, my Lord Jesus wants me to take that blessed position as a worker, and morning by morning and day by day and hour by hour and step by step, in every work I have to go out to just to abide before Him in the simple utter helplessness of one who knows nothing, and is nothing, and can do nothing. Oh, beloved workers, study that word nothing. You sometimes sing: "Oh, to be nothing, nothing"; but have you really studied that word and prayed every day, and worshiped God, in the light of it? Do you know the blessedness of that word nothing?

If I am something, then God is not everything; but when I become nothing, God can become all, and the everlasting God in Christ can reveal Himself fully. That is the higher life. We need to become nothing. Someone has well said that the seraphim and cherubim are flames of fire because they know they are nothing, and they allow God to put His fullness and His glory and brightness into them. Oh, become nothing in deep reality, and, as a worker, study only one thing—to become poorer and lower and more helpless, that Christ may work all in you.

Workers, here is your first lesson: learn to be nothing, learn to be helpless. The man who has got something is not absolutely dependent; but the man who has got nothing is absolutely dependent. Absolute dependence upon God is the secret of all power in work. The branch has nothing but what it gets from the vine, and you and I can have nothing but what we get from Jesus.

Deep Restfulness

But second, the life of the branch is not only a life of entire dependence, but of deep restfulness.

That little branch, if it could think, and if it could feel, and if it could speak—that branch away in Hampton Court vine, or on some of the million vines that we have in South Africa, in our sunny land—if we could have a little branch here today to talk to us, and if we could say: "Come, branch of the vine, I want to learn from you how I can be a true branch of the living Vine," what would it answer? The little branch would whisper:

"Man, I hear that you are wise, and I know that you can do a great many wonderful things. I know you have much strength and wisdom given to you but I have one lesson for you. With all your hurry and effort in Christ's work you never prosper. The first thing you need is to come and rest in your Lord Jesus. That is what I do. Since I grew out of that vine I have spent years and years, and all I have done is just to rest in the vine. When the time of spring came I had no anxious thought or care. The vine began to pour its sap into me, and to give the bud and leaf. And when the time of summer came I had no care, and in the great heat I trusted the vine to bring moisture to keep me fresh. And in the time of harvest, when the owner came to pluck the grapes, I had no care. If there was anything in the grapes not good, the owner never blamed the branch, the blame was always on the vine. And if you would be a true branch of Christ, the living Vine, just rest on Him. Let Christ bear the responsibility."

You say: "Won't that make me slothful?"

I tell you it will not. No one who learns to rest upon the living Christ can become slothful, for the closer your contact with Christ the more of the Spirit of His zeal and love will be borne in upon you. But, oh, begin to work in the midst of your entire dependence by adding to that deep restfulness. A man sometimes tries and tries to be dependent upon Christ, but he worries himself about this absolute dependence; he tries and he cannot get it. But let him sink down into entire restfulness every day.

In Thy strong hand I lay me down.
So shall the work be done;
For who can work so wondrously
As the Almighty One?

Worker, take your place every day at the feet of Jesus, in the blessed peace and rest that come from the knowledge —

I have no care, my cares are His!
I have no fear, He cares for all my fears.

Come, children of God, and understand that it is the Lord Jesus who wants to work through you. You complain of the lack of fervent love. It will come from Jesus. He will give the divine love in your heart with which you can love people. That is the meaning of the assurance: "The love of God is shed abroad in our hearts by the Holy Spirit" (Rom. 5:5); and of that other word: "The love of Christ constraineth us" (2 Cor. 5:14). Christ can give you a fountain of love, so that you cannot help loving the most wretched and the most ungrateful, or those who have wearied you hitherto. Rest in Christ, who can give wisdom and strength, and you do not know how that restfulness will often prove to be the very best part of your message. You plead with people and you argue, and they get the idea: "There is a man arguing and striving with me." They only feel: "Here are two men dealing with each other." But if you will let the deep rest of God come over you, the rest in Christ Jesus, the peace and rest and holiness of Heaven, that restfulness will bring a blessing to the heart, even more than the words you speak.

Much Fruitfulness

But third, the branch teaches a lesson of much fruitfulness.

The Lord Jesus Christ repeated that word fruit often in that parable. He spoke, first, of fruit, and then of more fruit, and then of much fruit. Yes, you are ordained not only to bear fruit, but to bear much fruit. "Herein is my Father glorified, that ye bear much fruit" (John 15:8). In the first place, Christ said: "I am the Vine, and my Father is the Husbandman. My Father is the Husbandman who has charge of me and you." He who will watch over the connection between Christ and the branches is God; and it is in the power of God through Christ we are to bear fruit.

Oh, Christians, you know this world is perishing for the want of workers. And it lacks not only more workers—the workers are saying, some more earnestly than others: "We need not only more workers, but we need our workers to have a new power, a different life; that we workers should be able to bring more blessing." Children of God, I appeal to you. You know what trouble you take, say, in a case of sickness. You have a beloved friend apparently in danger of death, and nothing can refresh that friend so much as a few grapes, and they are out of season; but what trouble you will take to get the grapes that are to be the nourishment of this dying friend! And, oh, there are around you people who never go to church, and so many who go to church, but do not know Christ. And yet the heavenly grapes, the grapes of the heavenly Vine, are not to be had at any price, except as the child of God bears them out of his inner life in fellowship with Christ. Except the children of God are filled with the sap of the heavenly Vine, except they are filled with the Holy Spirit and the love of Jesus, they cannot bear much of the real heavenly grape. We all confess there is a great deal of work, a great deal of preaching and teaching and visiting, a great deal of machinery, a great deal of earnest effort of every kind; but there is not much manifestation of the power of God in it.

What is lacking? There is lacking the close connection between the worker and the heavenly Vine. Christ, the heavenly Vine, has blessings that He could pour on tens of thousands who are perishing. Christ, the heavenly Vine, has power to provide the heavenly grapes. But "Ye are the branches," and you cannot bear heavenly fruit unless you are in close connection with Jesus Christ.

Do not confound work and fruit. There may be a good deal of work for Christ that is not the fruit of the heavenly Vine. Do not seek for work only. Oh! study this question of fruit-bearing. It means the very life and the very power and the very spirit and the very love within the heart of the Son of God—it means the heavenly Vine Himself coming into your heart and mine.

You know there are different sorts of grapes, each with a different name, and every vine provides exactly that peculiar aroma and juice which gives the grape its particular flavor and taste. Just so, there is in the heart of Christ Jesus a life, and a love, and a Spirit, and a blessing, and a power for men, that are entirely heavenly and divine, and that will come down into our hearts. Stand in close connection with the heavenly Vine and say:

"Lord Jesus, nothing less than the sap that flows through Thyself, nothing less than the Spirit of Thy divine life is what we ask. Lord Jesus, I pray Thee let Thy Spirit flow through me in all my work for Thee."

I tell you again that the sap of the heavenly Vine is nothing but the Holy Spirit. The Holy Spirit is the life of the heavenly Vine, and what you must get from Christ is nothing less than a strong inflow of the Holy Spirit. You need it exceedingly, and you want nothing more than that. Remember that. Do not expect Christ to give a bit of strength here, and a bit of blessing yonder, and a bit of help over there. As the vine does its work in giving its own peculiar sap to the branch, so expect Christ to give His own Holy Spirit into your heart, and then you will bear much fruit. And if you have only begun to bear fruit, and are listening to the word of Christ in the parable, "more fruit," "much fruit," remember that in order that you should bear more fruit you just require more of Jesus in your life and heart.

We ministers of the Gospel, how we are in danger of getting into a condition of work, work, work! And we pray over it, but the freshness and buoyancy and joy of the heavenly life are not always present. Let us seek to understand that the life of the branch is a life of much fruit, because it is a life rooted in Christ, the living, heavenly Vine.

And fourth, the life of the branch is a life of close communion.

Let us again ask: What has the branch to do? You know that precious, inexhaustible word that Christ used: Abide. Your life is to be an abiding life. And how is the abiding to be? It is to be just like the branch in the vine, abiding every minute of the day. There are the branches, in close communion, in unbroken communion, with the vine, from January to December. And cannot I live every day—it is to me an almost terrible thing that we should ask the question—cannot I live in abiding communion with the heavenly Vine?

You say: "But I am so much occupied with other things."

You may have ten hours' hard work daily, during which your brain has to be occupied with temporal things; God orders it so. But the abiding work is the work of the heart, not of the brain, the work of the heart clinging to and resting in Jesus, a work in which the Holy Spirit links us to Christ Jesus. Oh, do believe that deeper down than the brain, deep down in the inner life, you can abide in Christ, so that every moment you are free the consciousness will come:

"Blessed Jesus, I am still in Thee."

If you will learn for a time to put aside other work and to get into this abiding contact with the heavenly Vine, you will find that fruit will come.

What is the application to our life of this abiding communion? What does it mean?

It means close fellowship with Christ in secret prayer. I am sure there are Christians who do long for the higher life, and who sometimes have got a great blessing, and have at times found a great inflow of heavenly joy and a great outflow of heavenly gladness; and yet after a time it has passed away. They have not understood that close personal actual communion with Christ is an absolute necessity for daily life. Take time to be alone with Christ. Nothing in Heaven or earth can free you from the necessity for that, if you are to be happy and holy Christians. Oh! how many Christians look upon it as a burden and a tax, and a duty, and a difficulty to be often alone with God! That is the great hindrance to our Christian life everywhere. We need more quiet fellowship with God, and I tell you in the name of the heavenly Vine that you cannot be healthy branches, branches into which the heavenly sap can flow, unless you take plenty of time for communion with God. If you are not willing to sacrifice time to get alone with Him, and to give Him time every day to work in you, and to keep up the link of connection between you and Himself, He cannot give you that blessing of His unbroken fellowship. Jesus Christ asks you to live in close communion with Him. Let every heart say: "O, Christ, it is this I long for, it is this I choose." And He will gladly give it to you.

Absolute Surrender

And then finally, the life of the branch is a life of absolute surrender. This word, absolute surrender, is a great and solemn word, and I believe we do not understand its meaning. But yet the little branch preaches it.

"Have you anything to do, little branch, besides bearing grapes?"

"No, nothing."

"Are you fit for nothing?"

Fit for nothing! The Bible says that a bit of vine cannot even be used as a pen; it is fit for nothing but to be burned.

"And now, what do you understand, little branch, about your relationship to the vine?"

"My relationship is just this: I am utterly given up to the vine, and the vine can give me as much or as little sap as it chooses. Here I am at its disposal and the vine can do with me what it likes."

Oh, friends, we need this absolute surrender to the Lord Jesus Christ. The more I speak, the more I feel that this is one of the most difficult points to make clear, and one of the most important and needful points to explain—what this absolute surrender is. It is often an easy thing for a man or a number of men to come out and offer themselves up to God for entire consecration, and to say: "Lord, it is my desire to give up myself entirely to Thee." That is of great value, and often brings very rich blessing. But the one question I ought to study quietly is What is meant by absolute surrender?

It means that, as literally as Christ was given up entirely to God, I am given up entirely to Christ. Is that too strong? Some think so. Some think that never can be; that just as entirely and absolutely as Christ gave up His life to do nothing but seek the Father's pleasure, and depend on the Father absolutely and entirely, I am to do nothing but to seek the pleasure of Christ. But that is actually true. Christ Jesus came to breathe His own Spirit into us, to make us find our very highest happiness in living entirely for God, just as He did. Oh, beloved brethren, if that is the case, then I ought to say:

"Yes, as true as it is of that little branch of the vine, so true, by God's grace, I would have it to be of me. I would live day by day that Christ may be able to do with me what He will."

Ah! here comes the terrible mistake that lies at the bottom of so much of our own religion. A man thinks:

"I have my business and family duties, and my relationships as a citizen, and all this I cannot change. And now alongside all this I am to take in religion and the service of God, as something that will keep me from sin. God help me to perform my duties properly!"

This is not right. When Christ came, He came and bought the sinner with His blood. If there was a slave market here and I were to buy a slave, I should take that slave away to my own house from his old surroundings, and he would live at my house as my personal property, and I could order him about all the day. And if he were a faithful slave, he would live as having no will and no interests of his own, his one care being to promote the well-being and honor of his master. And in like manner I, who have been bought with the blood of Christ, have been bought to live every day with the one thought—How can I please my Master?

Oh, we find the Christian life so difficult because we seek for God's blessing while we live in our own will. We should be glad to live the Christian life according to our own liking. We make our own plans and choose our own work, and then we ask the Lord Jesus to come in and take care that sin shall not conquer us too much, and that we shall not go too far wrong; we ask Him to come in and give us so much of His blessing. But our relationship to Jesus ought to be such that we are entirely at His disposal, and every day come to Him humbly and straightforwardly and say:

"Lord, is there anything in me that is not according to Thy will, that has not been ordered by Thee, or that is not entirely given up to Thee?" Oh, if we would wait and wait patiently, I tell you what the result would be. There would spring up a relationship between us and Christ so close and so tender that we should afterward be amazed at how we formerly could have lived with the idea: "I am surrendered to Christ." We should feel how far distant our intercourse with Him had previously been, and that He can, and does indeed, come and take actual possession of us, and gives unbroken fellowship all the day. The branch calls us to absolute surrender.

I do not speak now so much about the giving up of sins. There are people who need that, people who have got violent tempers, bad habits, and actual sins which they from time to time commit, and which they have never given up into the very bosom of the Lamb of God. I pray you, if you are branches of the living Vine, do not keep one sin back. I know there are a great many difficulties about this question of holiness. I know that all do not think exactly the same with regard to it. That would be to me a matter of comparative indifference if I could see that all are honestly longing to be free from every sin. But I am afraid that unconsciously there are in hearts often compromises with the idea that we cannot be without sin, we must sin a little every day; we cannot help it. Oh, that people would actually cry to God: "Lord, do keep me from sin!" Give yourself utterly to Jesus, and ask Him to do His very utmost for you in keeping you from sin.

There is a great deal in our work, in our church and our surroundings that we found in the world when we were born into it, and it has grown all around us, and we think that it is all right, it cannot be changed. We do not come to the Lord Jesus and ask Him about it. Oh! I advise you, Christians, bring everything into relationship with Jesus and say: "Lord, everything in my life has to be in most complete harmony with my position as a branch of Thee, the blessed Vine."

Let your surrender to Christ be absolute. I do not understand that word surrender fully; it gets new meanings every now and then; it enlarges immensely from time to time. But I advise you to speak it out: "Absolute surrender to Thee, O Christ, is what I have chosen." And Christ will show you what is not according to His mind, and lead you on to deeper and higher blessedness.

In conclusion, let me gather up all in one sentence. Christ Jesus said: "I am the Vine, ye are the branches." In other words: "I, the living One who have so completely given myself to you, am the Vine. You cannot trust me too much. I am the Almighty Worker, full of a divine life and power." You are the branches of the Lord Jesus Christ. If there is in your heart the consciousness that you are not a strong, healthy, fruit-bearing branch, not closely linked with Jesus, not living in Him as you should be—then listen to Him say: "I am the Vine, I will receive you, I will draw you to myself, I will bless you, I will strengthen you, I will fill you with my Spirit. I, the Vine, have taken you to be my branches, I have given myself utterly to you; children, give yourselves utterly to me. I have surrendered myself as God absolutely to you; I became man and died for you that I might be entirely yours. Come and surrender yourselves entirely to be mine."

What shall our answer be? Oh, let it be a prayer from the depths of our heart, that the living Christ may take each one of us and link us close to Himself. Let our prayer be that He, the living Vine, shall so link each of us to Himself that we shall go away with our hearts singing: "He is my Vine, and I am His branches—I want nothing more—now I have the everlasting Vine." Then, when you get alone with Him, worship and adore Him, praise and trust Him, love Him and wait for His love. "Thou art my Vine, and I am Thy branch. It is enough, my soul is satisfied."

Glory to His blessed name!

Humility

PREFACE

There are three great motives that urge us to humility. It becomes me as a creature, as a sinner, as a saint. The first we see in the heavenly hosts, in unfallen man, in Jesus as Son of Man. The second appeals to us in our fallen state, and points out the only way through which we can return to our right place as creatures. In the third we have the mystery of grace, which teaches us that, as we lose ourselves in the overwhelming greatness of redeeming love, humility becomes to us the consummation of everlasting blessedness and adoration.

In our ordinary religious teaching, the second aspect has been too exclusively put in the foreground, so that some have even gone to the extreme of saying that we must keep sinning if we are indeed to keep humble. Others again have thought that the strength of self-condemnation is the secret of humility. And the Christian life has suffered loss, where believers have not been distinctly guided to see that, even in our relation as creatures, nothing is more natural and beautiful and blessed than to be nothing, that God may be all; or where it has not been made clear that it is not sin that humbles most, but grace, and that it is the soul, led through its sinfulness to be occupied with God in His wonderful glory as God, as Creator and Redeemer, that will truly take the lowest place before Him.

In these meditations I have, for more than one reason, almost exclusively directed attention to the humility that becomes us as creatures. It is not only that the connection between humility and sin is so abundantly set forth in all our religious teaching, but because I believe that for the fullness of the Christian life it is indispensable that prominence be given to the other aspect. If Jesus is indeed to be our example in His lowliness, we need to understand the principles in which it was rooted, and in which we find the common ground on which we stand with Him, and in which our likeness to Him is to be attained. If we are indeed to be humble, not only before God but towards men, if humility is to be our joy, we must see that it is not only the mark of shame, because of sin, but, apart from all sin, a being clothed upon with the very beauty and blessedness of heaven and of Jesus. We shall see that just as Jesus found His glory in taking the form of a servant, so when He said to us, "Whosoever would be first among you, shall be your servant," He simply taught us the blessed truth that there is nothing so divine and heavenly as being the servant and helper of all. The faithful servant, who recognizes his position, finds a real pleasure in supplying the wants of the master or his guests. When we see that humility is something infinitely deeper than contrition, and accept it as our participation in the life of Jesus, we shall begin to learn that it is our true nobility, and that to prove it in being servants of all is the highest fulfillment of our destiny, as men created in the image of God.

When I look back upon my own religious experience, or round upon the Church of Christ in the world, I stand amazed at the thought of how little humility is sought after as the distinguishing feature of the discipleship of Jesus. In preaching and living, in the daily intercourse of the home and social life, in the more special fellowship with Christians, in the direction and performance of work for Christ,-alas! how much proof there is that humility is not esteemed the cardinal virtue, the only root from which the graces can grow, the one indispensable condition of true fellowship with Jesus. That it should have been possible for men to say of those who claim to be seeking the higher holiness, that the profession has not been accompanied with increasing humility, is a loud call to all earnest Christians, however much or little truth there be in the charge, to prove that meekness and lowliness of heart are the chief mark by which they who follow the meek and lowly Lamb of God are to be known.

Chapter 1--HUMILITY: THE GLORY OF THE CREATURE

"They shall cast their crowns before the throne, so saying: Worthy art Thou, our Lord and our God, to receive the gloty, and the honour and the power: for Thou didst create all things, and because of Thy will then are, and were created. " Rev. 4:11

When God created the universe, it was with the one object of making the creature partaker of His perfection and blessedness, and so showing forth in it the glory of His love and wisdom and power. God wished to reveal Himself in and through created beings by communicating to them as much of His own goodness and glory as they were capable of receiving. But this communication was not a giving to the creature something which it could possess in itself, a certain life or goodness, of which it had the charge and disposal.By no means. But as God is the ever-living, ever-present, ever-acting One, who upholdeth all things by the word of His power, and in whom all things exist, the relation of the creature to God could only be one of unceasing, absolute, universal dependence. As truly as God by His power once created, so truly by that same power must God every moment maintain. The creature has not only to look back to the origin and first beginning of existence, and acknowledge that it there owes everything to God; its chief care, its highest virtue, its only happiness, now and through all eternity, is to present itself an empty vessel, in which God can dwell and manifest His power and goodness.

The life God bestows is imparted not once for all, but each moment continuously, by the unceasing operation of His mighty power. Humility, the place of entire dependence on God, is, from the very nature of things, the first duty and the highest virtue of the creature, and the root of every virtue.

And so pride, or the loss of this humility, is the root of every sin and evil. It was when the now fallen angels began to look upon themselves with self-complacency that they were led to disobedience, and were cast down from the light of heaven into outer darkness. Even so it was, when the serpent breathed the poison of his pride, the desire to be as God, into the hearts of our first parents, that they too fell from their high estate into all the wretchedness in which man is now sunk. In heaven and earth, pride, self-exaltation, is the gate and the birth, and the curse, of hell. (See Note "A" at end of chapter.)

Hence it follows that nothing can be our redemption, but the restoration of the 'lost humility, the original and only true relation of the creature to its God. And so Jesus came to bring humility back to earth, to make us partakers of it, and by it to save us. In heaven He humbled Himself to become man. The humility we see in Him possessed Him in heaven; it brought Him, He brought it, from there. Here on earth "He humbled

Himself, and became obedient unto death"; His humility gave His death its value, and so became our redemption. And now the salvation He imparts is nothing less and nothing else than a communication of His own life and death, His own disposition and spirit, His own humility, as the ground and root of His relation to God and His redeeming work. Jesus Christ took the place and fulfilled the destiny of man, as a creature, by His life of perfect humility. His humility is our salvation. His salvation is our humility.

And so the life of the saved ones, of the saints, must needs bear this stamp of deliverance from sin, and full restoration to their original state; their whole relation to God and man marked by an allpervading humility. Without this there can be no true abiding in God's presence, or experience of His favor and the power of His Spirit; without this no abiding faith, or love or joy or strength. Humility is the only soil in which the graces root; the lack of humility is the sufficient explanation of every defect and failure. Humility is not so much a grace or virtue along with others; it is the root of all, because it alone takes the right attitude before God, and allows Him as God to do all.

God has so constituted us as reasonable beings, that the truer the insight into the real nature or the absolute need of a command, the readier and fuller will be our obedience to it. The call to humility has been too little regarded in the Church because its true nature and importance has been too little apprehended. It is not a something which we bring to God, or He bestows; it is simply the sense of entire nothingness, which comes when we see how truly God is all, and in which we make way for God to be all. When the creature realizes that this is the true nobility, and consents to be with his will, his mind, and his affections, the form, the vessel in which the life and glory of God are to work and manifest themselves, he sees that humility is simply acknowledging the truth of his position as creature, and yielding to God His place.

In the life of earnest Christians, of those who pursue and profess holiness, humility ought to be the chief mark of their uprightness. It is often said that it is not so. May not one reason be that in the teaching and example of the Church, it has never had that place of supreme importance which belongs to it? And that this, again, is owing to the neglect of this truth, that strong as sin is as a motive to humility, there is one of still wider and mightier influence, that which makes the angels, that which made Jesus, that which makes the holiest of saints in heaven, so humble; that the first and chief mark of the relation of the creature, the secret of his blessedness, is the humility and nothingness which leaves God free to be all?

I am sure there are many Christians who will confess that their experience has been very much like my own in this, that we had long known the Lord without realizing that meekness and lowliness of heart are to be the distinguishing feature of the disciple as they were of the Master. And further, that this humility is not a thing that will come of itself, but that it must be made the object of special desire and prayer and faith and practice. As we study the word, we shall see what very distinct and oft-repeated instructions Jesus gave His disciples on this point, and how slow they were in understanding Him. Let us, at the very commencement of our meditations, admit that there is nothing so natural to man, nothing so insidious and hidden from our sight, nothing so difficult and dangerous, as pride. Let us feel that nothing but a very determined and persevering waiting on God and Christ will discover how lacking we are in the grace of humility, and how impotent to obtain what we seek. Let us study the character of Christ until our souls are filled with the love and admiration of His lowliness. And let us believe that, when we are broken down under a sense of our pride, and our impotence to cast it out, Jesus Christ Himself will come in to impart this grace too, as a part of His wondrous life within us.

NOTE A--

"All this is to make it known the region of eternity that pride can degrade the highest angels into devils, and humility raise fallen flesh and blood to the thrones of angels. Thus, this is the great end of God raising a new creation out of a fallen kingdom of angels: for this end it stands in its state of war betwixt the fire and pride of fallen angels, and the humility of the Lamb of God, that the last trumpet may sound the great truth through the depths of eternity, that evil can have no beginning but from pride, and no end but from humility. The truth is this: Pride may die in you, or nothing of heaven can live in you. Under the banner of the truth, give yourself up to the meek and humble spirit of the holy Jesus. Humility must sow seed, or there can be no reaping in Heaven. Look not at pride only as an unbecoming temper, nor at humility only as a decent virtue: for the one is death, and the other is life; the one is all hell, the other is all heaven. So much as you have of pride within you, you have of the fallen angels alive in you; so much as you have of true humility, so much you have of the Lamb of God within you. Could you see what every stirring of pride does to your soul, you would beg of everything you meet to tear the viper from you, though with the loss of a hand or an eye. Could you see what a sweet, divine, transforming power there is in humility, how it expels the poison of your nature, and makes room for the Spirit of God to live in you, you would rather wish to be the footstool of all the world than want the smallest degree of it." --Spirit of Prayer, Pt.II, p.73, Edition of Moreton, Canterbury, 1893.

Chapter 2--HUMILITY: THE SECRET OF REDEMPTION

"Have this mind in you which was also in Christ Jesus: who emptied Himself; taking the form of a servant; and humbled Himself; becoming obedient even unto death. Wherefore God also highly exalted Him. "Phil. 2: 5-9.

No tree can grow except on the root from which it sprang. Through all its existence it can only live with the life that was in the seed that gave it being. The full apprehension of this truth in its application to the first and the Second Adam cannot but help us greatly to understand both the need and the nature of the redemption there is in Jesus.

The Need.- When the Old Serpent, he who had been cast out from heaven for his pride, whose whole nature as devil was pride, spoke his words of temptation into the ear of Eve, these words carried with them the very poison of hell. And when she listened, and yielded her desire and her will to the prospect of being as God, knowing good and evil, the poison entered into her soul and blood and life, destroying forever that blessed humility and dependence upon God which would have been our everlasting happiness. And instead of this, her life and the life of the race that sprang from her became corrupted to its very root with that most terrible of all sins and all curses, the poison of Satan's own pride. All the wretchedness of which this world has been the scene, all its wars and bloodshed among the nations, all its selfishness and suffering, all its ambitions and jealousies, all its broken hearts and embittered lives, with all its daily unhappiness, have their origin in what this cursed, hellish pride, either our own, or that of others, has brought us. It is pride that made redemption needful; it is from our pride we need above everything to be redeemed. And our insight into the need of redemption will largely depend upon our knowledge of the terrible nature of the power that has entered our being.

No tree can grow except on the root from which it sprang. The power that Satan brought from hell, and cast into man's life, is working daily, hourly, with mighty power throughout the world. Men suffer from it; they fear and fight and flee it; and yet they know not whence it comes, whence it has its terrible supremacy. No wonder they do not know where or how it is to be overcome. Pride has its root and strength in a terrible spiritual power, outside of us as well as within us; as needful as it is that we confess and deplore it as our very own, is to know it in its Satanic origin. If this leads us to utter despair of ever conquering or casting it out, it will lead us all the sooner to that supernatural power in which alone our deliverance is to be found - the redemption of the Lamb of God. The hopeless struggle against the workings of self and pride within us may indeed become still more hopeless as we think of the power of darkness behind it all; the utter despair will fit us the better for realizing and accepting a power and a life outside of ourselves too, even the humility of heaven as brought down and brought nigh by the Lamb of God, to cast out Satan and his pride.

No tree can grow except on the root from which it sprang. Even as we need to look to the first Adam and his fall to know the power of the sin within us, we need to know well the Second Adam and His power to give within us a life of humility as real and abiding and overmastering as has been that of pride. We have our life from and in Christ, as truly, yea more truly, than from and in Adam. We are to walk "rooted in Him," "holding fast the Head from whom the whole body increaseth with the increase of God." The life of God which in the incarnation entered human nature, is the root in which we are to stand and grow; it is the same almighty power that worked there, and thence onward to the resurrection, which works daily in us. Our one need is to study and know and trust the life that has been revealed in Christ as the life that is now ours, and waits for our consent to gain possession and mastery of our whole being.

In this view it is of inconceivable importance that we should have right thoughts of what Christ is, of what really constitutes Him the Christ, and specially of what may be counted His chief characteristic, the root and essence of all His character as our Redeemer. There can be but one answer: it is His humility. What is the incarnation but His heavenly humility, His emptying Himself and becoming man? What is His life on earth but humility; His taking the form of a servant? And what is His atonement but humility? "He humbled Himself and became obedient unto death." And what is His ascension and His glory, but humility exalted to the throne and crowned with glory? "He humbled Himself, therefore God highly exalted Him." In heaven, where He was with the Father, in His birth, in His life, in His death, in His sitting on the throne, it is all, it is nothing but humility. Christ is the humility of God embodied in human nature; the Eternal Love humbling itself, clothing itself in the garb of meekness and gentleness, to win and serve and save us. As the love and condescension of God makes Him the benefactor and helper and servant of all, so Jesus of necessity was the Incarnate Humility. And so He is still in the midst of the throne, the meek and lowly Lamb of God.

If this be the root of the tree, its nature must be seen in every branch and leaf and fruit. If humility be the first, the all-including grace of the life of Jesus,- if humility be the secret of His atonement,-then the health and strength of our spiritual life will entirely depend upon our putting this grace first too, and making humility the chief thing we admire in Him, the chief thing we ask of Him, the one thing for. which we sacrifice all else. 1-See Note B (at end of this chapter)

Is it any wonder that the Christian life is so often feeble and fruitless, when the very root of the Christ life is neglected, is unknown? Is it any wonder that the joy of salvation is so little felt, when that in which Christ found it and brings it, is so little sought? Until a humility which will rest in nothing less than the end and death of self; which gives up all the honor of men as Jesus did, to seek the honor that comes from God alone; which absolutely makes and counts itself nothing, that God may be all, that the Lord alone may be exalted,-until such a humility be what we seek in Christ above our chief joy, and welcome at any price, there is very little hope of a religion that will conquer the world.

I cannot too earnestly plead with my reader, if possibly his attention has never yet been specially directed to the want there is of humility within him or around him, to pause and ask whether he sees much of the spirit of the meek and lowly Lamb of God in those who are called by His name. Let him consider how all want of love, all indifference to the needs, the feelings, the weakness of others; all sharp and hasty judgments and utterances, so often excused under the plea of being outright and honest; all manifestations of temper and touchiness and irritation; all feelings of bitterness and estrangement,have their root in nothing but pride, that ever seeks itself, and his eyes will be opened to see how a dark, shall I not say a devilish pride, creeps in almost everywhere, the assemblies of the saints not excepted. Let him begin to ask what would be the effect, if in himself and around him, if towards fellow saints and the world, believers were really permanently guided by the humility of Jesus; and let him say if the cry of our whole heart, night and day, ought not to be, Oh for the humility of Jesus in myself and all around me! Let him honestly fix his heart on his own lack of the humility which has been revealed in the likeness of Christ's life, and in the whole character of His redemption, and he will begin to feel as if he had never yet really known what Christ and His salvation is.

Believer! study the humility of Jesus. This is the secret, the hidden root of thy redemption. Sink down into it deeper day by day. Believe with thy whole heart that this Christ, whom God has given thee, even as His divine humility wrought the work for thee, will enter in to dwell and work within thee too, and make thee what the Father would have thee be.

Note B.-

"We need to know two things: 1. That our salvation consists wholly in being saved from ourselves, or that which we are by nature; 2. That in the whole nature of things nothing could be this salvation or saviour to us but such a humility of God as is beyond all expression. Hence the first unalterable term of the Saviour to fallen man: Except a man denies himself, he cannot be My disciple. Self is the whole evil of fallen nature; selfdenial is our capacity of being saved; humility is our saviour ... Self is the root, the branches, the tree, of all the evil of our fallen state. All the evils of fallen angels and men have their birth in the pride of self. On the other hand, all the virtues of the heavenly life are the virtues of humility. It is humility alone that makes the unpassable gulf between heaven and hell. What is then, or in what lies, the great struggle for eternal life? It all lies in the strife between pride and humility: pride and humility are the two master powers, the two kingdoms in strife for the eternal possession of man. There never was, nor ever will be, but one humility, and that is the one humility of Christ. Pride and self have the all of man, till man has his all from Christ. He therefore only fights the good fight whose strife is that the self-idolatrous nature which he hath from Adam may be brought to death by the supernatural humility of Christ brought to life in him."-W. Law, Address to the Clergy, p. 52. [I hope that this book of Law on the Holy Spirit may be issued by my publisher in the course of the year.]

Chapter 3 --HUMILITY IN THE LIFE OF JESUS

"I am in the midst of you as he that serveth." Luke 22: 27.

In the Gospel of John we have the inner life of our Lord laid open to us. Jesus speaks frequently of His relation to the Father, of the motives by which He is guided, of His consciousness of the power and spirit in which He acts. Though the word humble does not occur, we shall nowhere in Scripture see so clearly wherein His humility consisted. We have already said that this grace is in truth nothing but that simple consent of the creature to let God be all, in virtue of which it surrenders itself to His working alone. In Jesus we shall see how both as the Son of God in heaven, and as man upon earth, He took the place of entire subordination, and gave God the honor and the glory which is due to Him- And what He taught so often was made true to Himself: "He that humbleth him: shall be exalted." As it is written, "He humbled Himself, therefore God highly exalted Him."

Listen to the words in which our Lord speaks of His relation to the Father, and how unceasingly He uses the words not, and nothing, of Himself. The not I, in which Paul expresses his relation to Christ, is the very spirit of what Christ says of His relation the Father.

"The Son can do nothing of Himself" (John 5: 19).

"I can of My own self do nothing; My judgment is just, because I seek not Mine own will" (John 5: 30).

"I receive not glory from men" (John 5: 41).

"I am come not to do Mine own will" (John 6:38).

"My teaching is not Mine" (John 7:16)

"I am not come of Myself" (John 7:28)

"I do nothing of Myself" (John 8:28)

"I have not come of Myself, but He sent Me" (John 8: 42).

"I seek not Mine own glory" (John 8:50)

"The words that I say, I speak not from Myself" (John 14: 10).

"The word which ye hear is not Mine" (John 14: 24).

These words open to us the deepest roots of Christ's life and work. They tell us how it was that the Almighty God was able to work His mighty redemptive work through Him. They show what Christ counted the state of heart which became Him as the Son of the Father. They teach us what the essential nature and life is of that redemption which Christ accomplished and now communicates. It is this: He was nothing, that God might be all. He resigned Himself with His will and His powers entirely for the Father to work in Him. Of His own power, His own will, and His own glory, of His whole mission with all His works and His teaching,of all this He said, It is not I; I am nothing; I have given Myself to the Father to work; I am nothing, the Father is all.

This life of entire self-abnegation, of absolute submission and dependence upon the Father's will, Christ found to be one of perfect peace and joy. He lost nothing by giving all to God. God honored His trust, and did all for Him, and then exalted Him to His own right hand in glory. And because Christ had thus humbled Himself before God, and God was ever before Him, He found it possible to humble Himself before men too, and to be the Servant of all. His humility was simply the surrender of Himself to God, to allow Him to do in Him what He pleased, whatever men around might say of Him, or do to Him.

It is in this state of mind, in this spirit and disposition, that the redemption of Christ has its virtue and efficacy. It is to bring us to this disposition that we are made partakers of Christ. This is the true self-denial to which our Saviour calls us, the acknowledgment that self has nothing good in it, except as an empty vessel which God must fill, and that its claim to be or do anything may not for a moment be allowed. It is in this, above and before everything, in which the conformity to Jesus consists, the being and doing nothing of ourselves, that God may be all.

Here we have the root and nature of true humility. It is because this is not understood or sought after, that our humility is so superficial and so feeble. We must learn of Jesus, how He is meek and lowly of heart. He teaches us where true humility takes its rise and finds its strength-in the knowledge that it is God who worketh all in all, that our place is to yield to Him in perfect resignation and dependence, in full consent to be and to do nothing of ourselves. This is the life Christ came to reveal and to impart -a life to God that came through death to sin and self. If we feel that this life is too high for us and beyond our reach, it must but the more urge us to seek it in Him; it is the indwelling Christ who will live in us this life, meek and lowly. If we long for this, let us, meantime, above everything, seek the holy secret of the knowledge of the nature of God, as He every moment works all in all; the secret, of which all nature and every creature, and above all, every child of God, is to be the witness,-that it is nothing but a vessel, a channel, through which the living God can manifest the riches of His wisdom, power, and goodness. The root of all virtue and grace, of all faith and acceptable worship, is that we know that we have nothing but what we receive, and bow in deepest humility to wait upon God for it.

It was because this humility was not only a temporary sentiment, wakened up and brought into exercise when He thought of God, but the very spirit of His whole life, that Jesus was just as humble in His intercourse with men as with God. He felt Himself the Servant of God for the men whom God made and loved; as a natural consequence, He counted Himself the Servant of men, that through Him God might do

His work of love. He never for a moment thought of seeking His honor, or asserting His power to vindicate Himself. His whole spirit was that of a life yielded to God to work in. It is not until Christians study the humility of Jesus as the very essence of His redemption, as the very blessedness of the life of the Son of God, as the only true relation to the Father, and therefore as that which Jesus must give us if we are to have any part with Him, that the terrible lack of actual, heavenly, manifest humility will become a burden and a sorrow, and our ordinary religion be set aside to secure this, the first and the chief of the marks of the Christ within us.

Brother, are you clothed with humility? Ask your daily life. Ask Jesus. Ask your friends. Ask the world. And begin to praise God that there is opened up to you in Jesus a heavenly humility of which you have hardly known, and through which a heavenly blessedness you possibly have never yet tasted can come in to you.

Chapter 4--HUMILITY IN THE TEACHING OF JESUS

"Learn of Me, for I am meek and lowly of heart. "-Matt. xi. 29.
"Whosoever will be chief among you, let him be your servant, even as the Son of Man came to server." Matt.10:27.

We have seen humility in the life of Christ, as He laid open His heart to us: let us listen to His teaching. There we shall hear how He speaks of it, and how far He expects men, and specially His disciples, to be humble as He was. Let us carefully study the passages, which I can scarce do more than quote, to receive the full impression of how often and how earnestly He taught it: it may help us to realize what He asks of us.

I. Look at the commencement of His ministry. In the Beatitudes with which the Sermon on the Mount opens, He speaks:"Blessed are the poor in spirit; for theirs is the kingdom of heaven. Blessed are the meek; for they shall inherit the earth." The very first words of His proclamation of the kingdom of heaven reveal the open gate through which alone we enter. The poor, who have nothing in themselves, to them the kingdom comes. The meek,who seek nothing in themselves, theirs the earth shall be. The blessings of heaven and earth are for the lowly. For the heavenly and the earthly life, humility is the secret of blessing.

2. "Learn of Me; for I am meek and lowly of heart, and ye shall find rest for your souls."Jesus offers Himself as Teacher. He tells what the spirit both is, which we shall find Him as Teacher, and which we can learn receive from Him. Meekness and lowliness the one thing He offers us; in it we shall find perfect rest of soul. Humility is to be a salvation.

3. The disciples had been disputing who would be the greatest in the kingdom, and had agreed to ask the Master (Luke 9:46; Matt. 18:3). He set a child in their midst and said, "Whosoever shall humble himself as this little child, shall be exalted. " "Who the greatest in the kingdom of heaven?" The question is indeed a far-reaching one. What will be the chief distinction in the heavenly kingdom? The answer, none but Jesus would have given. The chief glory of heaven, the true heavenly-mindedness, the chief of the graces, is humility. "He that is least among you, the same shall be great. "

4. The sons of Zebedee had asked Jesus to sit on His right and left, the highest place in the kingdom. Jesus said it was not His to give, but the Father's, who would give it to those for whom it was prepared. They must not look or ask for it. Their thought must be of the cup and the baptism of humiliation. And then He added, "Whosoever will be chief among you, let him be your servant. Even as the Son of Man came to serve. " Humility, as it is the mark of Christ the heavenly, will be the

one standard of glory in heaven: the lowliest is the nearest to God. The primacy in the Church is promised to the humblest.

5. Speaking to the multitude and the disciples, of the Pharisees and their love of the chief seats, Christ said once again (Matt. 23:11), "He that is greatest among you shall be your servant." Humiliation is the only ladder to honor in God's kingdom.

6. On another occasion, in the house of a Pharisee, He spoke the parable of the guest who would be invited to come up higher (Luke 14:1-11), and added, "For whosoever exalteth himself shall be abased; and he that humbleth himself shall be exalted." The demand is inexorable; there is no other way. Self-abasement alone will be exalted.

7. After the parable of the Pharisee and the Publican, Christ spake again (Luke18: 14), "Everyone that exalteth himself shall be abased; and he that humbleth himself shall be exalted." In the temple and presence and worship of God, everything is worthless that is not pervaded by deep, true humility towards God and men.

8. After washing the disciples' feet, Jesus said (John 13:14), "If I then, the Lord and Master, have washed your feet, ye also ought to wash one another's feet." The authority of command, and example, every thought, either of obedience or conformity, make humility the first and most essential element of discipleship.

9. At the Holy Supper table, the disciples still disputed who should be greatest (Luke 22:26). Jesus said, "He that is greatest among you, let him be as the younger; and he that is chief, as he that doth serve. I am among you as he that serveth." The path in which Jesus walked, and which He opened up for us, the power and spirit in which He wrought out salvation, and to which He saves us, is ever the humility that makes me the servant of all.

How little this is preached. How little it is practised. How little the lack of it is felt or confessed. I do not say, how few attain to it, some recognizable measure of likeness to Jesus in His humility. But how few ever think, of making it a distinct object of continual desire or prayer. How little the world has seen it. How little has it been seen even in the inner circle of the Church.

"Whosoever will be chief among you, let him be your servant." Would God that it might be given us to believe that Jesus means this! We all know what the character of a faithful servant or slave implies. Devotion to the master's interests, thoughtful study and care to please him, delight in his prosperity and honor and happiness. There are servants on earth in whom these dispositions have been seen, and to whom the name of servant has never been anything but a glory. To how many of us has it not been a new joy in the Christian life to know that we may yield ourselves as servants, as slaves to God, and to find that His service is our highest liberty,-the liberty from sin and self? We need now to learn another lesson,-that Jesus calls us to be servants of one another, and that, as we accept it heartily, this service too will be a most blessed one, a new and fuller liberty too from sin and self. At first it may appear hard; this is only because of the pride which still counts itself something. If once we learn that to be nothing before God is the glory of the creature, the spirit of Jesus, the joy of heaven, we shall welcome with our whole heart the discipline we may have in serving even those who try to vex us. When our own heart is set upon this, the true sanctification, we shall study each word of Jesus on self-abasement with new zest, and no place will be too low, and no stooping too deep, and no service too mean or too long continued, if we may but share and prove the fellowship with Him who spake, "I am among you as he that serveth".

Brethren, here is the path to the higher life. Down, lower down! This was what Jesus ever said to the disciples who were thinking of being great in the kingdom, and of sitting on His right hand and His left. Seek not, ask not for exaltation; that is God's work. Look to it that you abase and humble yourselves, and take no place before God or man but that of servant; that is your work; let that be your one purpose and prayer. God is faithful. Just as water ever seeks and fills the lowest place, so the moment God finds the creature abased and empty, His glory and power flow in to exalt and to bless. He that humbleth himself-that must be our one care shall be exalted; that is God's care; by His mighty power and in His great love He will do it.

Men sometimes speak as if humility and meekness would rob us of what is noble and bold and manlike. Oh that all would believe that this is the nobility of the kingdom of heaven, that this is the royal spirit that the King of heaven displayed, that this is Godlike, to humble oneself, to become the servant of all! This is the path to the gladness and the glory of Christ's presence ever in us, His power ever resting on us. Jesus, the meek and lowly One, calls us to learn of Him the path to God. Let us study the words we have been reading, until our heart is filled with the thought: My one need is humility. And let us believe that what He shows, He gives; what He is, He imparts. As the meek and lowly One, He will come in and dwell in the longing heart.

Chapter 5--HUMILITY IN THE DISCIPLES OF JESUS

"Let him that is chief among you be as he that doth serve." -Luke 22:26.

We have studied humility in the person and teaching of Jesus; let us now look for it in the circle of His chosen companions---the twelve apostles. If, in the lack of it we find in them, the contrast between Christ and men is brought out more clearly, it will help us to appreciate the mighty change which Pentecost wrought in them, and prove how real our participation can be in the perfect triumph of Christ's humility over the pride Satan had breathed into man.

In the texts quoted from the teaching of Jesus, we have already seen what the occasions were on which the disciples had proved how entirely wanting they were in the grace of humility. Once, they had been disputing the way which of them should be the greatest Another time, the sons of Zebedee with their mother had asked for the first places--the seat on the right hand and the left. And, later on, at the Supper table on the last night, there was again a contention which should be accounted the greatest. Not that there were not moments when they indeed humbled themselves before their Lord. So it was with Peter when he cried out, "Depart from me, Lord, for I am a sinful man." So, too, with the disciples when they fell down and worshipped Him who had stilled the storm. But such occasional expressions of humility only bring out into stronger relief what was the habitual tone of their mind, as shown in the natural and spontaneous revelation given at other times of the place and the power of self. The study of the meaning of all this will teach us most important lessons.

First, How much there may be of earnest and active, religion while humility is still sadly wanting.- See it in the disciples. There was in them fervent attachment to Jesus. They had forsaken all for Him. The Father had revealed to them that He was the Christ of God. They believed in Him, they loved Him, they obeyed His commandments. They had forsaken all to follow Him. When others went back, they clave to Him. They were ready to die with Him. But deeper down than all this there was a dark power, of the existence and the hideousness of which they were hardly conscious, which had to be slain and cast out, ere they could be the witnesses of the power of Jesus to save. It is even so still. We may find professors and ministers, evangelists and workers, missionaries and teachers, in whom the gifts of the Spirit are many and manifest, and who are the channels of blessing to multitudes, but of whom, when the testing time comes, or closer intercourse gives fuller knowledge, it is only too painfully manifest that the grace of humility, as an abiding characteristic, is scarce to be seen. All tends to confirm the lesson that humility is one of the chief and the highest graces; one of the most difficult of attainment; one to which our first and chiefest efforts ought to be directed; one that only comes in power, when the fullness of the Spirit makes us partakers of the indwelling Christ, and He lives within us.

Second, How impotent all external teaching and all personal effort is, to conquer pride or give the meek and lowly heart.-For three years the disciples had been in the training school of Jesus. He had told them what the chief lesson was He wished to teach them: "Learn of Me, for I am meek and lowly in heart." Time after time He had spoken to them, to the Pharisees, to the multitude, of humility as the only path to the glory of God.He had not only lived before them as the Lamb of God in His divine humility, He had more than once unfolded to them the inmost secret of His life: "The Son of Man came not to be served, but to serve"; "I am among you as one that serveth." He had washed their feet, and told them they were to follow His example. And yet all had availed but little. At the Holy Supper there was still the contention as to who should be greatest. They had doubtless often tried to learn His lessons, and firmly resolved not again to grieve Him. But all in vain. To teach them and us the much needed lesson, that no outward instruction,not even of Christ Himself; no argument however convincing; no sense of the beauty of humility, however deep; no personal resolve or effort, however sincere and earnest,-can cast out the devil of pride. When Satan casts out Satan, it is only to enter afresh in a mightier, though more hidden power. Nothing can avail but this, that the new nature in its divine humility be revealed in power to take the place of the old, to become as truly our very nature as that ever was.

Third, It is only by the indwelling of Christ in His divine humility that we become truly humble.We have our pride from another, from Adam; we must have our humility from Another too. Pride is ours, and rules in us with such terrible power, because it is ourself, our very nature. Humility must be ours in the same way; it must be our very self, our very nature. As natural and easy as it has been to be proud, it must be, it will be, to be humble. The promise is, "Where," even in the heart, "sin abounded, grace did abound more exceedingly." All Christ's teaching of His disciples, and all their vain efforts, were the needful preparation for His entering into them in divine power, to give and be in them what He had taught them to desire. In His death He destroyed the power of the devil, He put away sin, and effected an everlasting redemption. In His resurrection He received from the Father an entirely new life, the life of man in the power of God, capable of being communicated to men, and entering and renewing and filling their lives with His divine power. In His ascension He received the Spirit of the Father, through whom He might do what He could not do while upon earth, make Himself one with those He loved, actually live their life for them, so that they could live before the Father in a humility like His, because it was Himself who lived and breathed in them. And on Pentecost He came and took possession. The work of preparation and conviction, the awakening of desire and hope which His teaching had effected,was perfected by the mighty change that Pentecost wrought. And the lives and the epistles of James and Peter and John bear witness that all was changed, and that the spirit of the meek and suffering Jesus had indeed possession of them.

What shall we say to these things? Among my readers I am sure there is more than one class. There may be some who have never yet thought very specially of the matter, and cannot at once realize its immense importance as a life question for the Church and its every member. There are others who have felt condemned for their shortcomings, and have put forth very earnest efforts, only to fail and be discouraged. Others, again, may be able to give joyful testimony of spiritual blessing and power, and yet there has never been the needed conviction of what those around them still see as wanting. And still others may be able to witness that in regard to this grace too the Lord has given deliverance and victory, while He has taught them how much they still need and may expect out of the fullness of Jesus. To whichever class we belong, may I urge the pressing need there is for our all seeking a still deeper conviction of the unique place that humility holds in the religion of Christ, and the utter impossibility of the Church or the believer being what Christ would have them be, as long as His humility is not recognized as His chief glory, His first command, and our highest blessedness. Let us consider deeply how far the disciples were advanced while this grace was still so terribly lacking, and let us pray to God that other gifts may not so satisfy us, that we never grasp the fact that the absence of this grace is the secret cause why the power of God cannot do its mighty work. It is only where we, like the Son, truly know and show that we can do nothing of ourselves, that God will do all.

It is when the truth of an indwelling Christ takes the place it claims in the experience of believers, that the Church will put on her beautiful garments and humility be seen in her teachers and members as the beauty of holiness.

Chapter 6 --HUMILITY IN DAILY LIFE

"He that loveth not his brother whom he hath seen, how can he love God whom he hath not seen?"-1 John 4:20.

What a solemn thought, that our love to God will be measured by our everyday intercourse with men and the love it displays; and that our love to God will be found to be a delusion, except was its truth is proved in standing the test of daily life with our fellowmen. It is even so with our humility. It is easy to think we humble ourselves before God: humility towards men will be the only sufficient proof that our humility before God is real; that humility has taken up its abode in us; and become our very nature; that we actually, like Christ, have made ourselves of no reputation. When in the presence of God lowliness of heart has become, not a posture we pray to Him, but the very spirit of our life, it will manifest itself in all our bearing towards our brethren. The lesson is one of deep import: the only humility that is really ours is not that which we try to show before God in prayer, but that which we carry with us, and carry out, in our ordinary conduct; the insignficances of daily life are the importances and the tests of eternity, because they prove what really is the spirit that possesses us. It is in our most unguarded moments that we really show and see what we are. To know the humble man, to know how the humble man behaves, you must follow him in the common course of daily life.

Is not this what Jesus taught? It was when the disciples disputed who should be greatest; when He saw how the Pharisees loved the chief place at feasts and the chief seats in the synagogues; when He had given them the example of washing their feet,- that He taught His lessons of humility. Humility before God is nothing if not proved in humility before men.

It is even so in the teaching of Paul. To the Romans He writes: "In honor preferring one another"; "Set not your mind on high things, but condescend to those that are lowly." "Be not wise in your own conceit." To the Corinthians: "Love," and there is no love without humility as its root, "vaunteth not itself, is not puffed up, seeketh not its own, is not provoked." To the Galatians: "Through love be servants one of another. Let us not be desirous of vainglory, provoking one another, envying one another." To the Ephesians, immediately after the three wonderful chapters on the heavenly life: "Therefore, walk with all lowliness and meekness, with long-suffering, forbearing one another in love"; "Giving thanks always, subjecting yourselves one to another in the fear of Christ." To the Philippians: "Doing nothing through faction or vainglory, but in lowliness of mind, each counting other better than himself. Have the mind in you which was also in Christ Jesus, who emptied Himself, taking the form of a servant, and humbled Himself."

And to the Colossians: "Put on a heart of compassion, kindness, humility, meekness, long-suffering, forebearing one another, and forgiving each other, even as the Lord forgave you." It is in our relation to one another, in our treatment of one another, that the true lowliness of mind and the heart of humility are to be seen. Our humility before God has no value, but as it prepares us to reveal the humility of Jesus to our fellow-men. Let us study humility in daily life in the light of these words.

The humble man seeks at all times to act up to the rule, "In honor preferring one another; Servants one of another; Each counting others better than himself Subjecting yourselves one to another." The question is often asked, how we can count others better than ourselves, when we see that they are far below us in wisdom and in holiness, in natural gifts, or in grace received. The question proves at once how little we understand what real lowliness of mind is. True humility comes when, in the, light of God, we have seen ourselves to be nothing, have consented to part with and cast away self, to let God be all. The soul that has done this, sand can say, So have I lost myself in finding Thee, no longer compares itself with others. It has given up forever every thought of self in God's presence; it meets its fellow-men as one who is nothing, and seeks nothing for itself; who is a servant of God, and for His sake a servant of all. A faithful servant may be wiser than the master, and yet retain the true spirit and posture of the servant. The humble man looks upon every, the feeblest and unworthiest, child of God, and honors him and prefers him in honor as the son of a King. The spirit of Him who washed the disciples' feet, makes it a joy to us to be indeed the least, to be servants one of another.

The humble man feels no jealousy-or envy. He can praise God when others are preferred and blessed before him. He can bear to hear others praised and himself forgotten, because in God's presence he has learnt to say with Paul, "I am nothing." He has received the spirit of Jesus, who pleased not Himself, and sought not His own honor, as the spirit of his life.

Amid what are considered the temptations to impatience and touchiness, to hard thoughts and sharp words, which come from the failings and sins of fellow-Christians, the humble man carries the oftrepeated injunction in his heart, and shows it in his life, "Forbearing one another, and forgiving one another, even as the Lord forgave you." He has learnt that in putting on the Lord Jesus he has put on the heart of compassion, kindness, humility, meekness, and long-suffering. Jesus has taken the place of self, and it is not an impossibility to forgive as Jesus forgave. His humility does not consist merely in thoughts or words of selfdepreciation, but, as Paul puts it, in "a heart of humility," encompassed by compassion and kindness, meekness and longsuffering,-the sweet and lowly gentleness recognized as the mark of the Lamb of God.

In striving after the higher experiences of the Christian life, the believer is often in danger of aiming at and rejoicing in what one might call the more human, the manly, virtues, such as boldness, joy, contempt of the world, zeal, self-sacrifice,-even the old Stoics taught and practised these,-while the deeper and gentler, the diviner and more heavenly graces, those which Jesus first taught upon earth, because He brought them from heaven; those which are more distinctly connected with His cross and the death of self,-poverty of spirit, meekness, humility, lowliness,-are scarcely thought of or valued. Therefore, let us put on a heart of compassion, kindness, humility, meekness,long-suffering; and let us prove our Christlikeness, not only in our zeal for saving the lost, but before all in our intercourse with the brethren, forbearing and forgiving one another, even as the Lord forgave us.

Fellow-Christians, do let us study the Bible portrait of the humble man. And let us ask our brethren, and ask the world, whether they recognize in us the likeness to the original. Let us be content with nothing less than taking each of these texts as the promise of what God will work in us, as the revelation in words of what the Spirit of Jesus will give as a birth within us. And let each failure and shortcoming simply urge us to turn humbly and meekly to the meek and lowly Lamb of God, in the assurance that where He is enthroned in the heart, His humility and gentleness will be one of the streams of living water that flow from within us. 1

(1- I knew Jesus, and He was very precious to my soul: but I found something in me that would not keep sweet and patient and kind. I did what I could to keep it down, but it was there. I besought Jesus to do something for me, and when I gave Him my will, He came to my heart, and took out all that would not be sweet, all that would not be kind, all that would not be patient, and then He shut the door."-George Foxe)

Once again I repeat what I have said before. I feel deeply that we have very little conception of what the Church suffers from the lack of this divine humility,-the nothingness that makes room for God to prove His power. It is not long since a Christian, of an humble, loving spirit, acquainted with not a few mission stations of various societies, expressed his deep sorrow that in some cases the spirit of love and forbearance was sadly lacking. Men and women, who in Europe could each choose their own circle of friends, brought close together with others of uncongenial minds, find it hard to bear, and to love, and to keep the unity of the Spirit in the bond of peace. And those who should have been fellow-helpers of each other's joy, became a hindrance and a weariness. And all for the one reason, the lack of the humility which counts itself nothing, which rejoices in becoming and being counted the least, and only seeks, like Jesus, to be the servant, the helper and comforter of others, even the lowest and unworthiest.

And whence comes it that men who have joyfully given up themselves for Christ, find it so hard to give up themselves for their brethren? Is not the blame with the Church? It has so little taught its sons that the humility of Christ is the first of the virtues, the best of all the graces and powers of the Spirit. It has so little proved that a Christlike humility is what it, like Christ, places and preaches first, as what is in very deed needed, and possible too. But let us not be discouraged. Let the discovery of the lack of this grace stir us to larger expectation from God. Let us look upon every brother who tries or vexes us, as God's means of grace, God's instrument for our purification, for our exercise of the humility Jesus our Life breathes within us. And let us have such faith in the All of God, and the nothing of self, that, as nothing in our own eyes, we may, in God's power, only seek to serve one another in love.

Chapter 7--HUMILITY AND HOLINESS

"Which say, Stand by thyself;-,for I am holier than thou. " -Isa. 65: 5.
We speak of the Holiness movement in our times, and praise God for
it. We hear a great deal of seekers after holiness and professors of
holiness, of holiness teaching and holiness meetings. The blessed truths
of holiness in Christ, and holiness by faith, are being emphasized as
never before. The great test of whether the holiness we profess to seek
or to attain, is truth and life, will be whether it be manifest in the
increasing humility it produces. In the creature, humility is the one
thing needed to allow God's holiness to dwell in him and shine through
him. In Jesus, the Holy One of God who makes us holy, a divine
humility was the secret of His life and His death and His exaltation; the
one infallible test of our holiness will be the humility before God and
men which marks us. Humility is the bloom and the beauty of holiness.
The chief mark of counterfeit holiness is its lack of humility. Every
seeker after holiness needs to be on his guard, lest unconsciously what
was begun in the spirit be perfected in the flesh, and pride creep in
where its presence is least expected. Two men went up into the temple
to pray: the one a Pharisee, the other a publican. There is no place or
position so sacred but the Pharisee can enter there. Pride can lift its
head in the very temple of God, and make His worship the scene of its
self exaltation. Since the time Christ so exposed his pride, the Pharisee
has put on the garb of the publican, and the confessor of deep
sinfulness equally with the professor of the highest holiness, must be
on the watch. Just when We are most anxious to have our heart the
temple of God, we shall find the two men coming up to pray. And the
publican will find that his danger is not from the Pharisee beside him,
who despises him, but the Pharisee within who commends and exalts.
In God's temple, when we think we are in the holiest of all, in the
presence of His holiness, let us beware of pride. "Now there was a day
when the sons of God came to present themselves before the Lord, and
Satan came also among them."

"God, I thank thee, I am not as the rest of men, or even as this
publican." It is in that which is just cause for thanksgiving, it is in the
very thanksgiving which we render to God, it may be in the very
confession that God has done it all, that self finds its cause of
complacency. Yes, even when in the temple the language of penitence
and trust in God's mercy alone is heard, the Pharisee may take up the
note of praise, and in thanking God be congratulating himself. Pride
can clothe itself in the garments of praise or of penitence. Even though
the words, "I am not as the rest of men" are rejected and condemned,
their spirit may too often be found in our feelings and language towards
our fellowworshippers and fellow-men. Would you know if this really

is so, just listen to the way in which Churches and Christians often speak of one another. How little of the meekness and gentleness of Jesus is to be seen. It is so little remembered that deep humility must be the keynote of what the servants of Jesus say of themselves or each other. Is there not many a Church or assembly of the saints, many a mission or convention, many a society or committee, even many a mission away in heathendom, where the harmony has been disturbed and the work of God hindered, because men who are counted saints have proved in touchiness and haste and impatience, in self-defense and selfassertion, in sharp judgments and unkind words, that they did not each reckon others better than themselves, and that their holiness has but little in it of the meekness of the saints?l In their spiritual history men may have had times of great humbling and brokenness, but what a different thing this is from being clothed with humility, from having an humble spirit, from having that lowliness of mind in which each counts himself the servant of others, and so shows forth the very mind which was also in Jesus Christ.

"Stand by; for I am holier than thou!" What a parody on holiness! Jesus the Holy One is the humble One: the holiest will ever be the humblest. There is none holy but God: we have as much of holiness as we have of God. And according to what we have of God will be our real humility, because humility is nothing but the disappearance of self in the vision that God is all. The holiest will be the humblest. Alas! though the bare-faced boasting Jew of the days of Isaiah is not often to be found, even our manners have taught us not to speak thus, how often his spirit is still seen, whether in the treatment of fellowsaints or of the children of the world. In the spirit in which opinions are given, and work is undertaken, and faults are exposed, how often, though the garb be that of the publican, the voice is still that of the Pharisee: "Oh God, I thank Thee that I am not as other men."

And is there, then, such humility to be found, that men shall indeed still count themselves "less than the least of all saints," the servants of all? There is. "Love vaunteth not itself, is not puffed up, seeketh not its own." Where the spirit of love is shed abroad in the heart, where the divine nature comes to a full birth where Christ the meek and lowly Lamb of God is truly formed within, there is given the power of a perfect love that forgets itself and finds its blessedness in blessing others, in bearing with them and honoring them, however feeble they be. Where this love enters, there God enters. And where God has entered in His power, and reveals Himself as All, there the creature becomes nothing. And where the creature becomes nothing before God; it cannot be anything but humble towards the fellow-creature. The presence of God becomes not a thing of times and seasons, but the covering under which the soul ever dwells, and its deep abasement before God becomes the holy place of His presence whence all its words and works proceed.

May God teach us that our thoughts and words and feelings concerning our fellowmen are His test of our humility towards Him, and that our humility before Him is the only power that can enable us to be always humble with our fellow-men. Our humility must be the life of Christ, the Lamb of God, within us.

Let all teachers of holiness, whether in the pulpit or on the platform, and all seekers after holiness, whether in the closet or the convention, take warning. There is no pride so dangerous, because none so subtle and insidious, as the pride of holiness. It is not that a man ever says, or even thinks, "Stand by; I am holier than thou." No, indeed, the thought would be regarded with abhorrence. But there grows up, all unconsciously, a hidden habit of soul, which feels complacency its attainments, and cannot help seeing how far it is in advance of others. It can be recognized, not always in any special selfassertion or self-laudation, but simply in the absence of that deep self-abasement which cannot but be the mark of the soul that has seen the glory of God (Job 42: 5, 6; Isa.6: 5). It reveals itself, not only in words or thoughts, but in a tone, a way of speaking of others, in which those who have the gift of spiritual discernment cannot but recognize the power of self. Even the world with its keen eyes notices it, and points to it as a proof that the profession of a heavenly life does not bear any specially heavenly fruits. O brethren! let us beware. Unless we make, with each advance in what we think holiness, the increase of humility our study, we may find that we have been delighting in beautiful thoughts and feelings, in solemn acts of consecration and faith,while the only sure mark of the presence of God, the disappearance of self, was all the time wanting. Come and let us flee to Jesus, and hide ourselves in Him until we be clothed upon with His humility. That alone is our holiness.

Chapter 8--HUMILITY AND SIN

"Sinners, of whom I am chief."-1 Tim.1:15

Humility is often identified with penitence and contrition. As a consequence, there appears to be no way of fostering humility but by keeping the soul occupied with its sin. We have learned, I think, that humility is something else and something more. We have seen in the teaching of our Lord Jesus and the Epistles how often the virtue is inculcated without any reference to sin. In the very nature of things, in the whole relation of the creature to the Creator, in the life of Jesus as He lived it and imparts it to us, humility is the very essence of holiness as of blessedness. It is the displacement of self by the enthronement of God. Where God is all, self is nothing.

But though it is this aspect of the truth I have felt it specially needful to press, I need scarce say what new depth and intensityman's sin and God's grace give to the humility of the saints. We have only to look at a man like the Apostle Paul, to see how, through his life as a ransomed and a holy man, the deep consciousness of having been a sinner lives inextinguishably. We all know the passages in which he refers to his life as a persecutor and blasphemer. "I am the least of the apostles, that am not worthy to be called an apostle, because I persecuted the Church of God ...I labored more abundantly than they all; yet not I, but the grace of God which was with me" (I Cor. 15: 9,10). "Unto me, who am less than the least of all saints, was this grace given, to preach to the heathen" (Eph.3: 8). "I was before a blasphemer, and a persecutor, and injurious; howbeit I obtained mercy, because I did it ignorantly in unbelief ...Christ Jesus came into the world to save sinners, of whom I am chief" (1 Tim. 1. 13, 15). God's grace had saved him; God remembered his sins no more for ever; but never, never could he forget how terribly he had sinned. The more he rejoiced in God's salvation, and the more his experience of God's grace filled him with joy unspeakable, the clearer was his consciousness that he was a saved sinner, and that salvation had no meaning or sweetness except as the sense of his being a sinner made it precious and real to him. Never for a moment could he forget that it was a sinner God had taken up in His arms and crowned with His love.

The texts we have just quoted are often appealed to as Paul's confession of daily sinning. One has only to read them carefully in their connection, to see how little this is the case. They have a far deeper meaning, they refer to that which lasts throughout eternity, and which will give its deep undertone of amazement and adoration to the humility with which the ransomed bow before the throne, as those who have been washed from their sins in the blood of the Lamb.Never, never, even in, glory, can they be other than ransomed sinners; never for a moment in this life can God's child live in the full light of His love, but as he feels that the sin, out of which he has been saved, is his one only right and title to all that grace has promised to do. The humility with which first he came as a sinner, acquires a new meaning when he learns how it becomes him as a creature. And then ever again, the humility, in which he was born as a creature, has its deepest, richest tones of adoration, in the memory of what it is to be a monument of God's wondrous redeeming love.

The true import of what these expressions of St. Paul teach us comes out all the more strongly when we notice the remarkable fact that, through his whole Christian course, we never find from his pen, even in those epistles in which we have the most intensely personal unbosomings, anything like confession of sin. Nowhere is there any mention of shortcoming or defect, nowhere any suggestion to his readers that he has failed in duty, or sinned against the law of perfect love. On the contrary, there are passages not a few in which he vindicates himself in language that means nothing if it does not appeal to a faultless life before God and men. "Ye are witnesses, and God also, how holily, and righteously, and unblameably we behaved ourselves toward you" (1 Thess.2:10). "Our glorying is this, this testimony of our conscience, that in holiness and sincerity of God we .behaved ourselves in the world, and more abundantly to you ward" (2 Cor.1:12). This is not an ideal or an aspiration; it is an appeal to what his actual life had been. However we may account for this absence of confession of sin, all will admit that it must point to a life in the power of the Holy Ghost, such as is but seldom realized or expected in these our days.

The point which I wish to emphasize is this-that the very fact of the absence of such confession of sinning only gives the more force to the truth that it is not in daily sinning that the secret of the deeper humility will be found, but in the habitual, never for a moment to be forgotten position, which just the more abundant grace will keep more distinctly alive, that our only place,, the only place of blessing, our one abiding position before God, must be that of those whose highest joy it is to confess that they are sinners saved by grace.

With Paul's deep remembrance of having sinned so terribly in the past, ere grace had met him, and the consciousness of being kept from present sinning, there was ever coupled the abiding remembrance of the dark hidden power of sin ever ready to come in, and only kept out by the presence and power of the indwelling Christ. "In me, that is, in my flesh, dwelleth no good thing;" - these words of Rom. 7 describe the flesh as it is to the end. The glorious deliverance of Rom.8 - "The law of the Spirit of life in Christ Jesus hath now made me free from the law of sin, which once led me captive" - is neither the annihilation nor the sanctification of the flesh, but a continuous victory given by the Spirit as He mortifies the deeds of the body. As health expels disease, and light swallows up darkness, and life conquers death, the indwelling of Christ through the Spirit is the health and light and life of the soul. But with this, the conviction of helplessness and danger ever tempers the faith in the momentary and unbroken action of the Holy Spirit into that chastened sense of dependence which makes the highest faith and joy the handmaids of a humility that only lives by the grace of God.

The three passages above quoted all show that it was the wonderful grace bestowed upon Paul, and of which he felt the need every moment, that humbled him so deeply. The grace of God that was with him, and enabled him to labor more abundantly than they all; the grace to preach to the heathen the unsearchable riches of Christ; the grace that was exceeding abundant with faith and love which is in Christ Jesus, it was this grace of which it is the very nature and glory that it is for sinners, that kept the consciousness of his having once sinned, and being liable to sin, so intensely alive. "Where sin abounded, grace did abound more exceedingly." This reveals how the very essence of grace is to deal with and take away sin, and how it must ever be the more abundant the experience of grace, the more intense the consciousness of being a sinner. It is not sin, but God's grace showing a man and ever reminding him what a sinner he was, that, will keep him truly humble. It is not sin, but grace, that will make me indeed know myself a sinner, and make the sinner's place of deepest self-abasement the place I never leave.

I fear that there are not a few who, by strong expressions of self-condemnation and self-denunciation, have sought to humble themselves, and have to confess with sorrow that a humble spirit, a "heart of humility," with its accompaniments of kindness and compassion, of meekness and forbearance, is still as far off as ever. Being occupied with self, even amid the deepest self-abhorrence, can never free us from self. It is the revelation of God, not only by the law condemning sin but by His grace delivering from it, that will make us humble. The law may break the heart with fear; it is only grace that works that sweet humility which becomes a joy to the soul as its second nature. It was the revelation of God in His holiness, drawing nigh to make Himself known in His grace, that made Abraham and Jacob, Job and Isaiah, bow so low. It is the soul in which God the Creator, as the All of the creature in its nothingness, God the Redeemer in His grace, as the All of the sinner in his sinfulness, is waited for and trusted and worshipped, that will find itself so filled with His presence, that there will be no place for self. So alone can the promise be fulfilled: "The haughtiness of man shall be brought low, and the Lord alone be exalted in that day."

It is the sinner dwelling in the full light of God's holy, redeeming love, in the experience of that full indwelling of divine love, which comes through Christ and the Holy Spirit, who cannot but be humble. Not to be occupied with thy sin, but to be occupied with God, brings deliverance from self.

Chapter 9 -- HUMILITY AND FAITH

"How can ye believe, which receive glory from one another, and the glory that cometh from the only God ye seek not?" John 5: 44.

In an address I lately heard, the speaker said that the blessings of the higher Christian life were often like the objects exposed in a shop window,-one could see them clearly and yet could not reach them. If told to stretch out his hand and take, a man would answer, I cannot; there is a thick pane of plate-glass between me and them. And even so Christians may see clearly the blessed promises of perfect peace and rest, of overflowing love and joy, of abiding communion and fruitfulness, and yet feel that there was something between hindering the true possession. And what might that be? Nothing but pride. The promises made to faith are so free and sure; the invitations and encouragements so strong; the mighty power of God on which it may count is so near and free,-that it can only be something that hinders faith that hinders the blessing being ours. In our text Jesus discovers to us that it is indeed pride that makes faith impossible. "How can ye believe, which receive glory from one another?" As we see how in their very nature pride and faith are irreconcilably at variance, we shall learn that faith and humility are at root one, and that we never can have more of true faith than we have of true humility; we shall see that we may indeed have strong intellectual conviction and assurance of the truth while pride is kept in the heart, but that it makes the living faith, which has power with God, an impossibility.

We need only think for a moment what faith is. Is it not the confession of nothingness and helplessness, the surrender and the waiting to let God work? Is it not in itself the most humbling thing there can be, the acceptance of our place as dependents,who can claim or get or do nothing but what grace bestows?! Humility is 'simply the disposition which prepares the soul for living on trust. And every, even the most secret breathing of pride, in self-seeking, self-will, selfconfidence, or self exaltation, is just the strengthening of that self which cannot enter the kingdom, or possess the things of the kingdom, because it refuses to allow God to be what He is and must be there-- the All in All.

Faith is the organ or sense for the perception and apprehension of the heavenly world and its blessings. Faith seeks .the glory that comes from God, that only comes where God is All. As long as we take glory from one another, as long as ever we seek and love and jealously guard the glory of this life, the honor and reputation that comes from men, we do not seek, and cannot receive the glory that comes from God. Pride renders faith impossible. Salvation comes through a cross and a crucified Christ. Salvation is the fellowship with the crucified Christ in the Spirit of His cross. Salvation is union with and delight in, salvation is participation in, the humility of Jesus. Is it wonder that our faith is so feeble when pride still reigns so much, and we have scarce learnt even to long or pray for humility as the most needful and blessed part of salvation?

Humility and faith are more nearly allied in Scripture than many know. See it in the life of Christ. There are two cases in which He spoke of a great faith. Had not the centurion, at whose faith He marvelled, saying, "I have not found so great faith, no, not in Israel !" spoken, "I am not worthy that Thou shouldst come under my roof"? And had not the mother to whom He spoke, "O woman,great is thy faith!" accepted the name of dog, and said, "Yea, Lord, yet the dogs eat of the crumbs'? It is the humility that brings a soul to be nothing before God, that also removes every hindrance to faith, and makes it only fear lest it should dishonor Him by not trusting Him wholly.

Brother, have we not here the cause of failure in the pursuit of holiness? Is it not this, though we knew it not, that made our consecration and our faith so superficial and so short-lived? We had no idea to what an extent pride and self were still secretly working within us, and how alone God by His incoming and His mighty power could cast them out. We understood not how nothing but the new and divine nature, taking entirely the place of the old self, could make us really humble. We knew not that absolute, unceasing, universal humility must be the rootdisposition of every prayer and every approach to God as well as of every dealing with man; and that we might as well attempt to see without eyes, or live without breath, as believe or draw nigh to God or dwell in His love, without an all-prevading humility and lowliness of heart.

Brother, have we not been making a mistake in taking so much trouble to believe, while all the time there was the old self in its pride seeking to possess itself of God's blessing and riches? No wonder we could not believe. Let us change our course. Let us seek first of all to humble ourselves under the mighty hand of God: He will exalt us. The cross, and the death, and the grave, into which Jesus humbled Himself, were His path to the glory of God. And they are our path. Let our one desire and our fervent prayer be, to be humbled with Him and like Him; let us accept gladly whatever can humble us before God or men;-this alone is the path to the glory of God.

You perhaps feel inclined to ask a question. I have spoken of some who have blessed experiences, or are the means of bringing blessing to others, and yet are lacking in humility. You ask whether these do not prove that they have true, even strong faith, though they show too clearly that they still seek too much the honor that cometh from men. There is more than one answer can be given. But the principal answer in our present connection is this: They indeed have a measure of faith, in proportion to which, with the special gifts bestowed upon them, is the blessing they bring to others. But in that very blessing the work of their faith is hindered, through the lack of humility. The blessing is often superficial or transitory, just because they are not the nothing that opens the way for God to be all. A deeper humility would without doubt bring a deeper and fuller blessing. The Holy Spirit not only working in them as a Spirit of power, but dwelling in them in the fullness of His grace, and specially that of humility, would through them communicate Himself to these converts for a life of power and holiness and steadfastness now all too little seen.

"How can ye believe, which receive glory from one another?" Brother! nothing can cure you of the desire of receiving glory from men, or of the sensitiveness and pain and anger which come when it is not given, but giving yourself to seek only the glory that comes from God. Let the glory of the All-glorious God be everything to you. You will be freed from the glory of men and of self, and be content and glad to be nothing. Out of this nothingness you will grow strong in faith, giving glory to God, and you will find that the deeper you sink in humility before Him, the nearer He is to fulfill the every desire of your Faith.

Chapter 10- HUMILITY AND DEATH TO SELF

"He humbled Himself and became obedient unto death." -Phil.2: 8.

Humility is the path to death, because in death it gives the highest proof of its perfection. Humility is the blossom of which death to self, is the ,perfect. fruit. Jesus humbled Himself unto death, and opened the path in which we too must walk. As there was no way for Him to prove His surrender to God to the very uttermost, or to give up and rise out of our human nature to the glory of the Father but through death, so with us too. Humility must lead us to die to self: so we prove how wholly we have given ourselves up to it and to God; so alone we are freed from fallen nature, and find the path that leads to life in God, to that full birth of the new nature, of which humility is the breath and the joy.

We have spoken of what Jesus did for His disciples when He communicated His resurrection life to them, when in the descent of the Holy Spirit He, the glorified and enthroned Meekness, actually came from heaven Himself to dwell in them. He won the power to do this through death: in its inmost nature the life He imparted was a life out of death, a life that had been surrendered to death, and been won through death. He who came to dwell in them was Himself One who had been dead and now lives for evermore. His life, His person, His presence, bears the marks of death, of being a life begotten out of death. That life in His disciples ever bears the deathmarks too; it is only as the Spirit of the death, of the dying One, dwells and works in the soul, that the power of His life can be known. The first and chief of the marks of the dying of the Lord Jesus, of the death-marks that show the true follower of Jesus, is humility. For these two reasons: Only humility leads to perfect death; Only death perfects humility. Humility and death are in their very nature one: humility is the bud; in death the fruit is ripened to perfection.

Humility leads to perfect death. Humility means the giving up of self and the taking of the place of perfect nothingness before God. Jesus humbled Himself, and became obedient unto death. In death He gave the highest, the perfect proof of having given up His will to the will of God. In death He gave up His self, with its natural reluctance to drink the cup; He gave up the life He had in union with our human nature; He died to self, and the sin that tempted Him; so, as man, He entered into the perfect life of God. If it had not been for His boundless humility, counting Himself as nothing except as a servant to do and suffer the will of God, He never would have died.

This gives us the answer to the question so often asked, and of which the meaning is so seldom clearly apprehended: How can I die to self? The death to self is not your work, it is God's work. In Christ you are dead to sin the life there is in you has gone through the process of death and resurrection; you may be sure you are indeed dead to sin. But the full manifestation of the power of this death in your disposition and conduct. depends upon the measure in which the Holy Spirit imparts the power of the death of Christ And here it is that the teaching is needed: if you would enter into full fellowship with Christ in His death, and know the full deliverance from self, humble yourself. This is your one duty. Place yourself before God in your utter helplessness; consent heartily to the fact of your impotence to slay or make alive yourself; sink down into your own nothingness, in the spirit of meek and patient and trustful surrender to God. Accept every humiliation,look upon every fellow-man who tries or vexes you, as a means of grace to humble you. Use every opportunity of humbling' yourself before your fellow-men as a help to abide humble before God. God will accept such humbling of yourself as the proof that your whole heart desires it, as the very best prayer for it, as your preparation for His mighty work of grace, when, by the mighty strengthening of His Holy Spirit, He reveals Christ fully in you, so that He, in His form of a servant, is truly formed in you, and dwells in your heart. It is the path of humility which leads to perfect death, the full and perfect experience that we are dead in Christ.

Then follows: Only this death leads to perfect humility. Oh, beware of the mistake so many make, who would fain be humble, but are afraid to be too humble. They have so many qualifications and limitations, so many reasonings and questionings, as to what true humility is to be and to do, that they never unreservedly yield themselves to it. Beware of this. Humble yourself unto the death. It is in the death to self that humility is perfected. Be sure that at the root of all real experience of more grace, of all true advance in consecration, of all actually increasing conformity to the likeness of Jesus, there must be a deadness to self that proves itself to God and men in our dispositions and habits. It is sadly possible to speak of the death-life and the Spirit-walk, while even the tenderest love cannot but see how much there is of self. The death to self has no surer deathmark than a humility which makes itself of no reputation, which empties out itself, and takes the form of a servant. It is possible to speak much and honestly of fellowship with a despised and rejected Jesus, and of bearing His cross, while the meek and lowly, the kind and gentle humility of the Lamb of God is not seen, is scarcely sought. The Lamb of God means to two things--meekness and death. Let us seek to receive Him in both forms. In Him they are inseparable: they must be in us too.

What a hopeless task if we had to do the work! Nature never can overcome nature, not even with the help of grace. Self can never cast out self, even in the regenerate man. Praise God! the work has been done, and finished and perfected for ever. The death of Jesus, once and forever, is our death to self. And the ascension of Jesus, His entering once and for ever into the Holiest, has given us the Holy Spirit to communicate to us in power, and make our very own, the power of the death-life. As the soul, in the pursuit and practice of humility, follows in the steps of Jesus, its consciousness of the need of something more is awakened, its desire and hope is quickened, its faith is strengthened, and it learns to look up and claim and receive that true fullness of the Spirit of Jesus, which can daily maintain His death to self and sin in its full power, and make humility the all pervading spirit of our life.(See note "C" at end of this chapter.)

"Are ye ignorant that all we who were baptized into Jesus Christ were baptized into His death? Reckon yourselves to be dead unto sin, but alive unto God in Christ Jesus. Present yourself unto God, as alive from the dead. " The whole self consciousness of the Christian is to be imbued and characterized by the spirit that animated the death of Christ. He has ever to present himself to God as one who has died in Christ, and in Christ is alive from the dead, bearing about in his body the dying of the Lord Jesus. His life ever bears the two-fold mark: its roots striking in true humility deep into the grave of Jesus, the death to sin and self; its head lifted up in resurrection power to the heaven where Jesus is.

Believer, claim in faith the death and the life of Jesus as thine. Enter in His grave into the rest from self and its work - the rest of God. With Christ, who committed His spirit into the Father's hands, humble thyself and descend each day into that perfect, helpless dependence upon God. God will raise thee up and exalt thee. Sink every morning in deep, deep nothingness into the grave of Jesus; every day the life of Jesus will be manifest inthee, Let a willing, loving, restful, happy humility be the mark that thou hast indeed claimed thy birthright - the baptism into the death of Christ. "By one offering He has perfected for ever them that are sanctified."The souls that enter into His humiliation will find in Him the power to see and count self dead, and, as those who have learned and received of Him, to walk with all lowliness and meekness, forbearing one another in love. The death-life is seen in a meekness and lowliness like that of Christ.

Note C

"To die to self, or come from under its power, is not, cannot be done, by any active resistance we can make to it by the powers of nature. The one true way of dying to self is the way of patience, meekness, humility, and resignation to God. This is the truth and perfection of dying to self ...For if I ask you what the Lamb of God means, must you not tell me that it is and means the perfection of patience, meekness, humility, and resignation to God? Must you not therefore say that a desire and faith of these virtues is an application to Christ, is a giving up yourself to Him and the perfection of faith in Him? And then, because this inclination of your heart to sink down in patience, meekness, humility, and resignation to God, is truly giving up all that you are and all thatyou have from fallen Adam, it is perfectly leaving all you have to follow Christ; it is your highest act of faith in Him. Christ is nowhere but in these virtues; when they are there, He is in His own kingdom. Let this be the Christ you follow.

"The Spirit of divine love can have no birth in any fallen creature, till it wills and chooses to be dead to all self, in a patient, humble resignation to the power and mercy of God. "I seek for all my salvation through the merits and mediation of the meek, humble, patient, suffering Lamb of God, who alone hath power to bring forth the blessed birth of these heavenly virtues in my soul. There is no possibility of salvation but in and by the birth of the meek, humble, patient, resigned Lamb of God in our souls. When the Lamb of God hath brought forth a real birth of His own meekness, humility, and full resignation to God in our souls, then it is the birthday of the Spirit of love in our souls, which, whenever we attain, will feast our souls with such peace and joy in God as will blot out the remembrance of everything that we called peace or joy before. "This way to God is infallible. This infallibility is grounded in the twofold character of our Saviour: 1. As He is the Lamb of God, a principle of all meekness and humility in the soul; 2. As He is the Light of heaven, and blesses eternal nature, and turns it into a kingdom of heaven, - when we are willing to get rest to our souls in meek, humble resignation to God, then it is that He, as the Light of God and heaven, joyfully breaks in upon us, turns our darkness into light, and begins that kingdom of God and of love within us, which will never have an end."
---See Wholly For God. (The whole passage deserves careful study, showing most remarkably how the continual sinking down in humility before God is, from man's side, the only way to die to self.)

Chapter 11--HUMILITY AND HAPPINESS

"Most gladly therefore will I rather glory in my weaknesses, that the strength of Christ may rest upon me. Wherefore I take pleasure in weakness: for when I am weak then am I strong. " -2 Cor. 12:9,10.

Lest Paul should exalt himself, by reason of the exceeding greatness of the revelations, a thorn in the flesh was sent him to keep him humble. Paul's first desire was to have it removed, and he besought the Lord thrice that it might depart. The answer came that the trial was a blessing; that, in the weakness and humiliation it brought, the grace and strength of the Lord could be the better manifested. Paul at once entered upon a new stage in his relation to the trial: instead of simply enduring it, he most gladly gloried in it; instead of asking for deliverance, he took pleasure in it. He had learned that the place of humiliation is the place of blessing, of power, of joy.

Every Christian virtually passes through these two stages in his pursuit of humility. In the first he fears and flees and seeks deliverance from all that can humble him. He has not yet learnt to seek humility at any cost. He has accepted the command to be humble, and seeks to obey it, though only to find how utterly he fails. He prays for humility, at times very earnestly; but in his secret heart he prays more, if not in word, then in wish, to be kept from the very things that will make him humble. He is not yet so in love with humility as the beauty of the Lamb of God, and the joy of heaven, that he would sell all to procure it. In his pursuit of it, and his prayer for it, there is still somewhat of a sense of burden and of bondage; to humble himself has not yet become the spontaneous expression of a life and a nature that is essentially humble. It has not yet become his joy and only pleasure. He cannot yet say, "Most gladly do I glory in weakness, I take pleasure in whatever humbles me."

But can we hope to reach the stage in which this will be the case? Undoubtedly. And what will it be that brings us there? That which brought Paul there - a new revelation of the Lord Jesus. Nothing but the presence of God can reveal and expel self. A clearer insight was to be given to Paul into the deep truth that the presence of Jesus will banish every desire to seek anything in ourselves, and will make us delight in every humiliation that prepares us for His fuller manifestation. Our humiliations lead us, in the experience of the presence and power of Jesus, to choose humility as our highest blessing. Let us try to learn the lessons the story of Paul teaches us.

We may have advanced believers, eminent teachers, men of heavenly experiences, who have not yet fully learnt the lesson of perfect humility, gladly glorying in weakness. We see this in Paul. The danger of exalting himself was coming very near. He knew not yet perfectly what it was to be nothing; to die, that Christ alone might live in him; to take pleasure in all that brought him low. It appears as if this were the highest lesson that he had to learn, full conformity to his Lord in that self-emptying where he gloried in weakness that God might be all. The highest lesson a believer has to learn is humility. Oh that every Christian who seek to advance in holiness may remember this well! There may be intense consecration, and fervent zeal and heavenly experience, and yet, if it is not prevented by very special dealings of the Lord, there may be an unconscious self-exaltation with it all. Let us learn the lesson,--the highest holiness is the deepest humility; and let us remember that comes not of itself, but only as it is made matter of special dealing on the part of our faithful Lord and His faithful servant. Let us look at our lives in the light of this experience, and see whether we gladly glory in weakness, whether we take pleasure, as Paul did, in injuries, in necessities, in distresses. Yes, let us ask whether we have learnt to regard a reproof, just or unjust, a reproach from friend or enemy, an injury, or trouble, or difficulty into which others bring us, as above all an opportunity of proving Jesus is all to us, how our own pleasure or honor are nothing, and , how humiliation is in very truth what we take pleasure in. It is indeed blessed, the deep happiness of heaven, to be so free from self that whatever is said of us or done to us is lost and swallowed up, in the thought that Jesus is all.

Let us trust Him who took charge of Paul to take charge of us too. Paul needed special discipline, and with it special instruction, to learn, what was more precious than even the unutterable things he had heard in heaven what it is to glory in weakness and lowliness. We need it, too, oh so much. He who cared for him will care for us too. He watches over us with a jealous, loving care, "lest we exalt ourselves". When we are doing so, He seeks to discover to us the evil, and deliver us from it. In trial and weakness and trouble He seeks to bring us low, until we so learn that His grace is all, as to take pleasure in the very thing that brings us and keeps us low. His strength made perfect in our weakness, His presence filling and satisfying our emptiness, becomes the secret of a humility that need never fail. It can, as Paul, in full sight of what God works in us, and through us, ever say, "In nothing was I behind the chiefest apostles, though I am nothing." His humiliations had led him to true humility, with its wonderful gladness and glorying and pleasure in all that humbles.

"Most gladly will I glory in my weaknesses, that the power of Christ may rest upon me;wherefore I take pleasure in weaknesses. "The humble man has learnt the secret of abiding gladness. The weaker he feels, the lower he sinks;the greater his humiliations appear, the more the power and the presence of Christ are his portion, until,as he says, "

I am nothing," the word of his Lord brings ever deeper joy: "My grace is sufficient for thee."

I feel as if I must once again gather up all in the two lessons: the danger of pride is greater and nearer than we think, and the grace for humility too.

The danger of pride is greater and nearer than we think, and that especially at the time of our highest experiences. The preacher of spiritual truth with an admiring congregation hanging on his lips, the gifted speaker on a Holiness platform expounding the secrets of the heavenly life, the Christian giving testimony to a blessed experience, the evangelist moving on as in triumph, and made a blessing to rejoicing multitudes,-no man knows the hidden, the unconscious danger to which these are exposed. Paul was in danger without knowing it; what Jesus did for him is written for our admonition, that we may know our danger and know our only safety. If ever it has been said of a teacher or professor of holiness,he is so full of self; or, he does not practise what he preaches; or, his blessing has not made him humbler or gentler,-let it be said no more. Jesus, in whom we trust, can make us humble.

Yes, the grace for humility is greater and nearer, too, than we think. The humility of Jesus is our salvation: Jesus Himself is our humility. Our humility is His care and His work. His grace is sufficient for us, to meet the temptation of pride too. His strength will be perfected in our weakness. Let us choose to be weak, to be low, to be nothing. Let humility be to us joy and gladness. Let us gladly glory and take pleasure in weakness, in all that can humble us and keep us low; the power of Christ will rest upon us. Christ humbled Himself, therefore God exalted Him. Christ will humble us, and keep us humble; let us heartily consent, let us trustfully and joyfully accept all that humbles; the power of Christ will rest upon us. We shall find that the deepest humility is the secret of the truest happiness, of a joy that nothing can destroy.

Chapter 12--HUMILITY AND EXALTATION

"He that humbleth himself shall be exalted. "Luke 14:11, 18:14.

"God giveth grace to the humble. Humble yourself in the sight of the Lord, and He shall exalt you." Jas. 4:10.

"Humble yourselves therefore under the mighty hand of God, that He may exalt you in due time. "1 Pet.5:6.

Just yesterday I was asked the question, How am I to conquer this pride? The answer; was simple. Two things are needed. Do what; God says is your work:humble yourself. Trust Him to do what He says is His work: He will exalt you.

The command is clear: humble yourself. That does not mean that it is your work to conquer and cast out the pride of your nature, and to form within yourself the lowliness of the holy Jesus. No, this is God's work;the very essence of that exaltation, wherein He lifts you up into the real likeness of the beloved Son. What the command does mean is this: take every opportunity of humbling yourself before God and man. In the faith of the grace that is already working in you; in the assurance of the more grace for victory that is coming; up to the light that conscience each time flashes upon the pride of the heart and its workings; notwithstanding all there may be of failure and falling, stand persistently as under the unchanging command: humble yourself. Accept with gratitude everything that God allows from within or without, from friend or enemy, in nature or in grace, to remind you of your need of humbling, and to help you to it. Reckon humility to be indeed the mother-virtue, your very first duty before God, the one perpetual safeguard of the soul, and set your heart upon it as the source of all blessing. The promise is divine and sure: He that humbleth himself shall be exalted. See that you do the one thing God asks: humble yourself. God will see that does the one thing He has promised. He will give more grace; He will exalt you in due time.

All God's dealings with man are characterized by two stages. There is the time of preparation, when command and promise, with the mingled experience of effort and impotence, of failure and partial success, with the holy expectancy of something better which these waken, train and discipline men for a higher stage. Then comes the time of fulfillment, when faith inherits the promise, and enjoys what it had so often struggled for in vain. This law holds good in every part of the Christian life, and in the pursuit of every separate virtue. And that because it is grounded in the very nature of things. In all that concerns our redemption, God must needs take the initiative. When that has been done, man's turn comes. In the effort after obedience and attainment, he must learn to know his impotence, in self-despair to die to himself, and so be fitted voluntarily and intelligently to receive from God the end, the completion of that of which he had accepted the beginning in ignorance. So, God who had been the Beginning, ere man rightly knew Him, or fully understood what His purpose was, is longed for and.welcomed as the End, as the All in All.

It is even thus, too, in the pursuit of humility. To every Christian the command comes from the throne of God Himself: humble yourself. The earnest attempt to listen and obey will be rewardedyes, rewarded- with the painful discovery of two things. The one,what depth of pride, that is of unwillingness to count oneself and to be counted nothing, to submit absolutely to God, there was, that one never knew. The other, what utter impotence there is in all our efforts, and in all our prayers too for God's help, to destroy the hideous monster. Blessed the man who now learns to put his hope in God, and to persevere, notwithstanding all the power of pride within him, in acts of humiliation before God and Men. We know the law of human nature: acts produce habits, habits breed dispositions, dispositions form the will, and the rightly-formed will is character. It is no otherwise in the work of grace. As acts, persistently repeated, beget habits and dispositions, and these strengthened the will, He who works both to will and to do comes with His mighty power and Spirit; and the humbling of the proud heart with which the' penitent saint cast himself so often before God, is rewarded with the "more grace" of the humble heart, in which the Spirit of Jesus has conquered, and brought the new nature to its maturity, and He the meek and lowly One now dwells for ever.

Humble yourselves in the sight of the Lord, and He will exalt you. And wherein does the exaltation consist? The highest glory of the creature is in being only a vessel, to receive and enjoy and show forth the glory of God. It can do this only as it is willing to be nothing in itself, that God may be all. Water always fills first the lowest places. The lower, the emptier a man lies before God, the speedier and the fuller will be the inflow of the divine glory.The exaltation God promises is not, cannot be, any external thing apart from Himself: all that He has to give or can give is only more of Himself, Himself to take more complete possession. The exaltation is not, like an earthly prize, something arbitrary, in no necessary connection with the conduct to be rewarded.No, but it is in its very nature the effect and result of the humbling of ourselves. It is nothing but the gift of such a divine indwelling humility, such a conformity to and possession of the humility of the Lamb of God,as fits us for receiving fully the indwelling of God.

He that humbleth himself shall be exalted. Of the truth of these words Jesus Himself is the proof; of the certainty of their fulfillment to us He is the pledge. Let us take His yoke upon us and learn of Him, for He is meek and lowly of heart. If we are but willing to stoop to Him, as He has stooped to us, He will yet stoop to each one of us again, and we shall find ourselves not unequally yoked with Him. As we enter deeper into the fellowship of His humiliation, and either humble ourselves or bear the humbling of men, we can count upon it that the Spirit of His exaltation, "the Spirit of God and of glory," will rest upon us. The presence and the power of the glorified Christ will come to them that are of an humble spirit. When God can again have His rightful place in us, He will lift us up. Make His glory thy care in humbling thyself; He will make thy glory His care in perfecting thy humility, and breathing into thee, as thy abiding life, the very Spirit of His Son. As the all-pervading life of God possesses thee, there will be nothing so natural, and nothing so sweet, as to be nothing, with not a thought or wish for self, because all is occupied with Him who filleth all. "Most gladly will I glory in my weakness, that the strength of Christ may rest upon me." Brother, have we not here the reason that our consecration and our faith have availed so little in the pursuit of holiness? It was by self and its strength that the work was done under the name of faith; it was for self and its happiness that God was called in; it was, unconsciously, but still truly, in self and its holiness that the soul rejoiced. We never knew that humility, absolute, abiding, Christlike humility and self-effacement, pervading and marking our whole life with God and man, was the most essential element of the life of the holiness we sought for.

It is only in the possession of God that I lose myself. As it is in the height and breadth and glory of the sunshine that the littleness of the mote playing in its beams is seen, even so humility is the taking our place in God's presence to be nothing but a mote dwelling in the sunlight of His love.

"How great is God! how small am I! .Lost, swallowed up in Love's immensity! God only there, not I."

May God teach us to believe that to be humble, to be nothing in His presence, is the highest attainment, and the fullest blessing of the Christian life. He speaks to us: "I dwell in the high and holy place, and with him the is of a contrite and humble spirit." Be this our portion!

"Oh, to be emptier, lowlier,
Mean, unnoticed, and unknown,
And to God a vessel holier,
Filled with Christ, and Christ alone!"

Note D.-A Secret of Secrets: Humility the Soul of True Prayer.--Till the spirit of the heart be renewed, till it is emptied of all earthly desires, and stands in an habitual hunger and thirst after God, which is the true spirit of prayer; till then, all our prayer will be, more or less, but too much like lessons given to scholars; and we shall mostly say them, only because we dare not neglect them. But be not discouraged; take the following advice, and then you may go to church without any danger of mere lip-labor or hypocrisy, although there should be a hymn or a prayer, whose language is higher than that of your heart. Do this: go to the church as the publican went to the temple; stand inwardly in the spirit of your mind in that form which he outwardly expressed, when he cast down his eyes, and could only say, "God be merciful to me, a sinner." Stand unchangeably, at least in your desire, in this form or state of heart; it will sanctify every petition that comes out of your mouth; and when anything is read or sung or prayed, that is more exalted than your heart is, if you make this an occasion of further sinking down in the spirit of the publican, you will then be helped, and highly blessed, by those prayers and praises which seem only to belong to a heart better than yours.

This, my friend, is a secret of secrets; it will help you to reap where you have not sown, and be a continual source of grace in your soul; for everything that inwardly stirs in you, or outwardly happens to you, becomes a real good to you, if it finds or excites in you this humble state of mind. For nothing is in vain, or without profit to the humble soul; it stands always in a state of divine growth; everything that falls upon it is like a dew of heaven to it. Shut up yourself, therefore, in this form of Humility; all good is enclosed in it; it is a water of heaven, that turns the fire of the fallen soul into the meekness of the divine life, and creates that oil, out of which the love to God and man gets its flame. Be enclosed, therefore,always in it; let it be as a garment wherewith you are always covered, and a girdle with which you are girt; breathe nothing but in and from its spirit; see nothing but with its eyes; hear nothing but with its ears. And then, whether you are in the church or out of the church, hearing the praises of God or receiving wrongs from men and the world, all will be edification, and everything will help forward your growth in the life of God. (The Spirit of Prayer, PtII, p. 121)

A PRAYER FOR HUMILITY

I will here give you an infallible touchstone, that will try all to the truth. It is this: retire from the world and all conversation, only for one month; neither write, nor read, nor debate anything with yourself; stop all the former workings of your heart and mind: and, with all the strength of your heart, stand all this month, as continually as you can, in the following form of prayer to God. Offer it frequently on your knees; but whether sitting, walking, or standing, be always inwardly longing, and earnestly praying this one prayer to God: "That of His great goodness He would make known to you, and take from your heart, every kind and form and degree of Pride, whether it be from evil spirits, or your own corrupt nature; and that He would awaken in you the deepest depth and truth of that Humility, which can make you capable of His light and Holy Spirit." Reject every thought, but that of waiting and praying in this matter from the bottom of your heart,with such truth and earnestness, as people in torment wish to pray and be delivered from it ...If you can and will give yourself up in truth and sincerity to this spirit of prayer, I will venture to affirm that, if you had twice as many evil spirits in you as Mary Magdalene had, they will all be cast out of you, and you will be forced with her to weep tears of love at the feet of the holy Jesus.-The Spirit of Prayer, Pt. II, p. 124

With Christ in the School of Prayer

PREFACE

OF ALL THE PROMISES CONNECTED WITH THE COMMAND, ABIDE IN ME,' there is none higher, and none that sooner brings the confession, `Not that I have already attained, or am already made perfect,' than this: `If ye abide in me, ask whatsoever ye will, and it shall be done unto you.' Power with God is the highest attainment of the life of full abiding.

And of all the traits of a life like CHRIST there is none higher and more glorious than conformity to Him in the work that now engages Him without ceasing in the Father's presence-His all-prevailing intercession. The more we abide in Him, and grow unto His likeness, will His priestly life work in us mightily, and our life become what His is, a life that ever pleads and prevails for men.

Thou hast made us kings and priests unto God. Both in the king and the priest the chief thing is power, influence, blessing. In the king it is the power coming downward; in the priest the power rising upward, prevailing with God. In our blessed Priest-King, Jesus Christ, the kingly power is founded on the priestly `He is able to save to the uttermost, because He ever liveth to make intercession.' in us, His priests and kings, it is no otherwise: it is in intercession that the Church is to find and wield its highest power, that each member ofthe, Church is to prove his descent from Israel, who as a prince had power with God and with men, and prevailed

It is under a deep impression that the place and power of prayer in the Christian life is too little understood that this book has been written. I feel sure that as long as we look on prayer chiefly as the means of maintaining our own Christian life, we shall not know fully what it is meant to be. But when we learn to regard it as the highest part of the work entrusted to us, the root and strength of all other work, we shall see that there is nothing that we so need to study and practice as the art of praying aright. If I have at all succeeded in pointing out the progressive teaching of our Lord in regard to prayer and the distinct reference the wonderful promises , of the last night (John 16:16) have to the works we are to do in His name, to the greater works, and to the bearing much fruit, we shall all admit that it is only when the Church gives herself up to this holy work of intercession that we can expect the power of Christ to manifest itself in her behalf. It is my prayer that God may use this little book to make clearer to some of His children the wonderful place of power and influence which He is waiting for them to occupy, and for which a weary world is waiting too.

In connection with this there is another truth that has come to me with wonderful clearness as I studied the teaching of Jesus on prayer. It is this: that the Father waits to hear every prayer of faith,: to give us whatsoever we will and whatsoever we ask in Jesus' name. We have become so accustomed to limit the wonderful love and the large promises of our God, that we cannot read the simplest and clearest statements of our Lord without the qualifying clauses by which we guard and expound them. If there is one thing I think the Church needs to learn, it is that God means prayer to have an answer, and that it hath not entered into the heart of man to conceive what God will do for His child who gives himself to believe that his prayer will be heard. God hears prayer; this is a truth universally admitted, but of which very few understand the meaning, or experience the power. If what I have written stirs my reader to go to the Master's words, and take His wondrous promises simply and literally as they stand, my object has been attained.

And then just one thing more. Thousands have in these last years found an unspeakable blessing in learning how completely Christ is our life, and how He undertakes to be and to do all in us that we need. I know not if we have yet learned to apply this truth to our prayerlife. Many complain that they have not the power to pray in faith, to pray the effectual prayer that availeth much. The message I would fain bring them is that the blessed Jesus is waiting, is longing, to teach them this. Christ is our life: in heaven He ever liveth to pray; His life in us is an ever-praying life, if we will but trust Him for it. Christ teaches us to pray not only by example, by instruction, by command, by promises, but by showing us HIMSELF the ever-living Intercessor, as our Life. It is when we believe this, and go and abide in Him for our prayer-life too, that our fears of not being able to pray aright will vanish, and we shall joyfully and triumphantly trust our Lord to teach us to pray, to be Himself the life and the power of our prayer.

May God open our eyes to see what the holy ministry of intercession is, to which, as His royal priesthood, we have been set apart. May He give us a large and strong heart to believe what mighty influence our prayers can exert. And may all fear as to our being able to fulfil our vocation vanish as we see Jesus, living ever to pray, living and standing surety for our prayer-life.

ANDREW MURRAY

And it came to pass, as He was praying in a certain place, that when He ceased, one of His disciples said to Him, Lord, teach us to pray. Luke 11:1

THE DISCIPLES HAD BEEN WITH CHRIST, AND SEEN HIM pray. They had learnt to understand something of the connection between His wondrous life in public, and His secret life of prayer. They had learnt to believe in Him as a Master in the art of prayer-none could pray like Him. And so they came to Him with the request, `Lord, teach us to pray.' And in after years they would have told us that there were few things more wonderful or blessed that He taught them than His lessons on prayer.

And now still it comes to pass, as He is praying in a certain place, that disciples who see Him thus engaged feel the need of repeating the same request, `Lord, teach us to pray.' As we grow in the Christian life, the thought and the faith of the Beloved Master in His never-failing intercession becomes ever more precious, and the hope of being Like Christ in His intercession gains an attractiveness before unknown. And as we see Him pray, and remember that there is none who can pray like Him, and none who can teach like Him, we feel the petition of the disciples, `Lord, teach us to pray,' is just what we need. And as we think how all He is and has, how He Himself is our very own, how He is Himself our life, we feel assured that we have but to ask, and He will be delighted to take us up into closer fellowship with Himself, and teach us to pray even as He prays.

Come, my brothers! Shall we not go to the Blessed Master and ask Him to enroll our names too anew in that school which He always keeps open for those who long to continue their studies in the Divine art of prayer and intercession? Yes, let us this very day say to the Master, as they did of old `Lord, teach us to pray.' As we meditate we shall find each word of the petition we bring to be full of meaning.

'Lord, teach us to pray.' Yes, to pray. This is what we need to be taught. Though in its beginnings prayer is so simple that the feeblest child can pray, yet it is at the same time the highest and holiest work to which man can rise. It is fellowship with the Unseen and Most Holy One. The powers of the eternal world have been placed at its disposal. It is the very essence of true religion the channel of all blessings, the secret of power and life. Not only for ourselves, but for others, for the Church for the world, it is to prayer that God has given the right to take hold of Him and His strength. It is on prayer that the promises wait for their fulfilment the kingdom for its coming, the glory of God for its full revelation. And for this blessed work, how slothful and unfit we are. It is only the Spirit of God can enable us to do it aright. How speedily we are deceived into a resting in the form, while the power is wanting. Our early training, the teaching of the Church, the influence , of habit, the stirring of the emotions-how easily these lead to prayer which has no Spiritual power, and avails but little. True prayer, -that takes hold of God's strength; 'that availeth much, to which the gates of heaven are really opened wide-who would not cry, Oh for some one to teach me thus to pray?

Jesus has opened a school, in which He trains His redeemed ones, who specially desire it, to have power in prayer. Shall we not enter it with the petition, Lord! it is just this we need to be taught! O teach us to pray.

'Lord, teach us to pray.' Yes, us, Lord. We have read in Thy Word with what power Thy believing people of old used to pray, and what mighty wonders were done in answer to their prayers. And if this took place under the Old Covenant, in the time of preparation, how much more wilt Thou not now, in these days of fulfilment, give Thy people this sure sign of Thy presence in their midst. We have heard the promises given to Thine apostles of the power of prayer in Thy name, and have seen how gloriously they experienced their truth: we know for certain. they can become true to us too. We hear continually even in these days what glorious tokens of Thy power Thou dost still give to those who trust Thee fully. Lord! these all are men of like passions with ourselves; teach us to pray so too. The promises are for us, the powers and gifts of the heavenly world are for us. O teach us to pray so that we may receive abundantly. To us too Thou hast entrusted Thy work, on our prayer too the coming of Thy kingdom depends, in our prayer too Thou canst glorify Thy name; 'Lord, teach us to pray.' Yes, us, Lord; we offer ourselves as learners; we would indeed be taught of Thee. 'Lord, teach us to pray.'

'Lord, teach us to pray.' Yes, we feel the need now of being taught to pray. At first there is no work appears so simple; later on, none that is more difficult; and the confession is forced from us: We know not how to pray as we ought. It is true we have God's Word, with its clear and sure promises; but sin has so darkened our mind, that we know not always how to apply the Word. In spiritual things we do not always seek the most needful things, or fail in praying according to the law of the sanctuary. In temporal things we are still less able to avail ourselves of the wonderful liberty our Father has given us to ask what we need. And even when we know what to ask, how much there is still needed to make prayer acceptable. It must be to the glory of God, in full surrender to His will, in full assurance of faith, in the name of Jesus, and with a perseverance that, if need be, refuses to be denied. All this must be learned. It can only be learned in the school of much prayer, for practice makes perfect. Amid the painful consciousness of ignorance and unworthiness, in the struggle between believing and doubting, the heavenly art of effectual prayer is learned. Because, even when we do not remember it, there is One, the Beginner and Finisher of faith and prayer, who watches over our praying, and sees to it that in all who trust Him for it their education in the school of prayer shall be carried on to perfection. Let but the deep undertone of all our prayer be the teachable- that comes from a sense of ignorance, and from faith in Him as a perfect teacher, and we may be sure we shall be taught, we shall learn to pray in power. Yes, we may depend upon it, HE teaches to pray.

'Lord, teach us to pray.' None can teach like Jesus, none but Jesus; therefore we call on Him, `LORD, teach us to pray.' A pupil needs a teacher, who knows his work, who has the gift of teaching, who in patience and love will descend to the pupil's needs. Blessed be God! Jesus is a this and much more. He knows what prayer is. It is Jesus, praying Himself, who teaches to pray. He knows what prayer is. He learned it amid the trials and tears of His earthly life. In heaven it is still His beloved work: His life there is prayer. Nothing delights Him more than to find those whom He can take with Him into the Father's presence, whom He can clothe with power to pray down God's blessing on those around them, whom He can train to be His fellow-workers in the intercession by which the kingdom is to be revealed on earth. He knows how to teach.Now the urgency of felt need, then by the confidence with which joy inspires. Here by the teaching of the Word, there by the testimony of another believer who knows what it is to have prayer beard. By His Holy Spirit, He has access to our heart, and teaches us to pray by showing us the sin that hinders the prayer, or giving us the assurance than we please God. He teaches, by giving not only thoughts of what to ask or how to ask, but by breathing within us the very spirit of prayer, by living within us as the Great Intercessor. We may indeed and most joyfully say, `Who teacheth like Him?' Jesus never taught His disciples how to preach, only how to pray. He did not speak much of what was needed to preach well but much of praying well. To know how to speak to God is more than knowing how to speak to man. Not power with men; 'but power with God is,the first thing. Jesus loves to teach us how to pray:

What think you, my beloved fellow-disciples! would it not be just what we need, to ask the Master for a month to give us a course of special lessons on the art of prayer? As we meditate on the words He spake on earth, let us yield ourselves to His teaching in the fullest confidence that, with such a teacher, we shall make progress. Let us take time not only to meditate, but to pray, to tarry at the foot of the throne, and be trained to the work of intercession. Let us do so in the assurance that amidst our, stammerings and fears He is carrying on His work most beautifully. He will breathe His own life which is all prayer, into us. As he makes us partakers of His righteousness and His life, He will of His intercession too. As the members of His body, as a holy priesthood, we shall take part in His priestly work of pleading and prevailing with God for men. Yes, let us joyfully say, ignorant and feeble though we be, 'Lord, teach us to pray:

Blessed Lord! who ever livest to pray, Thou canst teach me too to pray, me too to live ever to pray. In this Thou lovest to make me share Thy glory in heaven, that I should pray without ceasing, and ever stand as a priest in the presence of my God.

Lord Jesus! I ask Thee this day to enroll my name among those who confess that they know not how to pray as they ought, and specially ask Thee for a course of teaching in prayer. Lord! teach me to tarry with Thee in the school, and give Thee time to train me. May a deep sense of my ignorance, of the wonderful privilege and power of prayer, of the need of the Holy Spirit as the Spirit of prayer, lead me to cast away my thoughts of what I think I know, and make me kneel before Thee in true teachableness and poverty of spirit.

And fill me, Lord, with the confidence that with such a teacher as Thou art I shall learn to pray. In the assurance that I have as my teacher, Jesus, who is ever praying to the Father, and by His prayer rules the destinies of His Church and the world, I will not be afraid. As much as I need to know of the mysteries of the prayer-world, Thou wilt unfold for me. And when I may not know, Thou wilt teach me to be strong in faith, giving glory to God.

Blessed Lord! Thou wilt not put to shame Thy scholar who trusts Thee, nor, by Thy grace, would he Thee either. Amen.

The hour cometh, and now is, when the true worshippers shall worship the Father in spirit and in truth: for such doth the Father seek to be worshippers. God is a Spirit: and they that worship Him must worship Him in spirit and truth. John 4:23-24

THESE WORDS OF JESUS TO THE WOMAN OF SAMARIA ARE His first recorded teaching on the subject of prayer. They give us some wonderful first glimpses into the word prayer. The Father seeks worshippers: our worship satisfies His loving heart and is a joy to Him. He seeks true worshippers, but finds many not as He would have them. True worship is that which is in spirit and truth. The Son has come to open the way for this worship in spirit and truth, and teach it to us. And so one of our first lessons in the school of prayer must be to understand what it is to pray in spirit and in truth and to know how we can attain to it.

To the woman of Samaria our Lord spoke of a threefold worship. There is first, the ignorant worship of the Samaritans: 'Ye worship that which ye know not.' The second, intelligent worship of the Jew, having the true knowledge of God: ' We worship that which we know; for salvation is of the Jews. And then the new, the spiritual worship which He Himself has come to introduce: `The hour is coming, and is now, when the true worshippers shall worship the Father in spirit and truth.' From the connection it is evident that the words `in spirit and truth do not mean, as is often thought, earnestly., from the heart, in sincerity. The Samaritans had the five books of Moses and some knowledge of God: there was doubtless more than one among them who honestly and earnestly sought God in prayer. The Jews had the true full revelation of God in His word, as thus given; there were among them godly men, who called upon God with their whole heart. And yet not `in spirit and truth,' in the full meaning of the words. Jesus says, `The hour is coming, and now is:' it is only in and through Him that the worship of God will be in spirit and truth.

Among Christians one still finds the three classes of worshippers. Some who in their ignorance hardly know what they ask: they pray earnestly, and yet receive but little.Others there are, who have more correct knowledge, who try to pray with all their mind and heart, and often pray more earnestly, and yet do not attain to the full blessedness of worship in spirit and truth. It is into this third class we must ask our Lord Jesus to take us; we must be taught of them how to worship in spirit and truth. This alone is spiritual worship; this makes us worshippers such as the Father seeks. In prayer everything will depend on our understanding well and practising the worship in spirit and truth.

'God is a Spirit, and they that worship Him, must worship Him in spirit and truth.' The first thought suggested here by the Master is that there must be harmony between God and His worshipers; -such as God is; must His worship be. This is according to a principle which prevails throughout the universe: we look for correspondence between an object and the organ to which it reveals or yields itself. The eye has an inner fitness for the light, the ear for sound. The man who would truly worship God, who would find and know and possess and enjoy God, must be in harmony with Him, must have the capacity for receiving Him. Because God is Spirit, we must worship in spirit. As God is, so His worshipper.

And what does this mean? The woman had asked our Lord whether Samaria or Jerusalem was the true place of worship. He answers that henceforth worship is no longer to be limited to a certain place: 'Woman, believe Me, the hour cometh, when neither in this mountain, nor in Jerusalem shall ye worship the Father.' As God is Spirit, not bound by space or time but in His infinite perfection always and everywhere the same, so His worship would henceforth no longer be confined by place or form, but importance. How much our Christianity suffers from this, that it is confined to certain times and places. A man, who seeks to pray earnestly in the church or in the closet,spends the greater part of the week or the day in a spirit entirely at variance with that in which he prayed. His worship was the work of a fixed place or hour, not of his whole being. God is a Spirit: He is the Everlasting and Unchangeable One; what He is, He is always and in truth. Our worship must even so be in spirit and truth: His worship must be the spirit of our life; our life must be worship in spirit as God is Spirit.

God is a Spirit: and they that worship Him must worship Him in spirit and truth.' The second thought comes to us is that this worship in the spirit must come from God Himself. God is Spirit: He alone has Spirit to give: It was for this He sent His Son, to fit us for spiritual worship, by giving us the Holy Spirit. It is of His own work that Jesus speaks when He says twice, 'The hour cometh,' and then adds, 'and is now.' He came to baptize with the Holy Spirit; the Spirit could not stream forth until He was glorified (John 1.33, 7.37, 38, 16.7). It was when He had made an end of sin, and entering into the Holiest of all with His blood, had there on our behalf received the Holy Spirit (Acts 2.33), that He could send Him down to us as the Spirit of the Father. It was when Christ redeemed us, and we in Him had received the position of children, that the Father sent forth the Spirit of His Son into our hearts to cry, 'Abba, Father.' The worship in spirit is the worship of the Father in the Spirit of Christ, the Spirit of Sonship.

This is the reason why Jesus here uses the name Father. We never find one of the Old Testament saints personally appropriate the name of child or call God Father. The worship of the Father is only possible to those to whom the Spirit of the Son has been given. The worship in spirit is only possible to those to whom Son has revealed the Father, and who have received the spirit of Sonship. It is only Christ who opens the way and, teaches the worship in spirit.

And in truth. That does not only mean, in sincerity. Nor does it only signify, in accordance with the truth of God's Word. The expression is one of deep and Divine meaning. Jesus is `the only-begotten of the Father, full of grace and truth: `The law was given by Moses, grace and truth came by Jesus Christ: Jesus says, `I am the truth and the life: In the Old Testament all was shadow and promise;Jesus brought and gives the reality, the substance, of things hoped for. In Him the blessings and powers of the eternal life are our actual possession and experience. Jesus is full of grace and truth; the Holy Spirit is the Spirit of truth;through Him the grace that is in Jesus is ours in deed and truth, a positive communication out of the Divine life. And so worship in spirit is worship in truth; actual living fellowship with God, a real correspondence and harmony-between the Father, who is a Spirit, and the child praying in the spirit.

What Jesus said to the woman of Samaria, she could not at once understand. Pentecost was needed to reveal its full meaning. We are hardly prepared at our first entrance into the school of prayer to grasp such teaching. We shall understand it better later on. Let us only begin and take the lesson as He gives it. We are carnal and cannot bring God the worship He seeks. But Jesus came to give the Spirit: He has given Him to us. Let the disposition in which we set ourselves to pray be what Christ's words have taught us. Let there be the deep confession of our inability to bring God the worship that is pleasing to Him; the childlike teachableness that waits on Him to instruct us; the simple faith that yields itself to the breathing of the Spirit. Above all, let us hold fast the blessed truth-we shall find that the Lord has more to say to us about it-that the knowledge of the Fatherhood of God, the revelation of His infinite Fatherliness in our hearts, the faith in the infinite love that gives us His Son and His Spirit to make us children, is indeed the secret of prayer in spirit and truth. This is the new and living way Christ opened up for us. To have Christ the Son, and the Spirit of the Son, dwelling within us, and revealing the Father, this makes us true, spiritual worshippers.

Blessed Lord! I adore the love with which Thou didst teach a woman, who had refused Thee a cup of water, what the worship of God must be. I rejoice in the assurance that Thou wilt no less now instruct Thy disciple, who comes to Thee with a heart that longs to pray in spirit and in truth. O my Holy Master! do teach me this blessed secret. Teach me that the worship in spirit and truth is not of man, but only comes from Thee; that it is not only a thing of times and seasons, but the outflowing of a life in Thee. Teach me to draw near to God in prayer under the deep impression of my ignorance and my having nothing in myself to offer Him, and at the same time of the provision Thou my Saviour, makest for the Spirit's breathing in my childlike stammerings. I do bless Thee that in Thee I am a child, and have a child's liberty of access; that in Thee I have the spirit of Sonship and of worship in truth. Teach me, above all, Blessed Son of the Father, how it is the revelation of the Father that gives confidence in prayer; and let the infinite Fatherliness of God's Heart be my joy and strength for a life of prayer and of worship. Amen.

But thou, when thou prayest, enter into thine inner chamber, and having shut thy door, pray to thy Father which is in secret, and thy Father which seeth in secret shall recompense thee. -MATTHEW 6.6. After Jesus had called His first disciples, He gave them their first public teaching in the Sermon on the Mount. He there expounded to them the kingdom of God, its laws and its life. In that kingdom God is not only King, but Father; He not only gives all, but is Himself all. In the knowledge and fellowship of Him alone is its blessedness. Hence it came as a matter of course that the revelation of prayer and the prayer-life was a part of His teaching concerning the New Kingdom He came to set up. Moses gave neither command nor regulation with regard to prayer: even the prophets say little directly of the duty of prayer; it is Christ who teaches to pray.

And the first thing the Lord teaches His disciples is that they must have a secret place for prayer ; every one must have some solitary spot where he can be alone with his God. Every teacher must have a schoolroom. We have learned to know and accept Jesus as our only teacher in the school of prayer. He has already taught us at Samaria that worship is no longer confined to times and places; that worship, spiritual true worship, is a thing of the spirit and the life; the whole man must in his whole life be worshipping in spirit and truth. And yet He wants each one to choose for himself the fixed spot where He can daily meet him. That inner chamber, that solitary place, is Jesus' schoolroom. That spot may be anywhere; that spot may change from day to day if we have to change our abode; but that secret place there must be, with the quiet time in which the pupil places himself in the Master's presence, to be by Him prepared to worship the Father. There alone, but there most surely, Jesus comes to us to teach us to pray.

A teacher is always anxious that his schoolroom should be bright and attractive, filled with the light and air of heaven, a place where pupils long to come, and love to stay. In His first words on prayer in the Sermon on the Mount, Jesus seeks to set the inner chamber before us in its most attractive light. If we listen carefully, we soon notice what the chief thing He has to tell us is of our tarrying there. Three times He uses the name of Father: `Pray to thy Father;' 'Thy Father shall recompense thee;' `Your Father knoweth what things ye have need of.' The first thing in closet-prayer is: I must meet my Father. The light that shines in the closet must be: the light of the Father's countenance. The fresh air from heaven with which Jesus would have it filled, the atmosphere in which I am to breathe and pray, is: God's Father-love,

God's infinite Fatherliness. Thus each thought or petition we breathe out will be simple, hearty, childlike trust in the Father. This is how the Master teaches us to pray: He brings us into the Father's living presence. What we pray there must avail. Let us listen carefully to hear what the Lord has to say to us.

First `Pray to thy Father which is in secret.' God is a God who hides Himself to the carnal eye. As long as in our worship of God, we are chiefly occupied with our own thoughts and , exercises; we shall not meet Him who is a Spirit, the unseen One. But to the man who withdraws himself from all that is of the world and man, and prepares to wait upon God alone, the Father will reveal Himself. As he forsakes and gives up and shuts out the world, and the life of the world, and surrenders himself to be led of Christ into the secret of God's presence, the light of the Father's love will rise upon him. The secrecy of the inner chamber and the closed door, the entire separation from all around us, is an image of, and so a help to that inner spiritual sanctuary, the secret of God's tabernacle, within the veil, where our spirit truly comes into contact with the invisible One. And so we are taught, at the very outset of our search after the secret of effectual prayer, to remember that it is in the inner chamber; where we are alone with the Father, that we shall learn to pray aright. The Father is in secret: in these words Jesus teaches us where He is waiting for us, where He is always to be found. Christians often complain that private prayer is not what it should be. They feel weak and sinful, the heart is cold and dark; it is as if they have so little to pray, and in that little no faith or joy. They are discouraged and kept from prayer by the thought that they cannot come to the Father as they ought or as they wish. Child of God! listen to your Teacher. He tells you that when you go to private prayer your first thought must be: The Father is in secret, the Father awaits me there. Just because your heart is cold and prayerless, get into the presence of the loving Father. As a father pitieth his children so the Lord pitieth you. Do not be thinking of how little you have to bring God, but of how much He wants to give you. Just place yourself before, and look up into, His face; think of His love, His wonderful, tender, pitying love. Just tell Him how sinful and cold and dark all is: it is the Father's loving heart that will give light and warmth to yours. O do what Jesus says: Just shut the door, and pray to thy Father which is in secret. Is it not wonderful? to be able to go alone with God the infinite God,and then to look up and say: My Father!

`And thy Father, which seeth in secret, will recompense thee.' Here Jesus assures us that secret prayer cannot be fruitless: its blessing will show itself in our life. We have but in secret, alone with God, to entrust our life before men to Him; He will reward us openly; He will see to it that the answer to prayer be made manifest in His blessing upon us. Our Lord would thus teach us that as infinite Fatherliness and Faithfulness is that with which God meets us in secret, so on our part there should be the childlike simplicity of faith, the confidence that our prayer does bring down a blessing. He that cometh to God must believe that He is a rewarder of them that seek Him.' Not on the strong or the fervent feeling with which I pray does the blessing of the closet depend, but upon the love and the power of the Father to whom I there entrust my needs. And therefore the Master has but one desire: Remember your Father is, and sees and hears in secret; go there and stay there, and go again from there in the confidence: He will recompense. Trust Him for it; depend upon Him: prayer to the Father cannot be vain; He will reward you openly.

Still further to confirm this faith in the Father-love of God, Christ speaks a third word: `Your Father knoweth what things ye have need of before ye ask Him.' At first sight it might appear as if this thought made prayer less needful: God knows far better than we what we need. But as we get a deeper insight into what prayer really is, this truth will help much to strengthen our faith. It will teach us that we do not need, as the heathen, with the multitude and urgency of our words, to compel an unwilling God to listen to us. It will lead to a holy thoughtfulness and silence in prayer as it suggests the question: Does my Father really know that I need this? It will, when once we have been led by the Spirit to the certainty that our request is indeed something that, according to the Word, we do need for God's glory, give us wonderful confidence to say, My Father knows I need it and must have it. And if there be any delay in the answer, it will teach us in quiet perseverance to hold on: Father thou knowest I need it. O the blessed liberty and simplicity of a child that Christ our Teacher would fain cultivate in us as we draw near to God: let us look up to the Father until His Spirit works it in us. Let us sometimes in our prayers, when we are in danger of being so occupied with our fervent, urgent petitions, as to forget that the Father knows and hears, let us hold still and just quietly say: My Father sees, my Father hears, my Father knows; it will help our faith to take the answer, and to say: We know that we have the petitions we have asked of Him.

And now, all ye who have anew entered the school of Christ to be taught to pray, take these lessons, practise them, and trust Him to perfect you in them. Dwell much in the inner chamber, with the door shut-shut in from men, shut up with God; it is there the Father waits you, it is there Jesus will teach you to pray. To be alone in secret with THE FATHER: this be your highest joy. To be assured that THE FATHER will openly reward the secret prayer, so that it cannot remain unblessed: this be your strength day by day. And to know that the Father knows that you need what you ask: this be your liberty to bring every need, in the assurance that your God will supply it according to His riches in glory in Christ Jesus.

Blessed Saviour! with my whole heart I do bless Thee for the appointment of the inner chamber, as the school where Thou meetest each of Thy pupils alone, and revealest to him the Father. O my Lord! strengthen my faith so in the Father's tender love and kindness, that as often as I feel sinful or troubled, the first instinctive thought may be to go where I know the Father wafts me, and where prayer never can go unblessed. Let the thought that He knows my need before I ask, bring me, in great restfulness Of faith, to trust that He will give what His child requires. O let the place of secret prayer become to me the most beloved spot of earth.

And, Lord! hear me as I pray that Thou wouldest everywhere bless the closets of Thy believing people. Let Thy wonderful revelation of a Father's tenderness free all young Christians from every thought of secret prayer as a duty or a burden, and lead them to regard it as the highest privilege of their life, a joy and a blessing. Bring back all who are discouraged, because they cannot find ought to bring Thee in prayer. O give them to understand that they have only to come with their emptiness to Him who has all to give, and delights to do it. Not, what they have to bring the Father, but what the Father waits to give them, be their one thought.

And bless especially the inner chamber of all Thy servants who are working for Thee, as the place where God's truth and God's grace are revealed to them, where they are daily anointed with fresh oil, where their strength is renewed, and the blessings are received in faith, with which they are to bless their fellow-men. Lord; draw us all in the closet nearer to Thyself and the Father. Amen.

After this manner therefore pray ye: Our Father, which art in heaven.- MATTHEW 6.9.

EVERY TEACHER KNOWS THE POWER OF EXAMPLE. HE NOT only tells the child what to do and how to do it, but shows him how it really can be done. In condescension to our weakness, our Heavenly Teacher has given us the very words we are to take with us as we draw near to our Father. We have in them a form of prayer in which there breathe the freshness and fulness of the Eternal Life. So simple that the child can lisp it, so divinely rich that it comprehends all that God can give. A form of prayer that becomes the model and inspiration for all other prayer, and yet always draws us back to itself as the deepest utterance of our souls before our God.

`Our Father which art in heaven!' To appreciate this word of adoration aright, I must remember that none of the saints had in Scripture ever ventured to address God as their Father. The invocation places us at once in the centre of the wonderful revelation the Son came to make of His Father as our Father too. It comprehends the mystery of redemption-Christ delivering us from the curse that we might become the children of God. The mystery of regeneration-the Spirit in the new birth giving us the new life. And the mystery of faith-ere yet the redemption is accomplished or understood the word is given on the lips of the disciples to prepare them for the blessed experience still to come. The words are the key to the whole prayer, to all prayer. It takes time, it takes life to study them; it will take eternity to understand them fully. The knowledge of God's Father-love is the first and simplest, but also the last and highest lesson in the school of prayer. It is in the personal relation to the living God, and the personal conscious fellowship of love with Himself, that prayer begins. It is in the knowledge of God's Fatherliness, revealed by the Holy Spirit, that the power of prayer will be found to root and grow. In the infinite tenderness and pity and patience of the infinite Father, in His loving readiness to hear and to help, the life of prayer has its joy. O let us take time, until the Spirit has made these words to us spirit and truth, filling heart and life: Our Father which art in heaven.' Then we are indeed within the veil, in the secret place of power where prayer always prevails.

`Hallowed be Thy name.' There is something here that strikes us at once. While we ordinarily first bring our own needs to God in prayer, and then think of what belongs to God and His interests, the Master reverses the order. First, Thy name, Thy kingdom, Thy will; then, give us, forgive us, lead us, deliver us. The lesson is of more importance than we think. In true worship the Father must be first,must be all. The sooner I learn to forget myself in the desire that HE may be glorified, the richer will the blessing be that prayer will bring to myself. No one ever loses by what he sacrifices for the Father.

This must influence all our prayer. There are two sorts of prayer: personal and intercessory. The latter ordinarily occupies the lesser part of our time and energy. This may not be. Christ has opened the school of prayer specially to train intercessors for the great work of bringing down, by their faith and prayer, the blessings of His work and love on the world around. There can be no deep growth in prayer unless this be made our aim. The little child may ask of the father only what it needs for itself; and yet it soon learns to say, give some for sister too. But the grownup son, who only lives for the father's interest and takes charge of the father's business, asks more largely, and gets all that is asked. And Jesus would train us to the blessed life of consecration and service, in which our interests are all subordinate to the Name, and the Kingdom, and the Will of the Father. O let us live for this and let, on each act of adoration, Our Father! there follow in the same breath, Thy Name, Thy Kingdom, Thy Will;-for this we look up and long.

Hallowed be Thy name.' What name? This new name of Father. The word Holy is the central word of the Old Testament; the name Father of the New. In this name of Love all the holiness and glory of God are now to be revealed. And how is the name to be hallowed? By God Himself: `I will hallow My great name which ye have profaned.' Our prayer must be that in ourselves in all God's children, in presence of the world, God Himself would reveal the holiness, the Divine power, the hidden glory of the name of Father. The Spirit of the Father is the Holy Spirit: it is only when we yield ourselves to be led of Him, that the name will be hallowed in our prayers and our lives. Let us learn the prayer: `Our Father, hallowed be Thy name.'

'Thy kingdom come.' The Father is a King and has a kingdom. The son and heir of a king has no higher ambition than the glory of his father's kingdom. In time of war or danger this becomes his passion; he can think of nothing else. The children of the Father are here in the enemy's territory, where the kingdom, which is in heaven, is not yet fully manifested. What more natural than that, when they learn to hallow the Father-name, they should long and cry with deep enthusiasm: 'Thy kingdom come. The coming of the kingdom is the one great event on which the revelation of the Father's glory, the blessedness of His children, the salvation of the world depends. On our prayers too the coming of the kingdom waits. Shall we not join in the deep longing cry of the redeemed: 'Thy kingdom come'? Let us learn it in the school of Jesus.

'Thy will be done, as in heaven, so on earth.' This petition is too frequently applied alone to the suffering of the will of God. In heaven God's will is done, and the Master teaches the child to ask that the will may be done on earth just as in heaven: in the spirit of adoring submission and ready obedience. Because the will of God is the glory of heaven the doing of it is the blessedness of heaven. As the will is done,- the kingdom of heaven comes into the heart. And whereever faith has accepted the Father's love, obedience accepts the Father's will. The surrender to, and the prayer for a life of heaven-like obedience, is the spirit of childlike prayer.

`Give us this day our daily bread! When first the child has yielded himself to the Father in the care for His Name, His Kingdom, and His Will, he has full liberty to ask for his daily bread. A master cares for the food of his servant, a general of his soldiers, a father of his child. And will not the Father in heaven care for the child who has in prayer given himself up to His interests? We may indeed in full confidence say: Father, I live for Thy honour and Thy work; I know Thou carest for me. Consecration to God and His will gives wonderful liberty in prayer for temporal things: the whole earthly life is given to the Father's loving care.

`And forgive us our debts, as we also have forgiven our debtors. As bread is the first need of the body, so forgiveness for the soul, And the provision for the one is as sure as for the other. We are children, but sinners too; our right of access to the Father's presence we owe to the precious blood and the forgiveness it has won for us. Let us beware of the prayer for forgiveness becoming a formality: only what is really confessed is really forgiven. Let us in faith accept the forgiveness as promised: as a spiritual reality, an actual transaction between God and us, it is the entrance into all the Father's love and all the privileges of children. Such forgiveness, as a living experience, is impossible without a forgiving spirit to others: as forgiven expresses the heavenward, so forgiving the earthward, relation of God's child. In each prayer to the Father I must be able to say that I know of no one whom I do not heartily love.

`And lead us not into temptation, but deliver us from the evil one.' Our daily bread, the pardon of our sins, and then our being kept from all sin and the power of the evil one, in these three petitions all our personal need is comprehended. The prayer for bread and pardon must be accompanied by the surrender to live in all things in holy obedience to the Father's will, and the believing prayer in everything to be kept by the power of the indwelling Spirit from the power of the evil one. Children of God! it is thus Jesus would have us to pray to the Father in heaven. O let His Name, and Kingdom, and Will, have the first place in our love; His providing, and pardoning, and keeping love will be our sure portion, So the prayer will lead us up to the true childlife: the Father all to the child, the Father all for the child. We shall understand how Father and child, the Thine and the our, are all one, and how the heart that begins its prayer with the God-devoted Thine, will have the power in faith to speak out the Our too. Such prayer will, indeed, be the fellowship and interchange of love, always bringing us back in trust and worship to Him who is not only the Beginning but the End:' For Thine is the Kingdom and the Power, and the Glory, for ever Amen.' Son of the Father, teach us to pray, 'Our Father'.

O Thou who art the only-begotten Son, teach us, we beseech Thee, to pray, 'Our FATHER.' We thank Thee, Lord, for these Living Blessed Words which Thou hast given us. We thank Thee for the millions who in them have learnt to know and worship the Father, and for what they have been to us. Lord! it is as if we needed days and weeks in Thy school with each separate petition; so deep and full are they. But we look to Thee to lead us deeper into their meaning: do it, we pray Thee, for Thy Name's sake; Thy name is Son of the Father.

Lord! Thou didst once say: `No man knoweth the Father save the Son, and he to whom the Son willeth to reveal Him.' And again: `I made known unto them Thy name, and will make it known, that the love wherewith Thou hast loved Me may be in them.' Lord Jesus! reveal to us the Father. Let His name, His infinite Father-love, the love with which He loved Thee, according to Thy prayer, BE IN us. Then shall we say aright, `OUR Father!'

Then shall we apprehend Thy teaching and the first spontaneous breathing of our heart will be: `Our Father, Thy Name, Thy Kingdom, Thy Will.' And we shall bring our needs and our sins and our temptations to Him in the confidence that the love of such a Father cares for all.

Blessed Lord! we are Thy scholars, we trust Thee; do teach us to pray, 'Our Father.' Amen.

CHAPTER 5: Ask and It Shall be Given You or The Certainty of the Answer to Prayer

' Ask, and it shall be given you; seek, and ye shall find; knock and it shall be opened unto you :for every one that asketh receiveth and he that seeketh findeth ; and to him that knocketh it shall opened.'- Matthew 7:7-8

Ye ask, and receive not, because ye ask amiss.'-James 4:3

0UR Lord returns here in the Sermon the Mount a second time to speak of prayer. The first time He had spoken of the Father who is to be found in secret, and rewards openly, and has given us the pattern prayer (Matt. 6:5). Here He wants to teach us what in all Scripture is considered the chief thing in prayer: the assurance that prayer will be heard and answered. Observe how He uses words which mean almost the same thing, and each time repeats the promise distinctly: ` Ye shall receive, ye shall find, it shall be opened unto you;' and then gives us ground for such assurance the law of the kingdom: ` He that asketh receiveth ; he that seeketh, findeth to him that knocketh, it shall he opened. We cannot but feel how in this sixfold repetition He wants to impress deep on our minds this one truth, that we may and must most confidently expect an answer to our prayer. Next to the revelation of the Father's love, there is, in the whole course of the school of prayer, not a more important lesson than this: Every one that asketh, receiveth. In the three words the Lord uses, ask, seek, knock, a difference in meaning has been sought. If such was indeed His purpose, then the first, ASK, refers to the gifts we pray for. But I may ask and receive the gift without the Giver. Seek is the word Scripture uses of God Himself; Christ assures me that I can find Himself. But it is not enough to find God in time of need, without coming to abiding fellowship: KNOCK speaks of admission to dwell with Him and in Him. Asking and receiving the gift would thus lead to seeking and finding the Giver, and this again to the knocking and opening of the door of the Father's home and love. One thing is sure : the Lord does want us to count most certainly on it that asking, seeking, knocking, cannot be in vain: receiving an answer, finding God, the opened heart and home of God, are the certain fruit of prayer.

That the Lord should have thought it needful in so many forms to repeat the truth, is a lesson of deep import. It proves that He knows our heart, how doubt and distrust toward God are natural to us, and how easily we are inclined to rest in prayer as a religious work without an answer. He knows too how even when we believe that God is the Hearer of prayer, believing prayer that lays hold of the promise, is something spiritual, too high and difficult for the halfhearted disciple.

He therefore at the very outset of His instruction to those who would learn to pray, seeks to lodge this truth deep into their hearts: prayer does avail much; ask and ye shall receive; every one that asketh, receiveth. This is the fixed eternal law of the kingdom: if you ask and receive not, it must be because there is something amiss or wanting in the prayer. Hold on; let the word and Spirit teach you to pray aright, but do not let go the confidence He seeks to waken: Every one that asketh, receiveth.

'Ask, and it shall be given you.' Christ has no mightier stimulus to persevering prayer in His school than this. As a child has to prove a sum to be correct, so the proof that we have prayed aright is, the answer. If we ask and receive not, it is because we have not learned to pray aright. Let every learner in the school of Christ therefore take the Master's word in all simplicity: Every one that asketh, receiveth. He had good reasons for speaking so unconditionally. Let us beware of weakening the Word with our human wisdom. When He tells us heavenly things, let us believe Him. His Word will explain itself to him who believes it fully. If questions and difficulties arise, let us not seek to have them settled before we accept the Word. No; let us entrust them all to Him: it is His to solve them: our work is first and fully to accept and hold fast His promise. Let in our inner chamber, in the inner chamber of our heart too, the Word be inscribed in letters of light, Every one that asketh, receiveth.

According to this teaching of the Master, prayer consists of two parts, has two sides, a human and a Divine. The human is the asking, the Divine is the giving. Or, to look at both from the human side, there is the asking and the receiving-the two halves that make up a whole. It is as if He would tell us that we are not to rest without an answer, because it is the will of God, the rule in the Father's family : every childlike believing petition is granted. If no answer comes, we are not to sit down in the cloth that calls itself resignation, and suppose that it is not God's will to give an answer. No; there must be something in the prayer that is not as God would have it, childlike and believing; we must seek for grace to pray so that the answer may come. It is far easier to the flesh to submit without the answer than to yield itself to be searched and purified by the Spirit, until it has learnt to pray the prayer of faith. It is one of the terrible marks of the diseased state of Christian life in these days, that there are so many who rest content without the distinct experience of answer to prayer. They pray daily, they ask many things, and trust that some of them will be heard, but know little of direct definite answer to prayer as the rule of daily life. And it is this the Father wills ; He seeks daily intercourse with His children in listening to and granting their petitions.He wills that I should come to Him day by day with distinct requests; He wills day by day to do for me what I ask.It was in His answer to prayer that the saints of old learned to know God as the Living One, and were stirred to praise and love (Psalm 34, Psalm 66:19, Psalm 116:1) Our Teacher waits to imprint this upon our minds; prayer and its answer, the child asking and the father giving, belong to each other.

There may be cases in which the answer is a refusals, because the request is not according to God's Word, as when Moses asked to enter Canaan. But still there was an answer: God did not leave His servant in uncertainty as to His will. The gods of the heathen are dumb and cannot speak. Our Father lets His child know when He cannot give him what he asks, and he withdraws his petition, even as the Son did in Gethsemane. Both Moses the servant and Christ the Son knew that what they asked was not according to what 'the Lord had spoken: their prayer was the humble supplication whether it was not possible for the decision to be changed. God will teach those who are teach able and give Him time, by His Word and Spirit, whether their request be according to His will or not. Let us withdraw the request, if it be not according God's mind, or persevere till the answer come. Prayer is appointed to obtain the answer. It is in prayer and its answer that the interchange of love between .the Father and His child takes place.

How deep the estrangement of our heart from God must be, that we find it so difficult to grasp such promises, even while we accept the words and believe their truth, the faith of the heart, that fully has them and rejoices in them, comes so slowly. It is because our spiritual life is still so weak, and the capacity for taking God's thoughts is so feeble. But let us look to Jesus to teach us as none but He can teach. If we take His words in simplicity, and trust Him by his Spirit to make them within us life and power, they will so enter into our inner being, to the spiritual Divine reality of the truth they contain will indeed take possession of us, and we shall not rest content until every petition we offer is borne heavenward on Jesus' own words ` Ask, and it shall be given you.'

Beloved fellow-disciples in the school of Jesus, let us set ourselves to learn this lesson well. Let us take these words just as they were spoken. Let us not suffer human reason to weaken their force. Let us take these words as Jesus gives them, and believe them. He will teach us in due time how to understand them fully: let us begin by implicitly believing them. Let us take time, often as we pray, to listen to His voice: Every one that asketh, receiveth. Let. us not make the feeble experiences of our unbelief the measure of what our faith may expect. Let us seek, not only just in our seasons of prayer, but at all times, to hold fast the joyful assurance: man's prayer on earth and God's answer in heaven are meant for each other. Let us trust Jesus to teach us so too pray,that the answer can come. He will do it, if we hold fast the word He gives today : ` Ask, and ye shall receive.'

LORD, TEACH UP TO PRAY!

0 Lord Jesus! teach me to understand and believe what Thou hast now promised me. It is not hid from Thee, 0 my Lord, with what reasonings my heart seeks to satisfy itself, when no answer comes. There is the thought that my prayer is not in harmony with the Father's secret counsel ; that there is perhaps something better Thou wouldest give me; or that prayer as fellowship with God is blessing enough without an answer And yet, my blessed Lord, I find in Thy teaching on prayer that Thou didst not speak of these things, but didst say so plainly, that prayer may and must expect an answer. Thou doth assure us that this is the fellowship of a child with the Father; the child asks and the Father gives.

Blessed Lord ! Thy words are faithful and true. It must be, because I pray amiss, that my experience of answered prayer is not clearer. It must be, because I live too little in the Spirit, that my prayer is too little in the Spirit, and that the power for the prayer of faith is wanting. Lord ! teach me to pray. Lord Jesus! I trust Thee for it; teach me to pray in faith. Lord teach me this lesson of to-day! Every one that asketh, receiveth. Amen.

'Or what man is there of you, who, if his son ask him for a loaf, will give him a stone; or if he shall ask for a fish, will give him a serpent! If ye then, being evil, know how to give good gifts unto your children, how much more shall your Father which is in Heaven give good things to them that ask Him!' Matthew 7:9-11

In these words our Lord proceeds further to confirm what He said of the certainty of an answer to prayer. To remove all doubt, and show us on what sure ground His promise rests, He appeals to what every one has seen and experienced here on earth. We are all children, and know what we expected of our fathers. We are fathers, or continually see them ; and everywhere we look upon it as the most natural thing there can be, for a father to hear his child. And the Lord asks us to look up from earthly parents, of whom the best are but evil, and to calculate How much more the heavenly Father will give good gifts to them that ask Him. Jesus would lead us up to see, that as much greater as God is than sinful man, so much greater our assurance ought to be that He will more surely than any earthly father grant our childlike petitions. As much greater as God is than man, so much surer is that prayer will be heard with the Father in heaven than with a father on earth.

As simple and intelligible as this parable is, so deep and spiritual is the teaching it contains. The Lord would remind us that the prayer of a child owes its influence entirely to the relation in which he stands to the parent. The prayer can exert that influence only when the child is really living in that relationship, in the home, in the love, in the service of the Father. The power of the promise, 'Ask, and it shall be given you,' lies in the loving relationship between us as children and the Father in heaven; when we live and walk in that relationship, the prayer of faith and its answer will be the natural result. And so the lesson we have today in the school of prayer is this : Live as a child of God,then you will be able to pray as a child, and as a child you will most assuredly be heard.

And what is the true child-life ? The answer can be found in any home. The child that by preference forsakes the father's house, that finds no pleasure in the presence and love and obedience of the father, and still thinks to ask and obtain what he will, will surely be disappointed. On the contrary, he to whom the intercourse and will and honour and love of the father are the joy of his life, will find that it is the father's joy to grant his requests. Scripture says, ' As many as are led by the Spirit of God, they are the children of God:' the childlike privilege of asking all is inseparable from the childlike life under the leading of the Spirit. He that gives himself to be led by the Spirit in his life, will be led by Him in his prayers too. And he will find that Fatherlike giving is the Divine response to childlike living.

To see what this childlike living is, in which childlike asking and believing have their ground, we have only to notice what our Lord teaches in the Sermon on the Mount of the Father and His children. In it the prayer-promises are imbedded in the life-precepts; the two are inseparable. They form one whole; and He alone can count on the fulfilment of the promise, who accepts too all that the Lord has connected with it. It is as if in speaking the word, `.Ask, and ye shall receive,' He says: I give these promises to those whom in the beatitudes I have pictured in their childlike poverty and purity, and of whom I have said, 'They shall be called the children of God' (Matt. 5: 3-9): to children, who 'let your light shine before men, so that they may glorify your Father in heaven:' to those who walk in love, 'that ye may be children of your Father which is in heaven,' and who seek to be perfect ` even as your Father in heaven is perfect' (v. 45) : to those whose fasting and praying and almsgiving (6: 1-18) is not before men, but ' before your Father which seeth in secret;' who forgive even as your Father forgiveth you' (6:15);who trust the heavenly Father in righteousness (6:26-32); who not only say, Lord,

Lord, but do the will of my Father which is in heaven (7:21). Such are the children of the Father, and such is the life in the Father's love and service; in such a child-life, answered prayers are certain and abundant. But will not such teaching discourage the feeble one? If we are first to answer to this portrait of a child, must not many give up all hope of answers to prayer? The difficulty is removed if we think again of the blessed name of father and child. A child is weak; there is a great difference among children in age and gift. The Lord does not demand of us a perfect fulfilment of the law; no, but ony the childlike and whole-hearted surrender to live as a child with Him in obedience and truth. Nothing more. But also,nothing less. The Father must have the whole heart. When this is given, and He sees the child with honest purpose and steady will seeking in everything to be and live as a child, then our prayer will count with Him as the prayer of a child. Let any one simply and honestly begin to study the sermon on the Mount and take it as his guide in life, and he will find, notwithstanding weakness and failure, an ever-growing liberty to claim the fulfilment of its promises in regard to prayer. In the names of father and child he has the pledge that his petitions will be granted.

This is the one chief thought on which Jesus dwells here, and which He would have all His scholars take in. He would have us see that the secret of effectual prayer is: to have the heart filled with the Father-love of God. It is not enough for us to know that God is a Father: He would have us take time to come under the full impression of what that name implies. We must take the best earthly father we know; we must think of the tenderness and love with which he regards the request of his child, the love and joy with which he grants every reasonable desire; we must then, as we think in adoring worship of the infinite Love and Fatherliness of God, consider with how much more tenderness and joy He sees us come to Him, and gives us what we ask aright. And then, when we see how much this Divine arithmetic is beyond our comprehension, and feel how impossible it is for us to apprehend God's readiness to hear us, then He would have us come and open our heart for the Holy Spirit to shed abroad God's Father-love there. Let us do this not only when we want to pray, but let us yield heart and life to dwell in that love. The child who only wants to know the love of the father when he has something to ask, will be disappointed. But he who lets God be Father always and in everything, who would fain live his whole life in the Father's presence and love, who allows God in all the greatness of His love to be a Father to him, oh! he will experience most gloriously that a life in God's infinite Fatherliness and continual answers to prayer are inseparable.

Beloved fellow-disciple! we begin to see what the reason is that we know so little of daily answers to prayer, and what the chief lesson is which the Lord has for us in His school. It is all in the name of Father. We thought of new and deeper insight into some of the mysteries of the prayerworld as what we should get in Christ's school; He tells us the first is the highest lesson; we must learn to say well, ' Abba, Father!' 'Our Father which art in heaven.' He that can say this, has the key to all prayer. In all the compassion with which a father listens to his weak or sickly child, in all the joy with which he hears his stammering child, in all the gentle patience with which he bears with a thoughtless child, we must, as in so many mirrors, study the heart of our Father, until every prayer be borne upward on the faith of this Divine word: `How much more shall your heavenly Father give good gifts to them that ask Him.'

' LORD, TEACH US TO PRAY.'

Blessed Lord! Thou knowest that this, though it be one of the first and simplest and most glorious lessons in Thy school, is to our hearts one of the hardest to learn: we know so little of the love of the Father. Lord! teach us so to live with the Father that His love may be to us nearer, clearer, dearer, than the love of any earthly father. And let the assurance of His hearing our prayer be as much greater than the confidence in an earthly parent, as the heavens are higher than earth, as God is infinitely greater than man. Lord! show us that it is only our unchildlike distance from the Father that hinders the answer to prayer,

and lead us on to the true life of God's children. Lord Jesus ! it is
fatherlike love that wakens childlike trust. O reveal to us the Father,
and His tender, pitying love, that we may become childlike, and
experience how in the child-life lies the power of prayer.

Blessed Son of God! the Father loveth Thee and hath given Thee all
things. And Thou lovest the Father, and hast done all things He
commanded Thee, and therefore hast the power to ask all things. Lord!
give us Thine own Spirit, the Spirit of the Son. Make us childlike, as
Thou wert on earth. And let every prayer be breathed in the faith that as
the heaven is higher than the earth, so God's Father-love, and His
readiness to give us what we ask, surpasses all we can think or
conceive. Amen,

If ye then, being evil, know how to give good gifts unto your children, how much more shall the heavenly Father give the Holy Spirit to them that ask Him! Luke 11:13

In the Sermon on the Mount, the Lord had already given utterance to His wonderful How much more? Here in Luke, where He repeats the question, there is a difference. Instead of speaking, as then, of giving good gifts, He says, `How much more shall the heavenly Father give THE HOLY SPIRIT ?' He thus teaches us that the chief and the best of these gifts is the Holy Spirit, or rather, that in this gift all others are comprised. The Holy Spirit is the first of the Father's gifts, and the one He delights most to bestow. The Holy Spirit is therefore the gift we ought first and chiefly to seek.

The unspeakable worth of this gift we can easily understand. Jesus spoke of the Spirit as `the promise of the Father;' the one promise in which God's Fatherhood revealed itself. The best gift a good and wise father can bestow on a child on earth is his own spirit. This is the great object of a father in education---.to reproduce in his child his own disposition and character. If the child is to know and understand his father; if, as he grows up, he is to enter into all his will and plans; if he is to have his highest joy in the father, and the father in him,--he must be of one mind and spirit with him. And so it is impossible to conceive of God bestowing any higher gift on His child than this, His own Spirit. God is what He is through His Spirit; the Spirit is the very life of God. Just think what it means--God giving His own Spirit to His child on earth.

Or was not this the glory of Jesus as a Son upon earth, that the Spirit of the Father was in Him ? At His baptism in Jordan the two things were united,---.the voice, proclaiming Him the Beloved Son, and the Spirit, descending upon Him, And so the apostle says of us, ` Because ye are sons, God sent forth the Spirit of His Son into your hearts, crying, Abba, Father.' A king seeks in the whole education of his son to call forth in him a kingly spirit. Our Father in heaven desires to educate us as His children for the holy, heavenly life in which He dwells, and for this gives us, from the depths of His heart, His own Spirit. It was this which was the whole aim of Jesus when, after having made atonement with His own blood, He entered for us into God's presence. that He might obtain for us, and send down to dwell in us, the Holy Spirit. As the Spirit of the Father, and the Son, the whole life and love of the Father and the Son are in Him ; and coming down into us, He lifts us up into their fellowship. As Spirit of the Father, He sheds abroad the

Father's love, with which He loved the Son, in our hearts, and teaches us to live in it. As Spirit of the Son, He breaths in us the childlike liberty, and devotion, and obedience in which the Son lived upon earth. The Father can bestow no higher or more wonderful gift than this: His own Holy Spirit, the Spirit of sonship.

This truth naturally suggests the thought that this first and chief gift of God must be the first and chief object of all prayer. For every need of the spiritual life this is the one thing needful:the Holy Spirit. All the fulness is in Jesus; the fulness of grace and truth, out of which we receive, grace for grace. The Holy Spirit is the appointed conveyancer, whose special work it is to make Jesus and all there is in Him for us ours in personal appropriation, in blessed experience. He is the Spirit of life in Christ Jesus; as wonderful as the life is, so wonderful is the provision by which such an agent is provided to communicate it to us. If we but yield ourselves entirely to the disposal of the Spirit,and let Him have His way with us, He will manifest the life of Christ within us. He will do this with a Divine power, maintaining the life of Christ in us in uninterrupted continuity. Surely, if there is one prayer that should draw us to the Father's throne and keep us there, it is this: for the Holy Spirit, whom we as children have received, to stream into us and out from us in greater fulness.

In the variety of the gifts which the Spirit has to dispense, He meets the believer's every need: Just think of the names He bears. The Spirit of grace, to reveal and impart all of grace there is in Jesus. The Spirit of faith, teaching us to begin,and go on and increase in ever believing. The Spirit of adoption and assurance, who witnesses that we are God's children, and inspires the confiding and confident Abba Father! The Spirit of truth, to lead into all truth, to make each word of God ours in deed and in truth. The Spirit of prayer, through whom we speak with the Father;prayer that must be heard. The Spirit of judgment and burning, to search the heart, and convince of sin. The Spirit of holiness, manifesting and communicating the Father's holy presence within us. The Spirit of power, through whom we are strong to testify boldly and work effectually in the Father's service. The Spirit of glory, the pledge of our inheritance, the preparation and the foretaste of the glory to come. Surely the child of God needs but one thing to be able really to live as a child: it is, to be filled with this Spirit.

And now, the lesson Jesus teaches us today in His school is this: That the Father is just longing to give Him to us if we will but ask in the childlike dependence on what He says: ' If ye know to give good gifts unto your children, HOW MUCH MORE shall your heavenly Father gave the holy Spirit to them that ask Him.' In the words of God's promise, 'I will pour out my Spirit abundantly; 'and of His command, '

Be ye filled with the Spirit,' we have the measure of what God is ready to give, and what we may obtain. As God's children, we have already received the Spirit. But we still need to ask and pray for His special gifts and operations as we require them. And not only this, but for Himself to take complete and entire possession; for His unceasing momentary guidance. Just as the branch, already filled with the sap of the vine, is ever crying for the continued and increasing flow of that sap, that it may bring its fruit to perfection, so the believer, rejoicing in the possession of the Spirit, ever thirsts and cries for more. And what the great Teacher would have us learn is, that nothing less than God's promise and God's command may be the measure of our expectation and our prayer; we must be filled abundantly. He would have us ask this in the assurance that the wonderful How much more of God's Father-love is the pledge that, when we ask, we do most certainly receive.

Let us now believe this. As we pray to be filled with the Spirit, let us not seek for the answer in our feelings. All spiritual blessings must be received, that is, accepted or taken in faith.' Let me believe, the Father gives the Holy Spirit to His praying child. Even now, while I pray, I must say in faith:I have what I ask, the fulness of the Spirit is mine. Let us continue stedfast in this faith. On the strength of God's Word we know that we have what we ask. Let us, with thanksgiving that we have been heard, with thanksgiving for what we have received and taken and now hold as ours, continue stedfast in believing prayer that the blessing, which has already been given us, and which we hold in faith, may break through and fill our whole being. It is in such believing thanksgiving and prayer, that our soul opens up for the Spirit to take entire and undisturbed possession. It is such prayer that not only asks and hopes, but takes and holds, that inherits the full blessing. In all our prayer let us remember the lesson the Saviour would teach us this day; that, if there is one thing on earth we can be sure of, it is this, that the Father desires to have us filled' with His Spirit, that He delights to give us His Spirit.

And when once we have learned thus to believe for ourselves, and each day to take out of the treasure, we hold in heaven, what liberty and power to pray for the outpouring of the Spirit on the Church of God, on all flesh, on individuals, or on special efforts! He that has once learned to know the Father in prayer for himself, learns to pray most confidently for others too. The Father gives the Holy Spirit to them that asks Him, not least, but most, when they ask for others.

LORD, TEACH US TO PRAY!

Father in heaven ! Thou didst send Thy Son to reveal Thyself to us, Thy Father-love, and all that that love has for us. And He has taught us, that the gift above all gifts which Thou wouldest bestow in answer to prayer is, the Holy Spirit.

O my Father! I come to Thee with this prayer; there is nothing I would- -may I not say, I do-- desire so much as to be filled with the Spirit, the Holy Spirit. The blessings He brings are so unspeakable and just what I need. He sheds abroad Thy love in the heart, and fills it with Thyself. I long for this. He breathes the mind and life of Christ in me, so that I live as He did, in and for the Father's love. I long for this. He endues with power from on high for all my walk and work. I long for this, O Father ! I beseech Thee,give me this day the fulness of Thy Spirit. Father! I ask this, resting on the words of my Lord : ` How much more the Holy Spirit!' I do believe that Thou hearest my prayer; I receive now what I ask; Father! I claim and I take it: the fulness of Thy Spirit as mine. I receive the gift this day again as a faith gift; in faith I reckon my Father works through the Spirit all He has promised. The Father delights to breathe His Spirit into His waiting child as He tarries in fellowship with Himself. Amen

CHAPTER 8: Because of his Importunity or The Boldness of God's Friends

And He said unto them, Which of you shall have a friend,and shall go to him at midnight, and say to him, Friend, lend me three loaves; for a friend of mine is come to me from a journey, and I have nothing to set before him; and he from within shall answer and say, Trouble me not: the door is now shut, and my children are with me in bed; I cannot rise and give thee. 1 say unto you though he will not rise and give him because he is his friend, yet because of his importunity he will rise and give him as many as he needeth: --LUKE 11.5-8.

THE FIRST TEACHING TO HIS DISCIPLES WAS GIVEN BY OUR Lord in the Sermon on the Mount. It was nearly a year later that the disciples asked Jesus to teach them to pray. In answer He gave them a second time the Lord's prayer, so teaching them what to pray. He then speaks of how they ought to pray, and repeats what he formerly said of God's Fatherliness and the certainty of an answer. But in between He adds the beautiful parable of the friend at midnight, to teach them the twofold lesson, that God does not only want us to pray for ourselves, but for the perishing around us, and that in such intercession great boldness of entreaty is often needful, and always lawful yea, pleasing to God.

The parable is a perfect storehouse of instruction in regard to true intercession. There is, first, the love which seeks to help the needy around us: `my friend is come to me.' Then the need which urges to the cry: I have nothing to set before him.' Then follows the confidence that help is to be had: `which of you shall ask a friend and say, Friend, lend me three loaves.' Then comes the unexpected refusal; `I cannot rise and give thee.' Then again the Perseverance that takes no refusal: `because of his importunity. And lastly, the reward of such prayer: `he will give him as many as he needeth.' A wonderful setting forth of the way of prayer and faith in which the blessing of God has so often been sought and found.

Let us confine ourselves to the chief thought: prayer as an appeal to the friendship of God; and we shall find that two lessons are specially suggested. The one, that if we are God's friends and come as such to Him we must prove ourselves the friends of the needy; God's friendship to us and ours to others go hand in hand. The other, that when we come thus we may use the utmost liberty in claiming an answer.

There is a twofold use of prayer: the one, to obtain strength and blessing for our own life; the other, the higher, the true glory of prayer, for which Christ has taken us into His fellowship and teaching, is intercession, where prayer is the royal power a child of God exercises in heaven on behalf of others and even of the kingdom. We see it in Scripture how it was in intercession for others that Abraham and Moses, Samuel and Elijah, with all the holy men of old, proved that they had power with God and prevailed. It is when we give ourselves to be a blessing that we can specially count on the blessing of God. It is when we draw near to God as the friend of the poor and the perishing that we may count on His friendliness; the righteous man who is the friend of the poor is very specially the friend of God. This gives wonderful liberty in prayer. Lord! I have a needy friend whom I must help. As a friend I have undertaken to help him. In Thee I have a Friend, whose kindness and riches I know to be infinite: I am sure Thou wilt give me what I ask. If I, being evil, am ready to do for my friend what I can, how much more wilt Thou, O my heavenly Friend, now do for Thy friend what he asks?

The question might suggest itself, whether the Fatherhood of God does not give such confidence in prayer, that the thought of His Friendship can hardly teach us anything more: a father is more than a friend. And yet, if we consider it, this pleading the friendship of God opens new wonders to us. That a child obtains what he asks of his father looks so perfectly natural, we almost count it the father's duty to give. But with a friend it is as if the kindness is more free, dependent, not on nature, but on sympathy and character. And then the relation of a child is more that of perfect dependence; two friends are more nearly on a level. And so our Lord, in seeking to unfold to us the spiritual mystery of prayer, would fain have us approach God in this relation too, as those whom He has acknowledged as His friends, whose mind and life are in sympathy with His.

But then we must be living as His friends. I am still a child even when a wanderer; but friendship depends upon the conduct. 'Ye are my friends if ye do whatsoever I command you.' 'Thou seest that faith wrought with his works, and by works was faith made perfect; and the scripture was fulfilled which saith, And Abraham believed God and he was called the friend of God.' It is the Spirit, `the same Spirit,' that leads us that also bears witness to our acceptance With God; `likewise, also,' the same Spirit helpeth us in prayer. It is a life as the friend of God that gives the wonderful liberty to say: I have a friend to whom I can go even at midnight. And how much more when I go in the very spirit of that friendliness, manifesting myself the very kindness I look for in God, seeking to help my friend as I want God to help me. When I come to God in prayer, He always looks to what the aim is of my petition. If it be merely for my own comfort or joy I seek His grace, I do not receive. But if I can say that it is that He may be glorified in my dispensing His blessings to others, I shall not ask in vain. Or if I ask for others, but want to wait until God has made me so rich, that it is no sacrifice or act of faith to aid them, I shall not obtain. But if I can say that I have already undertaken for my needy friend, that in my poverty I have already begun the work of love, because I know I had a friend Who would help me, my prayer will be heard. Oh, we know not how much the plea avails: the friendship of earth looking in its need to the friendship of heaven: 'He will give him as much as he needeth.'

But not always at once. The one thing by which man can honour and enjoy his God is faith. Intercession is part of faith's training-school. There our friendship with men and with God is tested. There it is seen whether my friendship with the needy is so real, that I will take time and sacrifice my rest, will go even at midnight and not cease until I have obtained for them what I need. There it is seen whether my friendship with God is so clear, that I can depend on Him not to turn me away and therefore pray on until He gives.

O what a deep heavenly mystery this is of perseverance prayer. The God who has promised, who longs, whose fixed purpose it is to give the blessing, holds it back. It is to Him a matter of such deep importance that His friends on earth should know and fully trust their rich Friend in heaven, that He trains them, in the school of answer delayed, to find out how their perseverance really does prevail, and what the mighty power is they can wield in heaven, if they do but set themselves to it. There is a faith that sees the promise, and embraces it, and yet does not receive it (Hebrews 11:13,39). It is when the answer to prayer does not come, and the promise we are most firmly trusting appears to be of none effect, that the trial of faith, more precious than of gold, takes place. It is in this trial that the faith that has embraced the promise is purified and strengthened and prepared in personal, holy fellowship with the living God, to see the glory of God. It takes and holds the promise until it has received the fulfilment of what it had claimed in a living truth in the unseen but living God.

Let each child of God who is seeking to work the work of love in his Father's service take courage. The parent with his child, the teacher with his class, the visitor with his district, the Bible reader with his circle, the preacher with his hearers, each one who, in his little circle, has accepted and is bearing the burden of hungry, perishing souls-let them all take courage. Nothing is at first so strange to us as that God should really require persevering prayer, that there should be a real spiritual needs-be for importunity. To teach it us, the Master uses this almost strange parable. If the unfriendliness of a selfish earthly friend can be conquered by importunity, how much more will it avail with the heavenly Friend, who does so love to give, but is held back by our spiritual unfitness, our incapacity to possess what He has to give. O let us thank Him that in delaying His answer He is educating us up to our true position and the exercise of all our power with Him, training us to live with Him in the fellowship of undoubting faith and trust, to be indeed the friends of God. And let us hold fast the threefold cord that cannot be broken: the hungry friend needing the help, and the praying friend seeking the help, and the Mighty Friend, loving to give as much as he needeth.

O my Blessed Lord and Teacher! I must come to Thee in prayer. Thy teaching is so glorious, and yet too high for me to grasp. I must confess that my heart is too little to take in these thoughts of the wonderful boldness I may use with Thy Father as my Friend. Lord Jesus I trust Thee to give me Thy Spirit with Thy Word, and to make the Word quick and powerful in my heart. I desire to keep Thy Word of this day: `Because of his importunity he will give him as many as he needeth.' Lord! teach me more to know the power of persevering prayer. I know that in it the Father suits Himself to our need of time for the inner life to attain its growth and ripeness, so that His grace may indeed be assimilated and made our very own. I know that He would fain thus train us to the exercise of that strong faith that does not let Him go even in the face of seeming disappointment. I know He wants to lift us to that wonderful liberty, in which we understand how really He has made the dispensing of His gift dependent on our prayer. Lord! I know this: 0 teach me to see it in spirit and truth.

And may it now be the joy of my life to become the almoner of my Rich Friend in heaven, to care for all the angry and perishing, even at midnight, because I know my friend who always gives to him who perseveres, because of his importunity, as many as he needeth. Amen.

"Then saith he unto his disciples, The harvest truly is 'plenteous, but the laborers are few. Pray ye therefore the Lord of the harvest, that he will send forth laborers into his harvest" (Matthew 9:37-38).

The Lord frequently taught His disciples that they must pray and how they should pray. But He seldom told them what to pray. This He left to their sense of need and the leading of the Spirit. But in the above scripture He expressly directs them to remember one thing. In view of the abundant harvest, and the need for reapers, they must cry to the Lord of the harvest to send laborers. Just as in the parable of the friend at midnight, He wants them to understand that prayer is not to be selfish; it is the power through which blessing can come to others. The Father is Lord of the harvest. When we pray for the Holy Spirit, we must pray for Him to prepare and send laborers for the work.

Why does He ask His disciples to pray for this? Could He not pray Himself? Would not one prayer of His achieve more than a thousand of theirs? Is God, the Lord of the harvest, not aware of the need? And would He not, in His own good time, send laborers without the disciples' prayers? Such questions lead us into the deepest mysteries of prayer and its power in the Kingdom of God. The answer to such questions will convince us that prayer is indeed a power on which the gathering of the harvest and the coming of the Kingdom do in very truth depend.

Prayer is no form or show. The Lord Jesus was Himself the truth; everything He spoke was the truth. It was when "He saw the multitude, and was moved with compassion on them, because they were scattered abroad, as sheep having no shepherd," that He called on the disciples to pray for laborers to be sent to them (see Matthew 9:36). He did so because He really believed that their prayer was needed and would help.

The veil which hides the invisible world from us was wonderfully transparent to the holy human soul of Jesus. He had looked long and deep and far into the hidden connection of cause and effect in the spiritual world. He had marked in God's Word how God called men like Abraham, Moses, Joshua, Samuel, and Daniel, giving them authority over men in His Name. God also gave these men the authority to call the powers of heaven to their aid as they needed them. Jesus knew that the work of God had been entrusted to these men of old and to Himself for a time here upon earth. Now it was about to pass over into the hands of His disciples. He knew that where they were given responsibility for this work, it would not be a mere matter of form or show. The success of the work would actual depend on them and their faithfulness.

As a single individual, within the limitations of a human body and a human life, Jesus feels how little a short visit can accomplish among these wandering sheep He sees around Him. He longs for help to have them properly cared for. He therefore tells His disciples to begin to pray. When they have taken over the work from Him on earth, they are to make this one of their chief petitions in prayer: that the Lord of the harvest Himself would send laborer into His harvest. But since He entrusted them with the work and made it to a large extent dependent on them, He gives them authority to apply to Him for laborers and makes the supply dependent on their prayer.

How little Christians really feel and mourn the need of laborers in the fields of the world, so ripe for the harvest. How little they believe that our labor supply depends on prayer and that prayer will really provide "as many as he needeth." The dearth of labor is known and discussed. Efforts are sometimes made to supply the need. But how little the burden of the sheep wandering without a Shepherd is really assumed in the faith that the Lord of the harvest will send forth the laborers in answer to prayer. Without this prayer, fields ready for reaping will be left to perish. And yet it is so. The Lord has surrendered His work to His Church. He has made Himself dependent on them as His Body, through whom His work must be done. The power which the Lord gives His people to exercise in heaven and earth is real; the number of laborers and the measure of the harvest does actually depend on their prayer.

Why don't we obey the Master's instruction more heartily and cry more earnestly for laborers? There are two reasons. The one is: We miss the compassion of Jesus which gave rise to this request for prayer. Believers must learn to love their neighbors as themselves and to live entirely for God's glory in their relationships with fellow-men. The Father's first commandment to His redeemed ones is that they accept those who are perishing as the charge entrusted to them by their Lord. Accept them not only as a field of labor, but as the objects of loving care and interest. Soon, compassion towards the hopelessly perishing will touch your heart, and the cry will ascend with a new sincerity.

The other reason for the neglect of the command is: We believe too little in the power of prayer to bring about definite results. We do not live close enough to God to be capable of the confidence that He will answer. We have not surrendered entirely to His service and Kingdom. But our lack of faith will be overcome as we plead for help. Let us pray for a life in union with Christ, so that His compassion streams into us and His Spirit assures us that our prayer is heard.

Such prayer will obtain a twofold blessing. There will first be a desire for an increase in the number of men entirely given up to the service of God. That there are times when men actually cannot be found for the service of the Master as ministers, missionaries, or teachers of God's Word is a terrible blot upon the Church of Christ. As God's children make this a matter of supplication in their own circles or churches, it will be given. The Lord Jesus is now Lord of the harvest. He has been exalted to bestow the gifts of the Spirit. He wants to make gifts of men filled with the Spirit. But His supply and distribution of these gifts depend on the cooperation of the members with Him. Prayer will lead to such cooperation and will stir those praying to believe that they will find the men and the means for the work.

The other blessing will be equally great. Every believer is a laborer. As God's children, we have been redeemed for service and have our work waiting. It must be our prayer that the Lord would fill all His people with the spirit of devotion, so that no one may be found standing idle in the vineyard. Wherever there is a complaint about the lack of fit helpers for God's work, prayer has the promise of a supply. God is always ready and able to provide. It may take time and importunity, but Christ's command to ask the Lord of the harvest is the pledge that the prayer will be heard. "I say unto you, he will arise and give him as many as he needeth."

This power to provide for the needs of the world and secure the servants for God's work has been given to us in prayer. The Lord of the harvest will hear. Christ Who taught us to pray this way will support the prayers offered ire His Name and interest. Let us set apart time and give all of ourselves to this part of our intercessory work. It will lead us into the fellowship of that compassionate heart of His that led Him to call for our prayers. It will give us the insight of our royal position as children of the King whose will counts for something with the great God in the advancement of His Kingdom. We will feel that we really are God's fellowworkers on earth, that we have earnestly been entrusted with a share in His work. We will become partakers in the work of the soul. But we will also share in the satisfaction of the soul as we learn how, in answer to prayer, blessing has been given that otherwise would not have come.

Lord, teach us to pray.

Blessed Lord! Once again You have given us another wondrous lesson to learn. We humbly ask that you let us see these spiritual realities. There is a large harvest which is perishing as it waits for sleepy disciples to give the signal for laborers to come. Lord, teach us to view it with a heart full of compassion and pity. There are so few laborers, Lord. Show us what terrible sin the lack of prayer and faith is, considering there is a Lord of the harvest so able and ready to send them forth. Show us how He does indeed wait for the prayer to which He has promised an answer. We are the disciples to whom the commission to pray has been given. Lord, show us how You can breathe Your Spirit into us, so that Your compassion and the faith in Your promise will rouse us to unceasing, prevailing prayer.

O Lord! We cannot understand how You can entrust such work and give such power to men so slothful and unfaithful. We thank You for all those whom You are teaching day and night to cry for laborers to be sent. Lord, breathe Your Spirit into all Your children. Let them learn to live only for the Kingdom and glory of their Lord and become fully awake to the faith in what their prayer can accomplish. And let our hearts be filled with the assurance that prayer offered in living faith in the living God will bring certain and abundant answer. Amen.

"And Jesus answered and said unto him, What would thou that I should do unto thee?"(Mark 10:51; Luke 18:41).

The blind man had been crying out loud repeatedly, "Thou Son of David, have mercy on me." The cry had reached the ear of the Lord. He knew what the man wanted and was ready to grant it to him. But before He did it, He asked him, "What wilt thou that I should do unto thee?" He wanted to hear not only the general petition for mercy, but the distinct expression of what the man's desire was that day. Until he verbalized it, he was not healed.

There are still petitioners to whom the Lord puts the same question who cannot get the aid they need until they answer that question. Our prayers must be a distinct expression of definite need, not a vague appeal to His mercy or an indefinite cry for blessing. It isn't that His loving heart does not understand or is not ready to hear our cry. Rather, Jesus desires such definite prayer for our own sakes because it teaches us to know our own needs better. Time; thought, and self-scrutiny are required to find out what our greatest need really is. Our desires are put to the test to see whether they are honest and real and are according to God's Word. We also consider whether we really believe we will receive the things we ask. Such reflective prayer helps us to wait for the special answer and to mark it when it comes.

So much of our prayer is vague and pointless. Some cry for mercy, but do not take the trouble to know exactly why they want it. Others ask to be delivered from sin, but do not name any sin from which a deliverance can be claimed. Still others pray for God's blessing on those around them-for the outpouring of God's Spirit on their land or on the world-and yet have no special field where they can wait and expect to see the answer. To everyone the Lord says, "What do you really want, and what do you expect Me to do?"

Every Christian has only limited power. Just as he must have his own specific field of labor in which to serve God, he must also make his prayers specific. Each believer has his own circle, family, friends, and neighbors. If he were to take one or more of these by name, he would find himself entering the training school of faith which leads to personal dealing with his God. When we have faithfully claimed and received answers in such distinct matters, our more general prayers will be believing and effectual. Not many prayers will reach the mark if we just pour out our hearts in a multitude of petitions, without taking time to see whether every petition is sent with the purpose and expectation of getting an answer.

Bow before the Lord with silence in your soul and ask such questions as these:

What is really my desire?

Do I desire it in faith, expecting to receive an answer?

Am I ready to present it to the Father and leave it there in His bosom?

Is there agreement between God and me that I will get an answer?

We should learn to pray in such a way that God will see, and we will know what we really expect.

The Lord warns us against the vain repetitions of the Gentiles, who expect to be heard because they pray so much. We often hear prayers of great earnestness and fervor, in which a multitude of petitions are poured forth. The Savior would undoubtedly have to respond to some of them by asking: "What do you want?"

If I am in a foreign country on business for my father, I would certainly write two different sorts of letters home. There will be family letters with typical affectionate expressions in them, and there will be business letters containing orders for what I need. There may also be letters in which both are found. The answers will correspond to the letters. To each sentence of the letters containing the family news I do not expect a special answer. But for each order I send I am confident of an answer regarding the forwarding of the desired article. In our dealings with God, the business element must be present. Our expressions of need, sin, love, faith, and consecration must be accompained by an explicit statement of what we are asking for and what we expect to receive. In response, the Father loves to give us a token of His approval and acceptance.

But the word of the Master teaches us more. He does not say, "What dost thou wish?" but, "What dost thou will?" One often wishes for a thing without willing it. I wish to have a certain article but the price is too high, so I decide not take it. I wish, but do not will to have it. The lazy man wishes to be rich, but does not will it: Many people wish to be saved, but perish because they do not will it.

The will rules the whole heart and life. If I really will to have something that is within my reach, I do not rest until I have it. When Jesus asks us, "What wilt thou?" He asks whether it is our intention to get what we ask for at any price, however great the sacrifice. Do you really will to have it enough to pray continuously until He hears you, no matter how long it takes? How many prayers are wishes sent up for a short time and then forgotten! And how many are sent up year after year as a matter of duty, while we complacently wait without the answer.

One may ask if it wouldn't be better to make our wishes known to God, leaving it to Him to decide what is best, without our seeking to assert our wills. The answer is: by no means. The prayer of faith which Jesus sought to teach His disciples does not simply proclaim its desire and then leave the decision to God. That would be the prayer of submission for cases in which we cannot know God's will. But the prayer of faith, finding God's will in some promise of the Word, pleads for that promise until it comes.

In Matthew 9:28, Jesus said to the blind man, "Believe ye that I can do this?" In Mark He said, "What wilt thou that I should do?"(Mark 10:51). In both cases He said that faith had saved them. And He said to the Syrophenician woman, too, "Great is thy faith: be it unto thee even as thou wilt." Faith is nothing but the purpose of the will resting on God's Word and saying, "I must have it." To believe truly is to will firmly.

Such a will is not at variance with our dependence on God and our submission to Him. Rather, it is the true submission that honors God. It is only when the child has yielded his own will in entire surrender to the Father that he receives from the Father the liberty and power to will what he desires. Once the believer has accepted the will of God, as revealed through the Word and the Spirit, as his will, too, then it is the desire of God that His child use this renewed will in His service. The will is the highest power of the soul. Grace desires above everything to sanctify and restore this will to full and free exercise because it is one of the chief traits of God's image. God's child is like a son who lives only for his father's interests, seeks his father's will rather than his own, and is trusted by the father with his business. God speaks to that child in all truth, "What wilt thou?"

It is often spiritual sloth that, under the appearance of humility, professes to have no will. It fears the trouble of searching for the will of God, or, when found, the struggle of claiming it in faith. True humility is always accompanied by strong faith. Seeking to know only the will of God, that faith then boldly claims the fulfillment of the promise, "Ye shall ask what ye will, and it shall be done unto you."

Lord, teach us to pray.

Lord Jesus! Teach me to pray with all my heart and strength that there may be no doubt with You or with me about what I have asked. I want to know what I desire so well that as my petitions are being recorded in heaven, I can also record them here on earth and note each answer as it comes. Make my faith in what Your Word has promised so clear that the Spirit may work within me the liberty to will that it will come.

Lord! Renew, strengthen, and sanctify my entire will for the work of effectual prayer.

Blessed Savior! I pray that You reveal to me the wonderful grace You show us, the grace that asks us to say what we desire and then promises to do it. Son of God! I cannot fully understand it. I can only believe that You have indeed redeemed us wholly for Yourself, and that You want to mold our wills, making them Your most efficient servant. Lord! I unreservedly yield my will to You as the channel through which Your Spirit is to rule my whole being. Let Him take possession of it, lead it into the truth of Your promises, and make it so strong in prayer that I may always hear Your voice saying, "Great is thy faith: be it unto thee even as thou wilt." Amen.

"Therefore I say unto you, All things whatsoever ye pray and ask for, believe that ye have received them, and ye shall have them"(Mark 11:24).

What a promise! It is so large, so Divine, that our little hearts cannot comprehend it. In every possible way we seek to limit it to what we think is safe or probable. We don't allow it to come in just as He gave it to us with its quickening power and energy. If we would allow it, that promise would enlarge our hearts to receive all of what His love and power are really ready to do for us.

Faith is very far from being a mere conviction of the truth of God's Word or a conclusion drawn from certain premises. It is the ear which has heard God say what He will do and the eye which has seen Him doing it. Therefore, where there is true faith it is impossible for the answer not to come. We must do this one thing that He asks of us as we pray: "Believe that ye have received. "He will see to it that He does the thing He has promised: "Ye shall have them. "

The essence of Solomon's prayer (2 Chronicles 6:4) is, "Blessed be the Lord God of Israel, who hath with His hands fulfilled that which He spake with His mouth to my father David." This should be the essence of all true prayer. It is the joyful adoration of a God whose hand always secures the fulfillment of what His mouth has spoken. Let us in this spirit listen to the promise Jesus gives because each part of it has a Divine message.

"All things whatsoever. "From the first word our human wisdom begins to doubt and say, "This can't possibly be literally true." But if it isn't, why did the Master say it? He used the very stongest expression He could find: "All things whatsoever." And He said it more than once: "If thou canst believe, all things are possible to him that believeth" (Mark 9:23); "If ye have faith as a grain of mustard seed... nothing shall be impossible to you" (Matthew 17:20). Faith is completely the work of God's Spirit through His Word in the prepared heart of the believing disciple. It is impossible for the fulfillment not to come, because faith is the pledge and forerunner of the coming answer.

"All things whatsoever ye shall ask in prayer believing, ye receive. " The tendency of human reason is to intervene here with certain qualifiers, such as "if expedient," "if according to God's will," to break the force of a statement which appears dangerous. Beware of dealing this way with the Master's words. His promise is most literally true. He wants His frequently repeated "all things" to enter our hearts and reveal how mighty the power of faith is. The Head truly calls the members of His Body to share His power with Him. Our Father places His power at the disposal of the child who completely trusts Him. Faith gets its food and strength from the "all things" of Christ's promise. As we weaken it, we weaken faith.

The whatsoever is unconditional except for what is implied in the believing. Before we can believe, we must find out and know what God's will is. Believing is the exercise of a soul surrendered to the influence of the Word and the Spirit. Once we do believe, nothing is impossible. Let us pray that we do not limit Christ's "all things" with what we think is possible. Rather, His "whatsoever" should determine the boundaries of our hope and faith. It is seed-word which we should take just as He gives it and keep it in our hearts. It will germinate and take root, filling our lives with its fullness and bearing abundant fruit. "All things whatsoever ye pray and ask for." It is in prayer that these" all things" are to be brought to God. The faith that receives them is the fruit of the prayer. There must be a certain amount of faith before there can be prayer, but greater faith is the result of prayer. In the personal presence of the Savior and in conversation with Him, faith rises to grasp what at first appeared too high. Through prayer we hold up our desires to the light of God's Holy Will, our motives are tested, and proof is given whether we are indeed asking in the Name of Jesus and only for the glory of God. The leading of the Spirit shows us whether we are asking for the right thing and in the right spirit. The weakness of our faith becomes obvious as we pray. But we are encouraged to say to the Father that we do believe and that we prove the reality of our faith by the confidence with which we persevere. It is in prayer that Jesus teaches and inspires faith. Whoever waits to pray, or loses heart in prayer because he doesn't feel the faith needed to get an answer, will never learn that faith. Whoever begins to pray and ask will find the Spirit of faith is given nowhere so surely as at the foot of the throne. "Believe that ye have received." Clearly we are to believe that we receive the very things we ask. The Savior does not say that the Father may give us something else because He knows what is best. The very mountain that faith wants to remove is cast into the sea.

There is one kind of prayer in which we make known our request in everything, and the reward is the sweet peace of God in our hearts and minds. This is the prayer of trust. It makes reference to the countless desires of daily life which we cannot find out if God will give. We leave it to Him to decide whether or not to give, as He knows best. But the prayer of faith of which Jesus speaks is something higher and different. Nothing honors the Father like the faith that is assured that He will do what He has said in giving us whatever we ask. Such faith takes its stand on the promise delivered by the Spirit. It knows most certainly that it receives exactly what it asks, whether in the greater interest of the Master's work or in the lesser concerns of daily life. Notice how clearly the Lord states this in Mark 11:23: "Whosoever shall not doubt in his heart, but shall believe that what he saith cometh to pass, he shall have it." This is the blessing of the prayer of faith of which Jesus speaks.

"Believe that ye have received." This word of central importance is too often misunderstood. Believe that you have received what you're asking for now, while praying! You may not actually see it manifested until later. But now, without seeing it, you are to believe that it has already been given to you by the Father in heaven. Receiving or accepting an answer to prayer is just like receiving or accepting Jesus. It is a spiritual thing, an act of faith separate from all feeling. When I go to Jesus, asking Him for forgiveness for a sin, I believe He is in heaven for just that purpose, and I accept His forgiveness. In the same way, when I go to God asking for any special gift which is according to His Word, I must believe that what I desire is mine. I believe that I have it; I hold it in faith; and I thank God that it's mine. "If we know that He hear us, whatsoever we ask, we know that we have the petitions that we desired of Him"(I John 5:15).

"And ye shall have them. "The gift which we first hold in faith as ours from heaven will become ours in personal experience. But will it be necessary to pray longer once we know we have been heard and have received what we asked? Additional prayer will not be necessary when the blessing is on its way. In these cases we should maintain our confidence, proving our faith by praising God for what we have received, even though we haven't experienced it yet.

There are other cases in which faith needs to be further tried and strengthened in persevering prayer. Only God knows when everything is fully ripe for the manifestation of the blessing that has been given to faith. Elijah knew for certain that rain would come. God had promised it. And yet he had to pray the seven times. That prayer was not just for show. It was an intense spiritual reality both in the heart of Elijah as he lay there pleading and in heaven where it has its effectual work to do. It is through faith and patience we inherit the promises (Hebrews 6:12). Faith says most confidently, "I have received it." Patience perseveres in prayer until the gift bestowed in heaven is seen on earth. "Believe that ye have received, and ye shall have. " Between the have received in heaven, and the shall have of earth, the key word is believe. Believing praise and prayer is the link. Remember that it is Jesus Who said this. As we see heaven opened to us and the Father on the throne offering to give us whatever we ask for in faith, we are ashamed that we have so little availed ourselves of the privilege. We feel afraid that our feeble faith will still not be able to grasp what is so clearly placed within our reach. One thing must make us strong and full of hope: It is Jesus Who brought us this message from the Father. He Himself lived the life of faith and prayer when He was on earth. When the disciples expressed their surprise at what He had done to the fig tree, He told them that the very same life He led could be theirs. They could command not only the fig tree, but the very mountain, and they would obey.

Jesus is our life. In us He is everything now that He was on earth. He really gives everything He teaches. He is the Author and the Perfecter of our faith. He gives the spirit of faith. Don't be afraid that such faith isn't meant for us. Meant for every child of the Father, it is within the reach of anyone who will be childlike, yielding himself to the Father's will and love and trusting the Father's Word and power. Dear fellow Christian! Have courage! This word comes through Jesus, Who is God's Son and our Brother. Let our answer be, "Yes, blessed Lord, we do believe Your Word that we receive whatever we ask."

Lord, teach us to pray.

Blessed Lord! The Father sent You to show us all His Love and all the treasures of blessing that Love is waiting to bestow. Lord! You've given us such abundant promises concerning our liberty in prayer. We are ashamed that our poor hearts have accepted so little of it. It has simply seemed too much for us to believe.

Lord! Teach us to take and keep and use Your precious Word: "All things whatsoever ye ask, believe that ye have received." Blessed Jesus! It is in You that our faith must be rooted if it is to grow strong. Your work has completely freed us from the power of sin and has opened the way to the Father. Your love is longing to bring us into the full fellowship of Your glory and power. Your Spirit is constantly drawing us into a life of perfect faith and confidence. We are sure that through Your teaching we will learn to pray the prayer of faith. You will train us to pray so that we will believe that we really have what we ask for. Lord! Teach me to know and trust and love You in such a way that I live and dwell in You. Through You, may all my prayers rise up and go before God, and may my soul have the assurance that I am heard. Amen.

"Jesus, answering, saith unto them, Have faith in God. For verily I say unto you,... Whosoever shall not doubt in his heart, but shall believe that those things which he saith shall come to pass; he shall have whatsoever he saith"(Mark 11:22-23).

Answer to prayer is one of the most wonderful lessons in all Scripture. In many hearts it must raise the question, "How can I ever attain the faith that knows it receives everything it asks for?" It is this question our Lord will answer today.

Before He gave that wonderful promise to His disciples, Christ shows where faith in the answer to prayer originates and finds its strength. Have faith in God. This faith precedes the faith in the promise of an answer to prayer. The power to believe a promise depends entirely on faith in the promiser. Trust in the person engenders trust in what he says. We must live and associate with God in personal, loving communication. God Himself should be everything to us. His Holy Presence is revealed where our whole being is opened and exposed to His mighty influence. There the capacity for believing His promises will be developed.

The connection between faith in God and faith in His promise will become clear to us if we consider what faith really is. It is often compared to the hand or the mouth, by which we take and use what is given to us. But it is important that we understand that faith is also the ear by which we hear what is promised and the eye by which we see what is offered. The power to take depends on this. I must hear the person who gives me the promise because the very tone of his voice gives me courage to believe. I must see him because the light of his face melts all my qualms about my right to take. The value of the promise depends on the promiser. It is on my knowledge of what the promiser is that faith in the promise depends.

For this reason Jesus says, "Have faith in God, " before He gives the wonderful prayer-promise. Let your eye be open to the living God. Through this eye we yield ourselves to God's influence. Just allow it to enter and leave its impression on our minds. Believing God is simply looking at God and what He is, allowing Him to reveal His presence to us. Give Him time and completely yield to Him, receiving and rejoicing in His love. Faith is the eye through which the light of God's presence and the vigor of His power stream into the soul. As that which I see lives in me, so by faith God lives in me, too.

Faith is also the ear through which the voice of God is always heard. The Father speaks to us through the Holy Spirit. The Son is the Word-the substance of what God says-and the Spirit is the living voice. The child of God needs this secret voice from heaven to guide him, and teach him, as it taught Jesus, what to say and what to do. An ear opened towards God is a believing heart that waits to hear what He says.

The words of God will be not only the words of a book, they will be spirit, truth, life, and power. They will make mere thoughts come to life. Through this opened ear, the soul abides under the influence of the life and power of God Himself. As His words enter the mind, dwelling and working there, through faith God enters the heart, dwelling and working there.

When faith is in full use as eye and ear-the faculties of the soul by which we see and hear God-then it will be able to exercise its full power as hand and mouth-the faculties by which we take God and His blessings. The power of reception will depend entirely on the power of spiritual perception. For this reason, before Jesus gave the promise that God would answer believing prayer, He said, "Have faith in God." Faith is simply surrender. I yield myself to the suggestions I hear. By faith I yield myself to the living God. His glory and love fill my heart and have mastery over my life.

Faith is fellowship. I give myself up to the influence of the friend who makes me a promise and become linked to him by it. When we enter into living fellowship with God Himself, in a faith that always sees and hears Him, it becomes easy and natural to believe His promise regarding prayer. Faith in the promise is the fruit of faith in the promiser. The prayer of faith is rooted in the life of faith. And in this way the faith that prays effectively is indeed a gift of God. It is not something He bestows or infuses all at once, but is far deeper and truer. It is the blessed disposition or habit of soul which grows up in us through a life of communion with Him. Surely for one who knows his Father well and lives in constant close communion with Him, it is a simple thing to believe the promise that He will do what His child wishes.

Because very many of God's children do not understand this connection between the life of faith and the prayer of faith, their experience of the power of prayer is limited. Sincerely desiring to obtain an answer from God, they concentrate wholeheartedly on the promise and try their utmost to grasp that promise in faith. When they do not succeed, they are ready to give up hope. The promise is true, but it is beyond their power to accept it in faith.

Listen to the lesson Jesus teaches us: Have faith in God, the Living God. Let faith focus on God more than on the thing promised, because it is His love, His power, His living presence that will awaken and work the faith. To someone asking to develop more strength in his hands and arms, a physician would say that his whole constitution must be built up. So the cure of feeble faith can be found only in the invigoration of our whole spiritual lives through communication with God. Learn to believe in God, hold on to God, and to let God take possession of our life. It will become easy to grasp the promise. Whoever knows and trusts God finds it easy to also trust the promise. Note how distinctly this comes out in former saints. Every exhibition of the power of faith was the fruit of a special revelation from God. We see it in Abraham: "And the word of the Lord came unto Abram in a vision, saying, Fear not, Abram; I am thy shield .... And He brought him forth abroad, and said.....And he believed the Lord" (Genesis 15:1,5,6). And later again: "The Lord appeared to Abram, and said unto him, I am the Almighty God ....And Abram fell on his face, and God talked with him, saying, As for me, behold my convenant is with thee" (Genesis 17:1,3,4). It was the revelation of God Himself that gave the promise its living power to enter the heart and cultivate the faith. Because they knew God, these men of faith could not do anything but trust His promise. God's promise will be to us what God Himself is. The man who walks before the Lord and falls on his face to listen while the living God speaks to him will receive the promise. We have God's promises in the Bible with full liberty to claim them. Our spiritual power depends on God Himself speaking those promises to us. He speaks to those who walk and live with Him.

Therefore, have faith in God. Let faith be all eyes and ears. Surrender to God and let Him make His full impression on you, revealing Himself fully in your soul. Consider it a blessing of prayer that you can exercise faith in God as the living mighty God Who is waiting to give us the good pleasure of His will and faith with power. Regard Him as the God of love, Whose delight it is to bless and impart His love. In such faithful worship of God, the power will speedily come to believe the promise, too. "What things soever ye desire, when ye pray, believe that ye receive." Make God your own through faith; the promise will become yours, also.

Jesus is teaching us a precious lesson today. We seek God's gifts, but God wants to give us Himself first. We think of prayer as the means of extracting good gifts from heaven, and we think of Jesus as the means to draw ourselves up to God. We want to stand at the door and cry. Jesus wants us to enter in and realize that we are friends and children. Accept His teaching. Let every experience of the weakness of our faith in prayer incite us to have and exercise more faith in the living God, and in such faith to yield ourselves to Him. A heart full of God has power for the prayer of faith. Faith in God fosters faith in the promise, including the promise of an answer to prayer.

Therefore, child of God, take time to bow before Him and wait for Him to reveal Himself. Take time to let your soul exercise and express its faith in the Infinite One in holy worship. As He shares Himself with and takes possession of you, the prayer of faith will crown your faith in God.

Lord, teach us to pray.

O my God! I do believe in You. I believe You are the Father, infinite in Your love and power. As the Son, You are my redeemer and my life. And as the Holy Spirit, You are my comforter, my guide, and my strength. I have faith that You will share everything You are with me and that You will do everything You promise.

Lord Jesus! Increase my faith! Teach me to take time to wait and worship in God's Holy presence until my faith absorbs everything there is in Him for me. Let my faith see Him as the fountain of all life, working with almighty strength to accomplish His will in the world and in me. Let me see Him in His love longing to meet and fulfill my desires. Let faith take possession of my heart and life to the extent that through it God may dwell there. Lord Jesus, help me! I want with my whole heart to believe in God. Fill me every moment with faith in God. O my Blessed Savior! How can Your Church glorify You and fulfill the work of intercession through which Your Kingdom will come unless our whole lives consist of faith in God. Blessed Lord! Speak Your Word, "Have faith in God," into the depths of our souls. Amen.

"Then came the disciples to Jesus apart, and said Why could not we cast him out? And Jesus said unto them, Because of your unbelief. For verily I say unto you, If ye have faith as a grain of mustard seed, ye shall say unto this mountain, Remove hence to yonder place, and it shall remove; and nothing shall be impossible unto you. Howbeit this kind goeth nor out but by prayer and fasting"(Matthew 17:19-21). When the disciples saw Jesus cast the evil spirit out of the epileptic whom they could not cure, they asked the Master why they had failed. He had given them "power and authority over all devils, and to cure all diseases." They had often exercised that power, and joyfully told how the devils were subject to them. And yet now, while He was on the Mount, they had utterly failed. Christ's casting the evil spirit out proved that there had been nothing in the will of God or in the nature of the case to make the miracle impossible. From their expression, "Why could we not?", it is evident that the disciples had wanted and tried to cast the spirit out. They had probably called upon it, using the Master's Name. But their efforts had been in vain. They had been put to shame in front of the crowd.

Christ's answer was direct and plain: "Because of your unbelief." Christ's success was not a result of His having a special power to which the disciples had no access. He had so often taught them that there is one power-the power of faith-to which, in the kingdom of darkness as in the Kingdom of God, everything must bow. In the spiritual world failure has only one cause: lack of faith. Faith is the one condition on which all Divine power can enter man and work through him. It is the sensitivity of man's will yielded to and molded by the will of God.

The power the disciples had received to cast out devils did not belong to them as a permanent gift or possession. The power was in Christ, to be received, held, and used by faith alone, living faith in Himself. Had they been full of faith in Him as Lord and Conqueror in the spirit world, had they been full of faith in Him as having given them authority to cast out in His Name, their faith would have given them the victory. "Because of your unbelief" was, for all time, the Master's explanation and reproof of impotence and failure in His Church.

Such a deficiency of faith must have a cause. The disciples may have asked, "Why couldn't we believe? Our faith has cast out devils before this. Why did we fail in believing this time?" The Master answers them before they can ask, "This kind goeth not out but by prayer and fasting."

Though faith is the simplest exercise of the spiritual life, it is also the highest. 'The spirit must yield itself in perfect receptivity to God's

Spirit and become strengthened for this activity. Such faith depends entirely on the state of the spiritual life. Only when this is strong and in good health when the Spirit of God has total influence in our lives does faith have the power to do its mighty deeds.

Therefore Jesus adds, "Howbeit this kind goeth not out but by prayer and fasting." The faith than can overcome stubborn resistance such as you have just seen in this evil spirit, Jesus tells them, is not possible except for men living in very close fellowship with God and in very special separation from the world-in prayer and fasting. And so He teaches us two lessons in regard to prayer of deep importance. The one is that faith needs a life of prayer in which to grow and keep strong. The other is that prayer needs fasting for its full and perfect development.

Faith needs a life of prayer for its full growth. In all the different parts of the spiritual life there is a close union between unceasing action and reaction, so that each may be both cause and effect. Thus it is with faith. There can be no true prayer without faith; some measure of faith must precede prayer. And yet prayer is also the way to more faith: There can be no higher degrees of faith except through much prayer. This is the lesson Jesus teaches here.

Nothing needs to grow as much as our faith. "Your faith groweth exceedingly" is said of one church. When Jesus spoke the words,"According to your faith be it unto you" (Matthew 9:29), He announced the law of the Kingdom, which tells us that different people have different degrees of faith, that one person may have varying degrees, and that the amount of faith will always determine the amount of one's power and blessing. If we want to know where and how our faith is to grow, the Master points us to the throne of God. It is in prayer, exercising one's faith in fellowship with the living God, that faith can increase. Faith can only live by feeding on what is Divine, on God Himself.

It is in the adoring worship of God-the waiting on Him and for Him in the deep silence of soul that yields itself for God to reveal Himself-that the capacity for knowing and trusting God will be developed. As we take His Word from the Blessed Book and ask Him to speak it to us with His living, loving voice, the power to believe and receive the Word as God's own word to us will emerge in us. It is in prayer, in living contact with God in living faith, that faith will become strong in us. Many Christians cannot understand, nor do they feel the need, of spending hours with God. But the Master says (and the experience of His people has confirmed) that men of strong faith are men of much prayer.

This brings us back again to the lesson we learned when Jesus, before telling us to believe that we receive what we ask for, first said,"Have faith in God." It is God-the living God-into Whom our faith must strike its roots deeply and broadly. Then it will be strong enough to remove mountains and cast out devils. "If ye have faith, nothing shall be impossible to you." If we could only give ourselves up to the work God has for us in the world! As we came into contact with the mountains and the devils that are to be cast away and cast out, we would soon comprehend how much we need great faith and prayer. They alone are the soil in which faith can be cultivated. Christ Jesus is our life and the life of our faith. It is His life in us that makes us strong and ready to believe. The dying to self which much prayer implies allows a closer union to Jesus in which the spirit of faith will come in power. Faith needs prayer for its full growth.

The second lesson is that prayer needs fasting for its full growth. Prayer is the one hand with which we grasp the invisible. Fasting is the other hand, the one with which we let go of the visible. In nothing is man more closely connected with the world of sense than in his need for, and enjoyment of, food. It was the fruit with which man was tempted and fell in Paradise. It was with bread that Jesus was tempted in the wilderness. But He triumphed in fasting.

The body has been redeemed to be a temple of the Holy Spirit. In body as well as spirit, Scripture says, we are to glorify God in eating and drinking. There are many Christians to whom this eating for the glory of God has not yet become a spiritual reality. The first thought suggested by Jesus' words in regard to fasting and prayer is that only in a life of moderation and self-denial will there be sufficient heart and strength to pray much.

There is also a more literal meaning to His words. Sorrow and anxiety cannot eat, but joy celebrates its feasts with eating and drinking. There may come times of intense desire, when it is strongly felt how the body and its appetites still hinder the spirit in its battle with the powers of darkness. The need is felt of keeping it subdued. We are creatures of the senses. Our minds are helped by what comes to us in concrete form. Fasting helps to express, to deepen, and to confirm the resolution that we are ready to sacrifice anything, even ourselves, to attain the Kingdom of God. And Jesus, Who Himself fasted and sacrificed, knows to value, accept, and reward with spiritual power the soul that is thus ready to give up everything for Him and His Kingdom.

There is still a wider application of Christ's words. Prayer is reaching out for God and the unseen. Fasting is letting go of everything that can be seen and touched. Some Christians imagine that everything that isn't positively forbidden and sinful is permissible to them. So they try to retain as much as possible of this world with its property, its literature, and its enjoyments. The truly consecrated soul, however, is like a soldier who carries only what he needs for battle. Because he frees himself of all unnecessary weight, he is easily capable of combatting sin. Afraid of entangling himself with the affairs of a worldly life, he tries to lead a Nazarite life as one specially set apart for the Lord and His service. Without such voluntary separation, even from what is lawful, no one will attain power in prayer. Such power comes only through fasting and prayer.

Disciples of Jesus!-You have asked the Master to teach you to pray, so come now and accept His lessons! He tells you that prayer is the path to faithstrong faith that can cast out devils. He tells you: "If ye have faith, nothing shall be impossible to you." Let this glorious promise encourage you to pray much. Isn't the prize worth the price? Give up everything to follow Jesus in the path He opens to us! Fast if you need to! Do anything you must so that neither the body nor the world can hinder us in our great life-work-talking to God in prayer, so that we may become men of faith whom He can use in His work of saving the world.

Lord, teach us to pray.

O Lord Jesus! How continually You must reprimand us for our unbelief. Our terrible inability to trust our Father and His promises must appear quite strange to You. Lord! Let Your words, "Because of your unbelief," sink into the very depths of our hearts and reveal how much of the sin and suffering around us is our fault. Then teach us, Blessed Lord,that faith can be gained and learned in the prayer and fasting that brings us into living fellowship with Yourself and the Father.

O Savior! You are the Author and the Perfecter of our faith. Teach us what it means to let You live in us by Your Holy Spirit. Lord! Our efforts and prayers for grace to believe have been so ineffective. We know it is because we want You to give us strength in ourselves. Holy Jesus! Teach us the mystery of Your life in us-how You, by Your Spirit, live the life of faith in us, insuring that our faith will not fail. Make our faith a part of that wonderful prayer-life which You give to those who expect their training for the ministry of intercession to come from not only words and thoughts, but from the Spirit of Your own life. And teach us how, in fasting and prayer, we can mature in the faith for which nothing will be impossible. Amen.

"And when ye stand praying, forgive, if ye have ought against any; that your Father also which is in heaven may forgive you your trespasses" (Mark 11:25).

These words immediately follow the great prayer promise, "What things soever ye desire, when ye pray, believe that ye receive them, and ye shall have them" (Mark 11:24). We have already seen how the words that preceded that promise, 'Have faith in God,' taught us that, in prayer, everything depends: on the clarity of our relationship with God. These words that follow it remind us that our relationships: with our fellow-men must be clear, too. Love of God and love of our neighbor are inseparable. The prayer from a heart that is not right with God or with men will not succeed.

Faith and love are essential to each other. This is thought to which our Lord frequently gave expression. In the Sermon on the Mount, when speaking of the sixth commandment, He taught His disciples that acceptable worship of the Father was impossible if everything was not right with one's brother: "If thou art offering thy gift at the altar, and there rememberest that thy brother hath aught against thee, leave there thy gift before the altar, and go thy way; first be reconciled to thy brother, and then come and offer thy gift" (Matthew 5:23-24). After having taught us to pray, "Forgive us our debts, as we also have forgiven our debtors," Christ added, "If you forgive not men their trespasses, neither will your Father forgive your trespasses." At the close of the parable of the unmerciful servant, He applies His teaching in the words, "So likewise shall my heavenly Father do also unto you, if ye from your hearts forgive not every one his brother their trespasses" (Matthew 18:35).

Here, in Mark 11, beside the dried-up fig tree, as Jesus speaks of the power and the prayer of faith, He abruptly introduces the thought, "When ye stand praying, forgive, if ye have aught against any; that your Father also which is in heaven may forgive you your trespasses" (Mark 11:25). Perhaps the Lord had learned during His life that disobedience to the law of brotherly love was the great sin of even praying people, and the great cause of the ineffectiveness of their prayer. It is as if He wanted to lead us into His own blessed experience that nothing strengthens faith as much as the consciousness that we have given ourselves in love and compassion for those whom God loves.

The first lesson we are taught here is to have a forgiving disposition. We should pray, "Forgive us just as we have forgiven others." Scripture says, "Forgive one another, even as God also in Christ forgave you."

God's full and free forgiveness should be the model of our forgiveness of men. Otherwise our reluctant, half-hearted forgiveness, which is not forgiveness at all, will be God's rule with us. All of our prayers depend on our faith in God's pardoning grace. If God dealt with us while keeping our sins in mind, not one prayer would be heard. Pardon open the door to all God's love and blessing. Because God has pardoned all our sins, our prayers can go through to obtain all we need.

The deep sure ground of answer to prayer is God's forgiving love. When it has taken possession of our hearts, we pray in faith. But also, when it has taken possession of our hearts, we live in love. God's forgiving nature, revealed to us in His love, becomes our nature. With the power of His forgiving love dwelling in us, we forgive just as He forgives.

If great injury or injustice occurs, try first of all to assume a Godlike disposition. Avoid the sense of wounded honor, the desire to maintain your rights, and the need to punish the offender. In the little annoyances of daily life, never excuse a hasty temper, a sharp word, or a quick judgment with the thought that we mean no harm, or that it is too much to expect feeble human nature to really forgive the way God and Christ do. Take the command literally: "Even as Christ forgave, so also do ye." The blood cleanses selfishness from the conscience. The love it reveals is a pardoning love that takes possession of us and flows through us to others. Our forgiving love toward men is the evidence of God's forgiving love in us. It is a necessary condition of the prayer of faith.

There is a second, more general lesson: Our daily life in the world is the test of our communication with God in prayer. How often the Christian, when he comes to pray, does his utmost to cultivate certain frames of mind which he thinks will be pleasing. He doesn't understand (or he forgets) that life does not consist of a lot of loose pieces which can be picked up at random and then be discarded. Life is a whole. The hour of prayer is only a small part of daily life. God's opinion of what I really am and desire is not based on the feeling I conjure up, but on the tone of my life during the day.

My relationship with God is part of my relationships with men. Failure in one will cause failure in the other. It isn't necessary that it be a distinct consciousness of something wrong between my neighbor and myself. An ordinary current of thinking and judging-the unloving thoughts and words I allow to pass unnoticed-can hinder my prayer.

The effective prayer of faith comes from a life given up to the will and the love of God. Not as a result of what I try to be when praying, but because of what I am when I'm not praying, is my prayer answered by God.

All these thoughts can be gathered into a third lesson: In life among human beings, the one thing on which everything depends is love. The spirit of forgiveness is the spirit of love. Because God is love, He forgives. It is only when we are dwelling in love that we can forgive as God forgives. In love for our brothers we have the evidence of love for the Father, the basis for our confidence before God, and the assurance that our prayer will be heard. "Let us love in deed and truth; hereby shall we assure our heart before Him. If our heart condemn us not, we have boldness toward God, and whatever we ask, we receive of Him" (1 John 4:20; 3:18-22,23). Neither faith nor work will profit if we don't have love. Love unites us with God; it proves the reality of faith. "Have faith in God" and "Have love to men" are both essential commandments. The right relationships with the living God above me and the living men around me are the conditions for effective prayer. This love is of special consequence when we are praying for our fellowmen. We sometimes commit ourselves to work for Christ out of zeal for His cause or for our own spiritual health, without giving ourselves in personal self-sacrificing love for those whose souls we seek. No wonder our faith is powerless and without victory! View each wretched one, however unlovable he is, in the light of the tender love of Jesus the Shepherd searching for the lost. Look for Jesus Christ in him and take him into a heart that really loves, for Jesus' sake. This is the secret of believing prayer and successful effort. Jesus speaks of love as the root of forgiveness. It is also the root of believing prayer. There is nothing as heart-searching as believing prayer, or even the honest effort to pray in faith. Don't deflect that self-examination by the thought that God does not hear your prayer. "Ye ask and receive not, because ye ask amiss" (James 4:3). Let that Word of God search us. Ask whether our prayer is indeed the expression of a life completely given over to the will of God and the love of man. Love is the only soil in which faith can take root and thrive. Only in the love of fixed purpose and sincere obedience can faith obtain the blessing. Whoever gives himself to let the love of God dwell in him, whoever in daily life loves as God loves, will have the power to believe in the love that hears his every prayer. That almighty love is the Lamb Who is in the midst of the throne. It is suffering and enduring love that exists with God in prayer. The merciful shall obtain mercy; the meek shall inherit the earth.

Lord, teach us to pray.

Blessed Father! You are love, and only he who dwells in love can come into fellowship with You. Your blessed Son has taught me again how deeply true this. O my God! Let the Holy Spirit flood my heart with Your love. Be a fountain of love inside me that flows out to everyone around me. Let the power of believing prayer spring out of this life of love. O my Father! Grant by the Holy Spirit that this love may be the gate through which I find life in Your love. Let the joy with which I daily forgive whom ever might offend me be the proof that Your forgiveness is my power and life.

Lord Jesus! Blessed Teacher! Teach me how to forgive and to love. Let the power of Your blood make the pardon of my sins a reality, so that Your forgiveness of me and my forgiveness of others may be the very joy of heaven. Point out the weaknesses in my relationships with others that might hinder my fellowship with God. May my daily life at home and in society be the school in which strength and confidence are gathered for the prayer of faith. Amen.

CHAPTER 15: The Power of United Prayer

"Again I say unto you, That if two of you shall agree on earth as touching any thing that they shall risk, it shall be done for them of my Father which is in heaven. For where two or three are gathered together in my name, there am I in the midst of them" (Matthew 18:19-20). One of the first lessons of our Lord in His school of prayer was not to pray visibly. Go into your closet and be alone with the Father. When He has taught us that the meaning of prayer is personal, individual contact with God, He gives us a second lesson: You also need public, united prayer. He gives us a very special promise for the united prayer of two or three who agree in what they ask. As a tree has its root hidden in the ground and its stem growing up into the sunlight, so prayer needs secrecy in which the soul meets God alone and public fellowship with those who find their common meeting place in the Name of Jesus.

The reason why this must be so is plain. The bond that unites a man with his fellow-men is no less real and close than that which unites him to God: He one with them. Grace renews not only our relationship with God, but our relationships with our fellow human beings, too. We not only learn to say "My Father." It would be unnatural for the children of family to always meet their father separately, never expressing their desires or their love jointly. Believers are not only members of one family, but of one Body. Just as each member of the Body depends on the other, the extent to which the Spirit can dwell in the Body depends on the union and cooperation of everyone. Christians cannot reach the full blessing God is ready to bestow through His Spirit until they seek and receive it in fellowship with each other. It was to the hundred and twenty praying together in total agreement under the same roof that the Spirit came from the throne of the glorified Lord. In the same way, it is in the union and fellowship of believers that the Spirit can manifest His full power.

The elements of true, united prayer are given to us in these words of our Lord. The first is agreement as to the thing asked. It isn't enough to generally; consent to agree with anything another may ask. The object prayed for must be some special thing,a matter of distinct, united desire. The agreement must be, as in all prayer, in spirit and in truth. In such agreement exactly what we are asking for becomes very clear. We find out whether we can confidently ask for it according to God's will, and whether we are ready to believe that we have received it.

The second element is the gathering in the Name of Jesus. Later, we will learn much more about the necessity and the power of the Name of Jesus in prayer. Here our Lord teaches us that His Name must be the center and the bond of the union that makes them one, just as a home contains and unites all who are in it. "The Name of the Lord is a strong tower: the righteous runneth into it, and is safe" (Proverbs 18:10). That Name is such a reality to those who understand and believe in it, that to meet within it is to have Him present. Jesus is powerfully attracted by the love and unity of His disciples: "Where two or three are gathered in my Name, there am I in the midst of them" (Matthew 18:20). The presence of Jesus, alive in the fellowship of His loving, praying disciples, gives united prayer its power.

The third element is the sure answer: "It shall be done for them of my Father." Although a prayer meeting for maintaining religious fellowship, or for our own edification, may have its use, this was not the Savior's reason for recommending it. He meant it as a means of securing special answer to prayer. A prayer meeting without recognized answer to prayer ought to be the exception to the rule. When we feel too weak to exercise the faith necessary to attain a distinct desire, we ought to seek strength in the help of others. In the unity of faith, love, and the Spirit, the power of the Name and the presence of Jesus acts more freely, and the answer comes more surely. The evidence that there has been true, united prayer is the fruit-the answer, the receiving of the thing for which we have asked. "I say unto you, It shall be done for them of my Father which is in heaven."

What an extraordinary privilege united prayer is! What a potential power it has! Who can say why blessing might be gained:

if the believing husband and wife knew they were joined together in the Name of Jesus to experience His presence and power in united prayer (I Peter 33);

if friends were aware of the mighty help two or three praying in concert could give each other;

if in every prayer meeting the coming together in the Name, the faith in His presence, and the expectation of the answer stood in the foreground;

if in every church united, effective prayer were regarded as one of the chief purposes for which they are banded together;

if in the universal Church the coming of the Kingdom and of the King Himself were really matter of unceasing, united crying to God!

The Apostle Paul had great faith in the power of united prayer. To the Romans he writes, "I beseech you, brethren, by the love of the Spirit, that ye strive together with me in your prayer to God for me (Romans 15:30). He expects in answer to be delivered from his enemies and to prosper in his work. To the Corinthians he declares, "God will still deliver us, ye also helping together on our behalf by your supplications" (2 Corinthians 1:11). He expects their prayer to have a real share in his deliverance. To the Ephesians he writes, "With all prayer and supplication, praying at all seasons in the Spirit for all the saints and on my behalf, that utterance may be given unto me" (Ephesians 6:18-19). He makes the power and success in his ministry dependent on their prayers. With the Philippians he expects that his trials will become his salvation and increase the progress of the gospel, "through your supplications and the supply of the Spirit of Jesus Christ" (Philippians 1:19). When telling the Colossians to continue praying constantly, he adds, "Withal praying for us too, that God may open unto us a door for the word" (Colossians 4:3). And to the Thessalonians he writes, "Finally, brethren, pray for us, that the word of the Lord may run and be glorified, and that we may be delivered from unreasonable men" (2 Thessalonians 3:1-2).

It is quite evident that Paul perceived himself as the member of a Body whose sympathy and cooperation he depended on. He counted on the prayers of these churches to gain for him what otherwise might not be given. The prayers of the Church were to him as real a factor in the work of the Kingdom as the power of God.

Who can say what power a church could develop and exercise if it would assume the work of praying day and night for the coming of the Kingdom, for God's power, or for the salvation of souls? Most churches think their members gather simply to take care of and edify each other. They don't know that God rules the world by the prayers of His saints, that prayer is the power by which Satan is conquered,and that through prayer the Church on earth has access to the powers of the heavenly world. They do not remember that Jesus has, by His promise, made every assembly in His Name a gate to heaven, where His presence is to be felt, and His power experience by the Father fulfilling their desires.

We cannot sufficiently thank God for the blessed work of united prayer, with which Christendom, in our days, opens every year. It is of unspeakable value as proof of our unity and our faith in the power of united prayer, as a training school for the enlargement of our hearts to take in all the needs of the Church, and as a help to united persevering prayer. But it has been a special blessing as stimulus to continued union in prayer in the smaller circles. When God's people realize what it means to meet as one in the Name of Jesus, with His presenc in the midst of a Body united in the Holy Spirit, they will boldly claim the promise that the Father will do what they agree to request.

Lord, teach us to pray.

Blessed Lord! You ask so earnestly for the unity of Your people. Teach us how to encourage our unity with Your precious promise regarding united prayer. Show us how to join together in love any desire, so that Your presence is in our faith in the Father's answer.

O Father! We pray for those smaller circles of people who meet together so that they may become one. Remove all selfishness and self-interest, all narrowness of heart and estrangement that hinders their unity. Cast out the spirit of the world and the flesh through which Your promise loses all its power. Let the thought of Your presence and the Father's favor draw us all nearer to each other.

Grant especially, blessed Lord, that Your Church may believe that it is by the power of united prayer that she can bind and loose in heaven, cast out Satan, save souls, remove mountains, and hasten the coming of the Kingdom. And grant, good Lord, that my prayer circle may indeed pray with the power through which Your Name and Word are glorified. Amen.

"And he spake a parable unto them to this end, that men ought always to pray, and not to faint; saying there was in a city a judge, which feared not God neither regarded man: And there was a widow in that city; and she came unto him, saying, Avenge me of mine adversary. And he would not for a while but afterward he said within himself, Though I fear not God, nor regard man; Yet because this widow troubleth me, I will avenge her, lest by her continual coming she weary me. And the Lord said, Hear what the unjust judge saith. And shall not God avenge his own elect, which cry day and night unto him, though he bear long with them? I tell you that he will avenge them speedily. Nevertheless, when the Son of may cometh, shall he find faith on the earth?" (Luke18:1-8).

Of all the mysteries of the prayer world, the need for persevering prayer is one of the greatest. We cannot easily understand why the Lord, Who is so loving and longing to bless us, should have to be petitioned time after time, sometimes year after year, before the answer comes. It is also one of the greatest practical difficulties in the exercise of believing prayer. When our repeated prayers remain unanswered, it is easy for our lazy flesh maintaining the appearance of pious submission-to think that we must stop praying because God may have a secret reason for withholding His answer to our request. Faith alone can overcome difficulty. Once faith has taken its stand on God's Word and the Name of Jesus, and has yielded itself to the leading of the Spirit to seek only God's will and honor in its prayer, it need not be discouraged by delay. It knows from Scripture that the power of believing, prayer is considerable; real faith can never be disappointed. It knows that to exercise its power, it must he gathered up, just like water, until the stream carp come down in full force. Prayer must often be "heaped up" until God sees that its measure is full. Then the answer comes. Just as each of ten thousand seeds is a part of the final harvest, frequently be repeated, persevering prayer is necessary to acquire a desired blessing. Every single believing prayer has its influence. It is stored up toward an answer which comes in due time to whomever perseveres to the end. Human thoughts and possibilities have nothing to do with it; only the Word of the living God matters. Abraham for so long "in hope believed against hope" and then "through faith and patience inherited the promise." Wait and pray often for the coming of the Lord to fulfill His promise.

When the answer to our prayer does not come at once we should combine quiet patience and joyful as confidence in our persevering prayer. To enable us to do this, we must try to understand two words in which our Lord describes the character and conduct of our God and Father towards those who cry day and night to Him: "He is long-suffering over them. He will avenge them speedily."

The Master uses the word speedily. The blessing is all prepared. The Father is not only willing, but most anxious to give them what they ask. His everlasting love burns with His longing desire to reveal itself fully to His beloved and to satisfy their need. God will not delay one moment longer than is absolutely necessary. He will do everything in His power to hasten the answer.

But why-if this is true and God's power is infinite does it often take so long to get an answer to prayer? And why must God's own elect so often, in the midst of suffering and conflict, cry day an night? "He is long-suffering over them." "Behold! the husbandman waiteth for the precious fruit of the earth, being long-suffering over it, till he receive the early and the latter rain" (James 5:7). Of course the husbandman longs for his harvest. But he knows it must have its full term of sunshine and rain, so he has plenty of patience. A child so often wants to pick the half-ripe fruit, while the farmer knows to wait until the proper time.

In his spiritual nature, man, too, is under the law of gradual growth that reigns in all created life. Only on the path of development can he reach his divine destiny. And only the Father, Who determines the times and seasons, knows the moment when the soul , or the Church is ripened to that fullness of faith in which it can really take and keep a blessing . As a father who longs to have his only child home from school, and yet waits patiently until the time of , training is completed, so it is with God and His children.

Insight into this truth should lead the believer to cultivate the corresponding attitudes of patience, faith, waiting, and praise, which are the secret of his perseverance. By faith in the promise of God, we know that we have the petitions we have asked of Him. Faith holds the answer in the promise as an unseen spiritual possession. It rejoices in it and praises God for it. But there is a difference between this kind of faith and the clearer, fuller, riper faith that obtains the promise as a present experience. It is in persevering, confident, and praising prayer that the soul grows up into full union with its Lord in which it can possess the blessing in Him.

There may be things around us that have to be corrected through prayer before the answer can fully happen. The faith that has, according to the command, believed that it has received, can allow God to take His time. It knows it has and must succeed. In quiet, persistent, and determined perseverance it continues in prayer and thanksgiving until the blessing comes. And so we see a combination of what at first sight appears to be so contradictory: the faith that rejoices in God's answer as a present possession combined with the patience that cries day and night until that answer comes. The waiting child meets God triumphantly with his patient faith.

The great danger in this school is the temptation to think that it may not be God's will to give us what we desire. If our prayer agrees with God's Word and is led by the Spirit, don't give way to these fears.

Learn to give God time. He needs time with us. In daily fellowship with Him, we must give Him time to exercise the full influence of His presence in us. Day by day, as we are kept waiting, it is necessary that faith be given time to prove its reality and fill our beings entirely. God will lead us from faith to vision; we will see His glory.

Don't let delay shake your faith, for it is faith that will provide the answer in time. Each believing prayer is a step nearer to the final victory! It ripens the fruit, conquers hindrances in the unseen world, and hastens the end. Child of God! Give the Father time! He is long-suffering over you. He wants your blessing to be rich, full, and sure. Give Him time, but continue praying day and night. And above all, remember the promise: "I say unto you, He will avenge them speedily." The blessing of such persevering prayer is indescribable. There is nothing that examines the heart more closely than the prayer of faith. It teaches you to discover, confess, and give up everything that hinders the coming of the blessing everything that is not in accordance with the Father's will. It leads to closer fellowship with Him, Who alone can teach you to pray. Complete surrender becomes possible under the covering of the blood and the Spirit. Christian! Give God time! He will perfect whatever concerns you!

Let your attitude be the same whether you are praying for yourself or for others. All labor, bodily or mental, needs time and effort. We must give ourselves up to it. Nature reveals her secrets and yields her treasures only to diligent and thoughtful labor. However little we can understand it, spiritual husbandry is always the same: The seed we sow in the soil of heaven, the efforts we put forth, and the influence we seek to exert in the world above all require our complete surrender in prayer. Maintain great confidence that when the time is right, we will reap abundantly if we don't give up (Galatians 6:9).

Let us especially learn this lesson as we pray for the Church of Christ. She is indeed like a poor widow in the absence of her Lord, apparently at the mercy of her adversary and helpless to correct the situation. When we pray for His Church or any portion of it that is under the power of the world, let us ask Him to visit her with mighty workings of His Spirit to prepare her for His coming. Pray in the assured faith that prayer does help. Unceasing prayer will bring the answer. Just give

God time. And remember this day and night: "Hear what the unrighteous judge saith. And shall not God avenge His own elect, which cry to Him day and night, and He is longsuffering over them. I say unto you, He will avenge them speedily."

Lord, teach us to pray.

O Lord my God! Teach me how to know Your way and in faith to learn what Your beloved Son has taught: "He will avenge them speedily." Let Your tender love, and the delight You have in hearing and blessing Your children, lead me implicitly to accept the promise that we may have whatever we ask for, and that the answer will be seen in due time. Lord! We understand nature's seasons; we know how to wait for the fruit we long for. Fill us with the assurance that You won't delay one moment longer than is necessary, and that our faith will hasten the answer.

Blessed Master! You have said that God's elect appeal to Him day and night. Please teach us to understand this. You know how quickly we become tired. Perhaps we feel that the Divine Majesty of the Father is so far beyond the reach of our continued prayer that is isn't becoming for us to plead with Him too much. O Lord! Teach me how real the labor of prayer is! I know that here on earth, when I fail at something, I can often succeed by renewed and more continuous effort, and by taking more time and thought. Show me how, by giving myself more entirely to prayer-by actually living in prayer I can obtain what I have asked for.

Above all, O blessed Teacher, Author and Perfecter of my faith, let my whole life be one of faith in the Son of God Who loved me and gave Himself for me! In You my prayer gains acceptance and I have the assurance of the answer. Lord Jesus! In such faith I will pray always, ceasing never. Amen.

AUTHOR'S NOTE

The need of persevering prayer appears to be at variance with the faith which knows that it has received what it asks (Mark 11:24). One of the mysteries of the Divine life is the harmony between sudden, complete possession and slow, imperfect appropriation. Here persevering prayer appears to be the school in which the soul is strengthened for the boldness of faith. Considering the diversity of operations of the Spirit, there may be some in whom faith takes the form of persistent waiting. For others, triumphant thanksgiving appears the only proper expression of the assurance of having been heard.

"Father, I thank thee that thou hast heard me. And I knew that thou hearest me always" (John 11:41-42).

"Thou art my Son; this day have I begotten thee. Ask of me, and I shall give thee" (Psalm 2:7-8).

In the New Testament we find a distinction made between faith and knowledge. "To one is given, through the Spirit, the word of wisdom; to another the word of knowledge, according to the same Spirit; to another faith, in the same Spirit" (1 Corinthians 12:8-9). In a child or an uninformed Christian there may be much faith with little knowledge. Childlike simplicity accepts the truth without difficulty, and often cares little to give any reason for its faith but this: God said it. But it is the will of God that we should love and serve Him, not only with all the heart but also with all the mind. He wants us to develop an insight into the Divine wisdom and beauty of all His ways, words, and works. Only in this way will the believer be able to fully approach and rightly adore the glory of God's grace. And only thus can our hearts intelligently understand the treasures of wisdom and knowledge, that exist in redemption, preparing us to join in the,highest note of the song that rises before the throne: "O the depth of the riches both of the wisdom and knowledge of God!"

This truth has its full application in our prayer life. While prayer and faith are so simple that the newborn convert can pray with power, more mature Christians may find in the doctrine of prayer some of their deepest questions. How extensive is the power of prayer? How can God grant to prayer such mighty power? How can prayer be harmonized with the will of God? How can God's sovereignty and our will God's liberty and ours-be reconciled? These and similar questions are appropriate subjects for Christian meditation and inquiry. The more earnestly and reverently we approach such mysteries, the more we will fall down in adoring wonder to praise Him Who has in prayer given such power to man.

One of the difficulties with regard to prayer is the result of the perfection of God. He is absolutely independent of everything outside of Himself. He is an infinite being Who owes what He is to Himself alone. With His wise and holy will, He has determined Himself and everything that is to be. How can our prayer influence Him? How can He be moved by prayer to do what He otherwise would not do? Isn't the promise of an answer to prayer simply a condescension to our weakness? Is the power of prayer anything more than an accommodation of our mode of thought, because the accomplishments of Deity are never dependent of any outside action? And isn't the real blessing of prayer simply the influence it exerts on us?

Seeking answers to such questions provides the key to the very being of God in the mystery of the Holy Trinity. If God were only one Person, shut up within Himself, there could be no thought of nearness to Him or influence on Him. But in God there are three Persons: Father and Son, Who have in the Holy Spirit their living bond of unity and fellowship. When the Father gave the Son a place next to Himself as His equal and His counselor, He opened a way for prayer and its influence into the very inmost life of Deity itself.

On earth, just as in heaven, the whole relationship between Father and Son is that of giving and taking. If the taking is to be as voluntary and self-determined as the giving, the Son must ask and receive. "Thou art my Son; this day I have begotten thee. Ask of me, and I shall give thee" (Psalm 2:7-8). The Father gave the Son the place and the power to influence Him. The Son's asking wasn't just for show. It was one of those life-movements in which the love of the Father and the Son met and completed each other. The Father had determined that He would not be alone in His counsels. Their fulfillment would depend on the Son's asking and receiving. Thus asking was in the very Being and Life of God. Prayer on earth was to be the reflection and the outflow of this. Jesus said, "I knew that Thou hearest me always" (John 11:42). Just as the Sonship of Jesus on earth cannot be separated from His Sonship in heaven, His prayer on earth is the continuation and the counterpart of His asking in heaven. His prayer is the link between the eternal asking of the only begotten Son in the bosom of the Father and the prayer of men on earth. Prayer has its rise and its deepest source in the very Being of God. In the bosom of Deity nothing is ever done without prayer-the asking of the Son and the giving of the Father.

This may help us to understand how the prayer of man, coming through the Son, can have an effect on God. God's decrees are not made without reference to the Son, His petition, or a petition sent up through Him. The Lord Jesus is the first-begotten, the Head and Heir of all things. As the Representative of all creation, He always has a voice in the Father's decisions. In the decrees of the eternal purpose, room was always left for the liberty of the Son as Mediator and Intercessor. The same holds true for the petitions of all who draw near to the Father through the Son.

If Christ's liberty and power to influence the Father seems to be at variance with the immutability of the Divine decrees, remember that God doesn't leave a past, as man does, to which He is irrevocably bound. The distinctions of time have no meaning to Him Who inhabits eternity. Eternity is an everpresent now, in which the past never passes and the future is always present. To meet our human comprehension of time, Scripture must speak of past decrees and a coming future.

In reality, the unchanging nature of God's plan is still in perfect harmony with His liberty to do whatever He wills. The prayers of the Son and His people weren't included in the eternal decrees simply for show. Rather, the Father listens with His heart to every prayer that rises through the Son. God really does allow Himself to be moved by prayer to do what He otherwise would not have done.

This perfect, harmonious union of Divine sovereignty and human liberty is an unfathomable mystery because God as the Eternal One transcends all our thoughts. But let it be our comfort and strength to know that in the eternal fellowship of the Father and the Son, the power of prayer has its origin and certainty. Through our union with the Son, our prayer is taken up and can have its influence in the inner life of the Blessed Trinity. God's decrees are no iron framework against which man's liberty struggles vainly. God Himself is living love, Who in His Son as man has entered into the tenderest relationship with all that is human. Through the Holy Spirit, He takes up everything human into the Divine life of love, leaving Himself free to give every human prayer its place in His government of the world.

In the light of such thoughts, the doctrine of the Blessed Trinity is no longer an abstract speculation, but the living manifestation of how man is taken up into the fellowship of God, his prayer becoming a real factor in God's rule of this earth. We can catch a glimpse of the light shining out from the eternal world in words such as these: "Through Him, we have access by one Spirit unto the Father."

Lord, teach us to pray.

Everlasting God! In deep reverence I worship before the holy mystery of Your Divine being. If it pleases You, most glorious God, to reveal some of that mystery to me, I would bow with fear and trembling rather than sin against You as I meditated on Your glory.

Father! I thank You for being not only the Father of Your children here on earth, but the Father of Jesus Christ through eternity. Thank You for hearing our prayers and for having given Christ's asking a place in Your eternal plan. Thank You also for sending Christ to earth and for His blessed communication with You in heaven. There has always been room in Your counsel for His prayers and the answers to those prayers. And I thank You above all that through Christ's true human nature on Your throne above, and through Your Holy Spirit in our human nature here below, a way has been opened by which every human cry of need can be received into the life and love of God, always obtaining an answer.

Blessed Jesus! As the Son, You have opened this path of prayer and assured us of an answer. We beseech You to teach us how to pray. Let our prayers be the sign of our sonship, so that we, like You, know that the Father always hears us. Amen.

"And he saith unto them, Whose is this image and superscription?" (Matthew 22:20).

"And God said, Let us make man in our image, after our likeness" (Genesis 1:26).

"Whose is this image?" It was with this question that Jesus foiled His enemies when they tried to trick Him, settling the matter of responsibility in regard to paying taxes. The question and the principle it involves are universally applicable, particularly to man himself. Bearing God's image decides man's destiny. He belongs to God and prayer to God is what he was created for. Prayer is part of the wondrous likeness he bears to His Divine original. It is the earthly likeness of the deep mystery of the fellowship of love in which the Trinity has its blessedness.

The more we meditate on what prayer is and on the wonderful power it has with God, the more we have to ask how man is so special, that such a place in God's plan has been allotted to him. Sin has so degraded him that we can't conceive of what he was meant to be based on what he is now. We must turn back to God's own record of man's creation to find what God's purpose was, and what capacities man was given to fulfill that purpose.

Man's destiny appears clearly in God's language at creation. It was to fill, to subdue, and to have dominion over the earth and everything in it. These three expressions show us that man was intended, as God's representative, to rule here on earth. As God's deputy, he was to fill God's place, keeping everything in subjection to Him. It was the will of God that everything done on earth should be done through man, i.e., the history of the earth was to be entirely in his hands.

In accordance with such a destiny was the position he was to occupy and the power at his disposal. When an earthly sovereign sends a representative to a distant province, that representative advises the sovereign as to the policy to be adopted there. The sovereign follows that advice, doing whatever is necessary to inact the policy and maintain the dignity of his empire. If the sovereign, however, doesn't approve of the policy, he replaces the representative with someone who better understands his desires for the empire. But as long as the representative is trusted, his advice is carried out.

As God's representative, man was to have ruled. Everything was to have been done according to his will. On his advice and at his request, heaven was to have bestowed its blessing on earth. His prayer was to have been the natural channel through which the Lord in heaven and man, as lord of this world, communicated. The destinies of the world were given into the power of the wishes, the will, and the prayers of man.

With the advent of sin, all this underwent a terrible change: Man's fall brought all creation under the curse. Redemption brought the beginning of a glorious restoration. In Abraham, God began to make Himself a people from whom kings (not to mention the Great King) would emerge. We see how Abraham's prayer power affected the destinies of those who came into contact with him. In Abraham we see how prayer is not only the means of obtaining blessing for ourselves. It is the exercise of a royal prerogative to influence the destinies of men and the will of God which rules them. We do not once find Abraham praying for himself. His prayers for Sodom and Lot, for Abimelech, and for Ishmael prove that a man who is God's friend has the power to control the history of those around him.

This had been man's destiny from the first. But Scripture tells us more: God could entrust man with such a high calling because He had created him in His own image and likeness. The external responsibility was not committed to him without the inner fitness. The root of man's inner resemblance to God was in his nature to have dominion, to be lord of all. There was an inner agreement and harmony between God and man, an embryonic Godlikeness, which gave man a real fitness for being the mediator between God and His world.

Man was to be prophet, priest, and king, to interpret God's will, to represent nature's needs, to receive and dispense God's bounty. It was in bearing God's image that he could bear God's rule. He was indeed so much like God-so capable of entering into God's purposes and carrying out His plans that God could trust him with the wonderful privilege of asking for and obtaining what the world might need.

Although sin has for a time frustrated God's plans, prayer still remains what it would have been if man had never fallen: the proof of man's Godlikeness, the vehicle of his communication with the Father, and the power that is allowed to hold the hand that holds the destinies of the universe. Man is of Divine origin, created for and capable of possessing kinglike liberty. His prayer is not merely a cry for mercy. It is the greatest execution of his will.

What sin destroyed, grace has restored. What the first Adam lost, the second has won back. In Christ, man regains his original position, and the Church, abiding in Christ, inherits the promise: "Ask what ye will, and it shall be done unto you."

To begin with, such a promise does by no means refer to the grace or blessing we need for ourselves. It has reference to our position as the fruit-bearing branches of the heavenly Vine, who, like Him, only live for the work and glory of the Father. It is for those who abide in Him, who have forsaken themselves for a life of obedience and self-sacrifice in Him, who have completely surrendered to the interests of the Father and His Kingdom. They understand how their redemption through Christ has brought them back to their original destiny, restoring God's image and the power to have dominion.

Such men indeed have the power-each in his own area-to obtain and dispense the powers of heaven here on earth. With holy boldness they may make known what they will. They live as priests in God's presence. They are kings possessing the powers of the world to come. 1- {1- "God is seeking priests among the sons of men. A human priesthood is one of the essential parts of His eternal plan. To rule creation by man is His design.} They enter upon the fulfillment of the promise: "Ask whatsoever ye will, and it shall be done unto you." Church of the living God! Your calling is higher and holier than you know! God wants to rule the world through your members. He wants you to be His kings and priests. Your prayers can bestow and withhold the blessings of heaven. In His elect who are not content just to be saved, but who surrender themselves completely, the Father will fulfill all His glorious counsel through them just as He does through the Son. In His elect, who cry day and night to Him, God wants to prove how wonderful man's original destiny was. Man was the image-bearer of God on earth, which was indeed given to him to rule. When he fell, everything fell with him. Now the whole creation groans and travails in pain together.

But now man is redeemed. The restoration of the original dignity has begun. It is God's purpose that the fulfillment of His eternal purpose and the coming of His Kingdom should depend on His people. They abide in Christ and are ready to accept Him as their Head, their great Priest-King. In their prayers they boldly say what they desire God to do for them. As God's image-bearer and representative on earth, redeemed man has the power to determine the history of this earth through his prayers. Man was created and then redeemed to pray, and by his prayer to have dominion.

"Priesthood is the appointed link between heaven and earth, the channel of communication between the sinner and God. Such a priesthood, insofar as expiation is concerned, is in the hands of the Son of God alone; insofar as it is to be the medium of communication between Creator and creature, is also in the hands of redeemed men-of the Church of God.

"God is seeking kings. Not out of the ranks of angels. Fallen man must furnish Him with the rulers of His universe. Human hands must wield the scepter, human heads must wear the crown." (The Rent Veil, by Dr. H. Bonar.)

Lord, teach us to pray.

"Lord! What is man, that thou art mindful of him? and the son of man, that thou visitest him? for thou hast made him a little lower than the angels, and hast crowned him with glory and honor. Thou madest him to have dominion over the works of thy lands; thou hast put all things under his feet .... 0 Lord our Lord, how excellent is thy name in all the earth!" (Psalm 8:4-6,9).

Lord God! Man has sunk so low because of sin. And how terribly it has darkened his mind. He doesn't even know his Divine destiny: to be Your servant and representative. How sad it is that, even when their eyes are opened, men are so unready to accept their calling! They could have such power with God and with men, too!

Lord Jesus! Through You, the Father has again crowned man with glory and honor; opening the way for us to be what He wants us to be. O Lord! Have mercy on Your people-Your heritage! Work mightily with us in Your Church! Teach Your believing disciples to accept and to go forth in their royal priesthood. Teach us to use the power of prayer to which You have given such wonderful promises, to serve Your Kingdom, to have rule over the nations, and to make the Name of God glorious on the earth. Amen.

"Verily, verily, I say unto you, He that believeth on me, the works that I do shall he do also; and greater works than these shall he do; because I go unto my Father. And whatsoever ye shall ask in my name, that will l do, that the Father may be glorified in the Son. If ye shall ask any thing in my name, I will do it" (John 14:12-14).

The Savior opened His public ministry in the Sermon on the Mount with the same subject He uses here in His parting address from the Gospel of John: prayer. But there is a difference. The Sermon on the Mount is directed to disciples who have just entered His school, scarcely knowing that God is their Father, whose prayers have reference chiefly to their personal needs. In His closing address, He speaks to disciples whose training time is coming to an end, who are ready as His messengers to take over His place and His work.

Christ's first lesson had been: Be childlike, pray believingly, and trust the Father to give you everything good. Here He points to something higher. The disciples are now His friends. He has told then everything He knows about the Father. They are His messengers into whose hands the care of His work and Kingdom on earth is to be entrusted. Now they must assume that role, performing even greater works than Christ in the power of His approaching exaltation. Prayer is to be the channel through which that power is received. With Christ's ascension to the Father, a new epoch for both their working and their praying commences.

This connection comes out clearly in our text from John, chapter fourteen. As His Body here of earth, as those who are one with Him in heaven, the disciples are now to do greater works than He had done. Their successes and their victories are to be greater than His. Christ mentions two reasons for this. One is that He was going to the Father to receive all power; the other is that they could now ask for and expect that power in His Name "Because I go to the Father, and' (notice this and "and whatever ye shall ask, I will do." His going to the Father brings a double blessing: The disciple; could ask for and receive everything in His Name and as a consequence, would do the greater works This first mention of prayer in our Savior's parting words teaches us two most importantlessons. Whoever wants to do the works of Jesus must pray in His Name. Whoever prays in His Name must work in His Name.

In prayer the power for work is obtained. When Jesus was here on earth, He did the greatest works Himself. Devils that the disciples could not cast out fled at His word. When He went to be with the Fether, He was no longer here in body to work directly. The disciples were now His Body. All His work from the throne in heaven must and could be done here on earth through them.

Now that Christ was leaving the scene and could only work through commissioners, it might have been expected that the works would be fewer and weaker. He assures us of the contrary: "Verily, verily I say unto you, He that believeth on me, the works that I do shall he do also; and greater works than these shall he do; because I go unto my Father" (John 14:12). His approaching death was to be a breaking down of the power of sin. With the resurrection, the powers of the eternal life were to take possession of the human body and obtain supremacy over human life. With His ascension, Christ was to receive the power to communicate the Holy Spirit completely to His Body. The union-the oneness between Himself on the throne and those on earth was to be so intensely and divinely perfect, that He meant it as the literal truth: "Greater works than these shall he do, because I go to the Father."

And how true it was! Jesus, during three years of personal labor on earth, gathered little more than five hundred disciples, most of whom were so powerless that they weren't much help to His cause. Men like Peter and Paul did much greater things than He had done. From the throne He could do through them what He Himself in His humiliation could not yet do. He could ask the Father, receiving and bestowing new power for the greater works. And what was true for the disciples is true for us: As we believe and ask in His Name, the power comes and takes possession of us also to do the greater works.

Alas! There is little or nothing to be seen of the power to do anything like Christ's works, not to mention anything greater. There can only be one reason: the belief in Him and the believing prayer in His Name are absent. Every child of God must learn this lesson: Prayer in the Name of Jesus is the only way to share in the mighty power which Jesus has received from the Father for His people. It is in this power alone that the believer can do greater works. To every complaint about difficulties or lack of success, Jesus gives this one answer: "He that believeth on me shall do greater works, because I go to the Father, and whatsoever ye shall ask in my Name, that will I do." If you want to do the work of Jesus, believe and become linked to Him, the Almighty One. Then pray the prayer of faith in His Name. Without this our work is just human and carnal. It may have some use in restraining sin or in preparing the way for a blessing, but the real power is missing. Effective working first needs effective praying.

The second lesson is this: Whoever prays must work. It is for power to work that prayer has such great promises. Power for the effective prayer of faith is gained through working. Our blessed Lord repeats no less than six times (John 14:13-14; 15:7,16; 16:23-24) those unlimited prayer-promises which evoke anxious questions as to their real meaning: "whatsoever," "anything," "what ye will," "ask and ye shall receive."Many a believer has read these with joy and hope, and in deep earnestness of soul has attempted to plead them for his own need, arid has come out disappointed. The simple reason was that he separated the promise from its context.

The Lord gave the wonderful promise of the free case of His Name with the Father in conjunction with doing His works. The disciple who lives only for Jesus' work and Kingdom, for His will and honor, vain be given the power to appropriate the promise. Anyone grasping the promise only when he wants something very special for himself will be disappointed, because he is making Jesus the servant of his own comfort. But whoever wants to pray the effective prayer of faith because he needs it for the work of the Master will learn it, because he has made himself the servant of his Lord's interests. Prayer not only teaches and strengthens one for work, work teaches and strengthens one for prayer.

This is true in both the natural and the spiritual worlds. "Unto every one which hath (more) shall be given" (Luke 19:26). Whoever is "faithful over a few things, I will make ....ruler over many things" (Matthew 25:21). With the small amount of grace we have already received, let us give ourselves to the Master for His work! It will be to us a real school of prayer. When Moses had to take full charge of a rebellious people, he felt the need, but also the courage, to speak boldly to God and to ask grea things of Him (Exodus 33:12,15,18). As you give yourself entirely to God for His work, you will feel that these great promises are exactly what you need and that you may most confidently expect nothing less.

Believer in Jesus! You are called-you are appointed -to do the works of Jesus, and even greater works He has gone to the Father to get the power to do them in and through you. Remember His promise "Whatsoever ye shall ask in my Name, that will I do. "Give yourself and live to do the works of Christ and you will learn how to obtain wonderful answers to prayer. You will learn to do not only what He did but much more. With disciples full of faith in Himself, boldly asking great things in prayer, Christ can conquer the world.

Lord, teach us to pray.

O my Lord! Once again, I am hearing You say things that are beyond my comprehension. I can do nothing but accept them and keep them in simple childlike faith as Your gift to me. You have said than because of Your going to be with the Father, anyone who believes in You can do not only the things You have done, but greater things as well.

Lord! I worship You as the Glorified One and eagerly await the fulfillment of Your promise. May my whole life be one of continued believing in You. Purify and sanctify my heart. Make it so tenderly susceptible to Yourself and Your love that believing in You will become its very breath.

You have said that because You went to the Father, You will do whatever we ask You to do. You want Your people to share Your power. From Your throne, You want to work through them, as members of Your Body, in response to their believing prayer in Your Name. You have promised us power in our prayers to You and power in our work here on earth.

Blessed Lord! Forgive us for not believing You and Your promise more. Because of our lack of faith, we have failed to demonstrate how You are faithful to fulfill that promise. Please forgive us for so little honoring Your all-prevailing Name in heaven or on earth.

Lord! Teach me to pray so that I can prove Your Name is all powerful with God, with men, and with devils. Teach me to work and to pray in a way that glorifies You, and do Your great works through me. Amen.

"I go unto my Father. And whatsoever ye shall ask in my name, that will I do, that the Father may be glorified in the Son" (John 14:12-13). "That the Father may be glorified in the Son': It is to this end that Jesus on His throne in glory will do everything we ask in His Name. Every answer to prayer He gives will have this as its object. When there is no prospect of this object being obtained, He will not answer. It follows as a matter of course that with us, as with Jesus, this must be the essential element in our petitions. The glory of the Father must be the aim-the very soul and life-of our prayer.

This was Jesus' goal when He was on earth: "I seek not mine own honor: I seek the honor of Him that sent me." In such words we have the keynote of His life. The first words of His High-Priestly prayer voice it: "Father glorify Thy Son, that Thy Son may glorify Thee. I have glorified Thee on earth: glorify me with Thyself" (John 17:1,4). His reason for asking to be taken up into the glory He had with the Father is a twofold one: He has glorified Him on earth; He will still glorify Him in heaven. All He asks is to be able to glorify the Father more.

As we begin to share Jesus' feeling on this point, ratifying Him by making the Father's glory our chief object in prayer, too, our prayer cannot fail to get an answer. The Beloved Son has said that nothing glorifies the Father more than His doing what we ask. Therefore, Jesus won't miss any opportunity to do what we request. Let us make His aim ours! Let the glory of the Father be the link between our asking and His doing!

Jesus' words come indeed as a sharp two-edged word, dividing the soul and the spirit, and quickly discerning the thoughts and intents of the heart. In His prayers on earth, His intercession in heaven, and His promise of an answer to our prayers, Jesus makes His first object the glory of His Father. Is this our object, too? Or are self-interest and selfwill the strongest motives urging us to pray? A distinct, conscious longing for the glory of the Father must animate our prayers.

The believer does at times desire it. But he doesn't desire it enough. The reason for this failure is that the separation between the spirit of his daily life and the spirit of his hour of prayer is too wide. Desire for the glory of the Father is not something we can arouse and present to our Lord when we prepare ourselves to pray. Only when the whole life in all its parts is given up to God's glory can we really pray to Christ's glory, too. "Do all to the glory of God," and "Ask all to the glory of God." These twin commands are inseparable. Obedience to the former is the secret of grace for the latter. Living for the glory of God is the condition of the prayers that Jesus can answer.

This demand that prayer be to the glory of God is quite right and natural. Only the Lord is glorious. There is no glory but His, and what He allots to His creations. Creation exists to show forth His glory. Everything that doesn't glorify Him is sinful, dark, and dead. It is only in the glorifying of God that creatures can find glory. What the Son of Man did-giving Himself wholly to glorify the Father-is nothing but the simple duty of every redeemed one. He will also receive Christ's reward.

We cannot attain a life with God's glory as our only aim by any effort of our own. It is only in the man Christ Jesus that such a life can be found. Yes, blessed be God! His life is our life. He gave Himself for us. He is now our life. It is essential to discover, confess, and deny the self because it takes God's place. Only the presence and rule of the Lord Jesus in our hearts can cast out all self-glorification, replacing it with His own God-glorifying life and Spirit. It is Jesus, Who longs to glorify the Father in hearing our prayers, Who will teach us to live and to pray to the glory of God.

What power is there that can urge our slothful hearts to yield themselves to our Lord to work this in us? Surely nothing more is needed than a glimpse of how worthy of glory the Father is. Our faith should learn to bow before Him in adoring worship, ascribing to Him alone the Kingdom, the power, and the glory, yielding ourselves to life in His light. Surely we will be stirred to say, "To Him alone be glory." And we will look to our Lord Jesus with new intensity of desire for a life that refuses to recognize anything but the glory of God. When there isn't enough prayer to be answered, the Father is not glorified. It is our duty to live and pray so that our prayer can be answered. For the sake of God's glory, let us learn to pray well.

What a humbling thought it is, that so often there is earnest prayer in which the desire for our own joy or pleasure is far stronger than many desire for God's glory. No wonder there are so many unanswered prayers! Here we have the secret. God cannot be glorified when that glory is not the object of our prayers. Whoever wants to pray the prayer of faith must give himself to live literally so that the Father in all things is glorified in him. This must be his aim; without it there cannot be a prayer of faith.

"How can ye believe," said Jesus, "which receive honor of one another, and seek not the honor that cometh from God only?" (John 5:44). When we seek our own glory among men, we make faith impossible. Only the deep, intense self-sacrifice that gives up its own glory and seeks the glory of God wakens in the soul that spiritual susceptibility to Divine faith. The surrender to God and the expectation that He will show His glory in hearing us are essential. Only he who seeks God's glory will see it in the answer to his prayer.

How do we accomplish this? Let us begin with a confession. The glory of God hasn't really been an all-absorbing passion in our lives and our prayers. How little we have lived in the likeness of the Son and in sympathy with Him for God and His glory alone. Take time to allow the Holy Spirit to reveal how deficient we have been in this. True knowledge and confession of sin are the sure path to deliverance.

And then let us look to Jesus. In death He glorified God; through death He was glorified with Him. It is by dying-being dead to self and living for God-that we can glorify Him. This death to self, this life to the glory of God, is what Jesus gives and lives in each one who can trust Him for it. Let the spirit of our daily lives consist of the decision to live only for the glory of the Father as Christ did, the acceptance of Him with His life and strength working it in us, and the joyful assurance that we can live for the glory of God because Christ lives in us. Jesus helps us to live this way. The Holy Spirit is waiting to make it our experience, if we will only trust and let Him. Don't hold back through unbelief! Confidently do everything for the glory of God! Our obedience will please the Father. The Holy Spirit will seal us within with the consciousness that we are living for God and His glory.

What quiet peace and power will be in our prayers when we know that we are in perfect harmony with Christ, Who promises to do what we ask, "That the Father may be glorified in the Son." With our whole beings consciously yielded to the inspiration of the Word and Spirit, our desires will no longer be ours. They will be His, and their main purpose will be the glory of God. With increasing liberty we will be able in prayer to say, "Father! You know we ask it only for Your glory. Answers to prayer, instead of being mountains we cannot climb, will give us greater confidence that we are heard. And the privilege of prayer will become doubly precious because it brings us into perfect unison with the Beloved Son in the wonderful partnership He proposes: "You ask, and I do, that the father may be glorified in the Son."

Lord, teach us to pray.

Blessed Lord Jesus! Once again I am coming to You. Every lesson you give me convinces me all the more deeply that I don't know hove to pray properly. But every lesson also inspires me with hope that You are going to teach me What prayer should be. O my Lord! I look to You with courage. You are the Great Intercessor. You alone pray and hear prayer for the sole purpose of glorifying the Father. Teach me to pray as You do.

Savior! I want to be nothing, yielding my totally to You. I am giving myself to be crucified with You. Through the Spirit the works of self will be made dead. Let your life and Your love of the Father take Possession of me. A new longing is filling my soul that every day and every hour prayer to the glory of the Father will become everything to me. O my Lord! Please teach me this!

My God and my Father! Accept the desire of Your child who has seen that Your glory is alone worth living for. Show me Your glory. Let it overshadow me and fill my heart! May I dwell in it as Christ did. Tell me what pleases You, fulfill in me Your own good pleasure, so that I may find my glory in seeking the glory of my Father. Amen.

"If ye abide in me, and my words abide in you, ye shall ask what ye will, and it shall be done unto you" (John 15:7).

In all God's relations with us, the promise and its conditions are inseparable. If we fulfill the conditions He fulfills the promise. What He is to be to us depends on what we are willing to be to Him: "Draw near to God, and He will draw near to you." Therefore, in prayer the unlimited promise, "Ask what ye will, " has one simple and natural condition, "if ye abide in me." It is Christ Whom the Father always hears. God is in Christ.To reach God, we must be in Christ, too. Fully abiding in Him, we have the right to ask whatever we want and the promise that we will get an answer.

There is a terrible discrepancy between this promise and the experience of most believers. How many prayers bring no answer? The cause must be either that we do not fulfill the condition, or God does not fulfill the promise. Believers are not willing to admit either, and therefore have devised a way of escape from the dilemma. They put a qualifying clause into the promise that our Savior did not put there-if it be God's will. This maintains both God's integrity and their own. If they could only accept it and hold fast to it as it stands, trusting Christ to make it true! And if only they would confess their failure in fulfilling the condition as the one explanation for unanswered prayer. God's Spirit would then lead them to see how appropriate such a promise is to those who really believe that Christ means it. The Holy Spirit would then make our weakness in prayer a mighty motivation for us to discover the secret and obtain the blessing of fully abiding in Christ.

"If ye abide in me. "As a Christian grows in grace and knowledge of the Lord Jesus, he is often surprised to find how God's words grow, too, into new and deeper meaning. He can look back to the day when some word of God was opened up to him, and he rejoiced in the blessing he had found in it. After a time, some deeper experience gave it a new meaning, and it was as if he never had seen what it contained. And yet once again, as he advanced in the Christian life, the same word stood before him as a great mystery, until the Holy Spirit led him still more deeply into its Divine fullness.

The Master's precious "Abide in me" is one of these evergrowing, never-exhausted words. Step by step, it opens the fullness of the Divine life to us. As the union of the branch with the vine is one of never-ceasing growth, so our abiding in Christ is a life process in which the Divine life takes more and more complete possession of us. The young believer may really be abiding in Christ to the limited extent which is possible for him. If he reaches onward to attain what the Master means by full abiding,he will inherit all the promises connected with it.

In the growing life of abiding in Christ, the first stage is that of faith. As the believer sees that Christ's command is really meant for him, his great aim is simply to believe that abiding in Christ is his immediate duty and a blessing within his reach. He is especially occupied with the love, power, and faithfulness of the Savior. He feels his one basic need is to believe.

It isn't long before he sees something more is needed. Obedience and faith must go together. But faith can't simply be added to obedience; it must be revealed in obedience. Faith is obedience at home, looking to the Master; obedience is faith going out to do His will.

The privilege and the blessings of this abiding are often of more interest than its duties and its fruit. Much self-will passes unnoticed. The peace which a young disciple enjoys in believing leaves him. In practical obedience the abiding must be maintained: "If ye keep my commands, ye shall abide in my love." Before, the truth that the mind believed was enough to let the heart rest on Christ and His promises. Now, in this stage, his chief effort is to get his will united with the will of his Lord, with his heart and life brought entirely under Christ's rule. And yet there still seems to be something missing The will and the heart are on Christ's side; the disciple obeys and loves his Lord. But why does the fleshly nature still have so much power? Why aren't his spontaneous actions and emotions what they should be? Where is the beauty of holiness, the zeal of love, and the conformity with Jesus and His death, in which the life of self is lost? There must surely be something which he has not yet experienced through abiding in Christ. Faith and obedience are just the pathway to blessing. Before giving us the parable of the vine and the branches, Jesus had very distinctly told what that full blessing is. Three times over He said, "If ye love me, keep my commandments," promising threefold blessing with which He would crown such obedient love: the indwelling of the Holy Spirit, the manifestation of the Son, the Father and Son coming to make Their abode within us.

As our faith grows into obedience, and in obedience and love our whole being reaches out and clings to Christ, our inner life opens up. The capacity is formed within us of receiving the life and the Spirit of the glorified Jesus, through a distinct and conscious union with Christ and with the Father. The word is fulfilled in us: "In that day ye shall know that I am in my Father and ye in me, and I in you" (John 14:20) God and Christ exist in each other, not only in will and in love, but in identity of nature and life. We come to understand that because of this union between the Father and the Son, so we are in Christ and Christ is in us in exactly the same way.

After Jesus had spoken thus, He said, "Abide in me, and I in you. Accept, consent to receive that Divine life of union with myself, in virtue of which, as you abide in me, I also abide in you, even as I abide in the Father. So that your life is mine and mine is yours." True abiding consists of two parts: occupying a position into which Christ can come and abide, and abiding in Him so that the soul lets Him take the place of the self to become our life. Like little children who have no cares, we find happiness in trusting and obeying the love that has done everything for us.

To those who thus abide, the promise, "Ask whatsoever ye will," comes as their rightful heritage. It cannot be otherwise. Christ has full possession of them. He dwells in their love, their wills, and their lives. Not only have their wills been given up, Christ has entered them, dwelling and breathing there by His Spirit. These people pray in Him. He prays in them, and the Father always hears Him. What they ask will be done for them.

Beloved fellow-believer! Let us confess that because we do not abide in Christ as He would like us to, the Church is impotent in the face of infidelity, worldliness, and heathendom. In the midst of such enemies, the Lord could make her more than a conqueror. We must believe that He means what He promises, and accept the conviction the confession implies.

But don't be discouraged. The abiding of the branch in the Vine is a life of never-ceasing growth. The abiding (as the Master meant it) is within our reach, for He lives to give it to us. Let us but be ready to count all things as loss and to say, "What I have attained so far is hardly anything. I want to learn to perceive Christ the same way He perceives me." It is not be occupied so much with the abiding as with Him to Whom the abiding links us and His fullness. Let it be Christ-the whole Christ, in His obedience and humiliation, in His exaltation and power, Whom our soul moves and acts. He Himself will fulfill His promise in us.

As we abide and grow into fuller and fuller abiding, let us exercise our right-the will to enter into God's will. Obeying what that will commands, let us claim what it promises. Let us yield to the teaching of the Holy Spirit. He will show each of us what the will of God is so that we may claim it prayer. And let us be content with nothing less than the personal experience of what Jesus gave when said, "If ye abide in me, ye shall ask what ye will, and it shall be done unto you."

Lord, teach us to pray.

Beloved Lord! Make Your promise in all simplicity new to men. Teach me to accept it, letting the only limitation on Your holy giving be my own willingness. Lord! Let each word of Your promise be, in a new way, made quick and powerful in soul.

You say, "Abide it? me!" O my Master, my Life my All-I do abide in You. Allow me to grow up in all your fullness. It is not the effort of faith, trying to cling to You and trusting You to protect me; nor my will, obeying You and keeping Your commandments, that alone can satisfy me. Only You Yourself, living in me as You do in the Father, can satisfy me. It is You, my Lord, no longer before me and above me, but united with me, that I need. I trust You for this.

You say, "Ask whatever you will."Lord! I know that a life of complete, deep abiding will renew, sanctify, and strengthen my will in such a way that I will have the desire and the liberty to ask for great things. Lord! Let my will-dead in Your death, living in Your life-be bold and large in its petitions.

You say, "It shall be done. "O Jesus! You are the Amen, the Faithful and True Witness. Give me in Yourself the joyous confidence that You will make this promise even more wonderfully true to me than ever before, because it has not entered into the heart of man to conceive what God has prepared for those who love Him. Amen.

AUTHOR'S NOTE

Many books and sermons on prayer emphasize the blessing of prayer as a spiritual exercise, even if there is no answer. God's fellowship ought to be more important to us than the gift we ask for. But a careful examination of what Christ said about prayer reveals that He wanted us to think of prayer more as the means to an end. The answer was to be the proof that we and our prayer are acceptable to the Father in heaven. It is not that Christ would have us consider the gifts of higher value than the fellowship and favor of the Father. By no means. But the Father intends the answer to be a token of His favor and of the reality of our fellowship with Him.

Daily answer to prayer is the proof of our spiritual maturity. It shows that we have attained the true abiding in Christ, that our will is truly one with God's will. It also reveals that our faith is strong enough to see and take what God has prepared for us, that the Name of Christ and His nature have taken full possession of us, and that we have been found fit to take a place among those whom God admits to His counsels, according to whose prayer He rules the world. Prayer is very blessed; the answer is more blessed still. It is the response from the Father that our prayer, our faith, and our will are indeed as He would wish them to be.

I make these remarks with the one desire of leading my readers to put together for themselves everything that Christ has said about prayer. Accept the truth that when prayer is what it should be, or rather when we are what we should be, the answer must be expected. It will bring us out from those refuges where we have comforted ourselves with unanswered prayer. It will show us the place of power to which Christ has appointed His Church, that place which it occupies so little. It will reveal the terrible weakness of our spiritual life as the cause of our not praying boldly in Christ's Name. It will urge us mightily to rise to a life in full union with Christ and in the fullness of the Spirit as the secret of effective prayer. And it will so lead us to realize our destiny: "At that day: Verily, verily I say unto you, If ye shall ask anything of the Father, He will give it you in my Name: ask, and ye shall receive, that your joy may be fulfilled." Prayer that is really, spiritually, in union with Jesus is always answered.

"If ye abide in me, and my words abide in you, ye shall ask what ye will, and it shall be done unto you " (John 15:7).

The vital connection between the Word and prayer is one of the simplest and earliest lessons of the Christian life. As that newly-converted heathen put it: "I pray-I speak to my Father; I read-my Father speaks to me." Before prayer, God's Word strengthens me by giving my faith its justification and its petition. And after prayer, God's Word prepares me by revealing what the Father wants me to ask. In prayer, God's Word brings me the answer, for in it the Spirit allows me to hear the Father's voice.

Prayer is not monologue, but dialogue. Its most essential part is God's voice in response to mine. Listening to God's voice is the secret of the assurance that He will listen to mine. "Incline thine ear and hear," "Give ear to me," and "Hearken to my voice," are words which God speaks to man as well as man to God. His hearkening will depend on ours. My willingness to accept His words will determine the power my words have with Him. What God's words are to me is the test of what He Himself is to me. It shows the uprightness of my desire to meet Him in prayer.

It is this connection between His Word and our prayer that Jesus points to when He says, "If ye abide in me, and my words abide in you, ye shall ask what ye will, and it shall be done unto you." The deep importance of this truth becomes clear if we notice the expression which this one replaces. More than once Jesus had said, "Abide in me and I in you. "His abiding in us was the complement and the crown of our abiding in Him. But here, instead of "Ye in me and I in you, "He says, "Ye in me and my words in you." The abiding of His words is the equivalent of Himself abiding.

What a view this opens up to us of the place the words of God in Christ are to have in our spiritual lives, especially in our prayer. A man's words reveal himself. In his promises, he gives himself away, binding himself to the one who receives his promises. In his commands, he proclaims his will, seeking to make himself master of those whose obedience he claims, to guide and use them as if they were part of himself. Through our words, spirit holds fellowship with spirit. If a man's words are heard, accepted, held fast, and obeyed, he can impart himself to someone else through them. But with human beings, this can happen only in a limited sense.

God, however, is the infinite Being in Whom everything is life, power, spirit, and truth, in the very deepest meaning of the words. When God reveals Himself in His words, He does indeed give Himself- love and

His life, His will and His power to those who receive these words, in a reality passing comprehension. In every promise, He gives us the power to grasp and possess Himself. In every command, He allows us to share His will, His holiness, and His perfection. God's Word gives us God Himself. That Word is nothing less than the Eternal Son, Christ Jesus. Therefore, all of Christ's words are God's words, full of a Divine, quickening life and power. "The words that I speak unto you, they are spirit and they are life."

Those who study the deaf and mute tell us how much the power of speaking depends on that of hearing, and how the loss of hearing in children is followed by a loss of speaking, too. This is also true in a broader sense: Our speech is based on what we hear. In the highest sense, this is true of our conversation with God. To offer a prayer-to utter certain wishes and appeal to certain promises-is an easy thing that man can learn with human intelligence.But to pray in the Spirit-to speak words that reach and touch God, affecting and influencing the powers of the unseen world-depends entirely on our hearing God's voice. We must listen to the voice and language that God uses and, through the words of God, receive His thoughts, His mind, and His life into our hearts. The extent to which we listen will determine the extent to which we learn to speak in the voice and the language that God hears. The ear of the learner, wakened morning by morning, prepares him to speak to God. (Isaiah 1:4).

This hearing the voice of God is something more than the thoughtful study of the Word. One can study and gain knowledge of the Word having little real fellowship with the living God. But there is also a reading of the Word, in the very presence of the Father and under the leading of the Spirit, in which the Word comes to us in living power from God Himself. It is to us the very voice of the Father, a real, personal fellowship with Himself. The living voice of God enters the heart, bringing blessing and strength, and awakening the response of a living faith that reaches back to the heart of God.

The power both to obey and believe depends on hearing God's voice this way. The chief thing isn't knowing what God has said we must do, but that God Himself says it to us. Neither the law nor the book nor the knowledge of what is right works obedience. This can be accomplished only by the personal influence of God through His living fellowship. The presence of God Himself as the Promiser, not the knowledge of what He has promised, awakens faith and trust in prayer. It is only in the full presence of God that disobedience and unbelief become impossible.

"If ye abide in me, and my words abide in you, ye shall ask what ye will, and it shall be done unto you." In these words, the Savior gives

Himself. We must have the words in us taken up into our wills and lives, reproduced in our inner natures and conduct. They must abide in us. Our lives must be one continuous display of the words that fill us. The words reveal Christ inside and our lives reveal Him outside. As the words of Christ enter our very hearts, becoming and influencing our lives, our words will enter His heart and influence Him. My prayer will depend on my life: Whatever God's words are to me and in me will determine what my words will be to God and in God. If I do what God says, God will do what I say.

The Old Testament saints understood this connection between God's words and ours quite well. Their prayer really was a loving response to what they had heard God speak. If the word were a promise, they counted on God to do as He had spoken. "Do as Thou hast said"; "For Thou, Lord, hast spoken it"; "According to Thy promise"; "According to Thy word": In such expressions they showed that what God spoke in promise was the root and the life of what they spoke in prayer. If the word was a command, they simply did as the Lord had spoken: "So Abram departed as the Lord had spoken." Their lives were fellowship with God, the exchange of word and thought. What God spoke they heard and did; what they spoke God heard and did. In each word, He speaks to us, and the whole Christ gives Himself to fulfill it. For each word, He asks no less than that we give the whole man to keep that word and to receive its fulfillment."If my words abide in you." The condition is simple and clear. In His words His will is revealed. As the words abide in me, His will rules me. My will becomes the empty vessel which His will fills, and the willing instrument which His will rules. He fills my inner being. In the exercise of obedience and faith, my will becomes stronger and is brought into deeper inner harmony with Him. Because He can fully trust it to will nothing but what He wills, He is not afraid to give the promise, "If my words abide in you, ye shall ask what ye will, and it shall be done unto you." To all who believe it and act upon it, He will make it literally true. Disciples of Christ! While we have been excusing our unanswered prayers with a fancied submission to God's wisdom and will, the real reason has been that our own feeble lives have been the cause of our feeble prayers! Nothing can make men strong but the word coming from God's mouth. By that we must live. The word of Christ makes us one with Him and fits us spiritually for touching and taking hold of God. We must love and live in that Word, letting it abide in and become part of us. All that is of the world passes away. Whoever does God's will lives forever. Let us yield heart and life to the words of Christ, the words in which He gives Himself, the personal living Savior. His promise will become our rich experience: "If ye abide in me, and my words abide in you, ye shall ask what ye will, and it shall be done unto you."

Lord, teach us to pray.

Blessed Lord! I see why my prayer has not been more believing and effective. I was more occupied with my speaking to You than with Your speaking to me. I did not understand that the secret of faith is this: There can be only as much faith as there is of the living Word dwelling in the soul.

Your Word taught me so clearly to be swift to hear and slow to speak, and not to be hasty to say just anything to God. Lord, teach me that it is only when I take Your Word into my life that my words can be taken into Your heart. Teach me that if Your Word is a living power within me, it will be a living power with You, also. Show me that what Your mouth has spoken Your hand will perform.

Lord Jesus! Deliver me from the uncircumcised ear! Give me the opened ear of the learner, wakened morning by morning to hear the Father's voice. Just as You speak only what You hear from the Father, may my speaking be the echo of Your speaking to me. "When Moses went into the tabernacle to speak with Him, he heard the voice of One speaking unto him from off the mercy seat." Lord, may it be so with me, too. Let my life and character reveal that Your words abide and are seen in me. May this be my preparation for the complete blessing: "Ye shall ask what ye will, and it shall be done unto you." Amen.

"Ye have not chosen me, but I have chosen you, and ordained you, that ye should go and bring forth fruit, and that your fruit should remain; that whatsoever ye shall ask of the father in my name, he may give it you" (John 15:16).

"The effectual fervent prayer of a righteous man availeth much" (James 5:16).

The promise of the Father's giving whatsoever we ask is here once again renewed, showing us to whom such wonderful influence in the council chamber of the Most High is to be granted. "I chose you," the Master says, "and appointed you that ye should go and bear fruit, and that your fruit should remain." He then adds, to the end "that whatsoever ye," (the fruit bearing ones) "shall ask of the Father in my name, He may give it you." This is nothing but a fuller expression of what He meant by the words, "If ye abide in me." He had spoken of the object of this abiding as the bearing of "fruit," "more fruit," and "much fruit." In this, God would be glorified and the mark of discipleship would be seen. He now adds that the reality of the abiding, as seen in fruit abounding and abiding, is the qualification for our praying so as to obtain what we ask. Entire dedication to the fulfillment of our calling is the key to effective prayer and the unlimited blessings of Christ's wonderful prayer-promises.

There are Christians who fear that such a statement is at variance with the doctrine of free grace. But surely it doesn't disagree with free grace rightly understood or the many express statements of God's blessed Word. Take the words of St. John, "Let us love in deed and truth; hereby shall we assure our heart before Him. And whatsoever we ask, we receive of Him because we keep His commandments, and do the things that are pleasing in His sight" (1 John 3:18-19,22). Or take the often-quoted words of James:"The effectual fervent prayer of a righteous man availeth much" (James 5:16). This describes a man of whom, according to the definition of the Holy Spirit, it can be said, "He that doeth righteousness, is righteous even as He is righteous." Mark the spirit of so many of the Psalms, with their confident appeal to the integrity and righteousness of the supplicant. In Psalm 18 David says: "The Lord rewarded me according to my righteousness; according to the cleanness of my hands hath he recompensed me... I was also upright before him, and I kept myself from mine iniquity. Therefore hath the Lord recompensed me according to my righteousness" (Psalm 18:20,23). See also Psalms 7:3-5; 15:1-2; 17:3,6; 26:16; 119:121, 153). If we carefully consider these scriptures in the light of the New Testament, we find them in perfect harmony with the explicit teaching of the Savior's parting words: "If ye keep my commandments, ye shall abide in my love"; "Ye are my friends if ye do what I command you." The words are indeed meant literally: "I appointed you that ye should go and bear fruit, that, "then, "whatsoever ye shall ask of the Father in my name, He may give it you."

Let us seek to enter into the spirit of what the Savior teaches us here. There is a danger in our evangelical religion of looking too much at what it offers from one side, as a certain experience obtained in prayer and faith. There is another side which God's Word puts very strongly, that of obedience as the only path to blessing. What we need to realize is that in our relationship to God He is the Infinite Being Who created and redeemed us. The first sentiment that ought to motivate us is that of subjection ,surrender to His supremacy, His glory, His will, and His pleasure.This ought to be the first and uppermost thought of our lives. The question is not, however, how we are to obtain and enjoy His favor, for in this the main thing may still be self. What this Being in the very nature of things rightfully claims, and is infinitely and unspeakably worthy of, is that His glory and pleasure should be my only object. Surrender to His perfect and blessed will-a life of service and obedience-is the beauty and the charm of heaven. Service and obedience were the thoughts that were uppermost in the mind of the Son when He was on earth. Service and obedience must become the chief objects of our desires and aims, even more so than rest, light, joy, or strength.In them we will find the path to all the higher blessedness that awaits us.

Note what a prominent place the Master gives it, not only in this fifteenth chapter, in connection with the abiding, but in the fourteenth, where He speaks of the indwelling of the Trinity. John 14:15 says: "If ye love me, keep my commandments," and the Spirit will be given to you by the Father. Then verse 21:"He that hath my commandments and keepeth them,he it is that loveth me." He will have the special love of the Father and the special manifestation of Christ. Verse 23 is one of the highest of all the great and precious promises: "If a man loves me he will keep my words, and the Father and I will come and take up our abode with him." Could words put it more clearly that obedience is the way to the indwelling of the Spirit, to His revealing the Son within us, and to His preparing us to be the abode, the home of the Father? The indwelling of the Trinity is the heritage of those who obey.

Obedience and faith are simply two parts of one act-surrender to God and His will. As faith strengthens itself in order to be obedient, it is in turn strengthened by obedience. Faith is made perfect by works. Often our efforts to believe are unsuccessful because we don't assume the only position in which a large faith is legitimate or possible-that of entire surrender to the honor and the will of God. The man who is entirely consecrated to God and His will finds the power to claim everything that His God has promised to be for him.

The application of this in the school of prayer is very simple but very solemn. "I chose you, " the Master says, "and appointed you that ye should go and bear fruit, " much fruit (verses 5,8), "and that your fruit should abide, "that your life might be one of abiding fruit and abiding fruitfulness, "that" as fruitful branches abiding in me, "whatsoever ye shall ask of the Father in my name, He may give it you. "

How often we've tried to pray an effective prayer for grace to bear fruit and have wondered why the answer didn't come. It was because we were reversing the Master's order. We wanted to have the comfort, the joy, and the strength first, so we could do the work easily and without any feeling of difficulty or self-sacrifice. But He wanted us to do what He said in the obedience of faith, without worrying about whether we felt weak or strong, or whether the work was hard or easy. The path of fruit-bearing leads us to the place and the power of successful prayer. Obedience is the only path that leads to the glory of God. Obedience doesn't replace faith or supply its shortcomings. But faith's obedience gives access to all the blessings our God has for us. In the Gospel of John, the baptism of the Spirit (John 14:16), the manifestation of the Son (14:21), the indwelling of the Father (14:23), the abiding in Christ's love (15:10), the privilege of His holy friendship (15:14), and the power of effective prayer (15:16), all wait for the obedient.

Now we know the great reason why we have not had power in faith to pray successfully. Our lives weren't as they should have been. Simple obedience-abiding fruitfulness-was not its chief mark. We whole-heartedly approve of the Divine appointment of men to whom God gives the power to rule the world. At their request, He does what otherwise would not have taken place. Their will guides the path in which God's will is to work. These men must have learned obedience themselves. Their loyalty and submission to authority must be above all suspicion. If we approve the law, that obedience and fruit-bearing are the path to prevailing prayer, we must with shame acknowledge how little our lives have exemplified this.

Let us yield ourselves to take up the appointment the Savior gives us. If we concentrate on our relationship to Him as our Master, we should no longer begin each new day with thoughts of comfort, joy, or blessing. Our first thought should be: "I belong to the Master." Every moment I must act as His property, as a part of Himself, as one who only seeks to know and do His will. I am a servant, a slave of Jesus Christ. Let this be the spirit that animates me. If He says, "No longer do I call you servants, but I have called you friends," let us accept the place of friends, because, "Ye are my friends if ye do the things which I command you."

The one thing He commands us as His branches is to bear fruit. Live to bless others, to testify of the life and the love there is in Jesus. In faith and obedience give your whole life to that which Jesus chose us for and appointed us to-fruitbearing. Think of His electing us to this, accepting your appointment as coming from Him Who always gives us everything He demands of us. We will grow strong in the confidence that a life of fruit-bearing and abiding is within our reach. And we will understand why this fruit-bearing alone can be the path to the place of all effective prayer. The man who, in obedience to Christ, proves that he is doing what his Lord wills, will receive whatever he desires from the Father. "Whatsoever we ask we receive, because we keep His commandments, and do the things that are pleasing in His sight."

Lord, teach us to pray.

Blessed Master! Teach me to understand fully what I only partly realize, that only by obeying the will of God can we obtain His promises and use them effectively in our prayers. Show me how bearing fruit perfects the deeper growth of the branch into the Vine, allowing us to experience that perfect union with- God in which we can ask for whatever we want.

O Lord! Reveal to us how with all the hosts of heaven, with all the saints here on earth, and even with Yourself on earth, that obedience to God is the highest privilege. It gives access to oneness with the Father Himself in that which is His highest glory-His all-perfect will. And show us how, if we keep Your commandments and bear fruit according to Your will, our spiritual natures will grow to the full stature of a perfect man, having power to ask and receive anything.

O Lord Jesus! Reveal Yourself to us! Through Your purpose and power, make Your wonderful promises the daily experience of everyone who completely yields himself to You and Your words. Amen.

CHAPTER 24: The All-Powerful Plea

"And whatsoever ye shall ask in my name, that will I do ....If ye shall ask anything in my name, I will do it....that whatsoever ye shall ask of the Father in my name, he may give it to you .... Verily, verily, I say unto you, Whatsoever ye shall ask the Father in my name, he will give it to you ....Hitherto have ye asked nothing in my name: ask, and ye shall receive ....At that day ye shall ask in my name" (John 14:13-14;15:16; 16:23-24,26).

Until now the disciples had not asked in the Name of Christ, nor had He Himself ever used the expression. Here in His parting words, He repeats the word unceasingly in connection with those promises of unlimited meaning: "Whatsoever," "Anything," "What ye will. "He wanted to teach them and us that His Name is our only, but also our completely sufficient, plea. The power of prayer and its answer depend on the right use of the Name.

What is a person's name? It is a word or expression in which a person is represented to us. When I mention,or hear a name,it brings to mind the whole man, what I know of him, and also the impression he has made on me. The name of a king includes his honor, his power, and his kingdom. His name is the symbol of his power. And so each name of God embodies and represents some part of the glory of the Unseen One. The Name of Christ is the expression of everything He has done and everything He is and lives to do as our Mediator.

What does it mean to do a thing in the name of another? It is to come with his power and authority, as his representative and substitute.

Using another's name always presupposes a common interest. No one would give another the free use of his name without first being assured that his honor and interests were as safe with that other person as with himself.

What does it mean when Jesus gives us power over His Name-the free use of it-with the assurance that whatever we ask in it will be given to us? The ordinary comparison of one person giving another, on some special occasion, the liberty to ask something in his name, comes altogether short here. Jesus solemnly gives to all His disciples a general and unlimited power to use His Name at all times for everything they desire. He could not do this if He did not know that He could trust us with His interests and that His honor would be safe in our hands.

The free use of someone else's name is always a token of great confidence and close union. Someone who gives his name to another stands aside to let that person act for him. Someone who takes the name of another gives up his own as of no value. When I go in the name of another, I deny myself. I take not only his name, but himself and what he is, instead of myself and what I am.

Such use of a person's name may be the result of a legal union. A merchant leaving his home and business gives his chief clerk a general power by which he can withdraw thousands of dollars in the merchant's name. The clerk does this, not for himself, but only in the interests of the business. Because the merchant knows and trusts him as wholly devoted to his interests and business, he dares put his name and property at his command.

When the Lord Jesus went to heaven, He left His work-the management of His Kingdom on earth in the hands of His servants. He also gave them His Name to draw all the supplies they needed for the due conduct of His business. Christ's servants have the spiritual power to use the Name of Jesus only insofar as they yield themselves to live only for the interests and the work of the Master. The use of the Name always supposes the surrender of our interests to Him Whom we represent.

Another use of a name may be because of a life union.(In the case of the merchant and his clerk, the union is temporary.) Oneness of life on earth gives oneness of name: A child has the father's name because he has his life. Often the child of a good father is honored or helped by others for the sake of the name he bears. But this would not last long if it were found that it was only a name, and that the father's character wasn't present in it. The name and the character or spirit must be in harmony. When such is the case, the child will have a double claim on the father's friends. The character secures and increases the love and esteem extended at first for the name's sake.

It is the same with Jesus and the believer: We are one; we have one life and one Spirit with Him. For this reason we may proceed in His Name. Our power in using that Name, whether with God, men, or devils, depends on the measure of our spiritual life union with Christ. Our use of His Name rests on the unity of our lives with Him.

The Name and the Spirit of Jesus are one. "Whatsoever ye shall ask in my Name" means "in my nature." With God, things are requested according to their nature. Asking in Christ's Name doesn't mean that at the end of some request we say, "This I ask in the Name of Jesus Christ." It means we are praying according to His nature, which is love that doesn't seek its own will, but only the will of God and the good of all creatures. Such asking is the cry of Christ's own Spirit in our hearts.

The union that gives power to the use of the Name may be the union of love. When a bride whose life has been one of poverty becomes united to the bridegroom, she gives up her own name to be called by his, and has the full right to use it. She purchases in his name, and that name is not refused. This is done because the bridegroom has chosen her for himself, counting on her to care for his interests because they are now one.

The heavenly Bridegroom does nothing less. Having loved us and made us one with Himself, what can He do but give those who bear His Name the right to present it before the Father, or to come with it to Himself for all they need? No one really gives himself up to live in the Name of Jesus without receiving in ever-increasing measure the spiritual capacity to ask for and receive in that Name whatever he desires. My bearing of the name of another shows that I have given up my own name and, with it, my own independent life. But just as surely, it shows I have possession of everything belonging to the name I have taken instead of my own.

The common comparison to a messenger sent to ask in the name of another, or a guilty person using the name of a guardian in his appeal, is defective. We are not praying in the name of someone who is absent. Jesus Himself is with the Father. When we pray to the Father, it must be in Jesus' Name. The Name represents the person. To ask in His Name is to ask in full union of interest, life, and love with Himself, as one who lives in and for Him.

Let the Name of Jesus have undivided supremacy in my heart and life! My faith will grow to the assurance that what I ask for in that Name cannot be refused. The Name and the power of asking go together. When the Name of Jesus has become the power that rules my life, its power in prayer with God will be seen, too.

Everything depends on my own relationship to the Name. The power it has on my life is the power it will have in my prayers. There is more than one expression in Scripture which can make this clear. "Do all in the Name of the Lord Jesus" is the counterpart of "Ask all. " To do all and ask all in His Name go together. "We shall walk in the Name of our God" means the power of the Name must rule in the whole life. Only then will it have power in prayer. God looks not to our lips, but to our lives to see what the Name is to us. When Scripture speaks of "men who have given their lives for the Name of the Lord Jesus," or of one "ready to die for the Name of the Lord Jesus," we see what our relationship to the Name must be. When it is everything to me, it will obtain everything for me. If I let it have all I have, it will let me have all it has.

" Whatsoever ye shall ask in my Name, that will I do." Jesus means that promise literally. Christians have sought to limit it because it looked too free. It was hardly safe to trust man so unconditionally. They did not understand that the phrase "in my Name" is its own safeguard. It is a spiritual power which no one can use further than his living and acting in that Name allows.

As we bear the Name before men, we have the power to use it before God. Let us plead for God's Holy Spirit to show us what the Name means, and what the right use of it is. It is through the Spirit that the Name, which is above every name in heaven, will take the place of supremacy in our hearts and lives, too. Disciples of Jesus! Let the lessons of this day go deeply into your hearts. The Master says, "Only pray in my Name; whatsoever ye ask will be given. Heaven is opened to you! The treasures and power of the spiritual world are placed at your disposal to help those around you.

Learn to pray in the Name of Jesus. He says to us as He said to the disciples, "Hitherto ye have not asked in my Name: ask, and ye shall receive." Let each disciple of Jesus seek to avail himself of the rights of his royal priesthood, to use the power placed at his disposal for his work. Let Christian awake and hear this message: Your prayers can obtain what would otherwise be withheld! They can accomplish what would otherwise remain undone O awake, and use the Name of Jesus to open the treasures of heaven for this perishing world!

Lord, teach us to pray!

Blessed Lord! It seems as if each lesson You give me has such depth of meaning that if I could just learn that one, I would be able to pray properly. Right now I feel as if I only need to pray for one thing: Lord, please teach me what it is to pray inYour Name. Teach me to live and act, to walk and speak, to do everything in the Name of Jesus, so that my prayer cannot be anything else but in that blessed Name, too.

Lord! Teach me to fully grasp the precious promise that whatever I ask in Your name You will do. and the Father will give. I realize that I haven't fully attained, and that I don't completely understand, the wondrous union You mean when You say, "In my Name." Let me hold on to the promise until it fills my heart with the undoubting assurance that I can ask for anything in the Name of Jesus.

O my Lord! Let the Holy Spirit teach me this! You did describe Him as "the Comforter, Whom the Father shall send in My Name. "He knows what it is to be sent from heaven in Your Name, to reveal and to honor the power of that Name in Your servants; and to use that Name alone to glorify You. Lord Jesus! Let Your Spirit dwell in me and fill me! I yield my whole being to His rule and leading. Your Name and Your Spirit are one. Through Him, Your Name will be the strength of my life and my prayer. Then I will be able to forsake everything for Your Name's sake, speaking to men and to God in Your Name, and proving that this, indeed, is the Name above every name.

Lord Jesus! Please teach me by Your Holy Spirit to pray in Your Name. Amen.

"And in that day ye shall ask me nothing. Verily, verily, I say unto you, Whatsoever ye shall ask the Farther in my name, he will give it you. Hitherto have ye asked nothing in my name: ask, and ye shall receive, that your joy may be full" (John 16:23-24).

"At that day ye shall ask in my name: and I say not unto you, that I will pray the Father for you: For the Father himself loveth you" (John 16:26-27).

"Praying in the Holy Ghost, keep yourselves in the love of God" (Jude 20-21).

The words of John (I John 2:12-14) to little children, young men, and fathers suggest the thought that often in the Christian life there are three great stages of experience. The first, that of the new-born child, is filled with the assurance and the joy of forgiveness. The second, the transition stage of struggle and growth in knowledge and strength, is comparable to young men growing strong. God's Word is doing its work in them and giving them victory over the evil one. The final stage of maturity and ripeness is that of the fathers, who have entered deeply into the knowledge and fellowship of the Eternal One.

In Christ's teaching on prayer, three similar stages in prayerlife are apparent. The Sermon on the Mount describes the initial stage. All of His teaching is comprised in one word: Father. Pray to your Father; your Father sees, hears, knows, and will reward. How much more than any earthly father He is! Simply be childlike and trustful.

Then comes something like a transition stage of conflict and conquest. Words like these refer to it: "This sort goeth not out but by prayer and fasting""Shall not God avenge His own elect who cry day and night unto Him?"

Finally, we have in the parting words a higher stage: The children have become men. They are now the Master's friends, from whom He has no secrets, and to whom He says, "All things that I heard from my Father I made known unto you." In the frequently repeated "whatsoever ye will," He hands them the keys of the Kingdom. Now the time has come for the power of prayer in His Name to be proved.

The contrast between this final stage and the previous preparatory ones is marked most distinctly in the words: "Hitherto ye have asked nothing in my Name"; "At that day ye shall ask in my Name." "At that day" means the day of the outpouring of the Holy Spirit. The great work Christ was to do on the cross-the mighty power and the complete victory to be manifested in His resurrection and ascension would allow the glory of God to come down from heaven as never before, to dwell in men. The Spirit of the glorified Jesus was to come and be the life of

His disciples. And one of the signs of that wonderful, new flow of the Spirit was to be a power in prayer that was up to that time unknown. Prayer in the Name of Jesus-asking for and obtaining everything-is to be the evidence of the reality of the Spirit's indwelling.

The coming of the Holy Spirit indeed began a new epoch in the prayer world. To understand this, we must remember Who He is, what His work is, and why His not being given until Jesus was glorified is significant. It is in the Spirit that God exists, for He is Spirit. It is in the Spirit that the Son was begotten of the Father, because in the fellowship of the Spirit, the Father and the Son are one. The Father's prerogative is eternal, continuous giving to the Son. The Son's right and blessedness is to ask and receive eternally. Through the Spirit, this communion of life and love is maintained. This has been true from all eternity.

It is especially true now, when the Son as Mediator lives to pray. The great work which Jesus began on earth of reconciling God and man in His own body, He carries on in heaven. To accomplish this, He took the conflict between God's righteousness and our sin into His own person. On the cross, He ended the struggle once and for all in His own body. Then He ascended to heaven, where He carries out the deliverance He obtained and manifests His victory in each member of His Body. This is why He lives to pray. In His unceasing intercession, He places Himself in living fellowship with the unceasing prayer of His redeemed ones. Or rather, it is His unceasing intercession which shows itself in their prayers, giving them a power they never had before.

He does this through the Holy Spirit. This Spirit of the glorified Jesus was not manifested and could not be until Jesus had been glorified (John 7:39). This gift of the Father was something distinctively new, entirely different from what the Old Testament saints had known. The work that the blood effected in heaven when Christ entered within the veil was totally true and new. The redemption of human nature into fellowship with His resurrection power and His glory was intensely real. The taking up of our humanity through Christ into the life of the triune God was an event of such inconceivable significance, that the Holy Spirit was indeed no longer only what He had been in the Old Testament.

That "the Holy Spirit was not yet, for Christ was not yet glorified" was literally true. The Holy Spirit had come from Christ's exalted humanity to testify in our hearts of what Christ had accomplished. Just as Jesus, after having come to earth as a man, returned to heaven with power He didn't have before, so the Holy Spirit came to us with a new life which He hadn't had before. He came to us with that new life-as the Spirit of the glorified Jesus. Under the Old Testament He was invoked as the Spirit of God.At Pentecost He descended as the Spirit of the glorified Jesus, bringing down and communicating to us the full fruit and power of the accomplished redemption.

Christ's continuing intercession maintains the effectiveness and application of His redemption. The Holy Spirit descending from Christ to us draws us up into the great stream of His ascending prayers. The Spirit prays for us without words in the depths of a heart where even thoughts are at times formless. He takes us up into the wonderful flow of the life of the triune God. Through the Spirit, Christ's prayers become ours, and ours are made His. We ask for what we desire, and it is given to us. We then understand from experience, "Hitherto ye have not asked in my Name. At that day ye shall ask in my Name."

Brother! What we need in order to pray in the Name of Christ to ask that we may receive that our joy may be full-is the baptism of this Holy Spirit. This is more than the Spirit of God under the Old Testament. This is more than the Spirit of conversion and regeneration the disciples had before Pentecost. This is more than the Spirit with a portion of Christ's influence and power. This is the Holy Spirit, the Spirit of the glorified Jesus in His exaltation and power, coming to us as the Spirit of the indwelling Jesus, revealing the Son and the Father within us (John 14:16-23). This Spirit cannot simply be the Spirit of our hours of prayer. It must be the Spirit of our whole life and walk, glorifying Jesus in us by revealing the completeness of His work and making us wholly one with Him and like Him. Then we can pray in His Name, because we are in very deed one with Him. Then we have that immediate access to the Father of which Jesus says, "I say not unto you, that I will pray the Father for you" (John 16:26).

Oh! We need to understand and believe that to be filled with the Spirit of the Glorified One is the one need of God's believing people. Then we will be able "with all prayer and supplication to be praying at all seasons in the Spirit," and "praying in the Holy Ghost, to keep ourselves in the love of God." "At that day ye shall ask in my Name." Once again, we learn this lesson: What our prayer achieves depends on what we are and what our lives are. Living in the Name of Christ is the secret of praying in the Name of Christ; living in the Spirit is necessary for praying in the Spirit. Abiding in Christ gives the right and power to ask for what we desire. The extent of our abiding is equivalent to our power in prayer. The Spirit dwelling within us prays, not always in words and thoughts, but in a breathing and a being that is deeper than utterance. There is as much real prayer in us as there is of Christ's Spirit. Let our lives be full of Christ and full of His Spirit, so that the wonderfully unlimited promises to our prayers will no longer appear strange. "Hitherto ye have asked nothing in my Name. Ask, and ye shall receive, that your joy may be full. At that day ye shall ask in my Name. Verily, verily, I say unto you, Whatsoever ye shall ask the Father in my Name, He will give it you."

Lord, teach us to pray.

O my God! In holy awe I bow before You, the Three in One. Again I see how the mystery of prayer is the mystery of the Holy Trinity. I adore the Father Who always hears. I adore the Son Who lives eternally to pray. And I love the Holy Spirit Who comes from the Father and the Son, lifting us up into the fellowship of that blessed, never-ceasing asking and receiving. I bow, my God, in adoring worship before the infinite power which, through the Holy Spirit, takes us and our prayers into Your Divine life and its fellowship of love.

O my blessed Lord Jesus! Teach me to understand this lesson: The indwelling Spirit streaming from You and uniting us to You is the Spirit of prayer. Teach me how, as an empty, wholly consecrated vessel, to yield myself to His being my life. Teach me to honor Him and to trust Him, as a living Person, to lead my life and my prayer. Teach me especially in prayer to wait in holy silence, giving Him time to breathe His unutterable intercession within me. And teach me that through Him it is possible to pray without ceasing and to pray without failing, because He makes me a partaker of the never-ceasing and never-failing intercession in which You appear before the Father.

O Lord! Fulfill in me Your promise, "At that day ye shall ask in my Name. Verily, verily, I say unto you, Whatsoever ye shall ask the Father in my Name, that will He give." Amen.

AUTHOR'S NOTE

Prayer has often been compared to breathing. We have to carry out the comparison fully to see how wonderful the place is which the Holy Spirit occupies. With every breath, we expel impure air which would soon cause our death, and inhale fresh air to which we owe our life. In confession we release our sins, and in prayer we release the needs and desires of our hearts. And we inhale the fresh air of the promises, the love, and the life of God in Christ. We do this through the Holy Spirit, Who is the breath of our life.

He is also the breath of God. The Father breathes Him into us to unite Himself with our life. Just as every expiration is followed by the inhaling of the next breath, so God inhales His breath, and the Spirit returns to Him laden with the desires and needs of our hearts.

Thus the Holy Spirit is the breath of the life of God and the breath of the new life in us. As God breathes Him out, we receive Him in answer to prayer: as we breathe Him back again, He rises to God carrying our petitions. It is though the Holy Spirit that the Father and the Son are one, and that the intercession of the Son reaches the Father. He is our Spirit of prayer. True prayer is the living experience of the truth of the Holy Trinity. The Spirit's breathing, the Son's intercession, and the Father's will become one in us.

"But I have prayed for thee, that thy faith fail not" (Luke 22:32).
"I say not unto you, that I will pray the Father for you"(John 16:26).
"He ever liveth to make intercession for them" (Hebrews 7:25).

All growth in the spiritual life is connected with clearer insight into what Jesus is to us. The more I realize that Christ must be everything to me and in me, that everything in Christ is indeed for me, the more I learn to live the real life of faith. This life dies to self and lives wholly in Christ. The Christian life is no longer a vain struggle to live right, but a resting in Christ to find strength in Him as life. He helps us fight and gain the victory of faith!

This is especially true of the life of prayer. It, too, comes under the law of faith alone, and is seen in the light of the fullness and completeness there is in Jesus. The believer understands that prayer is no longer a matter of strain or anxious care, but an experience of what Christ will do for him and in him. It is a participation in the life of Christ, which is the same on earth as in heaven, always ascending to the Father as prayer. So he begins to pray. Such a believer not only trusts the merits of Jesus, or His intercession, by which our unworthy prayers are made acceptable: He also trusts in that near and close union through which He prays in us and we in Him. Having Him within us, we abide in Him and He in us through the Holy Spirit perfecting our union with Him, so that we ourselves can come directly to the Father in His Name.

The whole of salvation is Christ Himself: He has given Himself to us. He Himself lives in us. Because He prays, we pray, too. Just like the disciples, when they saw Jesus praying and asked Him to make them partakers of what He knew of prayer, we know that He makes us participate with Himself in the life of prayer. He is now our Intercessor on the throne.

This comes out quite clearly in the last night of His life. In His high-priestly prayer (John 17), He shows us how and what He has to pray to the Father, and what He will pray when He ascends to heaven. He had in His parting address repeatedly connected His going to the Father with their new life of prayer. The two would be ultimately connected. His entrance on the work of His eternal intercession would be the commencement and the power of their new prayer-life in His Name. It is the sight of Jesus in His intercession that gives us power to pray in His Name. All right and power of prayer is Christ's; He makes us share in His intercession.

To understand this, think first of His intercession. He lives to intercede. The work of Christ on earth as Priest was just a beginning. As Aaron, who offered the blood sacrifice, Jesus shed His blood. As Melchizedek,

He now lives within the veil to continue His work for the power of the eternal life.

"It is Christ that died: yea rather, who is even at the right hand of God, who maketh intercession for us." That intercession is an intense reality-a work that is absolutely necessary-and without which the continued application of redemption cannot take place. Through the incarnation and resurrection of Jesus, the wondrous reconciliation took place, and man became partaker of the Divine life and blessedness.

But the real, personal use of this reconciliation cannot take place without the unceasing exercise of His Divine power by the Head in heaven. In all conversion and sanctification, in every victory over sin and the world, there is a real exercise of Christ's power. This exercise takes place only through His prayer: He asks of the Father and receives from the Father. "He is able to save them to the uttermost because He ever liveth to make intercession" (Hebrews 7:25). He receives every need of His people in intercession, extending to them what the Godhead has to give. His mediation on the throne is as real and indispensable as it was on the cross. Nothing takes place without Christ's intercession. It engages all His time and all His power. It is His unceasing occupation at the right hand of the Father.

We participate, not only in the benefits of HIS work, but in the work itself. This is because we are His Body. The Head and the members are one: "The head cannot say to the feet, I have no need of thee" (I Corinthians 12:21). We share with Jesus everything He is and has. "The glory which Thou gavest me, I have given them" (John 17:22). We are partakers of His life, His righteousness, and His work. We share His intercession, too. He cannot do it without us.

"Christ is our life"; "No longer I, but Christ liveth in me." The life in Him and in us is identical; it is one and the same. His life in heaven is a life of continuous prayer. When it descends and takes possession of us, it does not lose its character. It becomes a life of continuous prayer in us, too. It is a life that without ceasing asks and receives from God. This is not as if there were two separate currents of prayer rising upwards-one from Him and one from His people. A substantial life-union is also a prayer-union. What He prays passes though us, and what we pray passes through Him. He is the angel with the golden censer. "Unto Him there was given much incense"-the secret of acceptable prayer -"that He should offer it with the prayers of all the saints upon the golden altar" (Revelation 8:3). We live and abide in Him, the Interceding One.

The Only-begotten is the only One Who has the right to pray. To Him alone it was said, "Ask, and it shall be given Thee." Just as the fullness for all things dwells in Him, a true fullness in prayer dwells in Him, too. He alone has the power of prayer. Growth of the spiritual life consists of a deeper belief that all treasures are in Him, and that we, too, are in Him. We receive each moment what we possess in Him. Prayer-life is the same. Our faith in the intercession of Jesus must not only be in His praying for us when we do not or cannot pray. As the Author of our life and our faith, He draws us to pray in unison with Himself. Our prayer must be a work of faith in the sense that as we know that Jesus communicates His whole life in us, He also breathes our praying into us.

To many a believer, it was a new epoch in his spiritual life when it was revealed to him how truly and entirely Christ was his life, standing responsible for his remaining faithful and obedient. It was then, that he really began to live a life of faith. No less blessed will be the discovery that Christ is responsible for our prayer-life, too. As the center and embodiment of all prayer, it is communicated by Him through the Holy Spirit to His people.

"He ever liveth to make intercession" as the Head of the Body. He is the Leader in that new and living way which He has opened up as the Author and the Perfecter of our faith. He provides everything for the life of His redeemed ones by giving His own life in them. He cares for their life of prayer by taking them up into His heavenly prayer-life, giving and maintaining His prayer-life within them. "I have prayed for thee," not to render thy faith needless, but "that thy faith fail not." Our faith and prayer of faith is rooted in His. If we pray with and in the eternal Intercessor, abiding in Him, "ask whatsoever ye will, and it shall be done unto you."

The thought of our fellowship in the intercession of Jesus reminds us of what He has taught us more than once before. All these wonderful prayer-promises have the glory of God, in the manifestation of His Kingdom and the salvation of sinners, as their aim. As long as we pray chiefly for ourselves, the promises of the last night must remain a sealed book to us. The promises are given to the fruit-bearing branches of the Vine, to disciples sent into the world to live for perishing men as the Father sent Him, to His faithful servants and intimate friends who take up the work He leaves behind. Like their Lord, they have become seed-corn, losing their lives to multiply them.

Let us each find out what our work is, and which souls are entrusted to our special prayers. Let us make our intercession for them our life of fellowship with God. We will not only discover the truth to the promises of power in prayer. We will begin to realize how our abiding in Christ and His abiding in us makes us share in His own joy of blessing and saving men.

O most wonderful intercession of our Blessed Lord Jesus! We not only owe everything to that intercession, but in it we are taken up as active partners and fellow-workers! Now we understand what it is to pray in the Name of Jesus, and why it has such power. To pray in His Name, in His Spirit, in Himself, and in perfect union with Him is the active and effective intercession of Christ Jesus. When will we ever be wholly taken up into it?

Lord, teach us to pray!

Blessed Lord! In lowly adoration I again bow before You. All of Your work of redemption has now passed into prayer. You are completely occupied with praying, to maintain and dispense what You purchased with Your blood. You live to pray. And because we abide in You, we have direct access to the Father. Our lives can be lives of unceasing prayer, and the answer to our prayer is certain.

Blessed Lord! You have invited Your people to be Your fellow-workers in a life of prayer. You have united Yourself with Your people. As Your Body, they share the ministry of intercession with You. Only through this ministry can the world be filled with the fruit of Your redemption and the glory of the Father. With more liberty than ever I come to You, my Lord, and plead with You to teach me to pray. Your life is prayer; Your life is mine. Lord! Teach me to pray in You and like You.

And, O my Lord! Let me know, just as You promised Your disciples, that You are in the Father, I am in You, and You are in me. Let the uniting power of the Holy Spirit make my whole life an abiding in You and in Your intercession. May my prayer be its echo, so that the Father hears me in You and You in me. Lord Jesus! In everything, let Your mind be in me! In everything, let my life be in You! In this way, I will be prepared to be the channel, Through which Your intercession pours its blessing on the world. Amen.

"Father, I will that they also, whom thou hast given me, be with me where I am '(John 17:24).

In His parting address, Jesus gives His disciples the full revelation of what the new life was to be when the Kingdom of God had come in power. They were to find their calling and their blessedness in the indwelling of the Holy Spirit, in union with Jesus, the heavenly Vine, and in their witnessing and suffering for Him. As He described their future life, the Lord had repeatedly given the most unlimited promises as to the power their prayers might have.

Now in closing, He Himself proceeds to pray. To let His disciples have the joy Of knowing what His intercession for them in heaven as their High Priest will be, He gives them this precious legacy of His prayer to the Father. He does this because, as priests, they are to share in His work of intercession, and they must know how to perform this holy work.

In the teaching of our Lord on this last night (John, chapter 17), we recognize that these astonishing prayer-promises have not been given for our benefit, but in the interest of the Lord and His Kingdom. Only from the Lord Himself can we learn what prayer in His Name is to be and what it can obtain. To pray in His Name is to pray in perfect unity with Himself. The High-Priestly prayer will teach everyone that prayer in the Name of Jesus may ask for and expect everything. This prayer is ordinarily divided into three parts. Our Lord first prays for Himself (verses 1-5), then for His disciples (verses 6-19), and last for all the believing people of all ages (verses 20-26). The follower of Jesus who gives himself to the work of intercession, and who would like to know how much of a blessing he can pray down upon his circle in the Name of Jesus, should in all humility let himself be led of the Spirit to study this wonderful prayer as one of the most important lessons of the school of prayer.

First of all, Jesus prays for Himself, for His being glorified, so that He may glorify the Father. "Father! Glorify Thy Son. And now, Father, glorify Me." He presents reasons for His praying this way. A holy convenant was concluded between the Father and the Son in heaven. The Father promised Him power over all flesh as the reward for His work. Now Jesus had done the work, He had glorified the Father, and His one purpose was to further glorify Him. With the utmost boldness He asks the Father to glorify Him, so that He may now be and do for His people everything He has undertaken.

Disciple of Jesus! Here you have the first lesson in your work of priestly intercession, to be learned from the example of your great High

Priest. To pray in the Name of Jesus is to pray in unity and in sympathy with Him. The Son began His prayer by clarifying His relationship to the Father, speaking of His work and obedience and His desire to see the Father glorified. You should pray like this. Draw near to the Father in Christ. Plead His finished work. Say that you are one with it, that you trust it, and live in it. Say that you, too, have given yourself to finish the work the Father has given you to do, and to live alone for His glory. Then ask confidently that the Son may be glorified in you. This is praying in the Name, in the very words, and in the Spirit of Jesus, in union with Jesus Himself. Such prayer has power. If with Jesus you glorify the Father, the Father will glorify Jesus by doing what you ask in His Name. It is only when your own personal relationship, like Christ's, is clear with God-when you are glorifying Him and seeking everything for His glory-that, like Christ, you will have power to intercede for those around you.

Our Lord next prays for the circle of His disciples. He speaks of them as those whom the Father has given Him. Their distinguishing characteristic is that they have received Christ's Word. He says He is now sending them into the world in His place, just as the Father had sent Him. He asks two things for them: that the Father would keep them from the evil one, and that He would sanctify them through His Word.

Just like the Lord, each believing intercessor has his own immediate circle for whom he prays first. Parents have their children, teachers their pupils, pastors their flocks, and all believers have those whose care lies on their hearts. It is of great consequence that intercession should be personal, pointed, and definite. Our first prayer must always be that they receive the Word.

But this prayer will not work unless we say to the Lord, "I have given them Your Word." This gives us liberty and power in intercession for souls. Don't just pray for them, but speak to them. When they have received the Word, pray for their being kept from the evil one and for their being sanctified through that Word. Instead of being hopeless or judging, or giving up on those who fall, let us pray, "Father! Keep them in Your Name! Sanctify them through Your truth!" Prayer in the Name of Jesus accomplishes much: "What ye will shall be done unto you."

Next our Lord prays for a still wider circle. "I pray not only for these, but for them who through their word shall believe." His priestly heart enlarges itself to embrace all places and all time. He prays that everyone who belongs to Him may everywhere be one, as God's proof to the world of the divinity of His mission. He then prays that they may always be with Him in His glory. Until then, He asks "that the love wherewith Thou last loved me may be in them, and I in them."

The disciple of Jesus who has first proved the power of prayer in his own circle cannot confine himself within its limits. He then prays for the universal Church and its different branches. He prays especially for the unity of the Spirit and of love. He prays for its being one in Christ, as a witness to the world that Christ, Who has made love triumph over selfishness and separation, is indeed the Son of God sent from heaven. Every believer ought to pray that the unity of the Church, not in external organizations, but in spirit and in truth, is manifested.

Jesus says, "Father! I will (or I desire)." Based on His right as Son, the Father's promise to Him, and His finished work, He can do so. The Father had said to Him, "Ask of me, and I will give Thee." He simply availed Himself of the Father's promise. Jesus has given us a similar promise: "Whatsoever ye will shall be done unto you." He asks me in His Name to say what I will, what I desire. Abiding in Him, in a living union with Him in which man is nothing and Christ is everything, the believer has the liberty to take up that word of His High Priest. In answer to the question, "What wilt thou? "to say, "Father! I will all that You have promised."

This is nothing but true faith. It honors God that I have such confidence in saying what I desire is indeed acceptable to Him. At first sight, our hearts shrink from the expression. We feel neither the liberty nor the power to speak in such a manner. But grace will most assuredly be given to each one who loses his will in his Lord's. Whoever gives up his will entirely will find it again renewed and strengthened with a Divine strength.

"Father! I will. " This is the keynote of the everlasting, ever-active, all-powerful intercession of our Lord in heaven. It is only in union with Him that our prayer is effective and accomplishes much. If we abide in Him, living, walking, and doing all things in His Name; if we take each separate petition, tested and touched by His Word and Spirit, and cast it into the mighty stream of intercession that goes up from Him to be presented before the Father; then we will have the full confidence that we receive what we ask for. The cry "Father! I will "will be breathed into us by the Spirit Himself. We will lose ourselves in Him and become nothing, finding that in our impotence we have power to succeed.

Disciples of Jesus! You are called to be like your Lord in His priestly intercession! When will we awaken to the glory of our destiny to pray to God for perishing men and be answered? When will we shake off the sloth that clothes itself in the pretense of humility and yield ourselves wholly to God's Spirit, that He might fill our wills with light and power to know, to take, and to possess everything that our God is waiting to give?

Lord, teach us to pray.

O my Blessed High Priest! Who am I that You should invite me to share Your power of intercession? And why, O my Lord, am I so slow of heart to understand, believe, and exercise this wonderful privilege to which You have redeemed Your people? O Lord! Give me Your grace, that my life's work may become praying without ceasing, to draw down the blessing of heaven on all my surrroundings on earth.

Blessed Lord! I come now to accept my calling, for which I will give up everything and follow You. Into Your hands I will believingly yield my whole being. Form, train, and inspire me to be one of Your prayer force, those who watch and strive in prayer, who have power and victory. Take possession of my heart, and fill it with the desire to glorify God in the gathering, sanctification, and union of those whom the Father has given You. Take my mind and give me wisdom to know when prayer can bring a blessing. Take me wholly and prepare me as You would a priest, to stand always before God and to bless His Name.

Blessed Lord! Now and through all my spiritual life, let me want everything for You, and nothing for myself. Let it be my experience that the peson who has and asks for nothing for himself, receives everything, including the wonderful grace of sharing Your everlasting ministry of intercession. Amen.

"And he said, Abba, Father, all things are possible unto thee; take away this cup from me: nevertheless, not what I will, but what thou wilt" (Mark 14:36).

What a contrast within the space of a few hours! What a transition from the quiet elevation of that, "He lifted up His eyes to heaven, and said, Father! I will," to that falling on the ground and crying in agony, "My Father! not what I will." In the one we see the High Priest within the veil in His all powerful intercession; in the other, the sacrifice on the altar opening the way through the rent veil. The High-Priestly "Father! I will" precedes the sacrificial "Father! not what I will," but this was only to show what the intercession would be once the sacrifice was brought. The prayer before the throne, "Father! I will," had its origin and its power in the prayer at the altar, "Father! not what I will." From the entire surrender of His will in Gethsemane, the High Priest on the throne has the power to ask what He will, and the right to make His people share that power, asking what they will.

For everyone who wants to learn to pray in the school of Jesus, this Gethsemane lesson is one of the most sacred and precious. To a superficial scholar, it may appear to take away the courage to pray in faith. If even the earnest supplication of the Son was not heard, if even He had to say, "Not what I will!" how much more we must need to say it! Thus it appears impossible that the promises which the Lord had given only a few hours previously, "Whatsoever ye shall ask," "Whatsoever ye will," could have been meant literally.

A deeper insight into the meaning of Gethsemane would teach us the sure way to the assurance of an answer to our prayers. Gaze in reverent and adoring wonder on this great sight: God's Son praying through His tears, and not obtaining what He asks. He Himself is our Teacher and will open up to us the mystery of His holy sacrifice, as revealed in this wondrous prayer.

To understand the prayer, let us note the infinite difference between what our Lord prayed earlier as royal High Priest, and what He here prays in His weakness. There He prayed to glorify the Father and to glorify Himself and His people as the fulfillment of distinct promises that had been given to Him. He asked what He knew would be according to the Word and the will of the Father. He could boldly say, "Father! I will."

Here He prays for something in regard to which the Father's will is not yet clear to Him. As far as He knows, it is the Father's will that He should drink the cup. He had told His disciples of the cup He must drink. A little later He would again say, "The cup which my Father hath given me, shall I not drink it?" It was for this He had come to this earth. But in the unutterable agony of soul that gripped Him as the power of darkness overcame Him, He began to taste the first drops of death-the wrath of God against sin. His human nature, as it shuddered in the presence of the awful reality of being made a curse, gave utterance in this cry of anguish. Its desire was that, if God's purpose could be accomplished without it, He might be spared the awful cup: "Let this cup pass from me." That desire was the evidence of the intense reality of His humanity.

The "Not as I will" kept that desire from being sinful. He pleadingly cries, "All things are possible with Thee," and returns again to still more earnest prayer that the cup may be removed. "Not what I will," repeated three times, constitutes the very essence and worth of His sacrifice. He had asked for something of which He could not say, "I know it is Thy will." He had pleaded God's power and love, and had then withdrawn his plea in His final, "Thy will be done." The prayer that the cup should pass away could not be answered. The prayer of submission that God's will be done was heard and gloriously answered in His victory first over the fear, and then over the power of death.

In this denial of His will, this complete surrender of His will to the will of the Father, Christ's obedience reached its highest perfection. From the sacrifice of the will in Gethsemane, the sacrifice of the life on Calvary derives its value. It is here, as Scripture says, that He learned obedience and became the Author of everlasting salvation to everyone who obeys Him. Because in that prayer He became obedient until death-the death of the cross-God exalted Him highly and gave Him the power to ask what He will. It was in that"Father! not what I will," that He obtained the power for the "Father! I will." By Christ's submittal in Gethsemane, He secured for His people the right to say to them, "Ask whatsoever ye will."

Let us look at the deep mysteries that Gethsemane offers. First, the Father offers His Well-beloved the cup of wrath. Second, the Son, Who is always so obedient, shrinks back and implores that He may not have to drink it. Third, the Father does not grant the Son His request, but still gives the cup. And last, the Son yields His will, is content that His will be not done, and goes out to Calvary to drink the cup. O Gethsemane! In you I see how my Lord could give me such unlimited assurance of an answer to my prayers. He won it for me by His consent to have His petition unanswered.

This is in harmony with the whole scheme of redemption. Our Lord always wins for us the opposite of what He suffered. He was bound so that we could go free. He was made sin so that we could become the righteousness of God. He died so that we could live. He bore God's curse so that God's blessing would be ours. He endured God's not answering His prayer, so that our prayers could find an answer. He said, "Not as I will, "so that He could say to us, "If ye abide in me, ask what ye will, and it shall be done unto you."

"If ye abide in me": Here in Gethsemane the word acquires new force and depth. Christ is our Head, Who stands in our place and bears what we would otherwise have had to bear forever. We deserved that God should turn a deaf ear to us and never listen to our cries. Christ came and suffered for us. He suffered what we had merited. For our sins, He suffered beneath the burden of that unanswered prayer. But now His suffering succeeds for me. What He has borne is taken away from me. His merit has won for me the answer to every prayer, if I abide in Him. Yes, in Him, as He bows there in Gethsemane, I must abide. As my Head, He not only once suffered for me, but He always lives in me, breathing and working His own nature in me. The Spirit through which He offered Himself to God is the Spirit that dwells in me, too. He makes me a partaker of the very same obedience and the sacrifice of the will to God. That Spirit teaches me to yield my will entirely to the will of the Father, to give it up even unto death. He teaches me to distrust whatever is of my own mind, thought, and will, even though it may not be directly sinful. He opens my ear to wait in great gentleness and teachableness of soul for what the Father day by day has to speak and to teach. He shows me how union with God's will (and the love of it) is union with God Himself. Entire surrender to God's will is the Father's claim, the Son's example, and the true blessedness of the soul. The Spirit leads my will into the fellowship of Christ's death and resurrection. My will dies in Him, and in Him is made alive again. He breathes into it a holy insight into God's perfect will, a holy joy in yielding itself to be an instrument of that will, and a holy liberty and power to lay hold of God's will to answer prayer. With my whole will, I learn to live for the interests of God and His Kingdom and to exercise the power of that will-crucified but risen again -in nature and in prayer, on earth and in heaven, with men and with God.

The more deeply I enter into the "Father! not what I will" of Gethsemane, and into Him Who said it, the fuller is my spiritual access to the power of His "Father! I will." The soul experiences that the will has become nothing in order that God's will may be everything. It is now inspired with a Divine strength to really will what God wills, and to claim what has been promised to it in the Name of Christ.

Listen to Christ in Gethsemane as He calls, "If ye abide in me, ye shall ask what ye will, and it shall be done unto you." Be of one mind and spirit with Him in His giving up everything to God's will; live like Him in obedience and surrender to the Father. This is abiding in Him-the secret of power in prayer.

Lord, teach us to pray

Blessed Lord Jesus! Gethsemane was the school where You learned to pray and to obey. It is still Your school, where You lead all Your disciples who wish to learn to obey and to pray just like You Lord! Teach me there to pray, in the faith that You have atoned for and conquered our self-will and can indeed give us grace to pray like you. O Lamb of God! I want to follow You to Gethsemane! There I want to become one with You and abide in You, as You to the very death yield Your will to the Father. With You, through You, and in You, I yield my will in absolute and entire surrender to the will of the Father. Conscious of my own weakness and the secret power with which self-will would assert itself and again take its place on the throne, I claim in faith the power of Your victory. You have triumphed over it and delivered me from it. In Your death, I will daily live. In Your life, I will daily die. Abiding in You, may my will, through the power of Your eternal Spirit, become a finely tuned instrument which yields to every touch of the will of my God. With my whole soul, I say with You and in You. "Father! not as I will, but as Thou wilt."

Blessed Lord! Open my heart, and the hearts of all Your people, to fully take in the glory of the truth: That a will, given up to God, is a will God accepts for use in His service, to desire, determine, and will what is according to God's will. Let mine be a will which, by the power of the Holy Spirit, exercises its royal prerogative in prayer. Let it loose and bind in heaven and on earth, asking whatever it chooses, and saying it will be done.

O Lord Jesus! Teach me to pray. Amen.

"And this is the confidence that we have in him, that, if we ask any thing according to his will, he heareth us: And if we know that he hear us, whatsoever we ask, we know that we have the petitions that we desired of him"(1 John 5:14-15).

One of the greatest hindrances to believing prayer is undoubtedly this: Many don't know if what they ask is according to the will of God. As long as they are in doubt on this point, they cannot have the boldness to ask in the assurance that they will certainly receive. They soon begin to think that, once they have made known their requests and receive no answer, it is best to leave it to God to do according to His good pleasure. The words of John, "If we ask anything according to His will, He heareth us," as they understand them, make certainty as to an answer to prayer impossible, because they cannot be sure of what the will of God really may be. They think of God's will as His hidden counsel: How can man fathom the purpose of a God Who is wise in all things?

This is the very opposite of John's purpose writing this. He wanted to stir boldness and confidence in us, until we had the full assurance of faith in prayer. He says that we should have the boldness to the Father that we know we are asking according to His will, and we know that He hears us. With such boldness, He will hear us no matter what we ask for, as long as it is according to His will. In faith we should know that we have the answer. And even as we are praying, we should be able to receive what we have asked.

John supposes that when we pray, we first find if our prayers are according to the will of God. They may be according to God's will, and yet not answered at once, or without the persevering prayer of faith. It is to give us courage to persevere and to be strong in faith that He tells us we can have boldness or confidence in prayer, because if we ask anything according to His will, He hears us. It is evident that if we are uncertain whether our petitions are according to His will, we cannot have the comfort of His promise, "We know that we have the petitions which we have asked of Him."

But this is just the difficulty. More than one believer says, "I do not know if what I desire is according to the will of God. God's will is the purpose of His infinite wisdom. It is impossible for me to know whether He considers something else better for me than what I desire. He may have reasons for holding what I asked." Everyone should understand that with such thoughts the prayer of faith becomes an impossibility. There may still be a prayer of submission or of trust in God's wisdom. But there cannot be a prayer of faith.

The great mistake here is that God's children do not really believe that it is possible to know God's will. Or if they believe this, they do not take the time and trouble to find it out. What we need is to see clearly how the Father leads His waiting, teachable child to know that his petition is according to His will. Through God's holy Word-taken up and kept in the heart, the life, and the will-and through God's Holy Spirit accepted in His dwelling and leading we will learn to know that our petitions are according to His will.

First, let us consider the Word. There is a secret will of God, with which we often fear that our prayers may be at variance. But this is not the will of God that we should be concerned with in our prayers. His will as revealed in His Word should be our concern. Our notions of a secret will that makes decrees, rendering the answers to our prayers impossible, are erroneous. Childlike faith in what He is willing to do for His children simply accepts the Father's assurance that it is His will to hear prayer and to do what faith in His Word desires and accepts. In the Word, the Father has revealed in general promises the great principles of His will with His people. The child has to take the promise and apply it to the special circumstances in His life to which it has reference. Whatever he asks within the limits of that revealed will, he may confidently expect, knowing it to be according to the will of God.

In His Word, God has given us the revelation of His will. He shows us His plans for us, His people, and for the world. With the most precious promises of grace and power, He carries out these plans through His people. As faith becomes strong and bold enough to claim the fulfillment of the general promise in the special case, we may have the assurance that our prayers are heard, because they are according to God's will. Take the words of John the verse following our text as an illustration: "If any man sees his brother sinning a sin not unto death, he shall ask and God will give him life." This is the general promise. The believer who pleads on the grounds of this promise, prays according to the will of God, and John wants him to feel the boldness to know that he has the petition for which he asks.

God's will is something spiritual and must be spiritually discerned. It is not a matter of logic that we can argue about. Not every Christian has the same gift or calling. While the general will revealed in the promises is the same for everyone, each person has a specific, individual role to fulfill in God's purpose. The wisdom of the saints is in knowing the specific will of God according to the measure of grace given us, and to ask in prayer just what God has prepared and made possible for each. The Holy Spirit dwells in us to communicate this widsom. The personal application of the general promises of the Word to our specific personal needs is given to us by the leading of the Holy Spirit.

It is this union of the teaching of the Word and the Spirit that many do not understand. This causes a twofold difficulty in knowing what God's will may be. Some seek the will of God in an inner feeling or conviction, and expect the Spirit to lead them without the Word. Others seek it in the Word, without the living leading of the Holy Spirit. The two must be united. Only in the Word and in the Spirit can we know the will of God and learn to pray according to it. In the heart, the Word and Spirit must meet. Only by indwelling can we experience their teaching. The Word must abide in us; our heart and life must be under its influence daily.

The quickening of the Word by the Spirit comes from within, not from without. Only he who yields himself entirely, in his whole life, to the supremacy of the Word and the will of God can expect to discern what that Word and will permit him to ask boldly in specific cases. The same is true of the Spirit. If I desire His leading in prayer to assure me what God's will is, my whole life must be yielded to that leading. Only in this way can mind and heart become spiritual and capable of knowing God's holy will. He who through Word and Spirit lives in the will of God by doing it; will know to pray according to that will in the confidence that He hears.

If only Christians could see what incalculable harm they do themselves by thinking that because their prayer is possibly not according to God's will, they must be content without an answer. God's Word tells us that the great reason for unanswered prayer is that we do not pray right: Ye ask and receive not, because ye ask amiss." In not granting an answer, the Father tells us that there is something wrong in our praying. He wants us to discover it and confess it, and so to teach us true believing and effective prayer. He can only attain this object when He brings us to the place where we see that we are to blame for the withholding of the answer. Our aims, our faith, or our lives are not what they should be. God is frustrated as long as we are content to say "Perhaps it is because my prayer is not according to His will that He does not hear me."

O let us no longer throw the blame for our unanswered prayers on the secret will of God, but on our own faulty praying! Let that word, "Ye receive not because ye ask amiss," be a lantern of the Lord, searching heart and life to prove that we are indeed those to whom Christ gave His promises of certain answers! Let us believe that we can know if our prayers are according to God's will! Let us yield our hearts to the indwelling of the Word of the Father to have Christ's Word abiding in us. We should live day by day with the anointing that teaches all things. If we yield ourselves unreservedly to the Holy Spirit as He teaches us to abide in Christ and to dwell in the Father's presence, we will soon understand how the Father's love longs for the child to know His will. In the confidence that that will includes every thing His power and love have promised to do, we should know, too, that He hears all of our prayers. "This is the boldness which we have, that if we ask anything according to His will, He heareth us."

Lord, teach us to pray.

Blessed Master! With my whole heart I thank You for the blessed lesson that the path to a life full of answers to prayer is through the will of God. Lord! Teach me to know this blessed will by living it, loving it, and always doing it. In this way, I will learn to offer prayers according to that will. In their harmony with God's blessed will, I will find boldness in prayer and confidence in accepting the answer.

Father! It is Your will that Your child should enjoy Your presence and blessing. It is Your will that everything in Your child's life should be in accordance with Your will, and that the Holy Spirit should work this in him. It is Your will that Your child should live in the daily experience of distinct answers to prayer, in order to enjoy living and direct fellowship with Yourself. It is Your will that Your Name should be glorified in and through Your children, and that it will be in those who trust You. O my Father! Let this will of Yours be my confidence in everything I ask.

Blessed Savior! Teach me to believe in the glory of this will. That will is the eternal love that, with Divine power, works out its purpose in each human will that yields itself to it. Lord! Teach me this! You can make me see how every promise and every command of the Word is indeed the will of God, and that its fulfillment is given to me by God Himself. Let His will become the sure rock on which prayer and my assurance of an answer always rest Amen.

AUTHOR'S NOTE

There is often great confusion as to the will of God. People think that what God wills must inevitably take place. This is by no means the case. God wills a great deal of blessing to His people which never comes to them. He wills it most earnestly, but they do not will it. Hence, it cannot come to them. This is the great mystery of man's creation with a free will and the renewal of his will in redemption. God has made the execution of His will dependent on the will of man. God's will as revealed in His promises will be fulfilled as much as our faith allow. Prayer is the power by which something comes to pass which otherwise would not have taken place. And faith the power which determines how much of God's will is done in us. Once God reveals to a soul what He is willing to do for it, the responsibility for the execution of that will rests with us.

Some are afraid that this is putting too much power into the hands of man. But all power is put into the hands of man through Christ Jesus (Luke 10:19). The key to prayer and all power is His. When we learn to understand that He is just as much one with us as with the Father, see how natural, right, and safe it is that such power is given. Christ the Son has the right to ask whatever I chooses. Through our abiding in Him and His abiding in us, His Spirit breathes in us what He wants to ask and obtain through us. We pray in His Name. The prayers are as much ours as they are His.

Others fear that to believe that prayer has such power limits the liberty and the love of God. O if we only knew how we are limiting His liberty and His love by not allowing Him to act in the only way in which He chooses to act, now that He has taken us up into fellowship with Himself! Our prayer is like pipes, though which water is carried from a large mountain stream to a town some distance away. Such water pipes don't make the water willing to flow down from the hills, nor do they give it its power of blessing and refreshment. This is its very nature. All they do is to determine its direction.

In the same way, the very nature of God is to love and to bless. His love longs to come down to us with its quickening and refreshing streams. But He has left it to prayer to say where the blessing is channeled. He has committed it to His believing people to bring the living water to the desert places. The will of God to bless is dependent on the will of man to say where the blessing goes.

"A holy priesthood, to offer up spiritual sacrifices, acceptable to God by Jesus Christ" (I Peter 2:5)

"Ye shall be named the Priests of the Lord." (Isaiah 61:6).

"The Spirit of the Lord God is upon me: because the Lord hath anointed me." These are the words of Jesus in Isaiah, chapter sixty-one. As the fruit of His work, all redeemed ones are priests-fellow-partakers with Him of His anointing with the Spirit as High Priest. This anointing is "Like the precious ointment upon the beard of Aaron, that went down to the skirts of his garments" (Psalm 133:2). Like every son of Aaron, every member of Jesus' Body has a right to the priesthood. But not everyone exercises it.Many are still entirely ignorant of it. And yet it is the highest privilege of a child of God, the mark of greatest nearness and likeness to Him "Whoever liveth to pray." Do you doubt this? Think of what constitutes priesthood.

There is, first, the work of the priesthood. This has two sides: one Godward, the other manward. "Every priest is ordained for men in things pertaining to God" (Hebrews 5:1). Or, as it is said by Moses (Deuteronomy 10:8, 21:5, 33:10; Malachi 2:6): "The Lord separated the tribe of Levi, to stand before the Lord to minister unto Him, and to bless His Name. " On the one hand, the priest had the power to draw nigh to God, to dwell with Him in His house, and to present Him with the blood of the sacrifice or the burning incense. This work he did not do, however, on his own behalf, but for the sake of the people whose representative he was. This is the other side of his work. He received people's sacrifices, presented them to God, and then came out to bless in His Name, giving the assurance of His favor and teaching them His law.

A priest is thus a man who does not live for himself. He lives with God and for God. His work as God's servant is to care for His house, His honor,and His worship, making known to men His love and His will. He lives with men and for men (Hebrews 5:2). His work is to find out their sins and needs, bring these before God, offer sacrifice and incense in their names, obtain forgiveness and blessing for them, and then to come out and bless them in His Name.

This is the high calling of every believer. They have been redeemed with the one purpose of being God's priests in the midst of the perishing millions around them. In conformity to Jesus, the Great High Priest, they are to be the ministers and stewards of the grace of God.

Secondly, there is the walk of the priesthood, harmony with its work. As God is holy, so the priest was to be especially holy. This means not only separated from everything unclean, but holy unto God-being set apart and given up to God for His use. Separation from the world and being given to God were indicated in many ways.

It was seen in the clothing. The holy garment made according to God's own orders, marked the priests as His (Exodus 28). It was seen in the command as to their special purity and freedom from contact with death and defilement. Much that was allowed to an ordinary Israelite was forbidden them. Priests could have no bodily defects or blemishes. Bodily perfection was to be the model wholeness and holiness in God's service. The priestly tribes were to have no inheritance with the other tribes. God was to be their inheritance. Their life was to be one of faith-set apart unto God; they were to live on Him as well as for Him. All this symbolic of what the character of the New Testament priest is to be. Our priestly power with God depends on our personal life and walk. Jesus must be able to say of our walk on earth, "They have not defiled their garments."

In our separation from the world, we must prove that our desire to be holy to the Lord is whole-hearted and entire. The bodily perfection of the priest must have its counterpart in our also being "without spot or blemish." We must be "the man of God, perfect, thoroughly furnished unto all good works," "perfect and entire, wanting nothing" (Leviticus 21:17-21; Ephesians 5:27; 2 Timothy 3:17; James 1:4). Above all, we must consent to give up all inheritance on earth. We must forsake everything and like Christ have need only of God and keep everything for Him alone. This marks the true priest, the man who only lives for God and his fellow-men.

Thirdly, there is the way to the priesthood. God had chosen all of Aaron's sons to be priests. Each of them was a priest by birth. Yet he could not begin his work without a special act of ordinance-his consecration. Every child of God is a priest by right of his birth-his blood relationship to the Great High Priest. But he can exercise his power only as he accepts and realizes his consecration.

With Aaron and his sons it took place thus (Exodus 29): After being washed and clothed, they were anointed with the holy oil. Sacrifices were then offered, and the right ear, the right hand, and the right foot were touched with the blood. They and their garments were then sprinkled with the blood and the oil together. In the same way, as the blood and the Spirit work more fully in the child of God, the power of the Holy Priesthood will also work in him. The blood will take away all sense of unworthiness; the Spirit will take away all sense of unfitness. Notice what was new in the application of the blood to the priest. If he had ever as a penitent sought forgiveness by bringing a sacrifice for his sin, the blood was sprinkled on the altar, but not on his person. But now, for priestly consecration, there was to be closer contact with the blood. The ear, hand and foot were by a special act brought under its power, and the whole being sanctified for God. When the believer is led to seek full priestly access God, he feels the need of a fuller and more enduring experience of the power of the blood. Where he had previously been content to have the blood sprinkled only on the mercy seat as what he needed for pardon, he now needs a more personal sprinkling a cleansing of his heart from an evil conscience. Through this, he has "no more conscience of sin" (Hebrews 10:2); he is cleansed from all sin. As he gets to enjoy this, his consciousness is awakened to his wonderful right of intimate access to God, and the full assurance that his intercessions are acceptable.

As the blood gives the right, the Spirit gives the power for believing intercession. He breathes into the priestly spirit a burning love for God's honor and the saving of souls. He makes us one with Jesus to the extent that prayer in His Name is reality. The more the Christian is truly filled with the Spirit of Christ, the more spontaneous will be his giving himself up to the life of priestly intercession.

Beloved fellow-Christians! God needs priests who can draw close to Him, live in His presence, and by their intercession draw down the blessings of His grace on others. And the world needs priests who will bear the burden of the perishing ones and intercede on their behalf. Are you willing to offer yourself for this holy work? You know the surrender it demands-nothing less than the Christ-like giving up of everything, so that the salvation of God's love may be accomplished among men. Don't be one of those who are content with being saved, just doing enough work to keep themselves warm and lively! Let nothing keep you back from giving yourselves to be wholly and only priests of the Most High God!

The thought of unworthiness or of unfitness need not keep you back. In the blood, the objective power of the perfect redemption works in you. In the Spirit, the full, subjective, personal experience of a Divine life is secured. The blood provides an infinite worthiness to make your prayers acceptable. The Spirit provides a Divine fitness, teaching you to pray exactly according to the will of God.

Every priest knew that when he presented a sacrifice according to the law of the sanctuary, it was accepted. Under the covering of the blood and the Spirit, you have the assurance that all the wonderful promises of prayer in the Name of Jesus will be fulfilled in you. Abiding in union with the Great High Priest, "You shall ask what you will, and it shall be done unto you." You will have power to pray the effective prayer of the righteous man that accomplishes a great deal. You will not only join in the general prayer of the Church for the world, but be able in your own sphere to take up your own special work in prayer. As priests, you will work on a personal basis with God to receive and know the answer, and so to bless in His Name.

Come, brother, come! Be a priest, only a priest, and all priest! Walk before the Lord in the full consciousness that you have been set apart for the holy ministry of intercession. This is the true blessedness of conformity to the image of God's Son.

Lord, teach us to pray.

O my blessed High Priest! Accept the consecration in which my soul responds to Your message! I believe in the holy priesthood of Your saints I believe that I am a priest, having the power to appear before the Father in prayer that will bring down many blessings on the perishing souls around me.

I believe in the power of Your precious blood to cleanse me from all sin. It gives me perfect confidence in God and brings me near to Him in the full assurance of faith that my intercession will be heard.

I believe in the anointing of the Spirit. It comes down to me daily from You, my Great High Priest, to sanctify me. It fills me with the consciousness my priestly calling and with the love of souls. It also teaches me what is according to God's will and how to pray the prayer of faith.

I believe that, just as You are in all things in life, You are in my prayer life, drawing me up in it the fellowship of Your wondrous work of intercession.

In this faith, I yield myself today to my God as one of His anointed priests. I stand before Him to intercede on behalf of sinners, and then return to bless them in His Name.

Holy Lord Jesus! Accept and seal my consecration. Lay Your hands on me and consecrate me Yourself to this holy work. Let me walk among men with the consciousness and the character of a priest or the Most High God.

And to Him Who loved us-Who washed us from our sins in His own blood, and Who made us kings and priests before God, His Father-to Him be glory and power forever! Amen.

CHAPTER 31: A Life of Prayer

"Rejoice evermore. Pray without ceasing. In everything give thanks" (I Thessalonians 5:16-18).

Our Lord told the parable of the widow and the unjust judge to teach us that men ought to pray without ceasing. The widow persevered in seeking one definite thing. The parable appears to refer to persevering in prayer for some special blessing, when God delays or appears to refuse. The Epistles, which speak of continuing in prayer, watching for the answer, and praying always in the Spirit, appear to refer to something different-the whole life being one of prayer. As the soul longs for the manifestation of God's glory to us, in us, through us, and around us, the inmost life of the soul is continually rising upward in dependence, faith, longing desire, and trustful expectation.

What is needed to live such a life of prayer? The first thing is undoubtedly an entire sacrifice of one's life to God's Kingdom and glory. If you try to pray without ceasing because you want to be very pious and good, you will never succeed. Yielding ourselves to live for God and His honor enlarges the heart and teaches us to regard everything in the light of God and His will. We instinctively recognize in everything around us the need for God's help and blessing, and an opportunity for His being glorified.

Everything is weighed and tested by the one thing that fills the heart: the glory of God. The soul has learned that only what is of God can really glorify Him. Through the heart and soul, the whole life becomes a looking up, a crying from the inmost heart, for God to prove His power and love, and reveal His glory. The believer awakes to the consciousness that he is one of the watchmen on Zion's walls, whose call really does touch and move the King in heaven to do what would otherwise not be done. He understands how real Paul's exhortation was: "praying always with all prayer and supplication in the Spirit for all the saints and for me," and "continue in prayer, with all praying also for us." To forget oneself-to live for God and His Kingdom among men-is the way to learn to pray without ceasing.

This life devoted to God must be accompanied by the deep confidence that our prayer is effective. In His prayer lessons, our Blessed Lord insisted on faith in the Father as a God Who most certainly does what we ask. "Ask and ye shall receive." To count confidently on an answer is the beginning and the end of His teaching. (Compare Matthew 7:8 and John 16:24.)

As we gain the assurance that our prayers are effective and that God does what we ask, we dare not neglect the use of this wonderful power. Our souls should turn wholly to God, and our lives should become prayer. The Lord needs and takes time, because we and everyone around us are creatures of time, subject to the law of growth. But know that not one single prayer of faith can possibly be lost, and that sometimes there is a necessity for accumulating prayer. Know that persevering prayer pleases God. Prayer becomes the quiet, persistent living of our life of desire and faith in the presence of our God.

Don't limit such free and sure promises of the living God with your reasoning any longer! Don't rob them of their power, and ourselves of the wonderful confidence they are meant to inspire! The hindrance is not in God, not in His secret will, and not in the limitations of His promises. It is in us. We are not what we should be to obtain the promise. Open your whole heart to God's words of promise in all their simplicity and truth! They will search us and humble us. They will lift us up and make us glad and strong. To the faith that knows it gets what it asks for, prayer is not a work or a burden, but a joy and a triumph. It becomes a necessity and a second nature.

This union of strong desire and firm confidence is nothing but the life of the Holy Spirit within us. The Holy Spirit dwells in us, hides Himself in the depths of our being, and stirs our desire for the Unseen and the Divine-God Himself. It is always the Holy Spirit Who draws out the heart to thirst for God and to long for His being recognized and glorified. Sometimes He speaks through us in groanings that cannot be uttered, sometimes in clear and conscious assurance, sometimes in distinct petitions for the deeper revelation of Christ to ourselves, and sometimes in pleas for a soul, a work, the Church or the world. Where the child of God really lives and walks in the Spirit-where he is not content to remain carnal, but tries to be a fit, spiritual organ for the Divine Spirit to reveal the life of Christ and Christ Himself-there the neverceasing life of intercession of the Blessed Son must reveal and repeat itself. Because it is the Spirit of Christ Who prays in us, our prayers must be heard. Because it is we who pray in the Spirit, there is need of time, patience, and continual renewing of the prayer until every obstacle is conquered, and the harmony between God's Spirit and ours is perfect.

The chief thing we need for a life of unceasing prayer is to know that Jesus teaches us to pray. We have begun to understand a little of what His teaching is. It isn't the communication of new thoughts or views, the discovery of failure or error, nor the arousal of desire and faith, however important all this may be. Jesus' teaching takes us up into the fellowship of His own prayer-life before the Father. This is how Jesus really teaches. It was the sight of Jesus praying that made the disciples ask to be taught to pray. The faith of Jesus' continuous prayer truly teaches us to pray.

We know why: He Who prays is our Head and our life. All He has is ours and is given to us when we give ourselves completely to Him. By His blood, He leads us into the immediate presence of God. The inner sanctuary is our home; we live there. Living so close to God and knowing we have been taken there to bless those who are far away, we cannot help but pray.

Christ makes us partakers with Himself of His prayer-power and prayer-life. Our true aim must not be to work a great deal and pray just enough to keep the work right. We should pray a great deal and then work enough for the power and blessing obtained in prayer to find its way through us to men. Christ lives to pray eternally; He saves and reigns. He communicates His prayer-life to us and maintains it in us if we trust Him. He is responsible for our praying without ceasing. Christ teaches us to pray by showing us how He does it, by doing it in us, and by leading us to do it in Him and like Him. Christ is everything-the life and the strength-for a neverceasing prayer-life. Seeing Christ's continuous praying as our life enables us to pray without ceasing. Because His priesthood is the power of an endless life-that resurrection life that never fades and never fails-and because His life is our life, praying without ceasing can become the joy of heaven here on earth. The Apostle says, "Rejoice evermore: pray without ceasing: in everything give thanks." Supported by never-ceasing joy and neverceasing praise, never-ceasing prayer is the manifestation of the power of the eternal life where Jesus always prays.

The union between the Vine and the branch is indeed a prayer union. The highest conformity to Christ-the most blessed participation in the glory of His heavenly life-is that we take part in His work of intercession. He and we live forever to pray. In union with Him, praying without ceasing becomes a possibility-a reality, the holiest and most blessed part of our holy and blessed fellowship with God. We abide within the veil in the presence of the Father. What the Father says, we do. What the Son asks, the Father does. Praying without ceasing is the earthly manifestation of heaven, a foretaste of the life where they rest neither day nor night in their song of worship and adoration.

Lord, teach us to pray.

O my Father! With my whole heart I praise You for this wondrous life of continuous prayer, continuous fellowship, continuous answers, and continuous oneness with Him Who lives to pray forever! O my God! Keep me abiding and walking in the presence of Your glory, so that prayer may be the spontaneous expression of my life with You.

Blessed Savior! With my whole heart I praise You for coming from heaven to share my needs and my pleas, so that I could share Your all-powerful intercession. Thank You for taking me into Your school of prayer, teaching me the blessedness and the power of a life that is totally comprised of prayer. And most of all, thank You for taking me up into the fellowship of Your life of intercession. Now through me, too, Your blessings can be dispensed to those around me.

Holy Spirit! With deep reverence I thank You for Your work in me. Through You I am lifted up into communication with the Son and the Father, entering the fellowship of the life and love of the Holy Trinity. Spirit of God! Perfect Your work in me! Bring me into perfect union with Christ, My Intercessor! Let Your unceasing indwelling make my life one of unceasing intercession. And let my life unceasingly glorify the Father and bless those around me. Amen.

The True Vine

PREFACE

I have felt drawn to try to write what young Christians might easily apprehend, as a help to them to take up that position in which the Christian life must be a success. It is as if there is not one of the principal temptations and failures of the Christian life that is not met here. The nearness, the all-sufficiency, the faithfulness of the Lord Jesus, the naturalness, the fruitfulness of a life of faith, are so revealed, that it is as if one could with confidence say, Let the parable enter into the heart, and all will be right.

May the blessed Lord give the blessing. May He teach us to study the mystery of the Vine in the spirit of worship, waiting for God's own teaching.

I am the True Vine--John 15:1

All earthly things are the shadows of heavenly realities--the expression, in created, visible forms, of the invisible glory of God. The Life and the Truth are in Heaven; on earth we have figures and shadows of the heavenly truths. When Jesus says: "I am the true Vine," He tells us that all the vines of earth are pictures and emblems of Himself. He is the divine reality, of which they are the created expression. They all point to Him, and preach Him, and reveal Him. If you would know Jesus, study the vine.

How many eyes have gazed on and admired a great vine with its beautiful fruit. Come and gaze on the heavenly Vine till your eye turns from all else to admire Him. How many, in a sunny clime, sit and rest under the shadow of a vine. Come and be still under the shadow of the true Vine, and rest under it from the heat of the day. What countless numbers rejoice in the fruit of the vine! Come, and take, and eat of the heavenly fruit of the true Vine, and let your soul say: "I sat under His shadow with great delight, and His fruit was sweet to my taste."

I am the true Vine.--This is a heavenly mystery. The earthly vine can teach you much about this Vine of Heaven. Many interesting and beautiful points of comparison suggest themselves, and help us to get conceptions of what Christ meant. But such thoughts do not teach us to know what the heavenly Vine really is, in its cooling shade, and its life-giving fruit. The experience of this is part of the hidden mystery, which none but Jesus Himself, by His Holy Spirit, can unfold and impart.

I am the true Vine.--The vine is the living Lord, who Himself speaks, and gives, and works all that He has for us. If you would know the meaning and power of that word, do not think to find it by thought or study; these may help to show you what you must get from Him to awaken desire and hope and prayer, but they cannot show you the Vine. Jesus alone can reveal Himself. He gives His Holy Spirit to open the eyes to gaze upon Himself, to open the heart to receive Himself. He must Himself speak the word to you and me.

I am the true Vine.--And what am I to do, if I want the mystery, in all its heavenly beauty and blessing, opened up to me? With what you already know of the parable, bow down and be still, worship and wait, until the divine Word enters your heart, and you feel His holy presence with you, and in you. The overshadowing of His holy love will give you the perfect calm and rest of knowing that the Vine will do all.

I am the true Vine.--He who speaks is God, in His infinite power able to enter into us. He is man, one with us. He is the crucified One, who won a perfect righteousness and a divine life for us through His death. He is the glorified One, who from the throne gives His Spirit to make His presence real and true. He speaks--oh, listen, not to His words only, but to Himself, as He whispers secretly day by day: "I am the true Vine! All that the Vine can ever be to its branch, "I will be to you."

Holy Lord Jesus, the heavenly Vine of God's own planting, I beseech Thee, reveal Thyself to my soul. Let the Holy Spirit, not only in thought, but in experience, give me to know all that Thou, the Son of God, art to me as the true Vine.

THE HUSBANDMAN

And My Father is the Husbandman--John 15:1

A vine must have a husbandman to plant and watch over it, to receive and rejoice in its fruit. Jesus says: "My Father is the husbandman." He was "the vine of God's planting." All He was and did, He owed to the Father; in all He only sought the Father's will and glory. He had become man to show us what a creature ought to be to its Creator. He took our place, and the spirit of His life before the Father was ever what He seeks to make ours: "Of him, and through him, and to him are all things." He became the true Vine, that we might be true branches. Both in regard to Christ and ourselves the words teach us the two lessons of absolute dependence and perfect confidence.

My Father is the Husbandman.--Christ ever lived in the spirit of what He once said: "The Son can do nothing of himself." As dependent as a vine is on a husbandman for the place where it is to grow, for its fencing in and watering and pruning. Christ felt Himself entirely dependent on the Father every day for the wisdom and the strength to do the Father's will. As He said in the previous chapter (14:10): "The words that I say unto you, I speak not from Myself; but the Father abiding in Me doeth his works." This absolute dependence had as its blessed counterpart the most blessed confidence that He had nothing to fear: the Father could not disappoint Him. With such a Husbandman as His Father, He could enter death and the grave. He could trust God to raise Him up. All that Christ is and has, He has, not in Himself, but from the Father.

My Father is the Husbandman.--That is as blessedly true for us as for Christ. Christ is about to teach His disciples about their being branches. Before He ever uses the word, or speaks at all of abiding in Him or bearing fruit, He turns their eyes heavenward to the Father watching over them, and working all in them. At the very root of all Christian life lies the thought that God is to do all, that our work is to give and leave ourselves in His hands, in the confession of utter helplessness and dependence, in the assured confidence that He gives all we need. The great lack of the Christian life is that, even where we trust Christ, we leave God out of the count. Christ came to bring us to God. Christ lived the life of a man exactly as we have to live it. Christ the Vine points to God the Husbandman. As He trusted God, let us trust God, that everything we ought to be and have, as those who belong to the Vine, will be given us from above.

Isaiah said: "A vineyard of red wine; I the Lord do keep it, I will water it every moment; lest any hurt it, I will keep it night and day." Ere we begin to think of fruit or branches, let us have our heart filled with the faith: as glorious as the Vine, is the Husbandman. As high and holy as is our calling, so mighty and loving is the God who will work it all. As surely as the Husbandman made the Vine what it was to be, will He make each branch what it is to be. Our Father is our Husbandman, the Surety for our growth and fruit.

Blessed Father, we are Thy husbandry. Oh, that Thou mayest have honor of the work of Thy hands! O my Father, I desire to open my heart to the joy of this wondrous truth: My Father is the Husbandman. Teach me to know and trust Thee, and to see that the same deep interest with which Thou caredst for and delightedst in the Vine, extends to every branch, to me too.

Every Branch in me that Beareth Not Fruit, He taketh It away--John 15:2

Here we have one of the chief words of the parable--branch. A vine needs branches: without branches it can do nothing, can bear no fruit. As important as it is to know about the Vine, and the Husbandman, it is to realize what the branch is. Before we listen to what Christ has to say about it, let us first of all take in what a branch is, and what it teaches us of our life in Christ. A branch is simply a bit of wood, brought forth by the vine for the one purpose of serving it in bearing its fruit. It is of the very same nature as the vine, and has one life and one spirit with it. Just think a moment of the lessons this suggests.

There is the lesson of entire consecration. The branch has but one object for which it exists, one purpose to which it is entirely given up. That is, to bear the fruit the vine wishes to bring forth. And so the believer has but one reason for his being a branch--but one reason for his existence on earth --that the heavenly Vine may through him bring forth His fruit. Happy the soul that knows this, that has consented to it, and that says, I have been redeemed and I live for one thing--as exclusively as the natural branch exists only to bring forth fruit, I too; as exclusively as the heavenly Vine exists to bring forth fruit, I too. As I have been planted by God into Christ, I have wholly given myself to bear the fruit the Vine desires to bring forth.

There is the lesson of perfect conformity. The branch is exactly like the vine in every aspect--the same nature, the same life, the same place, the same work. In all this they are inseparably one. And so the believer needs to know that he is partaker of the divine nature, and has the very nature and spirit of Christ in him, and that his one calling is to yield himself to a perfect conformity to Christ. The branch is a perfect likeness of the vine; the only difference is, the one is great and strong, and the source of strength, the other little and feeble, ever needing and receiving strength. Even so the believer is, and is to be, the perfect likeness of Christ.

There is the lesson of absolute dependence. The vine has its stores of life and sap and strength, not for itself, but for the branches. The branches are and have nothing but what the vine provides and imparts. The believer is called to, and it is his highest blessedness to enter upon, a life of entire and unceasing dependence upon Christ. Day and night, every moment, Christ is to work in him all he needs.

And then the lesson of undoubting confidence. The branch has no cure; the vine provides all; it has but to yield itself and receive. It is the sight of this truth that leads to the blessed rest of faith, the true secret of growth and strength: "I can do all things through Christ which strengtheneth me."

What a life would come to us if we only consented to be branches! Dear child of God, learn the lesson. You have but one thing to do: Only be a branch--nothing more, nothing less! Just be a branch; Christ will be the Vine that gives all. And the Husbandman, the mighty God, who made the Vine what it is, will as surely make the branch what it ought to be.

Lord Jesus, I pray Thee, reveal to me the heavenly mystery of the branch, in its living union with the Vine, in its claim on all its fullness. And let Thy all-sufficiency, holding and filling Thy branches, lead me to the rest of faith that knows that Thou workest all.

Every Branch in me That Beareth Not Fruit, He Taketh It Away--John 15:2

   Fruit.--This is the next great word we have: the Vine, the Husbandman, the branch, the fruit. What has our Lord to say to us of fruit? Simply this--that fruit is the one thing the branch is for, and that if it bear not fruit, the husbandman takes it away. The vine is the glory of the husbandman; the branch is the glory of the vine; the fruit is the glory of the branch; if the branch bring not forth fruit, there is no glory or worth in it; it is an offense and a hindrance; the husbandman takes it away. The one reason for the existence of a branch, the one mark of being a true branch of the heavenly Vine, the one condition of being allowed by the divine Husbandman to share the life the Vine is-- bearing fruit.

   And what is fruit? Something that the branch bears, not for itself, but for its owner; something that is to be gathered, and taken away. The branch does indeed receive it from the vine sap for its own life, by which it grows thicker and stronger. But this supply for its own maintenance is entirely subordinate to its fulfillment of the purpose of its existence--bearing fruit. It is because Christians do not understand or accept of this truth, that they so fail in their efforts and prayers to live the branch life. They often desire it very earnestly; they read and meditate and pray, and yet they fail, they wonder why? The reason is very simple: they do not know that fruit-bearing is the one thing they have been saved for. Just as entirely as Christ became the true Vine with the one object, you have been made a branch too, with the one object of bearing fruit for the salvation of men. The Vine and the branch are equally under the unchangeable law of fruit-bearing as the one reason of their being. Christ and the believer, the heavenly Vine and the branch, have equally their place in the world exclusively for one purpose, to carry God's saving love to men. Hence the solemn word: Every branch that beareth not fruit, He taketh it away.

   Let us specially beware of one great mistake. Many Christians think their own salvation is the first thing; their temporal life and prosperity, with the care of their family, the second; and what of time and interest is left may be devoted to fruit-bearing, to the saving of men. No wonder that in most cases very little time or interest can be found. No, Christian, the one object with which you have been made a member of Christ's Body is that the Head may have you to carry out His saving work. The one object God had in making you a branch is that Christ may through you bring life to men. Your personal salvation, your business and care for your family, are entirely subordinate to this. Your first aim in life, your first aim every day, should be to know how Christ desires to carry out His purpose in you.

Let us begin to think as God thinks. Let us accept Christ's teaching and respond to it. The one object of my being a branch, the one mark of my being a true branch, the one condition of my abiding and growing strong, is that I bear the fruit of the heavenly Vine for dying men to eat and live. And the one thing of which I can have the most perfect assurance is that, with Christ as my Vine, and the Father as my Husbandman, I can indeed be a fruitful branch.

Our Father, Thou comest seeking fruit. Teach us, we pray Thee, to realize how truly this is the one object of our existence, and of our union to Christ. Make it the one desire of our hearts to be branches, so filled with the Spirit of the Vine, as to bring forth fruit abundantly.

And Every Branch That Beareth Fruit, He Cleanseth, That it May Bear More Fruit--John 15:2

The thought of fruit is so prominent in the eye of Him who sees things as they are, fruit is so truly the one thing God has set His heart upon, that our Lord, after having said that the branch that bears no fruit is taken away, at once adds: and where there is fruit, the one desire of the Husbandman is more fruit. As the gift of His grace, as the token of spiritual vigor, as the showing forth of the glory of God and of Christ, as the only way for satisfying the need of the world, God longs and fits for, more fruit.

More Fruit--This is a very searching word. As churches and individuals we are in danger of nothing so much as self-contentment. The secret spirit of Laodicea--we are rich and increased in goods, and have need of nothing--may prevail where it is not suspected. The divine warning--poor and wretched and miserable--finds little response just where it is most needed.

Let us not rest content with the thought that we are taking an equal share with others in the work that is being done, or that men are satisfied with our efforts in Christ's service, or even point to us as examples. Let our only desire be to know whether we are bearing all the fruit Christ is willing to give through us as living branches, in close and living union with Himself, whether we are satisfying the loving heart of the great Husbandman, our Father in Heaven, in His desire for more fruit.

More Fruit--The word comes with divine authority to search and test our life: the true disciple will heartily surrender himself to its holy light, and will earnestly ask that God Himself may show what there may be lacking in the measure or the character of the fruit he bears. Do let us believe that the Word is meant to lead us on to a fuller experience of the Father's purpose of love, of Christ's fullness, and of the wonderful privilege of bearing much fruit in the salvation of men.

More Fruit--The word is a most encouraging one. Let us listen to it. It is just to the branch that is bearing fruit that the message comes: more fruit. God does not demand this as Pharaoh the task-master, or as Moses the lawgiver, without providing the means. He comes as a Father, who gives what He asks, and works what He commands. He comes to us as the living branches of the living Vine, and offers to work the more fruit in us, if we but yield ourselves into His hands. Shall we not admit the claim, accept the offer, and look to Him to work it in us?

"That it may bear more fruit": do let us believe that as the owner of a vine does everything to make the fruitage as rich and large as possible, the divine Husbandman will do all that is needed to make us bear more fruit. All He asks is, that we set our heart's desire on it, entrust ourselves to His working and care, and joyfully look to Him to do His perfect work in us. God has set His heart on more fruit; Christ waits to work it in us; let us joyfully look up to our divine Husbandman and our heavenly Vine, to ensure our bearing more fruit.

Our Father which art in Heaven, Thou art the heavenly Husbandman. And Christ is the heavenly Vine. And I am a heavenly branch, partaker of His heavenly life, to bear His heavenly fruit. Father, let the power of His life so fill me, that I may ever bear more fruit, to the glory of Thy name.

THE CLEANSING

Every Branch That Beareth Fruit, He Cleanseth It, That It May Bear More Fruit--John 15:2

There are two remarkable things about the vine. There is not a plant of which the fruit has so much spirit in it, of which spirit can be so abundantly distilled as the vine. And there is not a plant which so soon runs into wild wood, that hinders its fruit, and therefore needs the most merciless pruning. I look out of my window here on large vineyards: the chief care of the vinedresser is the pruning. You may have a trellis vine rooting so deep in good soil that it needs neither digging, nor manuring, nor watering: pruning it cannot dispense with, if it is to bear good fruit. Some tree needs occasional pruning; others bear perfect fruit without any: the vine must have it. And so our Lord tells us, here at the very outset of the parable, that the one work the Father does to the branch that bears fruit is: He cleanseth it, that it may bear more fruit.

Consider a moment what this pruning or cleansing is. It is not the removal of weeds or thorns, or anything from without that may hinder the growth. No; it is the cutting off of the long shoots of the previous year, the removal of something that comes from within, that has been produced by the life of the vine itself. It is the removal of something that is a proof of the vigor of its life; the more vigorous the growth has been, the greater the need for the pruning. It is the honest, healthy wood of the vine that has to be cut away. And why? Because it would consume too much of the sap to fill all the long shoots of last year's growth: the sap must be saved up and used for fruit alone. The branches, sometimes eight and ten feet long, are cut down close to the stem, and nothing is left but just one or two inches of wood, enough to bear the grapes. It is when everything that is not needful for fruit-bearing has been relentlessly cut down, and just as little of the branches as possible has been left, that full, rich fruit may be expected.

What a solemn, precious lesson! It is not to sin only that the cleansing of the Husbandman here refers. It is to our own religious activity, as it is developed in the very act of bearing fruit. It is this that must be cut down and cleansed away. We have, in working for God, to use our natural gifts of wisdom, or eloquence, or influence, or zeal. And yet they are ever in danger of being unduly developed, and then trusted in. And so, after each season of work, God has to bring us to the end of ourselves, to the consciousness of the helplessness and the danger of all that is of man, to feel that we are nothing. All that is to be left of us is just enough to receive the power of the life-giving sap of the Holy Spirit. What is of man must be reduced to its very lowest measure. All that is inconsistent with the most entire devotion to Christ's service must be removed. The more perfect the cleansing and cutting away of all that is of self, the less of surface over which the Holy Spirit is to be spread, so much the more intense can be the concentration of our whole being, to be entirely at the disposal of the Spirit. This is the true circumcision of the heart, the circumcision of Christ. This is the true crucifixion with Christ, bearing about the dying of the Lord Jesus in the body.

Blessed cleansing, God's own cleansing! How we may rejoice in the assurance that we shall bring forth more fruit.

O our holy Husbandman, cleanse and cut away all that there is in us that would make a fair show, or could become a source of self-confidence and glorying. Lord, keep us very low, that no flesh may glory in Thy presence. We do trust Thee to do Thy work.

THE PRUNING KNIFE

Already Ye Are Clean Because of the Word I Have Spoken Unto You-- John 15:3

What is the pruning knife of this heavenly Husbandman? It is often said to be affliction. By no means in the first place. How would it then fare with many who have long seasons free from adversity; or with some on whom God appears to shower down kindness all their life long? No; it is the Word of God that is the knife, shaper than any two-edged sword, that pierces even to the dividing asunder of the soul and spirit, and is quick to discern the thoughts and intents of the heart. It is only when affliction leads to this discipline of the Word that it becomes a blessing; the lack of this heart-cleansing through the Word is the reason why affliction is so often unsanctified. Not even Paul's thorn in the flesh could become a blessing until Christ's Word--"My strength is made perfect in weakness"--had made him see the danger of self-exaltation, and made him willing to rejoice in infirmities.

The Word of God's pruning knife. Jesus says: "Ye are already clean, because of the word I have spoken unto you." How searchingly that word had been spoken by Him, out of whose mouth there went a sharp two-edged sword, as he had taught them! "Except a man deny himself, lose his life, forsake all, hate father and mother, he cannot be My disciple, he is not worthy of Me"; or as He humbled their pride, or reproved their lack of love, or foretold their all forsaking Him. From the opening of His ministry in the Sermon on the Mount to His words of warning in the last night, His Word had tried and cleansed them. He had discovered and condemned all there was of self; they were now emptied and cleansed, ready for the incoming of the Holy Spirit.

It is as the soul gives up its own thoughts, and men's thoughts of what is religion, and yields itself heartily, humbly, patiently, to the teaching of the Word by the Spirit, that the Father will do His blessed work of pruning and cleansing away all of nature and self that mixes with our work and hinders His Spirit. Let those who would know all the Husbandman can do for them, all the Vine can bring forth through them, seek earnestly to yield themselves heartily to the blessed cleansing through the Word. Let them, in their study of the Word, receive it as a hammer that breaks and opens up, as a fire that melts and refines, as a sword that lays bare and slays all that is of the flesh. The word of conviction will prepare for the word of comfort and of hope, and the Father will cleanse them through the Word.

All ye who are branches of the true Vine, each time you read or hear the Word, wait first of all on Him to use it for His cleansing of the branch. Set your heart upon His desire for more fruit. Trust Him as Husbandman to work it. Yield yourselves in simple childlike surrender to the cleansing work of His Word and Spirit, and you may count upon it that His purpose will be fulfilled in you.

Father, I pray Thee, cleanse me through Thy Word. Let it search out and bring to light all that is of self and the flesh in my religion. Let it cut away every root of self-confidence, that the Vine may find me wholly free to receive His life and Spirit. O my holy Husbandman, I trust Thee to care for the branch as much as for the Vine. Thou only art my hope.

ABIDE

Abide in Me, and I in You--John 15:4

When a new graft is placed in a vine and it abides there, there is a twofold process that takes place. The first is in the wood. The graft shoots its little roots and fibers down into the stem, and the stem grows up into the graft, and what has been called the structural union is effected. The graft abides and becomes one with the vine, and even though the vine were to die, would still be one wood with it. Then there is the second process, in which the sap of the vine enters the new structure, and uses it as a passage through which sap can flow up to show itself in young shoots and leaves and fruit. Here is the vital union. Into the graft which abides in the stock, the stock enters with sap to abide in it.

When our Lord says: "Abide in me, and I in you," He points to something analogous to this. "Abide in me": that refers more to that which we have to do. We have to trust and obey, to detach ourselves from all else, to reach out after Him and cling to Him, to sink ourselves into Him. As we do this, through the grace He gives, a character is formed, and a heart prepared for the fuller experience: "I in you," God strengthens us with might by the Spirit in the inner man, and Christ dwells in the heart by faith.

Many believers pray and long very earnestly for the filling of the Spirit and the indwelling of Christ, and wonder that they do not make more progress. The reason is often this, the "I in you" cannot come because the "abide in me" is not maintained. "There is one body and one spirit"; before the Spirit can fill, there must be a body prepared. The graft must have grown into the stem, and be abiding in it before the sap can flow through to bring forth fruit. It is as in lowly obedience we follow Christ, even in external things, denying ourselves, forsaking the world, and even in the body seeking to be conformable to Him, as we thus seek to abide in Him, that we shall be able to receive and enjoy the "I in you." The work enjoined on us: "Abide in me," will prepare us for the work undertaken by Him: "I in you."

In--The two parts of the injunction have their unity in that central deep-meaning word "in." There is no deeper word in Scripture. God is in all. God dwells in Christ. Christ lives in God. We are in Christ. Christ is in us: our life taken up into His; His life received into ours; in a divine reality that words cannot express, we are in Him and He in us. And the words, "Abide in me and I in you," just tell us to believe it, this divine mystery, and to count upon our God the Husbandman, and Christ the Vine, to make it divinely true. No thinking or teaching or praying can grasp it; it is a divine mystery of love. As little as we can effect the union can we understand it. Let us just look upon this infinite, divine, omnipotent Vine loving us, holding us, working in us. Let us in the faith of His working abide and rest in Him, ever turning heart and hope to Him alone. And let us count upon Him to fulfill in us the mystery: "Ye in me, and I in you."

Blessed Lord, Thou dost bid me abide in Thee. How can I, Lord, except Thou show Thyself to me, waiting to receive and welcome and keep me? I pray Thee show me how Thou as Vine undertaketh to do all. To be occupied with Thee is to abide in Thee. Here I am, Lord, a branch, cleansed and abiding--resting in Thee, and awaiting the inflow of Thy life and grace.

EXCEPT YE ABIDE

**As the Branch Cannot Bear Fruit of Itself, Except It Abide In the Vine;
No More Can Ye, Except Ye Abide in Me--John 15:4**

We know the meaning of the word except. It expresses some
indispensable condition, some inevitable law. "The branch cannot bear
fruit of itself, except it abide in the vine. No more can ye, except ye
abide in me." There is but one way for the branch to bear fruit, there is
no other possibility, it must abide in unbroken communion with the
vine. Not of itself, but only of the vine, does the fruit come. Christ had
already said: "Abide in me"; in nature the branch teaches us the lesson
so clearly; it is such a wonderful privilege to be called and allowed to
abide in the heavenly Vine; one might have thought it needless to add
these words of warning. But no--Christ knows so well what a
renunciation of self is implied in this: "Abide in me"; how strong and
universal the tendency would be to seek to bear fruit by our own
efforts; how difficult it would be to get us to believe that actual,
continuous abiding in Him is an absolute necessity! He insists upon the
truth: Not of itself can the branch bear fruit; except it abide, it cannot
bear fruit. "No more can ye, except ye abide in me."

But must this be taken literally? Must I, as exclusively, and
manifestly, and unceasingly, and absolutely, as the branch abides in the
vine, be equally given up to find my whole life in Christ alone? I must
indeed. The except ye abide is as universal as the except it abide. The
no more can ye admits of no exception or modification. If I am to be a
true branch, if I am to bear fruit, if I am to be what Christ as Vine
wants me to be, my whole existence must be as exclusively devoted to
abiding in Him, as that of the natural branch is to abiding in its vine.

Let me learn the lesson. Abiding is to be an act of the will and the
whole heart. Just as there are degrees in seeking and serving God, "not
with a perfect heart," or "with the whole heart," so there may be
degrees in abiding. In regeneration the divine life enters us, but does
not all at once master and fill our whole being. This comes as matter of
command and obedience. There is unspeakable danger of our not
giving ourselves with our whole heart to abide. There is unspeakable
danger of our giving ourselves to work for God, and to bear fruit, with
but little of the true abiding, the wholehearted losing of ourselves in
Christ and His life. There is unspeakable danger of much work with but
little fruit, for lack of this one thing needful. We must allow the words,
"not of itself," "except it abide," to do their work of searching and
exposing, of pruning and cleansing, all that there is of self-will and

self-confidence in our life; this will deliver us from this great evil, and so prepare us for His teaching, giving the full meaning of the word in us: "Abide in me, and I in you."

Our blessed Lord desires to call us away from ourselves and our own strength, to Himself and His strength. Let us accept the warning, and turn with great fear and self-distrust to Him to do His work. "Our life is hid with Christ in God!" That life is a heavenly mystery, hid from the wise even among Christians, and revealed unto babes. The childlike spirit learns that life is given from Heaven every day and every moment to the soul that accepts the teaching: "not of itself," "except it abide," and seeks its all in the Vine. Abiding in the Vine then comes to be nothing more nor less than the restful surrender of the soul to let Christ have all and work all, as completely as in nature the branch knows and seeks nothing but the vine.

Abide in Me. I have heard, my Lord, that with every command, Thou also givest the power to obey. With Thy "rise and walk," the lame man leaped, I accept Thy word, "Abide in me," as a word of power, that gives power, and even now I say, Yea, Lord, I will, I do abide in Thee.

THE VINE

I am The Vine, Ye Are The Branches--John 15:5

In the previous verse Christ had just said: "Abide in me." He had then announced the great unalterable law of all branch-life, on earth or in Heaven: "not of itself"; "except it abide." In the opening words of the parable He had already spoken: "I am the vine." He now repeats the words. He would have us understand--note well the lesson, simple as it appears, it is the key of the abiding life--that the only way to obey the command, "Abide in me," is to have eye and heart fixed upon Himself. "Abide in me...I am the true vine." Yea, study this holy mystery until you see Christ as the true Vine, bearing, strengthening, supplying, inspiring all His branches, being and doing in each branch all it needs, and the abiding will come of itself. Yes, gaze upon Him as the true Vine, until you feel what a heavenly Mystery it is, and are compelled to ask the Father to reveal it to you by His Holy Spirit. He to whom God reveals the glory of the true Vine, he who sees what Jesus is and waits to do every moment, he cannot but abide. The vision of Christ is an irresistible attraction; it draws and holds us like a magnet. Listen ever to the living Christ still speaking to you, and waiting to show you the meaning and power of His Word: "I am the vine."

How much weary labor there has been in striving to understand what abiding is, how much fruitless effort in trying to attain it! Why was this? Because the attention was turned to the abiding as a work we have to do, instead of the living Christ, in whom we were to be kept abiding, who Himself was to hold and keep us. we thought of abiding as a continual strain and effort--we forget that it means rest from effort to one who has found the place of his abode. Do notice how Christ said, "Abide in Me; I am the Vine that brings forth, and holds, and strengthens, and makes fruitful the branches. Abide in Me, rest in Me, and let Me do My work. I am the true Vine, all I am, and speak, and do is divine truth, giving the actual reality of what is said. I am the Vine, only consent and yield thy all to Me, I will do all in thee."

And so it sometimes comes that souls who have never been specially occupied with the thought of abiding, are abiding all the time, because they are occupied with Christ. Not that the word abide is not needful; Christ used it so often, because it is the very key to the Christian life. But He would have us understand it in its true sense--"Come out of every other place, and every other trust and occupation, come out of self with its reasonings and efforts, come and rest in what I shall do. Live out of thyself; abide in Me. Know that thou art in Me; thou needest no more; remain there in Me."

"I am the Vine." Christ did not keep this mystery hidden from His disciples. He revealed it, first in words here, then in power when the Holy Spirit came down. He will reveal it to us too, first in the thoughts and confessions and desires these words awaken, then in power by the Spirit. Do let us wait on Him to show us all the heavenly meaning of the mystery. Let each day, in our quiet time, in the inner chamber with Him and His Word, our chief thought and aim be to get the heart fixed on Him, in the assurance: all that a vine ever can do for its branches, my Lord Jesus will do, is doing, for me. Give Him time, give Him your ear, that He may whisper and explain the divine secret: "I am the vine."

Above all, remember, Christ is the Vine of God's planting, and you are a branch of God's grafting. Ever stand before God, in Christ; ever wait for all grace from God, in Christ; ever yield yourself to bear the more fruit the Husbandman asks, in Christ. And pray much for the revelation of the mystery that all the love and power of God that rested on Christ is working in you too. "I am God's Vine," Jesus says; "all I am I have from Him; all I am is for you; God will work it in you."

I am the Vine. Blessed Lord, speak Thou that word into my soul. Then shall I know that all Thy fullness is for me. And that I can count upon Thee to stream it into me, and that my abiding is so easy and so sure when I forget and lose myself in the adoring faith that the Vine holds the branch and supplies its every need.

I Am The Vine, Ye Are the Branches--John 15:5

Christ had already said much of the branch; here He comes to the personal application: "Ye are the branches of whom I have been speaking. As I am the Vine, engaged to be and do all the branches need, so I now ask you, in the new dispensation of the Holy Spirit whom I have been promising you, to accept the place I give you, and to be My branches on earth." The relationship He seeks to establish is an intensely personal one: it all hinges on the two little words I and You. And it is for us as intensely personal as for the first disciples. Let us present ourselves before our Lord, until He speak to each of us in power, and our whole soul feels it: "I am the Vine; you are the branch."

Dear disciple of Jesus, however young or feeble, hear the voice. "You are the branch." You must be nothing less. Let no false humility, no carnal fear of sacrifice, no unbelieving doubts as to what you feel able for, keep you back from saying: "I will be a branch, with all that may mean--a branch, very feeble, but yet as like the Vine as can be, for I am of the same nature, and receive of the same spirit. A branch, utterly helpless, and yet just as manifestly set apart before God and men, as wholly given up to the work of bearing fruit, as the Vine itself. A branch, nothing in myself, and yet resting and rejoicing in the faith that knows that He will provide for all. Yes, by His grace, I will be nothing less than a branch, and all He means it to be, that through me, He may bring forth His fruit."

You are the branch.--You need be nothing more. You need not for one single moment of the day take upon you the responsibility of the Vine. You need not leave the place of entire dependence and unbounded confidence. You need, least of all, to be anxious as to how you are to understand the mystery, or fulfill its conditions, or work out its blessed aim. The Vine will give all and work all. The Father, the Husbandman, watches over your union with and growth in the Vine. You need be nothing more than a branch. Only a branch! Let that be your watchword; it will lead in the path of continual surrender to Christ's working, of true obedience to His every command, of joyful expectancy of all His grace.

Is there anyone who now asks: "How can I learn to say this aright, `Only be a branch!' and to live it out?" Dear soul, the character of a branch, its strength, and the fruit it bears, depend entirely upon the Vine. And your life as branch depends entirely upon your apprehension of what our Lord Jesus is. Therefore never separate the two words: "I the Vine--you the branch." Your life and strength and fruit depend upon what your Lord Jesus is! Therefore worship and trust Him; let Him be your one desire and the one occupation of your heart. And when you feel that you do not and cannot know Him aright, then just remember it is part of His responsibility as Vine to make Himself known to you. He does this not in thoughts and conceptions--no--but in a hidden growth within the life that is humbly and restfully and entirely given up to wait on Him. The Vine reveals itself within the branch; thence comes the growth and fruit, Christ dwells and works within His branch; only be a branch, waiting on Him to do all; He will be to thee the true Vine. The Father Himself, the divine Husbandman, is able to make thee a branch worthy of the heavenly Vine. Thou shalt not be disappointed.

Ye are the branches. This word, too Lord! O speak it in power unto my soul. Let not the branch of the earthly vine put me to shame, but as it only lives to bear the fruit of the vine, may my life on earth have no wish or aim, but to let Thee bring forth fruit through me.

MUCH FRUIT

He That Abideth in Me, and I in Him, the Same Bringeth Forth Much Fruit--John 15:5

Our Lord had spoken of fruit, more fruit. He now adds the thought: much fruit. There is in the Vine such fullness, the care of the divine Husbandman is so sure of success, that the much fruit is not a demand, but the simple promise of what must come to the branch that lives in the double abiding--he in Christ, and Christ in him. "The same bringeth forth much fruit." It is certain.

Have you ever noticed the difference in the Christian life between work and fruit? A machine can do work: only life can bear fruit. A law can compel work: only love can spontaneously bring forth fruit. Work implies effort and labor: the essential idea of fruit is that it is the silent natural restful produce of our inner life. The gardener may labor to give his apple tree the digging and manuring, the watering and the pruning it needs; he can do nothing to produce the apple: "The fruit of the Spirit is love, peace, joy." The healthy life bears much fruit. The connection between work and fruit is perhaps best seen in the expression, "fruitful in every good work." (Col. 1:10). It is only when good works come as the fruit of the indwelling Spirit that they are acceptable to God. Under the compulsion of law and conscience, or the influence of inclination and zeal, men may be most diligent in good works, and yet find that they have but little spiritual result. There can be no reason but this-- their works are man's effort, instead of being the fruit of the Spirit, the restful, natural outcome of the Spirit's operation within us.

Let all workers come and listen to our holy Vine as He reveals the law of sure and abundant fruitfulness: "He that abideth in me, and I in him, the same bringeth forth much fruit." The gardener cares for one thing--the strength and healthy life of his tree: the fruit follows of itself. If you would bear fruit, see that the inner life is perfectly right, that your relation to Christ Jesus is clear and close. Begin each day with Him in the morning, to know in truth that you are abiding in Him and He in you. Christ tells that nothing less will do. It is not your willing and running, it is not by your might or strength, but--"by my Spirit, saith the Lord." Meet each new engagement, undertake every new work, with an ear and heart open to the Master's voice: "He that abideth in me, beareth much fruit." See you to the abiding; He will see to the fruit, for He will give it in you and through you.

O my brother, it is Christ must do all! The Vine provides the sap, and the life, and the strength: the branch waits, and rests, and receives, and bears the fruit. Oh, the blessedness of being only branches, through whom the Spirit flows and brings God's life to men!

I pray you, take time and ask the Holy Spirit to give you to realize the unspeakably solemn place you occupy in the mind of God. He has planted you into His Son with the calling and the power to bear much fruit. Accept that place. Look much to God, and to Christ, and expect joyfully to be what God has planned to make you, a fruitful branch.

Much fruit! So be it, blessed Lord Jesus. It can be, for Thou art the Vine. It shall be, for I am abiding in Thee. It must be, for Thy Father is the Husbandman that cleanses the branch. Yea, much fruit, out of the abundance of Thy grace.

YOU CAN DO NOTHING

Apart From Me Ye Can Do Nothing--John 15:5

In everything the life of the branch is to be the exact counterpart of that of the Vine. Of Himself Jesus had said: "The Son can do nothing of himself." As the outcome of that entire dependence, He could add: "All that the Father doeth, doeth the Son also likewise." As Son He did not receive His life from the Father once for all, but moment by moment. His life was a continual waiting on the Father for all He was to do. And so Christ says of His disciples: "Ye can do nothing apart from me." He means it literally. To everyone who wants to live the true disciple life, to bring forth fruit and glorify God, the message comes: You can do nothing. What had been said: "He that abideth in me, and I in him, the same beareth much fruit," is here enforced by the simplest and strongest of arguments: "Abiding in Me is indispensable, for, you know it, of yourselves you can do nothing to maintain or act out the heavenly life."

A deep conviction of the truth of this word lies at the very root of a strong spiritual life. As little as I created myself, as little as I could raise a man from the dead, can I give myself the divine life. As little as I can give it myself, can I maintain or increase it: every motion is the work of God through Christ and His Spirit. It is as a man believes this, that he will take up that position of entire and continual dependence which is the very essence of the life of faith. With the spiritual eye he sees Christ every moment supplying grace for every breathing and every deepening of the spiritual life. His whole heart says Amen to the word: You can do nothing. And just because he does so, he can also say: "I can do all things in Christ who strengtheneth me." The sense of helplessness, and the abiding to which it compels, leads to true fruitfulness and diligence in good works.

Apart from me ye can do nothing.--What a plea and what a call every moment to abide in Christ! We have only to go back to the vine to see how true it is. Look again at that little branch, utterly helpless and fruitless except as it receives sap from the vine, and learn that the full conviction of not being able to do anything apart from Christ is just what you need to teach you to abide in your heavenly Vine. It is this that is the great meaning of the pruning Christ spoke of--all that is self must be brought low, that our confidence may be in Christ alone. "Abide in me"--much fruit! "Apart from me"--nothing! Ought there to be any doubt as to what we shall choose?

The one lesson of the parable is--as surely, as naturally as the branch abides in the vine, You can abide in Christ. For this He is the true Vine; for this God is the Husbandman; for this you are a branch. Shall we not cry to God to deliver us forever from the "apart from me," and to make the "abide in me" an unceasing reality? Let your heart go out to what Christ is, and can do, to His divine power and His tender love to each of His branches, and you will say evermore confidently: "Lord! I am abiding; I will bear much fruit. My impotence is my strength. So be it. Apart from Thee, nothing. In Thee, much fruit."

Apart from Me--you nothing. Lord, I gladly accept the arrangement: I nothing--Thou all. My nothingness is my highest blessing, because Thou art the Vine, that givest and workest all. So be it, Lord! I, nothing, ever waiting on Thy fullness. Lord, reveal to me the glory of this blessed life.

WITHERED BRANCHES

If a Man Abide Not in Me, He is Cast Forth as a Branch, and is Withered; and They Gather Them, and Cast Them into the Fire, and They are Burned--John 15:6

The lessons these words teach are very simple and very solemn. A man can come to such a connection with Christ, that he counts himself to be in Him, and yet he can be cast forth. There is such a thing as not abiding in Christ, which leads to withering up and burning. There is such a thing as a withered branch, one in whom the initial union with Christ appears to have taken place, and in whom yet it is seen that his faith was but for a time. What a solemn call to look around and see if there be not withered branches in our churches, to look within and see whether we are indeed abiding and bearing fruit!

And what may be the cause of this "not abiding." With some it is that they never understood how the Christian calling leads to holy obedience and to loving service. They were content with the thought that they had believed, and were safe from Hell; there was neither motive nor power to abide in Christ--they knew not the need of it. With others it was that the cares of the world, or its prosperity, choked the Word: they had never forsaken all to follow Christ. With still others it was that their religion and their faith was in the wisdom of men, and not in the power of God. They trusted in the means of grace, or in their own sincerity, or in the soundness of their faith in justifying grace; they had never come even to seek an entire abiding in Christ as their only safety. No wonder that, when the hot winds of temptation or persecution blew, they withered away: they were not truly rooted in Christ.

Let us open our eyes and see if there be not withered branches all around us in the churches. Young men, whose confessions were once bright, but who are growing cold. Or old men, who have retained their profession, but out of whom the measure of life there once appeared to be has died out. Let ministers and believers take Christ's words to heart, and see, and ask the Lord whether there is nothing to be done for branches that are beginning to wither. And let the word Abide ring through the Church until every believer has caught it--no safety but in a true abiding in Christ.

Let each of us turn within. Is our life fresh, and green, and vigorous, bringing forth its fruit in its season? (See Ps. 1:3; 92:13, 14; Jer. 17:7, 8.) Let us accept every warning with a willing mind, and let Christ's "if a man abide not" give new urgency to His "abide in me." To the upright soul the secret of abiding will become ever simpler, just the consciousness of the place in which He has put me; just the childlike resting in my union with Him, and the trustful assurance that He will keep me. Oh, do let us believe there is a life that knows of no withering, that is ever green; and that brings forth fruit abundantly!

Withered! O my Father, watch over me, and keep me, and let nothing ever for a moment hinder the freshness that comes from a full abiding in the Vine. Let the very thought of a withered branch fill me with holy fear and watchfulness.

WHATSOEVER YE WILL

If Ye Abide in Me, and My Words Abide in You, Ask Whatsoever Ye Will, and it Shall be Done Unto You--John 15:7

The Whole place of the branch in the vine is one of unceasing prayer. Without intermission it is ever calling: "O my vine, send the sap I need to bear Thy fruit." And its prayers are never unanswered: it asks what it needs, what it will, and it is done.

The healthy life of the believer in Christ is equally one of unceasing prayer. Consciously or unconsciously, he lives in continual dependence. The Word of his Lord, "You can do nothing," has taught him that not more unbroken than the continuance of the branch in the vine, must be his asking and receiving. The promise of our text gives us infinite boldness: "Ask whatsoever ye will, and it shall be done unto you."

The promise is given in direct connection with fruit-bearing. Limit it to yourself and your own needs, and you rob it of its power; you rob yourself of the power of appropriating it. Christ was sending these disciples out, and they were ready to give their life for the world; to them He gave the disposal of the treasures of Heaven. Their prayers would bring the Spirit and the power they needed for their work.

The promise is given in direct connection with the coming of the Spirit. The Spirit is not mentioned in the parable, just as little as the sap of the vine is mentioned. But both are meant all through. In the chapter preceding the parable, our Lord had spoken of the Holy Spirit, in connection with their inner life, being in them, and revealing Himself within them (14:15-23). In the next chapter He speaks of the Holy Spirit in connection with their work, coming to them, convincing the world, and glorifying Him (16:7-14). To avail ourselves of the unlimited prayer promises, we must be men who are filled with the Spirit, and wholly given up to the work and glory of Jesus. The Spirit will lead us into the truth of its meaning and the certainty of its fulfillment.

Let us realize that we can only fulfill our calling to bear much fruit, by praying much. In Christ are hid all the treasures men around us need; in Him all God's children are blessed with all spiritual blessings; He is full of grace and truth. But it needs prayer, much prayer, strong believing prayer, to bring these blessings down. And let us equally remember that we cannot appropriate the promise without a life given up for men. Many try to take the promise, and then look round for what they can ask. This is not the way; but the very opposite. Get the heart burdened with the need of souls, and the command to save them, and the power will come to claim the promise.

Let us claim it as one of the revelations of our wonderful life in the Vine: He tells us that if we ask in His name, in virtue of our union with Him, whatsoever it be, it will be done to us. Souls are perishing because there is too little prayer. God's children are feeble because there is too little prayer. We bear so little fruit because there is so little prayer. The faith of this promise would make us strong to pray; let us not rest till it has entered into our very heart, and drawn us in the power of Christ to continue and labor and strive in prayer until the blessing comes in power. To be a branch means not only bearing fruit on earth, but power in prayer to bring down blessing from Heaven. Abiding fully means praying much.

Ask what ye will. O my Lord, why is it that our hearts are so little able to accept these words in their divine simplicity? Oh, give me to see that we need nothing less than this promise to overcome the powers of the world and Satan! Teach us to pray in the faith of this Thy promise.

If Ye Abide in Me, and My Words, Abide in You, Ask Whatsoever Ye Will, and it Shall be Done Unto You--John 15:7

The reason the Vine and its branches are such a true parable of the Christian life is that all nature has one source and breathes one spirit. The plant world was created to be to man an object lesson teaching him his entire dependence upon God, and his security in that dependence. He that clothes the lilies will much more cloth us. He that gives the trees and the vines their beauty and their fruits, making each what He meant it to be, will much more certainly make us what He would have us to be. The only difference is what God works in the trees is by a power of which they are not conscious. He wants to work in us with our consent. This is the nobility of man, that he has a will that can cooperate with God in understanding and approving and accepting what He offers to do.

If ye abide--Here is the difference between the branch of the natural and the branch of the spiritual Vine. The former abides by force of nature: the latter abides, not by force of will, but by a divine power given to the consent of the will. Such is the wonderful provision God has made that, what the power of nature does in the one case, the power of grace will do in the other. The branch can abide in the Vine.

If ye abide in me...ask whatsoever ye will--If we are to live a true prayer life, with the love and the power and the experience of prayer marking it, there must be no question about the abiding. And if we abide, there need be no question about the liberty of asking what we will, and the certainty of its being done. There is the one condition: "If ye abide in me." There must be no hesitation about the possibility or the certainty of it. We must gaze on that little branch and its wonderful power of bearing such beautiful fruit until we truly learn to abide.

And what is its secret? Be wholly occupied with Jesus. Sink the roots of your being in faith and love and obedience deep down into Him. Come away out of every other place to abide here. Give up everything for the inconceivable privilege of being a branch on earth of the glorified Son of God in Heaven. Let Christ be first. Let Christ be all. Do not be occupied with the abiding--be occupied with Christ! He will hold you, He will keep you abiding in Him. He will abide in you.

If ye abide in me, and my words abide in you--This He gives as the equivalent of the other expression: "I in you. If my words abide in you"--that is, not only in meditation, in memory, in love, in faith--all these words enter into your will, your being, and constitute your life--if they transform your character into their own likeness, and you become and are what they speak and mean--ask what ye will; it shall be done unto you. Your words to God in prayer will be the fruit of Christ and His words living in you.

Ask what ye will, and it shall be done unto you--Believe in the truth of this promise. Set yourself to be an intercessor for men; a fruit-bearing intercessor, ever calling down more blessing. Such faith and prayer will help you wonderfully to abide wholly and unceasingly.

If ye abide. Yes, Lord, the power to pray and the power to prevail must depend on this abiding in Thee. As Thou art the Vine, Thou art the divine Intercessor, who breathest Thy spirit in us. Oh, for grace to abide simply and wholly in Thee, and ask great things!

Herein is My Father Glorified, that Ye Bear Much Fruit--John 15:8

How can we glorify God? Not by adding to His glory or bringing Him any new glory that He has not. But simply by allowing His glory to shine out through us, by yielding ourselves to Him, that His glory may manifest itself in us and through us to the world. In a vineyard or a vine bearing much fruit, the owner is glorified, as it tells of his skill and care. In the disciple who bears much fruit, the Father is glorified. Before men and angels, proof is given of the glory of God's grace and power; God's glory shines out through him.

This is what Peter means when he writes: "He that ministers, let him minister as of the ability that God giveth, that God in all things may be glorified through Jesus Christ." As a man works and serves in a power which comes from God alone, God gets all the glory. When we confess that the ability came from God alone, he that does the work, and they who see it, equally glorify God. It was God who did it. Men judge by the fruit of a garden of what the gardener is. Men judge of God by the fruit that the branches of the Vine of His planting bears. Little fruit brings little glory to God. It brings no honor to either the Vine or the Husbandman. "That ye bear much fruit, herein is my Father glorified."

We have sometimes mourned our lack of fruit, as a loss to ourselves and our fellow men, with complaints of our feebleness as the cause. Let us rather think of the sin and shame of little fruit as robbing God of the glory He ought to get from us. Let us learn the secret of bringing glory to God, serving of the ability which God giveth. The full acceptance of Christ's Word, "You can do nothing"; the simple faith in God, who worketh all in all; the abiding in Christ through whom the divine Husbandman does His work and gets much fruit--this is the life that will bring glory to God.

Much fruit--God asks it; see that you give it. God can be content with nothing less; be you content with nothing less. Let these words of Christ--fruit, more fruit, much fruit--abide in you, until you think as He does, and you be prepared to take from Him, the heavenly Vine, what He has for you. Much fruit: herein is my Father glorified. Let the very height of the demand be your encouragement. It is so entirely beyond your power, that it throws you more entirely upon Christ, your true Vine. He can, He will, make it true in you.

Much fruit--God asks because he needs. He does not ask fruit from the branches of His Vine for show, to prove what He can do. No; He needs it for the salvation of men: it is in that He is to be glorified. Throw yourself in much prayer on your Vine and your Husbandman. Cry to God and your Father to give you fruit to bring to men. Take the burden of the hungry and the perishing on you, as Jesus did when He was moved with compassion, and your power in prayer, and your abiding, and your bearing much fruit to the glory of the Father will have a reality and a certainty you never knew before.

The Father glorified. Blessed prospect--God glorifying Himself in me, showing forth the glory of His goodness and power in what He works in me, and through me. What a motive to bear much fruit, just as much as He works in me! Father, glorify Thyself in me.

TRUE DISCIPLES

Herein is My Father Glorified, that Ye Bear Much Fruit: So Shall Ye Be My Disciples--John 15:8

And are those who do not bear much fruit not disciples? They may be, but in a backward and immature stage. Of those who bear much fruit, Christ says: "These are My disciples, such as I would have them be--these are true disciples." Just as we say of someone in whom the idea of manliness is realized: That is a man! So our Lord tells who are disciples after His heart, worthy of the name: Those who bear much fruit. We find this double sense of the word disciple in the Gospel. Sometimes it is applied to all who accepted Christ's teaching. At other times it includes only the inner circle of those who followed Christ wholly, and gave themselves to His training for service. The difference has existed throughout all ages. There have always been a smaller number of God's people who have sought to serve Him with their whole heart, while the majority have been content with a very small measure of the knowledge of His grace and will.

And what is the difference between this smaller inner circle and the many who do not seek admission to it? We find it in the words: much fruit. With many Christians the thought of personal safety, which at their first awakening was a legitimate one, remains to the end the one aim of their religion. The idea of service and fruit is always a secondary and very subordinate one. The honest longing for much fruit does not trouble them. Souls that have heard the call to live wholly for their Lord, to give their life for Him as He gave His for them, can never be satisfied with this. Their cry is to bear as much fruit as they possibly can, as much as their Lord ever can desire or give in them.

Bear much fruit: so shall ye be My disciples--Let me beg every reader to consider these words most seriously. Be not content with the thought of gradually doing a little more or better work. In this way it may never come. Take the words, much fruit, as the revelation of your heavenly Vine of what you must be, of what you can be. Accept fully the impossibility, the utter folly of attempting it in your strength. Let the words call you to look anew upon the Vine, an undertaking to live out its heavenly fullness in you. Let them waken in you once again the faith and the confession: "I am a branch of the true Vine; I can bear much fruit to His glory, and the glory of the Father."

We need not judge others. But we see in God's Word everywhere two classes of disciples. Let there be no hesitation as to where we take our place. Let us ask Him to reveal to us how He ask and claims a life wholly given up to Him, to be as full of His Spirit as He can make us. Let our desire be nothing less than perfect cleansing, unbroken abiding, closest communion, abundant fruitfulness--true branches of the true Vine.

The world is perishing, the church is failing, Christ's cause is suffering, Christ is grieving on account of the lack of wholehearted Christians, bearing much fruit. Though you scarce see what it implies or how it is to come, say to Him that you are His branch to bear much fruit; that you are ready to be His disciple in His own meaning of the word.

My disciples. Blessed Lord, much fruit is the proof that Thou the true Vine hast in me a true branch, a disciple wholly at Thy disposal. Give me, I pray Thee, the childlike consciousness that my fruit is pleasing to Thee, what Thou countest much fruit.

Even as the Father Hath Loved Me, I Also Have Loved you--John 15:9

Here Christ leaves the language of parable, and speaks plainly out of the Father. Much as the parable could teach, it could not teach the lesson of love. All that the vine does for the branch, it does under the compulsion of a law of nature: there is no personal living love to the branch. We are in danger of looking to Christ as a Saviour and a supplier of every need, appointed by God, accepted and trusted by us, without any sense of the intensity of personal affection in which Christ embraces us, and our life alone can find its true happiness. Christ seeks to point us to this.

And how does He do so? He leads us once again to Himself, to show us how identical His own life is with ours. Even as the Father loved Him, He loves us. His life as vine dependent on the Father was a life in the Father's love; that love was His strength and His joy; in the power of that divine love resting on Him He lived and died. If we are to live like Him, as branches to be truly like our Vine, we must share in this too. Our life must have its breath and being in a heavenly love as much as His. What the Father's love was to Him, His love will be to us. If that love made Him the true Vine, His love can make us true branches. "Even as the Father hath loved me, so have I loved you."

Even as the Father hath loved Me--And how did the Father love Him? The infinite desire and delight of God to communicate to the Son all He had Himself, to take the Son into the most complete equality with Himself, to live in the Son and have the Son live in Him--this was the love of God to Christ. It is a mystery of glory of which we can form no conception, we can only bow and worship as we try to think of it. And with such a love, with this very same love, Christ longs in an infinite desire and delight to communicate to us all He is and has, to make us partakers of His own nature and blessedness, to live in us and have us live in Himself.

And now, if Christ loves us with such an intense, such an infinite divine love, what is it that hinders it triumphing over every obstacle and getting full possession of us? The answer is simple. Even as the love of the Father to Christ, so His love to us is a divine mystery, too high for us to comprehend or attain to by any effort of our own. It is only the Holy Spirit who can shed abroad and reveal in its all-conquering power without intermission this wonderful love of God in Christ. It is the vine itself that must give the branch its growth and fruit by sending up its sap. It is Christ Himself must by His Holy Spirit dwell in the heart; then shall we know and have in us the love that passeth knowledge.

As the Father loved Me, so have I loved you--Shall we not draw near to the personal living Christ, and trust Him, and yield all to Him, that He may love this love into us? Just as he knew and rejoiced every hour--the Father loveth Me--we too may live in the unceasing consciousness--as the Father loved Him, so He loves me.

As the Father loved Me, so have I loved you. Dear Lord, I am only beginning to apprehend how exactly the life of the Vine is to be that of the branch too. Thou art the Vine, because the Father loved Thee, and poured His love through Thee. And so Thou lovest me, and my life as branch is to be like Thine, a receiving and a giving out of heavenly love.

ABIDE IN MY LOVE

Even as the Father Hath Loved Me, I Also Have Loved You: Abide Ye in My Love--John 15:9

Abide in My love--We speak of a man's home as his abode. Our abode, the home of our soul, is to be the love of Christ. We are to live our life there, to be at home there all the day: this is what Christ means our life to be, and really can make it. Our continuous abiding in the Vine is to be an abiding in His love.

You have probably heard or read of what is called the higher, or the deeper life, of the richer or the fuller life, of the life abundant. And you possibly know that some have told of a wonderful change, by which their life of continual failure and stumbling had been changed into a very blessed experience of being kept and strengthened and made exceeding glad. If you asked them how it was this great blessing came to them, many would tell you it was simply this, that they were led to believe that this abiding in Christ's love was meant to be a reality, and that they were made willing to give up everything for it, and then enabled to trust Christ to make it true to them.

The love of the Father to the Son is not a sentiment--it is a divine life, an infinite energy, an irresistible power. It carried Christ through life and death and the grave. The Father loved Him and dwelt in Him, and did all for Him. So the love of Christ to us too is an infinite living power that will work in us all He delights to give us. The feebleness of our Christian life is that we do not take time to believe that this divine love does really delight in us, and will possess and work all in us. We do not take time to look at the Vine bearing the branch so entirely, working all in it so completely. We strive to do for ourselves what Christ alone can, what Christ, oh, so lovingly, longs to do for us.

And this now is the secret of the change we spoke of, and the beginning of a new life, when the soul sees this infinite love willing to do all, and gives itself up to it. "Abide ye in my love." To believe that, it is possible so to live moment by moment; to believe that everything that makes it difficult or impossible will be overcome by Christ Himself; to believe that Love really means an infinite longing to give itself wholly to us and never leave us; and in this faith to cast ourselves on Christ to work it in us; this is the secret of the true Christian life.

And how to come to this faith? Turn away from the visible if you would see and possess the invisible. Take more time with Jesus, gazing on Him as the heavenly Vine, living in the love of the Father, wanting you to live in His love. Turn away from yourself and your efforts and your faith, if you would have the heart filled with Him and the certainty of His love. Abiding means going out from everything else, to occupy one place and stay there. Come away from all else, and set your heart on Jesus, and His love, that love will waken your faith and strengthen it. Occupy yourself with that love, worship it, wait for it. You may be sure it will reach out to you, and by its power take you up into itself as your abode and your home.

Abide in My love. Lord Jesus, I see it, it was Thy abiding in Thy Father's love that made Thee the true Vine, with Thy divine fullness of love and blessing for us. Oh, that I may even so, as a branch, abide in Thy love, for its fullness to fill me and overflow on all around.

OBEY AND ABIDE

If Ye Keep My Commandments, Ye Shall Abide In My Love--John 15:10

In our former meditation reference was made to the entrance into a life of rest and strength which has often come through a true insight into the personal love of Christ, and the assurance that that love indeed meant that He would keep the soul. In connection with that transition, and the faith that sees and accepts it, the word surrender or consecration is frequently used. The soul sees that it cannot claim the keeping of this wonderful love unless it yields itself to a life of entire obedience. It sees too that the faith that can trust Christ for keeping from sinning must prove its sincerity by venturing at once to trust Him for strength to obey. In that faith it dares to give up and cut off everything that has hitherto hindered it, and to promise and expect to live a life that is well pleasing to God.

This is the thought we have here now in our Saviour's teaching. After having in the words, "Abide in my love," spoken of a life in His love as a necessity, because it is at once a possibility and an obligation, He states what its one condition is: "If ye keep my commandments, ye shall abide in my love." This is surely not meant to close the door to the abode of His love which he had just opened up. Not in the most distant way does it suggest the thought which some are too ready to entertain, that as we cannot keep His commandments, we cannot abide in His love. No; the precept is a promise: "Abide in my love," could not be a precept if it were not a promise. And so the instruction as to the way through this open door points to no unattainable ideal; the love that invites to her blessed abode reaches out the hand, and enables us to keep the commandments. Let us not fear, in the strength of our ascended Lord, to take the vow of obedience, and give ourselves to the keeping of His commandments. Through His will, loved and done, lies the path to His love.

Only let us understand well what it means. It refers to our performance of all that we know to be God's will. There may be things doubtful, of which we are not sure. A sin of ignorance has still the nature of sin in it. There may be involuntary sins, which rise up in the flesh, which we cannot control or overcome. With regard to these God will deal in due tome in the way of searching and humbling, and if we be simple and faithful, give us larger deliverance than we dare expect. But all this may be found in a truly obedient soul. Obedience has reference to the positive keeping of the commandments of our Lord, and the performance of His will in everything in which we know it. This is a possible degree of grace, and it is the acceptance in Christ's strength of such obedience as the purpose of our heart, of which our Saviour speaks here. Faith in Christ as our Vine, in His enabling and sanctifying power, fits us for this obedience of faith, and secures a life of abiding in His love.

If ye keep My commandments, ye shall abide in My love--It is the heavenly Vine unfolding the mystery of the life He gives. It is to those abiding in Him to whom He opens up the secret of the full abiding in His love. It is the wholehearted surrender in everything to do His will, that gives access to a life in the abiding enjoyment of His love.

Obey and abide. Gracious Lord, teach me this lesson, that it is only through knowing Thy will one can know Thy heart, and only through doing that will one can abide in Thy love. Lord, teach me that as worthless as is the doing in my own strength, so essential and absolutely indispensable is the doing of faith in Thy strength, if I would abide in Thy love.

If Ye Keep My Commandments, Ye Shall Abide in My Love, Even as I have Kept My Father's Commandments, and Abide in His Love--John 15:10

We have had occasion more than once to speak of the perfect similarity of the vine and the branch in nature, and therefore in aim. Here Christ speaks no longer in a parable, but tells us plainly out of how His own life is the exact model of ours. He had said that it is alone by obedience we can abide in His love. He now tells that this was the way in which He abode in the Father's love. As the Vine, so the branch. His life and strength and joy had been in the love of the Father: it was only by obedience He abode in it. We may find our life and strength and joy in His love all the day, but it is only by an obedience like His we can abide in it. Perfect conformity to the Vine is one of the most precious of the lessons of the branch. It was by obedience Christ as Vine honored the Father as Husbandman; it is by obedience the believer as branch honors Christ as Vine.

Obey and abide--That was the law of Christ's life as much as it is to be that of ours. He was made like us in all things, that we might be like Him in all things. He opened up a path in which we may walk even as He walked. He took our human nature to teach us how to wear it, and show us how obedience, as it is the first duty of the creature, is the only way to abide in the favor of God and enter into His glory. And now He comes to instruct and encourage us, and asks us to keep His commandments, even as He kept His Father's commandments and abides in His love.

The divine fitness of this connection between obeying and abiding, between God's commandments and His love, is easily seen. God's will is the very center of His divine perfection. As revealed in His commandments, it opens up the way for the creature to grow into the likeness of the Creator. In accepting and doing His will, I rise into fellowship with Him. Therefore it was that the Son, when coming into the world, spoke: "I come to do thy will, O God"! This was the place and this would be the blessedness of the creature. This was what he had lost in the Fall. This was what Christ came to restore. This is what, as the heavenly Vine, He asks of us and imparts to us, that even as He by keeping His Father's commandments abode in His love, we should keep His commandments and abide in His love.

Ye, even as I--The branch cannot bear fruit except as it has exactly the same life as the Vine. Our life is to be the exact counterpart of Christ's life. It can be, just in such measure as we believe in Him as the Vine, imparting Himself and His life to His branches. "Ye, even as I," the Vine says: one law, one nature, one fruit. Do let us take from our Lord the lesson of obedience as the secret of abiding. Let us confess that simple, implicit, universal obedience has taken too little the place it should have. Christ died for us as enemies, when we were disobedient. He took us up into His love; now that we are in Him, His Word is: "Obey and abide; ye, even as I." Let us give ourselves to a willing and loving obedience. He will keep us abiding in His love.

Ye, even as I. O my blessed Vine, who makest the branch in everything partake of Thy life and likeness, in this too I am to be like Thee: as Thy life in the Father's love through obedience, so mine in Thy love! Saviour, help me, that obedience may indeed be the link between Thee and me.

These Things Have I Spoken Unto You, That My Joy May Be in You, and That Your Joy May Be Fulfilled--John 15:11

If any one asks the question, "How can I be a happy Christian?" our Lord's answer is very simple: "These things," about the Vine and the branches, "I have spoken to you, that my joy may be in you, and that your joy may be fulfilled." "You cannot have My joy without My life. Abide in Me, and let Me abide in you, and My joy will be in you." All healthy life is a thing of joy and beauty; live undividedly the branch life; you will have His joy in full measure.

To many Christians the thought of a life wholly abiding in Christ is one of strain and painful effort. They cannot see that the strain and effort only come, as long as we do not yield ourselves unreservedly to the life of Christ in us. The very first words of the parable are not yet opened up to them: "I am the true Vine; I undertake all and provide for all; I ask nothing of the branch but that it yields wholly to Me, and allows Me to do all. I engage to make and keep the branch all that it ought to be." Ought it not to be an infinite and unceasing joy to have the Vine thus work all, and to know that it is none less than the blessed Son of God in His love who is each moment bearing us and maintaining our life?

That My joy may be in you--We are to have Christ's own joy in us. And what is Christ's own joy? There is no joy like love. There is no joy but love. Christ had just spoken of the Father's love and His own abiding in it, and of His having loved us with that same love. His joy is nothing but the joy of love, of being loved and of loving. It was the joy of receiving His Father's love and abiding in it, and then the joy of passing on that love and pouring it out on sinners. It is this joy He wants us to share: the joy of being loved of the Father and of Him; the joy of in our turn loving and living for those around us. This is just the joy of being truly branches: abiding in His love, and then giving up ourselves in love to bear fruit for others. Let us accept His life, as He gives it in us as the Vine, His joy will be ours: the joy of abiding in His love, the joy of loving like Him, of loving with His love.

And that your joy may be fulfilled--That it may be complete, that you may be filled with it. How sad that we should so need to be reminded that as God alone is the fountain of all joy, "God our exceeding joy," the only way to be perfectly happy is to have as much of God, as much of His will and fellowship, as possible! Religion is meant to be in everyday life a thing of unspeakable joy. And why do so many complain that it is not so? Because they do not believe that there is no joy like the joy of abiding in Christ and in His love, and being branches through whom He can pour out His love on a dying world.

Oh, that Christ's voice might reach the heart of every young Christian, and persuade him to believe that His joy is the only true joy, that His joy can become ours and truly fill us, and that the sure and simple way of living in it is--only this--to abide as branches in Him our heavenly Vine. Let the truth enter deep into us--as long as our joy is not full, it is a sign that we do not yet know our heavenly Vine aright; every desire for a fuller joy must only urge us to abide more simply and more fully in His love.

My joy--your joy. In this too it is: as the Vine, so the branch; all the Vine in the branch. Thy joy is our joy--Thy joy in us, and our joy fulfilled. Blessed Lord, fill me with Thy joy--the joy of being loved and blessed with a divine love; the joy of loving and blessing others.

LOVE ONE ANOTHER

This is My Commandment, That Ye Love One Another--John 15:12

God is love. His whole nature and perfection is love, living not for Himself, but to dispense life and blessing. In His love He begat the Son, that He might give all to Him. In His love He brought forth creatures that He might make them partakers of His blessedness.

Christ is the Son of God's love, the bearer, the revealer, the communicator of that love. His life and death were all love. Love is His life, and the life He gives. He only lives to love, to live out His life of love in us, to give Himself in all who will receive Him. The very first thought of the true Vine is love--living only to impart His life to the branches.

The Holy Spirit is the Spirit of love. He cannot impart Christ's life without imparting His love. Salvation is nothing but love conquering and entering into us; we have just as much of salvation as we have of love. Full salvation is perfect love.

No wonder that Christ said: "A new commandment I give unto you"; "This is my commandment"--the one all-inclusive commandment-- "that ye love one another." The branch is not only one with the vine, but with all its other branches; they drink one spirit, they form one body, they bear one fruit. Nothing can be more unnatural than that Christians should not love one another, even as Christ loved them. The life they received from their heavenly Vine is nothing but love. This is the one thing He asks above all others. "Hereby shall all men know that ye are my disciples...love one another." As the special sort of vine is known by the fruit it bears, the nature of the heavenly Vine is to be judged of by the love His disciples have to one another.

See that you obey this commandment. Let your "obey and abide" be seen in this. Love your brethren as the way to abide in the love of your Lord. Let your vow of obedience begin here. Love one another. Let your intercourse with the Christians in your own family be holy, tender, Christlike love. Let your thoughts of the Christians round you be, before everything, in the spirit of Christ's love. Let your life and conduct be the sacrifice of love--give your self up to think of their sins or their needs, to intercede for them, to help and to serve them. Be in your church or circle the embodiment of Christ's love. The life Christ lives in you is love; let the life in which you live it out be all love.

But, man, you write as if all this was so natural and simple and easy. Is it at all possible thus to live and thus to love? My answer is: Christ commands it: you must obey. Christ means it: you must obey, or you cannot abide in His love.

But I have tried and failed. I see no prospect of living like Christ. Ah! that is because you have failed to take in the first word of the parable--"I am the true Vine: I give all you need as a branch, I give all I myself have." I pray you, let the sense of past failure and present feebleness drive you to the Vine. He is all love. He loves to give. He gives love. He will teach you to love, even as He loved.

Love one another. Dear Lord Jesus, Thou art all love; the life Thou gavest us is love; Thy new commandment, and Thy badge of discipleship is, "Love one another." I accept the charge: with the love with which Thou lovest me, and I love Thee, I will love my brethren.

EVEN AS I HAVE LOVED YOU

This is My Commandment, That Ye Love One Another, Even as I
Have Loved You--John 15:12

This is the second time our Lord uses the expression--Even as I. The
first time it was of His relation to the Father, keeping His
commandments, and abiding in His love. Even so we are to keep
Christ's commandments, and abide in His love. The second time He
speaks of His relation to us as the rule of our love to our brethren:
"Love one another, as I have loved you." In each case His disposition
and conduct is to be the law for ours. It is again the truth we have more
than once insisted on--perfect likeness between the Vine and the
branch.

Even as I--But is it not a vain thing to imagine that we can keep His
commandments, and love the brethren, even as He kept His Father's,
and as He loved us? And must not the attempt end in failure and
discouragement? Undoubtedly, if we seek to carry out the injunction in
our strength, or without a full apprehension of the truth of the Vine and
its branches. But if we understand that the "even as I" is just the one
great lesson of the parable, the one continual language of the Vine to
the branch, we shall see that it is not the question of what we feel able
to accomplish, but of what Christ is able to work in us. These high and
holy commands--"Obey, even as I! Love, even as I"--are just meant to
bring us to the consciousness of our impotence, and through that to
waken us to the need and the beauty and the sufficiency of what is
provided for us in the Vine. We shall begin to hear the Vine speaking
every moment to the branch: "Even as I. Even as I: My life is your life;
and have a share in all My fullness; the Spirit in you, and the fruit that
comes from you, is all just the same as in Me. Be not afraid, but let
your faith grasp each "Even as I" as the divine assurance that because I
live in you, you may and can live like Me."

But why, if this really be the meaning of the parable, if this really be
the life a branch may live,who do so few realize it? Because they do
not know the heavenly mystery of the Vine. They know much of the
parable and its beautiful lessons. But the hidden spiritual mystery of the
Vine in His divine omnipotence and nearness, bearing and supplying
them all the day--this they do not know, because they have not waited
on God's Spirit to reveal it to them.

Love one another, even as I have loved you--"Ye, even as I." How
are we to begin if we are really to learn the mystery? With the

confession that we need to be brought to an entirely new mode of life, because we have never yet known Christ as the Vine in the completeness of His quickening and transforming power. With the surrender to be cleansed from all that is of self, and detached from all that is in the world, to live only and wholly as Christ lived for the glory of the Father. And then with the faith that this "even as I" is in very deed what Christ is ready to make true, the very life the Vine will maintain in the branch wholly dependent upon Him.

Even as I. Ever again it is, my blessed Lord, as the Vine, so the branch--one life, one spirit, one obedience, one joy, one love.

Lord Jesus, in the faith that Thou art my Vine, and that I am Thy branch, I accept Thy command as a promise, and take Thy "even as I" as the simple revelation of what Thou dost work in me. Yea, Lord, as Thou hast loved, I will love.

Greater Love Hath No Man Than This, That a Man Lay Down His Life for His Friends--John 15:13

In the three following verses our Lord speaks of His relation to His disciples under a new aspect--that of friendship. He point us to the love in which it on His side has its origin (v.13): to the obedience on our part by which it is maintained (v.14); and then to the holy intimacy to which it leads (v.15).

Our relation to Christ is one of love. In speaking of this previously, He showed us what His love was in its heavenly glory; the same love with which the Father had loved Him. Here we have it in its earthly manifestation--lay down His life for us. "Greater love hath no man than this, that a man lay down his life for his friends." Christ does indeed long to have us know that the secret root and strength of all He is and does for us as the Vine is love. As we learn to believe this, we shall feel that here is something which we not only need to think and know about, but a living power, a divine life which we need to receive within us. Christ and His love are inseparable; they are identical. God is love, and Christ is love. God and Christ and the divine love can only be known by having them, by their life and power working within us. "This is eternal life, that they know thee"; there is no knowing God but by having the life; the life working in us alone gives the knowledge. And even so the love; if we would know it, we must drink of its living stream, we must have it shed forth by the Holy Spirit in us.

"Greater love hath no man than this, that a man give his life for his friends." The life is the most precious thing a man has; the life is all he is; the life is himself. This is the highest measure of love: when a man gives his life, he hold nothing back, he gives all he has and is. It is this our Lord Jesus wants to make clear to us concerning His mystery of the Vine; with all He has He has placed Himself at our disposal. He wants us to count Him our very own; He wants to be wholly our possession, that we may be wholly His possession. He gave His life for us in death not merely as a passing act, that when accomplished was done with; no, but as a making Himself ours for eternity. Life for life; He gave His life for us to possess that we might give our life for Him to possess. This is what is taught by the parable of the Vine and the branch, in their wonderful identification, in their perfect union.

It is as we know something of this, not by reason or imagination, but deep down in the heart and life, that we shall begin to see what ought to be our life as branches of the heavenly Vine. He gave Himself to death; He lost Himself, that we might find life in Him. This is the true Vine, who only lives to live in us. This is the beginning and the root of that holy friendship to which Christ invites us.

Great is the mystery of godliness! Let us confess our ignorance and unbelief. Let us cease from our own understanding and our own efforts to master it. Let us wait for the Holy Spirit who dwells within us to reveal it. Let us trust His infinite love, which gave its life for us, to take possession and rejoice in making us wholly its own.

His life for His friends. How wonderful the lessons of the Vine, giving its very life to its branches! And Jesus gave His life for His friends. And that love gives itself to them and in them. My heavenly Vine, oh, teach me how wholly Thou longest to live in me!

Ye Are My Friends, if Ye Do the Things Which I Command You--
John 15:14

Our Lord has said what He gave as proof of His friendship: He gave
His life for us. He now tells us what our part is to be--to do the things
which He commands. He gave His life to secure a place for His love in
our hearts to rule us; the response His love calls us to, and empowers
us for, is that we do what He commands us. As we know the dying
love, we shall joyfully obey its commands. As we obey the commands,
we shall know the love more fully. Christ had already said: "If ye keep
my commandments, ye shall abide in my love." He counts it needful to
repeat the truth again: the one proof of our faith in His love, the one
way to abide in it, the one mark of being true branches is--to do the
things which He commands us. He began with absolute surrender of
His life for us. He can ask nothing less from us. This alone is a life in
His friendship.

This truth, of the imperative necessity of obedience, doing all that
Christ commands us, has not the place in our Christian teaching and
living that Christ meant it to have. We have given a far higher place to
privilege than to duty. We have not considered implicit obedience as a
condition of true discipleship. The secret thought that it is impossible to
do the things He commands us, and that therefore it cannot be expected
of us, and a subtle and unconscious feeling that sinning is a necessity
have frequently robbed both precepts and promises of their power. The
whole relation to Christ has become clouded and lowered, the waiting
on His teaching, the power to hear and obey His voice, and through
obedience to enjoy His love and friendship, have been enfeebled by the
terrible mistake. Do let us try to return to the true position, take Christ's
words as most literally true, and make nothing less the law of our life:
"Ye are my friends, if ye do the things that I command you." Surely our
Lord asks nothing less than that we heartily and truthfully say: "Yea,
Lord, what Thou dost command, that will I do."

These commands are to be done as a proof of friendship. The power
to do them rests entirely in the personal relationship to Jesus. For a
friend I could do what I would not for another. The friendship of Jesus
is so heavenly and wonderful, it comes to us so as the power of a divine
love entering in and taking possession, the unbroken fellowship with
Himself is so essential to it, that it implies and imparts a joy and a love
which make the obedience a delight. The liberty to claim the friendship
of Jesus, the power to enjoy it, the grace to prove it in all its

blessedness--all come as we do the things He commands us.

Is not the one thing needful for us that we ask our Lord to reveal Himself to us in the dying love in which He proved Himself our friend, and then listen as He says to us: "Ye are My friends." As we see what our Friend has done for us, and what as unspeakable blessedness it is to have Him call us friends, the doing His commands will become the natural fruit of our life in his love. We shall not fear to say: "Yea, Lord, we are Thy friends, and do what Thou dost command us."

If ye do. Yes, it is in doing that we are blessed, that we abide in His love, that we enjoy His friendship. "If ye do what I command you!" O my Lord, let Thy holy friendship lead me into the love of all Thy commands, and let the doing of Thy commands lead me ever deeper into Thy friendship.

CHRIST'S FRIENDSHIP: ITS INTIMACY

No Longer Do I Call You Servants; for the Servant Knoweth Not What His Lord Doeth: But I Have Called You Friends; for All Things That I Heard From My Father, I Have Made Known Unto You--John 15:15

The highest proof of true friendship, and one great source of its blessedness, is the intimacy that holds nothing back, and admits the friend to share our inmost secrets. It is a blessed thing to be Christ's servant; His redeemed ones delight to call themselves His slaves. Christ had often spoken of the disciples as His servants. In His great love our Lord now says: "No longer do I call you servants"; with the coming of the Holy Spirit a new era was to be inaugurated. "The servant knoweth not what his Lord doeth"--he has to obey without being consulted or admitted into the secret of all his master's plans. "But, I have called you friends, for all things I heard from my Father I have made known unto you." Christ's friends share with Him in all the secrets the Father has entrusted to Him.

Let us think what this means. When Christ spoke of keeping His Father's commandments, He did not mean merely what was written in Holy Scripture, but those special commandments which were communicated to Him day by day, and from hour to hour. It was of these He said: "The Father loveth the Son, and showeth him all things that he doeth, and he will show him greater things." All that Christ did was God's working. God showed it to Christ, so that He carried out the Father's will and purpose, not, as man often does, blindly and unintelligently, but with full understanding and approval. As one who stood in God's counsel, He knew God's plan.

And this now is the blessedness of being Christ's friends, that we do not, as servants, do His will without much spiritual insight into its meaning and aim, but are admitted, as an inner circle, into some knowledge of God's more secret thoughts. From the Day of Pentecost on, by the Holy Spirit, Christ was to lead His disciples into the spiritual apprehension of the mysteries of the kingdom, of which He had hitherto spoken only by parables.

Friendship delights in fellowship. Friends hold council. Friends dare trust to each other what they would not for anything have others know. What is it that gives a Christian access to this holy intimacy with Jesus? That gives him the spiritual capacity for receiving the communications Christ has to make of what the Father has shown Him? "Ye are my friends if ye do what I command you." It is loving obedience that purifies the soul. That refers not only to the commandments of the Word, but to that blessed application of the Word to our daily life, which none but our Lord Himself can give. But as these are waited for in dependence and humility, and faithfully obeyed, the soul becomes fitted for ever closer fellowship, and the daily life may become a continual experience: "I have called you friends; for all things I have heard from my Father, I have made known unto you."

I have called you friends. What an unspeakable honor! What a heavenly privilege! O Saviour, speak the word with power into my soul: "I have called you My friend, whom I love, whom I trust, to whom I make known all that passes between my Father and Me."

Ye Did Not Choose Me, But I Chose You, and Appointed You That Ye Should Go and Bear Fruit--John 15:16

The branch does not choose the vine, or decide on which vine it will grow. The vine brings forth the branch, as and where it will. Even so Christ says: "Ye did not choose me, but I chose you." But some will say is not just this the difference between the branch in the natural and in the spiritual world, that man has a will and a power of choosing, and that it is in virtue of his having decided to accept Christ, his having chosen Him as Lord, that he is now a branch? This is undoubtedly true. And yet it is only half a truth. The lesson of the Vine, and the teaching of our Lord, points to the other half, the deeper, the divine side of our being in Christ. If He had not chosen us, we had never chosen Him. Our choosing Him was the result of His choosing us, and taking hold of us. In the very nature of things, it is His prerogative as Vine to choose and create His own branch. We owe all we are to "the election of grace." If we want to know Christ as the true Vine, the sole origin and strength of the branch life, and ourselves as branches in our absolute, most blessed, and most secure dependence upon Him, let us drink deep of this blessed truth: "Ye did not choose me, but I chose you."

And with what view does Christ say this? That they may know what the object is for which He chose them, and find, in their faith in His election, the certainty of fulfilling their destiny. Throughout Scripture this is the great object of the teaching of election. "Predestinated to be conformed to the image of his son." (to be branches in the image and likeness of the Vine). "Chosen that we should be holy." "Chosen to salvation, through sanctification of the Spirit." "Elect in sanctification of the Spirit unto obedience." Some have abused the doctrine of election, and others, for fear of its abuse, have rejected it, because they have overlooked this teaching. They have occupied themselves with its hidden origin in eternity, with the inscrutable mysteries of the counsels of God instead of accepting the revelation of its purpose in time, and the blessings it brings into our Christian life.

Just think what these blessings are. In our verse Christ reveals His twofold purpose in choosing us to be His branches: that we may bear fruit on earth, and have power in prayer in Heaven. What confidence the thought that He has chosen us for this gives, that He will not fail to fit us for carrying out His purpose! What assurance that we can bear fruit that will abide, and can pray so as to obtain! What a continual call to the deepest humility and praise, to the most entire dependence and expectancy! He would not choose us for what we are not fit for, or what He could not fit us for. He has chosen us; this is the pledge, He will do all in us.

Let us listen in silence of soul to our holy Vine speaking to each of us: "You did not choose Me!" And let us say, "Yea, Lord, but I chose You! Amen, Lord!" Ask Him to show what this means. In Him, the true Vine, your life as branch has its divine origin, its eternal security, and the power to fulfill His purpose. From Him to whose will of love you owe all, you may expect all. In Him, His purpose, and His power, and His faithfulness, in His love let me abide.

I chose you. Lord, teach me what this means--that Thou hast set Thy heart on me, and chosen me to bear fruit that will abide, and to pray prayer that will prevail. In this Thine eternal purpose my soul would rest itself and say: "What He chose me for I will be, I can be, I shall be."

ABIDING FRUIT

I Chose You, and Appointed You, That Ye Should Go and Bear Fruit, and That Your Fruit Should Abide--John 15:16

There are some fruits that will not keep. One sort of pears or apples must be used at once; another sort can be kept over till next year. So there is in Christian work some fruit that does not last. There may be much that pleases and edified, and yet there is no permanent impression made on the power of the world or the state of the Church. On the other hand, there is work that leaves its mark for generations or for eternity. In it the power of God makes itself lastingly felt. It is the fruit of which Paul speaks when he describes the two styles of ministry: "My preaching was not in persuasive words of wisdom, but in demonstrations of the Spirit and of power; that your faith should not stand in the wisdom of men, but in the power of God." The more of man with his wisdom and power, the less of stability; the more of God's Spirit, the more of a faith standing in God's power.

Fruit reveals the nature of the tree from which it comes. What is the secret of bearing fruit that abides? The answer is simple. It is as our life abides in Christ, as we abide in Him, that the fruit we bear will abide. The more we allow all that is of human will and effort to be cut down short and cleansed away by the divine Husbandman, the more intensely our being withdraws itself from the outward that God may work in us by His Spirit; that is, the more wholly we abide in Christ, the more will our fruit abide.

What a blessed thought! He chose you, and appointed you to bear fruit, and that your fruit should abide. He never meant one of His branches to bring forth fruit that should not abide. The deeper I enter into the purpose of this His electing grace, the surer my confidence will become that I can bring forth fruit to eternal life, for myself and others. The deeper I enter into this purpose of His electing love, the more I will realize what the link is between the purpose from eternity, and the fruit to eternity: the abiding in Him. The purpose is His, He will carry it out; the fruit is His, He will bring it forth; the abiding is His, He will maintain it.

Let everyone who professes to be a Christian worker, pause. Ask whether you are leaving your mark for eternity on those around you. It is not your preaching or teaching, your strength of will or power to influence, that will secure this. All depends on having your life full of God and His power. And that again depends upon your living the truly branchlike life of abiding--very close and unbroken fellowship with Christ. It is the branch, that abides in Him, that brings forth much fruit, fruit that will abide.

Blessed Lord, reveal to my soul, I pray Thee, that Thou hast chosen me to bear much fruit. Let this be my confidence, that Thy purpose can be realized--Thou didst choose me. Let this be my power to forsake everything and give myself to Thee. Thou wilt Thyself perfect what Thou hast begun. Draw me so to dwell in the love and the certainty of that eternal purpose, that the power of eternity may posses me, and the fruit I bear may abide.

That ye may bear fruit. O my heavenly Vine, it is beginning to dawn upon my soul that fruit, more fruit--much fruit--abiding fruit is the one thing Thou hast to give me, and the one thing as branch I have to give Thee! Here I am. Blessed Lord, work out Thy purpose in me; let me bear much fruit, abiding fruit, to thy glory.

PREVAILING PRAYER

I Appointed You That Ye Should Go and Bear Fruit, and That Your Fruit Should Abide: That Whatsoever Ye Shall Ask of the Father in My Name, He May Give It You--John 15:16

In the first verse of our parable, Christ revealed Himself as the true Vine, and the Father as the Husbandman, and asked for Himself and the Father a place in the heart. Here, in the closing verse, He sums up all His teaching concerning Himself and the Father in the twofold purpose for which He had chosen them. With reference to Himself, the Vine, the purpose was, that they should bear fruit. With reference to the Father, it was, that whatsoever they should ask in His name, should be done of the Father in Heaven. As fruit is the great proof of the true relation to Christ, so prayer is of our relation to the Father. A fruitful abiding in the Son, and prevailing prayer to the Father, are the two great factors in the true Christian life.

That whatsoever ye shall ask of the Father in my name, he may give it you.--These are the closing words of the parable of the Vine. The whole mystery of the Vine and its branches leads up to the other mystery--that whatsoever we ask in His name the Father gives! See here the reason of the lack of prayer, and of the lack of power in prayer. It is because we so little live the true branch life, because we so little lose ourselves in the Vine, abiding in Him entirely, that we feel so little constrained to much prayer, so little confident that we shall be heard, and so do not know how to use His name as the key to God's storehouse. The Vine planted on earth has reached up into Heaven; it is only the soul wholly and intensely abiding in it, can reach into Heaven with power to prevail much. Our faith in the teaching and the truth of the parable, in the truth and the life of the Vine, must prove itself by power in prayer. The life of abiding and obedience, of love and joy, of cleansing and fruit-bearing, will surely lead to the power of prevailing prayer.

Whatsoever ye shall ask--The promise was given to disciples who were ready to give themselves, in the likeness of the true Vine, for their fellow men. This promise was all their provision for their work; they took it literally, they believed it, they used it, and they found it true. Let us give ourselves, as branches of the true Vine, and in His likeness, to the work of saving men, of bringing forth fruit to the glory of God, and we shall find a new urgency and power to pray and to claim the "whatsoever ye ask." We shall waken to our wonderful responsibility of having in such a promise the keys to the King's storehouses given us, and we shall not rest till we have received bread and blessing for the perishing.

"I chose you, that ye may bring forth fruit, and that your fruit may abide; that whatsoever ye shall ask of the Father in my name, he may give it to you." Beloved disciple, seek above everything to be a man of prayer. Here is the highest exercise of your privilege as a branch of the Vine; here is the full proof of your being renewed in the image of God and His Son; here is your power to show how you, like Christ, live not for yourself, but for others; here you enter Heaven to receive gifts for men; here your abiding in Christ has led to His abiding in you, to use you as the channel and instrument of His grace. The power to bear fruit for men has been crowned by power to prevail with God.

"I am the vine, my Father is the Husbandman." Christ's work in you is to bring you so to the Father that His Word may be fulfilled in you: "At that day ye shall ask in my name; and I say not that I will pray the Father for you; for the Father himself loveth you." The power of direct access to the Father for men, the liberty of intercession claiming and receiving blessing for them in faith, is the highest exercise of our union with Christ. Let all who would truly and fully be branches give themselves to the work of intercession. It is the one great work of Christ the Vine in Heaven, the source of power for all His work. Make it your one great work as branch: it will be the power of all your work.

In My name. Yes, Lord, in Thy name, the new name Thou hast given Thyself here, the true Vine. As a branch, abiding in Thee in entire devotion, in full dependence, in perfect conformity, in abiding fruitfulness, I come to the Father, in Thee, and He will give what I ask. Oh, let my life be one of unceasing and prevailing intercession! Amen!

Waiting on God

"My soul waiteth only upon God [marg: is silent unto God]; from Him cometh my salvation." Ps. 62:1

If salvation indeed comes from God, and is entirely His work, just as creation was, it follows, as a matter of course, that our first and highest duty is to wait on Him to do the work that pleases Him. Waiting becomes then the only way to the experience of a full salvation, the only way, truly, to know God as the God of our salvation. All the difficulties that are brought forward as keeping us back from full salvation, have their cause in this one thing: the defective knowledge and practice of waiting upon God. All that the Church and its members need for the manifestation of the mighty power of God in the world, is the return to our true place, the place that belongs to us, both in creation and redemption, the place of absolute and unceasing dependence upon God. Let us strive to see what the elements are that make up this most blessed and needful waiting upon God: it may help us to discover the reasons why this grace is so little cultivated, and to feel how infinitely desirable it is that the Church, that we ourselves, should at any price learn its blessed secret.

The deep need for this waiting on God lies equally in the nature of man and the nature of God. God, as Creator, formed man, to be a vessel in which He could show forth His power and goodness. Man was not to have in himself a fountain of life, or strength, or happiness: the ever-living and only living One was each moment to be the Communicator to him of all that he needed. Man's glory and blessedness was not to be independent, or dependent upon himself, but dependent on a God of such infinite riches and love. Man was to have the joy of receiving every moment out of the fulness of God. This was his blessedness as an unfallen creature.

When he fell from God, he was still more absolutely dependent on Him. There was not the slightest hope of his recovery out of his state of death, but in God, His power and mercy. It is God alone who began the work of redemption; it is God alone who continues and carries it on each moment in each individual believer. Even in the regenerate man there is no power of goodness in himself: he has and can have nothing that he does not each moment receive; and waiting on God is just as indispensable, and must be just as continuous and unbroken, as the breathing that maintains his natural life.

It is, then, because Christians do not know their relation to God of absolute poverty and helplessness, that they have no sense of the need of absolute and unceasing dependence, or the unspeakable blessedness of continual waiting on God. But when once a believer begins to see it, and consent to it, that he by the Holy Spirit must each moment receive what God each moment works, waiting on God becomes his brightest hope and joy. As he apprehends how God, as God, as Infinite Love, delights to impart His own nature to His child as fully as He can, how God is not weary of each moment keeping charge of his life and strength, he wonders that he ever thought otherwise of God than as a God to be waited on all the day. God unceasingly giving and working; His child unceasingly waiting and receiving: this is the blessed life. "Truly my soul waiteth upon God; from Him cometh my salvation." First we wait on God for salvation. Then we learn that salvation is only to bring us to God, and teach us to wait on Him. Then we find what is better still, that waiting on God is itself the highest salvation. It is the ascribing to Him the glory of being All; it is the experiencing that He is All to us.

May God teach us the blessedness of waiting on Him.

"My soul, wait thou only upon God!"

I have waited for Thy salvation, O Lord! Gen 49:18.
It is not easy to say exactly in what sense Jacob used these words, in
the midst of his prophecies in regard to the future of his sons. But they
do certainly dictate that both for himself and for them his expectation
was from God alone. It was God's salvation he waited for; a salvation
which God had promised and which God Himself alone could work
out. He knew himself and his sons to be under God's charge. Jehovah
the Everlasting God would show in them what His saving power is and
does. The words point forward to that wonderful history of redemption
which is not yet finished, and to the glorious future in eternity whither
it is leading. They suggest to us how there is no salvation but God's
salvation, and how waiting on God for that, whether for our personal
experience, or in wider circles, is our first duty, our true blessedness.
Let us think of ourselves, and the inconceivably glorious salvation God
has wrought for us in Christ, and is now purposing to work out and to
perfect in us by His Spirit. Let us meditate until we somewhat realize
that every participation of this great salvation, from moment to
moment, must be the work of God Himself. God cannot part with His
grace, or goodness, or strength, as an external thing that He gives us, as
He gives the raindrops from heaven. No; He can only give it, and we
can only enjoy it, as He works it Himself directly and unceasingly. And
the only reason that He does not work it more effectually and
continuously is, that we do not let Him. We hinder Him either by our
indifference or by our self-effort, so that He cannot do what He would.
What He asks of us, in the way of surrender, and obedience, and desire,
and trust, is all comprised in this one word: waiting on Him, waiting
for His salvation. It combines the deep sense of our entire helplessness
of ourselves to work what is divinely good, and our perfect confidence
that our God will work it all in His divine power.
Again, I say, let us meditate on the divine glory of the salvation God
purposes working out in us, until we know the truths it implies. Our
heart is the scene of a divine operation more wonderful than Creation.
We can do as little towards the work as towards creating the world,
except as God works in us to will and to do. God only asks of us to
yield, to consent, to wait upon Him, and He will do it all. Let us
meditate and be still, until we see how meet and right and blessed it is
that God alone do all, and our soul will of itself sink down in deep
humility to say: "I have waited for Thy salvation, O Lord." And the
deep blessed background of all our praying and working will be: "Truly
my soul waiteth upon God."
The application of the truth to wider circles, to those we labor among

or intercede for, to the Church of Christ around us, or throughout the world, is not difficult. There can be no good but what God works; to wait upon God, and have the heart filled with faith in His working, and in that faith to pray for His mighty power to come down, is our only wisdom. Oh for the eyes of our heart to be opened to see God working in ourselves and in others, and to see how blessed it is to worship and just to wait for His salvation!

Our private and public prayer are our chief expression of our relation to God: it is in them chiefly that our waiting upon God must be exercised. If our waiting begin by quieting the activities of nature, and being still before God; if it bows and seeks to see God in His universal and almighty operation, alone able and always ready to work all good; if it yields itself to Him in the assurance that He is working and will work in us; if it maintains the place of humility and stillness, and surrenders until God's Spirit has quickened the faith that He will perfect His work: it will indeed become the strength and the joy of the soul. Life will become one deep blessed cry: "I have waited for Thy salvation, O Lord."

"My soul, wait thou only upon God"

"These wait all upon Thee; That Thou mayest give them their meat in due season. That Thou givest unto them, they gather: Thou openest Thine hand, they are satisfied with good." Ps.104:27-28

This Psalm, in praise of the Creator, has been speaking of the birds and the beasts of the forest; of the young lions, and man going forth to his work; of the great sea, wherein are things creeping innumerable, both small and great beasts. And it sums up the whole relation of all creation to its Creator, and its continuous and universal dependence upon Him in the one word: "These all wait upon Thee." Just as much as it was God's work to create, it is His work to maintain. As little as the creature could create itself, it is it left to provide for itself. The whole creation is ruled by the one unalterable law of — waiting upon God! The word is the simple expression of that for the sake of which alone the creature was brought into existence, the very groundwork of its constitution. The one object for which God gave life to creatures was that in them He might prove and show forth His wisdom, power, and goodness, in His being each moment their life and happiness, and pouring forth unto them, according to their capacity, the riches of His goodness and power. And just as this is the very place and nature of God, to be unceasingly the supplier of every want in the creature, so the very place and nature of the creature is nothing hut this - to wait upon God and receive from Him what He alone can give, what He delights to give.

If we are in this little book at all to apprehend what waiting on God is to be to the believer, to practice it and to experience its blessedness, it is of consequence that we begin at the very beginning, and see the deep reasonableness of the call that comes to us. We shall understand how the duty is no arbitrary command. We shall see how it is not only rendered necessary by our sin and helplessness. It is simply and truly our restoration to our original destiny and our highest nobility, to our true place and glory as creatures blessedly dependent on the All-Glorious God.

If once our eyes are opened to this precious truth, all Nature will become a preacher, reminding us of the, relationship which, founded in creation, is now taken in grace. As we read this Psalm, and learn to look upon all life in Nature as continually maintained by God Himself, waiting on God will be seen to be the very necessity of our being. As we think of the young lions and the ravens crying to Him, of the birds and the fishes and every insect waiting on Him, till He give them their meat in due season, we shall see that it is the very nature and glory of God that He is a God who is to be waited on. Every thought of what

Nature is, and what God is, will give new force to the call: "Wait thou only upon God."

"These all wait upon Thee, that thou mayest give." It is God who giveth all: let this faith enter deeply into our hearts. Ere yet we fully understand all that is implied in our waiting upon God, and ere we have even been able to cultivate the habit, let the truth enter our souls: waiting on God, unceasing and entire dependence upon Him, is, in heaven and earth, the one only true religion, the one unalterable and all-comprehensive expression for the true relationship to the ever-blessed one in whom we live.

Let us resolve at once that it shall be the one characteristic of our life and worship, a continual, humble, truthful waiting upon God. We may rest assured that He who made us for Himself, that He might give Himself to us and in us, that He will never disappoint us. In waiting on Him we shall find rest and joy and strength, and the supply of every need.

"My soul, wait thou only upon God."

"The Lord upholdeth all that fall, And raiseth up all those that be bowed down. The eyes of all wait upon Thee; And Thou givest them their meat in due season." Ps 145:14-15

PSALM 104 is a Psalm of Creation, and the words, "These all wait upon Thee," were used with reference to the animal creation. Here we have a Psalm of the Kingdom, and "The eyes of all wait upon Thee" appears specially to point to the needs of God's saints, of all that fall and them that be bowed down. What the universe and the animal creation do unconsciously, God's people are to do intelligently and voluntarily. Man is to be the interpreter of Nature. He is to prove that there is nothing more noble or more blessed in the exercise of our free will than to use it in waiting upon God.

If an army has been sent out to march into an enemy's country, and tidings are received that it is not advancing, the question is at once asked, what may be the cause of delay. The answer will very often be: "Waiting for supplies." All the stores of provisions or clothing or ammunition have not arrived; without these it dare not proceed. It is no otherwise in the Christian life: day by day, at every step, we need our supplies from above. And there is nothing so needful as to cultivate that spirit of dependence on God and of confidence in Him, which refuses to go on without the needed supply of grace and strength.

If the question be asked, whether this be anything different from what we do when we pray, the answer is, that there may be much praying with but very little waiting on God. In praying we are often occupied with ourselves, with our own needs, and our own efforts in the presentation of them. In waiting upon God, the first thought is of the God upon whom we wait. We enter His presence, and feel we need just to be quiet, so that He, as God, can overshadow us with Himself. God longs to reveal Himself, to fill us with Himself. Waiting on God gives Him time in His own way and divine power to come to us.

It is specially at the time of prayer that we ought to set ourselves to cultivate this spirit.

Before you pray, bow quietly before God, just t remember and realize who He is, how near He is, how certainly He can and will help. Just be still before Him, and allow His Holy Spirit to waken and stir up in your soul the child-like disposition of absolute dependence and confident expectation. Wait upon God as a Living Being, as the Living God, who notices you, and is just longing to fill you with His salvation. Wait on God till you know you have met Him; prayer will then be come so different.

And when you are praying, let there be intervals of silence, reverent stillness of soul, in which you yield yourself to God, in case He may have aught He wishes to teach you or to work in you. Waiting on Him will become the most blessed part of prayer, and the blessing thus obtained will be doubly precious as the fruit or such fellowship with the Holy One, God has so ordained it, in harmony with His holy nature, and with ours, that waiting on Him should be the honor we give Him. Let us bring Him the service gladly and truthfully; He will reward it abundantly.

"The eyes of all wait upon Thee, and Thou givest them their meat in due season." Dear soul, God provides in Nature for the creatures He has made: how much more will He provide in Grace for those He has redeemed. Learn to say of every want, and every failure, and every lack of needful grace: I have waited too little upon God, or He would have given me in due season all I needed. And say then too,

"My soul, wait thou only upon God!"

"Shew me thy ways, O Lord; Teach me Thy paths. Lead me in Thy truth, and teach me; For Thou art the God of my salvation; On Thee do I wait all the day." Ps. 25:4-5

I spoke of an army on the point of entering an enemy's territories. Answering the question as to the cause of delay: "Waiting for supplies." The answer might also have been: "Waiting for instructions," or "Waiting for orders." If the last despatch had not been received, with the final orders of the commander-in-chief, the army dared not move. Even so in the Christian life: as deep as the need of waiting for supplies, is that of waiting for instructions.

See how beautiful this comes out in Ps. 25. The writer knew and loved God's law exceedingly, and meditated in that law day and night. But he knew that this was not enough. He knew that for the right spiritual apprehension of the truth, and for the right personal application of it to his own peculiar circumstances, he needed a direct divine teaching. The psalm has at all times been a very peculiar one, because of its reiterated expression of the felt need of the Divine teaching, and of the childlike confidence that that teaching would be given. Study the psalm until your heart is filled with the two thoughts - the absolute need, the absolute certainty of divine guidance. And with these how entirely it is in this connection that he speaks, "On Thee do I wait all the day." Waiting for guidance, waiting for instruction, all the day, is a very blessed part of waiting upon God.

The Father in heaven is so interested in His child, and so longs to have his life at every step in His will and His love, that He is willing to keep his guidance entirely in His own hand. He knows so well that we are unable to do what is really holy and heavenly, except as He works it in us, that He means His very demands to become promises of what He will do, in watching over and leading us all the day. Not only in special difficulties and times of perplexity, but in the common course of everyday life, we may count upon Him to teach us His war, and show us His path.

And what is needed in us to receive this guidance? One thing: waiting for instructions, waiting on God. "On Thee do I wait all the day." We want in our times of prayer to give clear expression to our sense of need, and our faith in His help. We want definitely to become conscious of our ignorance as to what God's war may be, and the need of the Divine light shining within us, if our way is to be as of the sun, shining more and more unto the perfect day. And we want to wait quietly before God in prayer, until the deep, restful assurance fills us: It will be given - "the meek will He guide in the way."

"On Thee do I wait all the day." The special surrender to the Divine guidance in our seasons of prayer must cultivate, and be followed up by, the habitual looking upwards "all the day." As simple as it is, to one who has eyes, to walk all the day in the light of the sun, so simple and delightful can it become to a soul practiced in waiting on God, to walk all the day in the enjoyment of God's light and leading. What is needed to help us to such a life is just one thing: the real knowledge and faith of God as the one only source of wisdom and goodness, as ever ready, and longing much to be to us all that we can possibly require - yes! this is the one thing we need. If we but saw our God in His love, if we but believed that He waits to be gracious, that He waits to be our life and to work all in us, - how this waiting on God would become our highest joy, the natural and spontaneous response of our hearts to His great love and glory!

"My soul, wait thou only upon God!"

"Let none that wait on Thee be ashamed." Ps. 25:3

Let us now, in our meditation of today, each one forget himself, to think of the great company of God, saints throughout the world, who are all with us waiting on Him. And let us all join in the fervent prayer for each other, "Let none that wait on Thee be ashamed."

Just think for a moment of the multitude of waiting ones who need that prayer; how many there are, sick and weary and solitary, to whom it is as if their prayers are not answered, and who sometimes begin to fear that their hope will be put to shame. And then, how many servants of God, ministers or missionaries, teachers or workers, of various name, whose hopes in their work have been disappointed, and whose longing for power and blessing remains unsatisfied. And then, too, how many, who have heard of a life of rest and perfect peace, of abiding light and fellowship, of strength and victory, and who cannot find the path. With all these, it is nothing but that they have not yet learned the secret of full waiting upon God. They just need, what we all need, the living assurance that waiting on God can never be in vain. Let us remember all who are in danger of fainting or being weary, and all unite in the cry, "Let none that wait on Thee be ashamed!"

If this intercession for all who wait on God becomes part of our waiting on Him for ourselves, we shall help to bear each other's burdens, and so fulfil the law of Christ.

There will be introduced into our waiting on God that element of unselfishness and love, which is the path to the highest blessing, and the fullest communion with God. Love to the brethren and love to God are inseparably linked. In God, the love to His Son and to us are one: "That the love wherewith Thou hast loved Me, may be in them." In Christ, the love of the Father to Him, and His love to us, are one: "As the Father loved me, so have I loved you." In us, He asks that His love to us shall be ours to the brethren: "As I have loved you, that ye love one another." All the love of God, and of Christ, are inseparably linked with love to the brethren. And how can we, day by day, prove and cultivate this love otherwise than by daily praying for each other? Christ did not seek to enjoy the Father's love for Himself; He passed it all on to us. All true seeking of God and His love for ourselves, will be inseparably linked with the thought and the love of our brethren in prayer for them.

"Let none that wait on Thee be ashamed." Twice in the psalm David speaks of his waiting on God for himself; here he thinks of all who wait on Him. Let this page take the message to all God's tried and weary ones, that there are more praying for them than they know. Let it stir them and us in our waiting to make a point of at times forgetting ourselves, and to enlarge our hearts, and say to the Father, "These all wait upon Thee, and Thou givest them their meat in due season." Let it inspire us all with new courage-for who is there who is not at times ready to faint and be weary? "Let none that wait on Thee be ashamed" is a promise in a prayer, "They that wait on Thee shall not be ashamed!" From many and many a witness the cry comes to every one who needs the help, brother, sister, tried one, "Wait on the Lord; be of good courage, and He shall strengthen your heart; wait, I say, on the Lord. Be of good courage, and He shall strengthen your heart, all ye that wait on the Lord."

Blessed Father! We humbly beseech Thee, Let none that wait on Thee be ashamed; no, not one. Some are weary, and the time of waiting appears long. And some are feeble, and scarcely know how to wait. And some are so entangled in the effort of their prayers and their work, they think that they can find no time to wait continually. Father, teach us all how to wait. Teach us to think of each other, and pray for each other. Teach us to think of Thee, the God of all waiting ones. Father! Let none that wait on Thee be ashamed. For Jesus' sake. Amen.

"My soul, wait thou only upon God!"

"Let integrity and uprightness preserve me; for I wait on Thee." Ps 25:21

For the third time in this psalm we have the word wait. As before in verse 5, "On Thee do I wait all the day," so here, too, the believing supplicant appeals to God to remember that he is waiting on Him, looking for an answer. It is a great thing for a soul not only to wait upon God, but to be filled with such a consciousness that its whole spirit and position is that of a waiting one, that it can, in childlike confidence, say, Lord! Thou knowest, I wait on Thee. It will prove a mighty plea in prayer, giving ever-increasing boldness of expectation to claim the promise, "They that wait on Me shall not be ashamed!"

The prayer in connection with which the plea is put forth here is one of great importance in the spiritual life. If we draw nigh to God, it must be with a true heart. There must be perfect integrity, whole-heartedness, in our dealing with God. As we read in the next Psalm (26:1, 11). "Judge me, O Lord, for I have walked in mine integrity," "As for me, I walk in my integrity," there must be perfect uprightness or single-heartedness before God, as it is written, "His righteousness is for the upright in heart." The soul must know that it allows nothing sinful, nothing doubtful; if it is indeed to meet the Holy One, and receive His full blessing, it must be with a heart wholly and singly given up to His will. The whole spirit that animates us in the waiting must be, "Let integrity and uprightness" - Thou seest that I desire to come so to Thee, Thou knowest I am looking to Thee to work them perfectly in me; - let them "preserve me, for I wait on Thee."

And if at our first attempt truly to live the life of fully and always waiting on God, we begin to discover how much that perfect integrity is wanting, this will just be one of the blessings which the waiting was meant to work. A soul cannot seek close fellowship with God, or attain the abiding consciousness of waiting on Him all the day, without a very honest and entire surrender to all His will.

"For I wait on Thee": it is not only in connection with the prayer of our text but with every prayer that this plea may be used. To use it often will be a great blessing to ourselves. Let us therefore study the words well until we know all their bearings. It must be clear to us what we are waiting for. There may be very different things. It may be waiting for God in our times of prayer to take his place as God, and to work in us the sense of HIS holy presence and nearness. It may be a special petition, to which we are expecting an answer. It may be our whole inner life, in which we are on the lookout for God's putting forth of His power. It may be the whole state of His Church and saints, or some part of His work, for which our eyes are ever toward Him. It is good that we sometimes count up to ourselves exactly what the things are we are waiting for, and as we say definitely of each of them, "On Thee do I wait," we shall be emboldened to claim the answer, "For on Thee do I wait."

It must also be clear to us, on Whom we are waiting. Not an idol, a God of whom we have made an image by our conceptions of what He is. No, but the living God, such as He really is in His great glory, His infinite holiness, His power, wisdom, and goodness, in His love and nearness. It is the presence of a beloved or a dreaded master that wakens up the whole attention of the servant who waits on him. It is the presence of God, as He can in Christ by His Holy Spirit make Himself known, and keep the soul under its covering and shadow, that will waken and strengthen the true waiting spirit. Let us be still and wait and worship till we know how near He is, and then say, "On Thee do I wait."

And then, let it be very clear, too, that we are waiting. Let that become so much our consciousness that the utterance comes spontaneously, "On Thee I do wait all the day; I wait on Thee." This will indeed imply sacrifice and separation, a soul entirely given up to God as its all, its only joy. This waiting on God has hardly yet been acknowledged as the only true Christianity. And yet, if it be true that God alone is goodness and joy and love; if it be true that our highest blessedness is in having as much of God as we can; if it be true that Christ has redeemed us wholly for God, and made a life of continual abiding in His presence possible, nothing less ought to satisfy than to be ever breathing this blessed atmosphere, "I wait on Thee."

"My soul, wait thou only on God!"

"Wait on the Lord: be strong, And let your heart take courage Yea, wait thou on the Lord." Ps. 27:14

The psalmist had just said, "I had fainted, unless I had believed to see the goodness of the Lord in the land of the living." If it had not been for his faith in God, his heart had fainted. But in the confident assurance in God which faith gives, he urges himself and us to remember one thing above all, - to wait upon God. "Wait on the Lord: be strong, and let your heart take courage: yea, wait thou on the Lord." One of the chief needs in our waiting upon God, one of the deepest secrets of its blessedness and blessing, is a quiet, confident persuasion that it is not in vain; courage to believe that God will hear and help; we are waiting on a God who never could disappoint His people.

"Be strong and of good courage." These words are frequently found in connection with some great and difficult enterprise, in prospect of the combat with the power of strong enemies, and the utter insufficiency of all human strength. Is waiting on God a work so difficult, that, for that too, such words are needed, "Be strong, and let your heart take courage"? Yes, indeed. The deliverance for which we often have to wait is from enemies, in presence of whom we are impotent. The blessings for which we plead are spiritual and all unseen; things impossible with men; heavenly, supernatural, divine realities. Our heart may well faint and fail.

Our souls are so little accustomed to hold fellowship with God; the God on whom we wait so of ten appears to hide Himself. We who have to wait are often tempted to fear that we do not wait aright, that our faith is too feeble, that our desire is not as upright or as earnest as it should be, that our surrender is not complete. Amid all these causes of fear or doubt, how blessed to hear the voice of God, "Wait on the Lord! Be strong, and let thine heart take courage! YEA, WAIT THOU ON THE LORD!" Let nothing in heaven or earth or hell - let nothing keep thee from waiting on thy God in full assurance that it cannot be in vain. The one lesson our text teaches us is this, that when we set ourselves to wait on God we ought beforehand to resolve that it shall be with the most confident expectation of God's meeting and blessing us. We ought to make up our minds to this, that nothing was ever so sure, as that waiting on God will bring us untold and unexpected blessing. We are so accustomed to judge of God and His work in us by what we feel, that the great probability is that when we begin more to cultivate the waiting on Him, we shall be discouraged, because we do not find any special blessing from it. The message comes to us, "Above everything, when you wait on God, do so in the spirit of abounding hopefulness. It is God in His glory, in His power, in His love longing to bless you that you are waiting on."

If you say that you are afraid of deceiving yourself with vain hope, because you do not see or feel any warrant in your present state for such special expectations, my answer is, it is God, who is the warrant for your expecting great things. Oh, do learn the lesson. You are not going to wait on yourself to see what you feel and what changes come to you. You are going to WAIT ON GOD, to know first, WHAT HE IS, and then, after that, what He will do. The whole duty and blessedness of waiting on God has its root in this, that He is such a blessed Being, full, to overflowing, of goodness and power and life and joy, that we, however wretched, cannot for any time come into contact with Him, without that life and power secretly, silently beginning to enter into him and blessing him. God is Love! That is the one only and all-sufficient warrant of your expectation. Love seeketh out its own: God's love is just His delight to impart Himself and His blessedness to His children.

Come, and however feeble you feel, just wait in His presence. As a feeble, sickly invalid is brought out into the sunshine to let its warmth go through him, come with all that is dark and cold in you into the sunshine of God's holy, omnipotent love, and sit and wait there, with the one thought: Here I am, in the sunshine of His love. As the sun does its work in the weak one who seeks its rays, God will do His work in you. Oh, do trust Him fully. "Wait on the Lord! Be strong, and let your heart take courage! Yea, wait thou on the Lord!"

"My soul, wait thou only upon God!"

"Be strong, and let your heart take courage, All ye that wait for the Lord." Ps. 31:24

The words are nearly the same as in our last meditation. But I gladly avail myself of them again to press home a much-needed lesson for all who desire to learn truly and fully what waiting on God is. The lesson is this: It is with the heart we must wait upon God. "Let your heart take courage"

All our waiting depends upon the state of the heart. As a man's heart is, so is he before God. We can advance no further or deeper into the holy place of God's presence to wait on Him there, than our heart is prepared for it by the Holy Spirit. The message is, "Let your heart take courage, all ye that wait on the Lord."

The truth appears so simple, that some may ask, Do not all admit this? Where is the need of insisting on it so specially? Because very many Christians have no sense of the great difference between the religion of the mind and the religion of the heart, and the former is far more diligently cultivated than the latter. They know not how infinitely greater the heart is than the mind. It is in this that one of the chief causes must be sought of the feebleness of our Christian life, and it is only as this is understood that waiting on God will bring its full blessing.

A text in Proverbs (3:5) may help to make my meaning plain. Speaking of a life in the fear and favor of God, it says, "Trust in the Lord with all thine heart, and lean not upon thine own understanding." In all religion we have to use these two powers. The mind as to gather knowledge from God's word, and prepare the food by which the heart with the inner life is to be nourished. But here comes in a terrible danger, of our leaning to our own understanding, and trusting in our apprehension of divine things.

People imagine that if they are occupied with the truth, the spiritual life will as a matter of course be strengthened. And this is by no means the case. The understanding deals with conceptions and images of divine things, but it cannot reach the real life of the soul. Hence the command, "Trust in the Lord with all thine heart, and lean not upon thine own understanding." It is with the heart man believeth, and comes into touch with God. It is in the heart God has given His Spirit, to be there to us the presence and the power of God working in us. In all our religion it is the heart that must trust and love and worship and obey. My mind is utterly impotent in creating or maintaining the spiritual life within me: the heart must wait on God for Him to work it in me.

It is in this even as in the physical life. My reason may tell me what to eat and drink, and how the food nourishes me. But in the eating and feeding my reason I can do nothing: the body has its organs for that special purpose. Just so, reason may tell me what God's word says, but it can do nothing to the feeding of the soul on the bread of life - this the heart alone can do by its faith and trust in God. A man may be studying the nature and effects of food or sleep; when he wants to eat or sleep he sets aside his thoughts and study, and uses the power of eating or sleeping. And so the Christian needs ever, when he has studied or heard God's word, to cease from his thoughts, to put no trust in them, and to waken up his heart to open itself before God, and seek the living fellowship with Him.

This is now the blessedness of waiting upon God, that I confess the impotence of all my thoughts and efforts, and set myself still to bow my heart before Him in holy silence, and to trust Him to renew and strengthen His own work in me. And this is just the lesson of our text, "Let your heart take courage, all ye that wait on the Lord." Remember the difference between knowing with the mind and believing with the heart. Beware of the temptation of leaning upon your understanding, with its clear strong thoughts. They only help you to know what the heart must get from God: in themselves they are only images and shadows.

"Let your heart take courage, all ye that wait on the Lord." Present it before Him as that wonderful part of your spiritual nature in which God reveals Himself, and by which you can know Him. Cultivate the greatest confidence that, though you cannot see into your heart, God is working there by His Holy Spirit. Let the heart wait at times in perfect silence and quiet; in its hidden depths God will work. Be sure of this, and just wait on Him. Give your whole heart, with its secret workings, into God's hands continually. He wants the heart, and takes it, and as God dwells in it. "Be strong, and let your heart take courage, all ye that wait on the Lord."

"My soul, wait thou only upon God!"

"Behold, the eye of the Lord is upon them that fear Him, upon them that hope in His mercy; To deliver their soul from death, And to keep them alive in famine. Our soul hath waited for the Lord; He is our help and our shield. For our heart shall rejoice in Him, Because we have trusted in His holy name. Let thy mercy, O Lord, be upon us, According as we wait for thee." Ps. 33:18-22

God's eye is upon His people: their eye is upon Him. In waiting upon God, our eye, looking up to Him, meets His looking down upon us. This is the blessedness of waiting upon God, that it takes our eyes and thoughts away from ourselves, even our needs and desires, and occupies us with our God. We worship Him in His glory and love, with His all-seeing eye watching over us, that He may supply our every need. Let us consider this wonderful meeting between God and His people, and mark well what we are taught here of them on whom God's eye rests, and of Him on whom our eye rests.

"The eye of the Lord is on them that fear Him, on them that hope in His mercy." Fear and hope are generally thought to be in conflict with each other, in the presence and worship of God they are found side by side in perfect and beautiful harmony. And this because in God Himself all apparent contradictions are reconciled. Righteousness and peace, judgment and mercy, holiness and love, infinite power and infinite gentleness, a majesty that is exalted above all heaven, and a condescension that bows very low, meet and kiss each other.

There is indeed a fear that hath torment, that is cast out entirely by perfect love. But there is a fear that is found in the very heavens. In the song of Moses and the Lamb they sing, "Who shall not fear Thee, O Lord, and glorify Thy name?" And out of the very throne the voice came, "Praise our God, all ye His servants, and ye that fear Him." Let us in our waiting ever seek "to fear the glorious and fearful name, THE LORD THY GOD." The deeper we w bow before His holiness in holy fear and adoring awe, in deep reverence and humble self-abasement, even as the angels veil their faces before the throne, the more will His holiness rest upon us, and the soul be filled to have God reveal Himself; the deeper we enter into the truth "that no flesh glory in His presence," will it be given us to see His glory. "The eye of the Lord is on them that fear Him."

"On them that hope in His mercy." So far will the true fear of God be from keeping us back from hope, it will stimulate and strengthen it. The lower we bow, the deeper we feel we have nothing to hope in but His mercy. The lower we bow, the nearer God will come, and make our hearts bold to trust Him. Let every exercise of waiting, let our whole habit of waiting on God, be pervaded by abounding hope — a hope as bright and boundless as God's mercy. The fatherly kindness of God is such that, in whatever state we come to Him, we may confidently hope in His mercy.

Such are God's waiting ones. And now, think of the God on whom we wait. "The eye of the Lord is on them that fear Him, on them that hope in His mercy; to deliver their soul from death, and to keep them alive in famine." Not to prevent the danger of death and famine — this is often needed to stir the waiting on Him — but to deliver and to keep alive. For the dangers are often very real and dark; the situation, whether in the temporal or spiritual life, may appear to be utterly hopeless. There is always one hope: God's eye is on them.

That eye sees the danger, and sees in tender love His trembling waiting child, and sees the moment when the heart is ripe for the blessing, and sees the way in which it is to come. This living, mighty God, oh, let us fear Him and hope in His mercy. And let us humbly but boldly say, "Our soul waiteth for the Lord; He is our help and our shield. Let Thy mercy be upon us, O Lord, according as we wait for Thee."

Oh, the blessedness of waiting on such a God! a very present help in every time of trouble; a shield and defense against every danger. Children of God! will you not learn to sink down in entire helplessness and impotence and in stillness to wait and see the salvation of God?

In the utmost spiritual famine, and when death appears to prevail, oh, wait on God. He does deliver, He does keep alive. Say it not only in solitude, but say it to each other — the psalm speaks not of one but of God's people — "Our soul waiteth on the Lord: He is our help and our shield." Strengthen and encourage each other in the holy exercise of waiting, that each may not only say of it himself, but of his brethren, "We have waited for Him; we will be glad and rejoice in His salvation."

"My soul, wait thou only upon God!"

"Rest in the Lord, and wait patiently for Him, Those that wait upon the Lord, they shall inherit the land." Ps. 37:7, 9

"In patience possess your souls." "Ye have need of patience." "Let patience have its perfect work, that ye may be perfect and entire." Such words of the Holy Spirit show us what an important element in the Christian life and character patience is. And nowhere is there a better place for cultivating or displaying it than in waiting on God. There we discover how impatient we are, and what our impatience means. We confess at times that we are impatient with men, and circumstances that hinder us, or with ourselves and our slow progress in the Christian life. If we truly set ourselves to wait upon God, we shall find that it is with Him we are impatient, because He does not at once, or as soon as we could wish, do our bidding. It is in waiting upon God that our eyes are opened to believe in His wise and sovereign will, and to see that the sooner and the more completely we yield absolutely to it, the more surely His blessing can come to us.

"It is not of him that willeth, nor of him that runneth, but of God that sheweth mercy." Rom 9:16. We have as little power to increase or strengthen our spiritual life, as we had to originate it. We "were born not of the will of the flesh, nor of the will of man, but of the will of God." Even so, our willing and running, our desire and effort, avail nought; all is "of God that sheweth mercy."

All the exercises of the spiritual life, our reading and praying, our willing and doing, have their very great value. But they can go no farther than this, that they point the way and prepare us in humility to look to and to depend alone upon God Himself, and in patience to wait His good time and mercy. The waiting is to teach us our absolute dependence upon God's mighty working, and to make us in perfect patience place ourselves at His disposal. They that wait on the Lord shall inherit the land; the promised land and its blessing. The heirs must wait; they can afford to wait.

"Rest in the Lord, and wait patiently for Him." The margin gives for "Rest in the Lord," "Be silent to the Lord," or R. V., "Be still before the Lord." It is resting in the Lord, in His will, His promise, His faithfulness, and His love, that makes patience easy. And the resting in Him is nothing but being silent unto Him, still before Him. Having our thoughts and wishes, our fears and hopes, hushed into calm and quiet in that great peace of God which passeth all understanding. That peace keeps the heart and mind when we are anxious for anything, because we have made our request known to Him. The rest, the silence, the stillness, and the patient waiting, all find their strength and joy in God

Himself.

The need for patience, and the reasonableness, and the blessedness of patience will be opened up to the waiting soul. Our patience will be seen to be the counterpart of God's patience. He longs far more to bless us fully than we can desire it. But, as the husbandman has long patience till the fruit be ripe, so God bows Himself to our slowness and bears long with us. Let us remember this, and wait patiently: of each promise and every answer to prayer the word is true: "I the Lord will hasten it in its time." Isa 60:22.

"Rest in the Lord, and wait patiently for Him." Yes, for HIM. Seek not only the help, the gift, thou needest seek: HIMSELF; wait for HIM. Give God His glory by resting in Him, by trusting him fully, by waiting patiently for Him. This patience honors Him greatly; it leaves Him, as God on the throne, to do His work; it yields self wholly into His hands. It lets God be God. If thy waiting be for some special request, wait patiently. If thy waiting be more the exercise of the spiritual life seeking to know and have more of God, wait patiently. Whether it be in the shorter specific periods of waiting, or as the continuous habit of the souls. Rest in the Lord, be still before the Lord, and wait patiently. "They that wait on the Lord shall inherit the land."

"My soul, wait thou only upon God!"

"Wait on the Lord, and keep His way, And He shalt exalt thee to inherit the land." Ps. 37:34.

If we desire to find a man whom we long to meet, we inquire where the places and the ways are where he is to be found. When waiting on God, we need to be very careful that we keep His ways; out of these we never can expect to find Him. "Thou meetest him that rejoiceth and worketh righteousness; those that remember Thee in Thy ways." Isa 64:5. We may be sure that God is never and nowhere to be found but in His ways. And that there, by the soul who seeks and patiently waits, He is always most surely to be found. "Wait on the Lord, and keep His ways, and He shall exalt thee."

How close the connection between the two parts of the injunction, "Wait on the Lord," - that has to do with worship and disposition; "and keep His ways," - that deals with walk and work. The outer life must be in harmony with the inner; the inner must be the inspiration and the strength for the outer. It is our God who has made known His ways in His Word for our conduct, and invites our confidence for His grace and help in our heart. If we do not keep His ways, our waiting on Him can bring no blessing. The surrender to full obedience to all His will is the secret of full access to all the blessings of His fellowship.

Notice how strongly this comes out in the psalm. It speaks of the evildoer who prospereth in his way, and calls on the believer not to fret himself. When we see men around us prosperous and happy while they forsake God's ways, and ourselves left in difficulty or suffering, we are in danger of first fretting at what appears so strange, and then gradually yielding to seek our prosperity in their path. The psalm says, "Fret not thyself; trust in the Lord, and do good. Rest in the Lord, and wait patiently for Him; cease from anger, and forsake wrath. Depart from evil, and do good; the Lord forsaketh not His saints. The righteous shall inherit the land. The law of his God is in his heart; none of his steps shall slide." "And then follows - the word occurs for the third time in the psalm - "Wait on the Lord, and keep His way." Do what God asks you to do; God will do more than you can ask Him to do.

And let no one give way to the fear: I cannot keep His way; it is this robs one of every confidence. It is true you have not the strength yet to keep all His ways. But keep carefully those for which you have received strength already. Surrender yourself willingly and trustingly to keep all God's ways, in the strength which will come in waiting on Him. Give up your whole being to God without reserve and without doubt; He will prove Himself God to you, and work in you that which is pleasing in His sight through Jesus Christ.

Keep His ways, as you know them in the Word. Keep His ways, as nature teaches them, in always doing what appears right. Keep His ways, as Providence points them out. Keep His ways, as the Holy Spirit suggests. Do not think of waiting on God while you say you are not willing to work in His path. However weak you feel, only be willing, and He who has worked to will, will work to do by His power.

"Wait on the Lord, and keep His way." It may be that the consciousness of shortcoming and sin makes our text look more like a hindrance than a help in waiting on God. Let it not be so.

Have we not said more than once, the very starting-point and ground-work of this waiting is utter and absolute impotence? Why then not come with everything evil you feel in yourself, every memory of unwillingness, unwatchfulness, unfaithfulness, and all that causes such unceasing self-condemnation? Put your power in God's omni-potence, and find in waiting on God your deliverance.

Your failure has been owing to only one thing: you sought to conquer and obey in your own strength. Come and bow before God until you learn that He is the God who alone is good, and alone can work any good thing. Believe that in you, and all that nature can do, there is no true power. Be content to receive from God each moment the inworking of His mighty grace and life, and waiting on God will become the renewal of your strength to run in His ways and not be weary, to walk in His paths and never faint. "Wait on the Lord, and keep His way" will be command and promise in one.

"My soul, wait thou only upon God!"

"And now, Lord, what wait I for? My hope is in Thee. Deliver me from all my transgressions." Ps. 39:7, 8.

There may be times when we feel as if we knew not what we are waiting for. There may be other times we think we do know, and when it would just be so good for us to realize that we do not know what to ask as we ought. God is able to do for us exceeding abundantly above what we ask or think, and we are in danger of limiting Him, when we confine our desires and prayers to our own thoughts of them. It is a great thing at times to say, as our psalm says: "And now, Lord, what wait I for?" I scarce know or can tell; this only I can say - "My hope is in Thee."

How we see this limiting of God in the case of Israel! When Moses promised them meat in the wilderness, they doubted, saying, "Can God furnish a table in the wilderness? He smote the rock that the water gushed out; can He give bread also? Can He provide flesh for His people?" If they had been asked whether God could provide streams in the desert, they would have answered, Yes. God had done it: He could do it again. But when the thought came of God doing something new, they limited Him; their expectation could not rise beyond their past experience, or their own thoughts of what was possible.

Even so we may be limiting God by our conceptions of what He has promised or is able to do. Do let us beware of limiting the Holy one of Israel in our very prayer. Let us believe that the very promises of God we plead have a divine meaning, infinitely beyond our thoughts of them. Let us believe that His fulfilment of them can be, in a power and an abundance of grace, beyond our largest grasp of thought. And let us therefore cultivate the habit of waiting on God, not only for what we think we need, but for all His grace and power are ready to do for us.

In every true prayer there are two hearts in exercise. The one is your heart, with its little, dark, human thoughts of what you need and God can do. The other is God's great heart, with its infinite, its divine purposes of blessing. What think you? To which of these two ought the larger place to be given in your approach to Him? Undoubtedly, to the heart of God: every thing depends upon knowing and being occupied with that. But how little this is done. This is what waiting on God is meant to teach you. Just think of God's wonderful love and redemption, in the meaning these words must have to Him. Confess how little you understand what God is willing to do for you, and say each time as you pray: "And now, what wait I for?" My heart cannot say, God's heart knows and waits to give. "My hope is in Thee." Wait on God to do for you more than you can ask or think.

Apply this to the prayer that follows: "Deliver me from all my transgressions." You have prayed to be delivered from temper, or pride, or self-will. It is as if it is in vain. May it not be that you have had your own thoughts about the way or the extent of God's doing it, and have never waited on the God of glory, according to the riches of His glory, to do for you what hath not entered the heart of man to conceive? Learn to worship God as the God who doeth wonders, who wishes to prove in you that He can do something supernatural and divine. Bow before Him, wait upon Him, until your soul realizes that you are in the hands of a divine and almighty worker. Consent but to know what and how He will work; expect it to be something altogether godlike, something to be waited for in deep humility, and received only by His divine power. Let, the, "And now, Lord, what wait I for? My hope is in Thee" become the spirit of every longing and every prayer. He will in His time do His work.

Dear soul, in waiting on God you may often be ready to be weary, because you hardly know what you have to expect. I pray you, be of good courage — this ignorance is often one of the best signs. He is teaching you to leave all in His hands, and to wait on Him alone. "Wait on the Lord! Be strong, and let your heart take courage. Yea, wait thou on the Lord"

"My soul, wait thou only upon God!"

"I waited patiently for the Lord, and He inclined unto me, and heard my cry. . . and He hath put a new song in my mouth, even praise unto our God." Ps. 40:1-3.

Come and listen to the testimony of one who can speak from experience of the sure and blessed outcome of patient, waiting upon God. True patience is so foreign to our self-confident nature, it is so indispensable in our waiting upon God, it is such an essential element of true faith, that we may well once again meditate on what the word has to teach us.

The word patience is derived from the Latin word for suffering. It suggests the thought of being under the constraint of some power from which we fain would be free. At first we submit against our will; experience teaches us that when it is vain to resist, patient endurance is our wisest course. In waiting on God it is of infinite consequence that we not only submit, because we are compelled to, but because we lovingly and joyfully consent to be in the hands of our blessed Father. Patience then becomes our highest blessedness and our highest grace. It honors God, and gives Him time to have His way with us. It is the highest expression of our faith in His goodness and faithfulness. It brings the soul perfect rest in the assurance that God is carrying on His work. It is the token of our full consent that God should deal with us in such a way and time as He thinks best. True patience is the losing of our self-will in His perfect will.

Such patience is needed for the true and full waiting on God. Such patience is the growth and fruit of our first lessons in the school of waiting. To many a one it will appear strange how difficult it is truly to wait upon God. The great stillness of soul before God that sinks into its own helplessness and waits for Him to reveal Himself; the deep humility that is afraid to let own will or own strength work aught except as God works to will and to do; the meekness that is content to be and to know nothing except as God gives His light; the entire resignation of the will that only wants to be a vessel in which His holy will can move and mold: all these elements of perfect patience are not found at once. But they will come in measure as the soul maintains its position, and ever again says: "Truly my soul waiteth upon God; from HIM cometh my salvation: He only is my rock and my salvation."

Have you ever noticed what proof we have that patience is a grace for which very special grace is given, in these words of Paul: "Strengthened with all might, according to His glorious power, unto all" - what? "patience and long-suffering with joyfulness." Yes, we need to be strengthened with all God's might, and that according to the measure of His glorious power, if we are to wait on God in all patience. It is God revealing Himself in us as our life and strength, that will enable us with perfect patience to leave all in His hands. If any are inclined to despond, because they have not such patience, let them be of good courage; it is in the course of our feeble and very imperfect waiting that God Himself by His hidden power strengthens us and works out in us the patience of the saints, the patience of Christ Himself.

Listen to the voice of one who was deeply tried: "I waited patiently for the Lord, and He inclined unto me, and heard my cry." Hear what he passed through: "He brought me up also out of an horrible pit, out of the miry clay, and set my feet upon a rock, and established my goings. And He hath put a new song in my mouth, even praise unto our God." Patient waiting upon God brings a rich reward; the deliverance is sure; God Himself will put a new song into your mouth. O soul! be not impatient, whether it be in the exercise of prayer and worship that you find it difficult to wait, or in the delay in respect of definite requests, or in the fulfilling of your heart's desire for the revelation of God Himself in a deeper spiritual life - fear not, but rest in the Lord, and wait patiently for Him.

And if you sometimes feel as if patience is not your gift, then remember it is God's gift, and take that prayer (2 Thess. 3:5): "The Lord direct your hearts into the patience of Christ." Into the patience with which you are to wait on God, He Himself will guide you.

"My soul, wait thou only upon God!"

Day 15: WAITING ON GOD: FOR HIS COUNSEL

"They soon forgot His works: they waited not for His counsel." Ps. 106:13.

This is said of the sin of God's people in the wilderness. He had wonderfully redeemed them, and was prepared as wonderfully to supply their every need. But, when the time of need came, "they waited not for His counsel." They thought not that the Almighty God was their Leader and Provider; they asked not what His plans might be. They simply thought the thoughts of their own heart, and tempted and provoked God by their unbelief. "They waited not for His counsel." How this has been the sin of God's people in all ages! In the land of Canaan, in the days of Joshua, the only three failures of which we read were owing to this one sin. In going up against Ai, in making a covenant with the Gibeonites, in settling down without going up to possess the whole land, they waited not for His counsel. And so even the advanced believer is in danger from this most subtle of temptations — taking God's word and thinking his own thoughts of them, and not waiting for His counsel. Let us take the warning and see what Israel teaches us. And let us very specially regard it not only as a danger to which the individual is exposed, but as one against which God's people, in their collective capacity, need to be on their guard.

Our whole relation to God is ruled in this, that His will is to be done in us and by us as it is in heaven. He has promised to make known His will to us by His Spirit, the Guide into all truth. And our position is to be that of waiting for His counsel as the only guide of our thoughts and actions. In our church worship, in our prayer-meetings, in our conventions, in all our gatherings as managers, or directors, or committees, or helpers in any part of the work for God, our first object ought ever to be to ascertain the mind of God. God always works according to the counsel of His will; the more that counsel of His will is sought and found and honored, the more surely and mightily will God do His work for us and through us.

The great danger in all such assemblies is that in our consciousness of having our Bible, and our past experience of God's leading, and our sound creed, and our honest wish to do God's will, we trust in these, and do not realize that with every step we need and may have a heavenly guidance. There may be elements of God's will, application of God's word, experience of the close presence and leading of God, manifestations of the power of His Spirit, of which we know nothing as yet. God may be willing, nay, God is willing to open up these to the souls who are intently set upon allowing Him to have his way entirely, and who are willing in patience to wait for His making it known. When we come together praising God for all He has done and taught and given, we may at the same time be limiting Him by not expecting greater things. It was when God had given the water out of the rock that they did not trust Him for bread. It was when God had given Jericho into his hands that Joshua thought the victory over Ai was sure, and waited not for counsel from God. And so, while we think that we know and trust the power of God for what we may expect, we may be hindering Him by not giving time, and not definitely cultivating the habit of waiting for His counsel.

A minister has no more solemn duty than teaching people to wait upon God. Why was it that in the house of Cornelius, when "Peter spake these words, the Holy Ghost fell upon all that heard him"? They had said, "We are here before God to hear all things that are commanded thee of God." We may come together to give and to listen to the most earnest exposition of God's truth with little spiritual profit if there be not the waiting for God's counsel.

And so in all our gatherings we need to believe in the Holy Spirit as the Guide and Teacher of God's saints when they wait to be led by Him into the things which God hath prepared, and which the heart cannot conceive. More stillness of soul to realize God's presence; more consciousness of ignorance of what God's great plans may be; more faith in the certainty that God has greater things to show us; that He Himself will be revealed in new glory: these must be the marks of the assemblies of God's saints if they would avoid the reproach, "They waited not for His counsel."

"My soul, wait thou only upon God!"

"I wait for the Lord, my soul doth wait, And in His word do I hope. My soul waiteth for the Lord. More than they that watch for the morning: More than they that watch for the morning." Ps. 130:5-6.

With what intense longing the morning light is often waited for. By the mariners in a shipwrecked vessel; by a benighted traveler in a dangerous country; by an army that finds itself surrounded by an enemy. The morning light will show what hope of escape there may be. The morning may bring life and liberty. And so the saints of God in darkness have longed for the light of His countenance, more than watchmen for the morning. They have said, "More than watchmen for the morning, my soul waiteth for the Lord." Can we say that too? Our waiting on God can have no higher object than simply having His light shine on us, and in us, and through us, all the day.

God is Light. God is a Sun. Paul says: "God hath shined in our hearts to give the light," What light? "The light of the glory of God, in the face of Jesus Christ." Just as the sun shines its beautiful, life-giving light on and into our earth, so God shines into our hearts the light of His glory, of His love, in Christ His Son. Our heart is meant to have that light filling and gladdening it all the day. It can have it, because God is our sun, an it is written, "Thy sun shall no more go down for ever." God's love shines on us without ceasing.

But can we indeed enjoy it all the day? We can. And how can we? Let nature give us the answer. Those beautiful trees and flowers, with all this green grass, what do they do to keep the sun shining on them? They do nothing; they simply bask in the sunshine, when it comes. The sun is millions of miles away, but over all that distance it comes, its own light and joy; and the tiniest flower that lifts its little head upwards is met by the same exuberance of light and blessing as flood the widest landscape. We have not to care for the light we need for our day's work; the sun cares, and provides and shines the light around us all the day. We simply count upon it, and receive it, and enjoy it.

The only difference between nature and grace is this, that what the trees and the flowers do unconsciously, as they drink in the blessing of the light, is to be with us a voluntary and a loving acceptance. Faith, simple faith in God's word and love, is to be the opening of the eyes, the opening of the heart, to receive and enjoy the unspeakable glory of His grace. And just as the trees, day by day, and month by month, stand and grow into beauty and fruitfulness, just welcoming whatever sunshine the sun may give, so it is the very highest exercise of our Christian life just to abide in the light of God, and let it, and let Him, fill us with the life and the brightness it brings.

And if you ask, But can it really be, that just as naturally and heartily as I recognize and rejoice in the beauty of a bright sunny morning, I can rejoice in God's light all the day? It can, indeed. From my breakfast-table I look out on a beautiful valley, with trees and vineyards and mountains. In our spring and autumn months the light in the morning is exquisite, and almost involuntarily we say, How beautiful! And the question comes, Is it only the light of the sun that is to bring such continual beauty and joy? And is there no provision for the light of God being just as much an unceasing source of joy and gladness? There is, indeed, if the soul will but be still and wait on Him, ONLY LET GOD SHINE.

Dear soul! learn to wait on the Lord, more than watchers for the morning. All within you may be very dark; is that not the very best reason for waiting for the light of God? The first beginnings of light may be just enough to discover the darkness, and painfully to humble you on account of sin. Can you not trust the light to expel the darkness? Do believe it will. Just bow, even now, in stillness before God, and wait on Him to shine into you. Say, in humble faith, God is light, infinitely brighter and more beautiful than that of the sun. God is light: the Father. The eternal, inaccessible, and incomprehensible light: the Son. The light concentrated, and embodied, and manifested: the Spirit, the light entering and dwelling and shining in our hearts. God is light, and is here shining on my heart. I have been so occupied with the rushlights of my thoughts and efforts. I have never opened the shutters to let His light in. Unbelief has kept it out.

I bow in faith: God, light, is shining into my heart; the God of whom Paul wrote, "God hath shined into our heart," is my God. What would I think of a sun that could not shine? What shall I think of a God that does not shine? No, God shines! God is light! I will take time, and just be still, and rest in the light of God. My eyes are feeble, and the windows are not clean, but I will wait on the Lord. The light does shine, the light will shine in me, and make me full of light. And I shall learn to walk all the day in the light and joy of God. My soul waits on the light of the Lord, more than the watcher for the morning.

"My soul, wait thou only upon God"

"I will wait upon the Lord, that hideth His face from the house of Jacob; and I will look for Him." Isa 8:17.

Here we have a servant of God, waiting upon Him, not on behalf of himself, but of his people, from whom God was hiding His face. It suggests to us how our waiting upon God, though it commences with our personal needs, with the desire for the revelation of Himself, or for the answer to personal petitions, need not, may not, stop there. We may be walking in the full light of God's countenance, and God yet be hiding His face from His people around us; far from being content to think that this is nothing but the just punishment of their sin, or the consequence of their indifference, we are called with tender hearts to think of their sad estate, and to wait on God on their behalf. The privilege of waiting upon God is one that brings great responsibility. Even as Christ, when He entered God's presence, at once used His place of privilege and honor as intercessor, so we, no less, if we know what it is really to enter in and wait upon God, must use our access for our less favored brethren. "I will wait upon the Lord, who hideth His face from the house of Jacob."

You worship with a certain congregation. Possibly there is not the spiritual life or joy either in the preaching or in the fellowship that you could desire. You belong to a Church, with its many congregations. There is so much of error or worldliness, of seeking after human wisdom and culture, or trust in ordinances and observances, that you do not wonder that God hides His face, in many cases, and that there is but little power for conversion or true edification.

Then there are branches of Christian work with which you are connected - a Sunday school, a gospel hall, a young men's association, a mission work abroad - in which the feebleness of the Spirit's working appears to indicate that God is hiding His face. You think, too, you know the reason, There is too much trust in men and money; there is too much formality and self-indulgence; there is too little faith and prayer; too little love and humility; too little of the spirit of the crucified Jesus. At times you feel as if things were hopeless; nothing will help.

Do believe that God can help and will help. Let the spirit of the prophet come into you, as you value his words, and set yourself to wait on God, on behalf of His erring children. Instead of the tone of judgment or condemnation, of despondency or despair, realize your calling to wait upon God. If others fail in doing it, give yourself doubly to it. The deeper the darkness, the greater the need of appealing to the one only Deliverer. The greater the self-confidence around you, that knows not that it is poor and wretched and blind, the more urgent the call on you who profess to see the evil and to have access to Him who alone can help, to be at your post waiting upon God. Say on each new occasion, when you are tempted to speak or to sigh: "I will wait on the Lord, who hideth His face from the house of Jacob."

There is a still larger circle - the Christian Church throughout the world. Think of Greek, Roman Catholic, and Protestant churches, and the state of the millions that belong to them. Or think only of the Protestant churches with their open Bible and orthodox creeds. How much nominal profession and formality, how much of the rule of the flesh and of man in the very temple of God! And what abundant proof that God does hide his face!

What are those who see and mourn this to do? The first thing to be done is this: "I will wait on the Lord, who hideth His face from the house of Jacob." Let us wait on God, in the humble confession of the sins of His people. Let us take time and wait on Him in this exercise. Let us wait on God in tender, loving intercession for all saints, our beloved brethren, however wrong their lives or their teaching may appear. Let us wait on God in faith and expectation, until He shows us that He will hear. Let us wait on God, with the simple offering of ourselves to Himself, and the earnest prayer that He would send us to our brethren. Let us wait on God, and give Him no rest till He makes Zion a joy in the earth.

Yes, let us rest in the Lord, and wait patiently for Him who now hides His face from so many of His children. And let us say of the lifting up of the light of His countenance we long for all His people, "I wait for the Lord, my soul doth wait, and my hope is in His word. My soul waiteth for the Lord, more than the watchers for the morning, the watchers for the morning."

"My soul, wait thou only upon God!"

And it shall be said in that day, Lo, this is our God; we have waited for him, and he will save us: this is the LORD; we have waited for Him, we will be glad and rejoice in his salvation.—Isaiah 25:9

In this passage, we have two precious thoughts. The one, that it is the language of God's people who have been unitedly waiting on Him. The other, that the fruit of their waiting has been that God has so revealed Himself, that they could joyfully say, "Lo, this is our God . . . this is the LORD." The power and the blessing of united waiting is what we need to learn.

Note that this phrase is repeated twice, "We have waited for him." In some time of trouble, the hearts of the people had been drawn together, and they had, ceasing from all human hope or help, with one heart set themselves to wait for their God. Is this not just what we need in our churches and conventions and prayer meetings? Is not the need of the church and the world great enough to demand it? Are there not in the church of Christ evils to which no human wisdom is equal? Have we not ritualism and rationalism, formalism and worldliness, robbing the church of its power? Have we not culture and money and pleasure threatening its spiritual life? Are not the powers of the church utterly inadequate to cope with the powers of infidelity and iniquity and wretchedness in Christian countries and in heathendom? And, is there not, in the promise of God and in the power of the Holy Spirit, a provision made that can meet the need and give the church the restful assurance that she is doing all her God expects of her? And would not united waiting upon God for the supply of His Spirit most certainly seem the needed blessing? We cannot doubt it.

The object of a more definite waiting upon God in our gatherings would be very much the same as in personal worship. It would mean a deeper conviction that God must and will do all. It would require a more humble and abiding entrance into our deep helplessness, and the need of entire and unceasing dependence upon Him. We need a more living consciousness that the essential thing is to give God His place of honor and of power. We must have a confident expectation that to those who wait on Him, God will, by His Spirit, give the secret of His acceptance and presence, and then, in due time, the revelation of His saving power. The great aim would be to bring everyone in a praying and worshiping company under a deep sense of God's presence, so that when they part there will be the consciousness of having met God Himself, of having left every request with Him, and of now waiting in stillness while He works out His salvation.

It is this experience that is indicated in our text. The fulfillment of the words may, at times, be in such striking interpositions of God's power that all can join in the cry, "Lo, this is our God . . . this is the LORD." They may equally become true in spiritual experience, when God's people, in their waiting times, become so conscious of His presence that, in holy awe, souls feel, "Lo, this is our God . . . this is the LORD." It is this, alas, that is too much missed in our meetings for worship. The godly minister has no more difficult, no more solemn, no more blessed task, than to lead his people out to meet God. And, before he preaches, he must bring each one into contact with Him. "We are now here in the presence of God"—these words of Cornelius show the way in which Peter's audience was prepared for the coming of the Holy Spirit. Waiting before God, waiting for God, and waiting on God are the conditions of God showing His presence.

A company of believers gathered with the one purpose, helping each other by little intervals of silence, to wait on God alone, opening the heart for whatever God may have of new discoveries of evil, of His will, of new openings in work or methods of work, would soon have reason to say, "Lo, this is our God; we have waited for him, and he will save us: this is the LORD; we have waited for him, we will be glad and rejoice in his salvation."

My soul, wait thou only upon God!

Yea, in the way of thy judgments, 0 LORD, have we waited for thee . .
. For when thy judgments are in the earth, the inhabitants of the world
will learn righteousness.—Isaiah 26:8–9

The LORD is a God of judgment: blessed are all they that wait upon
him.—Isaiah 30:18

God is a God of mercy and a God of judgment. Mercy and judgment
are forever together in His dealings. In the Flood, in the deliverance of
Israel out of Egypt, in the overthrow of the Canaanites, we ever see
mercy in the midst of judgment. I n these, the inner circle of His own
people, we see it, too. The judgment punishes the sin, while mercy
saves the sinner. Or, rather, mercy saves the sinner, not in spite of, but
by means of, the very judgment that came upon his sin. In waiting on
God, we must beware of forgetting this—as we wait we must expect
Him as a God of judgment.

"In the way of thy judgments, 0 LORD, have we waited for thee." That
will prove true in our inner experience. If we are honest in our longing
for holiness—in our prayers to be wholly the Lord's—His holy
presence will stir up and discover hidden sin. It, will bring us very low
in the bitter conviction of the evil of our nature, its opposition to God's
law, and its inability to fulfill that law. The words will come true:
"Who may abide the day of his coming? . . . For he is like a refiner's
fire" (Mal. 3:2). "Oh that thou wouldest . . . come down . . . As when
the melting fire burneth" (Isa. 64:1). In great mercy, God executes,
within the soul, His judgments upon sin, as He makes it feel its
wickedness and guilt. Many try to flee from these judgments. The soul
that longs for God, and for deliverance from sin, bows under them in
humility and in hope. In silence of soul, it says, "Rise up, LORD, and
let thine enemies be scattered" (Num. 10:35). "In the way of thy
judgments . . . have we waited for thee."

Let no one who seeks to learn the blessed art of waiting on God,
wonder if at first the attempt to wait on Him only reveals more of sin
and darkness. Let no one despair because unconquered sins, evil
thoughts, or great darkness appear to hide God's face. Was not, in His
own beloved Son, the gift and bearer of His mercy on Calvary, the
mercy as hidden and lost in the judgment? Oh, submit and sink down
deep under the judgment of your every sin. Judgment prepares the way
and breaks out in wonderful mercy. It is written, "Zion shall be
redeemed with judgment" (Isa. 1:27). Wait on God, in the faith that His
tender mercy is working out His redemption in the midst of judgment.
Wait for Him; He will be gracious to you.

There is another application still, one of unspeakable solemnity. We are expecting God, in the way of His judgments, to visit his earth; we are waiting for Him. What a thought! We know of these coming judgments. We know that there are tens of thousands of professing Christians who live on in carelessness, and who, if no change comes, must perish under God's hand. Oh, will we not do our utmost to warn them, to plead with and for them, if God may lave mercy on them! If we feel our lack of boldness, zeal, and cower, will we not begin to wait on God more definitely and persistently as a God of judgment? Will we not ask Him to so reveal Himself in the judgments that are coming on our very friends, that we may be inspired with a new fear of Him and them, and constrained to speak and pray as never yet before? Verily, waiting on God is not leant to be a spiritual self-indulgence. Its object is to let God and His holiness, Christ and the love that died on Calvary, the Spirit and fire that burns in heaven and came to earth, get possession of us to warn and arouse men with the message that we are waiting for God in the way of His judgments. Oh, Christian, prove that you really believe in the God of judgment!

My soul, wait thou only upon God!

And therefore will the LORD wait, that he may be gracious unto you, and therefore will He be exalted, that he may have mercy upon you: for the LORD is a God of judgment: blessed are all they that wait for him.—Isaiah 30:18

We must not only think of our waiting upon God, but also of what is more wonderful still, of God's waiting upon us. The vision of Him waiting on us will give new impulse and inspiration to our waiting upon Him. It will give us an unspeakable confidence that our waiting cannot be in vain. If He waits for us, then we may be sure that we are more than welcome—that He rejoices to find those He has been seeking for. Let us seek even now, at this moment, in the spirit of lowly waiting on God, to find out, something of what it means. "Therefore will the LORD wait, that he may be gracious unto you." We will accept and echo back the message, "Blessed are all they that wait for him." Look up and see the great God upon His throne. He is love an unceasing and inexpressible desire to communicate His own goodness and blessedness to all His creatures. He longs and delights to bless. He has inconceivably glorious purposes concerning every one of His children, by the power of His Holy Spirit, to reveal in them His love and power. He waits with all the longings of a father's heart. He waits that He may be gracious unto you. And, each time you come to wait upon Him, or seek to maintain in daily life the holy habit of waiting, you may look up and see Him ready to meet you. He will be waiting so that He may be gracious unto you. Yes, connect every exercise, every breath of the life of waiting, with faith's vision of your God waiting for you.

And if you ask: How is it, if He waits to be gracious, that even after I come and wait upon Him, He does not give the help I seek, but waits on longer and longer? There is a double answer. The one is this. God is a wise husbandman, who "waiteth for the precious fruit of the earth, and hath long patience for it (James 5:7). He cannot gather the fruit until it is ripe. He knows when we are spiritually ready to receive the blessing to our profit and His glory. Waiting in the sunshine of His love is what will ripen the soul for His blessing. Waiting under the cloud of trial, that breaks in showers of blessing, is as necessary. Be assured that if God waits longer than you could wish, it is only to make the blessing doubly precious. God waited four thousand years, until the fullness of time, before He sent His Son. Our times are in His hands. He will avenge His elect speedily. He will make haste for our help and not delay one hour too long.

The other answer points to what has been said before. The giver is more than the gift; God is more than the blessing. And our being kept waiting on Him is the only way for our learning to find our life and joy in Himself. Oh, if God's children only knew what a glorious God they have, and what a privilege it is to be linked in fellowship with Him, then they would rejoice in Him! Even when He keeps them waiting, they will learn to understand better than ever. "Therefore will the LORD wait, that he may be gracious unto you." His waiting will be the highest proof of His graciousness.

"Blessed are all they that wait for him." A queen has her ladies-in-waiting. The position is one of subordination and service, and yet it is considered one of the highest dignity and privilege, because a wise and gracious sovereign makes them companions and friends. What a dignity and blessedness to be attendants-in-waiting on the everlasting God, ever on the watch for every indication of His will or favor, ever conscious of His nearness, His goodness, and His grace! "The LORD is good unto them that wait for him" (Lam. 3:25). "Blessed are all they that wait for him." Yes, it is blessed when a waiting soul and a waiting God meet each other. God cannot do His work without His and our waiting His time. Let waiting be our work, as it is His. And, if His waiting is nothing but goodness and graciousness, let ours be nothing but a rejoicing in that goodness, and a confident expectancy of that grace. And, let every thought of waiting become to us the simple expression of unmingled and unutterable blessedness, because it brings us to a God who waits that He may make Himself known to us perfectly as the gracious One.

My soul, wait thou only upon God!

They that wait upon the LORD shall renew their strength; they shall mount up with wings as eagles; they shall run, and not be weary; and they shall walk, and not faint.—Isaiah 40:31

Our waiting on God will depend greatly on our faith of what He is. In our text, we have the close of a passage in which God reveals Himself as the everlasting and almighty One. It is as that revelation enters into our soul that the waiting will become the spontaneous expression of what we know Him to be--a God altogether most worthy to be waited upon.

Listen to the words, "Why sayest thou, 0 Jacob . . . My way is hid from the LORD . . .? Hast thou not known? hast thou not heard, that the everlasting God, the LORD, the Creator of the ends of the earth, fainteth not, neither is weary?" (Isa. 40:27-28). So far from it: "He giveth power to the faint; and to them that have no might he increaseth strength. Even the youths shall faint . . . and the young men shall utterly fall" (vv. 29-30). And consider that "the glory of young men is their strength" (Prov. 20:29). All that is deemed strong with man shall come to nothing. "But they that wait upon the LORD," on the Everlasting One, who does not faint, and is not weary, they "shall renew their strength; they shall mount up with wings as eagles; they shall run, and"—listen now, they will be strong with the strength of God, and, even as He, they will "not be weary; and they shall walk, and" even as He, they will "not faint."

Yes, "they shall mount up with wings as eagles." You know what eagles' wings mean. The eagle is the king of birds; it soars the highest into the heavens. Believers are to live a heavenly life, in the very presence and love and joy of God. They are to live where God lives; they need God's strength to rise there. It will be given to them that wait on Him.

You know how the eagles' wings are obtained. Only in one way—by the eagle birth. You are born of God. You have the eagles' wings. You may not have known it; you may not have used them; but God can and will teach you how to use them.

You know how the eagles are taught the use of their wings. See yonder cliff rising a thousand feet out of the sea. See high up a ledge on the rock, where there is an eagle's nest with its treasure of two young eaglets. See the mother bird come and stir up her nest, and with her beak push the timid birds over the precipice. See how they flutter and fall and sink toward the depth. See now how she "fluttereth over her young, spreadeth abroad her wings, taketh them, beareth them on her wings" (Deut. 32:11), and so, as they ride upon her wings, brings them to a place of safety. And so, she does this once and again, each time casting them out over the precipice, and then again taking and carrying them. "So the LORD alone did lead him" (v. 12). Yes, the instinct of that eagle mother was God's gift, a single ray of that love in which the Almighty trains His people to mount as on eagles' wings.

He stirs up your nest. He disappoints your hopes. He brings down your confidence. He makes you fear and tremble, as all your strength fails, and you feel utterly weary and helpless. And all the while He is spreading His strong wings for you to rest your weakness on and offering His everlasting Creator strength to work in you. And all He asks is that you sink down in your weariness and wait on Him. Allow Him in His Jehovah strength to carry you as you ride upon the wings of His omnipotence.

Dear child of God, I pray you, lift up your eyes, and behold your God! Listen to Him who says that He "fainteth not, neither is weary" (Isa. 40:28), who promises that you too will not faint or be weary, who asks nothing but this one thing, that you should wait on Him. And, let your answer be, With such a God, so mighty, so faithful, so tender,
My soul, wait thou only upon God!

Thou shalt know that I am the LORD: for they shall not be ashamed that wait for me.—Isaiah 49:23

Blessed are all they that wait for him.—Isaiah 30:18

What promises! How God seeks to draw us to waiting on Him by the most positive assurance that it never can be in vain; "they shall not be ashamed that wait for me." How strange that, though we should so often have experienced it, we are yet so slow to learn that this blessed waiting must and can be the very breath of our life—a continuous resting in God's presence and His love, an unceasing yielding of ourselves for Him to perfect His work in us. Let us once again listen and meditate, until our heart says with new conviction, "Blessed are all they that wait for him."

We found in the prayer of Psalm 25: "Let none that wait on thee be ashamed"(v. 3). The very prayer shows how we fear that it might be true. Let us listen to God's answer, until every fear is banished, and we send back to heaven the words God speaks, Yes, Lord, we believe what You say: "All they who wait for Me will not be ashamed." "Blessed are all they that wait for him."

The context of each of these two passages points us to times when God's church was in great straits, and to human eyes there were no possibilities of deliverance. But, God interposes with His word of promise, and pledges His almighty power for the deliverance of His people. And it is as the God who has Himself undertaken the work of their redemption that He invites them to wait on Him, and assures them that disappointment is impossible.

We, too, are living in days in which there is much in the state of the church, with its profession and its formalism, that is indescribably sad. Amid all we praise God for, there is, alas, much to mourn over! Were it not for God's promises, we might well despair. But, in His promises the living God has given and bound Himself to us. He calls us to wait on Him. He assures us we will not be put to shame. Oh, that our hearts might learn to wait before Him, until He Himself reveals to us what His promises mean. In the promises, He reveals Himself in His hidden glory! We will be irresistibly drawn to wait on Him alone. May God increase the company of those who say: "Our soul waiteth for the LORD: he is our help and our shield" (Ps. 33:20).

This waiting upon God on behalf of His church and people will depend greatly upon the place that waiting on Him has taken in our personal life. The mind may often have beautiful visions of what God has promised to do, and the lips may speak of them in stirring words, but these are not really the measure of our faith or power. No, it is what we really know of God in our personal experience, conquering the enemies within, reigning and ruling, revealing Himself in His holiness and power in our innermost being. It is this that will be the real measure of the spiritual blessing we expect from Him, and bring to our fellow men. It is as we know how blessed the waiting on God has become to our own souls, that we will confidently hope in the blessing to come on the church around us. The keyword of all our expectations will be, He has said: "All they who wait on Me will not be ashamed." From what He has done in us, we will trust Him to do mighty things around us. "Blessed are all they that wait for him." Yes, blessed even now in the waiting. The promised blessings for ourselves, or for others, may tarry. The unutterable blessedness of knowing and having Him who has promised—the divine Blesser, the living Fountain of the coming blessings—is even now ours. Do let this truth acquire full possession of your souls, that waiting on God is itself the highest privilege of man, the highest blessedness of His redeemed child.

Even as the sunshine enters with its light and warmth, with its beauty and blessing, into every little blade of grass that rises upward out of the cold earth, so the everlasting God meets, in the greatness and the tenderness of His love, each waiting child, to shine in his heart "the light of the knowledge of the glory of God in the face of Jesus Christ" (2 Cor. 4:6). Read these words again, until your heart learns to know what God waits to do to you. Who can measure the difference between the great sun and that little blade of grass? And yet, the grass has all of the sun it can need or hold.

Do believe that in waiting on God, His greatness and your littleness suit and meet each other most wonderfully. Just bow in emptiness and poverty and utter weakness, in humility and meekness, and surrender to His will before His great glory, and be still. As you wait on Him, God draws near. He will reveal Himself as the God who will mightily fulfill His every promise. And, let your heart continually take up the song: "Blessed are all they that wait for him."

My soul, wait thou only upon God

For since the beginning of the world men have not heard, nor perceived by the ear, neither hath the eye seen, 0 God, beside thee, what he hath prepared for him that waiteth for him—Isaiah 64:4

The American Standard Version has the thought: "Neither hath the eye seen a God besides thee, who worketh for him that waiteth for him." In the King James Version, the thought is that no eye has seen the thing that God has prepared. In the American Standard Version, no eye has seen a God, besides our God, who works for him who waits for Him. To both, the two thoughts are common: that our place is to wait upon God, and that what the human heart cannot conceive will be revealed to us. The difference is the following: in the American Standard Version, it is the God who works; in the King James Version, the thing He is to work. In 1 Corinthians 2:9, "But as it is written, Eye hath not seen, nor ear heard, neither have entered into the heart of man, the things which God hath prepared for them that love him," the reference is in regard to the things that the Holy Spirit is to reveal, as in the King James Version, and in this chapter we will keep to that.

The previous verses in Isaiah, especially Isaiah 63:15, refer to the low state of God's people. The prayer has been poured out, "Look down from heaven" (v. 15). "Why hast thou . . . hardened our heart from thy fear? Return for thy servants' sake" (v. 17). And 64:1-2, still more urgent, "Oh that thou wouldest rend the heavens, that thou wouldest come down . . . as when the melting fire burneth . . . to make thy name known to thine adversaries!" Then follows the plea from the past, "When thou didst terrible things which we looked not for, thou camest down, the mountains flowed down at thy presence" (v. 3). "For"—this is now the faith that has been awakened by the thought of things we looked not for, He is still the same God—"neither hath the eye seen, 0 God, beside thee, what he hath prepared for him that waiteth for him." God alone knows what He can do for His waiting people. As Paul expounds and applies it: "The things of God knoweth no man, but the Spirit of God" (1 Cor. 2:11). "But God hath revealed them unto us by his Spirit" (v. 10).

The need of God's people, and the call for God's intervention, is as urgent in our days as it was in the time of Isaiah. There is now, as there was then, as there has been at all times, a few who seek after God with their whole hearts. But, if we look at Christendom as a whole, at the state of the church of Christ, there is infinite cause for beseeching God to rend the heavens and come down. Nothing but a special interposition of almighty power will avail. I fear we do not have a proper conception of what the so-called Christian world is in the sight of God. Unless God comes down "as when the melting fire burneth . . . to make [His] name known to [His] adversaries" (Isa. 64:2), our labors are comparatively fruitless.

Look at the ministry: how much it is in the wisdom of man and of literary culture; how little in demonstration of the Spirit and of power. Think of the unity of the body: how little there is of the manifestation of the power of a heavenly love binding God's children into one. Think of holiness—the holiness of Christlike humility and crucifixion to the world. How little the world sees that they have men among them who live in Christ in heaven, in whom Christ and heaven live.

What is to be done? There is only one thing. We must wait upon God. And what for? We must cry, with a cry that never rests, "Oh that thou wouldest rend the heavens . . . [and] come down, that the mountains might flow down at thy presence" (Isa. 64:1). We must desire and believe, we must ask and expect, that God will do unlooked-for things. We must set our faith on a God of whom men do not know what He has prepared for them who wait for Him. The wonder-doing God, who can surpass all our expectations, must be the God of our confidence. Yes, let God's people enlarge their hearts to wait on a God able to do exceeding abundantly above what we can ask or think (Eph. 3:20). Let us band ourselves together as His elect who cry day and night to Him for things men have not seen. He is able to arise and to make His people a name and a praise in the earth. "The LORD will wait, that he may be gracious unto you . . . blessed are all they that wait for him" (Isa. 30:18).

My soul, wait thou only upon God!

_____

The LORD is good unto them that wait for him.—Lamentations 3:25

There is none good but God (Matt. 19:17). His goodness is in the heavens. "Oh how great is thy goodness, which thou hast laid up for them that fear thee" (Ps. 31:19). "0 taste and see that the LORD is good" (Ps. 34:8). And here is now the true way of entering into and rejoicing in this goodness of God—waiting upon Him. The Lord is good—even His children often do not know it, for they do not wait in quietness for Him to reveal it. But, to those who persevere in waiting, whose souls do wait, it will come true. One might think that it is just those who have to wait who might doubt it. But, this is only when they do not wait, but grow impatient. The truly waiting ones will all say, "The LORD is good unto them that wait for him." If you want to fully know the goodness of God, give yourself more than ever to a life of waiting on Him.

At our first entrance into the school of waiting upon God, the heart is mainly set on the blessings which we wait for. God graciously uses our needs and desires for help to educate us for something higher than we were thinking of. We were seeking gifts; He, the Giver, longs to give Himself and to satisfy the soul with His goodness. It is just for this reason that He often withholds the gifts, and that the time of waiting is made so long. He is constantly seeking to win the heart of His child for Himself. He wishes that we would not only say, when He bestows the gift, "How good is God!" but that long before it comes, and even if it never comes, we should all the time be experiencing: it is good that a man should quietly wait. "The LORD is good unto them that wait for him."

What a blessed life the life of waiting then becomes, the continual worship of faith, adoring, and trusting His goodness. As the soul learns its secret, every act or exercise of waiting becomes just a quiet entering into the goodness of God, to let it do its blessed work and satisfy our every need. And, every experience of God's goodness gives new attractiveness to the work of waiting. Instead of only taking refuge in time of need, there comes a great longing to wait continually and all day. And, however duties and engagements occupy the time and the mind, the soul gets more familiar with the secret art of always waiting. Waiting becomes the habit and disposition, the very second nature and breath of the soul.

Dear Christian, begin to see that waiting is not one among a number of Christian virtues, to be thought of from time to time. But, it expresses that disposition that lies at the very root of the Christian life. It gives a higher value and a new power to our prayers and worship, to our faith and surrender, because it links us, in unalterable dependence, to God

Himself. And, it gives us the unbroken enjoyment of the goodness of God: "The LORD is good unto them that wait for him."

Let me stress once again that you must take time and trouble to cultivate this much needed element of the Christian life. We get too much secondhand religion from the teaching of men. That teaching has great value, even as the preaching of John the Baptist sent his disciples away from himself to the living Christ, if it leads us to God Himself. What our faith needs is—more of God.

Many of us are too occupied with our work. As with Martha, the very service we want to render the Master separates us from Him. It is neither pleasing to Him nor profitable to ourselves. The more work, the more need of waiting upon God. The doing of God's will would then be, instead of exhausting, our meat and drink, our nourishment and refreshment and strength. "The LORD is good unto them that wait for him." How good is known only by those who prove it in waiting on Him. How good none can fully tell but those who have proved Him to the utmost.

My soul, wait thou only upon God!

It is good that a man should both hope and quietly wait for the salvation of the LORD - Lamentations 3:26

Take heed, and be quiet; fear not, neither be fainthearted" (Isa. 7:4). "In quietness and in confidence shall be your strength" (Isa. 30:15). Such words reveal to us the close connection between quietness and faith. They show us what a deep need there is of quietness, as an element of true waiting upon God. If we are to have our whole heart turned toward God, we must have it turned away from man, from all that occupies and interests, whether of joy or sorrow.

God is a being of such infinite greatness and glory, and our nature has become so estranged from Him, that it requires our whole heart and desires set upon Him, even in some little measure, to know and receive Him. Everything that is not God, that excites our fears or stirs our efforts or awakens our hopes or makes us glad, hinders us in our perfect waiting on Him. The message is one of deep meaning: "Take heed, and be quiet"; "In quietness...shall be your strength"; "It is good that a man should . . . quietly wait."

Scripture abundantly testifies how the very thought of God in His majesty and holiness should silence us: "The LORD is in his holy temple: let all the earth keep silence before him" (Hab. 2:20); "Hold thy peace at the presence of the Lord GOD" (Zeph. 1:7); "Be silent, 0 all flesh, before the LORD: for he is raised up out of his holy habitation" (Zech. 2:13).

As long as the waiting on God is chiefly regarded as an end toward more effectual prayer, and the obtaining of our petitions, this spirit of perfect quietness will not be obtained. But, when it is seen that waiting on God is itself an unspeakable blessedness—one of the highest forms of fellowship with the Holy One—the adoration of Him in His glory will of necessity humble the soul into a holy stillness, making way for God to speak and reveal Himself. Then, it comes to the fulfillment of the precious promise, that all of self and self-effort will be humbled: "The haughtiness of men shall be bowed down, and the LORD alone shall be exalted in that day" (Isa. 2:11).

Let everyone who wants to learn the art of waiting on God remember the lesson, "Take heed, and be quiet" (Isa. 7:4). "It is good that a man . . . quietly wait." Take time to be separate from all friends and all duties, all cares and all joys; time to be still and quiet before God. Take time not only to secure stillness from man and the world, but from self and its energy. Let the Word and prayer be very precious. But remember, even these may hinder the quiet waiting. The activity of the mind in studying the Word or giving expression to its thoughts in prayer, the activities of the heart, with its desires and hopes and fears, may so engage us that we do not come to the still waiting on the All-glorious One; our whole being is prostrate in silence before Him.

Though at first it may appear difficult to know how thus quietly to wait, with the activities of mind and heart for a time subdued, every effort after it will be rewarded. We will discover that it grows upon us, and the little season of silent worship will bring a peace and a rest that give a blessing not only in prayer, but all day.

"It is good that a man should . . . quietly wait for the salvation of the LORD." Yes, it is good. The quietness is the confession of our meekness. It will not be done with all our willing and running (Rom. 9:16), with all our thinking and praying. We must receive it from God. It is the confession of our trust that our God will, in His time, come to our help—the quiet resting in Him alone. It is the confession of our desire to sink into our nothingness and to let Him work and reveal Himself. Do let us wait quietly. In daily life, let there be, in the soul that is waiting for the great God to do His wondrous work, a quiet reverence, an abiding watching against too deep engrossment with the world. Then, the whole character will come to bear the beautiful stamp—quietly waiting for the salvation of God.

My soul, wait thou only upon God!

_____

Therefore I will look unto the LORD; I will wait for the God of my salvation: my God will hear me—Micah 7:7

Have you ever heard of a little book, "Expectation Corners"? It tells of a king who prepared a city for some of his poor subjects. Not far from them were large storehouses, where everything they could need was supplied if they sent in their requests. But, on one condition—that they should be on the lookout for the answer, so that when the king's messengers came with the answer to their petitions, they should always be found waiting and ready to receive them. The sad story is told of one desponding person who never expected to get what he asked, because he was too unworthy. One day, he was taken to the king's storehouses, and there, to his amazement, he saw, with his address on them, all the packages that had been made up for him and sent. There was the garment of praise and the oil of joy and the eye salve and so much more. They had been to his door but found it closed; he was not on the lookout. From that time on, he learned the lesson Micah would teach us today. "I will look unto the LORD; I will wait for the God of my salvation: my God will hear me."

We have said more than once: waiting for the answer to prayer is not the whole of waiting, but only a part. Today, I want to take in the blessed truth that it is a part, and a very important one. When we have special petitions, in connection with which we are waiting on God, our waiting must be very definitely in the confident assurance, "My God will hear me."

A holy, joyful expectancy is of the very essence of true waiting. And, this is not only true in reference to the many varied requests every believer has to make, but most especially to the one great petition which ought to be the chief thing every heart seeks for itself—that the life of God in the soul may have full sway, that Christ may be fully formed within, and that we may be filled to all the fullness of God. This is what God has promised. This is what God's people too little seek, very often because they do not believe it possible. This is what we ought to seek and dare to expect, because God is able and waiting to work it in us.

But, God Himself must work it. And for this end our working must cease. We must see how entirely it is to be the faith of the operation of God, who raised Jesus from the dead. Just as much as the resurrection, the perfecting of God's life in our souls is to be directly His work. And, waiting has to become, more than ever, a tarrying before God in stillness of soul, counting upon Him who raises the dead and calls the things that are not as though they were (Rom. 4:17).

Just notice how the threefold use of the name of God in our text points us to Himself as the one from whom alone is our expectation. "I will look unto the LORD; I will wait for the God of my salvation: my God will hear me." Everything that is salvation, everything that is good and holy, must be the direct, mighty work of God Himself within us. In every moment of a life in the will of God, there must be the immediate operation of God. And, the one thing I have to do is this: to look to the Lord, to wait for the God of my salvation, to hold fast the confident assurance, "my God will hear me."

God says, "Be still, and know that I am God" (Ps. 46:10).

There is no stillness like that of the grave. In the grave of Jesus, in the fellowship of His death, in death to self with its own will and wisdom, its own strength and energy—there is rest. As we cease from self and our soul becomes still to God, God will arise and show Himself. "Be still, and know"; then you will know "that I am God." There is no stillness like the stillness Jesus gives when He speaks. "Peace, be still" (Mark 4:39). In Christ, in His death, in His life, in His perfected redemption, the soul may be still, and God will come in, take possession, and do His perfect work.

My soul, be thou still only unto God!

"Simeon . . . was just and devout, waiting for the consolation of Israel: and the Holy Ghost was upon him. . . Anna, a prophetess . . . spoke of him to all them that looked for redemption in Jerusalem" —Luke 2:25, 36, 38.

Here we have the mark of a waiting believer. "Just," righteous in all his conduct; "devout," devoted to God, ever walking as in His presence; "waiting for the consolation of Israel," looking for the fulfillment of God's promises: "and the Holy Ghost was upon him." In the devout waiting, he had been prepared for the blessing. And Simeon was not the only one. Anna spoke to all who looked for redemption in Jerusalem. This was the one mark, amid surrounding formalism and worldliness, of a godly band of men and women in Jerusalem. They were waiting on God, looking for His promised redemption.

And now that the consolation of Israel has come, and the redemption has been accomplished, do we still need to wait? We do indeed. But, will not our waiting, who look back to it as come, differ greatly from those who looked forward to it as coming? It will, especially in two aspects. We now wait on God in the full power of the redemption, and we wait for its full revelation.

Our waiting is now in the full power of the redemption. Christ said, "In that day you will know that you are in Me. Abide in Me." The Epistles teach us to present ourselves to God as "dead indeed unto sin, but alive unto God through Jesus Christ" (Rom. 6:11), "blessed... with all spiritual blessings in heavenly places in Christ" (Eph. 1:3). Our waiting on God may now be in the wonderful consciousness maintained by the Holy Spirit within us, that we are accepted in the Beloved, that the love that rests on Him rests on us, that we are living in that love, in the very nearness and presence and sight of God.

The old saints took their stand on the Word of God, and waiting, hoping on that Word, we rest on the Word, too—but, oh, under what exceedingly greater privileges, as one with Christ Jesus! In our waiting on God, let this be our confidence: in Christ we have access to the Father. How sure, therefore, we may be that our waiting cannot be in vain.

Our waiting differs, too, in this, that while they waited for a redemption to come, we see it accomplished and now wait for its revelation in us. Christ not only said, "Abide in me" (John 15:4), but also "I in you" (v. 4). The Epistles not only speak of us in Christ, but of Christ in us, as the highest mystery of redeeming love. As we maintain our place in Christ day by day, God waits to reveal Christ in us in such a way that He is formed in us, that His mind and disposition and likeness acquire form and substance in us, so that by each it can in truth be said, "Christ liveth in me" (Gal. 2:20).

My life in Christ up there in heaven and Christ's life in me down here on earth—these two are the complement of each other. And, the more my waiting on God is marked by the living faith, I in Christ, the more the heart thirsts for and claims the Christ in me. The waiting on God, which began with special needs and prayer, will increasingly be concentrated, as far as our personal life is concerned, on this one thing: Lord, reveal Your redemption fully in me; let Christ live in me.

Our waiting differs from that of the old saints in the place we take, and the expectations we entertain. But, at root it is the same: waiting on God, from whom alone is our expectation.

Learn one lesson from Simeon and Anna. How utterly impossible it was for them to do anything toward the great redemption—toward the birth of Christ or His death. It was God's work. They could do nothing but wait. Are we as absolutely helpless in regard to the revelation of Christ in us? We are indeed. God did not work out the great redemption in Christ as a whole and leave its application in detail to us.

The secret thought that it is so is the root of all our feebleness. The revelation of Christ in every individual believer, and in each one the daily revelation, step by step and moment by moment, is as much the work of God's omnipotence as the birth or resurrection of Christ. Until this truth enters and fills us, and we feel that we are just as dependent upon God for each moment of our life in the enjoyment of redemption as they were in their waiting for it, our waiting upon God will not bring its full blessing. The sense of utter and absolute helplessness, the confidence that God can and will do all, are the marks of our waiting as of theirs. As gloriously as God proved Himself to them the faithful and wonder-working God, He will to us, too.

My soul, wait thou only upon God!

"[Be] ye yourselves like unto men that wait for their lord."—Luke 12:36. "Until the appearing of our Lord Jesus Christ: which in its own times he shall show, who is the blessed and only Potentate, the King of kings, and Lord of lords."—1 Timothy 6:14-15 (ASV). "Turned to God from idols to serve the living and true God; and to wait for his Son from heaven."—1 Thessalonians 1:9-10

Waiting on God in heaven, and waiting for His Son from heaven— these two God has joined together, and no man may put them asunder. The waiting on God for His presence and power in daily life will be the only true preparation for waiting for Christ in humility and true holiness. The waiting for Christ coming from heaven to take us to heaven will give the waiting on God its true tone of hopefulness and joy. The Father, who, in His own time, will reveal His Son from heaven, is the God who, as we wait on Him, prepares us for the revelation of His Son. The present life and the coming glory are inseparably connected in God and in us.

There is sometimes a danger of separating them. It is always easier to be engaged with the Christianity of the past or the future than to be faithful in the Christianity of today. As we look to what God has done in the past, or will do in time to come, the personal claim of present duty and present submission to His working may be avoided. Waiting on God must always lead to waiting for Christ as the glorious consummation of His work. And, waiting for Christ must always remind us of the duty of waiting upon God as our only proof that the waiting for Christ is in spirit and in truth.

There is such a danger of our being more occupied with the things that are coming than with Him who is to come. There is such scope in the study of coming events for imagination and reason and human ingenuity, that nothing but deeply humble waiting on God can save us from mistaking the interest and pleasure of intellectual study for the true love of Him and His appearing. All you who say you wait for Christ's coming, be sure that you wait on God now. All you who seek to wait on God now to reveal His Son in you, see to it that you do so as men waiting for the revelation of His Son from heaven. The hope of that glorious appearing will strengthen you in waiting upon God for what He is to do in you now. The same omnipotent love that is to reveal that glory is working in you even now to prepare you for it.

"The blessed hope and appearing of the glory of the great God and our Saviour Jesus Christ" (Titus 2:13 ASV), is one of the great bonds of union given to God's church throughout the ages. "He shall come to be glorified in his saints, and to be marveled at in all them that believed"

(2 Thess. 1:10 ASV). Then, we will all meet, and the unity of the body of Christ will be seen in its divine glory. It will be the meeting place and the triumph of divine love. Jesus receiving His own and presenting them to the Father. His own meeting Him and worshiping, in speechless love, that blessed face. His own meeting each other in the ecstasy of God's own love. Let us wait, long for, and love the appearing of our Lord and heavenly Bridegroom. Tender love to Him and tender love to each other is the true and only bridal spirit.

I am very afraid that this is sometimes forgotten. A beloved brother in Holland was speaking about the expectancy of faith being the true sign of the bride. I ventured to express a doubt. An unworthy bride, about to be married to a prince, might only be thinking of the position and the riches that she was to receive. The expectancy of faith might be strong and true love utterly lacking. It is not when we are most occupied with prophetic subjects, but when in humility and love we are clinging close to our Lord and His followers, that we are in the bride's place. Jesus refuses to accept our love except as it is love to His disciples. Waiting for His coming means waiting for the glorious coming manifestation of the unity of the body, while we seek here to maintain that unity in humility and love. Those who love most are the most ready for His coming. Love to each other is the life and beauty of His bride, the church.

And how is this to be brought about? Beloved child of God, if you want to learn how to properly wait for His Son from heaven, live even now waiting on God in heaven. Remember how Jesus lived ever waiting on God. He could do nothing of Himself. It was God who perfected His Son through suffering and then exalted Him. It is God alone who can give you the deep spiritual life of one who is really waiting for His Son: wait on God for it. Waiting for Christ Himself is so different from waiting for things that may come to pass! The latter any Christian can do; the former, God must work in you every day by His Holy Spirit. Therefore, all you who wait on God, look to Him for grace to wait for His Son from heaven in the Spirit which is from heaven. And, you who want to wait for His Son, wait on God continually to reveal Christ in you.

The revelation of Christ in us, as it is given to them who wait upon God, is the true preparation for the full revelation of Christ in glory. My soul, wait thou only upon God!

"He charged them not to depart from Jerusalem, but to wait for the promise of the Father." Acts1:4 ASV

In speaking of the saints in Jerusalem at Christ's birth—with Simeon and Anna—we saw how the call to waiting is no less urgent now, though the redemption they waited for has come, than it was then. We wait for the full revelation in us of what came to them, but what they could scarcely comprehend. In the same way, it is with waiting for the promise of the Father. In one sense, the fulfillment can never come again as it came at Pentecost. In another sense, and that in as deep a reality as with the first disciples, we need to wait daily for the Father to fulfill His promise in us.

The Holy Spirit is not a person distinct from the Father in the way two persons on earth are distinct. The Father and the Spirit are never without or separate from each other. The Father is always in the Spirit; the Spirit works nothing but as the Father works in Him. Each moment, the same Spirit that is in us is in God, too. And, he who is most full of the Spirit will be the first to wait on God most earnestly to further fulfill His promise and to still strengthen him mightily by His Spirit in the inner man. The Spirit in us is not a power at our disposal. Nor is the Spirit an independent power, acting apart from the Father and the Son. The Spirit is the real, living presence and the power of the Father working in us. Therefore, it is he who knows that the Spirit is in him who waits on the Father for the full revelation and experience of the Spirit's indwelling. It is he who waits for His increase and abounding more and more.

See this in the apostles. They were filled with the Spirit at Pentecost. When they, not long after, on returning from the council where they had been forbidden to preach, prayed afresh for boldness to speak in His name, a fresh coming down of the Holy Spirit was the Father's fresh fulfillment of His promise.

At Samaria, by the Word and the Spirit, many had been converted, and the whole city was filled with joy. At the apostles' prayer, the Father once again fulfilled the promise. (See Acts 8:14-7.) Even so to the waiting company—"We are all here before God"(see Acts 10:33)—in Cornelius' house. And so, too, in Acts 13. It was when men, filled with the Spirit, prayed and fasted, that the promise of the Father was afresh fulfilled, and the leading of the Spirit was given from heaven: "Separate me Barnabas and Saul" (Acts 13:2).

So also we find Paul, in Ephesians, praying for those who have been sealed with the Spirit, that God would grant them the spirit of illumination. And later on, that He would grant them, according to the riches of His glory, to be strengthened with might by the Spirit in the inner man.

The Spirit given at Pentecost was not something that God failed with in heaven, and sent out of heaven to earth. God does not, cannot, give away anything in that manner. When He gives grace or strength or life, He gives it by giving Himself to work it—it is all inseparable from Himself. Much more so is the Holy Spirit. He is God, present and working in us. The true position in which we can count upon that working with an unceasing power is as we, praising for what we have, still unceasingly wait for the Father's promise to be still more mightily fulfilled.

What new meaning and promise does this give to our lives of waiting! It teaches us to continually keep the place where the disciples tarried at the footstool of the throne. It reminds us that, as helpless as they were to meet their enemies, or to preach to Christ's enemies until they were endued with power, we, too, can only be strong in the life of faith, or the work of love, as we are in direct communication with God and Christ. They must maintain the life of the Spirit in us. This assures us that the omnipotent God will, through the glorified Christ, work in us a power that can bring unexpected things to pass, impossible things. Oh, what the church will be able to do when her individual members learn to live their lives waiting on God—when together, with all of self and the world sacrificed in the fire of love, they unite in waiting with one accord for the promise of the Father, once so gloriously fulfilled, but still unexhausted!

Come and let each of us be still in the presence of the inconceivable grandeur of this prospect: the Father waiting to fill the church with the Holy Spirit. And willing to fill me, let each one say.

With this faith, let a hush and a holy fear come over the soul, as it waits in stillness to take it all in. And, let life increasingly become a deep joy in the hope of the ever fuller fulfillment of the Father's promise.

My soul, wait thou only upon God!

"Therefore turn thou to thy God: keep mercy and judgment, and wait on thy God continually."—Hosea 12:6.

Continuity is one of the essential elements of life. Interrupt it for a single hour in a man, and it is lost; he is dead. Continuity, unbroken and ceaseless, is essential to a healthy Christian life. God wants me to be, and God waits to make me; I want to be, and I wait on Him to make me, every moment, what He expects of me—what is well pleasing in His sight. If waiting on God is the essence of true faith, the maintenance of the spirit of entire dependence must be continuous. The call of God, "wait on thy God continually," must be accepted and obeyed. Although there may be times of special waiting, the disposition and habit of soul must be there unchangeably and uninterrupted.

This continual waiting is indeed a necessity. To those who are content with a feeble Christian life, it appears to be a luxury beyond what is essential to be a good Christian. But, all who are praying the prayer, "Lord, make me as holy as a pardoned sinner can be made! Keep me as near to You as it is possible for me to be! Fill me as full of Your love as You are willing to do!" feel at once that it is something that must be had. They feel that there can be no unbroken fellowship with God, no full abiding in Christ, no maintaining of victory over sin and readiness for service, without waiting continually on the Lord.

The continual waiting is a possibility. Many think that with the duties of life it is out of the question. They cannot always be thinking of it. Even when they wish to, they forget.

They do not understand that it is a matter of the heart and that what the heart is full of, occupies it, even when the thoughts are otherwise engaged. A father's heart may be continuously filled with intense love and longing for a sick wife or child at a distance, even though pressing business requires all his thoughts. When the heart has learned how entirely powerless it is for one moment to keep itself or bring forth any good, when it has learned how surely and truly God will keep it, when it has, in despair of itself, accepted God's promise to do for it the impossible, it learns to rest in God. In the midst of occupations and temptations, it can wait continually.

This waiting is a promise. God's commands are enablings. Gospel precepts are all promises, a revelation of what our God will do for us. When you first begin waiting on God, it is with frequent intermission and failure. But, do believe God is watching over you in love and secretly strengthening you in it. There are times when waiting appears like just losing time, but it is not so. Waiting, even in darkness, is unconscious advance, because it is God you have to do with, and He is working in you. God, who calls you to wait on Him, sees your feeble efforts and works it in you. Your spiritual life is in no respect your own work; as little as you begin it, can you continue it. It is God's Spirit who has begun the work in you of waiting upon God. He will enable you to wait continually.

Waiting continually will be met and rewarded by God Himself working continually. We are coming to the end of our lessons. I hope that you and I might learn one thing: God must, God will work continually. He ever does work continually, but the experience of it is hindered by unbelief. But, He, who by His Spirit teaches you to wait continually, will bring you also to experience how, as the Everlasting One, His work is never ceasing. In the love and the life and the work of God, there can be no break, no interruption.

Do not limit God in this by your thoughts of what may be expected. Do fix your eyes upon this one truth: in His very nature, God, as the only Giver of life, cannot do anything other than work in His child every moment. Do not look only at the one side: "If I wait continually, God will work continually." No, look at the other side. Place God first and say, "God works continually; every moment I may wait on Him continually." Take time until the vision of your God working continually, without one moment's intermission, fills your being. Your waiting continually will then come of itself. Full of trust and joy, the holy habit of the soul will be: "on thee do I wait all the day" (Ps. 25:5). The Holy Spirit will keep you ever waiting.

My soul, wait thou only upon God!

"My soul, wait thou only upon God; for my expectation is from him. He only is my rock and my salvation."—Psalm 62:5-6.

It is possible to be waiting continually on God, but not only upon Him. There may be other secret confidences intervening and preventing the blessing that was expected. And so the word only must come to throw its light on the path to the fullness and certainty of blessing. "My soul, wait thou only upon God . . . He only is my rock."

Yes, "my soul, wait thou only upon God." There is but one God, but one source of life and happiness for the heart; "He only is my rock"; "My soul, wait thou only upon God." You desire to be good; "There is none good but . . . God" (Matt. 19:17), and there is no possible goodness but what is received directly from Him. You have sought to be holy; "There is none holy as the LORD" (1 Sam. 2:2), and there is no holiness but what He by His Spirit of holiness every moment breathes in you. You would gladly live and work for God and His kingdom, for men and their salvation. Hear how He says: "The everlasting God, the LORD, the Creator of the ends of the earth, fainteth not, neither is weary . . . He giveth power to the faint; and to them that have no might he increaseth strength . . . They that wait upon the LORD shall renew their strength. (Isa. 40:28-39, 31). He only is God; He only is your Rock: "my soul, wait thou only upon God."

"My soul, wait thou only upon God." You will not find many who can help you in this. There will be enough of your brothers to draw you to put trust in churches and doctrines, in schemes and plans and human appliances, in means of grace and divine appointments. But, "my soul, wait thou only upon God" Himself. His most sacred appointments become a snare when trusted in. The brazen serpent becomes Nehushtan (see 2 Kings 18:4); the ark and the temple a vain confidence. Let the living God alone, none and nothing but He, be your hope.

"My soul, wait thou only upon God." Eyes and hands and feet, mind and thought, may have to be intently engaged in the duties of this life. "My soul, wait thou only upon God." You are an immortal spirit, created not for this world but for eternity and for God. Oh, my soul, realize your destiny. Know your privilege, and "wait thou only upon God." Let not the interest of spiritual thoughts and exercises deceive you; they very often take the place of waiting upon God. "My soul, wait thou," your very self, your innermost being, with all its power, "wait thou only upon God." God is for you; you are for God. Wait only upon Him.

Yes, "my soul, wait thou only upon God." Beware of two great enemies: the world and self. Beware of allowing any earthly satisfaction or enjoyment, however innocent it appears, keep you back from saying, "I [will] go . . . unto God my exceeding joy" (Ps. 43:4). Remember and study what Jesus said about denying self: "Let [a man] deny himself" (Matt. 16:24). Tersteegen says: "The saints deny themselves in everything." Pleasing self in little things may be strengthening it to assert itself in greater things.

"My soul, wait thou only upon God." Let Him be all your salvation and all your desire. Say continually and with an undivided heart, "From him cometh my [expectation]. He only is my rock . . . I shall not be greatly moved" (Ps. 62:1-2). Whatever your spiritual or temporal needs are, whatever the desire or prayer of your heart, whatever your interest in connection with God's work in the church or the world—in solitude or in the rush of the world, in public worship or other gatherings of the saints, "my soul, wait thou only upon God." Let your expectations be from Him alone. "He only is my rock."

"My soul, wait thou only upon God." Never forget the two foundation truths on which this blessed waiting rests. If you are ever inclined to think this waiting only is too hard or too high, they will recall you at once. They are your absolute helplessness and the absolute sufficiency of your God. Oh, enter deeply into the entire sinfulness of all that is of self, and do not think of letting self have anything to say one single moment. Enter deeply into your utter and unceasing inability to ever change what is evil in you, or to bring forth anything that is spiritually good. Enter deeply into your relationship of dependence on God, to receive from Him every moment what He gives. Enter deeper still into His covenant of redemption, with His promise to restore more gloriously than ever what you have lost. And, by His Son and Spirit, He will unceasingly give you His actual divine presence and power. And thus, wait upon your God continually and only.

"My soul, wait thou only upon God." No words can tell, no heart can conceive, the riches of the glory of this mystery of the Father and of Christ. Our God, in the infinite tenderness and omnipotence of His love, waits to be our life and joy. Oh, my soul, let it no longer be necessary that I repeat the words, "Wait upon God." But, let all that is in me rise and sing, "Truly my soul waiteth upon God" (Ps. 62:1). "On thee do I wait all the day" (Ps. 25:5).

My soul, wait thou only upon God!

Moment by Moment

I the LORD do keep it; I will water it every moment—Isaiah 27:3

Dying with Jesus, by death reckoning mine;
Living with Jesus, a new life divine;
Looking to Jesus till glory doth shine,

Moment by moment, 0 Lord, I am Thine.
Chorus: Moment by moment I'm kept in His love;
Moment by moment I've life from above;
Looking to Jesus till glory doth shine;
Moment by moment, 0 Lord, I am Thine.
Never a battle with wrong for the right,
Never a contest that He doth not fight;
Lifting above us His banner so white,
Moment by moment, I'm kept in His sight.
Never a trial that He is not there,
Never a burden that He doth not bear,
Never a sorrow that He doth not share,
Moment by moment, I'm under His care.
Never a heartache, and never a groan,
Never a teardrop, and never a moan;
Never a danger but there on the throne,
Moment by moment, He thinks of His own.
Never a weakness that He doth not feel,
Never a sickness that He cannot heal;
Moment by moment, in woe or in weal,
Jesus, my Saviour, abides with me still.

The Ministry of Intercession

THE MINISTRY OF INTERCESSION

THERE is no holy service
But hath its secret bliss:
Yet, of all blessèd ministries,
Is one so dear as this?
The ministry that cannot be
A wondering seraph's dower,
Enduing mortal weakness
With more than angel-power;
The ministry of purest love
Uncrossed by any fear,
That bids us meet   At the Master's feet
And keeps us very near.
God's ministers are many,
For this His gracious will,
Remembrancers that day and night
This holy office fill.
While some are hushed in slumber,
Some to fresh service wake,
And thus the saintly number
No change or chance can break.
And thus the sacred courses
Are evermore fulfilled,
The tide of grace   By time or place
Is never stayed or stilled.
x
Oh, if our ears were opened
To hear as angels do
The Intercession-chorus
Arising full and true,
We should hear it soft up-welling
In morning's pearly light;
Through evening's shadows swelling
In grandly gathering might;
The sultry silence filling
Of noontide's thunderous glow,
And the solemn starlight thrilling
With ever-deepening flow.
We should hear it through the rushing
Of the city's restless roar,
And trace its gentle gushing
O'er ocean's crystal floor:

We should hear it far up-floating
Beneath the Orient moon,
And catch the golden noting
From the busy Western noon;
And pine-robed heights would echo
As the mystic chant up-floats,
And the sunny plain   Resound again
With the myriad-mingling notes.
Who are the blessèd ministers
Of this world-gathering band?
All who have learnt one language,
Through each far-parted land;
All who have learnt the story
Of Jesu's love and grace,
And are longing for His glory
To shine in every face.
All who have known the Father
In Jesus Christ our Lord,
And know the might   And love the light
Of the Spirit in the Word.
xi
Yet there are some who see not
Their calling high and grand,
Who seldom pass the portals,
And never boldly stand
Before the golden altar
On the crimson-stainèd floor,
Who wait afar and falter,
And dare not hope for more.
Will ye not join the blessèd ranks
In their beautiful array?
Let intercession blend with thanks
As ye minister to-day!
There are little ones among them
Child-ministers of prayer,
White robes of intercession
Those tiny servants wear.
First for the near and dear ones
Is that fair ministry,
Then for the poor black children,
So far beyond the sea.
The busy hands are folded,
As the little heart uplifts

In simple love,   To God above,
Its prayer for all good gifts.
There are hands too often weary
With the business of the day,
With God-entrusted duties,
Who are toiling while they pray.
They bear the golden vials,
And the golden harps of praise
Through all the daily trials,
Through all the dusty ways,
These hands, so tired, so faithful,
With odours sweet are filled,
And in the ministry of prayer
Are wonderfully skilled.
xii
There are ministers unlettered,
Not of Earth's great and wise,
Yet mighty and unfettered
Their eagle-prayers arise.
Free of the heavenly storehouse!
For they hold the master-key
That opens all the fulness
Of God's great treasury.
They bring the needs of others,
And all things are their own,
For their one grand claim   Is Jesu's name
Before their Father's throne.
There are noble Christian workers,
The men of faith and power,
The overcoming wrestlers
Of many a midnight hour;
Prevailing princes with their God,
Who will not be denied,
Who bring down showers of blessing
To swell the rising tide.
The Prince of Darkness quaileth
At their triumphant way,
Their fervent prayer availeth
To sap his subtle sway.
But in this temple service
Are sealed and set apart
Arch-priests of intercession,
Of undivided heart.

The fulness of anointing
On these is doubly shed,
The consecration of their God
Is on each low-bowed head.
They bear the golden vials
With white and trembling hand;
In quiet room   Or wakeful gloom
These ministers must stand,—

xiii

To the Intercession-Priesthood
Mysteriously ordained,
When the strange dark gift of suffering
This added gift hath gained.
For the holy hands uplifted
In suffering's longest hour
Are truly Spirit-gifted
With intercession-power.
The Lord of Blessing fills them
With His uncounted gold,
An unseen store,   Still more and more,
Those trembling hands shall hold.
Not always with rejoicing
This ministry is wrought,
For many a sigh is mingled
With the sweet odours brought.
Yet every tear bedewing
The faith-fed altar fire
May be its bright renewing
To purer flame, and higher.
But when the oil of gladness
God graciously outpours,
The heavenward blaze,   With blended praise,
More mightily upsoars.
So the incense-cloud ascendeth
As through calm, crystal air,
A pillar reaching unto heaven
Of wreathèd faith and prayer.
For evermore the Angel
Of Intercession stands
In His Divine High Priesthood
With fragrance-fillèd hands,
To wave the golden censer
Before His Father's throne,

With Spirit-fire intenser,
And incense all His own.
xiv
And evermore the Father
Sends radiantly down
All-marvellous responses,
His ministers to crown;
The incense-cloud returning
As golden blessing-showers,
We in each drop discerning
Some feeble prayer of ours,
Transmuted into wealth unpriced,
By Him who giveth thus
The glory all to Jesus Christ,
The gladness all to us!
F. R. Havergal.
September 1877.

INTRODUCTION

I HAVE been asked by a friend, who heard of this book being published, what the difference would be between it and the previous one on the same subject, With Christ in the School of Prayer. An answer to that question may be the best introduction I can give to the present volume.

Any acceptance the former work has had must be attributed, as far as the contents go, to the prominence given to two great truths. The one was, the certainty that prayer will be answered. There is with some an idea that to ask and expect an answer is not the highest form of prayer. Fellowship with God, apart from any request, is more than supplication. About the petition there is something of selfishness and bargaining—to worship is more than to beg. With others the thought that prayer is so often unanswered is so prominent, that they think more of the spiritual benefit derived from the exercise of prayer than 2 the actual gifts to be obtained by it. While admitting the measure of truth in these views, when kept in their true place, The School of Prayer points out how our Lord continually spoke of prayer as a means of obtaining what we desire, and how He seeks in every possible way to waken in us the confident expectation of an answer. I was led to show how prayer, in which a man could enter into the mind of God, could assert the royal power of a renewed will, and bring down to earth what without prayer would not have been given, is the highest proof of his having been made in the likeness of God's Son. He is found worthy of entering into fellowship with Him, not only in adoration and worship, but in having his will actually taken up into the rule of the world, and becoming the intelligent channel through which God can fulfil his eternal purpose. The book sought to reiterate and enforce the precious truths Christ preaches so continually: the blessing of prayer is that you can ask and receive what you will: the highest exercise and the glory of prayer is that persevering importunity can prevail and obtain what God at first could not and would not give.

With this truth there was a second one that came out very strongly as we studied the Master's words. In answer to the question, But why, if the answer to prayer is so positively promised, why are 3 there such numberless unanswered prayers? we found that Christ taught us that the answer depended upon certain conditions. He spoke of faith, of perseverance, of praying in His Name, of praying in the will of God. But all these conditions were summed up in the one central one: "If ye abide in Me, ask whatsoever ye will and it shall be done unto you." It became clear that the power to pray the effectual prayer of faith depended upon the life. It is only to a man given up to live as entirely in Christ and for Christ as the branch in the vine and for the vine, that these promises can come true. "In that day," Christ said, the day of Pentecost, "ye shall ask in My Name." It is only in a life full of the Holy Spirit that the true power to ask in Christ's Name can be known. This led to the emphasising the truth that the ordinary Christian life cannot appropriate these promises. It needs a spiritual life, altogether sound and vigorous, to pray in power. The teaching naturally led to press the need of a life of entire consecration. More than one has told me how it was in the reading of the book that he first saw what the better life was that could be lived, and must be lived, if Christ's wonderful promises are to come true to us.

In regard to these two truths there is no change in the present volume. One only wishes that one could put them with such clearness and force as to 4 help every beloved fellow-Christian to some right impression of the reality and the glory of our privilege as God's children: "Ask whatsoever ye will, and it shall be done unto you." The present volume owes its existence to the desire to enforce two truths, of which formerly I had no such impression as now.

The one is—that Christ actually meant prayer to be the great power by which His Church should do its work, and that the neglect of prayer is the great reason the Church has not greater power over the masses in Christian and in heathen countries. In the first chapter I have stated how my convictions in regard to this have been strengthened, and what gave occasion to the writing of the book. It is meant to be, on behalf of myself and my brethren in the ministry and all God's people, a confession of shortcoming and of sin, and, at the same time, a call to believe that things can be different, and that Christ waits to fit us by His Spirit to pray as He would have us. This call, of course, brings me back to what I spoke of in connection with the former volume: that there is a life in the Spirit, a life of abiding in Christ, within our reach, in which the power of prayer—both the power to pray and the power to obtain the answer—can be realised in a measure which we could not have thought possible before. Any failure in the prayer-life, any desire 5 or hope really to take the place Christ has prepared for us, brings us to the very root of the doctrine of grace as manifested in the Christian life. It is only by a full surrender to the life of abiding, by the yielding to the fulness of the Spirit's leading and quickening, that the prayer-life can be restored to a truly healthy state. I feel deeply how little I have been able to put this in the volume as I could wish. I have prayed and am trusting that God, who chooses the weak things, will use it for His own glory.

The second truth which I have sought to enforce is that we have far too little conception of the place that intercession, as distinguished from prayer for ourselves, ought to have in the Church and the Christian life. In intercession our King upon the throne finds His highest glory; in it we shall find our highest glory too. Through it He continues His saving work, and can do nothing without it; through it alone we can do our work, and nothing avails without it. In it He ever receives from the Father the Holy Spirit and all spiritual blessings to impart; in it we too are called to receive in ourselves the fulness of God's Spirit, with the power to impart spiritual blessing to others. The power of the Church truly to bless rests on intercession—asking and receiving heavenly gifts to carry to men. Because this is so, it is no wonder that where, owing to lack of teaching or spiritual insight, we 6 trust in our own diligence and effort, to the influence of the world and the flesh, and work more than we pray, the presence and power of God are not seen in our work as we would wish.

Such thoughts have led me to wonder what could be done to rouse believers to a sense of their high calling in this, and to help and train them to take part in it. And so this book differs from the former one in the attempt to open a practising school, and to invite all who have never taken systematic part in the great work of intercession to begin and give themselves to it. There are tens of thousands of workers who have known and are proving wonderfully what prayer can do. But there are tens of thousands who work with but little prayer, and as many more who do not work because they do not know how or where, who might all be won to swell the host of intercessors who are to bring down the blessings of heaven to earth. For their sakes, and the sake of all who feel the need of help, I have prepared helps and hints for a school of intercession for a month (see the Appendix). I have asked those who would join, to begin by giving at least ten minutes a day definitely to this work. It is in doing that we learn to do; it is as we take hold and begin that the help of God's Spirit will come. It is as we daily hear God's call, and at once put it into practice, that the consciousness will begin to 7 live in us, I too am an intercessor; and that we shall feel the need of living in Christ and being full of the Spirit if we are to do this work aright. Nothing will so test and stimulate the Christian life as the honest attempt to be an intercessor. It is difficult to conceive how much we ourselves and the Church will be the gainers, if with our whole heart we accept the post of honour God is offering us. With regard to the school of intercession, I am confident that the result of the first month's course will be to awake the feeling of how little we know how to intercede. And a second and a third month may only deepen the sense of ignorance and unfitness. This will be an unspeakable blessing. The confession, "We know not how to pray as we ought," is the introduction to the experience, "The Spirit maketh intercession for us"—our sense of ignorance will lead us to depend upon the Spirit praying in us, to feel the need of living in the Spirit.

We have heard a great deal of systematic Bible study, and we praise God for thousands on thousands of Bible classes and Bible readings. Let all the leaders of such classes see whether they could not open prayer classes—helping their students to pray in secret, and training them to be, above everything, men of prayer. Let ministers ask what they can do in this. The faith in God's word can nowhere be so exercised and perfected as in the intercession 8 that asks and expects and looks out for the answer. Throughout Scripture, in the life of every saint, of God's own Son, throughout the history of God's Church, God is, first of all, a prayer-hearing God. Let us try and help God's children to know their God, and encourage all God's servants to labour with the assurance: the chief and most blessed part of my work is to ask and receive from my Father what I can bring to others.

It will now easily be understood how what this book contains will be nothing but the confirmation and the call to put into practice the two great lessons of the former one. "Ask whatsoever ye will, and it shall be done to you"; "Whatever ye ask, believe that ye have received": these great prayer-promises, as part of the Church's enduement of power for her work, are to be taken as literally and actually true. "If ye abide in Me, and My words abide in you"; "In that day ye shall ask in My Name": these great prayer-conditions are universal and unchangeable. A life abiding in Christ and filled with the Spirit, a life entirely given up as a branch for the work of the vine, has the power to claim these promises and to pray the effectual prayer that availeth much. Lord, teach us to pray.

ANDREW MURRAY.

Wellington, 1st September 1897.

CHAPTER I. The Lack of Prayer

"Ye have not, because ye ask not."—Jas. iv. 2.

"And He saw that there was no man, and wondered that there was no intercessor."—Isa. lix. 16.

"There is none that calleth upon Thy name, that stirreth up himself to take hold of Thee."—Isa. lxiv. 7.

AT our last Wellington Convention for the Deepening of the Spiritual Life, in April, the forenoon meetings were devoted to prayer and intercession. Great blessing was found, both in listening to what the Word teaches of their need and power, and in joining in continued united supplication. Many felt that we know too little of persevering importunate prayer, and that it is indeed one of the greatest needs of the Church.

During the past two months I have been attending a number of Conventions. At the first, a Dutch Missionary Conference at Langlaagte, Prayer had been chosen as the subject of the addresses. At the next, at Johannesburg, a brother in business gave expression to his deep conviction that the great want of the Church of our day was, more of the spirit and practice of intercession. A week later we had a Dutch Ministerial Conference in the Free State, where three days were spent, after two days' services in the congregation on the work of the Holy Spirit, in considering the relation of the Spirit to prayer. At the ministerial meetings held at most of the succeeding conventions, we were led to take up the subject, and everywhere there was the confession: We pray too little! And with this there appeared to be a fear that, with the pressure of duty and the force of habit, it was almost impossible to hope for any great change.

I cannot say what a deep impression was made upon me by these conversations. Most of all, by the thought that there should be anything like hopelessness on the part of God's servants as to the prospect of an entire change being effected, and real deliverance found from a failure which cannot but hinder our own joy in God, and our power in His service. And I prayed God to give me words that might not only help to direct attention to the evil, but, specially, that might stir up faith, and waken the assurance that God by His Spirit will enable us to pray as we ought.

Let me begin, for the sake of those who have never had their attention directed to the matter, by stating some of the facts that prove how universal is the sense of shortcoming in this respect.

Last year there appeared a report of an address to ministers by Dr. Whyte, of Free St. George's, Edinburgh. In that he said that, as a young minister, he had thought that, of the time he had over from pastoral visitation, he ought to spend as much as possible with his books in his study. He wanted to feed his people with the very best he could prepare for them. But he had now learned that prayer was of more importance than study. He reminded his brethren of the election of deacons to take charge of the collections, that the twelve might "give themselves to prayer and the ministry of the word," and said that at times, when the deacons brought him his salary, he had to ask himself whether he had been as faithful in his engagement as the deacons had been to theirs. He felt as if it were almost too late to regain what he had lost, and urged his brethren to pray more. What a solemn confession and warning from one of the high places: We pray too little!

During the Regent Square Convention two years ago the subject came up in conversation with a well-known London minister. He urged that if so much time must be given to prayer, it would involve the neglect of the imperative calls of duty "There is the morning post, before breakfast, with ten or twelve letters which must be answered. Then there are committee meetings waiting, with numberless other engagements, more than enough to fill up the day. It is difficult to see how it can be done."

My answer was, in substance, that it was simply a question of whether the call of God for our time and attention was of more importance than that of man. If God was waiting to meet us, and to give us blessing and power from heaven for His work, it was a short-sighted policy to put other work in the place which God and waiting on Him should have.

At one of our ministerial meetings, the superintendent of a large district put the case thus: "I rise in the morning and have half an hour with God, in the Word and prayer, in my room before breakfast. I go out, and am occupied all day with a multiplicity of engagements. I do not think many minutes elapse without my breathing a prayer for guidance or help. After my day's work, I return in my evening devotions and speak to God of the day's work. But of the intense, definite, importunate prayer of which Scripture speaks one knows little." What, he asked, must I think of such a life?

We all know the difference between a man whose profits are just enough to maintain his family and keep up his business, and another whose income enables him to extend the business and to help others. There may be an earnest Christian life in which there is prayer enough to keep us from going back, and just maintain the position we have attained to, without much of growth in spirituality or Christlikeness. The attitude is more defensive, seeking to ward off temptation, than aggressive, reaching out after higher attainment. If there is indeed to be a going from strength to strength, with some large experience of God's power to sanctify ourselves and to bring down real blessing on others, there must be more definite and persevering 14 prayer. The Scripture teaching about crying day and night, continuing steadfastly in prayer, watching unto prayer, being heard for his importunity, must in some degree become our experience if we are really to be intercessors.

At the very next Convention the same question was put in somewhat different form. "I am at the head of a station, with a large outlying district to care for. I see the importance of much prayer, and yet my life hardly leaves room for it. Are we to submit? Or tell us how we can attain to what we desire?" I admitted that the difficulty was universal. I recalled the words of one of our most honoured South African missionaries, now gone to his rest: he had the same complaint. "In the morning at five the sick people are at the door waiting for medicine. At six the printers come, and I have to set them to work and teach them. At nine the school calls me, and till late at night I am kept busy with a large correspondence." In my answer I quoted a Dutch proverb: 'What is heaviest must weigh heaviest,'—must have the first place. The law of God is unchangeable: as on earth, so in our traffic with heaven, we only get as we give. Unless we are willing to pay the price, and sacrifice time and attention and what appear legitimate or necessary duties, for the sake of the heavenly gifts, we need not look for a large experience of the power of the heavenly world in our work. The whole company present joined in the sad confession; it had been thought over, and mourned over, times without number; and yet, somehow, there they were, all these pressing claims, and all the ineffectual resolves to pray more, barring the way. I need not now say to what further thoughts our conversation led; the substance of them will be found in some of the later chapters in this volume.

Let me call just one more witness. In the course of my journey I met with one of the Cowley Fathers, who had just been holding Retreats for clergy of the English Church. I was interested to hear from him the line of teaching he follows. In the course of conversation he used the expression—"the distraction of business," and it came out that he found it one of the great difficulties he had to deal with in himself and others. Of himself, he said that by the vows of his Order he was bound to give himself specially to prayer. But he found it exceedingly difficult. Every day he had to be at 16 four different points of the town he lived in; his predecessor had left him the charge of a number of committees where he was expected to do all the work; it was as if everything conspired to keep him from prayer.

All this testimony surely suffices to make clear that prayer has not the place it ought to have in our ministerial and Christian life; that the shortcoming is one of which all are willing to make confession; and that the difficulties in the way of deliverance are such as to make a return to a true and full prayer-life almost impossible. Blessed be God—"The things that are impossible with men are possible with God"! "God is able to make all grace abound toward you, that ye, always having all sufficiency in all things, may abound to all good work." Do let us believe that God's call to much prayer need not be a burden and cause of continual self-condemnation. He means it to be a joy. He can make it an inspiration, giving us strength for all our work, and bringing down His power to work through us in our fellowmen. Let us not fear to admit to the full the sin that shames us, and then to face it in the name of our Mighty Redeemer. The light that shows us our sin and condemns us for it, will show us the way out of it, into the life of liberty that is well-pleasing to God. If we allow this one matter, unfaithfulness in prayer, to convict us of the lack in our Christian life which lies at the root of it, God will use the discovery to bring us not only the power to pray that we long for, but the joy of a new and healthy life, of which prayer is the spontaneous expression.

And what is now the way by which our sense of the lack of prayer can be made the means of blessing, the entrance on a path in which the evil may be conquered? How can our intercourse with the Father, in continual prayer and intercession, become what it ought to be, if we and the world around us are to be blessed? As it appears to me, we must begin by going back to God's Word, to study what the place is God means prayer to have in the life of His child and His Church. A fresh sight of what prayer is according to the will of God, of what our prayers can be, through the grace of God, will free us from those feeble defective views, in regard to the absolute necessity of continual prayer, which lie at the root of our failure. As we get an insight into the reasonableness and rightness of this divine appointment, and come under the full conviction of how wonderfully it fits in with God's love and our own happiness, we shall be freed from the false impression of its being an arbitrary demand. We shall with our whole heart and soul consent to it and rejoice in it, as the one only possible way for the blessing of heaven to come to earth. All thought of task and burden, of self-effort and strain, will pass away in the blessed faith that as simple as breathing is in the healthy natural life, will praying be in the Christian life that is led and filled by the Spirit of God.

As we occupy ourselves with and accept this teaching of God's Word on prayer, we shall be led to see how our failure in the prayer-life was owing to failure in the Spirit-life. Prayer is one of the most heavenly and spiritual of the functions of the Spirit-life. How could we try or expect to fulfil it so as to please God, except as our soul is in perfect health, and our life truly possessed and moved by God's Spirit? The insight into the place God means prayer to take, and which it only can take, in a full Christian life, will show us that we have not been living the true, the abundant life, and that any thought of praying more and effectually will be vain, except as we are brought into a closer relation to our Blessed Lord Jesus. Christ is our life, Christ liveth in us, in such reality that His life of prayer on earth, and of intercession in heaven, is breathed into us in just such measure as our surrender and our faith allow and accept it. Jesus Christ is the Healer of all diseases, the Conqueror of all enemies, the Deliverer from all sin; if our failure teaches us to turn afresh to Him, and find in Him the grace He gives to pray as we ought, this humiliation may become our greatest blessing. Let us all unite in praying God that He would visit our souls and fit us for that work of intercession, which is at this moment the greatest need of the Church and the world. It is only by intercession that that power can be brought down from Heaven which will enable the Church to conquer the world. Let us stir up the slumbering gift that is lying unused, and seek to gather and train and band together as many as we can, to be God's remembrancers, and to give Him no rest till He makes His Church a joy in the earth. Nothing but intense believing prayer can meet the intense spirit of worldliness, of which complaint is everywhere made.

"If ye, being evil, know how to give good gifts to your children; how much more shall your Heavenly Father give the Holy Spirit to them that ask Him?"—Luke xi. 13.

CHRIST had just said (v. 9), "Ask, and it shall be given": God's giving is inseparably connected with our asking. He applies this especially to the Holy Spirit. As surely as a father on earth gives bread to his child, so God gives the Holy Spirit to them that ask Him. The whole ministration of the Spirit is ruled by the one great law: God must give, we must ask. When the Holy Spirit was poured out at Pentecost with a flow that never ceases, it was in answer to prayer. The inflow into the believer's heart, and His outflow in the rivers of living water, ever still depend upon the law: "Ask, and it shall be given." In connection with our confession of the lack of prayer, we have said that what we need is some due apprehension of the place it occupies in God's plan of redemption; we shall perhaps nowhere see this more clearly than in the first half of the Acts of the Apostles. The story of the birth of the Church in the outpouring of the Holy Spirit, and of the first freshness of its heavenly life in the power of that Spirit, will teach us how prayer on earth, whether as cause or effect, is the true measure of the presence of the Spirit of heaven.

We begin with the well-known words (i. 13), "These all continued with one accord in prayer and supplication." And then there follows: "And when the day of Pentecost was fully come, they were all with one accord in one place. And they were all filled with the Holy Ghost. And the same day there were added to them about three thousand souls." The great work of redemption had been accomplished. The Holy Spirit had been promised by Christ "not many days hence." He had sat down on His throne and received the Spirit from the Father. But all this was not enough. One thing more was needed: the ten days' united continued supplication of the disciples. It was intense, continued prayer that prepared the disciples' hearts, that opened the windows of heaven, that brought down the promised gift. As little as the power of the Spirit could be given without Christ sitting on the throne, could it descend without the disciples on the footstool of the throne. For all the ages the law is laid down here, at the birth of the Church, that whatever else may be found on earth, the power of the Spirit must be prayed down from heaven. The measure of believing, continued prayer will be the measure of the Spirit's working in the Church. Direct, definite, determined prayer is what we need.

See how this is confirmed in chapter iv. Peter and John had been brought before the Council and threatened with punishment. When they returned to their brethren, and reported what had been said to them, "all lifted up their voice to God with one accord," and prayed for boldness to speak the word. "And when they had prayed, the place was shaken, and they were all filled with the Holy Ghost, and they spake the word of God with boldness. And the multitude of them that believed were one heart and one soul. And with great power gave the apostles witness of the resurrection of the Lord Jesus; and great grace was upon them all." It is as if the story of Pentecost is repeated a second time over, with the prayer, the shaking of the house, the filling with the Spirit, the speaking God's word with boldness and power, the great grace upon all, the manifestation of unity and love—to imprint it ineffaceably on the heart of the Church: it is prayer that lies at the root of the spiritual life and power of the Church. The measure of God's giving the Spirit is our asking. He gives as a father to him who asks as a child.

Go on to the sixth chapter. There we find that, when murmurings arose as to the neglect of the Grecian Jews in the distribution of alms, the apostles proposed the appointment of deacons to serve the tables. "We," they said, "will give ourselves to prayer and the ministry of the word." It is often said, and rightly said, that there is nothing in honest business, when it is kept in its place as entirely subordinate to the kingdom, which must ever be first, that need prevent fellowship with God. Least of all ought a work like ministering to the poor hinder the spiritual life. And yet the apostles felt it would hinder them in their giving themselves to the ministry of prayer and the word. What does this teach? That the maintenance of the spirit of prayer, such as is consistent with the claims of much work, is not enough for those who are the leaders of the Church. To keep up the communication with the King on the throne and the heavenly world clear and fresh; to draw down the power and blessing of that world, not only for the maintenance of our own spiritual life, but for those around us; continually to receive instruction and empowerment for the great work to be done—the apostles, as the ministers of the word, felt the need of being free from other duties, that they might give themselves to much prayer. James writes: "Pure religion and undefiled before God and the Father is this, To visit the fatherless and widows in their affliction." If ever any work were a sacred one, it was that of caring for these Grecian widows. And yet, even such duties might interfere with the special calling to give themselves to prayer and the ministry of the word. As on earth, so in the kingdom of heaven, there is power in the division of labour; and while some, like the deacons, had specially to care for serving the tables and ministering the alms of the Church here on earth, others had to be set free for that steadfast continuance in prayer which would uninterruptedly secure the downflow of the powers of the heavenly world. The minister of Christ is set apart to give himself as much to prayer as to the ministry of the word. In faithful obedience to this law is the secret of the Church's power and success. As before, so after Pentecost, the apostles were men given up to prayer.

In chapter viii. we have the intimate connection between the Pentecostal gift and prayer, from another point of view. At Samaria, Philip had preached with great blessing, and many had believed. But the Holy Ghost was, as yet, fallen on none of them. The apostles sent down Peter and John to pray for them, that they might receive the Holy Ghost. The power for such prayer was a higher gift than preaching— the work of the men who had been in closest contact with the Lord in glory, the work that was essential to the perfection of the life that preaching and baptism, faith and conversion had only begun. Surely of all the gifts of the early Church for which we should long there is none more needed than the gift of prayer—prayer that brings down the Holy Ghost on believers. This power is given to the men who say: "We will give ourselves to prayer."

In the outpouring of the Holy Spirit, in the house of Cornelius at Cæsarea, we have another testimony to the wondrous interdependence of the action of prayer and the Spirit, and another proof of what will come to a man who has given himself to prayer. Peter went up at midday to pray on the housetop. And what happened? He saw heaven opened, and there came the vision that revealed to him the cleansing of the Gentiles; with that came the message of the three men from Cornelius, a man who "prayed alway," and had heard from an angel, "Thy prayers are come up before God"; and then the voice of the Spirit was heard saying, "Go with them." It is Peter praying, to whom the will of God is revealed, to whom guidance is given as to going to Cæsarea, and who is brought into contact with a praying and prepared company of hearers. No wonder that in answer to all this prayer a blessing comes beyond all expectation, and the Holy Ghost is poured out upon the Gentiles. A much-praying minister will receive an entrance into God's will he would otherwise know nothing of; will be brought to praying people where he does not expect them; will receive blessing above all he asks or thinks. The teaching and the power of the Holy Ghost are alike unalterably linked to prayer.

Our next reference will show us faith in the power that the Church's prayer has with its glorified King, as it is found, not only in the apostles, but in the Christian community. In chapter xii. we have the story of Peter in prison on the eve of execution. The death of James had aroused the Church to a sense of real danger, and the thought of losing Peter too, wakened up all its energies. It betook itself to prayer. "Prayer was made of the Church without ceasing to God for him." That prayer availed much; Peter was delivered. When he came to the house of Mary, he found "many gathered together praying." Stone walls and double chains, soldiers and keepers, and the iron gate, all gave way before the power from heaven that prayer brought down to his rescue. The whole power of the Roman Empire, as represented by Herod, was impotent in presence of the power the Church of the Holy Spirit wielded in prayer. They stood in such close and living communication with their Lord in heaven; they knew so well that the words, "all power is given unto Me," and "Lo I am with you alway," were absolutely true; they had such faith in His promise to hear them whatever they asked—that they prayed in the assurance that the powers of heaven could work on earth, and would work at their request and on their behalf. The Pentecostal Church believed in prayer, and practised it.

Just one more illustration of the place and the blessing of prayer among men filled with the Holy Spirit. In chapter xiii. we have the names of five men at Antioch who had given themselves specially to ministering to the Lord with prayer and fasting. Their giving themselves to prayer was not in vain: as they ministered to the Lord, the Holy Spirit met them, and gave them new insight into God's plans. He called them to be fellow-workers with Himself; there was a work to which He had called Barnabas and Saul; their part and privilege would be to separate these men with renewed fasting and prayer, and to let them go, "sent forth of the Holy Ghost." God in heaven would not send forth His chosen servants without the co-operation of His Church; men on earth were to have a real partnership in the work of God. It was prayer that fitted and prepared them for this; it was to praying men the Holy Ghost gave authority to do His work and use His name. It was to prayer the Holy Ghost was given. It is still prayer that is the only secret of true Church extension, that is guided from heaven to find and send forth God-called and God-empowered men. To prayer the Holy Spirit will show the men He has selected; to prayer that sets them apart under His guidance He will give the honour of knowing that they are men, "sent forth by the Holy Ghost." It is prayer which is the link between the King on the throne and the Church at His footstool—the human link that has its divine strength in the power of the Holy Ghost, who comes in answer to it.

As one looks back upon these chapters in the history of the Pentecostal Church, how clear the two great truths stand out: where there is much prayer there will be much of the Spirit; where there is much of the Spirit there will be ever-increasing prayer. So clear is the living connection between the two, that when the Spirit is given in answer to prayer it ever wakens more prayer to prepare for the fuller revelation and communication of His Divine power and grace. If prayer was thus the power by which the Primitive Church flourished and triumphed, is it not the one need of the Church of our days? Let us learn what ought to be counted axioms in our Church work:—

Heaven is still as full of stores of spiritual blessing as it was then. God still delights to give the Holy Spirit to them that ask Him. Our life and work are still as dependent on the direct impartation of Divine power as they were in Pentecostal times. Prayer is still the appointed means for drawing down these heavenly blessings in power on ourselves and those around us. God still seeks for men and women who will, with all their other work of ministering, specially give themselves to persevering prayer.

And we—you, my reader, and I—may have the privilege of offering ourselves to God to labour in prayer, and bring down these blessings to this earth. Shall we not beseech God to make all this truth so living in us that we may not rest till it has mastered us, and our whole heart be so filled with it, that the practice of intercession shall be counted by us our highest privilege, and we find in it the sure and only measure for blessing on ourselves, on the Church, and on the world?

CHAPTER III. A Model of Intercession

"And he said unto them, Which of you shall have a friend, and shall go unto him at midnight, and shall say unto him, Friend, lend me three loaves; for a friend of mine is come unto me from a journey, and I have nothing to set before him; and he from within shall answer and say, Trouble me not: I cannot rise and give thee? I say unto you, Though he will not rise and give him, because he is his friend, yet, because of his importunity, he will arise and give him as many as he needeth."—Luke xi. 5–8.

"I have set watchmen upon thy walls, O Jerusalem, which shall never hold their peace day nor night: ye that are the Lord's remembrancers, keep not silence, and give Him no rest."—Isa. lxii. 6, 7.

WE have seen in our previous chapter what power prayer has. It is the one power on earth that commands the power of heaven. The story of the early days of the Church is God's great object-lesson, to teach His Church what prayer can do, how it alone, but it most surely, can draw down the treasures and powers of heaven into the life of earth.

Just remember the lessons we learnt of how prayer is at once indispensable and irresistible. Did we not see how unknown and untold power and blessing is stored up for us in heaven?—how that power will make us a blessing to men, and fit us to do any work or face any danger? how it is to be sought in prayer continually and persistently? how they who have the heavenly power can pray it down upon others? how in all the intercourse of ministers and people, in all the ministrations of Christ's Church, it is the one secret of success? how it can defy all the power of the world, and fit men to conquer that world for Christ? It is the power of the heavenly life, the power of God's own Spirit, the power of Omnipotence, that waits for prayer to bring it down.

In all this prayer there was little thought of personal need or happiness. It was the desire to witness for Christ and bring Him and His salvation to others, it was the thought of God's kingdom and glory, that possessed these disciples. If we would be delivered from the sin of restraining prayer, we must enlarge our hearts for the work of intercession. The attempt to pray constantly for ourselves must be a failure; it is in intercession for others that our faith and love and perseverance will be aroused, and that power of the Spirit be found which can fit us for saving men. We are asking how we may become more faithful and successful in prayer; let us see how the Master teaches us, in the parable of the Friend at Midnight, that intercession for the needy calls forth the highest exercise of our power of believing and prevailing prayer. Intercession is the most perfect form of prayer: it is the prayer Christ ever liveth to pray on His throne. Let us learn what the elements of true intercession are.

1. Notice the urgent need: here intercession has its origin. The friend came at midnight—an untimely hour. He was hungry, and could not buy bread. If we are to learn to pray aright we must open eye and heart to the need around us.

We hear continually of the thousand millions of heathen and Mohammedans living in midnight darkness, perishing for lack of the bread of life. We hear of five hundred millions of nominal Christians, the great majority of them almost as ignorant and indifferent as the heathen. We see millions in the Christian Church, not ignorant or indifferent, and yet knowing little of a walk in the light of God or in the power of a life fed by bread from heaven. We have each of us our own circles—congregations, schools, friends, missions—in which the great complaint is that the light and life of God are too little known. Surely, if we believe what we profess, that God alone is able to help, that God certainly will help in answer to prayer,—all this need ought to make intercessors of us, people who give their lives to prayer for those around them.

Let us take time to consider and realise the need. Each Christless soul going down into outer darkness, perishing of hunger, with bread enough and to spare! Thirty millions a year dying without the knowledge of Christ! Our own neighbours and friends, souls intrusted to us, dying without hope! Christians around us living a sickly, feeble, fruitless life! Surely there is need for prayer. Nothing, nothing but prayer to God for help, will avail.

2. Note the willing love.—The friend took his weary, hungry friend into his house, and into his heart too. He did not excuse himself by saying he had no bread: he gave himself at midnight to seek it for him. He sacrificed his night's rest, his comfort, to find the needed bread. "Love seeketh not its own." It is the very nature of love to give up and forget itself for the sake of others. It takes their needs and makes them its own, it finds its real joy in living and dying for others as Christ did.

It is the love of a mother to her prodigal son that makes her pray for him. True love to souls will become in us the spirit of intercession. It is possible to do a great deal of faithful, earnest work for our fellowmen without true love to them. Just as a lawyer or a physician, from a love of his profession and a high sense of faithfulness to duty, may interest himself most thoroughly in clients or patients without any special love to each, so servants of Christ may give themselves to their work with devotion and even self-sacrificing enthusiasm without the Christlike love to souls being strong. It is this lack of love that causes so much shortcoming in prayer. It is as love of our profession and work, delight in thoroughness and diligence, sink away in the tender compassion of Christ, that love will compel us to prayer, because we cannot rest in our work if souls are not saved. True love must pray.

3. Note the sense of impotence.—We often speak of the power of love. In one sense this is true; and yet the truth has its limitations, which must not be forgotten. The strongest love may be utterly impotent. A mother might be willing to give her life for her dying child, and yet not be able to save it. The friend at midnight was most willing to give his friend bread, but he had none. It was this sense of impotence, of his inability to help, that sent him a-begging: "My friend is come to me, and I have nothing to set before him." It is this sense of impotence with God's servants that is the very strength of the life of intercession.

"I have nothing to set before them": as this consciousness takes possession of the minister or missionary, the teacher or worker, intercession will become their only hope and refuge. I may have knowledge and truth, a loving heart, and the readiness to give myself for those under my charge; but the bread of heaven I cannot give them. With all my love and zeal, "I have nothing to set before them." Blessed the man who has made that "I have nothing," the motto of his ministry. As he thinks of the judgment day and the danger of souls, as he sees what a supernatural power and life is needed to save men from sin, as he feels how utterly insufficient all he can ever do is to give them life, that "I have nothing" urges him to pray. Intercession appears to him, as he thinks of the midnight darkness and the hungry souls, as his only hope, the one thing in which his love can take refuge.

Let us take the lesson to heart, for a warning to all who are strong and wise to work, for the encouragement of all who are feeble. The sense of our impotence is the soul of intercession. The simplest, feeblest Christian can pray down blessing from an Almighty God.

4. Note the faith in prayer.—What he has not himself, another can

supply. He has a rich friend near, who will be both able and willing to give the bread. He is sure that if he only asks, he will receive. This faith makes him leave his home at midnight: if he has not the bread himself to give, he can ask another.

It is this simple, confident faith that God will give, that we need: where it really exists, there will surely be no mistake about our not praying. And in God's word we have everything that can stir and strengthen such faith in us. Just as the heaven our natural eye can see is one great ocean of sunshine, with its light and heat, giving beauty and fruitfulness to earth, Scripture shows us God's true heaven, filled with all spiritual blessings,—divine light and love and life, heavenly joy and peace and power, all shining down upon us. It reveals to us God waiting, delighting to bestow these blessings in answer to prayer. By a thousand promises and testimonies it calls and urges us to believe that prayer will be heard, that what we cannot possibly do ourselves for those whom we want to help, can be got by prayer. Surely there can be no question as to our believing that prayer will be heard, that through prayer the poorest and feeblest can dispense blessings to the needy, and each of us, though poor, may yet be making many rich.

5. Note the importunity that prevails.—The faith of the friend met a sudden and unexpected check: the rich friend refuses to hear—"I cannot rise and give thee." How little the loving heart had counted on this disappointment; it cannot consent to accept it. The supplicant presses his threefold plea: here is my needy friend, you have abundance, I am your friend; and refuses to accept a denial. The love that opened his house at midnight, and then left it to seek help, must win.

This is the central lesson of the parable. In our intercession we may find that there is difficulty and delay with the answer. It may be as if God says, "I cannot give thee." It is not easy, against all appearances, to hold fast our confidence that He will hear, and to persevere in full assurance that we shall have what we ask. And yet this is what God looks for from us. He so highly prizes our confidence in Him, it is so essentially the highest honour the creature can render the Creator, that He will do anything to train us in the exercise of this trust in Him. Blessed the man who is not staggered by God's delay, or silence, or apparent refusal, but is strong in faith, giving glory to God. Such faith perseveres, importunately, if need be, and cannot fail to inherit the blessing.

6. Note, last, the certainty of a rich reward.—"I say unto you, because of his importunity, he will give him as many as he needeth." Oh that we might learn to believe in the certainty of an abundant answer. A prophet said of old: "Let not your hands be weak; your work shall be rewarded." Would that all who feel it difficult to pray much, would fix their eye on the recompense of the reward, and in faith learn to count upon the Divine assurance that their prayer cannot be vain. If we will but believe in God and His faithfulness, intercession will become to us the very first thing we take refuge in when we seek blessing for others, and the very last thing for which we cannot find time. And it will become a thing of joy and hope, because, all the time we pray, we know that we are sowing seed that will bring forth fruit an hundredfold. Disappointment is impossible: "I say unto you, He will rise and give him as many as he needeth."

Let all lovers of souls, and all workers in the service of the gospel, take courage. Time spent in prayer will yield more than that given to work. Prayer alone gives work its worth and its success. Prayer opens the way for God Himself to do His work in us and through us. Let our chief work, as God's messengers, be intercession: in it we secure the presence and power of God to go with us.

"Which of you shall have a friend at midnight, and shall say to him, Friend, lend me three loaves?" This friend is none other but our God. Do let us learn that in the darkness of midnight, at the most unlikely time, and in the greatest need, when we have to say of those we love and care for, "I have nothing to set before them," we have a rich Friend in heaven, the Everlasting God and Father, who only waits to be asked aright. Let us confess before Him our lack of prayer. Let us admit that the lack of faith, of which it is the proof, is the symptom of a life that is not spiritual, that is yet all too much under the power of self and the flesh and the world. Let us in the faith of the Lord Jesus, who spake this parable, and Himself waits to make every trait of it true in us, give ourselves to be intercessors. Let every sight of souls needing help, let every stirring of the spirit of compassion, let every sense of our own impotence to bless, let every difficulty in the way of our getting an answer, just combine to urge us to do this one thing: with importunity to cry to the God who alone can help, who, in answer to our prayer, will help. And let us, if we indeed feel that we have failed, do our utmost to train a young generation of Christians, who profit by our mistake and avoid it. Moses could not enter the land of Canaan, but there was one thing he could do: he could at God's bidding "charge Joshua, and encourage him, and strengthen him" (Deut. iii. 28). If it is too late for us to make good our failure, let us at least encourage those who come after us to enter into the good land, the blessed life of unceasing prayer.

The Model Intercessor is the Model Christian Worker. First to get from God, and then to give to men what we ourselves secure from day to day, is the secret of successful work. Between our Impotence and God's Omnipotence intercession is the blessed link.

CHAPTER IV. Because of His Importunity

"I say unto you, Though he will not rise and give him, because he is his friend, yet because of his importunity he will arise and give him as many as he needeth."—Luke xi. 8.

"And He spake a parable unto them, to the end, they ought always to pray and not to faint.... Hear what the unrighteous judge saith. And shall not God avenge His own elect, which cry to Him day and night, and He is long-suffering with them? I tell you that He will avenge them speedily."—Luke xviii. 1–8.

OUR Lord Jesus thought it of such importance that we should know the need of perseverance and importunity in prayer, that He spake two parables to teach us this. This is proof sufficient that in this aspect of prayer we have at once its greatest difficulty and its highest power. He would have us know that in prayer all will not be easy and smooth; we must expect difficulties, which can only be conquered by persistent, determined perseverance.

In the parables our Lord represents the difficulty as existing on the side of the persons to whom the petition was addressed, and the importunity as needed to overcome their reluctance to hear. In our intercourse with God the difficulty is not on His side, but on ours. In connection with the first parable He tells us that our Father is more willing to give good things to those who ask Him than any earthly father to give his child bread. In the second, He assures us that God longs to avenge His elect speedily. The need of urgent prayer cannot be because God must be made willing or disposed to bless: the need lies altogether in ourselves. But because it was not possible to find any earthly illustration of a loving father or a willing friend from whom the needed lesson of importunity could be taught, He takes the unwilling friend and the unjust judge to encourage in us the faith, that perseverance can overcome every obstacle.

The difficulty is not in God's love or power, but in ourselves and our own incapacity to receive the blessing. And yet, because there is this difficulty with us, this lack of spiritual preparedness, there is a difficulty with God too. His wisdom, His righteousness, yea His love, dare not give us what would do us harm, if we received it too soon or too easily. The sin, or the consequence of sin, that makes it impossible for God to give at once, is a barrier on God's side as well as ours; to break through this power of sin in ourselves, or those for whom we pray, is what makes the striving and the conflict of prayer such a reality. And so in all ages men have prayed, and that rightly too, under a sense that there were difficulties in the heavenly world to overcome. As they pleaded with God for the removal of the unknown obstacles, and in that persevering supplication were brought into a state of utter brokenness and helplessness, of entire resignation to Him, of union with His will, and of faith that could take hold of Him, the hindrances in themselves and in heaven were together overcome. As God conquered them, they conquered God. As God prevails over us, we prevail with God.

God has so constituted us that the clearer our insight is into the reasonableness of a demand, the more hearty will be our surrender to it. One great cause of our remissness in prayer is that there appears to be something arbitrary, or at least something incomprehensible, in the call to such continued prayer. If we could be brought to see that this apparent difficulty is a Divine necessity, and in the very nature of things the source of unspeakable blessing, we should be more ready with gladness of heart to give ourselves to continue in prayer. Let us see if we cannot understand how the difficulty that the call to importunity throws in our way is one of our greatest privileges.

I do not know whether you have ever noticed what a part difficulties play in our natural life. They call out man's powers as nothing else can. They strengthen and ennoble character. We are told that one reason of the superiority of the Northern nations, like Holland and Scotland, in strength of will and purpose, over those of the sunny South, as Italy and Spain, is that the climate of the latter has been too beautiful, and the life it encourages too easy and relaxing—the difficulties the former had to contend with have been their greatest boon; how all nature has been so arranged by God that in sowing and reaping, as in seeking coal or gold, nothing is found without labour and effort. What is education but a daily developing and disciplining of the mind by new difficulties presented to the pupil to overcome? The moment a lesson has become easy, the pupil is moved on to one that is higher and more difficult. With the race and the individual, it is in the meeting and the mastering of difficulties that our highest attainments are found.

It is even so in our intercourse with God. Just imagine what the result would be if the child of God had only to kneel down and ask, and get, and go away. What unspeakable loss to the spiritual life would ensue. It is in the difficulty and delay that calls for persevering prayer, that the true blessing and blessedness of the heavenly life will be found. We there learn how little we delight in fellowship with God, and how little we have of living faith in Him. We discover how earthly and unspiritual our heart still is, how little we have of God's Holy Spirit. We there are brought to know our own weakness and unworthiness, and to yield to God's Spirit to pray in us, to take our place in Christ Jesus, and abide in Him as our only plea with the Father. There our own will and strength and goodness are crucified. There we rise in Christ to newness of life, with our whole will dependent on God and set upon His glory. Do let us begin to praise God for the need and the difficulty of importunate prayer, as one of His choicest means of grace.

Just think what our Lord Jesus owed to the difficulties in His path. In Gethsemane it was as if the Father would not hear: He prayed yet more earnestly, until "He was heard." In the way He opened up for us, He learned obedience by the things He suffered, and so was made perfect; His will was given up to God; His faith in God was proved and strengthened; the prince of this world, with all his temptation, was overcome. This is the new and living way He consecrated for us; it is in persevering prayer we walk with and are made partakers of His very Spirit. Prayer is one form of crucifixion, of our fellowship with Christ's Cross, of our giving up our flesh to the death. O Christians! shall we not be ashamed of our reluctance to sacrifice the flesh and our own will and the world, as it is seen in our reluctance to pray much? Shall we not learn the lesson which nature and Christ alike teach? The difficulty of importunate prayer is our highest privilege; the difficulties to be overcome in it bring us our richest blessings.

In importunity there are various elements. Of these the chief are perseverance, determination, intensity. It begins with the refusal to at once accept a denial. It grows to the determination to persevere, to spare no time or trouble, till an answer comes. It rises to the intensity in which the whole being is given to God in supplication, and the boldness comes to lay hold of God's strength. At one time it is quiet and restful; at another passionate and bold. Now it takes time and is patient; then again it claims at once what it desires. In whatever different shape, it always means and knows—God hears prayer: I must be heard.

Remember the wonderful instances we have of it in the Old Testament saints. Think of Abraham, as he pleads for Sodom. Time after time he renews his prayer until the sixth time he has to say, "Let not my Lord be angry." He does not cease until he has learnt to know God's condescension in each time consenting to his petition, until he has learnt how far he can go, has entered into God's mind, and now rests in God's will. And for his sake Lot was saved. "God remembered Abraham, and delivered Lot out of the midst of the overthrow." And shall not we, who have a redemption and promises for the heathen which Abraham never knew, begin to plead more with God on their behalf.

Think of Jacob, when he feared to meet Esau. The angel of the Lord met him in the dark, and wrestled with him. And when the angel saw that he prevailed not, he said, "Let me go." And Jacob said, "I will not let thee go." And he blessed him there. And that boldness that said, "I will not," and forced from the reluctant angel the blessing, was so pleasing in God's sight, that a new name was there given to him: "Israel, he who striveth with God, for thou hast striven with God and with men, and hast prevailed." And through all the ages God's children have understood, what Christ's two parables teach, that God holds Himself back, and seeks to get away from us, until what is of flesh and self and sloth in us is overcome, and we so prevail with Him that He can and must bless us. Oh! why is it that so many of God's children have no desire for this honour—being princes of God, strivers with God, and prevailing? What our Lord taught us, "What things soever ye desire, believe that ye have received," is nothing but His putting of Jacob's words, "I will not let Thee go except thou bless me." This is the importunity He teaches, and we must learn: to claim and take the blessing.

Think of Moses when Israel had made the golden calf. Moses returned to the Lord and said, "Oh, this people have sinned a great sin. Yet now, if Thou wilt forgive their sin—; and if not, blot me, I pray Thee, out of Thy book which Thou hast written." That was importunity, that would rather die than not have his people given him. Then, when God had heard him, and said He would send His angel with the people, Moses came again, and would not be content until, in answer to his prayer that God Himself should go with them (xxxiii. 12, 17, 18), He had said, "I will do this thing also that thou hast spoken." After that, when in answer to his prayer, "Show me Thy glory," God made His goodness pass before him, he at once again began pleading, "Let my Lord, I pray Thee, go among us." And he was there with the Lord forty days and forty nights (Ex. xxxiv. 28). Of these days he says, "I fell down before the Lord, as at the first, forty days and forty nights, I did neither eat bread, nor drink water, because of all your sin which ye sinned." As an intercessor Moses used importunity with God, and prevailed. He proves that the man who truly lives near to God, and with whom God speaks face to face, becomes partaker of that same power of intercession which there is in Him who is at God's right hand and ever lives to pray.

Think of Elijah in his prayer, first for fire, and then for rain. In the former you have the importunity that claims and receives an immediate answer. In the latter, bowing himself down to the earth, his face between his knees, his answer to the servant who had gone to look toward the sea, and come with the message, "There is nothing," was "Go again seven times." Here was the importunity of perseverance. He had told Ahab there would be rain; he knew it was coming; and yet he prayed till the seven times were fulfilled. And it is of this Elijah and this prayer we are taught, "Pray for one another. Elijah was a man of like passions with ourselves. The effectual fervent prayer of a righteous man availeth much." Will there not be some who feel constrained to cry out, "Where is the Lord God of Elijah?"—this God who draws forth such effectual prayer, and hears it so wonderfully. His name be praised: He is still the same. Let His people but believe that He still waits to be inquired of! Faith in a prayer-hearing God will make a prayer-loving Christian.

We remember the marks of the true intercessor as the parable taught us them. A sense of the need of souls; a Christlike love in the heart; a consciousness of personal impotence; faith in the power of prayer; courage to persevere in spite of refusal; and the assurance of an abundant reward;—these are the dispositions that constitute a Christian an intercessor, and call forth the power of prevailing prayer. These are the dispositions that constitute the beauty and the health of the Christian life, that fit a man for being a blessing in the world, that make him a true Christian worker, who does indeed get from God the bread of heaven to dispense to the hungry. These are the dispositions that call forth the highest, the heroic virtues of the life of faith. There is nothing to which the nobility of natural character owes so much as the spirit of enterprise and daring which in travel or war, in politics or science, battles with difficulties and conquers. No labour or expense is grudged for the sake of 54 victory. And shall we who are Christians not be able to face the difficulties that we meet in prayer? It is as we "labour" and "strive" in prayer that the renewed will asserts its royal right to claim in the name of Christ what it will, and wields its God-given power to influence the destinies of men. Shall men of the world sacrifice ease and pleasure in their pursuits, and shall we be such cowards and sluggards as not to fight our way through to the place where we can find liberty for the captive and salvation for the perishing? Let each servant of Christ learn to know his calling. His King ever lives to pray. The Spirit of the King ever lives in us to pray. It is from heaven the blessings, which the world needs, must be called down in persevering, importunate, believing prayer. It is from heaven, in answer to prayer, the Holy Spirit will take complete possession of us to do His work through us. Let us acknowledge how vain our much work has been owing to our little prayer. Let us change our method, and let henceforth more prayer, much prayer, unceasing prayer, be the proof that we look for all to God, and that we believe that He heareth us.

CHAPTER V. The Life that can Pray

"If ye abide in Me, and My words abide in you, ask whatsoever ye will, and it shall be done unto you."—John xv. 7.

"The supplication of a righteous man availeth much in its working."—James v. 16.

"Beloved, if our heart condemn us not, we have boldness toward God; and whatsoever we ask, we receive of Him, because we keep His commandments, and do the things that are pleasing in His sight."—1 John iii. 21, 22.

HERE on earth the influence of one who asks a favour for others depends entirely on his character, and the relationship he bears to him with whom he is interceding. It is what he is that gives weight to what he asks. It is no otherwise with God. Our power in prayer depends upon our life. Where our life is right we shall know how to pray so as to please God, and prayer will secure the answer. The texts quoted above all point in this direction. "If ye abide in Me," our Lord says, ye shall ask, and it shall be done unto you. It is the prayer of a righteous man, according to James, that availeth much. We receive whatsoever we ask, John says, because we obey and please God. All lack of power to pray aright and perseveringly, all lack of power in prayer with God, points to some lack in the Christian life. It is as we learn to live the life that pleases God, that God will give what we ask. Let us learn from our Lord Jesus, in the parable of the vine, what the healthy, vigorous life is that may ask and receive what it will. Hear His voice, "If ye abide in Me, and My words abide in you, ye shall ask what ye will, and it shall be done unto you." And again at the close of the parable: "Ye did not choose Me, but I chose you, and appointed you, that you should go and bear fruit, and that your fruit should abide: that whatsoever ye shall ask the Father in My name, He may give it you."

And what is now, according to the parable, the life that one must lead to bear fruit, and then ask and receive what we will? What is it we are to be or do, that will enable us to pray as we should, and to receive what we ask? The answer is in one word: it is the branch-life that gives power for prayer. We are branches of Christ, the Living Vine. We must simply live like branches, and abide in Christ, then we shall ask what we will, and it shall be done unto us.

We all know what a branch is, and what its essential characteristic. It is simply a growth of the vine, produced by it and appointed to bear fruit. It has only one reason of existence; it is there at the bidding of the vine, that through it the vine may bear and ripen its precious fruit. Just as the vine only and solely and wholly lives to produce the sap that makes the grape, so the branch has no other aim and object but this alone, to receive that sap and bear the grape. Its only work is to serve the vine, that through it the vine may do its work.

And the believer, the branch of Christ the Heavenly Vine, is it to be understood that he is as literally, as exclusively, to live only that Christ may bear fruit through him? Is it meant that a true Christian as a branch is to be just as absorbed in and devoted to the work of bearing fruit to the glory of God as Christ the Vine was on earth, and is now in heaven? This, and nothing less, is indeed what is meant. It is to such that the unlimited prayer promises of the parable are given. It is the branch-life, existing solely for the Vine, that will have the power to pray aright. With our life abiding in Him, and His words abiding, kept and obeyed, in our heart and life, transmuted into our very being, there will be the grace to pray aright, and the faith to receive the whatsoever we will.

Do let us connect the two things, and take them both in their simple, literal truth, and their infinite, divine grandeur. The promises of our Lord's farewell discourse, with their wonderful six-fold repetition of the unlimited, anything, whatsoever (John xiv. 13, 14; xv. 7, 16; xvi. 23, 24), appear to us altogether too large to be taken literally, and they are qualified down to meet our human ideas of what appears seemly. It is because we separate them from that life of absolute and unlimited devotion to Christ's service to which they were given. God's covenant is ever: Give all and take all. He that is willing to be wholly branch, and nothing but branch, who is ready to place himself absolutely at the disposal of Jesus the Vine of God, to bear His fruit through him, and to live every moment only for Him, will receive a Divine liberty to claim Christ's whatsoever in all its fulness, and a Divine wisdom and humility to use it aright. He will live and pray, and claim the Father's promises, even as Christ did, only for God's glory in the salvation of men. He will use his boldness in prayer only with a view to power in intercession, and getting men blessed. The unlimited devotion of the branch-life to fruitbearing, and the unlimited access to the treasures of the Vine life, are inseparable. It is the life abiding wholly in Christ that can pray the effectual prayer in the name of Christ.

Just think for a moment of the men of prayer in Scripture, and see in them what the life was that could pray in such power. We spoke of Abraham as intercessor. What gave Him such boldness? He knew that God had chosen and called him away from his home and people to walk before Him, that all nations might be blessed in him. He knew that he had obeyed, and forsaken all for God. Implicit obedience, to the very sacrifice of his son, was the law of his life. He did what God asked: he dared trust God to do what he asked. We spoke of Moses as intercessor. He too had forsaken all for God, "counting the reproach of Christ greater riches than all the treasures of Egypt." He lived at God's disposal: "as a servant he was faithful in all His house." How often it is written of him, "According to all that the Lord commanded Moses, so did he." No wonder that he was very bold: his heart was right with God: he knew God would hear him. No less true is this of Elijah, the man who stood up to plead for the Lord God of Israel. The man who is ready to risk all for God can count upon God to do all for him.

It is as men live that they pray. It is the life that prays. It is the life that, with whole-hearted devotion, gives up all for God and to God, that can claim all from God. Our God longs exceedingly to prove Himself the Faithful God and Mighty Helper of His people. He only waits for hearts wholly turned from the world to Himself, and open to receive His gifts. The man who loses all will find all; he dare ask and take it. The branch that only and truly lives abiding in Christ, the Heavenly Vine, entirely given up, like Christ, to bear fruit in the salvation of men, and has His words taken up into and abiding in its life, may and dare ask what it will—it shall be done. And where we have not yet attained to that full devotion to which our Lord had trained His disciples, and cannot equal them in their power of prayer, we may, nevertheless, take courage in remembering that, even in the lower stages of the Christian life, every new onward step in the striving after the perfect branch-life, and every surrender to live for others in intercession, will be met from above by a corresponding liberty to draw nigh with greater boldness, and expect larger answers. The more we pray, and the more conscious we become of our unfitness to pray in power, the more we shall be urged and helped to press on towards the secret of power in prayer—a life abiding in Christ entirely at His disposal.

And if any are asking, with somewhat of a despair of attainment, what the reason may be of the failure in this blessed branch-life, so simple and yet so mighty, and how they can come to it, let me point them to one of the most precious lessons of the parable of the Vine. It is one that is all too little noticed. Jesus spake, "I am the true Vine, and my

Father is the Husbandman." We have not only Himself, the glorified Son of God, in His divine fulness, out of whose fulness of life and grace we can draw,—this is very wonderful,—but there is something more blessed still. We have the Father, as the Husbandman, watching over our abiding in the Vine, over our growth and fruitbearing. It is not left to our faith or our faithfulness to maintain our union with Christ: the God, who is the Father of Christ, and who united us with Him,—God Himself will see to it that the branch is what it should be, will enable us to bring forth just the fruit we were appointed to bear. Hear what Christ said of this, "Every branch that beareth fruit, He cleanseth it, that it may bear more fruit." More fruit is what the Father seeks; more fruit is what the Father will Himself provide. It is for this that He, as the Vinedresser, cleanses the branches.

Just think a moment what this means. It is said that of all fruitbearing plants on earth there is none that produces fruit so full of spirit, from 63 which spirit can be so abundantly distilled, as the vine. And of all fruitbearing plants there is none that is so ready to run into wild wood, and for which pruning and cleansing are so indispensable. The one great work that a vinedresser has to do for the branch every year is to prune it. Other plants can for a time dispense with it, and yet bear fruit: the vine must have it. And so the one thing the branch that desires to abide in Christ and bring forth much fruit, and to be able to ask whatsoever it will, must do, is to trust in and yield itself to this Divine cleansing. What is it that the vinedresser cuts away with his pruning-knife? Nothing but the wood that the branch has produced—true, honest wood, with the true vine nature in it. This must be cut away. And why? Because it draws away the strength and life of the vine, and hinders the flow of the juice to the grape. The more it is cut down, the less wood there is in the branch, the more all the sap can go to the grape. The wood of the branch must decrease, that the fruit for the vine may increase; in obedience to the law of all nature, that death is the way to life, that gain comes through sacrifice, the rich and luxuriant growth of wood must be cut off and cast away, that the life more abundant may be seen in the cluster.

Even so, child of God, branch of the Heavenly Vine, there is in thee that which appears perfectly innocent and legitimate, and which yet so draws out thy interest and thy strength, that it must be pruned and cleansed away. We saw what power in prayer men like Abraham and Moses and Elijah had, and we know what fruit they bore. But we also know what it cost them; how God had to separate them from their surroundings, and ever again to draw them from any trust in themselves, to seek their life in Him alone. It is only as our own will, and strength and effort and pleasure, even where these appear perfectly natural and sinless, are cut down, so that the whole energies of our being are free and open to receive the sap of the Heavenly Vine, the Holy Spirit, that we shall bear much fruit. It is in the surrender of what nature holds fast, it is in the full and willing submission to God's holy pruning-knife, that we shall come to what Christ chose and appointed us for—to bear fruit, that whatsoever we ask the Father in Christ's name, He may give to us.

What the pruning-knife is, Christ tells us in the next verse. "Ye are clean through the word which I have spoken to you." As He says later, "Sanctify them through Thy truth; Thy word is truth." "The word of God is sharper than any two-edged sword, piercing even to the dividing of soul and spirit." What heart-searching words Christ had spoken to His disciples on love and humility, on being the least, and, like Himself, the servant of all, on denying self, and taking the cross, and losing the life. Through His word the Father had cleansed them, cut away all confidence in themselves or the world, and prepared them for the inflowing and filling of the Spirit of the Heavenly Vine. It is not we who can cleanse ourselves: God is the Vinedresser: we may confidently intrust ourselves to His care.

Beloved brethren,—ministers, missionaries, teachers, workers, believers old and young,—are you mourning your lack of prayer, and, as a consequence, your lack of power in prayer? Oh! come and listen to your beloved Lord as He tells you, "only be a branch, united to, identified with, the Heavenly Vine, and your prayers will be effectual and much availing." Are you mourning that just this is your trouble— you do not, cannot, live this branch-life, abiding in Him? Oh! come and listen again. "More fruit" is not only your desire, but the Father's too. He is the Husbandman who cleanseth the fruitful branch, that it may bear more fruit. Cast yourself upon God, to do in you what is impossible to man. Count upon a Divine cleansing, to cut down and take away all that self-confidence and self-effort, that has been the cause of your failure. The God who gave you His beloved Son to be your Vine, who made you His branch, will He not do His work of cleansing to make you fruitful in every good work, in the work of prayer and intercession too?

Here is the life that can pray. A branch entirely given up to the Vine and its aims, with all responsibility for its cleansing cast on the Vinedresser; a branch abiding in Christ, trusting and yielding to God for His cleansing, can bear much fruit. In the power of such a life we shall love prayer, we shall know how to pray, we shall pray, and receive whatsoever we ask.

CHAPTER VI. Restraining Prayer: is it Sin?

"Thou restrainest prayer before God."—Job xv. 4.

"What profit should we have, if we pray unto Him?"—Job xxi. 15.

"God forbid that I should sin against the Lord in ceasing to pray for you."—1 Sam. xii. 23.

"Neither will I be with you any more, except ye destroy the accursed from among you."—Josh. vii. 12.

ANY deep quickening of the spiritual life of the Church will always be accompanied by a deeper sense of sin. This will not begin with theology; that can only give expression to what God works in the life of His people. Nor does it mean that that deeper sense of sin will only be seen in stronger expressions of self-reproach or penitence: that is sometimes found to consist with a harbouring of sin, and unbelief as to deliverance. But the true sense of the hatefulness of sin, the hatred of it, will be proved by the intensity of desire for deliverance, and the struggle to know to the very utmost what God can do in saving from it—a holy jealousy, in nothing to sin against God.

If we are to deal effectually with the lack of prayer we must look at it from this point of view and ask, Restraining prayer, is it sin? And if it be, how is it to be dealt with, to be discovered, and confessed, and cast out by man, and cleansed away by God? Jesus is a Saviour from sin. It is only as we know sin truly that we can truly know the power that saves from sin. The life that can pray effectually is the life of the cleansed branch—the life that knows deliverance from the power of self. To see that our prayer-sins are indeed sins, is the first step to a true and Divine deliverance from them.

In the story of Achan we have one of the strongest proofs in Scripture that it is sin that robs God's people of His blessing, and that God will not tolerate it; and at the same time the clearest indication of the principles under which God deals with it, and removes it. Let us see in the light of the story if we can learn how to look at the sin of prayerlessness, and at the sinfulness that lies at the root of it. The words I have quoted above, "Neither will I be with you any more, except ye put away the accursed thing from among you," take us into the very heart of the story, and suggest a series of the most precious lessons around the truth they express, that the presence of sin makes the presence of God impossible.

1. The presence of God is the great privilege of God's people, and their only power against the enemy.—God had promised to Moses, I will bring you in unto the land. Moses proved that he understood this when God, after the sin of the golden calf, spoke of withdrawing His presence and sending an angel. He refused to accept anything less than God's presence. "For whereby shall it be known that I and Thy people have found grace in Thy sight? Is it not that Thou goest with us?" It was this gave Caleb and Joshua their confidence: The Lord is with us. It was this gave Israel their victory over Jericho: the presence of God. This is throughout Scripture the great central promise: I am with thee. This marks off the whole-hearted believer from the worldling and worldly Christians around him: he lives consciously hidden in the secret of God's presence.

2. Defeat and failure are always owing to the loss of God's presence.— It was thus at Ai. God had brought His people into Canaan with the promise to give them the land. When the defeat at Ai took place Joshua felt at once that the cause must be in the withdrawal of God's power. He had not fought for them. His presence had been withheld.

In the Christian life and the work of the Church, defeat is ever a sign of the loss of God's presence. If we apply this to our failure in the prayer-life, and as a result of that to our failure in work for God, we are led to see that all is simply owing to our not standing in clear and full fellowship with God. His nearness, His immediate presence, has not been the chief thing sought after and trusted in. He could not work in us as He would. Loss of blessing and power is ever caused by the loss of God's presence.

3. The loss of God's presence is always owing to some hidden sin.— Just as pain is ordered in nature to warn of some hidden evil in the system, defeat is God's voice telling us there is something wrong. He has given Himself so wholly to His people, He delights so in being with them, and would so fain reveal in them His love and power, that He never withdraws Himself unless they compel Him by sin.

Throughout the Church there is a complaint of defeat. The Church has so little power over the masses, or the educated classes. Powerful conversions are comparatively rare. The fewness of holy, consecrated, spiritual Christians, devoted to the service of God and their fellowmen, is felt everywhere. The power of the Church for the preaching of the gospel to the heathen is paralysed by the scarcity of money and men; and all owing to the lack of the effectual prayer which brings the Holy Spirit in power, first on ministers and believers, then on missionaries and the heathen. Can we deny it that the lack of prayer is the sin on account of which God's presence and power are not more manifestly seen among us?

4. God Himself will discover the hidden sin.—We may think we know what the sin is: it is only God who can discover its real deep meaning. When He spoke to Joshua, before naming the sin of Achan, God first said, "They have transgressed My covenant which I commanded them." God had commanded (vi. 19) that all the booty of Jericho, gold and silver and all that was in it, was to be a devoted thing, consecrated unto the Lord, and to come into His treasury. And Israel had broken this consecration vow: it had not given God His due; it had robbed God.

It is this we need: God must discover to us how the lack of prayer is the indication of unfaithfulness to our consecration vow, that God should have all our heart and life. We must see that this restraining prayer, with the excuses we make for it, is greater sin than we have thought; for what does it mean? That we have little taste or relish for fellowship with God; that our faith rests more on our own work and efforts than on the power of God; that we have little sense of the heavenly blessing God waits to shower down; that we are not ready to sacrifice the ease and confidence of the flesh for persevering waiting on God; that the spirituality of our life, and our abiding in Christ, is altogether too feeble to make us prevail in prayer. When the pressure of work for Christ is allowed to be the excuse for our not finding time to seek and secure His own presence and power in it, as our chief need, it surely proves that there is no right sense of our absolute dependence upon God; no deep apprehension of the Divine and supernatural work of God in which we are only His instruments, no true entrance into the heavenly, altogether other-worldly, character of our mission and aims, no full surrender to and delight in Christ Jesus Himself.

If we were to yield to God's Spirit to show us that all this is in very deed the meaning of remissness in prayer, and of our allowing other things to crowd it out, all our excuses would fall away, and we should fall down and cry, "We have sinned! we have sinned!" Samuel once said, "As for me, God forbid that I should sin against the Lord in ceasing to pray for you." Ceasing from prayer is sin against God. May God discover this to us. (Note A.)

5. When God discovers sin, it must be confessed and cast out.—When the defeat at Ai came, Joshua and Israel were ignorant of the cause. God dealt with Israel as a nation, as one body, and the sin of one member was visited on all. Israel as a whole was ignorant of the sin, and yet suffered for it. The Church may be ignorant of the greatness of this sin of restraining prayer, individual ministers or believers may never have looked upon it as actual transgression, none the less does it bring its punishment. But when the sin is no more hidden, when the Holy Spirit begins to convince of it, then comes the time of heart-searching. In our story the combination of individual and united responsibility is very solemn. The individual: as we find it in the expression, "man for man"; each man felt himself under the eye of God, to be dealt with. And when Achan had been taken, he had to make confession. The united: as we see it in all Israel first suffering and dealt with by God, then taking Achan, and his family, and the accursed thing, and destroying them out of their midst.

If we have reason to think this is the sin that is in the camp, let us begin with personal and united confession. And then let us come before God to put away and destroy the sin. Here stands at the very threshold of Israel's history in Canaan the heap of stones in the valley of Achor, to tell us that God cannot bear sin, that God will not dwell with sin, and that if we really want God's presence in power, sin must be put away. Let us look the solemn fact in the face. There may be other sins, but here is certainly one that causes the loss of God's presence—we do not pray as Christ and Scripture teach us. Let us bring it out before God, and give up this sin to the death. Let us yield ourselves to God to obey His voice. Let no fear of past failure, let no threatening array of temptations, or duties, or excuses, keep us back. It is a simple question of obedience. Are we going to give up ourselves to God and His Spirit to live a life in prayer, well-pleasing to Him? Surely, if it is God who has been withholding His presence, who has been discovering the sin, who is calling for its destruction, and a return to obedience, surely we can count upon His grace to accept and strengthen for the life He asks of us. It is not a question of what you can do; it is the question of whether you now, with your whole heart, turn to give God His due, and give yourself to let His will and grace have their way with you.

6. With sin cast out God's presence is restored.—From this day onwards there is not a word in Joshua of defeat in battle. The story shows them going on from victory to victory. God's presence secured gives power to overcome every enemy.

This truth is so simple that the very ease with which we acquiesce in it robs it of its power. Let us pause and think what it implies. God's presence restored means victory secured. Then, we are responsible for defeat. Then, there must be sin somewhere causing it. Then, we ought at once to find out and put away the sin. We may confidently expect God's presence the moment the sin is put away. Surely each one is under the solemn obligation to search his life and see what part he may have in this evil.

God never speaks to His people of sin except with a view to saving them from it. The same light that shows the sin will show the way out of it. The same power that breaks down and condemns will, if humbly yielded to and waited on in confession and faith, give the power to rise up and conquer. It is God who is speaking to His Church and to us about this sin: "He wondered that there was no intercessor." "I wondered that there was none to uphold." "I sought for a man that should stand in the gap before Me, and found none." The God who speaks thus is He who will work the change for His children who seek His face. He will make the valley of Achor, of trouble and shame, of sin confessed and cast out, a door of hope. Let us not fear, let us not cling to the excuses and explanations which circumstances suggest, but simply confess, "We have sinned; we are sinning; we dare not sin longer." In this matter of prayer we are sure God does not demand of us impossibilities. He does not weary us with an impracticable ideal. He asks us to pray no more than He gives grace to enable us to. He will give the grace to do what He asks, and so to pray that our intercessions shall, day by day, be a pleasure to Him and to us, a source of strength to our conscience and our work, and a channel of blessing to those for whom we labour.

God dealt personally with Joshua, with Israel, with Achan. Let each of us allow Him to deal personally with us concerning this sin, of restraining prayer, and its consequences in our life and work; concerning the deliverance from sin, its certainty and blessedness. Just bow in stillness and wait before God, until, as God, He overshadow you with His presence, lead you out of that region of argument as to human possibilities, where conviction of sin can never be deep, and full deliverance can never come. Take quiet time, and be still before God, that He may take this matter in hand. "Sit still, for He will not be in rest until He have finished this thing this day." Leave yourself in God's hands.

CHAPTER VII. Who shall Deliver?

"Is there no balm in Gilead; is there no physician there? why then is not the health of the daughter of my people recovered?"—Jer. viii. 22.

"Return, ye backsliding children, and I will heal your backslidings. Behold, we come unto Thee; for Thou art the Lord our God."—Jer. iii. 22.

"Heal me, O Lord, and I shall be healed."—Jer. xii. 14.

"O wretched man that I am! who shall deliver me out of the body of this death? I thank God through Jesus Christ our Lord. The law of the Spirit of life in Christ Jesus made me free from the law of sin and death."—Rom. vii. 24, viii. 2.

DURING one of our conventions a gentleman called upon me to ask advice and help. He was evidently an earnest and well-instructed Christian man. He had for some years been in most difficult surroundings, trying to witness for Christ. The result was a sense of failure and unhappiness. His complaint was that he had no relish for the Word, and that though he prayed, it was as if his heart was not in it. If he spoke to others, or gave a tract, it was under a sense of duty: the love and the joy were not present. He longed to be filled with God's Spirit, but the more he sought it, the farther off it appeared to be. What was he to think of his state, and was there any way out of it?

My answer was, that the whole matter appeared to me very simple; he was living under the law and not under grace. As long as he did so, there could be no change. He listened attentively, but could not exactly see what I meant.

I reminded him of the difference, the utter contrariety, between law and grace. Law demands; grace bestows. Law commands, but gives no strength to obey; grace promises, and performs, does all we need to do. Law burdens, and casts down and condemns; grace comforts, and makes strong and glad. Law appeals to self, to do its utmost; grace points to Christ to do all. Law calls to effort and strain, and urges us towards a goal we never can reach; grace works in us all God's blessed will. I pointed out to him how his first step should be, instead of striving against all this failure, fully to accept of it, and the lesson of his own impotence, as God had been seeking to teach it him, and, with this confession, to sink down before God in utter helplessness. There would be the place where he would learn that, unless grace gave him deliverance and strength, he never could do better than he had done, and that grace would indeed work all for him. He must come out from under law and self and effort, and take his place under grace, allowing God to do all.

In later conversations he told me the diagnosis of the disease had been correct. He admitted grace must do all. And yet, so deep was the thought that we must do something, that we must at least bring our faithfulness to secure the work of grace, he feared that his life would not be very different; he would not be equal to the strain of new difficulties into which he was now going. There was, amid all the intense earnestness, an undertone of despair; he could not live as he knew he ought to. I have already said, in the opening chapter, that in some of our meetings I had noticed this tone of hopelessness. And no minister who has come into close contact with souls seeking to live wholly for God, to "walk worthy of the Lord unto all well pleasing," but knows that this renders true progress impossible. To speak specially of the lack of prayer, and the desire of living a fuller prayer-life, how many are the difficulties to be met! We have so often resolved to pray more and better, and have failed. We have not the strength of will some have, with one resolve to turn round and change our habits. The press of duty is as great as ever it was; it is so difficult to find time for more prayer; real enjoyment in prayer, which would enable us to persevere, is what we do not feel; we do not possess the power to supplicate and to plead, as we should; our prayers, instead of being a joy and a strength, are a source of continual self-condemnation and doubt. We have at times mourned and confessed and resolved; but, to tell the honest truth, we do not expect, for we do not see the way to, any great change.

It is evident that as long as this spirit prevails, there can be very little prospect of improvement. Discouragement must bring defeat. One of the first objects of a physician is ever to waken hope; without this he knows his medicines will often profit little. No teaching from God's Word as to the duty, the urgent need, the blessed privilege of more prayer, of effectual prayer, will avail, while the secret whisper is heard: There is no hope. Our first care must be to find out the hidden cause of the failure and despair, and then to show how divinely sure deliverance is. We must, unless we are to rest content with our state, listen to and join in the question, "Is there no balm in Gilead; is there no physician there? why then is not the health of the daughter of my people restored?" We must listen, and receive into our heart, the Divine promise with the response it met with: "Return, ye backsliding children, and I will heal your backslidings. Behold, we come unto Thee, for Thou art the Lord our God." We must come with the personal prayer, and the faith that there will be a personal answer. Shall we not even now begin to claim it in regard to the lack of prayer, and believe that God will help us: "Heal me, O Lord, and I shall be healed."

It is always of consequence to distinguish between the symptoms of a disease and the disease itself. Feebleness and failure in prayer is a sign of feebleness in the spiritual life. If a patient were to ask a physician to give him something to stimulate his feeble pulse, he would be told that this would do him little good. The pulse is the index of the state of the heart and the whole system: the physician strives to have health restored. What everyone who would fain pray more faithfully and effectually must learn is this, that his whole spiritual life is in a sickly state, and needs restoration. It is as he comes to look, not only at his shortcomings in prayer, but at the lack in the life of faith, of which this is the symptom, that he will become fully alive to the serious nature of the disease. He will then see the need of a radical change in his whole life and walk, if his prayer-life, which is simply the pulse of the spiritual system, is to indicate health and vigour. God has so created us that the exercise of every healthy function causes joy. Prayer is meant to be as simple and natural as breathing or working to a healthy man. The reluctance we feel, and the failure we confess, are God's own voice calling us to acknowledge our disease, and to come to Him for the healing He has promised.

And what is now the disease of which the lack of prayer is the symptom? We cannot find a better answer than is pointed out in the words, "Ye are not under the law, but under grace."

Here we have suggested the possibility of two types of Christian life. There may be a life partly under the law and partly under grace; or, a life entirely under grace, in the full liberty from self-effort, and the full experience of the Divine strength which it can give. A true believer may still be living partly under the law, in the power of self-effort, striving to do what he cannot accomplish. The continued failure in his Christian life to which he confesses is owing to this one thing: he trusts in himself, and tries to do his best. He does, indeed, pray and look to God for help, but still it is he in his strength, helped by God, who is to do the work. In the Epistles to the Romans, and Corinthians, and Galatians, we know how Paul tells them that they have not received the spirit of bondage again, that they are free from the law, that they are no more servants but sons; that they must beware of nothing so much as to be entangled again with the yoke of bondage. Everywhere it is the contrast between the law and grace, between the flesh, which is under the law, and the Spirit, who is the gift of grace, and through whom grace does all its work. In our days, just as in those first ages, the great danger is living under the law, and serving God in the strength of the flesh. With the great majority of Christians it appears to be the state in which they remain all their lives. Hence the lack to such a large extent of true holy living and power in prayer. They do not know that all failure can have but one cause: Men seek to do themselves what grace alone can do in them, what grace most certainly will do.

Many will not be prepared to admit that this is their disease, that they are not living "under grace." Impossible, they say. "From the depth of my heart," a Christian cries, "I believe and know that there is no good in me, and that I owe everything to grace alone." "I have spent my life," a minister says, "and found my glory in preaching and exalting the doctrines of free grace." "And I," a missionary answers, "how could I ever have thought of seeing the heathen saved, if my only confidence had not been in the message I brought, and the power I trusted, of God's abounding grace." Surely you cannot say that our failures in prayer, and we sadly confess to them, are owing to our not living "under grace"? This cannot be our disease.

We know how often a man may be suffering from a disease without knowing it. What he counts a slight ailment turns out to be a dangerous complaint. Do not let us be too sure that we are not, to a large extent, still living "under the law," while considering ourselves to be living wholly "under grace." Very frequently the reason of this mistake is the limited meaning attached to the word "grace." Just as we limit God Himself, by our little or unbelieving thoughts of Him, so we limit His grace at the very moment that we are delighting in terms like the "riches of grace," "grace exceeding abundant." Has not the very term, "grace abounding," from Bunyan's book downward, been confined to the one great blessed truth of free justification with ever renewed pardon and eternal glory for the vilest of sinners, while the other equally blessed truth of "grace abounding" in sanctification is not fully known. Paul writes: "Much more shall they which receive the abundance of grace reign in life through Jesus Christ." That reigning in life, as conqueror over sin, is even here on earth. "Where sin abounded" in the heart and life, "grace did abound more exceedingly, that grace might reign through righteousness" in the 87 whole life and being of the believer. It is of this reign of grace in the soul that Paul asks, "Shall we sin because we are under grace?" and answers, "God forbid." Grace is not only pardon of, but power over, sin; grace takes the place sin had in the life, and undertakes, as sin had reigned within in the power of death, to reign in the power of Christ's life. It is of this grace that Christ spoke, "My grace is sufficient for thee," and Paul answered, "I will glory in my weakness; for, when I am weak, then am I strong." It is of this grace, which, when we are willing to confess ourselves utterly impotent and helpless, comes in to work all in us, that Paul elsewhere teaches, "God is able to make all grace abound unto you, that ye, always having all sufficiency in all things, may abound unto all good works."

It has often happened that a seeker after God and salvation has read his Bible long, and yet never seen the truth of a free and full and immediate justification by faith. When once his eyes were opened, and he accepted it, he was amazed to find it everywhere. Even so many believers, who hold the doctrines of free grace as applied to pardon, have never seen its wondrous meaning as it undertakes to work our whole life in us, and actually give us strength every moment for whatever the Father would have us be and do. When God's light shines into our heart with this blessed truth, we know what Paul means, "Not I, but the grace of God." There again you have the twofold Christian life. The one, in which that "Not I"—I am nothing, I can do nothing— has not yet become a reality. The other, when the wondrous exchange has been made, and grace has taken the place of our effort, and we say and know, "I live, yet no longer I, but Christ liveth in me." It may then become a lifelong experience: "The grace of our Lord was exceeding abundant, with faith and love which is in Christ Jesus."

Beloved child of God! what think you, is it not possible that this has been the want in your life, the cause of your failure in prayer? You knew not how grace would enable you to pray, if once the whole life were under its power. You sought by earnest effort to conquer your reluctance or deadness in prayer, but failed. You strove by every motive of shame or love you could think of to stir yourself to it, but it would not help. Is it not worth while asking the Lord whether the message I bring you as His servant may not be more true for you than you think? Your lack of prayer is owing to a diseased state of life, and the disease is nothing but this—you have not accepted, for daily life and every duty, the full salvation which the word brings: "Ye are not under the law, but under grace." As universal and deep-reaching as the demand of the law and the reign of sin, yea, more exceeding abundant, is the provision of grace and the power by which it makes us reign in life. (Note B.)

In the chapter that follows that in which Paul wrote, "Ye are not under the law, but under grace," he gives us a picture of a believer's life under law, with the bitter experience in which it ends: "O wretched man that I am! who shall deliver me from the body of this death?" His answer to the question, "I thank God through Jesus Christ our Lord," shows that there is deliverance from a life held captive under evil habits that have been struggled against in vain. That deliverance is by the Holy Spirit giving the full experience of what the life of Christ can work in us: "The law of the Spirit of life in Christ Jesus hath made me free from the law of sin and death." The law of God could only deliver us into the power of the law of sin and death. The grace of God can bring us into, and keep us in, the liberty of the Spirit. We can be made free from the sad life under the power that led us captive, so that we did not what we would. The Spirit of life in Christ can free us from our continual failure in prayer, and enable us in this, too, to walk worthy of the Lord unto all well-pleasing.

Oh! be not hopeless, be not despondent; there is a balm in Gilead; there is a Physician there; there is healing for our sickness. What is impossible with man is possible with God. What you see no possibility of doing, grace will do. Confess the disease; trust the Physician; claim the healing; pray the prayer of faith, "Heal me, and I shall be healed." You too can become a man of prayer, and pray the effectual prayer that availeth much.1

1 I ought to say, for the encouragement of all, that the gentleman of whom I spoke, at a Convention a fortnight later, saw and claimed the rest of faith in trusting God for all, and a letter from England tells that he has found that His grace is sufficient.

CHAPTER VIII. Wilt Thou be made Whole?

"Jesus saith unto him, Wilt thou be made whole? The impotent man answered him, Sir, I have no man to put me into the pool. Jesus saith unto him, Rise and walk. Immediately the man was made whole, and walked."—John v. 6–9.

"Peter said, In the name of Jesus Christ of Nazareth, rise up and walk.... The faith which is by Him hath given this man this perfect soundness in the presence of you all."—Acts iii. 6, 16.

"Peter said, Æneas, Jesus Christ maketh thee whole: arise. And he arose immediately."—Acts ix. 34.

FEEBLENESS in prayer is the mark of disease. Impotence to walk is, in the Christian, as in the natural life, a terrible proof of some evil in the system that needs a physician. The lack of power to walk joyfully in the new and living way that leads to the Father and the throne of grace is specially grievous. Christ is the great Physician, who comes to every Bethesda where impotent folk are gathered, and speaks out his loving, searching question, Wilt thou be made whole? For all who are still clinging to their hope in the pool, or are looking for some man to put them in, who are hoping, in course of time, somehow to be helped by just continuing in the use of the ordinary means of grace, His question points to a better way. He offers them healing in a way of power they have never understood. And to all who are willing to confess, not only their own impotence, but their failure to find any man to help them, His question brings the sure and certain hope of a near deliverance. We have seen that our weakness in prayer is part of a life smitten with spiritual impotence. Let us listen to our Lord as He offers to restore our spiritual strength, to fit us for walking like healthy, strong men in all the ways of the Lord, and so be fit rightly to fill our place in the great work of intercession. As we see what the wholeness is He offers, how He gives it, and what He asks of us, we shall be prepared for giving a willing answer to His question.

What the Health that Jesus Offers.

I might mention many marks of spiritual health. Our text leads us to take one,—walking. Jesus said to the sick man, Rise and walk, and with that restored him to his place among men in full health and vigour, able to take his part in all the work of life. It is a wonderfully suggestive picture of the restoration of spiritual health. To the healthy, walking is a pleasure; to the sick, a burden, if not an impossibility. How many Christians there are to whom, like the maimed and the halt and the lame and the impotent, movement and progress in God's way is indeed an effort and a weariness. Christ comes to say, and with the word He gives the power, Rise and walk.

Just think of this walk to which He restores and empowers us. It is a life like that of Enoch and Noah, who "walked with God." A life like that of Abraham, to whom God said, "Walk before Me," and who himself spake, "The Lord before whom I walk." A life of which David sings, "They shall walk in the light of Thy countenance," and Isaiah prophesies, "They that wait on the Lord shall renew their strength; they shall run and not be weary, they shall walk and not faint." Even as God the Creator fainteth not nor is weary, shall they who walk with Him, waiting on Him, never be exhausted or feeble. It is a life concerning which it could be said of the last of the Old Testament saints, Zacharias and Elisabeth, "They were both righteous before God, walking in all the commandments and ordinances of the Lord blameless." This is the walk Jesus came to make possible and true to His people in greater power than ever before.

Hear what the New Testament speaks of it: "That like as Christ was raised from the dead by the glory of the Father, so we also should walk in newness of life." It is the Risen One who says to us, Rise and walk: He gives the power of the resurrection life. It is a walk in Christ. "As ye have received Christ Jesus the Lord, so walk ye also in Him." It is a walk like Christ. "He that saith he abideth in Him ought so to walk even as He walked." It is a walk by the Spirit and after the Spirit. "Walk by the Spirit, and ye shall not fulfil the lusts of the flesh." "Who walk not after the flesh, but after the Spirit." It is a walk worthy of God and well pleasing to Him. "That ye would walk worthy of the Lord, unto all well pleasing, being fruitful in every good work." "I beseech you, that as ye received of us, how ye should walk and please God, even as ye do walk, that ye would abound more and more." It is a walk in heavenly love. "Walk in love, even as Christ loved you." It is a "walk in the light, as He is in the light." It is a walk of faith, all its power coming simply from God and Christ and the Holy Spirit, to the soul turned away from the world. "We walk by faith, and not by sight."

How many believers there are who regard such a walk as an impossible thing—so impossible that they do not feel it a sin that they "walk otherwise"; and so they do not long for this walk in newness of life. They have become so accustomed to the life of impotence, that the life and walk in God's strength has little attraction. But some there are with whom it is not thus. They do wonder if these words really mean what they say, and if the wonderful life each one of them speaks of is simply an unattainable ideal, or meant to be realised in flesh and blood. The more they study them, the more they feel that they are spoken as for daily life. And yet they appear too high. Oh that they would believe that God sent his Almighty Son, and His Holy Spirit, indeed to bring us and fit us for a life and walk from heaven beyond all that man could dare to think or hope for.

How Jesus Makes Us Whole.

When a physician heals a patient, he acts on him from without, and does something which is, if possible, ever after to render him independent of his aid. He restores him to perfect health, and leaves him. With the work of our Lord Jesus it is in both respects the very opposite. Jesus works not from without, but from within, by entering Himself in the power of His Spirit into our very life. And instead of, as in the bodily healing, being rendered, if possible, independent of a physician for the future, Christ's one purpose in healing is, as we said, the exact opposite. His one condition of success, is to bring us into such dependence upon Himself as that we shall not be able one single moment to do without Him. Christ Jesus Himself is our life, in a sense that many Christians have no conception of. The prevailing feeble and sickly life is entirely owing to the lack of the apprehension of the Divine truth, that as long as we expect Christ continually to do something for us from heaven, in single acts of grace from time to time, and each time trust Him to give us what will last a little while, we cannot be restored to perfect health. But when once we see how there is to be nothing of our own for a single moment, and it is to be all Christ moment by moment, and learn to accept it from Him and trust Him for it, the life of Christ becomes the health of our soul. Health is nothing but life in its normal, undisturbed action. Christ gives us health by giving us Himself as our life; so He becomes our strength for our walk. Isaiah's words find their New Testament fulfilment: They that wait on the Lord shall walk and not faint, because Christ is now the strength of their life.

It is strange how believers sometimes think this life of dependence too great a strain, and a loss of our personal liberty. They admit a need of dependence, of much dependence, but with room left for our own will and energy. They do not see that even a partial dependence makes us debtors, and leaves us nothing to boast of. They forget that our relationship to God, and co-operation with Him, is not that He does the larger part and we the lesser, but that God does all and we do all—God all in us, we all through God. This dependence upon God secures our true independence; when our will seeks nothing but the Divine will, we reach a Divine nobility, the true independence of all that is created. He that has not seen this must remain a sickly Christian, letting self do part and Christ part. He that accepts the life of unceasing dependence on Christ, as life and health and strength, is made whole. As God, Christ can enter and become the life of His creature. As the Glorified One who received the Holy Spirit from the Father to bestow, He can renew the heart of the sinful creature and make it His home, and by His presence maintain it in full health and strength.

O ye all who would fain walk and please God, and in your prayer-life not have your heart condemn you, listen to Christ's words: "Wilt thou be made whole?" He can give soul-health. He can give a life that can pray, and know that it is well-pleasing to the Father. If you would have this, come and hear how you can receive it.

What Christ asks of us.

The story invites us to notice three things very specially. Christ's question first appeals to the will, and asks for the expression of its consent. He then listens to man's confession of his utter helplessness. Then comes the ready obedience to Christ's command, that rises up and walks.

1. Wilt thou be made whole? About the answer of the impotent man there could be no doubt. Who would not be willing to have his sickness removed? But, alas, in the spiritual life what need to press the question. Some will not admit that they are so sick. And some will not believe that Christ can make a man whole. And some will believe it for others, but they are sure it is not for them. At the root of all lies the fear of the self-denial and the sacrifice which will be needed. They are not willing to forsake entirely the walk after the course of this world, to give up all self-will, and self-confidence, and self-pleasing. The walk in Christ and like Christ is too straight and hard: they do not will it, they do not will to be made whole. My brother, if thou art willing, speak it out: "Lord! at any price, I will!" From Christ's side the act is one of the will: "I will, be thou clean." From your side equally: "Be it unto thee as thou wilt." If you would be delivered from your impotence—oh, fear not to say, "I will, I will!"

Then comes the second step. Christ wants us to look up to him as our only Helper. "I have no man to put me in," must be our cry. Here on earth there is no help for me. Weakness may grow into strength in the ordinary use of means, if all the organs and functions are in a sound state. Sickness needs special measures. Your soul is sick; your impotence to walk joyfully the Christian walk in God's way is a sign of disease; fear not to confess it, and to admit that there is no hope for restoration unless by an act of Christ's mercy healing you. Give up the idea of growing out of your sickly into a healthy state, of growing out from under the law into a life under grace. A few days ago I heard a student plead the cause of the Volunteer Pledge. "The pledge calls you," he said, "to a decision. Do not think of growing into a missionary: unless God forbids you, take the step; the decision will bring joy and strength, will set you free to grow up in all needed for a missionary, and will be a help to others." It is even so in the Christian life. Delay and struggle will equally hinder you; do confess that you cannot bring yourself to pray as you would, because you cannot give yourself the healthy, heavenly life that loves to pray, and that knows to count upon God's Spirit to pray in us. Come to Christ to heal you. He can in one moment make you whole. Not in the sense of working a sudden change in your feelings, or in what you are in yourself, but in the heavenly reality of coming in, in response to your surrender and faith, and taking charge of your inner life, and filling it with Himself and Spirit.

The third thing Christ asks is this, the surrender of faith. When He spoke to the impotent man His word of command had to be obeyed. The man believed that there was truth and power in Christ's word; in that faith he rose and walked. By faith he obeyed. And what Christ said to others was for him too—"Go thy way; thy faith hath made thee whole." Of us, too, Christ asks this faith, that His word changes our impotence into strength, and fits us for that walk in newness of life for which we have been quickened in Him. If we do not believe this, if we will not take courage and say, with Paul, "I can do all things in Christ, which strengtheneth me," we cannot obey. But if we will listen to the word that tells us of the walk that is not only possible, but has been proved and seen in God's saints from of old, if we will fix our eye on the mighty, living, loving Christ, who speaks in power, "Rise and walk," we shall take courage and obey. We shall rise and begin to walk in Him and His strength. In faith, apart from and above all feeling, we shall accept and trust an unseen Christ as our strength, and go on in the strength of the Lord God. We shall know Christ as the strength of our life. We shall know, and tell, and prove that Jesus Christ hath made us whole.

Can it indeed be? Yes, it can. He has done it for many: He will do it for you. Beware of forming wrong conceptions of what must take place. When the impotent man was made whole he had still all to learn as to the use of his new-found strength. If he wanted to dig, or build, or learn a trade, he had to begin at the beginning. Do not expect at once to be a proficient in prayer or any part of the Christian life. No; but expect and be confident of this one thing, that, as you have trusted yourself to Christ to be your health and strength, He will lead and teach you. Begin to pray in a quiet sense of your ignorance and weakness, but in a joyful assurance that He will work in you what you need. Rise and walk each day in a holy confidence that He is with you and in you. Just accept Jesus Christ the Living One, and trust Him to do His work.

Will you do it? Have you done it? Even now Jesus speaks, "Rise and walk." "Amen, Lord! at Thy word I come. I rise to walk with Thee, and in Thee, and like Thee."

"What things soever ye desire, when ye pray, believe that ye have received them, and ye shall have them."—Mark xi. 24.

HERE we have a summary of the teaching of our Lord Jesus on prayer. Nothing will so much help to convince us of the sin of our remissness in prayer, to discover its causes, and to give us courage to expect entire deliverance, as the careful study and then the believing acceptance of that teaching. The more heartily we enter into the mind of our blessed Lord, and set ourselves simply just to think about prayer as He thought, the more surely will His words be as living seeds. They will grow and produce in us their fruit,—a life and practice exactly corresponding to the Divine truth they contain. Do let us believe this: Christ, the living Word of God, gives in His words a Divine quickening power which brings what they say, which works in us what He asks, which actually fits and enables for all He demands. Learn to look upon His teaching on prayer as a definite promise of what He, by His Holy Spirit dwelling in you, is going to work into your very being and character.

Our Lord gives us the five marks, or essential elements, of true prayer. There must be, first, the heart's desire; then the expression of that desire in prayer; with that, the faith that carries the prayer to God; in that faith, the acceptance of God's answer; then comes the experience of the desired blessing. It may help to give definiteness to our thought, if we each take a definite request in regard to which we would fain learn to pray believingly. Or, perhaps better still, we might all unite and take the one thing that has been occupying our attention. We have been speaking of failure in prayer; why should we not take as the object of desire and supplication the "grace of supplication," and say, I want to ask and receive in faith the power to pray just as, and as much as, my God expects of me? Let us meditate on our Lord's words, in the confidence that He will teach us how to pray for this blessing.

1. "What things soever ye desire."—Desire is the secret power that moves the whole world of living men, and directs the course of each. And so desire is the soul of prayer, and the cause of insufficient or unsuccessful prayer is very much to be found in the lack or feebleness of desire. Some may doubt this: they are sure that they have very earnestly desired what they ask. But if they consider whether their desire has indeed been as whole-hearted as God would have it, as the heavenly worth of these blessings demands, they may come to see that it was indeed the lack of desire that was the cause of failure. What is

true of God is true of each of his blessings, and is the more true the more spiritual the blessing: "Ye shall seek Me, and shall find, when ye shall search for Me with all your heart" (Jer. xxix. 13). Of Judah in the days of Asa it is written, "They sought Him with their whole desire" (2 Chron. xv. 15). A Christian may often have very earnest desires for spiritual blessings. But alongside of these there are other desires in his daily life occupying a large place in his interests and affections. The spiritual desires are not all-absorbing. He wonders that his prayer is not heard. It is simply that God wants the whole heart. "The Lord thy God is one Lord, therefore thou shalt love the Lord thy God with all thy heart." The law is unchangeable: God offers Himself, gives Himself away, to the whole-hearted who give themselves wholly away to Him. He always gives us according to our heart's desire. But not as we think it, but as He sees it. If there be other desires which are more at home with us, which have our heart more than Himself and His presence, He allows these to be fulfilled, and the desires that engage us at the hour of prayer cannot be granted.

We desire the gift of intercession, grace and power to pray aright. Our hearts must be drawn away from other desires: we must give ourselves wholly to this one. We must be willing to live wholly in intercession for the kingdom. By fixing our eye on the blessedness and the need of this grace, by thinking of the certainty that God will give it us, by giving ourselves up to it, for the sake of the perishing world, desire may be strengthened, and the first step taken towards the possession of the coveted blessing. Let us seek the grace of prayer, as we seek the God with whom it will link us, "with our whole desire"; we may depend upon the promise, "He will fulfil the desire of them that fear Him." Let us not fear to say to Him, "I desire it with my whole heart."

2. "What things soever ye desire when ye pray."—The desire of the heart must become the expression of the lips. Our Lord Jesus more than once asked those who cried to Him for mercy, "What wilt thou?" He wanted them to say what they would. To speak it out roused their whole being into action, brought them into contact with Him, and wakened their expectation. To pray is to enter into God's presence, to claim and secure His attention, to have distinct dealing with Him in regard to some request, to commit our need to His faithfulness and to leave it there: it is in so doing that we become fully conscious of what we are seeking.

There are some who often carry strong desires in their heart, without bringing them to God in the clear expression of definite and repeated prayer. There are others who go to the Word and its promises to strengthen their faith, but do not give sufficient place to that pointed asking of God which helps the soul to the assurance that the matter has been put into God's hands. Still others come in prayer with so many requests and desires, that it is difficult for themselves to say what they really expect God to do. If you would obtain from God this great gift of faithfulness in prayer and power to pray aright, begin by exercising yourself in prayer in regard to it. Say of it to yourself and to God: "Here is something I have asked, and am continuing to ask till I receive. As plain and pointed as words can make it, I am saying, 'My Father! I do desire, I do ask of Thee, and expect of Thee, the grace of prayer and intercession.'"

3. "What things soever ye desire, when ye pray, believe."—As it is only by faith that we can know God, or receive Jesus Christ, or live the Christian life, so faith is the life and power of prayer. If we are to enter upon a life of intercession, in which there is to be joy and power and blessing, if we are to have our prayer for the grace of prayer answered, we must learn anew what faith is, and begin to live and pray in faith as never before.

Faith is the opposite of sight, and the two are contrary the one to the other. "We walk by faith, and not by sight." If the unseen is to get full possession of us, and heart and life and prayer are to be full of faith, there must be a withdrawal from, a denial of, the visible. The spirit that seeks to enjoy as much as possible of what is innocent or legitimate, that gives the first place to the calls and duties of daily life, is inconsistent with a strong faith and close intercourse with the spiritual world. "We look not at the things that are seen"—the negative side needs to be emphasised if the positive, "but at the things which are not seen," is to become natural to us. In praying, faith depends upon our living in the invisible world.

This faith has specially to do with God. The great reason of our lack of faith is our lack of knowledge of God and intercourse with Him. "Have faith in God," Jesus said when He spoke of removing mountains. It is as a soul knows God, is occupied with His power, love, and faithfulness, comes away out of self and the world, and allows the light of God to shine on it, that unbelief will become impossible. All the mysteries and difficulties connected with answers to prayer will, however little we may be able to solve them intellectually, be swallowed up in the adoring assurance: "This God is our God. He will bless us. He does indeed answer prayer. And the grace to pray I am asking for He will delight to give." (Note C.)

4. "What things soever ye desire, when ye pray, believe that ye have received," now as you pray.—Faith has to accept the answer, as given by God in heaven, before it is found or felt upon earth. This point causes difficulty, and yet it is of the very essence of believing prayer, its real secret. Try and take it in. Spiritual things can only be spiritually apprehended or appropriated. The spiritual heavenly blessing of God's answer to your prayer must be spiritually recognised and accepted before you feel anything of it. It is faith does this. A soul that not only seeks an answer, but seeks first the God who gives the answer, receives the power to know that it has what it has asked of Him. If it knows that it has asked according to His will and promises, and that it has come to and found Himself to give it, it does believe that it has received. "We know that He heareth us."

There is nothing so heart-searching as this faith, "Believe that ye have received." As we strive to believe, and find we cannot, it leads us to discover what there is that hinders. Blessed is the man who holds nothing back, and lets nothing hold him back, but, with his eye and heart on God alone, refuses to rest till he has believed what our Lord bids him, "that he has received." Here is the place where Jacob becomes Israel, and the power of prevailing prayer is born out of human weakness and despair. Here comes in the real need for persevering and ever-importunate prayer, that will not rest, or go away, or give up, till it knows it is heard, and believes that it has received.

You pray for "the Spirit of grace and supplication"? As you ask for it in strong desire, and believe in God who hears prayer, do not be afraid to press on and believe that your life can indeed be changed, that the world with its press of duties, whether religious or not, hindering prayer, can be overcome, and that God gives you your heart's desire, grace to pray both in measure and in spirit, just as the Father would have His child do. "Believe that you have received."

5. "What things soever ye desire, when ye pray, believe that ye have received, and ye shall have them."—The receiving from God in faith, the believing acceptance of the answer with the perfect, praising assurance that it has been given, is not necessarily the experience or subjective possession of the gift we have asked for. At times there may be a considerable, or even a long, interval. In other cases the believing supplicant may at once enter upon the actual enjoyment of what he has received. It is specially in the former case that we have need of faith

and patience: faith to rejoice in the assurance of the answer bestowed and received, and to begin and act upon that answer though nothing be felt; patience to wait if there be for the present no sensible proof of its presence. We can count upon it: Ye shall have, in actual enjoyment.

If we apply this to the prayer for the power of faithful intercession, the grace to pray earnestly and perseveringly for souls around us, let us learn to hold fast the Divine assurance that, as surely as we believe we receive, and that faith therefore, apart from all failing, may rejoice in the certainty of an answered prayer. The more we praise God for it, the sooner will the experience come. We may begin at once to pray for others, in the confidence that grace will be given us to pray more perseveringly and more believingly than we have done before. If we do not find any special enlargement or power in prayer, this must not hinder or discourage us. We have accepted, apart from feeling, a spiritual Divine gift by faith; in that faith we are to pray, nothing doubting. The Holy Spirit may for a little time be hiding Himself within us; we may count upon Him, even though it be with groanings which cannot find expression, to pray in us; in due time we shall become conscious of His presence and power. As sure as there is desire and prayer and faith, and faith's acceptance of the gift, there will be, too, the manifestation and experience of the blessing we sought.

Beloved brother! do you truly desire that God should enable you so to pray that your life may be free from continual self-condemnation, and that the power of His Spirit may come down in answer to your petition? Come and ask it of God. Kneel down and pray for it in a single definite sentence. When you have done so, kneel still in faith, believing in God who answers. Believe that you do now receive what you have prayed: believe that you have received. If you find it difficult to do this, kneel still, and say that you do it on the strength of His own word. If it cost time, and struggle, and doubt—fear not; at His feet, looking up into His face, faith will come. "Believe that you have received": at His bidding you dare claim the answer. Begin in that faith, even though it be feeble, a new prayer-life, with this one thought as its strength: "You have asked and received grace in Christ to prepare you, step by step, to be faithful in prayer and intercession. The more simply you hold to this, and expect the Holy Spirit to work it in you, the more surely and fully will the word be made true to you: Ye shall have it. God Himself who gave the answer will work it in you."

CHAPTER X. The Spirit of Supplication

"I will pour upon the house of David the Spirit of grace and of supplication."—Zech. xii. 10.

"The Spirit also helpeth our infirmity; for we know not how to pray as we ought: but the Spirit Himself maketh intercession for us with groanings which cannot be uttered. And He that searcheth the hearts knoweth what is the mind of the Spirit, because He maketh intercession for the saints according to God."—Rom. viii. 26, 27.

"With all prayer and supplication praying at all seasons in the Spirit, and watching thereunto in all perseverance and supplication for all the saints."—Eph. vi. 18.

"Praying in the Holy Spirit."—Jude 20.

THE Holy Spirit has been given to every child of God to be his life. He dwells in him, not as a separate Being in one part of his nature, but as his very life. He is the Divine power or energy by which his life is maintained and strengthened. All that a believer is called to be or to do, the Holy Spirit can and will work in him. If he does not know or yield to the Holy Guest, the Blessed Spirit cannot work, and his life is a sickly one, full of failure and of sin. As he yields, and waits, and obeys the leading of the Spirit, God works in him all that is pleasing in His sight.

This Holy Spirit is, in the first place, a Spirit of prayer. He was promised as a "Spirit of grace and supplication," the grace for supplication. He was sent forth into our hearts as "the Spirit of adoption, whereby we cry, Abba, Father." He enables us to say, in true faith and growing apprehension of its meaning, Our Father which art in heaven. "He maketh intercession for the saints according to God." And as we pray in the Spirit, our worship is as God seeks it to be, "in spirit and in truth." Prayer is just the breathing of the Spirit in us; power in prayer comes from the power of the Spirit in us, waited on and trusted in. Failure in prayer comes from feebleness of the Spirit's work in us. Our prayer is the index of the measure of the Spirit's work in us. To pray aright, the life of the Spirit must be right in us. For praying the effectual, much-availing prayer of the righteous man everything depends on being full of the Spirit.

There are three very simple lessons that the believer, who would enjoy the blessing of being taught to pray by the Spirit of prayer, must know. The first is: Believe that the Spirit dwells in you (Eph. i. 13). Deep in the inmost recesses of his being, hidden and unfelt, every child of God has the Holy, Mighty Spirit of God dwelling in him. He knows it by faith, the faith that, accepting God's word, realises that of which he sees as yet no sign. "We receive the promise of the Spirit by faith." As long as we measure our power, for praying aright and perseveringly, by what we feel, or think we can accomplish, we shall be discouraged when we hear of how much we ought to pray. But when we quietly believe that, in the midst of all our conscious weakness, the Holy Spirit as a Spirit of supplication is dwelling within us, for the very purpose of enabling us to pray in such manner and measure as God would have us, our hearts will be filled with hope. We shall be strengthened in the assurance which lies at the very root of a happy and fruitful Christian life, that God has made an abundant provision for our being what He wants us to be. We shall begin to lose our sense of burden and fear and discouragement about our ever praying sufficiently, because we see that the Holy Spirit Himself will pray, is praying, in us.

The second lesson is: Beware above everything of grieving the Holy Spirit (Eph. iv. 30). If you do, how can He work in you the quiet, trustful, and blessed sense of that union with Christ which makes your prayers well pleasing to the Father? Beware of grieving Him by sin, by unbelief, by selfishness, by unfaithfulness to His voice in conscience. Do not think grieving Him a necessity: that cuts away the very sinews of your strength. Do not consider it impossible to obey the command, "Grieve not the Holy Spirit." He Himself is the very power of God to make you obedient. The sin that comes up in you against your will, the tendency to sloth, or pride, or self-will, or passion that rises in the flesh, your will can, in the power of the Spirit, at once reject, and cast upon Christ and His blood, and your communion with God is immediately restored. Accept each day the Holy Spirit as your Leader and Life and Strength; you can count upon Him to do in your heart all that ought to be done there. He, the Unseen and Unfelt One, but known by faith, gives there, unseen and unfelt, the love and the faith and the power of obedience you need, because He reveals Christ unseen within you, as actually your Life and Strength. Grieve not the Holy Spirit by distrusting Him, because you do not feel His presence in you.

Especially in the matter of prayer grieve Him not. Do not expect, when you trust Christ to bring you into a new, healthy prayer-life, that you will be able all at once to pray as easily and powerfully and joyfully as you fain would. No; it may not come at once. But just bow quietly before God in your ignorance and weakness. That is the best and truest prayer, to put yourself before God just as you are, and to count on the hidden Spirit praying in you. "We know not what to pray as we ought"; ignorance, difficulty, struggle, marks our prayer all along. But, "the Spirit helpeth our infirmities." How? "The Spirit Himself," deeper down than our thoughts or feelings, "maketh intercession for us with groanings which cannot be uttered." When you cannot find words, when your words appear cold and feeble, just believe: The Holy Spirit is praying in me. Be quiet before God, and give Him time and opportunity; in due season you will learn to pray. Beware of grieving the Spirit of prayer, by not honouring Him in patient, trustful surrender to His intercession in you.

The third lesson: "Be filled with the Spirit" (Eph. v. 18). I think that we have seen the meaning of the great truth: It is only the healthy spiritual life that can pray aright. The command comes to each of us: "Be filled with the Spirit." That implies that while some rest content with the beginning, with a small measure of the Spirit's working, it is God's will that we should be filled with the Spirit. That means, from our side, that our whole being ought to be entirely yielded up to the Holy Spirit, to be possessed and controlled by Him alone. And, from God's side, that we may count upon and expect the Holy Spirit to take possession and fill us. Has not our failure in prayer evidently been owing to our not having accepted the Spirit of prayer to be our life; to our not having yielded wholly to Him, whom the Father gave as the Spirit of His Son, to work the life of the Son in us? Let us, to say the very least, be willing to receive Him, to yield ourselves to God and trust Him for it. Let us not again wilfully grieve the Holy Spirit by declining, by neglecting, by hesitating to seek to have Him as fully as He is willing to give Himself to us. If we have at all seen that prayer is the great need of our work and of the Church, if we have at all desired or resolved to pray more, let us turn to the very source of all power and blessing—let us believe that the Spirit of prayer, even in His fulness, is for us.

We all admit the place the Father and the Son have in our prayer. It is to the Father we pray, and from whom we expect the answer. It is in the merit, and name, and life of the Son, abiding in Him and He in us, that we trust to be heard. But have we understood that in the Holy Trinity all the Three Persons have an equal place in prayer, and that the faith in the Holy Spirit of intercession as praying in us is as indispensable as the faith in the Father and the Son? How clearly we have this in the words, "Through Christ we have access by one Spirit to the Father." As much as prayer must be to the Father, and through the Son, it must be by the Spirit. And the Spirit can pray in no other way in us, than as He lives in us. It is only as we give ourselves to the Spirit living and praying in us, that the glory of the prayer-hearing God, and the ever-blessed and most effectual mediation of the Son, can be known by us in their power. (Note D.)

Our last lesson: Pray in the Spirit for all saints (Eph. vi. 18). The Spirit, who is called "the Spirit of supplication," is also and very specially the Spirit of intercession. It is said of Him, "the Spirit Himself maketh intercession for us with groanings that cannot be uttered." "He maketh intercession for the saints." It is the same word as is used of Christ, "who also maketh intercession for us." The thought is essentially that of mediation—one pleading for another. When the Spirit of intercession takes full possession of us, all selfishness, as if we wanted Him separate from His intercession for others, and have Him for ourselves alone, is banished, and we begin to avail ourselves of our wonderful privilege to plead for men. We long to live the Christ-life of self-consuming sacrifice for others, as our heart unceasingly yields itself to God to obtain His blessing for those around us. Intercession then becomes, not an incident or an occasional part of our prayers, but their one great object. Prayer for ourselves then takes its true place, simply as a means for fitting us better for exercising our ministry of intercession more effectually.

May I be allowed to speak a very personal word to each of my readers? I have humbly besought God to give me what I may give them—Divine light and help truly to forsake the life of failure in prayer, and to enter, even now, and at once, upon the life of intercession which the Holy Spirit can enable them to lead. It can be done by a simple act of faith, claiming the fulness of the Spirit, that is, the full measure of the Spirit which you are capable in God's sight of receiving, and He is therefore willing to bestow. Will you not, even now, accept of this by faith?

Let me remind you of what takes place at conversion. Most of us, you probably too, for a time sought peace in efforts and struggles to give up sin and please God. But you did not find it thus. The peace of God's pardon came by faith, trusting God's word concerning Christ and His salvation. You had heard of Christ as the gift of His love, you knew that He was for you too, you had felt the movings and drawings of His grace; but never till in faith in God's word you accepted Him as God's gift to you, did you know the peace and joy that He can give. Believing in Him and His saving love made all the difference, and changed your relation from one who had ever grieved Him, to one who loved and served Him. And yet, after a time, you have a thousand times wondered you love and serve Him so ill.

At the time of your conversion you knew little about the Holy Spirit. Later on you heard of His dwelling in you, and His being the power of God in you for all the Father intends you to be, and yet His indwelling and inworking have been something vague and indefinite, and hardly a source of joy or strength. At conversion you did not yet know your need of Him, and still less what you might expect of Him. But your failures have taught it you. And now you begin to see how you have been grieving Him, by not trusting and not following Him, by not allowing Him to work in you all God's pleasure.

All this can be changed. Just as you, after seeking Christ, and praying to Him, and trying without success to serve Him, found rest in accepting Him by faith, just so you may even now yield yourself to the full guidance of the Holy Spirit, and claim and accept Him to work in you what God would have. Will you not do it? Just accept Him in faith as Christ's gift, to be the Spirit of your whole life, of your prayer-life too, and you can count upon Him to take charge. You can then begin, however feeble you feel, and unable to pray aright, to bow before God in silence, with the assurance that He will teach you to pray.

My dear brother, as you consciously by faith accepted Christ, to pardon, you can consciously now in the like faith accept of Christ who gives the Holy Spirit to do His work in you. "Christ redeemed us that we might receive the promise of the Spirit by faith." Kneel down, and simply believe that the Lord Christ, who baptizeth with the Holy Spirit, does now, in response to your faith, begin in you the blessed life of a full experience of the power of the indwelling Spirit. Depend most confidently upon Him, apart from all feeling or experience, as the Spirit of supplication and intercession to do His work. Renew that act of faith each morning, each time you pray; trust Him, against all appearances, to work in you,—be sure He is working,—and He will give you to know what the joy of the Holy Spirit is as the power of your life.

"I will pour out the Spirit of supplication." Do you not begin to see that the mystery of prayer is the mystery of the Divine indwelling. God in heaven gives His Spirit in our hearts to be there the Divine power praying in us, and drawing us upward to our God. God is a Spirit, and nothing but a like life and Spirit within us can hold communion with Him. It was for this man was created, that God might dwell and work in Him, and be the life of his life. It was this Divine indwelling that sin lost. It was this that Christ came to exhibit in His life, to win back for us in His death, and then to impart to us by coming again from heaven in the Spirit to live in His disciples. It is this, the indwelling of God through the Spirit, that alone can explain and enable us to appropriate the wonderful promises given to prayer. God gives the Spirit as a Spirit of Supplication, too, to maintain His Divine life within us as a life out of which prayer ever rises upward.

Without the Holy Spirit no man can call Jesus Lord, or cry, Abba, Father; no man can worship in spirit and truth, or pray without ceasing. The Holy Spirit is given the believer to be and do in him all that God wants him to be or do. He is given him especially as the Spirit of prayer and supplication. Is it not clear that everything in prayer depends upon our trusting the Holy Spirit to do His work in us; yielding ourselves to His leading, depending only and wholly on Him?

We read, "Stephen was a man full of faith and the Holy Spirit." The two ever go together, in exact proportion to each other. As our faith sees and trusts the Spirit in us to pray, and waits on Him, He will do His work; and it is the longing desire, and the earnest supplication, and the definite faith the Father seeks. Do let us know Him, and in the faith of Christ who unceasingly gives Him, cultivate the assured confidence, we can learn to pray as the Father would have us.

"Whatsoever ye shall ask in My Name, that will I do. If ye shall ask anything in My Name, I will do it. I have appointed you, that whatsoever ye shall ask of the Father in My Name, He may give it you. Verily, verily I say unto you, whatsoever ye shall ask the Father in My Name, He will give it you. Hitherto have ye asked nothing in My Name; ask, and ye shall receive, that your joy may be full. At that day ye shall ask in My Name."—John xiv. 13, 14, xv. 16, xvi. 23, 24, 26.

IN MY NAME—repeated six times over. Our Lord knew how slow our hearts would be to take it in, and He so longed that we should really believe that His Name is the power in which every knee should bow, and in which every prayer could be heard, that He did not weary of saying it over and over: In My Name! Between the wonderful whatsoever ye shall ask, and the Divine I will do it, the Father will give it, this one word is the simple link: In My Name. Our asking and the Father's giving are to be equally in the Name of Christ. Everything in prayer depends upon our apprehending this—In My Name.

We know what a name is: a word by which we call up to our mind the whole being and nature of an object. When I speak of a lamb or a lion, the name at once suggests the different nature peculiar to each. The Name of God is meant to express His whole Divine nature and glory. And so the Name of Christ means His whole nature, His person and work, His disposition and Spirit. To ask in the Name of Christ is to pray in union with Him. When first a sinner believes in Christ, he only knows and thinks of His merit and intercession. And to the very end that is the one foundation of our confidence. And yet, as the believer grows in grace and enters more deeply and truly into union with Christ—that is, as he abides in Him—he learns that to pray in the Name of Christ also means in His Spirit, and in the possession of His nature, as the Holy Spirit imparts it to us. As we grasp the meaning of the words, "At that day ye shall ask in My Name"—the day when in the Holy Spirit Christ came to live in His disciples—we shall no longer be staggered at the greatness of the promise: "Whatsoever ye shall ask in My Name, I will do it." We shall get some insight into the unchangeable necessity and certainty of the law: what is asked in the Name of Christ, in union with Him, out of His nature and Spirit, must be given. As Christ's prayer-nature lives in us, His prayer-power becomes ours too. Not that the measure of our attainment or experience is the ground of our confidence, but the honesty and whole-heartedness of our surrender to all that we see that Christ seeks to be in us, will be the measure of our spiritual fitness and power to pray in His Name. "If ye abide in Me," He says, "ye shall ask what ye will." As we live in Him, we get the spiritual power to avail ourselves of His Name. As the branch wholly given up to the life and service of the Vine can count upon all its sap and strength for its fruit, so the believer, who in faith has accepted the fulness of the Spirit to possess his whole life, can indeed avail himself of all the power of Christ's Name.

Here on earth Christ as man came to reveal what prayer is. To pray in the Name of Christ we must pray as He prayed on earth; as He taught us to pray; in union with Him, as He now prays in heaven. We must in love study, and in faith accept, Him as our Example, our Teacher, our Intercessor.

Christ our Example.

Prayer in Christ on earth and in us cannot be two different things. Just as there is but one God, who is a Spirit, who hears prayer, there is but one spirit of acceptable prayer. When we realise what time Christ spent in prayer, and how the great events of His life were all connected with special prayer, we learn the necessity of absolute dependence on and unceasing direct communication with the heavenly world, if we are to live a heavenly life, or to exercise heavenly power around us. We see how foolish and fruitless the attempt must be to do work for God and heaven, without in the first place in prayer getting the life and the power of heaven to possess us. Unless this truth lives in us, we cannot avail ourselves aright of the mighty power of the Name of Christ. His example must teach us the meaning of His Name.

Of His baptism we read, "Jesus having been baptized, and praying, the heaven was opened." It was in prayer heaven was opened to Him, that heaven came down to Him with the Spirit and the voice of the Father. In the power of these He was led into the wilderness, in fasting and prayer to have them tested and fully appropriated. Early in His ministry Mark records (i. 35), "And in the morning, a great while before day, He rose and departed into a desert place, and there prayed." And somewhat later Luke tells (v. 16), "Multitudes came together to hear and to be healed. But He withdrew Himself into the desert, and prayed." He knew how the holiest service, preaching and healing, can exhaust the spirit; how too much intercourse with men could cloud the fellowship with God; how time, time, full time, is needed if the spirit is to rest and root in Him; how no pressure of duty among men can free from the absolute need of much prayer. If anyone could have been satisfied with always living and working in the spirit of prayer, it would have been our Master. But He could not; He needed to have His supplies replenished by continual and long-continued seasons of prayer. To use Christ's Name in prayer surely includes this, to follow His example and to pray as He did.

Of the night before choosing His apostles we read (Luke vi. 12), "He went out into the mountain to pray, and continued all night in prayer to God." The first step towards the constitution of the Church, and the separation of men to be His witnesses and successors, called Him to special long-continued prayer. All had to be done according to the pattern on the mount. "The Son can do nothing of Himself: the Father showeth Him all things that Himself doeth." It was in the night of prayer it was shown Him.

In the night between the feeding of the five thousand, when Jesus knew that they wanted to take Him by force and make Him King, and the walking on the sea, "He withdrew again into the mountain, Himself alone, to pray" (Matt. xiv. 23; Mark vi. 46; John vi. 15). It was God's will He was come to do, and God's power He was to show forth. He had it not as a possession of His own; it had to be prayed for and received from above. The first announcement of His approaching death, after He had elicited from Peter the confession that He was the Christ, is introduced by the words (Luke ix. 15), "And it came to pass that He was praying alone." The introduction to the story of the Transfiguration is (Luke ix. 28), "He went up into the mountain to pray." The request of the disciples, "Lord, teach us to pray" (Luke xi. 1), follows on, "It came to pass as He was praying in a certain place." In His own personal life, in His intercourse with the Father, in all He is and does for men, the Christ whose name we are to use is a Man of prayer. It is prayer gives Him His power of blessing, and transfigures His very body with the glory of heaven. It is His own prayer-life makes Him the teacher of others how to pray. How much more must it be prayer, prayer alone, much prayer, that can fit us to share His glory of a transfigured life, or make us the channel of heavenly blessing and teaching to others. To pray in the Name of Christ is to pray as He prays.

As the end approaches, it is still more prayer. When the Greeks asked to see Him, and He spoke of His approaching death, He prayed. At Lazarus' grave He prayed. In the last night He prayed His prayer as our High-Priest, that we might know what His sacrifice would win, and what His everlasting intercession on the throne would be. In

Gethsemane He prayed His prayer as Victim, the Lamb giving itself to the slaughter. On the Cross it is still all prayer—the prayer of compassion for His murderers; the prayer of atoning suffering in the thick darkness; the prayer in death of confiding resignation of His spirit to the Father. Note E.)

Christ's life and work, His suffering and death—it was all prayer, all dependence on God, trust in God, receiving from God, surrender to God. Thy redemption, O believer, is a redemption wrought out by prayer and intercession: thy Christ is a praying Christ: the life He lived for thee, the life He lives in thee, is a praying life, that delights to wait on God and receive all from Him. To pray in His Name is to pray as He prayed. Christ is only our example because He is our Head, our Saviour, and our Life. In virtue of His Deity and of His Spirit He can live in us: we can pray in His Name, because we abide in Him and He in us.

Christ our Teacher.

Christ was what He taught. All His teaching was just the revelation of how He lived, and—praise God—of the life He was to live in us. His teaching of the disciples was first to awaken desire, and so prepare them for what He would by the Holy Spirit be and work in them. Let us believe very confidently: all He was in prayer, and all He taught, He Himself will give. He came to fulfil the law; much more will He fulfil the gospel in all He taught us, as to what to pray, and how.

What to pray.—It has sometimes been said that direct petitions, as compared with the exercise of fellowship with God, are but a subordinate part of prayer, and that "in the prayer of those who pray best and most, they occupy but an inconsiderable place." If we carefully study all that our Lord spoke of prayer, we shall see that this is not His teaching. In the Lord's Prayer, in the parables on prayer, in the illustration of a child asking bread, of our seeking and knocking, in the central thought of the prayer of faith, "Whatsoever ye pray, believe that ye have received," in the oft-repeated "whatsoever" of the last evening—everywhere our Lord urges and encourages us to offer definite petitions, and to expect definite answers. It is only because we have too much confined prayer to our own needs, that it has been thought needful to free it from the appearance of selfishness, by giving the petitions a subordinate place. If once believers were to awake to the glory of the work of intercession, and to see that in it, and the definite pleading for definite gifts on definite spheres and persons, lie our highest fellowship with our glorified Lord, and our only real power to bless men, it would be seen that there can be no truer fellowship with God than these definite petitions and their answers, by which we become the channel of His grace and life to men. Then our fellowship with the Father is even such as the Son has in His intercession.

How to pray.—Our Lord taught us to pray in secret, in simplicity, with the eye on God alone, in humility, in the spirit of forgiving love. But the chief truth He reiterated was ever this: to pray in faith. And He defined that faith, not only as a trust in God's goodness or power, but as the definite assurance that we have received the very thing we ask. And then, in view of the delay in the answer, He insisted on perseverance and urgency. We must be followers of those "who through faith and patience inherit the promises"—the faith that accepts the promise, and knows it has what it has asked—the patience that obtains the promise and inherits the blessing. We shall then learn to understand why God, who promises to avenge His elect speedily, bears with them in seeming delay. It is that their faith may be purified from all that is of the flesh, and tested and strengthened to become that spiritual power that can do all things—can even cast mountains into the heart of the sea.

Christ as our Intercessor.

We have gazed on Christ in His prayers; we have listened to His teaching as to how we must pray; to know fully what it is to pray in His Name, we must know Him too in His heavenly intercession.

Just think what it means: that all His saving work wrought from heaven is still carried on, just as on earth, in unceasing communication with, and direct intercession to the Father, who worketh all in all, who is All in All. Every act of grace in Christ has been preceded by, and owes its power to, intercession. God has been honoured and acknowledged as its Author. On the throne of God, Christ's highest fellowship with the Father, and His partnership in His rule of the world, is in intercession. Every blessing that comes down to us from above bears upon it the stamp from God: through Christ's intercession. His intercession is nothing but the fruit and the glory of His atonement. When He gave Himself a sacrifice to God for men, He proved that His whole heart had the one object: the glory of God, in the salvation of men. In His intercession this great purpose is realised: He glorifies the Father by asking and receiving all of Him; He saves men by bestowing what He has obtained from the Father. Christ's intercession is the Father's glory,

His own glory, our glory.

And now, this Christ, the Intercessor, is our life; He is our Head, and we are His body; His Spirit and life breathe in us. As in heaven so on earth, intercession is God's chosen, God's only channel of blessing. Let us learn from Christ what glory there is in it; what the way to exercise this wondrous power; what the part it is to take in work for God.

The glory of it.—By it, beyond anything, we glorify God. By it we glorify Christ. By it we bring blessing to the Church and the world. By it we obtain our highest nobility—the Godlike power of saving men.

The way to it.—Paul writes, "Walk in love, even as Christ loved us, and gave Himself a sacrifice to God for us." If we live as Christ lived, we will, as He did, give ourselves, for our whole life, to God, to be used by Him for men. When once we have done this, given ourselves, no more to seek anything for ourselves, but for men, and that to God, for Him to use us, and to impart to us what we can bestow on others, intercession will become to us, as it is in Christ in heaven, the great work of our life. And if ever the thought comes that the call is too high, or the work too great, the faith in Christ, the Interceding Christ, who lives in us, will give us the victory. We will listen to Him who said, "The works that I do, shall ye do; and greater works shall ye do." We shall remember that we are not under the law, with its impotence, but under grace with its omnipotence, working all in us. We shall believe again in Him who said to us, Rise and walk, and gave us—and we received it—His life as our strength. We shall claim afresh the fulness of God's Spirit as His sufficient provision for our need, and count Him to be in us the Spirit of Intercession, who makes us one with Christ in His. Oh! let us only keep our place—giving up ourselves, like Him, in Him, to God for men.

Then we shall understand the part intercession is to take in God's work through us. We shall no longer try to work for God, and ask Him to follow it with His blessing. We shall do what the friend at midnight did, what Christ did on earth, and ever does in heaven—we shall first get from God, and then turn to men to give what He gave us. As with Christ, we shall make our chief work, we shall count no time or trouble too great, to receive from the Father; giving to men will then be in power.

Servants of Christ! children of God! be of good courage. Let no fear of feebleness or poverty make you afraid—ask in the Name of Christ. His

Name is Himself, in all His perfection and power. He is the living Christ, and will Himself make His Name a power in you. Fear not to plead the Name; His promise is a threefold cord that cannot be broken: Whatsoever ye ask—in My Name—it shall be done unto you.

CHAPTER XII. My God will hear Me

"Therefore will the Lord wait, that He may be gracious unto you. Blessed are all they that wait for Him. He will be very gracious unto thee at the voice of thy cry; when He shall hear it, He will answer thee."—Isa. xxx. 18, 19.

"The Lord will hear when I call upon Him."—Ps. iv. 3.

"I have called upon Thee, for Thou wilt hear me, O God!"—Ps. xvii. 6.

"I will look unto the Lord; I will wait for the God of my salvation: my God will hear me."—Mic. vii. 7.

THE power of prayer rests in the faith that God hears it. In more than one sense this is true. It is this faith that gives a man courage to pray. It is this faith that gives him power to prevail with God. The moment I am assured that God hears me too, I feel drawn to pray and to persevere in prayer. I feel strong to claim and to take in faith the answer God gives. One great reason of lack of prayer is the want of the living, joyous assurance: "My God will hear me." If once God's servants got a vision of the living God waiting to grant their request, and to bestow all the heavenly gifts of the Spirit they are in need of, for themselves or those they are serving, how everything would be set aside to make time and room for this one only power that can ensure heavenly blessing— the prayer of faith!

When a man can, and does say, in living faith, "My God will hear me!" surely nothing can keep him from prayer. He knows that what he cannot do or get done on earth, can and will be done for him from heaven. Let each one of us bow in stillness before God, and wait on Him to reveal Himself as the prayer-hearing God. In His presence the wondrous thoughts gathering round the central truth will unfold themselves to us.

1. "My God will hear me."—What a blessed certainty!—We have God's word for it in numberless promises. We have thousands of witnesses to the fact that they have found it true. We have had experience of it in our lives. We have had the Son of God come from heaven with the message that if we ask, the Father will give. We have had Himself praying on earth, and being heard. And we have Him in heaven now, sitting at the right hand of God and making intercession for us. God hears prayer—God delights to hear prayer. He has allowed

His people a thousand times over to be tried, that they might be compelled to cry to Him, and learn to know Him as the Hearer of Prayer.

Let us confess with shame how little we have believed this wondrous truth, in the sense of receiving it into our heart, and allowing it to possess and control our whole being. That we accept a truth is not enough; the living God, of whom the truth speaks, must in its light so be revealed, that our whole life is spent in His presence, with the consciousness as clear as in a little child towards its earthly parent—I know for certain my father hears me.

Beloved child of God! you know by experience how little an intellectual apprehension of truth has profited you. Beseech God to reveal Himself to you. If you want to live a different prayer-life, bow each time ere you pray in silence to worship this God; to wait till there rests on you some right sense of His nearness and readiness to answer. So will you begin to pray with the words, "My God will hear me!"

2. "My God will hear me." What a wondrous grace!—Think of God in His infinite majesty, His altogether incomprehensible glory, His unapproachable holiness, sitting on a throne of grace, waiting to be gracious, inviting, encouraging you to pray with His promise: "Call upon Me, and I will answer thee." Think of yourself, in your nothingness and helplessness as a creature; in your wretchedness and transgressions as a sinner; in your feebleness and unworthiness as a saint; and praise the glory of that grace which allows you to say boldly of your prayer for yourself and others, "My God will hear me." Think of how you are not left to yourself, and what you can accomplish, in this wonderful intercourse with God. God has united you with Christ; in Him and His Name you have your confidence; on the throne He prays with you and for you; on the footstool of the throne you pray with Him and in Him. His worth, and the Father's delight in hearing Him, are the measure of your confidence, your assurance of being heard. There is more. Think of the Holy Spirit, the Spirit of God's own Son, sent into your heart to cry, Abba, Father, and to be in you a Spirit of Supplication, when you know not what to pray as you ought. Think, in all your insignificance and unworthiness, of your being as acceptable as Christ Himself. Think in all your ignorance and feebleness, of the Spirit making intercession according to God within you, and cry out, "What wondrous grace! Through Christ I have access to the Father, by the Spirit. I can, I do believe it: 'My God will hear me.'"

3. "My God will hear me."—What a deep mystery!—There are difficulties that cannot but at times arise and perplex even the honest heart. There is the question as to God's sovereign, all-wise, all-disposing will. How can our wishes, often so foolish, and our will, often so selfish, overrule or change that perfect will? Were it not better to leave all to His disposal, who knows what is best, and loves to give us the very best? Or how can our prayer change what He has ordained before? Then there is the question as to the need of persevering prayer, and long waiting for the answer. If God be Infinite Love, and delighting more to give than we to receive, where the need for the pleading and wrestling, the urgency, and the long delay of which Scripture and experience speak? Arising out of this there is still another question—that of the multitude of apparently vain and unanswered prayers. How many have pleaded for loved ones, and they die unsaved. How many cry for years for spiritual blessing, and no answer comes. To think of all this tries our faith, and makes us hesitate as we say, "My God will hear me."

Beloved! prayer, in its power with God, and His faithfulness to His promise to hear it, is a deep spiritual mystery. To the questions put above answers can be given that remove some of the difficulty. But, after all, the first and the last that must be said is this: As little as we can comprehend God can we comprehend this, one of the most blessed of His attributes, that He hears prayer. It is a spiritual mystery—nothing less than the mystery of the Holy Trinity. God hears because we pray in His Son, because the Holy Spirit prays in us. If we have believed and claimed the life of Christ as our health, and the fulness of the Spirit as our strength, let us not hesitate to believe in the power of our prayer too. The Holy Spirit can enable us to believe and rejoice in it, even where every question is not yet answered. He will do this, as we lay our questionings in God's bosom, trust His faithfulness, and give ourselves humbly to obey His command to pray without ceasing. Every art unfolds its secrets and its beauty only to the man who practises it. To the humble soul who prays in the obedience of faith, who practises prayer and intercession diligently, because God asks it, the secret of the Lord will be revealed, and the thought of the deep mystery of prayer, instead of being a weary problem, will be a source of rejoicing, adoration, and faith, in which the unceasing refrain is ever heard: "My God will hear me!"

4. "My God will hear me." What a solemn responsibility!—How often we complain of darkness, of feebleness, of failure, as if there was no help for it. And God has promised in answer to our prayer to supply

our every need, and give us His light and strength and peace. Would that we realised the responsibility of having such a God, and such promises, with the sin and shame of not availing ourselves of them to the utmost. How confident we should feel that the grace, which we have accepted and trusted to enable us to pray as we should, will be given.

There is more. This access to a prayer-hearing God is specially meant to make us intercessors for our fellowmen. Even as Christ obtained His right of prevailing intercession by His giving Himself a sacrifice to God for men, and through it receives the blessings He dispenses, so, if we have truly with Christ given ourselves to God for men, we share His right of intercession, and are able to obtain the powers of the heavenly world for them too. The power of life and death is in our hands (1 John v. 16). In answer to prayer the Spirit can be poured out, souls can be converted, believers can be established. In prayer the kingdom of darkness can be conquered, souls brought out of prison into the liberty of Christ, and the glory of God be revealed. Through prayer, the sword of the Spirit, which is the Word of God, can be wielded in power, and, in public preaching as in private speaking, the most rebellious made to bow at Jesus' feet.

What a responsibility on the Church to give herself to the work of intercession! What a responsibility on every minister, missionary, worker, set apart for the saving of souls, to yield himself wholly to act out and prove his faith: "My God will hear me!" And what a call on every believer, instead of burying and losing this talent, to seek to the very utmost to use it in prayer and supplication for all saints and for all men. My God will hear me: The deeper our entrance into the truth of this wondrous power God hath given to men, the more whole-hearted will be our surrender to the work of intercession.

5. "My God will hear me." What a blessed prospect!—I see it—all the failures of my past life have been owing to the lack of this faith. My failure, especially in the work of intercession, has had its deepest root in this—I did not live in the full faith of the blessed assurance, "My God will hear me!" Praise God! I begin to see it—I believe it. All can be different. Or, rather, I see Him, I believe Him. "My God will hear me!" Yes, me, even me! Commonplace and insignificant though I be, filling but a very little place, so that I will scarce be missed when I go—even I have access to this Infinite God, with the confidence that He heareth me. One with Christ, led by the Holy Spirit, I dare to say: "I will pray for others, for I am sure my God will listen to me: 'My God

will hear me.'" What a blessed prospect before me—every earthly and spiritual anxiety exchanged for the peace of God, who cares for all and hears prayer. What a blessed prospect in my work—to know that even when the answer is long delayed, and there is a call for much patient, persevering prayer, the truth remains infallibly sure—"My God will hear me!"

And what a blessed prospect for Christ's Church if we could but all give prayer its place, give faith in God its place, or, rather, give the prayer-hearing God His place! Is not this the one great thing, those, who in some little measure begin to see the urgent need of prayer, ought in the first place to pray for. When God, at the first, time after time, poured forth the Spirit on His praying people, He laid down the law for all time: as much of prayer, so much of the Spirit. Let each one who can say, "My God will hear me," join in the fervent supplication, that throughout the Church that truth may be restored to its true place, and the blessed prospect will be realised: a praying Church endued with the power of the Holy Ghost.

6. "My God will hear me." What a need of Divine teaching!—We need this, both to enable us to hold this word in living faith, and to make full use of it in intercession. It has been said, and it cannot be said too often or too earnestly, that the one thing needful for the Church of our day is, the power of the Holy Spirit. It is just because this is so, from the Divine side, that we may also say as truly that, from the human side, the one thing needful is, more prayer, more believing, persevering prayer. In speaking of lack of the Spirit's power, and the condition for receiving it, someone used the expression—the block is not on the perpendicular, but on the horizontal line. It is to be feared that it is on both. There is much to be confessed and taken away in us if the Spirit is to work freely. But it is specially on the perpendicular line that the block is—the upward look, and the deep dependence, and the strong crying to God, and the effectual prayer of faith that avails—all this is sadly lacking. And just this is the one thing needful.

Shall we not all set ourselves to learn the lesson which will make prevailing prayer possible—the lesson of a faith that always sings, "My God will hear me"? Simple and elementary as it is, it needs practice and patience, it needs time and heavenly teaching, to learn it aright. Under the impression of a bright thought, or a blessed experience, it may look as if we knew the lesson perfectly. But ever again the need will recur of making this our first prayer—that God who hears prayer would teach us to believe it, and so to pray aright. If we desire it we can count upon Him He who delights in hearing prayer and answering it, He who gave His Son that He might ever pray for us and with us, and His Holy Spirit to pray in us, we can be sure there is not a prayer that He will hear more certainly than this: that He so reveal Himself as the prayer-hearing God, that our whole being may respond, "My God will hear me."

CHAPTER XIII. Paul a Pattern of Prayer

"Go and inquire for one called Saul of Tarsus: for, behold, he prayeth."—Acts ix. 11.

"For this cause I obtained mercy, that in me first Jesus Christ might show forth all long-suffering, for a pattern to them which should hereafter believe on Him to life everlasting."—1 Tim. i. 16.

GOD took His own Son, and made Him our Example and our Pattern. It sometimes is as if the power of Christ's example is lost in the thought that He, in whom is no sin, is not man as we are. Our Lord took Paul, a man of like passions with ourselves, and made him a pattern of what he could do for one who was the chief of sinners. And Paul, the man who, more than any other, has set his mark on the Church, has ever been appealed to as a pattern man. In his mastery of Divine truth, and his teaching of it; in his devotion to his Lord, and his self-consuming zeal in His service; in his deep experience of the power of the indwelling Christ and the fellowship of his cross; in the sincerity of his humility, and the simplicity and boldness of his faith; in his missionary enthusiasm and endurance—in all this, and so much more, "the grace of our Lord Jesus was exceeding abundant in him." Christ gave him, and the Church has accepted him, as a pattern of what Christ would have, of what Christ would work. Seven times Paul speaks of believers following him: (1 Cor. iv. 16), "Wherefore I beseech you, be ye followers of me"; (xi. 1), "Be ye followers of me, even as I am of Christ"; Phil, iii. 17, iv. 9; 1 Thess. i. 6; 2 Thess. iii. 7–9.

If Paul, as a pattern of prayer, is not as much studied or appealed to as he is in other respects, it is not because he is not in this too as remarkable a proof of what grace can do, or because we do not, in this respect, as much stand in need of the help of his example. A study of Paul as a pattern of prayer will bring a rich reward of instruction and encouragement. The words our Lord used of him at his conversion, "Behold he prayeth," may be taken as the keynote of his life. The heavenly vision which brought him to his knees ever after ruled his life. Christ at the right hand of God, in whom we are blessed with all spiritual blessings, was everything to him; to pray and expect the heavenly power in his work and on his work, from heaven direct by prayer, was the simple outcome of his faith in the Glorified One. In this, too, Christ meant him to be a pattern, that we might learn that, just in the measure in which the heavenliness of Christ and His gifts, the unworldliness of the powers that work for salvation, are known and believed, will prayer become the spontaneous rising of the heart to the only source of its life. Let us see what we know of Paul.

Paul's Habits of Prayer.

These are revealed almost unconsciously. He writes (Rom. i. 9), "God is my witness, that without ceasing I make mention of you always in my prayers. For I long to see you, that I may impart unto you some spiritual gift, to the end ye may be established." Rom. x. 1, ix. 2, 3: "My heart's desire and prayer to God for Israel is, that they may be saved"; "I have great heaviness and continual sorrow of heart; for I could wish that myself were accursed from Christ for my brethren." 1 Cor. i. 4: "I thank my God always on your behalf, for the grace of God which is given you by Jesus Christ." 2 Cor. vi. 4, 6: "Approving ourselves as the ministers of Christ, in watchings, in fastings." Gal. iv. 19: "My little children, of whom I travail in birth again till Christ be formed in you." Eph. i. 16: "I cease not to give thanks for you, making mention of you in my prayers." Eph. iii. 14: "I bow my knees to the Father, that He would grant you to be strengthened with might by His Spirit in the inner man." Phil. i. 3, 4, 8, 9: "I thank my God upon every remembrance of you, always in every prayer of mine making request for you all with joy. For God is my record, how greatly I long after you all in the bowels of Jesus Christ. And this I pray"—Col. i. 3, 9: "We give thanks to God, praying always for you. For this cause also, since the day we heard it, we do not cease to pray for you, and to desire"— Col. ii. 1: "I would that ye knew what great conflict I have for you, and for as many as have not seen my face in the flesh." 1 Thess. i. 2: "We give thanks to God always for you all, making mention of you in our prayers." iii. 9: "We joy for your sakes before God; night and day praying exceedingly that we might perfect that which is lacking in your faith." 2 Thess. i. 3: "We are bound to thank God always for you. Wherefore also we always pray for you." 2 Tim. i. 3: "I thank God, that without ceasing I have remembrance of thee night and day." Philem. 4: "I thank my God, making mention of thee always in my prayers."

These passages taken together give us the picture of a man whose words, "Pray without ceasing," were simply the expression of his daily life. He had such a sense of the insufficiency of simple conversion; of the need of the grace and the power of heaven being brought down for the young converts in prayer; of the need of much and unceasing prayer, day and night, to bring it down; of the certainty that prayer would bring it down—that his life was continual and most definite prayer. He had such a sense that everything must come from above, and such a faith that it would come in answer to prayer, that prayer was neither a duty nor a burden, but the natural turning of the heart to the only place whence it could possibly obtain what it sought for others.

The Contents of Paul's Prayers.

It is of as much importance to know what Paul prayed, as how frequently and earnestly he did so. Intercession is a spiritual work. Our confidence in it will depend much on our knowing that we ask according to the will of God. The more distinctly we ask heavenly things, which we feel at once God alone can bestow, which we are sure He will bestow, the more direct and urgent will our appeal be to God alone. The more impossible the things are that we seek, the more we will turn from all human work to prayer and to God alone.

In the Epistles, in addition to expressions in which he speaks of his praying, we have a number of distinct prayers in which Paul gives utterance to his heart's desire for those to whom he writes. In these we see that his first desire was always that they might be "established" in the Christian life. Much as he praised God when he heard of conversion, he knew how feeble the young converts were, and how for their establishing nothing would avail without the grace of the Spirit prayed down. If we notice some of the principal of these prayers we shall see what he asked and obtained.

Take the two prayers in Ephesians—the one for light, the other for strength. In the former (i. 15), he prays for the Spirit of wisdom to enlighten them to know what their calling was, what their inheritance, what the mighty power of God working in them. Spiritual enlightenment and knowledge was their great need, to be obtained for them by prayer. In the latter (iii. 15) he asks that the power they had been led to see in Christ might work in them, and they be strengthened with Divine might, so as to have the indwelling Christ, and the love that passeth knowledge, and the fulness of God actually come on them. These were things that could only come direct from heaven; these were things he asked and expected. If we want to learn Paul's art of intercession, we must ask nothing less for believers in our days.

Look at the prayer in Philippians (i. 9–11). There, too, it is first for spiritual knowledge; then comes a blameless life, and then a fruitful life to the glory of God. So also in the beautiful prayer in Colossians (i. 9–11). First, spiritual knowledge and understanding of God's will, then the strengthening with all might to all patience and joy.

Or take the two prayers in 1 Thessalonians (iii. 12, 13, and v. 23). The one: "God so increase your love to one another, that He may stablish your hearts unblameable in holiness." The other: "God sanctify you wholly, and preserve you blameless." The very words are so high that we hardly understand, still less believe, still less experience what they mean. Paul so lived in the heavenly world, he was so at home in the holiness and omnipotence of God and His love, that such prayers were the natural expression of what he knew God could and would do. "God stablish your hearts unblameable in holiness," "God sanctify you wholly"—the man who believes in these things and desires them, will pray for them for others. The prayers are all a proof that he seeks for them the very life of heaven upon earth. No wonder that he is not tempted to trust in any human means, but looks for it from heaven alone. Again, I say, the more we take Paul's prayers as our pattern, and make his desires our own for believers for whom we pray, the more will prayer to the God of heaven become as our daily breath.

Paul's Requests for Prayer.

These are no less instructive than his own prayers for the saints. They prove that he does not count prayer any special prerogative of an apostle; he calls the humblest and simplest believer to claim his right. They prove that he does not think that only the new converts or feeble Christians need prayer; he himself is, as a member of the body, dependent upon his brethren and their prayers. After he had preached the gospel for twenty years, he still asks for prayer that he may speak as he ought to speak. Not once for all, not for a time, but day by day, and that without ceasing, must grace be sought and brought down from heaven for his work. United, continued waiting on God is to Paul the only hope of the Church. With the Holy Spirit a heavenly life, the life of the Lord in heaven, entered the world; nothing but unbroken communication with heaven can keep it up.

Listen how he asks for prayer, and with what earnestness—Rom. xv. 30: "I beseech you, brethren, for the Lord Jesus Christ's sake, and for the love of the Spirit, that ye strive together with me in your prayers to God for me; that I may be delivered from them which do not believe in Judæa; and may come unto you with joy by the will of God." How remarkably both prayers were answered: Rom. xv. 5, 6, 13. The remarkable fact that the Roman world-power, which in Pilate with Christ, in Herod with Peter, at Philippi, had proved its antagonism to God's kingdom, all at once becomes Paul's protector, and secures him a safe convoy to Rome, can only be accounted for by these prayers.

2 Cor. i. 10, 11: "In whom we trust that He will yet deliver us, ye also helping together by prayer for us." Eph. vi. 18, 19: "Praying always with all prayer and supplication in the Spirit, for all saints; and for me that I may open my mouth boldly, that therein I may speak boldly as I ought to speak." Phil. i. 19: "I know that this (trouble) shall turn to my salvation, through your prayer, and the supply of the Spirit of Jesus Christ." Col. iv. 2, 3, 4: "Continue in prayer; withal also praying for us, that God would open unto us a door of utterance, to speak the mystery of Christ: that I may make it manifest as I ought to speak." 1 Thess. v. 25: "Brethren, pray for us." Philem. 22: "I trust that through your prayers I shall be given to you."

We saw how Christ prayed, and taught His disciples to pray. We see how Paul prayed, and taught the churches to pray. As the Master, so the servant calls us to believe and to prove that prayer is the power alike of the ministry and the Church. Of his faith we have a summary in these remarkable words concerning something that caused him grief: "This shall turn to my salvation through your prayer, and the supply of the Spirit of Jesus Christ." As much as he looked to his Lord in heaven did he look to his brethren on earth, to secure the supply of that Spirit for him. The Spirit from heaven and prayer on earth were to him, as to the twelve after Pentecost, inseparably linked. We speak often of apostolic zeal and devotion and power—may God give us a revival of apostolic prayer.

Let me once again ask the question: Does the work of intercession take the place in the Church it ought to have? Is it a thing commonly understood in the Lord's work, that everything depends upon getting from God that "supply of the Spirit of Christ" for and in ourselves that can give our work its real power to bless. This is Christ's Divine order for all work, His own and that of His servants; this is the order Paul followed: first come every day, as having nothing, and receive from God "the supply of the Spirit" in intercession—then go and impart what has come to thee from heaven.

In all His instructions, our Lord Jesus spake much oftener to His disciples about their praying than their preaching. In the farewell discourse, He said little about preaching, but much about the Holy Spirit, and their asking whatsoever they would in His Name. If we are to return to this life of the first apostles and of Paul, and really accept the truth every day—my first work, my only strength is intercession, to secure the power of God on the souls entrusted to me—we must have the courage to confess past sin, and to believe that there is deliverance. To break through old habits, to resist the clamour of pressing duties that have always had their way, to make every other call subordinate to this one, whether others approve or not, will not be easy at first. But the men or women who are faithful will not only have a reward themselves, but become benefactors to their brethren. "Thou shalt be called the repairer of the breach, the restorer of paths to dwell in."

But is it really possible? Can it indeed be that those who have never been able to face, much less to overcome the difficulty, can yet become mighty in prayer? Tell me, was it really possible for Jacob to become Israel—a prince who prevailed with God? It was. The things that are impossible with men are possible with God. Have you not in very deed received from the Father, as the great fruit of Christ's redemption, the Spirit of supplication, the Spirit of intercession? Just pause and think what that means. And will you still doubt whether God is able to make you "strivers with God," princes who prevail with Him? Oh, let us banish all fear, and in faith claim the grace for which we have the Holy Spirit dwelling in us, the grace of supplication, the grace of intercession. Let us quietly, perseveringly believe that He lives in us, and will enable us to do our work. Let us in faith not fear to accept and yield to the great truth that intercession, as it is the great work of the King on the throne, is the great work of His servants on earth. We have the Holy Spirit, who brings the Christ-life into our hearts, to fit us for this work. Let us at once begin and stir up the gift within us. As we set aside each day our time for intercession, and count upon the Spirit's enabling power, the confidence will grow that we can, in our measure, follow Paul even as he followed Christ.

CHAPTER XIV. God seeks Intercessors

"I have set watchmen upon thy walls, O Jerusalem, which shall never hold their peace day nor night. Ye that are the Lord's remembrancers, keep not silence, and give Him no rest till He make Jerusalem a praise in the earth."—Isa. lxii. 6, 7.

"And He saw that there was no man, and wondered that there was no intercessor."—Isa. lix. 16.

"And I looked, and there was none to help; and I wondered, and there was none to uphold."—Isa. lxiii. 5.

"There is none that calleth upon Thy name, that stirreth himself to take hold of Thee."—Isa. lxiv. 7.

"And I sought for a man that should stand in the gap before Me for the land, that I should not destroy it; but I found none."—Ezek. xxii. 30.

"I chose you, and appointed you, that ye should go and bear fruit: that whatsoever ye shall ask of the Father in My name, He may give it you."—John xv. 16.

IN the study of the starry heavens, how much depends upon a due apprehension of magnitudes. Without some sense of the size of the heavenly bodies, that appear so small to the eye, and yet are so great, and of the almost illimitable extent of the regions in which they move, though they appear so near and so familiar, there can be no true knowledge of the heavenly world or its relation to this earth. It is even so with the spiritual heavens, and the heavenly life in which we are called to live. It is specially so in the life of intercession, that most wondrous intercourse between heaven and earth. Everything depends upon the due apprehension of magnitudes.

Just think of the three that come first: There is a world, with its needs entirely dependent on and waiting to be helped by intercession; there is a God in heaven, with His all-sufficient supply for all those needs, waiting to be asked; there is a Church, with its wondrous calling and its sure promises, waiting to be roused to a sense of its wondrous responsibility and power.

God seeks intercessors.—There is a world with its perishing millions, with intercession as its only hope. How much of love and work is comparatively vain, because there is so little intercession. A thousand millions living as if there never had been a Son of God to die for them. Thirty millions every year passing into the outer darkness without hope. Fifty millions bearing the Christian name, and the great majority living in utter ignorance or indifference. Millions of feeble, sickly Christians; thousands of wearied workers, who could be blessed by intercession, could help themselves to become mighty in intercession. Churches and missions sacrificing life and labour often with little result, for lack of intercession. Souls, each one worth more than worlds, worth nothing less than the price paid for them in Christ's blood, and within reach of the power that can be won by intercession. We surely have no conception of the magnitude of the work to be done by God's intercessors, or we should cry to God above everything to give from heaven the spirit of intercession.

God seeks intercessors.—There is a God of glory able to meet all these needs. We are told that He delights in mercy, that He waits to be gracious, that He longs to pour out His blessing; that the love that gave the Son to death is the measure of the love that each moment hovers over every human being. And yet He does not help. And there they perish, a million a month in China alone, and it is as if God does not move. If He does so love and long to bless, there must be some inscrutable reason for His holding back. What can it be? Scripture says, because of your unbelief. It is the faithlessness and consequent unfaithfulness of God's people. He has taken them up into partnership with Himself; He has honoured them, and bound Himself, by making their prayers one of the standard measures of the working of His power. Lack of intercession is one of the chief causes of lack of blessing. Oh, that we would turn eye and heart from everything else and fix them upon this God who hears prayer, until the magnificence of His promises, and His power, and His purpose of love overwhelmed us! How our whole life and heart would become intercession.

God seeks intercessors.—There is a third magnitude to which our eyes must be opened: the wondrous privilege and power of the intercessors. There is a false humility, which makes a great virtue of self-depreciation, because it has never seen its utter nothingness. If it knew that, it would never apologise for its feebleness, but glory in its utter weakness, as the one condition of Christ's power resting on it. It would judge of itself, its power and influence before God in prayer, as little by what it sees or feels, as we judge of the size of the sun or stars by what the eye can see. Faith sees man created in God's image and likeness to be God's representative in this world and have dominion over it. Faith sees man redeemed and lifted into union with Christ, abiding in Him, identified with Him, and clothed with His power in intercession. Faith sees the Holy Spirit dwelling and praying in the heart, making, in our sighings, intercession according to God. Faith sees the intercession of the saints to be part of the life of the Holy Trinity—the believer as God's child asking of the Father, in the Son, through the Spirit. Faith sees something of the Divine fitness and beauty of this scheme of salvation through intercession, wakens the soul to a consciousness of its wondrous destiny, and girds it with strength for the blessed self-sacrifice it calls to.

God seeks intercessors.—When He called His people out of Egypt, He separated the priestly tribe, to draw nigh to Him, and stand before Him, and bless the people in His name. From time to time He sought and found and honoured intercessors, for whose sake He spared or blessed His people. When our Lord left the earth He said to the inner circle He had gathered around Him—an inner circle of special devotion to His service, to which access is still free to every disciple: "I chose you, and appointed you, that whatsoever ye shall ask of the Father in My Name, He may give it you." We have already noticed the six times repeated three wonderful words—Whatsoever—In My Name—It shall be done. In them Christ placed the powers of the heavenly world at their disposal—not for their own selfish use, but in the interests of His kingdom. How wondrously they used it we know. And since that time, down through the ages, these men have had their successors, men who have proved how surely God works in answer to prayer. And we may praise God that, in our days too, there is an ever-increasing number who begin to see and prove that in church and mission, in large societies and little circles and individual effort, intercession is the chief thing, the power that moves God and opens heaven. They are learning, and long to learn better, and that all may learn, that in all work for souls intercession must take the first place, and that those who in it have received from heaven, in the power of the Holy Ghost, what they are to communicate to others, will be best able to do the Lord's work.

God seeks intercessors.—Though God had His appointed servants in Israel, watchmen set by Himself to cry to Him day and night and give Him no rest, He often had to wonder and complain that there was no intercessor, none to stir himself up to take hold of His strength. And He still waits and wonders in our day, that there are not more intercessors, that all His children do not give themselves to this highest and holiest work, that many of them who do so, do not engage in it more intensely and perseveringly. He wonders to find ministers of His gospel complaining that their duties do not allow them to find time for this, which He counts their first, their highest, their most delightful, their alone effective work. He wonders to find His sons and daughters, who have forsaken home and friends for His sake and the gospel's, come so short in what He meant to be their abiding strength—receiving day by day all they needed to impart to the dark heathen. He wonders to find multitudes of His children who have hardly any conception of what intercession is. He wonders to find multitudes more who have learned that it is their duty, and seek to obey it, but confess that they know but little of taking hold upon God or prevailing with Him.

God seeks intercessors.—He longs to dispense larger blessings. He longs to reveal His power and glory as God, His saving love, more abundantly. He seeks intercessors in larger number, in greater power, to prepare the way of the Lord. He seeks them. Where could He seek them but in His Church? And how does He expect to find them? He intrusted to His Church the task of telling of their Lord's need, the task of encouraging and training, and preparing them for His holy service. And He ever comes again, seeking fruit, seeking intercessors. In His Word He has spoken of the "widows indeed, who trust in God, and continue in supplication night and day." He looks if the Church is training the great army of aged men and women, whose time of outward work is past, but who can strengthen the army of the "elect, who cry to Him day and night." He looks to the great host of the Christian Endeavour, the three or four million of young lives that have given themselves away in the solemn pledge, "I promise the Lord Jesus Christ that I will strive to do whatever He would like to have me do," and wonders how many are being trained to pass from the brightness of the weekly prayer-meeting and its confession of loyalty, to swell the secret intercession that is to save souls. He looks to the thousands of young men and young women in training for the work of ministry and mission, and gazes longingly to see if the Church is teaching them that intercession, power with God, must be their first care, and in seeking to train and help them to it. He looks to see whether ministers and missionaries are understanding their opportunity, and labouring to train the believers of their congregation into those who can "help together" by their prayer, and can "strive with them in their prayers." As Christ seeks the lost sheep until He find it, Gods seeks intercessors. (Note F.)

God seeks intercessors.—He will not, He cannot, take the work out of the hands of His Church. And so He comes, calling and pleading in many ways. Now by a man whom He raises up to live a life of faith in His service, and to prove how actually and abundantly He answers prayer. Then by the story of a church which makes prayer for souls its starting-point, and bears testimony to God's faithfulness. Sometimes in a mission which proves how special prayer can meet special need, and bring down the power of the Spirit. And sometimes again by a season of revival coming in answer to united urgent supplication. In these and many other ways God is showing us what intercession can do, and beseeching us to waken up and train His great host to be, every one, a people of intercessors.

God seeks intercessors.—He sends His servants out to call them. Let ministers make this a part of their duty. Let them make their church a training school of intercession. Give the people definite objects for prayer. Encourage them to take a definite time to it, if it were only ten minutes every day. Help them to understand the boldness they may use with God. Teach them to expect and look out for answers. Show them what it is first to pray and get an answer in secret, and then carry the answer and impart the blessing. Tell everyone who is master of his own time that he is as the angels, free to tarry before the throne and then go out and minister to the heirs of salvation. Sound out the blessed tidings that this honour is for all God's people. There is no difference. That servant girl, this day labourer, that bedridden invalid, this daughter in her mother's home, these men and young men in business—all are called, all, all are needed. God seeks intercessors.

God seeks intercessors.—As ministers take up the work of finding and training them it will urge themselves to pray more. Christ gave Paul to be a pattern of His grace before He made him a preacher of it. It has been well said, "The first duty of a clergyman is humbly to beg of God that all he would have done in his people may be first truly and fully done in himself." The effort to bring this message of God may cause much heart-searching and humiliation. All the better. The best practice in doing a thing is helping others to do it. O ye servants of Christ, set as watchmen to cry to God day and night, let us awake to our holy calling. Let us believe in the power of intercession. Let us practise it. Let us seek on behalf of our people to get from God Himself the Spirit and the Life we preach. With our spirit and life given up to God in intercession, the Spirit and Life that God gives them through us cannot fail to be the Life of Intercession too.

CHAPTER XV. The Coming Revival

"Wilt Thou not revive us again: that Thy people may rejoice in Thee?"—Ps. lxxxv. 6.

"O Lord, revive Thy work in the midst of the years."—Hab. iii. 2.

"Though I walk in the midst of trouble, Thou wilt revive me: Thy right hand shall save me."—Ps. cxxxviii. 7.

"I dwell with him that is of a humble and contrite heart, to revive the heart of the contrite ones."—Isa. lvii. 15.

"Come, and let us return to the Lord: for He hath torn, and He will heal us. He will revive us."—Hos. vi. 1, 2.

THE COMING REVIVAL—one frequently hears the word. There are teachers not a few who see the tokens of its approach, and confidently herald its speedy appearance. In the increase of mission interest, in the tidings of revivals in places where all were dead or cold, in the hosts of our young gathered into Students' and other Associations or Christian Endeavour Societies, in doors everywhere opened in the Christian and the heathen world, in victories already secured in the fields white unto the harvest, wherever believing, hopeful workers enter, they find the assurance of a time of power and blessing such as we have not known. The Church is about to enter on a new era of increasing spirituality and larger extension.

There are others who, while admitting the truth of some of these facts, yet fear that the conclusions drawn from them are one-sided and premature. They see the interest in missions increased, but point out to how small a circle it is confined, and how utterly out of proportion it is to what it ought to be. To the great majority of Church members, to the greater part of the Church, it is as yet anything but a life question. They remind us of the power of worldliness and formality, of the increase of the money-making and pleasure-loving spirit among professing Christians, to the lack of spirituality in so many, many of our churches, and the continuing and apparently increasing estrangement of multitudes from God's Day and Word, as proof that the great revival has certainly not begun, and is hardly thought of by the most. They say that they do not see the deep humiliation, the intense desire, the fervent prayer which appear as the forerunners of every true revival.

There are right-hand and left-hand errors which are equally dangerous. We must seek as much to be kept from the superficial Optimism, which never is able to gauge the extent of the evil, as from the hopeless Pessimism which can neither praise God for what He has done, nor trust Him for what He is ready to do. The former will lose itself in a happy self-gratulation, as it rejoices in its zeal and diligence and apparent success, and never see the need of confession and great striving in prayer, ere we are prepared to meet and conquer the hosts of darkness. The latter virtually gives over the world to Satan, and almost prays and rejoices to see things get worse, to hasten the coming of Him who is to put all right. May God keep us from either error, and fulfil the promise, "Thine ears shall hear a word behind thee, saying, This is the way, walk ye in it, when ye turn to the right hand, and when ye turn to the left." Let us listen to the lessons suggested by the passages we have quoted; they may help us to pray the prayer aright: "Revive Thy work, O Lord!"

1. "Revive Thy work, O Lord!"—Read again the passages of Scripture, and see how they all contain the one thought: Revival is God's work; He alone can give it; it must come from above. We are frequently in danger of looking to what God has done and is doing, and to count on that as the pledge that He will at once do more. And all the time it may be true that He is blessing us up to the measure of our faith or self-sacrifice, and cannot give larger measure, until there has been a new discovery and confession of what is hindering Him. Or we may be looking to all the signs of life and good around us, and congratulating ourselves on all the organisations and agencies that are being created, while the need of God's mighty and direct interposition is not rightly felt, and the entire dependence upon Him not cultivated. Regeneration, the giving of Divine life, we all acknowledge to be God's act, a miracle of His power. The restoring or reviving of the Divine life, in a soul or a Church, is as much a supernatural work. To have the spiritual discernment that can understand the signs of the heavens, and prognosticate the coming revival, we need to enter deep into God's mind and will as to its conditions, and the preparedness of those who pray for it or are to be used to bring it about. "Surely the Lord God will do nothing, but He revealeth His secret unto his servants the prophets." It is God who is to give the revival; it is God who reveals His secret; it is the spirit of absolute dependence upon God, giving Him the honour and the glory, that will prepare for it.

2. "Revive Thy work, O Lord!"—A second lesson suggested is, that the revival God is to give will be given in answer to prayer. It must be

asked and received direct from God Himself. Those who know anything of the history of revivals will remember how often this has been proved—both larger and more local revivals have been distinctly traced to special prayer. In our own day there are numbers of congregations and missions where special or permanent revivals are—all glory be to God—connected with systematic, believing prayer. The coming revival will be no exception. An extraordinary spirit of prayer, urging believers to much secret and united prayer, pressing them to "labour fervently" in their supplications, will be one of the surest signs of approaching showers and floods of blessing.

Let all who are burdened with the lack of spirituality, with the low state of the life of God in believers, listen to the call that comes to all. If there is to be revival,—a mighty, Divine revival,—it will need, on our part, corresponding whole-heartedness in prayer and faith. Let not one believer think himself too weak to help, or imagine that he will not be missed. If he first begin, the gift that is in him may be so stirred that, for his circle or neighbourhood, he shall be God's chosen intercessor. Let us think of the need of souls, of all the sins and failings among God's people, of the little power there is in so much of the preaching, and begin to cry every day, "Wilt Thou not revive us again, that Thy people may rejoice in Thee?" And let us have the truth graven deep in our hearts: every revival comes, as Pentecost came, as the fruit of united, continued prayer. The coming revival must begin with a great prayer revival. It is in the closet, with the door shut, that the sound of abundance of rain will be first heard. An increase of secret prayer with ministers and members, will be the sure harbinger of blessing.

3. "Revive Thy work, O Lord!"—A third lesson our texts teach is that it is to the humble and contrite that the revival is promised. We want the revival to come upon the proud and the self-satisfied, to break them down and save them. God will give this, but only on the condition that those who see and feel the sin of others take their burden of confession and bear it, and that all who pray for and claim in faith God's reviving power for His Church, shall humble themselves with the confession of its sins. The need of revival always points to previous decline; and decline was always caused by sin. Humiliation and contrition have ever been the conditions of revival. In all intercession confession of man's sin and God's righteous judgment is ever an essential element.

Throughout the history of Israel we continually see this. It comes out in the reformations under the pious Kings of Judah. We hear it in the prayer of men like Ezra and Nehemiah and Daniel. In Isaiah and

Jeremiah and Ezekiel, as well as in the minor prophets, it is the keynote of all the warning as of all the promise. If there be no humiliation and forsaking of sin there can be no revival or deliverance: "These men have set up their idols in their hearts. Shall I at all be inquired of by them?" "To this man will I look, even to him that is poor and of a contrite spirit, and that trembleth at My word." Amid the most gracious promises of Divine visitation there is ever this note: "Be ashamed and confounded for your ways, O House of Israel."

We find the same in the New Testament. The Sermon on the Mount promises the kingdom to the poor and them that mourn. In the Epistles to the Corinthians and Galatians the religion of man, of worldly wisdom and confidence in the flesh, is exposed and denounced; without its being confessed and forsaken, all the promises of grace and the Spirit will be vain. In the Epistles to the seven churches we find five of which He, out of whose mouth goes the sharp, two-edged sword, says, that He has something against them. In each of these the keyword of His message is—not to the unconverted, but to the Church—Repent! All the glorious promises which each of these Epistles contain, down to the last one, with its "Open the door and I will come in"; "He that overcometh shall sit with Me on My throne," are dependent on that one word—Repent!

And if there is to be a revival, not among the unsaved, but in our churches, to give a holy, spiritual membership, will not that trumpet sound need to be heard—Repent? Was it only in Israel, in the ministry of kings and prophets, that there was so much evil in God's people to be cleansed away? Was it only in the Church of the first century, that Paul and James and our Lord Himself had to speak such sharp words? Or is there not in the Church of our days an idolatry of money and talent and culture, a worldly spirit, making it unfaithful to its one only Husband and Lord, a confidence in the flesh which grieves and resists God's Holy Spirit? Is there not almost everywhere a confession of the lack of spirituality and spiritual power? Let all who long for the coming revival, and seek to hasten it by their prayers, pray this above everything, that the Lord may prepare His prophets to go before Him at His bidding: "Cry aloud and spare not, lift up thy voice like a trumpet, and show My people their transgression." Every deep revival among God's people must have its roots in a deep sense and confession of sin. Until those who would lead the Church in the path of revival bear faithful testimony against the sins of the Church, it is to feared that it will find people unprepared. Men would fain have a revival as the outgrowth of their agencies and progress. God's way is the opposite: it is out of death, acknowledged as the desert of sin, confessed as utter helplessness, that He revives. He revives the heart of the contrite one.

4. "Revive Thy work, O Lord!"—There is a last thought, suggested by the text from Hosea. It is as we return to the Lord that revival will come; for if we had not wandered from Him, His life would be among us in power. "Come and let us return to the Lord: for He hath torn, He will heal us: He hath smitten; He will bind us up: He will revive us, and we shall live in His sight." As we have said, there can be no return to the Lord, where there is no sense or confession of wandering. Let us return to the Lord must be the keynote of the revival. Let us return, acknowledging and forsaking whatever there has been in the Church that is not entirely according to His mind and spirit. Let us return, yielding up and casting out whatever there has been in our religion or along with it of the power of God's two great enemies—confidence in the flesh or the spirit of the world. Let us return, in the acknowledgment of how undividedly God must have us, to fill us with His Spirit, and use us for the kingdom of His Son. Oh, let us return, in the surrender of a dependence and a devotion which has no measure but the absolute claim of Him who is the Lord! Let us return to the Lord with our whole heart, that He may make and keep us wholly His. He will revive us, and we shall live in His sight. Let us turn to the God of Pentecost, as Christ led his disciples to turn to Him, and the God of Pentecost will turn to us.

It is for this returning to the Lord that the great work of intercession is needed. It is here the coming revival must find its strength. Let us begin as individuals in secret to plead with God, confessing whatever we see of sin or hindrance, in ourselves or others. If there were not one other sin, surely in the lack of prayer there is matter enough for repentance and confession and returning to the Lord. Let us seek to foster the spirit of confession and supplication and intercession in those around us. Let us help to encourage and to train those who think themselves too feeble. Let us lift up our voice to proclaim the great truths. The revival must come from above; the revival must be received in faith from above and brought down by prayer; the revival comes to the humble and contrite, for them to carry to others; if we return to the Lord with our whole heart, He will revive us. On those who see these truths, rests the solemn responsibility of giving themselves up to witness for them and to act them out.

And as each of us pleads for the revival throughout the Church, let us specially, at the same time, cry to God for our own neighbourhood or sphere of work. Let, with every minister and worker, there be "great searchings of heart," as to whether they are ready to give such proportion of time and strength to prayer as God would have. Let them, even as in public they are leaders of their larger or smaller circles, give themselves in secret to take their places in the front rank of the great intercession host, that must prevail with God, ere the great revival, the floods of blessing can come. Of all who speak or think of, or long for, revival, let not one hold back in this great work of honest, earnest, definite pleading: Revive Thy work, O Lord! Wilt Thou not revive us again?

Come and let us return to the Lord: He will revive us! And let us know, let us follow on to know the Lord. "His going forth is sure as the morning; and He shall come unto us as the rain, as the latter rain that watereth the earth." Amen. So be it.

NOTES

NOTE A, Chap. VI. p. 73

Just this day I have been meeting a very earnest lady missionary from India. She confesses and mourns the lack of prayer. But—in India at least—it can hardly be otherwise. You have only the morning hours, from six to eleven, for your work. Some have attempted to rise at four, and get the time they think they need, and have suffered, and had to give it up. Some have tried to take time after lunch, and been found asleep on their knees. You are not your own master, and must act with others. No one who has not been in India can understand the difficulty; sufficient time for much intercession cannot be secured.

Were it only in the heat of India the difficulty existed, one might be silent. But, alas! in the coldest winter in London, and in the moderate climate of South Africa, there is the same trouble everywhere. If once we really felt—intercession is the most important part of our work, the securing of God's presence and power in full measure is the essential thing, this is our first duty—our hours of work would all be made subordinate to this one thing.

May God show us all whether there indeed be an insuperable difficulty for which we are not responsible, whether it be only a mistake we are making, or a sin by which we are grieving Him and hindering His Spirit!

If we ask the question George Muller once asked of a Christian, who complained that he could not find time sufficient for the study of the Word and prayer, whether an hour less work, say four hours, with the soul dwelling in the full light of God, would not be more prosperous and effective than five hours with the depressing consciousness of unfaithfulness, and the loss of the power that could be obtained in prayer, the answer will not be difficult. The more we think of it the more we feel that when earnest, godly workers allow, against their better will, the spiritual to be crowded out by incessant occupation and the fatigue it brings, it must be because the spiritual life is not sufficiently strong in them to bid the lever stand aside till the presence of God in Christ and the power of the Spirit have been fully secured.

Let us listen to Christ saying, "Render unto Cæsar the things that are Cæsar's"—let duty and work have their place—"and unto God the things that are God's." Let the worship in the Spirit, the entire dependence and continued waiting upon God for the full experience of His presence and power every day, and the strength of Christ working in us, ever have the first place. The whole question is simply this, Is God to have the place, the love, the trust, the time for personal fellowship He claims, so that all our working shall be God working in us?

NOTE B, Chap. VII. p. 89

Let me tell here a story that occurs in one of Dr. Boardman's works. He had been invited by a lady of good position, well known as a successful worker among her husband's dependents, to come and address them. "And then," she added, "I want to speak to you about a bit of bondage of my own." When he had addressed her meeting, and found many brought to Christ through her, he wondered what her trouble might be. She soon told him. God had blessed her work, but, alas, the enjoyment she once had had in God's word and secret prayer had been lost. And she had tried her utmost to get it back, and had failed. "Ah! that is just your mistake," he said. "How that? Ought I not to do my best to have the coldness removed?" "Tell me," he said, "were you saved by doing your best?" "Oh, no! I tried long to do that, but only found rest when I ceased trying, and trusted Christ." "And that is what you need to do now. Enter your closet at the appointed time, however dull you feel, and place yourself before your Lord. Do not try to rouse an earnestness you do not feel; but quietly say to Him that He sees how all is wrong, how helpless you are, and trust Him to bless you. He will do it; as you trust quietly, His Spirit will work."

The simple story may teach many a Christian a most blessed lesson in the life of prayer. You have accepted of Christ Jesus to make you whole, and give you strength to walk in newness of life; you have claimed the Holy Spirit to be in you the Spirit of Supplication and Intercession; but do not wonder if your feelings are not all at once changed, or if your power of prayer does not come in the way you would like. It is a life of faith. By faith we receive the Holy Spirit and all His workings. Faith regards neither sight nor feeling, but rests, even when there appears to be no power to pray, in the assurance that the Spirit is praying in us as we bow quietly before God. He that thus waits in faith, and honours the Holy Spirit, and yields himself to Him, will soon find that prayer will begin to come. And he that perseveres in the faith that through Christ and by the Spirit each prayer, however feeble, is acceptable to God, will learn the lesson that it is possible to be taught by the Spirit, and led to walk worthy of the Lord to all well pleasing.

NOTE C, Chap. IX. p. 111

Just yesterday again—three days after the conversation mentioned in the note to chap. vii.—I met a devoted young missionary lady from the interior. As a conversation on prayer was proceeding, she interposed unasked with the remark, "But it is really impossible to find the time to pray as we wish to." I could only answer, "Time is a quantity that accommodates itself to our will; what our hearts really consider of first importance in the day, we will soon succeed in finding time for." It must surely be that the ministry of intercession has never been put before our students in Theological Halls and Missionary Training Homes as the most important part of their life-work. We have thought of our work in preaching or visiting as our real duty, and of prayer as a subordinate means to do this work successfully. Would not the whole position be changed if we regarded the ministry of intercession as the chief thing—getting the blessing and power of God for the souls entrusted to us? Then our work would take its right place, and become the subordinate one of really dispensing blessings which we had received from God. It was when the friend at midnight, in answer to his prayer, had received from Another as much as he needed, that he could supply his hungry friend. It was the intercession, going out and importuning, that was the difficult work; returning home with his rich supply to impart was easy, joyful work. This is Christ's divine order for all thy work, my brother: First come, in utter poverty, every day, and get from God the blessing in intercession, go then rejoicingly to impart it.

NOTE D, Chap. X. p. 123

Let me once again refer my readers to William Law, and repeat what I have said before, that no book has so helped me to an insight into the place and work of the Holy Spirit in the economy of redemption as his Address to the Clergy.2

The way in which he opens up how God's one object was to dwell in man, making him partaker of His goodness and glory, other way than by himself living and working in him, gives one the key to what Pentecost and the sending forth of the Spirit of God's Son into our hearts really means. It is Christ in God's name really regaining and retaking possession of the home He had created for Himself. It is God entering into the secret depths of our nature there to "work to will and to do," to "work that which is pleasing in His sight in Christ Jesus." It is as this truth enters into us, and we see that there is and can be no good in us but what God works, that we shall see light on the Divine mystery of prayer, and believe in the Holy Spirit as breathing within us desires which God will fulfil when we yield to them, and believingly present them in the name of Christ. We shall then see that just as wonderful and prevailing as the intercession and prayer passing from the Incarnate Son to the Father in heaven is our intercourse with God; the Spirit, who is God, breathing and praying in us amid all our feebleness His heaven-born Divine petitions: what a heavenly thing prayer becomes.

The latter part of the above-mentioned book consists of extracts from Law's letters. These have been published separately as a little shilling volume.3 No one who will take the time quietly to read and master the so simple but deep teaching they contain, without being wonderfully strengthened in the confidence which is needed, if we are to pray much and boldly. As we learn that the Holy Spirit is within us to reveal Christ there, to make us in living reality partakers of His death, His life, His merit, His disposition, so that He is formed within us, we will begin to see how Divinely right and sure it is that our intercessions in His name must be heard; his own Spirit maintains the living union with Himself, in whom we are brought nigh to God, and gives us boldness of access; what I have so feebly said in the chapter on the Spirit of Supplication will get new meaning; and, what is more, the exercise of prayer a new attractiveness; its solemn Divine mystery will humble us, its unspeakable privilege lift us up in faith and adoration.

2 The Power of the Spirit: An Address to the Clergy. By William Law. With additional Extracts and an Introduction by Rev. A. M. James Nisbet & Co. 2s. 6d.
3 The Divine Indwelling. Selections from the Letters of William Law. With Introduction by A. M. James Nisbet & Co.
NOTE E, Chap. XI. p. 136

There is a question, the deepest of all, on which I have not entered in this book. I have spoken of the lack of prayer in the individual Christian as a symptom of a disease. But what shall we say of it, that there is such a widespread prevalence of this failure to give a due proportion of time and strength to prayer? Do we not need to inquire, How comes it that the Church of Christ, endued with the Holy Ghost, cannot train its ministers and workers and members to place first what is first? How comes it that the confession of too little prayer, and the call for more prayer, is so frequently heard, and yet the evil continues?

The Spirit of God, the Spirit of Supplication and Intercession, is in the Church and in every believer. There must surely be some other spirit of great power resisting and hindering this Spirit of God. It is indeed so. The spirit of the world, which under all its beautiful and even religious activities is the spirit of the god of this world, is the great hindrance. Everything that is done on earth, whether within or without the Church, is done by either of these two spirits. What is in the individual the flesh, is in mankind as a whole the spirit of the world; and all the power the flesh has in the individual is owing to the place given to the spirit of this world in the Church and in Christian life. It is the spirit of the world is the great hindrance to the spirit of prayer. All our most earnest calls to men to pray more will be vain except this evil be acknowledged and combated and overcome. The believer and the Church must be entirely freed from the spirit of the world.

And how is this to be done? There is but one way—the Cross of Christ, "by which," as Paul says, "the world is crucified unto me, and I unto the world." It is only through death to the world that we can be freed from its spirit. The separation must be vital and entire. It is only through the acceptance of our crucifixion with Christ that we can live out this confession, and, as crucified to the world, maintain the position of irreconcilable hostility to whatever is of its spirit and not of the Spirit of God; and it is only God Himself who, by His Divine power, can lead us into and keep us daily dead to sin, and alive unto God in Christ Jesus. The cross, with its shame and its separation from the world, and its death to all that is of flesh and of self, is the only power that can conquer the spirit of the world.

I have felt so strongly that the truth needs to be anew asserted, that I hope, if it please God, to publish a volume, The Cross of Christ, with the inquiry into what God's word teaches as to our actual participation with Christ in His crucifixion. Christ prayed on the way to the cross. He prayed Himself to the cross. He prayed on the cross. He prays ever as the fruit of the cross. As the Church lives on the cross, and the cross lives in the Church, the spirit of prayer will be given. In Christ it was the crucifixion spirit and death that was the source of the Intercession Spirit and Power. With us it can be no otherwise.

NOTE F, Chap. XIV. p. 177

I have more than once spoken of the need of training Christians to the work of intercession. In a previous note I have asked the question whether, in the teaching of our Theological Halls and Mission Training

Houses, sufficient attention is given to prayer as the most important, and in some senses the most difficult part of the work for which the students are being prepared. I have wondered whether it might not be possible to offer those who are willing, during their student life, to put themselves under a course of training, some help in the way of hints and suggestions as to what is needed to give prayer the place and the power in our ministry it ought to have.

As a rule, it is in the student life that the character must be formed for future years, and it is in the present student world that the Church of the future must be influenced. If God allows me to carry out a plan that is hardly quite mature yet, I would wish to publish a volume, The Student's Prayer Manual, combining the teaching of Scripture as to what is most needed to make men of prayer of us, with such practical directions as may help a young Christian, preparing to devote his life to God's service successfully, to cultivate such a spirit and habit of prayer as shall abide with him through all his coming life and labours.

Lord, Teach Us to Pray

The disciples had been with Christ, and seen Him pray. They had learnt to understand something of the connection between His wondrous life in public, and His secret life of prayer. They had learnt to believe in Him as a Master in the art of prayer—none could pray like Him. And so they came to Him with the request, 'Lord, teach us to pray.' And in after years they would have told us that there were few things more wonderful or blessed that He taught them than His lessons on prayer.

And now still it comes to pass, as He is praying in a certain place, that disciples who see Him thus engaged feel the need of repeating the same request, 'Lord, teach us to pray.' As we grow in the Christian life, the thought and the faith of the Beloved Master in His never-failing intercession becomes evermore precious, and the hope of being Like Christ in His intercession gains an attractiveness before unknown. And as we see Him pray, and remember that there is none who can pray like Him, and none who can teach like Him, we feel the petition of the disciples, 'Lord, teach us to pray,' is just what we need. And as we think how all He is and has, how He Himself is our very own, how He is Himself our life, we feel assured that we have but to ask, and He will be delighted to take us up into closer fellowship with Himself, and teach us to pray even as He prays.

Come, my brothers! Shall we not go to the Blessed Master and ask Him to enrol our names too anew in that school which He always keeps open for those who long to continue their studies in the Divine art of prayer and intercession? Yes, let us this very day say to the Master, as they did of old, 'Lord, teach us to pray.' As we meditate we shall find each word of the petition we bring to be full of meaning.

'Lord, teach us to pray.' Yes, to pray. This is what we need to be taught. Though in its beginnings prayer is so simple that the feeble child can pray, yet it is at the same time the highest and holiest work to which man can rise. It is fellowship with the Unseen and Most Holy One. The powers of the eternal world have been placed at its disposal. It is the very essence of true religion, the channel of all blessings, the secret of power and life. Not only for ourselves, but for others, for the Church, for the world, it is to prayer that God has given the right to take hold of Him and His strength. It is on prayer that the promises wait for their fulfilment, the kingdom for its coming, the glory of God for its full revelation. And for this blessed work, how slothful and unfit we are. It is only the Spirit of God can enable us to do it aright. How speedily we are deceived into a resting in the form, while the power is wanting. Our early training, the teaching of the Church, the influence of habit, the stirring of the emotions—how easily these lead to prayer which has no spiritual power, and avails but little. True prayer, that takes hold of God's strength, that availeth much, to which the gates of heaven are really opened wide—who would not cry, Oh for some one to teach me thus to pray?

Jesus has opened a school, in which He trains His redeemed ones, who specially desire it, to have power in prayer. Shall we not enter it with the petition, Lord! it is just this we need to be taught! O teach us to pray.

'Lord, teach us to pray.' Yes, us, Lord. We have read in Thy Word with what power Thy believing people of old used to pray, and what mighty wonders were done in answer to their prayers. And if this took place under the Old Covenant, in the time of preparation, how much more wilt Thou not now, in these days of fulfilment, give Thy people this sure sign of Thy presence in their midst. We have heard the promises given to Thine apostles of the power of prayer in Thy name, and have seen how gloriously they experienced their truth: we know for certain, they can become true to us too. We hear continually even in these days what glorious tokens of Thy power Thou dost still give to those who trust Thee fully. Lord! these all are men of like passions with ourselves; teach us to pray so too. The promises are for us, the powers and gifts of the heavenly world are for us. O teach us to pray so that we may receive abundantly. To us too Thou hast entrusted Thy work, on our prayer too the coming of Thy kingdom depends, in our prayer too Thou canst glorify Thy name; 'Lord, teach us to pray.' Yes, us, Lord; we offer ourselves as learners; we would indeed be taught of Thee. 'Lord, teach us to pray.'

'Lord, teach us to pray.' Yes, we feel the need now of being taught to pray. At first there is no work appears so simple; later on, none that is more difficult; and the confession is forced from us: We know not how to pray as we ought. It is true we have God's Word, with its clear and sure promises; but sin has so darkened our mind, that we know not always how to apply the Word. In spiritual things we do not always seek the most needful things, or fail in praying according to the law of the sanctuary. In temporal things we are still less able to avail ourselves of the wonderful liberty our Father has given us to ask what we need. And even when we know what to ask, how much there is still needed to make prayer acceptable. It must be to the glory of God, in full surrender to His will, in full assurance of faith, in the name of Jesus, and with a perseverance that, if need be, refuses to be denied. All this must be learned. It can only be learned in the school of much prayer, for practice makes perfect. Amid the painful consciousness of ignorance and unworthiness, in the struggle between believing and doubting, the heavenly art of effectual prayer is learnt. Because, even when we do not remember it, there is One, the Beginner and Finisher of faith and prayer, who watches over our praying, and sees to it that in all who trust Him for it their education in the school of prayer shall be carried on to perfection. Let but the deep undertone of all our prayer be the teachableness that comes from a sense of ignorance, and from faith in Him as a perfect teacher, and we may be sure we shall be taught, we shall learn to pray in power. Yes, we may depend upon it, He teaches to pray.

'Lord, teach us to pray.' None can teach like Jesus, none but Jesus; therefore we call on Him, 'Lord, teach us to pray.' A pupil needs a teacher, who knows his work, who has the gift of teaching, who in patience and love will descend to the pupil's needs. Blessed be God! Jesus is all this and much more. He knows what prayer is. It is Jesus, praying Himself, who teaches to pray. He knows what prayer is. He learned it amid the trials and tears of His earthly life. In heaven it is still His beloved work: His life there is prayer. Nothing delights Him more than to find those whom He can take with Him into the Father's presence, whom He can clothe with power to pray down God's blessing on those around them, whom He can train to be His fellow-workers in the intercession by which the kingdom is to be revealed on earth. He knows how to teach. Now by the urgency of felt need, then by the confidence with which joy inspires. Here by the teaching of the Word, there by the testimony of another believer who knows what it is to have prayer heard. By His Holy Spirit, He has access to our heart, and teaches us to pray by showing us the sin that hinders the prayer, or giving us the assurance that we please God. He teaches, by giving not only thoughts of what to ask or how to ask, but by breathing within us the very spirit of prayer, by living within us as the Great Intercessor. We may indeed and most joyfully say, 'Who teacheth like Him?' Jesus never taught His disciples how to preach, only how to pray. He did not speak much of what was needed to preach well, but much of praying well. To know how to speak to God is more than knowing how to speak to man. Not power with men, but power with God is the first thing. Jesus loves to teach us how to pray.

What think you, my beloved fellow-disciples! would it not be just what we need, to ask the Master for a month to give us a course of special lessons on the art of prayer? As we meditate on the words He spake on earth, let us yield ourselves to His teaching in the fullest confidence that, with such a teacher, we shall make progress. Let us take time not only to meditate, but to pray, to tarry at the foot of the throne, and be trained to the work of intercession. Let us do so in the assurance that amidst our stammerings and fears He is carrying on His work most beautifully. He will breathe His own life, which is all prayer, into us. As He makes us partakers of His righteousness and His life, He will of His intercession too. As the members of His body, as a holy priesthood, we shall take part in His priestly work of pleading and prevailing with God for men. Yes, let us most joyfully say, ignorant and feeble though we be, 'Lord, teach us to pray.'

'Lord, Teach Us To Pray.'

Blessed Lord! who ever livest to pray, Thou canst teach me too to pray, me to live ever to pray. In this Thou lovest to make me share Thy glory in heaven, that I should pray without ceasing, and ever stand as a priest in the presence of my God.

Lord Jesus! I ask Thee this day to enrol my name among those who confess that they know not how to pray as they ought, and especially ask Thee for a course of teaching in prayer. Lord! teach me to tarry with Thee in the school, and give Thee time to train me. May a deep sense of my ignorance, of the wonderful privilege and power of prayer, of the need of the Holy Spirit as the Spirit of prayer, lead me to cast away my thoughts of what I think I know, and make me kneel before Thee in true teachableness and poverty of spirit.

And fill me, Lord, with the confidence that with such a teacher as Thou art I shall learn to pray. In the assurance that I have as my teacher, Jesus, who is ever praying to the Father, and by His prayer rules the destinies of His Church and the world, I will not be afraid. As much as I need to know of the mysteries of the prayer-world, Thou wilt unfold for me. And when I may not know, Thou wilt teach me to be strong in faith, giving glory to God.

Blessed Lord! Thou wilt not put to shame Thy scholar who trusts Thee, nor, by Thy grace, would he Thee either. Amen.

'IN SPIRIT AND TRUTH;' OR THE TRUE WORSHIPPERS.

'The hour cometh, and now is, when the true worshippers shall worship the Father in spirit and truth: for such doth the Father seek to be His worshippers. God is a Spirit: and they that worship Him must worship Him in spirit and truth.'—John iv. 23, 24.

These words of Jesus to the woman of Samaria are His first recorded teaching on the subject of prayer. They give us some wonderful first glimpses into the world of prayer. The Father seeks worshippers: our worship satisfies His loving heart and is a joy to Him. He seeks true worshippers, but finds many not such as He would have them. True worship is that which is in spirit and truth. The Son has come to open the way for this worship in spirit and in truth, and teach it us. And so one of our first lessons in the school of prayer must be to understand what it is to pray in spirit and in truth, and to know how we can attain to it.

To the woman of Samaria our Lord spoke of a threefold worship. There is, first, the ignorant worship of the Samaritans: 'Ye worship that which ye know not.' The second, the intelligent worship of the Jew, having the true knowledge of God: 'We worship that which we know; for salvation is of the Jews.' And then the new, the spiritual worship which He Himself has come to introduce: 'The hour is coming, and is now, when the true worshippers shall worship the Father in spirit and truth.' From the connection it is evident that the words 'in spirit and truth' do not mean, as is often thought, earnestly, from the heart, in sincerity. The Samaritans had the five books of Moses and some knowledge of God; there was doubtless more than one among them who honestly and earnestly sought God in prayer. The Jews had the true full revelation of God in His word, as thus far given; there were among them godly men, who called upon God with their whole heart. And yet not 'in spirit and truth,' in the full meaning of the words. Jesus says, 'The hour is coming, and now is:' it is only in and through Him that the worship of God will be in spirit and truth.

Among Christians one still finds the three classes of worshippers. Some who in their ignorance hardly know what they ask: they pray earnestly, and yet receive but little. Others there are, who have more correct knowledge, who try to pray with all their mind and heart, and often pray most earnestly, and yet do not attain to the full blessedness of worship in spirit and truth. It is into this third class we must ask our Lord Jesus to take us; we must be taught of Him how to worship in spirit and truth. This alone is spiritual worship; this makes us worshippers such as the Father seeks. In prayer everything will depend on our understanding well and practising the worship in spirit and truth.

'God is a Spirit and they that worship Him must worship Him in spirit and truth.' The first thought suggested here by the Master is that there must be harmony between God and His worshippers; such as God is, must His worship be. This is according to a principle which prevails throughout the universe: we look for correspondence between an object and the organ to which it reveals or yields itself. The eye has an inner fitness for the light, the ear for sound. The man who would truly worship God, would find and know and possess and enjoy God, must be in harmony with Him, must have a capacity for receiving Him. Because God is Spirit, we must worship in spirit. As God is, so His worshipper.

And what does this mean? The woman had asked our Lord whether Samaria or Jerusalem was the true place of worship. He answers that henceforth worship is no longer to be limited to a certain place: 'Woman, believe Me, the hour cometh when neither in this mountain, nor in Jerusalem, shall ye worship the Father.' As God is Spirit, not bound by space or time, but in His infinite perfection always and everywhere the same, so His worship would henceforth no longer be confined by place or form, but spiritual as God Himself is spiritual. A lesson of deep importance. How much our Christianity suffers from this, that it is confined to certain times and places. A man who seeks to pray earnestly in the church or in the closet, spends the greater part of the week or the day in a spirit entirely at variance with that in which he prayed. His worship was the work of a fixed place or hour, not of his whole being. God is a spirit: He is the Everlasting and Unchangeable One; what He is, He is always and in truth. Our worship must even so be in spirit and truth: His worship must be the spirit of our life; our life must be worship in spirit as God is Spirit.

'God is a Spirit: and they that worship Him must worship Him in spirit and truth.' The second thought that comes to us is that this worship in the spirit must come from God Himself. God is Spirit: He alone has Spirit to give. It was for this He sent His Son, to fit us for such spiritual worship, by giving us the Holy Spirit. It is of His own work that Jesus speaks when He says twice, 'The hour cometh,' and then adds, 'and is now.' He came to baptize with the Holy Spirit; the Spirit could not stream forth till He was glorified (John i. 33, vii. 37, 38, xvi. 7). It was when He had made an end of sin, and entering into the Holiest of all with His blood, had there on our behalf received the Holy Spirit (Acts

ii. 33), that He could send Him down to us as the Spirit of the Father. It was when Christ had redeemed us, and we in Him had received the position of children, that the Father sent forth the Spirit of His Son into our hearts to cry, 'Abba, Father.' The worship in spirit is the worship of the Father in the Spirit of Christ, the Spirit of Sonship.

This is the reason why Jesus here uses the name of Father. We never find one of the Old Testament saints personally appropriate the name of child or call God his Father. The worship of the Father is only possible to those to whom the Spirit of the Son has been given. The worship in spirit is only possible to those to whom the Son has revealed the Father, and who have received the spirit of Sonship. It is only Christ who opens the way and teaches the worship in spirit.

And in truth. That does not only mean, in sincerity. Nor does it only signify, in accordance with the truth of God's Word. The expression is one of deep and Divine meaning. Jesus is 'the only-begotten of the Father, full of grace and truth.' 'The law was given by Moses; grace and truth came by Jesus Christ.' Jesus says, 'I am the truth and the life.' In the Old Testament all was shadow and promise; Jesus brought and gives the reality, the substance, of things hoped for. In Him the blessings and powers of the eternal life are our actual possession and experience. Jesus is full of grace and truth; the Holy Spirit is the Spirit of truth; through Him the grace that is in Jesus is ours indeed, and truth a positive communication out of the Divine life. And so worship in spirit is worship in truth; actual living fellowship with God, a real correspondence and harmony between the Father, who is a Spirit, and the child praying in the spirit.

What Jesus said to the woman of Samaria, she could not at once understand. Pentecost was needed to reveal its full meaning. We are hardly prepared at our first entrance into the school of prayer to grasp such teaching. We shall understand it better later on. Let us only begin and take the lesson as He gives it. We are carnal and cannot bring God the worship He seeks. But Jesus came to give the Spirit: He has given Him to us. Let the disposition in which we set ourselves to pray be what Christ's words have taught us. Let there be the deep confession of our inability to bring God the worship that is pleasing to Him; the childlike teachableness that waits on Him to instruct us; the simple faith that yields itself to the breathing of the Spirit. Above all, let us hold fast the blessed truth—we shall find that the Lord has more to say to us about it—that the knowledge of the Fatherhood of God, the revelation of His infinite Fatherliness in our hearts, the faith in the infinite love that gives us His Son and His Spirit to make us children, is indeed the secret of prayer in spirit and truth. This is the new and living way Christ opened up for us. To have Christ the Son, and The Spirit of the Son, dwelling within us, and revealing the Father, this makes us true, spiritual worshippers.

'Lord, Teach Us To Pray.'

Blessed Lord! I adore the love with which Thou didst teach a woman, who had refused Thee a cup of water, what the worship of God must be. I rejoice in the assurance that Thou wilt no less now instruct Thy disciple, who comes to Thee with a heart that longs to pray in spirit and in truth. O my Holy Master! do teach me this blessed secret.

Teach me that the worship in spirit and truth is not of man, but only comes from Thee; that it is not only a thing of times and seasons, but the outflowing of a life in Thee. Teach me to draw near to God in prayer under the deep impression of my ignorance and my having nothing in myself to offer Him, and at the same time of the provision Thou, my Saviour, makest for the Spirit's breathing in my childlike stammerings. I do bless Thee that in Thee I am a child, and have a child's liberty of access; that in Thee I have the spirit of Sonship and of worship of truth. Teach me, above all, Blessed Son of the Father, how it is the revelation of the Father that gives confidence in prayer; and let the infinite Fatherliness of God's Heart be my joy and strength for a life of prayer and of worship. Amen.

PRAY TO THY FATHER WHICH IS IN SECRET OR ALONE WITH GOD.

'But thou, when thou prayest, enter into thine inner chamber, and having shut thy door, pray to thy Father which is in secret, and thy Father which seeth in secret shall recompense thee.'—Matt. vi. 6.

After Jesus had called His first disciples He gave them their first public teaching in the Sermon on the Mount. He there expounded to them the kingdom of God, its laws and its life. In that kingdom God is not only King, but Father; He not only gives all, but is Himself all. In the knowledge and fellowship of Him alone is its blessedness. Hence it came as a matter of course that the revelation of prayer and the prayer-life was a part of His teaching concerning the New Kingdom He came to set up. Moses gave neither command nor regulation with regard to prayer: even the prophets say little directly of the duty of prayer; it is Christ who teaches to pray.

And the first thing the Lord teaches His disciples is that they must have a secret place for prayer; every one must have some solitary spot where he can be alone with his God. Every teacher must have a schoolroom. We have learnt to know and accept Jesus as our only teacher in the school of prayer. He has already taught us at Samaria that worship is no longer confined to times and places; that worship, spiritual true worship, is a thing of the spirit and the life; the whole man must in his whole life be worship in spirit and truth. And yet He wants each one to choose for himself the fixed spot where He can daily meet him. That inner chamber, that solitary place, is Jesus' schoolroom. That spot may be anywhere; that spot may change from day to day if we have to change our abode; but that secret place there must be, with the quiet time in which the pupil places himself in the Master's presence, to be by Him prepared to worship the Father. There alone, but there most surely, Jesus comes to us to teach us to pray.

A teacher is always anxious that his schoolroom should be bright and attractive, filled with the light and air of heaven, a place where pupils long to come, and love to stay. In His first words on prayer in the Sermon on the Mount, Jesus seeks to set the inner chamber before us in its most attractive light. If we listen carefully, we soon notice what the chief thing is He has to tell us of our tarrying there. Three times He uses the name of Father: 'Pray to thy Father;' 'Thy Father shall recompense thee;' Your Father knoweth what things ye have need of.' The first thing in closet-prayer is: I must meet my Father. The light that shines in the closet must be: the light of the Father's countenance. The fresh air from heaven with which Jesus would have filled the atmosphere in which I am to breathe and pray, is: God's Father-love, God's infinite Fatherliness. Thus each thought or petition we breathe out will be simple, hearty, childlike trust in the Father. This is how the Master teaches us to pray: He brings us into the Father's living presence. What we pray there must avail. Let us listen carefully to hear what the Lord has to say to us.

First, 'Pray to thy Father which is in secret.' God is a God who hides Himself to the carnal eye. As long as in our worship of God we are chiefly occupied with our own thoughts and exercises, we shall not meet Him who is a Spirit, the unseen One. But to the man who withdraws himself from all that is of the world and man, and prepares to wait upon God alone, the Father will reveal Himself. As he forsakes and gives up and shuts out the world, and the life of the world, and surrenders himself to be led of Christ into the secret of God's presence, the light of the Father's love will rise upon him. The secrecy of the inner chamber and the closed door, the entire separation from all around us, is an image of, and so a help to, that inner spiritual sanctuary, the secret of God's tabernacle, within the veil, where our spirit truly comes into contact with the Invisible One. And so we are taught, at the very outset of our search after the secret of effectual prayer, to remember that it is in the inner chamber, where we are alone with the Father, that we shall learn to pray aright. The Father is in secret: in these words Jesus teaches us where He is waiting us, where He is always to be found. Christians often complain that private prayer is not what it should be. They feel weak and sinful, the heart is cold and dark; it is as if they have so little to pray, and in that little no faith or joy. They are discouraged and kept from prayer by the thought that they cannot come to the Father as they ought or as they wish. Child of God! listen to your Teacher. He tells you that when you go to private prayer your first thought must be: The Father is in secret, the Father waits me there. Just because your heart is cold and prayerless, get you into the presence of the loving Father. As a father pitieth his children, so the Lord pitieth you. Do not be thinking of how little you have to bring God, but of how much He wants to give you. Just place yourself before, and look up into, His face; think of His love, His wonderful, tender, pitying love. Just tell Him how sinful and cold and dark all is: it is the Father's loving heart will give light and warmth to yours. O do what Jesus says: Just shut the door, and pray to thy Father, which is in secret. Is it not wonderful? to be able to go alone with God, the infinite God. And then to look up and say: My Father!

'And thy Father, which seeth in secret, will recompense thee.' Here Jesus assures us that secret prayer cannot be fruitless: its blessing will show itself in our life. We have but in secret, alone with God, to entrust our life before men to Him; He will reward us openly; He will see to it that the answer to prayer be made manifest in His blessing upon us. Our Lord would thus teach us that as infinite Fatherliness and Faithfulness is that with which God meets us in secret, so on our part there should be the childlike simplicity of faith, the confidence that our prayer does bring down a blessing. 'He that cometh to God must believe that He is a rewarder of them that seek Him.' Not on the strong or the fervent feeling with which I pray does the blessing of the closet depend, but upon the love and the power of the Father to whom I there entrust my needs. And therefore the Master has but one desire: Remember your Father is, and sees and hears in secret; go there and stay there, and go again from there in the confidence: He will recompense. Trust Him for it; depend upon Him: prayer to the Father cannot be vain; He will reward you openly.

Still further to confirm this faith in the Father-love of God, Christ speaks a third word: 'Your Father knoweth what things ye have need of before ye ask Him.' At first sight it might appear as if this thought made prayer less needful: God knows far better than we what we need. But as we get a deeper insight into what prayer really is, this truth will help much to strengthen our faith. It will teach us that we do not need, as the heathen, with the multitude and urgency of our words, to compel an unwilling God to listen to us. It will lead to a holy thoughtfulness and silence in prayer as it suggests the question: Does my Father really know that I need this? It will, when once we have been led by the Spirit to the certainty that our request is indeed something that, according to the Word, we do need for God's glory, give us wonderful confidence to say, My Father knows I need it and must have it. And if there be any delay in the answer, it will teach us in quiet perseverance to hold on: Father! Thou knowest I need it. O the blessed liberty and simplicity of a child that Christ our Teacher would fain cultivate in us, as we draw near to God: let us look up to the Father until His Spirit works it in us. Let us sometimes in our prayers, when we are in danger of being so occupied with our fervent, urgent petitions, as to forget that the Father knows and hears, let us hold still and just quietly say: My Father sees, my Father hears, my Father knows; it will help our faith to take the answer, and to say: We know that we have the petitions we have asked of Him.

And now, all ye who have anew entered the school of Christ to be taught to pray, take these lessons, practise them, and trust Him to perfect you in them. Dwell much in the inner chamber, with the door shut—shut in from men, shut up with God; it is there the Father waits you, it is there Jesus will teach you to pray. To be alone in secret with the Father: this be your highest joy. To be assured that the Father will openly reward the secret prayer, so that it cannot remain unblessed: this be your strength day by day. And to know that the Father knows that you need what you ask, this be your liberty to bring every need, in the assurance that your God will supply it according to His riches in glory in Christ Jesus.

'Lord, teach us to pray.'

Blessed Saviour! with my whole heart I do bless Thee for the appointment of the inner chamber, as the school where Thou meetest each of Thy pupils alone, and revealest to him the Father. O my Lord! strengthen my faith so in the Father's tender love and kindness, that as often as I feel sinful or troubled, the first instinctive thought may be to go where I know the Father waits me, and where prayer never can go unblessed. Let the thought that He knows my need before I ask, bring me, in great restfulness of faith, to trust that He will give what His child requires. O let the place of secret prayer become to me the most beloved spot on earth.

And, Lord! hear me as I pray that Thou wouldest everywhere bless the closets of Thy believing people. Let Thy wonderful revelation of a Father's tenderness free all young Christians from every thought of secret prayer as a duty or a burden, and lead them to regard it as the highest privilege of their life, a joy and a blessing. Bring back all who are discouraged, because they cannot find aught to bring Thee in prayer. O give them to understand that they have only to come with their emptiness to Him who has all to give, and delights to do it. Not, what they have to bring the Father, but what the Father waits to give them, be their one thought.

And bless especially the inner chamber of all Thy servants who are working for Thee, as the place where God's truth and God's grace is revealed to them, where they are daily anointed with fresh oil, where their strength is renewed, and the blessings are received in faith, with which they are to bless their fellow-men. Lord, draw us all in the closet nearer to Thyself and the Father. Amen.

'AFTER THIS MANNER PRAY;' OR THE MODEL PRAYER.

'After this manner therefore pray ye: Our Father which art in heaven.'— Matt. vi. 9.

Every teacher knows the power of example. He not only tells the child what to do and how to do it, but shows him how it really can be done. In condescension to our weakness, our Heavenly Teacher has given us the very words we are to take with us as we draw near to our Father. We have in them a form of prayer in which there breathe the freshness and fulness of the Eternal Life. So simple that the child can lisp it, so divinely rich that it comprehends all that God can give. A form of prayer that becomes the model and inspiration for all other prayer, and yet always draws us back to itself as the deepest utterance of our souls before our God.

'Our Father which art in heaven!' To appreciate this word of adoration aright, I must remember that none of the saints had in Scripture ever ventured to address God as their Father. The invocation places us at once in the centre of the wonderful revelation the Son came to make of His Father as our Father too. It comprehends the mystery of redemption—Christ delivering us from the curse that we might become the children of God. The mystery of regeneration—the Spirit in the new birth giving us the new life. And the mystery of faith—ere yet the redemption is accomplished or understood, the word is given on the lips of the disciples to prepare them for the blessed experience still to come. The words are the key to the whole prayer, to all prayer. It takes time, it takes life to study them; it will take eternity to understand them fully. The knowledge of God's Father-love is the first and simplest, but also the last and highest lesson in the school of prayer. It is in the personal relation to the living God, and the personal conscious fellowship of love with Himself, that prayer begins. It is in the knowledge of God's Fatherliness, revealed by the Holy Spirit, that the power of prayer will be found to root and grow. In the infinite tenderness and pity and patience of the infinite Father, in His loving readiness to hear and to help, the life of prayer has its joy. O let us take time, until the Spirit has made these words to us spirit and truth, filling heart and life: 'Our Father which art in heaven.' Then we are indeed within the veil, in the secret place of power where prayer always prevails.

'Hallowed be Thy name.' There is something here that strikes us at once. While we ordinarily first bring our own needs to God in prayer, and then think of what belongs to God and His interests, the Master reverses the order. First, Thy name, Thy kingdom, Thy will; then, give us, forgive us, lead us, deliver us. The lesson is of more importance than we think. In true worship the Father must be first, must be all. The sooner I learn to forget myself in the desire that He may be glorified, the richer will the blessing be that prayer will bring to myself. No one ever loses by what he sacrifices for the Father.

This must influence all our prayer. There are two sorts of prayer: personal and intercessory. The latter ordinarily occupies the lesser part of our time and energy. This may not be. Christ has opened the school of prayer specially to train intercessors for the great work of bringing down, by their faith and prayer, the blessings of His work and love on the world around. There can be no deep growth in prayer unless this be made our aim. The little child may ask of the father only what it needs for itself; and yet it soon learns to say, Give some for sister too. But the grown-up son, who only lives for the father's interest and takes charge of the father's business, asks more largely, and gets all that is asked. And Jesus would train us to the blessed life of consecration and service, in which our interests are all subordinate to the Name, and the Kingdom, and the Will of the Father. O let us live for this, and let, on each act of adoration, Our Father! there follow in the same breath, Thy Name, Thy Kingdom, Thy Will;—for this we look up and long.

'Hallowed be Thy name..' What name? This new name of Father. The word Holy is the central word of the Old Testament; the name Father of the New. In this name of Love all the holiness and glory of God are now to be revealed. And how is the name to be hallowed? By God Himself: 'I will hallow My great name which ye have profaned.' Our prayer must be that in ourselves, in all God's children, in presence of the world, God Himself would reveal the holiness, the Divine power, the hidden glory of the name of Father. The Spirit of the Father is the Holy Spirit: it is only when we yield ourselves to be led of Him, that the name will be hallowed in our prayer and our lives. Let us learn the prayer: 'Our Father, hallowed be Thy name.'

'Thy kingdom come.' The Father is a King and has a kingdom. The son and heir of a king has no higher ambition than the glory of his father's kingdom. In time of war or danger this becomes his passion; he can think of nothing else. The children of the Father are here in the enemy's territory, where the kingdom, which is in heaven, is not yet fully manifested. What more natural than that, when they learn to hallow the Father-name, they should long and cry with deep enthusiasm: 'Thy kingdom come.' The coming of the kingdom is the one great event on which the revelation of the Father's glory, the blessedness of His children, the salvation of the world depends. On our prayers too the coming of the kingdom waits. Shall we not join in the deep longing cry of the redeemed: 'Thy kingdom come'? Let us learn it in the school of Jesus.

'Thy will be done, as in heaven, so on earth.' This petition is too frequently applied alone to the suffering of the will of God. In heaven God's will is done, and the Master teaches the child to ask that the will may be done on earth just as in heaven: in the spirit of adoring submission and ready obedience. Because the will of God is the glory of heaven, the doing of it is the blessedness of heaven. As the will is done, the kingdom of heaven comes into the heart. And wherever faith has accepted the Father's love, obedience accepts the Father's will. The surrender to, and the prayer for a life of heaven-like obedience, is the spirit of childlike prayer.

'Give us this day our daily bread.' When first the child has yielded himself to the Father in the care for His Name, His Kingdom, and His Will, he has full liberty to ask for his daily bread. A master cares for the food of his servant, a general of his soldiers, a father of his child. And will not the Father in heaven care for the child who has in prayer given himself up to His interests? We may indeed in full confidence say: Father, I live for Thy honor and Thy work; I know Thou carest for me. Consecration to God and His will gives wonderful liberty in prayer for temporal things: the whole earthly life is given to the Father's loving care.

'And forgive us our debts as we also have forgiven our debtors.' As bread is the first need of the body, so forgiveness for the soul. And the provision for the one is as sure as for the other. We are children, but sinners too; our right of access to the Father's presence we owe to the precious blood and the forgiveness it has won for us. Let us beware of the prayer for forgiveness becoming a formality: only what is really confessed is really forgiven. Let us in faith accept the forgiveness as promised: as a spiritual reality, an actual transaction between God and us, it is the entrance into all the Father's love and all the privileges of children. Such forgiveness, as a living experience, is impossible without a forgiving spirit to others: as forgiven expresses the heavenward, so forgiving the earthward, relation of God's child. In each prayer to the Father I must be able to say that I know of no one whom I do not heartily love.

'And lead us not into temptation, but deliver us from the evil one.' Our daily bread, the pardon of our sins, and then our being kept from all sin and the power of the evil one, in these three petitions all our personal need is comprehended. The prayer for bread and pardon must be accompanied by the surrender to live in all things in holy obedience to the Father's will, and the believing prayer in everything to be kept by the power of the indwelling Spirit from the power of the evil one.

Children of God! it is thus Jesus would have us to pray to the Father in heaven. O let His Name, and Kingdom, and Will, have the first place in our love; His providing, and pardoning, and keeping love will be our sure portion. So the prayer will lead us up to the true child-life: the Father all to the child, the Father all for the child. We shall understand how Father and child, the Thine and the Our, are all one, and how the heart that begins its prayer with the God-devoted Thine, will have the power in faith to speak out the Our too. Such prayer will, indeed, be the fellowship and interchange of love, always bringing us back in trust and worship to Him who is not only the Beginning but the End: 'For thine is the kingdom, and the power, and the glory, for ever, Amen.' Son of the Father, teach us to pray, 'Our Father.'

'Lord, teach us to pray.'

O Thou who art the only-begotten Son, teach us, we beseech Thee, to pray, 'Our Father.' We thank Thee, Lord, for these Living Blessed Words which Thou hast given us. We thank Thee for the millions who in them have learnt to know and worship the Father, and for what they have been to us. Lord! it is as if we needed days and weeks in Thy school with each separate petition; so deep and full are they. But we look to Thee to lead us deeper into their meaning: do it, we pray Thee, for Thy Name's sake; Thy name is Son of the Father.

Lord! Thou didst once say: 'No man knoweth the Father save the Son, and he to whom the Son willeth to reveal Him.' And again: 'I made known unto them Thy name, and will make it known, that the love wherewith Thou hast loved Me may be in them.' Lord Jesus! reveal to us the Father. Let His name, His infinite Father-love, the love with which He loved Thee, according to Thy prayer, BE IN US. Then shall we say aright, 'Our Father!' Then shall we apprehend Thy teaching, and the first spontaneous breathing of our heart will be: 'Our Father, Thy Name, Thy Kingdom, Thy Will.' And we shall bring our needs and our sins and our temptations to Him in the confidence that the love of such a Father cares for all.

Blessed Lord! we are Thy scholars, we trust Thee; do teach us to pray, 'Our Father.' Amen.

"Jesus Himself"

Their eyes were opened, and they knew Him."

I

THE words, from which I want to present a simple message, will be found in the Gospel according to St. Luke, the 24th chapter and the 31st verse: "And their eyes were opened, and they knew Him." Some time since, I preached a sermon with the words "Jesus Himself" as the text; and as I went home I said to those who were walking with me: "How possible it is to have Jesus Himself with us and never to know it, and how possible to preach of, and to listen to, all the truth about Jesus Himself and yet not to know Him." I cannot say what a deep impression was made upon me as I thought over it.

Now these disciples had spent a most blessed time with Jesus, but if they had gone away before He revealed Himself that evening, they would never have been sure that it was Jesus, for their eyes were holden that they should not know Him. That is, alas, the condition of a great multitude in the Church of Christ. They know that Christ has risen from the dead. They believe, and they very often have blessed experiences that come from the risen Christ. Very often in a time of Convention, or in time of silent Bible reading, or in a time of the visitation of God's grace, their hearts burn; and yet it can be said of a people whose hearts are burning within them, that they did not know it was Jesus Himself.

And now if you ask me what is to be the great blessing to be sought, my answer is this: Not only should we think about Jesus Himself and speak about Him and believe in Him, but we should come to the point that the disciples in the text arrived at, "and they knew Him." Everything is to be found in that.

If I read that story of the disciples on the way to Emmaus, I get from it four stages in the Christian life. Just think! How did they begin the morning that day? With

Hearts sad and troubled,

because they thought Jesus was dead. They did not know that He was alive, and that is the state of very many Christians. They look to the

Cross, and they struggle to trust Christ, but they have never yet learned the blessedness of believing that there is a living Christ to do everything for them. Oh! that word of the angel to the women! "Why seek ye the living among the dead?" What is the difference between a dead Christ, whom the women went to anoint, and a living Christ? A dead Christ, I must do everything for; a living Christ does everything for me.

The disciples began the morning with a sad heart. I fancy very possibly they spent a sleepless night. Oh! the terrible disappointment! They had hoped that Christ would be the Deliverer of Israel, and they had seen Him die an accursed death. On the morning of that first day of the week, they rose with sad hearts—the bitter sadness cannot be expressed. That is just the life of many Christians. They try to believe in Jesus and to trust Him, and to hope in Him, but there is no joy. Why? Because they do not know that there is a living Christ to reveal Himself.

Then there is the second stage. What is that? The stage of which Christ speaks:

"Slow of heart to believe."

They had the message from the women. They told the stranger who walked with them: "Certain women have astonished us, telling us they have seen an angel, who says He is alive." And Christ replied to them: "Oh! fools, and slow of heart to believe." Yes! there are many Christians to-day who have heard and who know that they must not only believe in a crucified Christ, but in a living Christ, and they try to grasp it and take it in, but it does not bring them a blessing, and why? Because they want to feel it and not to believe it. They want to work for it, and with efforts get hold of it, instead of just quietly sinking down and believing, "Christ, the living Jesus, He will do everything for us." That is the second stage. The first stage is that of ignorance, the second stage is that of unbelief—the doubting heart that cannot take in the wonderful truth that Jesus lives.

Then comes the third stage—

The burning heart.

Jesus came to the two disciples, and after He had reproved them and said: "Oh! fools, and slow of heart to believe," He began to open the

Scriptures to them, and to tell them of all the wonderful things the prophets had taught. Then their eyes were opened, and they began to understand the Scriptures. They saw that it was true that it was prophesied that Christ must rise. As He talked, there came out from Him—the living risen One—a mighty influence, and it rested upon them, and they began to feel their hearts burn within them with joy and gladness.

You still say perhaps: "That is the stage we want to come to." No; God forbid you should stop there. You may get in that third stage—the burning heart—and yet something is still wanting—the revelation of Christ. The disciples had had a blessed experience of His divine powers, but He had not revealed Himself, and oh! how often it is that at Conventions and in churches, and in meetings and in blessed fellowship with God's saints, our hearts burn within us. These are precious experiences of the working of God's grace and Spirit, and yet there is something wanting. What is that? Jesus Himself has been working upon us, and the power of his risen life has touched us, but we cannot say, "I have met Him. He has made Himself known to me." Oh, the difference between a burning heart, which becomes cold after a time, which comes by fits and starts, and the blessed revelation of Jesus Himself as my Saviour, taking charge of me and blessing me and keeping me every day! This is the stage of

The satisfied heart.

Oh my brother, my sister! It is what I ask for you, and it is what I am sure you ask for yourself. I ask it for myself. Lord Jesus! may we know Thee in thy divine glory as the risen One, our Jesus, our Beloved and our mighty One. Oh! if there are any sad ones who cannot take this in, and who say, "I have never known the joy of religion yet"—listen, we are going to tell you how you can. All will center round this one thing, that just as a little child lives day by day in the arms of its mother, and grows up year by year under a mother's eye, it is a possibility that you can live every day and hour of your life in fellowship with the Holy Jesus.

He will do it for you.

Come, and let your sad heart begin to hope. Will He reveal Himself? He did it to the disciples and He will do it to you. Perhaps there are some who have got beyond the sad heart and who yet feel, "I have not got what I want." If you throw open your heart and give up everything but just believing and allowing Him to do what He wants, it will come. God be praised! it will come.

Jesus will reveal Himself.

Perhaps you have arrived at the stage of the burning heart, and can tell of many blessed experiences, but somehow there is a worm at the root. The experiences do not last, and the heart is so changeable. Oh come, my beloved! Follow Christ. Say, "Jesus, reveal Thyself that we may know Thee Thyself. We ask not only to drink of the living water, we want the fountain. We ask not only to bathe ourselves in the light, we want the Sun of Righteousness within our hearts. We ask not only to know Thee, who hast touched us and warmed our hearts and blessed us, but we want to know that we have the unchangeable Jesus dwelling within our hearts and abiding with us forevermore."

Now comes the question which I really wanted to put,—What are the conditions under which our blessed Lord reveals Himself? Or, put it this way,—To whom is it that Jesus will reveal Himself? We have only to see how he dealt with these disciples, and we get the answer. What is the answer? First of all I think I find here that Christ revealed Himself to those disciples

Who had given up everything for Him.

He had said to them: "Forsake all and follow Me," and they had done it. With all their feebleness and all their unfaithfulness they followed Christ to the end. He said to them: "Ye have continued with Me in My temptations, and I appoint you a kingdom, as I have received a kingdom from My Father." They were not perfect men, but they would have died for Him. They loved Him, they obeyed Him, they followed Him. They had left all, and for three years they had been following hard after Christ. You say "Tell me what Christ wants of me, if I am to have his wonderful presence. Tell me what is the character of the man to whom Christ will reveal Himself in this highest and fullest way?" I answer: "It is the one who is ready to forsake all and to follow Him." If Christ is to give Himself wholly to me, He must know that He has me wholly for Himself; and I trust God will give grace that these words spoken about the consecration and the surrender, not only of all evil, but of many lawful things, and even, if necessary, of life itself, may lead us to understand what the demand is that Jesus makes upon us.

The motto of the Cape General Mission is,

"God first."

In one sense that is a beautiful motto, and yet I am not always satisfied with it, because it is a motto that is often misunderstood. God first may mean "I" second, something else third, and something else fourth. God is thus first in order, but still God becomes one of a series of powers, and that is not the place God wants. The meaning of the words, "God first" is really "God all; God everything;" and that is what Christ wants. To be willing to give up everything, to submit to Christ to teach him what to say and what to do, is the first mark of the man to whom Christ will come. Are you not ready to take this step and say: "Jesus! I do give up everything; I have given up everything; reveal Thyself."

Oh, brother! oh, sister! do not hesitate. Speak it out in your heart, and let this be the time in which a new sacrifice shall be laid at the feet of the blessed Lamb of God.

There is a second thought. There is first the idea of having forsaken all to follow Him; of having given up everything in obedience to Him, and living just a life of simple love and obedience. But there is a second thing needed in the man who is to have this full revelation of Christ. He must be

Convicted of his unbelief.

"Oh! fools, and slow of heart to believe what the prophets have said." Oh! brother, sister, if we could have a sight of the amount of unbelief in the hearts of God's children, barring the door and closing the heart against Christ, how we should stand astonished and ashamed! When there is not unbelief but where there is faith, Christ cannot help coming in. He cannot help coming where there is a living faith, a full faith. The heart is opened, the heart is prepared; and as naturally as water runs into a hollow place, so naturally Christ must come into a heart that is full of faith. What is the hindrance with some earnest souls, who say: "I have given myself up to the Lord Jesus. I have done it often, and by His grace I am doing it every day, and God knows how earnestly and really I am doing it, and I have the sanction of God upon it, I know God has blessed me"? They have not been convicted of their unbelief. "Oh! fools, and slow of heart to believe." Do you know what Christ said about a man calling his brother a fool? Yet here the loving Son of God could find no other word to speak to His beloved disciples: "Oh! fools, and slow of heart to believe." You want the Lord Jesus to give you this full revelation of Himself? Are you willing to acknowledge that you are a fool for never having believed in Him? "Lord Jesus, it is my own fault. There Thou art, longing to have possession of me. There Thou hast been with Thy faithful promises waiting to reveal Thyself."

Did you ever hear of a man loving another and not longing to reveal himself? Christ longs to reveal Himself, but He cannot on account of our unbelief. May God convict us of our unbelief that we may get utterly ashamed and broken down, and cry, "Oh, my God, what is this, this heart of unbelief actually throwing a barrier across the door that Christ cannot step in, blinding my eyes that I cannot see Jesus, though he is so near? Here He has been for ten or twenty years, from time to time giving me the burning heart, enjoying the experience of a little of His love and grace, and yet I have not had the revelation of Him, taking possession of my heart and dwelling with me in unbroken continuity." Oh! may God convict us of unbelief. Do let us believe because all things are possible to him that believes. That is God's word, and this blessing, receiving the revelation of Jesus, can come only to those who learn to believe and to trust him.

There is another mark of those to whom this special revelation of Christ will come, and that is,

"They do not rest until they obtain it."

You know the story. Their hearts were burning as they drew nigh to the place they were going to, and Christ made as if He were going farther. He put them to the test, and if they had allowed Him quietly to go on, if they had been content with the experience of the burning heart, they would have lost something infinitely better. But they were not content with it. They were not content to go home to the disciples that night and say, "Oh, what a blessed afternoon we have had! What wonderful teaching we have had!" No! The burning heart and the blessed experience just made them say, "Lord, abide with us," and they compelled Him to come in. They constrained Him to come in.

It always reminds me of the story of Jacob, "I will not let Thee go, except Thou bless me." That is the spirit that prepares us for the revelation of Jesus. Oh! my dear friend, has this been the spirit in which we have looked upon the wonderful blessing that we have sometimes heard of? "Oh! my Lord Jesus, though I do not understand it, though I cannot grasp it, though my struggles avail nothing, I am not going to let Thee go. If it is possible for a sinner on earth to have Jesus every day, every hour, and every moment in resurrection power dwelling in his heart, shining within him, filling him with love and joy,—if that is possible, I want it."

Is that your language?

Oh! come then and say: "Lord Jesus, I cannot let Thee go except Thou bless me." The question is asked so often: "What is the cause of the feeble life of so many Christians?" What is really the matter? What is actually the want?

How little the Church responds to Christ's call! how little the Church is what Christ would have her to be! What is the cause of all the trouble? Various answers may be given, but there is one answer which includes all the other answers, and that is, each believer wants the personal

Full revelation of a personal Christ

as an indwelling Lord, as a satisfying portion. When the Lord Jesus was here upon earth, what was it that distinguished His disciples from other people? He took them away from their fish-nets, and from their homes, and He gathered them about Himself, and they knew Jesus. He was their Master, and guarded them, and they followed Him. And what is to make a difference between Christ's disciples—not those who are just hoping to get to heaven, but Christ's whole-hearted disciples— what is to make a difference between them and other people? It is this, to be in fellowship with Jesus—every hour of the day; and just as Christ upon earth was able to keep those people with Him for three years, day by day, so

Christ is able

in heaven now to do what He could not do when He was on earth—to keep in the closest fellowship with every believer throughout the whole world. Glory be to God! You know that text in Ephesians: "He that descended is the same also that ascended, that He might fill all things." Why was my Lord Jesus taken up to heaven away from the life of earth? Because the life of earth is a life confined to localities, but the life in heaven is a life in which there is no limit and no bound and no locality, and Christ was taken up to heaven, that, in the power of God, of the omnipresent God, He might be able to fill every individual here and be with every individual believer.

That is what my heart wants to realize by faith; that is a possibility, that is a promise, that is my birthright, and I want to have it, and I want by the grace of God to say, "Jesus, I will not rest until Thou hast revealed Thyself fully to my soul."

There are often very blessed experiences in the Christian life in what I call the third stage—the stage of the burning heart. Do you know what another great mark of that stage is? Delight in God's word. How did the disciples get their burning hearts? By that strange opening of the Scripture to them. He made it all look different,—new,—and they saw what they had never seen before. They could not help feeling,

How wonderful,

how heavenly was that teaching. Oh! there are many Christians who find the best time of the day is the time when they can get with their Bibles, and who love nothing so much as to get a new thought; and as a diamond digger rejoices when he has found a diamond, or a gold digger when he has found a nugget, they delight when they get from the Bible some new thought, and they feed upon it. Yet with all that interest in God's word, and with all that stirring of the heart with joy, when they go into business or attend to their daily duties, there is still something wanting.

We must come away from all the manifold and multifarious blessings that Jesus can bestow from time to time, to the blessed unity of that one— that Jesus makes Himself known, Jesus Himself is willing to make Himself known. Oh! if I were to ask, "Is not this just what you and I want, and what many of us have been longing for?" I am sure you would answer,

"That is what I want."

Think what the blessedness will be that comes from it. You often sing:—

"Oh! the peace my Saviour gives!
Peace I never knew before,
And my way has brighter grown,
Since I've learnt to trust Him more."

I recently had a letter from some one in the Free State saying what a wonderful comfort and strength that little verse was in the midst of difficulties and troubles. Yes; but how can that peace be kept? It was the presence of Christ that brought the peace. When the storm was threatening to swallow up the disciples, it was the presence of Christ Himself that gave the peace.

Oh! Christian, do you want peace and rest? You must have Jesus Himself. You talk of purity, you talk of cleansing, you talk of deliverance from sin. Praise God, here is the deliverance and the cleansing, when the living Jesus comes and gives power. Then we have this resurrection of Christ, this heavenly Christ upon the throne, making Himself known to us. Surely that will be the secret of purity and the secret of strength.

Where does the strength of so many come from? From the joy of a personal friendship with Jesus. Those disciples, if they had gone away with their burning hearts to the other disciples, could have told them wonderful things of a man who had explained to them the Scriptures and the promises, but they could not have said, "We have seen Jesus." They might have said, "Jesus is alive. We are sure of that," but that would not have satisfied the others. But they could now go and say,

"We have seen Himself.

He has revealed Himself to us." We are all glad to work for Christ, but there is a complaint throughout the Church of Christ, from the ministers in the pulpit down to the feeblest worker, of lack of joy and lack of blessedness. Let us try and find out whether this is not the place where the secret will be discovered—that the Lord Jesus comes and shows Himself to us as our Master and speaks to us. When we have Jesus with us, and when we go every footstep with the thought that it is Jesus wants us to go, it is Jesus who sends us and is helping us, then there will be brightness in our testimony, and it will help other believers, and they will begin to understand; "I see why I have failed. I took the word, I took the blessing, and I took, as I thought, the life, but I was without the living Jesus."

And if you now ask, "How will this revelation come?" Brother, sister, that is the secret that no man may tell, that Jesus keeps to Himself. It is

In the power of the Holy Ghost;

Christ, the risen One, entered into a new life. His resurrection life is entirely different from His life before His death. You know what we read: "They knew Him." He revealed Himself, and then He passed away. And was that vision of Christ worth so much? It was lost in a moment. It was worth heaven, eternity, everything. Why? Because henceforth Christ was no longer to be known after the flesh. Christ was henceforth in the power of the Spirit, which fills Heaven; in the power of the Spirit which is the power of the Godhead; in the power of the Spirit, which fills our hearts. Christ was henceforth to live in the life of Heaven.

Thank God, Christ can by the power of the Holy Ghost reveal Himself to each one of us; but oh! brother, it is a secret thing between Christ and yourself. Take this assurance, "Their eyes were opened and they knew Him," and believe that it is written for you.

You say, "I have known the other three stages; the stage of the sad heart, mourning that I knew no living Christ; I have known the stage of the slow heart to believe, when I struggled with my unbelief; and I know the stage of the burning heart, when there are great times of joy and blessedness." You say that? Oh come then and know the fourth stage of

The satisfied heart,

of the heart made glad for eternity, of the heart that cannot keep its joy in, but goes away back to Jerusalem, and says, "It is true. Jesus has revealed Himself. I know it, I feel it." Oh! brother, oh! sister, how will this revelation come? Jesus will tell you. Just come to the Lord Jesus and breathe up before Him a simple child-like prayer, and I, His servant, will come and take you by the hand and say: "Come, now, my work is done. I have pointed to the Lamb of God, to the risen One. My work is done."

Let us enter into the Holy Presence and begin, if you have never yet sought it before, begin to plead: "Oh! Saviour, that I might have this blessedness every moment present with me—Jesus Himself, my portion forever."

"Jesus Himself."

"Lo, I am with you alway."

II

WHEN I think of all the struggles and difficulties and failures of which many complain, and know that many are trying to make a new effort to begin a holy life, their hearts fearing all the time that they would fail again, owing to so many difficulties and temptations and the natural weakness of their character, my heart longs to be able to tell them in words so simple that a little child could understand,

What the secret is of the Christian life.

And then the thought comes to me, Can I venture to hope that it will be given to me to take that glorious, heavenly, divine Lord Jesus and to show Him to these souls, so that they can see Him in His glory? And can it be given to me to open their eyes to see that there is a Divine, Almighty Christ, who does actually come into the heart and who faithfully promises, "I will come and dwell with you, and I will never leave you?" No; my words cannot do that. But then I thought, my Lord Jesus can use me as a simple servant to take such feeble ones by the hand and encourage and help them; to say, Oh, come, come, come, into the presence of Jesus and wait on Him, and He will reveal Himself to thee. I pray God that He may use His precious Word. It is simply

The presence of the Lord Jesus.

That is the secret of the Christian's strength and joy. You know that when He was upon earth, He was present in bodily form with his disciples. They walked about together all day, and at night they went into the same house, and sometimes slept together and ate and drank together. They were continually together. It was the presence of Jesus that was the training school of His disciples. They were bound to Him by that wonderful intercourse of love during three long years, and in that intercourse they learned to know Christ, and Christ instructed and corrected them, and prepared them for what they were afterward to receive. And now when He is going away, He says to them: "Lo, behold, I am with you always—all the days—even unto the end of the world."

What a promise! And just as really as Christ was with Peter in the boat, just as Christ sat with John at the table, as really can I have Christ with me. And more really, for they had their Christ in the body and He was to them a man, an individual separate from them, but I may have glorified Christ in the power of the throne of God, the omnipotent Christ, the omnipresent Christ.

What a promise! You ask me, How can that be? And my answer is, Because Christ is God, and because Christ after having been made man, went up into the throne and the Life of God. And now that blessed Christ Jesus, with His loving, pierced heart; that blessed Jesus Christ, who lived upon earth; that same Christ glorified into the glory of God, can be in me and

Can be with me all the days.

You say, Is it really possible for a man in business, for a woman in the midst of a large and difficult household, for a poor man full of care; is it possible? Can I always be thinking of Jesus? Thank God, you need not always be thinking of Him. You may be the manager of a bank, and your whole attention may be required to carry out the business that you have to do. But thank God, while I have to think of my business, Jesus will think of me, and He will come in and will take charge of me. That little child, three months old, as it sleeps in its mother's arms, lies helplessly there; it hardly knows its mother, it does not think of her, but the mother thinks of the child. And this is the blessed mystery of love, that Jesus the God-man waits to come in to me in the greatness of His love; and as He gets possession of my heart, He embraces me in those divine arms and tells me, "My child, I the Faithful One, I the Mighty One will abide with thee, will watch over thee and keep thee all the days." He tells me He will come into my heart, so that I can be a happy Christian, a holy Christian, and a useful Christian. You say, Oh! if I could only believe that, if I could think that it is possible to have Christ always, every hour, every moment with me,

Taking and keeping charge of me!

My brother, my sister, it is just literally this that is my message to you. When Jesus said to His disciples, "Lo, I am with you always," He meant it in the fullness of the divine Omnipresence, in the fullness of the divine love, and he longs to-night to reveal Himself to you and to me as we have never seen Him before.

And now just think a moment what a blessed life that must be—the presence of Jesus always abiding. Is not that the secret of peace and happiness? If I could just attain (that is what each heart says) to that blessed state in which every day and all the day I felt Jesus to be watching and ever keeping me, oh, what peace I would have in the thought, "I have no care if He cares for me, and I have no fear if He provides for me." Your heart says that this is too good to be true, and that it is too glorious to be for you. Still you acknowledge it must be most blessed. Fearful one, erring one, anxious one, I bring you God's promise, it is for me and for you. Jesus will do it; as God, He is able, and Jesus is willing and longing as the Crucified One to keep you in perfect peace. This is a wonderful fact, and it is the secret of joy unspeakable.

And this is also

The secret of Holiness.

Instead of indwelling sin, an indwelling Christ conquering it; instead of indwelling sin, the indwelling life and light and love of the blessed Son of God. He is the secret of holiness. "Christ is made unto us sanctification." Remember that it is Christ Himself who is made unto us sanctification. Christ coming into me, taking charge of my whole being; my nature and my thoughts and my affections and my will; ruling all things. It is this that will make me holy. We talk about holiness, but do you know what holiness is? You have as much holiness as you have of Christ, for it is written, "Both he that sanctifieth and they who are sanctified are all of one;" and Christ sanctifies by bringing God's life into me.

We read in Judges, "The Spirit of the Lord clothed Gideon." But you know that there is in the New Testament an equally wonderful text, where we read, "Put on the Lord Jesus Christ," that is, clothe yourself with Christ Jesus. And what does that mean? It does not only mean, by imputation of righteousness outside of me, but to clothe myself with the living character of the living Christ, with the living love of the living Christ.

Put on the Lord Jesus.

Oh! what a work. I cannot do it unless I believe and understand that He whom I have to put on is as a garment covering my whole being. I have to put on a living Christ who has said, "Lo, I am with you all the days." Just draw the folds closer round you, of that robe of light with which Christ would array you. Just come and acknowledge that Christ is with you, on you, in you. Oh, put Him on! And when you look at one characteristic of His after another; and you hear God's word, "Let this mind be in you which was also in Jesus Christ," and it tells you He was obedient unto the death; and then you answer, Christ the obedient one, Christ whose whole life was obedience, it is that Christ whom I have received and put on. He becomes my life and His obedience rests upon me, until I learn to whisper as Jesus did, "My Father, Thy will be done; lo, I come to do Thy will."

This, too, is the secret of influence in witness and work. How comes it that it is so

Difficult to be obedient,

and how comes it that I so often sin? People sing, "Oh, to be wholly Thine," and sing it from their hearts. How comes it then that they are disobedient again? Where does the disobedience come from? And the answer comes, It is because I am trying to obey a distant Christ, and thus His commands do not come with power. Look what I find in God's Word. When God wanted to send any man upon His service, He first met him and talked with him and cheered him time after time. God appeared to Abraham seven or eight times, and gave to him one command after another; and so Abraham learned to obey Him perfectly. God appeared to Joshua and to Gideon, and they obeyed. And why are we not obedient? Because we have so little of this near intercourse with Jesus. But, oh, if we knew

This blessed, heavenly secret

of having the presence of Christ with us every day, every hour, every minute, what a joy it would be to obey! We could not walk in this consciousness,—My Lord Jesus is with me and around me,—and not obey Him! Oh, do you not begin to long and say, This is what I must have, the ever-abiding presence of Jesus! There are some Christians who try not to be disobedient, who come to their Sunday and week-day duties most faithfully, and pray for grace and a blessing, and they complain of so little blessing and power, so little power! And why? Because there is not enough of the living Jesus in their hearts. I sometimes think of this as a most solemn truth. There is a great diversity of gifts amongst ministers and others who speak; but I am sure of this, that a man's gifts are not the measure of his real power. I am sure of this, that God can see what neither you nor I can see. Sometimes people feel something of it; but in proportion as a man has in reality, not as a sentiment or an aspiration, or a thought, but in reality, the very spirit and presence of Jesus upon him, there comes out from him an unseen silent influence. That secret influence is the

Holy presence of Jesus.

"Lo, I am with you always." And now, if what I have said has sufficed just to indicate what a desirable thing it is, what a blessed thing it is to live for, then let me now give you an answer to the question that arises in more than one heart. I can hear some one say, "Tell me how I can get this blessed abiding presence of Jesus; and when I have got it, how I can ever keep it. I think if I have this, I have all. The Lord Jesus has come very near to me. I have tried to turn away from everything that can hinder, and have had my Lord very near. But how can I know that He will be with me always?" If you were to ask the Lord, "Oh, my blessed Lord Christ, what must I do, how can I enjoy Thy never-failing presence?" His first answer would be, "Only believe. I have said it often, and you only partly understood it, but I will say it again—

My child, only believe."

It is by faith. We sometimes speak of faith as trust, and it is a very helpful thing to tell men that faith is trust: but when people say, as they sometimes do, that it is nothing else but trust, that is not the case. It is a far wider word than trust. It is by faith that I learn to know the invisible One, the invisible God, and that I see Him. Faith is my spiritual eye-sight for the unseen and heavenly. You often try hard to trust God, and you fail. Why? Because you have not taken time first to see God. How can you trust God fully until you have met Him and known Him? You ask, "Where ought I to begin?" You ought to begin with first believing; with presenting yourself before this God in the attitude of silent worship, and asking Him to let a sense of His greatness and His presence come upon you. You must ask Him to let your heart be covered over with his holy presence. You must seek to realize in your heart the presence of an Almighty and all-loving God, an unspeakably loving God. Take time to worship Him as the omnipotent God, to feel that the very power that created the world, the very power that raised Jesus from the dead, is at this moment working in your heart. We do not experience it because we do not believe. We must take time to believe. Jesus says, "Oh, my child, shut your eyes to the world, and shut out of your heart all these thoughts about religion, and begin to believe in God Himself." That is the first article of the Creed—"I believe in God."

By believing I open my heart,

to receive this glorious God, and I bow and worship. And then as I believe this, I look up and I see the Lamb upon the Throne, and I believe that the Almighty power of God is in Jesus for the very purpose of revealing His presence to my heart. Why are there two upon the Throne? Is not God enough? The Lamb of God is upon the Throne in your interest and in mine; the Lamb upon the Throne is Christ Himself, with power as God to take possession of me. Oh, do not think you cannot get that realization. And do not think of it as now only within your reach; but cultivate the habit of faith. "Jesus, I believe in Thy glory; I believe in Thine omnipotence; I believe in Thy power working within me. I believe in Thy living, loving presence with me, revealing itself in Divine power."

Do not be occupied with feelings or experiences. You will find it far simpler and easier just to trust and say, "I am sure He is all for me." Get rid of yourself for the time; don't think or speak about yourself; but

Think what Jesus is.

And then remember it is believe always. I sometimes feel that I cannot find words to tell how God wants His people to believe from morning till night. Every breath ought to be just believing. Yes, it is indeed true; the Lord Jesus loves us to be just believing from morning to evening, and you must begin to make that the chief thing in life. In the morning when you wake, let your heart go forth with a large faith in this; and in the watches of the night let this thought be present with you—my Saviour Jesus is round me and near me, and you can look up and say, "I want to trust Thee always." You know what trust is. It is so sweet to trust. And now cannot you trust Jesus; this presence, this keeping presence? He lives for you in Heaven. You are marked with His blood, and he loves you; and cannot you say, "My King, my King, He is with me all the days?" Oh, trust Jesus to fulfill His own promises.

There is a second answer that I think Christ would give if we come to Him believing, and say, "Is there anything more, my blessed Master?" I think I can hear His answer:

"My child, always obey."

Do not fail to understand the lesson contained in this one word. You must distinctly and definitely take that word obey and obedience, and learn to say for yourselves: "Now I have to obey, and by the grace of God I am going to obey in everything." At our recent exhibition at the Cape, Mr. Rhodes, our Prime Minister, went to the gate, thinking he had got the fee in his pocket. When he got to the gate, however, he found he had not enough money, and said to the door-keeper, "I am Mr. Rhodes; let me in and I will take care you do not suffer." But the man said, "I cannot help that, sir, I have my orders," and he refused to let Mr. Rhodes in. He had to borrow from a friend, and pay before he could pass the gate. At a dinner afterward Mr. Rhodes spoke about it, and said it was a real joy to see a man stick to his order like that. That is it. The man had his orders, and that was enough to him, and whoever came to the gate had to pay his fee before he could enter. God's children ought to be like soldiers, and be

Ready to say, "I must obey."

Oh! to have that thought in our hearts—"Jesus, I love to obey Thee." There must be personal intercourse with the Saviour, and then comes the joy of personal service and allegiance. Are you ready to obey in all feebleness and weakness and fear? Can you say, "Yes, Lord Jesus, I will obey?" If so, then give yourself up absolutely. Then your feeling will be, "I am not going to speak one word if I think that Jesus would not like to hear it. I am not going to have an opinion of my own, but my whole life is to be covered with the purity of His obedience to the Father and His self-sacrificing love to me. I want Christ to have my whole life, my whole heart, my whole character. I want to be like Christ and to obey." Give yourself up to this loving obedience.

The third thought is this: If I say, "My Master, blessed Saviour, tell me all, I will believe, I do obey, and I will obey. Is there anything more I need to secure the enjoyment of Thine abiding presence?" And I catch this answer:

"My child, close intercourse with me every day."

Ah, there is the fault of many who try to obey and try to believe; they do it in their own strength, and they do not know that if the Lord Jesus is to reign in their hearts, they must have close communion with Him every day. You cannot do all He desires, but Jesus will do it for you. There are many Christians who fail here, and on that account do not understand what it is to have fellowship with Jesus. Do let me try and impress this upon you: God has given you a loving, living Saviour, and how can He bless if you do not meet Him? The joy of friendship is found in intercourse; and Jesus asks for this every day, that he may have time to influence me, to tell me of Himself, to teach me, to breathe His Spirit unto me, to give me new life and joy and strength. And remember, intercourse with Jesus

Does not mean half-an-hour

or an hour in your closet. A man may study his Bible or his commentary carefully; he may look up all the parallel passages in the chapter; when he comes out of his closet he may be able to tell you all about it, and yet he has never met Jesus that morning at all. You have prayed for five or ten minutes, and you have never met Jesus. And so we must remember that though the Bible is most precious, and the reading of it most blessed and needful; yet prayer and Bible reading are not fellowship with Jesus. What we need every morning is to meet Jesus, and to say, "Lord, here is the day again, and I am just as weak in myself as ever I was; do Thou come and feed me this morning with Thyself and speak to my soul." Oh, friends, it is not your faith that will keep you standing, but it is a living Jesus, met

Every day in fellowship

and worship and love. Wait in His presence, however cold and faithless you feel. Wait before Him and say: "Lord, helpless as I am, I believe and rest in the blessed assurance that what Thou hast promised Thou wilt do for me."

I ask my Master once again, "Lord Jesus, is that all?" And his answer is: "No, my child; I have one thing more." "And what is that? Thou hast told me to believe, and to obey, and to abide near to Thee: what wouldst Thou have more?"

"Work for me my child.

Remember, I have redeemed thee for My service; I have redeemed thee to have a witness to go out into the world confessing Me before men." Oh, do not hide your treasure, or think that if Jesus is with you, you can hide it. One of two things will happen—either you must give all up, or it must come out. You have perhaps heard of the little girl, who, after one of Mr. Moody's meetings, was found to be singing some of the hymns we all know. The child's parents were in a good position in society, and while singing those hymns in the drawing-room her mother forbade her. One day she was singing the hymn "Oh, I'm so glad that Jesus loves me," when her mother said, "My child, how is it that you sing this when I have forbidden it?" She replied, "Oh, mother, I cannot help it; it comes out of itself." If Jesus Christ be in the heart, He must come out. Remember, it is not only our duty to confess Him; it is that, but it is something more. If you do not do it, it is just an indication that you have not given yourself up to Jesus; your character, your reputation, your all. You are holding back from Him. You must confess Jesus in the world, in your home; and in fact everywhere. You know the Lord's command, "Go ye into all the world, and preach the Gospel to every creature;" "and, lo, I am with you," meaning, "Any one may work for Me, and I will be with him." It is true of the minister, the missionary, and every believer who works for Jesus. The presence of Jesus is intimately connected with work for Him. You say, "I have never thought of that before. I have my Sunday work, but during the week I am not doing work for Him." You cannot have the presence of Jesus, and let this continue to be the case. I do not believe you could have the presence of Jesus all the week and yet do nothing for Him; therefore my advice is, work for Him who is worthy, His blessing and His presence will be found in the work. It is

A blessed privilege to work for Christ

in this perishing world. Oh, why is it that our hearts often feel so cold and closed up, and so many of us say, "I do not feel called to Christ's work"? Be willing to yield yourself for the Lord's service, and He will reveal Himself to you.

Christ comes with His wondrous promise, and what He says, He says to all believers: "Lo, I am with you always; that is My promise; this is what I in My power can do; this is what I faithfully engage to perform; will you have it?

I give Myself to thee, O soul."

To each of those who have come to Him, Christ says, "I give Myself to thee, to be absolutely and wholly thine every hour of every day; to be with thee and in thee every moment, to bless thee and sustain thee, and to give thee each moment the consciousness of My presence; I will be wholly, wholly, wholly thine."

And now, what is the other side? He wants me to be wholly His. Are you ready to take this as your motto now,

"Wholly for God"?

O God, breathe Thou Thy presence in my heart that Thou mayest shine forth from my life. "Wholly for God," let this be our motto. Come let us cast ourselves on our faces before His feet. Our missionary from Nyassaland says he has often been touched by seeing how the native Christians, when they are brought to Jesus, do not stand in prayer; they do not kneel; but they cast themselves upon the earth with their foreheads to the ground, and there they lie, and with loud voices cry unto God. I sometimes feel that I wish we could do that ourselves; but we need not do it literally. Let us do it in spirit, for the everlasting Son of God has come into our hearts. Are you going to take Him and to keep Him there, to give Him glory and let Him have His way? Come now and say, "I will seek Thee with my whole heart; I am wholly Thine." Yield yourself entirely to Him to have complete possession. He will take and keep possession. Come now. Jesus delights in the worship of His Saints. Our whole life can become one continuous act of worship and work of love and joy, if we only remember and value this, that Jesus has said, "Lo, I am with you all the days, even unto the end of the world."

The Power of Persevering Prayer

And the Lord said, "Men ought always to pray, and not to faint... There was in a city a judge, which feared not God, neither regarded man: And there was a widow in that city; and she came unto him, saying, Avenge me of mine adversary. And he would not for awhile: but afterward he said within himself, Though I fear not God, nor regard man; Yet because this widow troubleth me, I will avenge her, lest by her continual coming she weary me. And the Lord said, Hear what the unjust judge saith. And shall not God avenge His own elect, which cry day and night unto Him, though He bear long with them? I tell you that He will avenge them speedily. Nevertheless when the Son of man cometh, shall He find faith on the earth?" (Luke 18:1-8)

Of all the mysteries of the prayer world the need of persevering prayer is one of the greatest. That the Lord, who is so loving and longing to bless, should have to be asked, time after time, sometimes year after year, before the answer comes, we cannot easily understand. It is also one of the greatest practical difficulties in the exercise of believing prayer. When, after persevering pleading, our prayer remains unanswered, it is often easiest for our lazy flesh, and it has all the appearance of pious submission, to think that we must now cease praying, because God may have His secret reason for withholding His answer to our request.It is by faith alone that the difficulty is overcome. When once faith has taken its stand on God's word and the Name of Jesus, and has yielded itself to the leading of the Spirit to seek God's will and honor alone in its prayer, it need not be discouraged by delay. It knows from Scripture that the power of believing prayer is simply irresistible; real faith can never be disappointed. It knows that just as water, to exercise the irresistible power it can have, must be gathered up and accumulated until the stream can come down in full force, so there must often be a heaping up of prayer until God sees that the measure is full, when the answer comes. It knows that just as the peasant farmer has to take his ten thousand steps to sow his tens of thousands seeds, each one a part of the preparation for the final harvest, so there is a need for often repeated persevering prayer, all working out some desired blessing. It knows for certain that not a single believing prayer can fail of its effect in heaven, but has its influence, and is treasured up to work out an answer in due time to him who perseveres to the end. It knows that it has to do, not with human thoughts or possibilities, but with the word of the living God. And so, even as Abraham through so many years "who against hope believed in hope" (Romans 4:18), and then "followers of them who through faith and patience inherit the promises." (Hebrews 6:12)

To enable us, when the answer to our prayer does not come at once, to combine quiet patience and joyful confidence in our persevering prayer, we must especially try to understand the words in which our Lord sets forth the character and conduct, not of the unjust judge, but of our God and Father, toward those whom He allows to cry day and night to Him: "I tell you that He will avenge them speedily." (Luke 18:8) He will avenge them quickly, the Master says. The blessing is all prepared; He is not only willing, but most anxious, to give them what they ask; everlasting love burns with the longing desire to reveal itself fully to its beloved and to satisfy their needs. God will not delay one moment longer than is absolutely necessary; He will do all in His power to expedite and rush the answer.

But why, if this is true and His power is infinite, does it often take so long for the answer to prayer to come? And why must God's own elect so often, in the middle of suffering and conflict, cry day and night? He is waiting patiently while He listens to them. "Behold, the husbandman waiteth for the precious fruit of the earth, and hath long patience for it, until he receive the early and latter rain." (James 5:7) The farmer does, indeed, long for his harvest, but knows that it must have its full amount of sunshine and rain, and he has long patience. A child so often wants to pick the half-ripe fruit; the farmer knows how to wait until the proper time. Man, in his spiritual nature too, is under the law of gradual growth that reigns in all created life. It is only in the path of development that he can reach his divine destiny. And it is the Father, in whose hand are the times and seasons, who knows the moment when the soul or the Church is ripened to that fullness of faith in which it can really take and keep the blessing. Like a father who longs to have his only child home from school, and yet waits patiently until the time of training is completed, so it is with God and His children: He is the patient One, and answers quickly. The insight into this truth leads the believer to cultivate the corresponding dispositions: patience and faith, waiting and anticipating, are the secret of his perseverance. By faith in the promise of God, we know that we have the petitions we have asked of Him. Faith takes and holds the answer in the promise as an unseen spiritual possession, rejoices in it, and praises for it. But there is a difference between the faith that thus holds the word and knows that it has the answer and the clearer, fuller, riper faith that obtains the promise as a present experience. It is in persevering, not unbelieving, but confident and praising prayer, that the soul grows up into that full union with its Lord in which it can enter upon the possession of the blessing in Him. There may be in these around us, there may be in that great system of being of which we are part, there may be in God's government, things that have to be put right through our prayer before the answer can fully come: the faith that has, according to the command, believed that it has received, can allow God to take His time; it knows it has prevailed and must prevail. In quiet, persistent, and determined perseverance it continues in prayer and thanksgiving until the blessing comes. And so we see combined what at first sight appears contradictory--the faith that rejoices in the answer of the unseen God as a present possession and the patience that cries day and night until it be revealed. The quickness of God's patience is met by the triumphant but patient faith of His waiting child.

Our great danger, in this school of the answer delayed, is the temptation to think that, after all, it may not be God's will to give us what we ask. If our prayer be according to God's word, and under the leading of the Spirit, let us not give way to these fears. Let us learn to give God time. God needs time with us. If only we give Him time, that is, time in the daily fellowship with Himself, for Him to exercise the full influence of His presence on us, and time, day by day, in the course of our being kept waiting, for faith to prove its reality and to fill our whole being, He Himself will lead us from faith to vision; we shall see the glory of God. Let no delay shake our faith. Of faith it holds good: first the blade, then the ear, then the full corn in the ear. Each believing prayer brings a step nearer the final victory. Each believing prayer helps to ripen the fruit and bring us nearer to it; it fills up the measure of prayer and faith known to God alone; it conquers the hindrances in the unseen world; it hastens the end. Child of God, give the Father time. He is patiently listening to you. He wants the blessing to be rich, and full, and sure; give Him time, while you cry day and night. Only remember the word: "I tell you that He will avenge them speedily." (Luke 18:8)

The blessing of such persevering prayer is unspeakable. There is nothing so heart-searching as the prayer of faith. It teaches you to discover and confess, and to give up everything that hinders the coming of the blessing, everything there may not be in accordance with the Father's will. It leads to closer fellowship with Him who alone can teach us to pray, to a more entire surrender to draw near under no covering but that of the blood and the Spirit. It calls for a closer and more simple abiding in Christ alone. Christian, give God time. He will perfect that which concerns you.

Let it be thus whether you pray for yourself or for others. All labor, bodily or mental, needs time and effort: we must give up ourselves up to it. Nature discovers her secrets and yields her treasures only to diligent and thoughtful labor. However little we can understand it, in the spiritual farming it is the same: the seed we sow in the soil of heaven, the efforts we put forth, and the influence we seek to exert in the world above, need our whole being: we must give ourselves to prayer. But let us hold firm the great confidence that in due season we will reap if we don't give up.

And let us especially learn the lesson as we pray for the Christ's Church. She is, indeed, like the poor widow, in the absence of her Lord, apparently at the mercy of her adversary, helpless to obtain restitution. Let us, when we pray for His Church or any portion of it, under the power of the world, asking Him to visit her with the mighty workings of His Spirit and to prepare her for His coming—let us pray in the assured faith: prayer does help, praying always and not stopping will bring the answer. Only give God time. And then keep crying out day and night. "And the Lord said, Hear what the unjust judge saith. And shall not God avenge His own elect, which cry day and night unto Him, though He bear long with them?" (Luke 18:6-7)

.

THE END

'Jesus Himself'

Their eyes were opened, and they knew Him."

I

THE words, from which I want to present a simple message, will be found in the Gospel according to St. Luke, the 24th chapter and the 31st verse: "And their eyes were opened, and they knew Him." Some time since, I preached a sermon with the words "Jesus Himself" as the text; and as I went home I said to those who were walking with me: "How possible it is to have Jesus Himself with us and never to know it, and how possible to preach of, and to listen to, all the truth about Jesus Himself and yet not to know Him." I cannot say what a deep impression was made upon me as I thought over it.

Now these disciples had spent a most blessed time with Jesus, but if they had gone away before He revealed Himself that evening, they would never have been sure that it was Jesus, for their eyes were holden that they should not know Him. That is, alas, the condition of a great multitude in the Church of Christ. They know that Christ has risen from the dead. They believe, and they very often have blessed experiences that come from the risen Christ. Very often in a time of Convention, or in time of silent Bible reading, or in a time of the visitation of God's grace, their hearts burn; and yet it can be said of a people whose hearts are burning within them, that they did not know it was Jesus Himself.

And now if you ask me what is to be the great blessing to be sought, my answer is this: Not only should we think about Jesus Himself and speak about Him and believe in Him, but we should come to the point that the disciples in the text arrived at, "and they knew Him." Everything is to be found in that.

If I read that story of the disciples on the way to Emmaus, I get from it four stages in the Christian life. Just think! How did they begin the morning that day? With

Hearts sad and troubled,

because they thought Jesus was dead. They did not know that He was alive, and that is the state of very many Christians. They look to the Cross, and they struggle to trust Christ, but they have never yet learned the blessedness of believing that there is a living Christ to do everything for them. Oh! that word of the angel to the women! "Why seek ye the living among the dead?" What is the difference between a dead Christ, whom the women went to anoint, and a living Christ? A dead Christ, I must do everything for; a living Christ does everything for me.

The disciples began the morning with a sad heart. I fancy very possibly they spent a sleepless night. Oh! the terrible disappointment! They had hoped that Christ would be the Deliverer of Israel, and they had seen Him die an accursed death. On the morning of that first day of the week, they rose with sad hearts—the bitter sadness cannot be expressed. That is just the life of many Christians. They try to believe in Jesus and to trust Him, and to hope in Him, but there is no joy. Why? Because they do not know that there is a living Christ to reveal Himself.

Then there is the second stage. What is that? The stage of which Christ speaks:

"Slow of heart to believe."

They had the message from the women. They told the stranger who walked with them: "Certain women have astonished us, telling us they have seen an angel, who says He is alive." And Christ replied to them: "Oh! fools, and slow of heart to believe." Yes! there are many Christians to-day who have heard and who know that they must not only believe in a crucified Christ, but in a living Christ, and they try to grasp it and take it in, but it does not bring them a blessing, and why? Because they want to feel it and not to believe it. They want to work for it, and with efforts get hold of it, instead of just quietly sinking down and believing, "Christ, the living Jesus, He will do everything for us." That is the second stage. The first stage is that of ignorance, the second stage is that of unbelief—the doubting heart that cannot take in the wonderful truth that Jesus lives.

Then comes the third stage—

The burning heart.

Jesus came to the two disciples, and after He had reproved them and said: "Oh! fools, and slow of heart to believe," He began to open the Scriptures to them, and to tell them of all the wonderful things the prophets had taught. Then their eyes were opened, and they began to understand the Scriptures. They saw that it was true that it was prophesied that Christ must rise. As He talked, there came out from Him—the living risen One—a mighty influence, and it rested upon them, and they began to feel their hearts burn within them with joy and gladness.

You still say perhaps: "That is the stage we want to come to." No; God forbid you should stop there. You may get in that third stage—the burning heart—and yet something is still wanting—the revelation of Christ. The disciples had had a blessed experience of His divine powers, but He had not revealed Himself, and oh! how often it is that at Conventions and in churches, and in meetings and in blessed fellowship with God's saints, our hearts burn within us. These are precious experiences of the working of God's grace and Spirit, and yet there is something wanting. What is that? Jesus Himself has been working upon us, and the power of his risen life has touched us, but we cannot say, "I have met Him. He has made Himself known to me." Oh, the difference between a burning heart, which becomes cold after a time, which comes by fits and starts, and the blessed revelation of Jesus Himself as my Saviour, taking charge of me and blessing me and keeping me every day! This is the stage of

The satisfied heart.

Oh my brother, my sister! It is what I ask for you, and it is what I am sure you ask for yourself. I ask it for myself. Lord Jesus! may we know Thee in thy divine glory as the risen One, our Jesus, our Beloved and our mighty One. Oh! if there are any sad ones who cannot take this in, and who say, "I have never known the joy of religion yet"—listen, we are going to tell you how you can. All will center round this one thing, that just as a little child lives day by day in the arms of its mother, and grows up year by year under a mother's eye, it is a possibility that you can live every day and hour of your life in fellowship with the Holy Jesus.

He will do it for you.

Come, and let your sad heart begin to hope. Will He reveal Himself? He did it to the disciples and He will do it to you. Perhaps there are some who have got beyond the sad heart and who yet feel, "I have not got what I want." If you throw open your heart and give up everything but just believing and allowing Him to do what He wants, it will come.

God be praised! it will come.

Jesus will reveal Himself.

Perhaps you have arrived at the stage of the burning heart, and can tell of many blessed experiences, but somehow there is a worm at the root. The experiences do not last, and the heart is so changeable. Oh come, my beloved! Follow Christ. Say, "Jesus, reveal Thyself that we may know Thee Thyself. We ask not only to drink of the living water, we want the fountain. We ask not only to bathe ourselves in the light, we want the Sun of Righteousness within our hearts. We ask not only to know Thee, who hast touched us and warmed our hearts and blessed us, but we want to know that we have the unchangeable Jesus dwelling within our hearts and abiding with us forevermore."

Now comes the question which I really wanted to put,—What are the conditions under which our blessed Lord reveals Himself? Or, put it this way,—To whom is it that Jesus will reveal Himself? We have only to see how he dealt with these disciples, and we get the answer. What is the answer? First of all I think I find here that Christ revealed Himself to those disciples

Who had given up everything for Him.

He had said to them: "Forsake all and follow Me," and they had done it. With all their feebleness and all their unfaithfulness they followed Christ to the end. He said to them: "Ye have continued with Me in My temptations, and I appoint you a kingdom, as I have received a kingdom from My Father." They were not perfect men, but they would have died for Him. They loved Him, they obeyed Him, they followed Him. They had left all, and for three years they had been following hard after Christ. You say "Tell me what Christ wants of me, if I am to have his wonderful presence. Tell me what is the character of the man to whom Christ will reveal Himself in this highest and fullest way?" I answer: "It is the one who is ready to forsake all and to follow Him." If Christ is to give Himself wholly to me, He must know that He has me wholly for Himself; and I trust God will give grace that these words spoken about the consecration and the surrender, not only of all evil, but of many lawful things, and even, if necessary, of life itself, may lead us to understand what the demand is that Jesus makes upon us.

The motto of the Cape General Mission is,

"God first."

In one sense that is a beautiful motto, and yet I am not always satisfied with it, because it is a motto that is often misunderstood. God first may mean "I" second, something else third, and something else fourth. God is thus first in order, but still God becomes one of a series of powers, and that is not the place God wants. The meaning of the words, "God first" is really "God all; God everything;" and that is what Christ wants. To be willing to give up everything, to submit to Christ to teach him what to say and what to do, is the first mark of the man to whom Christ will come. Are you not ready to take this step and say: "Jesus! I do give up everything; I have given up everything; reveal Thyself."

Oh, brother! oh, sister! do not hesitate. Speak it out in your heart, and let this be the time in which a new sacrifice shall be laid at the feet of the blessed Lamb of God.

There is a second thought. There is first the idea of having forsaken all to follow Him; of having given up everything in obedience to Him, and living just a life of simple love and obedience. But there is a second thing needed in the man who is to have this full revelation of Christ. He must be

Convicted of his unbelief.

"Oh! fools, and slow of heart to believe what the prophets have said." Oh! brother, sister, if we could have a sight of the amount of unbelief in the hearts of God's children, barring the door and closing the heart against Christ, how we should stand astonished and ashamed! When there is not unbelief but where there is faith, Christ cannot help coming in. He cannot help coming where there is a living faith, a full faith. The heart is opened, the heart is prepared; and as naturally as water runs into a hollow place, so naturally Christ must come into a heart that is full of faith. What is the hindrance with some earnest souls, who say: "I have given myself up to the Lord Jesus. I have done it often, and by His grace I am doing it every day, and God knows how earnestly and really I am doing it, and I have the sanction of God upon it, I know God has blessed me"? They have not been convicted of their unbelief. "Oh! fools, and slow of heart to believe." Do you know what Christ said about a man calling his brother a fool? Yet here the loving Son of God could find no other word to speak to His beloved disciples: "Oh! fools, and slow of heart to believe." You want the Lord Jesus to give you this full revelation of Himself? Are you willing to acknowledge that you are a fool for never having believed in Him? "Lord Jesus, it is my own fault. There Thou art, longing to have possession of me. There Thou hast been with Thy faithful promises waiting to reveal Thyself."

Did you ever hear of a man loving another and not longing to reveal himself? Christ longs to reveal Himself, but He cannot on account of our unbelief. May God convict us of our unbelief that we may get utterly ashamed and broken down, and cry, "Oh, my God, what is this, this heart of unbelief actually throwing a barrier across the door that Christ cannot step in, blinding my eyes that I cannot see Jesus, though he is so near? Here He has been for ten or twenty years, from time to time giving me the burning heart, enjoying the experience of a little of His love and grace, and yet I have not had the revelation of Him, taking possession of my heart and dwelling with me in unbroken continuity." Oh! may God convict us of unbelief. Do let us believe because all things are possible to him that believes. That is God's word, and this blessing, receiving the revelation of Jesus, can come only to those who learn to believe and to trust him.

There is another mark of those to whom this special revelation of Christ will come, and that is,

"They do not rest until they obtain it."

You know the story. Their hearts were burning as they drew nigh to the place they were going to, and Christ made as if He were going farther. He put them to the test, and if they had allowed Him quietly to go on, if they had been content with the experience of the burning heart, they would have lost something infinitely better. But they were not content with it. They were not content to go home to the disciples that night and say, "Oh, what a blessed afternoon we have had! What wonderful teaching we have had!" No! The burning heart and the blessed experience just made them say, "Lord, abide with us," and they compelled Him to come in. They constrained Him to come in.

It always reminds me of the story of Jacob, "I will not let Thee go, except Thou bless me." That is the spirit that prepares us for the revelation of Jesus. Oh! my dear friend, has this been the spirit in which we have looked upon the wonderful blessing that we have sometimes heard of? "Oh! my Lord Jesus, though I do not understand it, though I cannot grasp it, though my struggles avail nothing, I am not going to let Thee go. If it is possible for a sinner on earth to have Jesus every day, every hour, and every moment in resurrection power dwelling in his heart, shining within him, filling him with love and joy,—if that is possible, I want it."

Is that your language?

Oh! come then and say: "Lord Jesus, I cannot let Thee go except Thou bless me." The question is asked so often: "What is the cause of the feeble life of so many Christians?" What is really the matter? What is actually the want?

How little the Church responds to Christ's call! how little the Church is what Christ would have her to be! What is the cause of all the trouble? Various answers may be given, but there is one answer which includes all the other answers, and that is, each believer wants the personal

Full revelation of a personal Christ

as an indwelling Lord, as a satisfying portion. When the Lord Jesus was here upon earth, what was it that distinguished His disciples from other people? He took them away from their fish-nets, and from their homes, and He gathered them about Himself, and they knew Jesus. He was their Master, and guarded them, and they followed Him. And what is to make a difference between Christ's disciples—not those who are just hoping to get to heaven, but Christ's whole-hearted disciples— what is to make a difference between them and other people? It is this, to be in fellowship with Jesus—every hour of the day; and just as Christ upon earth was able to keep those people with Him for three years, day by day, so

Christ is able

in heaven now to do what He could not do when He was on earth—to keep in the closest fellowship with every believer throughout the whole world. Glory be to God! You know that text in Ephesians: "He that descended is the same also that ascended, that He might fill all things." Why was my Lord Jesus taken up to heaven away from the life of earth? Because the life of earth is a life confined to localities, but the life in heaven is a life in which there is no limit and no bound and no locality, and Christ was taken up to heaven, that, in the power of God, of the omnipresent God, He might be able to fill every individual here and be with every individual believer.

That is what my heart wants to realize by faith; that is a possibility, that is a promise, that is my birthright, and I want to have it, and I want by the grace of God to say, "Jesus, I will not rest until Thou hast revealed Thyself fully to my soul."

There are often very blessed experiences in the Christian life in what I call the third stage—the stage of the burning heart. Do you know what another great mark of that stage is? Delight in God's word. How did the disciples get their burning hearts? By that strange opening of the Scripture to them. He made it all look different,—new,—and they saw what they had never seen before. They could not help feeling,

How wonderful,

how heavenly was that teaching. Oh! there are many Christians who find the best time of the day is the time when they can get with their Bibles, and who love nothing so much as to get a new thought; and as a diamond digger rejoices when he has found a diamond, or a gold digger when he has found a nugget, they delight when they get from the Bible some new thought, and they feed upon it. Yet with all that interest in God's word, and with all that stirring of the heart with joy, when they go into business or attend to their daily duties, there is still something wanting.

We must come away from all the manifold and multifarious blessings that Jesus can bestow from time to time, to the blessed unity of that one— that Jesus makes Himself known, Jesus Himself is willing to make Himself known. Oh! if I were to ask, "Is not this just what you and I want, and what many of us have been longing for?" I am sure you would answer,

"That is what I want."

Think what the blessedness will be that comes from it. You often sing:—

"Oh! the peace my Saviour gives!
Peace I never knew before,
And my way has brighter grown,
Since I've learnt to trust Him more."

I recently had a letter from some one in the Free State saying what a wonderful comfort and strength that little verse was in the midst of difficulties and troubles. Yes; but how can that peace be kept? It was the presence of Christ that brought the peace. When the storm was threatening to swallow up the disciples, it was the presence of Christ Himself that gave the peace.

Oh! Christian, do you want peace and rest? You must have Jesus Himself. You talk of purity, you talk of cleansing, you talk of deliverance from sin. Praise God, here is the deliverance and the cleansing, when the living Jesus comes and gives power. Then we have this resurrection of Christ, this heavenly Christ upon the throne, making Himself known to us. Surely that will be the secret of purity and the secret of strength.

Where does the strength of so many come from? From the joy of a personal friendship with Jesus. Those disciples, if they had gone away with their burning hearts to the other disciples, could have told them wonderful things of a man who had explained to them the Scriptures and the promises, but they could not have said, "We have seen Jesus." They might have said, "Jesus is alive. We are sure of that," but that would not have satisfied the others. But they could now go and say,

"We have seen Himself.

He has revealed Himself to us." We are all glad to work for Christ, but there is a complaint throughout the Church of Christ, from the ministers in the pulpit down to the feeblest worker, of lack of joy and lack of blessedness. Let us try and find out whether this is not the place where the secret will be discovered—that the Lord Jesus comes and shows Himself to us as our Master and speaks to us. When we have Jesus with us, and when we go every footstep with the thought that it is Jesus wants us to go, it is Jesus who sends us and is helping us, then there will be brightness in our testimony, and it will help other believers, and they will begin to understand; "I see why I have failed. I took the word, I took the blessing, and I took, as I thought, the life, but I was without the living Jesus."

And if you now ask, "How will this revelation come?" Brother, sister, that is the secret that no man may tell, that Jesus keeps to Himself. It is

In the power of the Holy Ghost;

Christ, the risen One, entered into a new life. His resurrection life is entirely different from His life before His death. You know what we read: "They knew Him." He revealed Himself, and then He passed away. And was that vision of Christ worth so much? It was lost in a moment. It was worth heaven, eternity, everything. Why? Because henceforth Christ was no longer to be known after the flesh. Christ was henceforth in the power of the Spirit, which fills Heaven; in the power of the Spirit which is the power of the Godhead; in the power of the Spirit, which fills our hearts. Christ was henceforth to live in the life of Heaven.

Thank God, Christ can by the power of the Holy Ghost reveal Himself to each one of us; but oh! brother, it is a secret thing between Christ and yourself. Take this assurance, "Their eyes were opened and they knew Him," and believe that it is written for you.

You say, "I have known the other three stages; the stage of the sad heart, mourning that I knew no living Christ; I have known the stage of the slow heart to believe, when I struggled with my unbelief; and I know the stage of the burning heart, when there are great times of joy and blessedness." You say that? Oh come then and know the fourth stage of

The satisfied heart,

of the heart made glad for eternity, of the heart that cannot keep its joy in, but goes away back to Jerusalem, and says, "It is true. Jesus has revealed Himself. I know it, I feel it." Oh! brother, oh! sister, how will this revelation come? Jesus will tell you. Just come to the Lord Jesus and breathe up before Him a simple child-like prayer, and I, His servant, will come and take you by the hand and say: "Come, now, my work is done. I have pointed to the Lamb of God, to the risen One. My work is done."

Let us enter into the Holy Presence and begin, if you have never yet sought it before, begin to plead: "Oh! Saviour, that I might have this blessedness every moment present with me—Jesus Himself, my portion forever."

"Jesus Himself."

"Lo, I am with you alway."

II

WHEN I think of all the struggles and difficulties and failures of which many complain, and know that many are trying to make a new effort to begin a holy life, their hearts fearing all the time that they would fail again, owing to so many difficulties and temptations and the natural weakness of their character, my heart longs to be able to tell them in words so simple that a little child could understand,

What the secret is of the Christian life.

And then the thought comes to me, Can I venture to hope that it will be given to me to take that glorious, heavenly, divine Lord Jesus and to show Him to these souls, so that they can see Him in His glory? And can it be given to me to open their eyes to see that there is a Divine, Almighty Christ, who does actually come into the heart and who faithfully promises, "I will come and dwell with you, and I will never leave you?" No; my words cannot do that. But then I thought, my Lord Jesus can use me as a simple servant to take such feeble ones by the hand and encourage and help them; to say, Oh, come, come, come, into the presence of Jesus and wait on Him, and He will reveal Himself to thee. I pray God that He may use His precious Word. It is simply

The presence of the Lord Jesus.

That is the secret of the Christian's strength and joy. You know that when He was upon earth, He was present in bodily form with his disciples. They walked about together all day, and at night they went into the same house, and sometimes slept together and ate and drank together. They were continually together. It was the presence of Jesus that was the training school of His disciples. They were bound to Him by that wonderful intercourse of love during three long years, and in that intercourse they learned to know Christ, and Christ instructed and corrected them, and prepared them for what they were afterward to receive. And now when He is going away, He says to them: "Lo, behold, I am with you always—all the days—even unto the end of the world."

What a promise! And just as really as Christ was with Peter in the boat, just as Christ sat with John at the table, as really can I have Christ with me. And more really, for they had their Christ in the body and He was to them a man, an individual separate from them, but I may have glorified Christ in the power of the throne of God, the omnipotent Christ, the omnipresent Christ.

What a promise! You ask me, How can that be? And my answer is,

Because Christ is God, and because Christ after having been made man, went up into the throne and the Life of God. And now that blessed Christ Jesus, with His loving, pierced heart; that blessed Jesus Christ, who lived upon earth; that same Christ glorified into the glory of God, can be in me and

Can be with me all the days.

You say, Is it really possible for a man in business, for a woman in the midst of a large and difficult household, for a poor man full of care; is it possible? Can I always be thinking of Jesus? Thank God, you need not always be thinking of Him. You may be the manager of a bank, and your whole attention may be required to carry out the business that you have to do. But thank God, while I have to think of my business, Jesus will think of me, and He will come in and will take charge of me. That little child, three months old, as it sleeps in its mother's arms, lies helplessly there; it hardly knows its mother, it does not think of her, but the mother thinks of the child. And this is the blessed mystery of love, that Jesus the God-man waits to come in to me in the greatness of His love; and as He gets possession of my heart, He embraces me in those divine arms and tells me, "My child, I the Faithful One, I the Mighty One will abide with thee, will watch over thee and keep thee all the days." He tells me He will come into my heart, so that I can be a happy Christian, a holy Christian, and a useful Christian. You say, Oh! if I could only believe that, if I could think that it is possible to have Christ always, every hour, every moment with me,

Taking and keeping charge of me!

My brother, my sister, it is just literally this that is my message to you. When Jesus said to His disciples, "Lo, I am with you always," He meant it in the fullness of the divine Omnipresence, in the fullness of the divine love, and he longs to-night to reveal Himself to you and to me as we have never seen Him before.

And now just think a moment what a blessed life that must be—the presence of Jesus always abiding. Is not that the secret of peace and happiness? If I could just attain (that is what each heart says) to that blessed state in which every day and all the day I felt Jesus to be watching and ever keeping me, oh, what peace I would have in the thought, "I have no care if He cares for me, and I have no fear if He provides for me." Your heart says that this is too good to be true, and that it is too glorious to be for you. Still you acknowledge it must be most blessed. Fearful one, erring one, anxious one, I bring you God's promise, it is for me and for you. Jesus will do it; as God, He is able, and Jesus is willing and longing as the Crucified One to keep you in perfect peace. This is a wonderful fact, and it is the secret of joy unspeakable.

And this is also

The secret of Holiness.

Instead of indwelling sin, an indwelling Christ conquering it; instead of indwelling sin, the indwelling life and light and love of the blessed Son of God. He is the secret of holiness. "Christ is made unto us sanctification." Remember that it is Christ Himself who is made unto us sanctification. Christ coming into me, taking charge of my whole being; my nature and my thoughts and my affections and my will; ruling all things. It is this that will make me holy. We talk about holiness, but do you know what holiness is? You have as much holiness as you have of Christ, for it is written, "Both he that sanctifieth and they who are sanctified are all of one;" and Christ sanctifies by bringing God's life into me.

We read in Judges, "The Spirit of the Lord clothed Gideon." But you know that there is in the New Testament an equally wonderful text, where we read, "Put on the Lord Jesus Christ," that is, clothe yourself with Christ Jesus. And what does that mean? It does not only mean, by imputation of righteousness outside of me, but to clothe myself with the living character of the living Christ, with the living love of the living Christ.

Put on the Lord Jesus.

Oh! what a work. I cannot do it unless I believe and understand that He whom I have to put on is as a garment covering my whole being. I have to put on a living Christ who has said, "Lo, I am with you all the days." Just draw the folds closer round you, of that robe of light with which Christ would array you. Just come and acknowledge that Christ is with you, on you, in you. Oh, put Him on! And when you look at one characteristic of His after another; and you hear God's word, "Let this mind be in you which was also in Jesus Christ," and it tells you He was obedient unto the death; and then you answer, Christ the obedient one, Christ whose whole life was obedience, it is that Christ whom I have received and put on. He becomes my life and His obedience rests upon me, until I learn to whisper as Jesus did, "My Father, Thy will be done; lo, I come to do Thy will."

This, too, is the secret of influence in witness and work. How comes it that it is so

Difficult to be obedient,

and how comes it that I so often sin? People sing, "Oh, to be wholly Thine," and sing it from their hearts. How comes it then that they are disobedient again? Where does the disobedience come from? And the answer comes, It is because I am trying to obey a distant Christ, and thus His commands do not come with power. Look what I find in God's Word. When God wanted to send any man upon His service, He first met him and talked with him and cheered him time after time. God appeared to Abraham seven or eight times, and gave to him one command after another; and so Abraham learned to obey Him perfectly. God appeared to Joshua and to Gideon, and they obeyed. And why are we not obedient? Because we have so little of this near intercourse with Jesus. But, oh, if we knew

This blessed, heavenly secret

of having the presence of Christ with us every day, every hour, every minute, what a joy it would be to obey! We could not walk in this consciousness,—My Lord Jesus is with me and around me,—and not obey Him! Oh, do you not begin to long and say, This is what I must have, the ever-abiding presence of Jesus! There are some Christians who try not to be disobedient, who come to their Sunday and week-day duties most faithfully, and pray for grace and a blessing, and they complain of so little blessing and power, so little power! And why? Because there is not enough of the living Jesus in their hearts. I sometimes think of this as a most solemn truth. There is a great diversity of gifts amongst ministers and others who speak; but I am sure of this, that a man's gifts are not the measure of his real power. I am sure of this, that God can see what neither you nor I can see. Sometimes people feel something of it; but in proportion as a man has in reality, not as a sentiment or an aspiration, or a thought, but in reality, the very spirit and presence of Jesus upon him, there comes out from him an unseen silent influence. That secret influence is the

Holy presence of Jesus.

"Lo, I am with you always." And now, if what I have said has sufficed just to indicate what a desirable thing it is, what a blessed thing it is to live for, then let me now give you an answer to the question that arises in more than one heart. I can hear some one say, "Tell me how I can get this blessed abiding presence of Jesus; and when I have got it, how I can ever keep it. I think if I have this, I have all. The Lord Jesus has come very near to me. I have tried to turn away from everything that can hinder, and have had my Lord very near. But how can I know that He will be with me always?" If you were to ask the Lord, "Oh, my blessed Lord Christ, what must I do, how can I enjoy Thy never-failing presence?" His first answer would be, "Only believe. I have said it often, and you only partly understood it, but I will say it again—

My child, only believe."

It is by faith. We sometimes speak of faith as trust, and it is a very helpful thing to tell men that faith is trust: but when people say, as they sometimes do, that it is nothing else but trust, that is not the case. It is a far wider word than trust. It is by faith that I learn to know the invisible One, the invisible God, and that I see Him. Faith is my spiritual eye-sight for the unseen and heavenly. You often try hard to trust God, and you fail. Why? Because you have not taken time first to see God. How can you trust God fully until you have met Him and known Him? You ask, "Where ought I to begin?" You ought to begin with first believing; with presenting yourself before this God in the attitude of silent worship, and asking Him to let a sense of His greatness and His presence come upon you. You must ask Him to let your heart be covered over with his holy presence. You must seek to realize in your heart the presence of an Almighty and all-loving God, an unspeakably loving God. Take time to worship Him as the omnipotent God, to feel that the very power that created the world, the very power that raised Jesus from the dead, is at this moment working in your heart. We do not experience it because we do not believe. We must take time to believe. Jesus says, "Oh, my child, shut your eyes to the world, and shut out of your heart all these thoughts about religion, and begin to believe in God Himself." That is the first article of the Creed—"I believe in God."

By believing I open my heart,

to receive this glorious God, and I bow and worship. And then as I believe this, I look up and I see the Lamb upon the Throne, and I believe that the Almighty power of God is in Jesus for the very purpose of revealing His presence to my heart. Why are there two upon the Throne? Is not God enough? The Lamb of God is upon the Throne in your interest and in mine; the Lamb upon the Throne is Christ Himself, with power as God to take possession of me. Oh, do not think you cannot get that realization. And do not think of it as now only within your reach; but cultivate the habit of faith. "Jesus, I believe in Thy glory; I believe in Thine omnipotence; I believe in Thy power working within me. I believe in Thy living, loving presence with me, revealing itself in Divine power."

Do not be occupied with feelings or experiences. You will find it far simpler and easier just to trust and say, "I am sure He is all for me." Get rid of yourself for the time; don't think or speak about yourself; but

Think what Jesus is.

And then remember it is believe always. I sometimes feel that I cannot find words to tell how God wants His people to believe from morning till night. Every breath ought to be just believing. Yes, it is indeed true; the Lord Jesus loves us to be just believing from morning to evening, and you must begin to make that the chief thing in life. In the morning when you wake, let your heart go forth with a large faith in this; and in the watches of the night let this thought be present with you—my Saviour Jesus is round me and near me, and you can look up and say, "I want to trust Thee always." You know what trust is. It is so sweet to trust. And now cannot you trust Jesus; this presence, this keeping presence? He lives for you in Heaven. You are marked with His blood, and he loves you; and cannot you say, "My King, my King, He is with me all the days?" Oh, trust Jesus to fulfill His own promises.

There is a second answer that I think Christ would give if we come to Him believing, and say, "Is there anything more, my blessed Master?" I think I can hear His answer:

"My child, always obey."

Do not fail to understand the lesson contained in this one word. You must distinctly and definitely take that word obey and obedience, and learn to say for yourselves: "Now I have to obey, and by the grace of God I am going to obey in everything." At our recent exhibition at the Cape, Mr. Rhodes, our Prime Minister, went to the gate, thinking he had got the fee in his pocket. When he got to the gate, however, he found he had not enough money, and said to the door-keeper, "I am Mr.

Rhodes; let me in and I will take care you do not suffer." But the man said, "I cannot help that, sir, I have my orders," and he refused to let Mr. Rhodes in. He had to borrow from a friend, and pay before he could pass the gate. At a dinner afterward Mr. Rhodes spoke about it, and said it was a real joy to see a man stick to his order like that. That is it. The man had his orders, and that was enough to him, and whoever came to the gate had to pay his fee before he could enter. God's children ought to be like soldiers, and be

Ready to say, "I must obey."

Oh! to have that thought in our hearts—"Jesus, I love to obey Thee." There must be personal intercourse with the Saviour, and then comes the joy of personal service and allegiance. Are you ready to obey in all feebleness and weakness and fear? Can you say, "Yes, Lord Jesus, I will obey?" If so, then give yourself up absolutely. Then your feeling will be, "I am not going to speak one word if I think that Jesus would not like to hear it. I am not going to have an opinion of my own, but my whole life is to be covered with the purity of His obedience to the Father and His self-sacrificing love to me. I want Christ to have my whole life, my whole heart, my whole character. I want to be like Christ and to obey." Give yourself up to this loving obedience.

The third thought is this: If I say, "My Master, blessed Saviour, tell me all, I will believe, I do obey, and I will obey. Is there anything more I need to secure the enjoyment of Thine abiding presence?" And I catch this answer:

"My child, close intercourse with me every day."

Ah, there is the fault of many who try to obey and try to believe; they do it in their own strength, and they do not know that if the Lord Jesus is to reign in their hearts, they must have close communion with Him every day. You cannot do all He desires, but Jesus will do it for you. There are many Christians who fail here, and on that account do not understand what it is to have fellowship with Jesus. Do let me try and impress this upon you: God has given you a loving, living Saviour, and how can He bless if you do not meet Him? The joy of friendship is found in intercourse; and Jesus asks for this every day, that he may have time to influence me, to tell me of Himself, to teach me, to breathe His Spirit unto me, to give me new life and joy and strength. And remember, intercourse with Jesus

Does not mean half-an-hour

or an hour in your closet. A man may study his Bible or his commentary carefully; he may look up all the parallel passages in the chapter; when he comes out of his closet he may be able to tell you all about it, and yet he has never met Jesus that morning at all. You have prayed for five or ten minutes, and you have never met Jesus. And so we must remember that though the Bible is most precious, and the reading of it most blessed and needful; yet prayer and Bible reading are not fellowship with Jesus. What we need every morning is to meet Jesus, and to say, "Lord, here is the day again, and I am just as weak in myself as ever I was; do Thou come and feed me this morning with Thyself and speak to my soul." Oh, friends, it is not your faith that will keep you standing, but it is a living Jesus, met

Every day in fellowship

and worship and love. Wait in His presence, however cold and faithless you feel. Wait before Him and say: "Lord, helpless as I am, I believe and rest in the blessed assurance that what Thou hast promised Thou wilt do for me."

I ask my Master once again, "Lord Jesus, is that all?" And his answer is: "No, my child; I have one thing more." "And what is that? Thou hast told me to believe, and to obey, and to abide near to Thee: what wouldst Thou have more?"

"Work for me my child.

Remember, I have redeemed thee for My service; I have redeemed thee to have a witness to go out into the world confessing Me before men." Oh, do not hide your treasure, or think that if Jesus is with you, you can hide it. One of two things will happen—either you must give all up, or it must come out. You have perhaps heard of the little girl, who, after one of Mr. Moody's meetings, was found to be singing some of the hymns we all know. The child's parents were in a good position in society, and while singing those hymns in the drawing-room her mother forbade her. One day she was singing the hymn "Oh, I'm so glad that Jesus loves me," when her mother said, "My child, how is it that you sing this when I have forbidden it?" She replied, "Oh, mother, I cannot help it; it comes out of itself." If Jesus Christ be in the heart, He must come out. Remember, it is not only our duty to confess Him; it is that, but it is something more. If you do not do it, it is just an indication that you have not given yourself up to Jesus; your character, your reputation, your all. You are holding back from Him. You must confess Jesus in the world, in your home; and in fact everywhere. You know the Lord's command, "Go ye into all the world, and preach the Gospel to every creature;" "and, lo, I am with you," meaning, "Any one may work for Me, and I will be with him." It is true of the minister, the missionary, and every believer who works for Jesus. The presence of Jesus is intimately connected with work for Him. You say, "I have never thought of that before. I have my Sunday work, but during the week I am not doing work for Him." You cannot have the presence of Jesus, and let this continue to be the case. I do not believe you could have the presence of Jesus all the week and yet do nothing for Him; therefore my advice is, work for Him who is worthy, His blessing and His presence will be found in the work. It is

A blessed privilege to work for Christ

in this perishing world. Oh, why is it that our hearts often feel so cold and closed up, and so many of us say, "I do not feel called to Christ's work"? Be willing to yield yourself for the Lord's service, and He will reveal Himself to you.

Christ comes with His wondrous promise, and what He says, He says to all believers: "Lo, I am with you always; that is My promise; this is what I in My power can do; this is what I faithfully engage to perform; will you have it?

I give Myself to thee, O soul."

To each of those who have come to Him, Christ says, "I give Myself to thee, to be absolutely and wholly thine every hour of every day; to be with thee and in thee every moment, to bless thee and sustain thee, and to give thee each moment the consciousness of My presence; I will be wholly, wholly, wholly thine."

And now, what is the other side? He wants me to be wholly His. Are you ready to take this as your motto now,

"Wholly for God"?

O God, breathe Thou Thy presence in my heart that Thou mayest shine forth from my life. "Wholly for God," let this be our motto. Come let us cast ourselves on our faces before His feet. Our missionary from

Nyassaland says he has often been touched by seeing how the native Christians, when they are brought to Jesus, do not stand in prayer; they do not kneel; but they cast themselves upon the earth with their foreheads to the ground, and there they lie, and with loud voices cry unto God. I sometimes feel that I wish we could do that ourselves; but we need not do it literally. Let us do it in spirit, for the everlasting Son of God has come into our hearts. Are you going to take Him and to keep Him there, to give Him glory and let Him have His way? Come now and say, "I will seek Thee with my whole heart; I am wholly Thine." Yield yourself entirely to Him to have complete possession. He will take and keep possession. Come now. Jesus delights in the worship of His Saints. Our whole life can become one continuous act of worship and work of love and joy, if we only remember and value this, that Jesus has said, "Lo, I am with you all the days, even unto the end of the world."

Made in the USA
Middletown, DE
30 November 2018